D0378884

EMPIRE OF FORTUNE

By Francis Jennings

The Covenant Chain

The Invasion of America: Indians, Colonialism, and the Cant of Conquest

The Ambiguous Iroquois Empire: The Covenant Chain Confederation of Indian Tribes with English Colonies from Its Beginnings to the Lancaster Treaty of 1744

Empire of Fortune: Crowns, Colonies, and Tribes in the Seven Years War in America

Edited

With William R. Swagerty:

The Newberry Library Center for the History of the American Indian Bibliographical Series

With William N. Fenton and Mary A. Druke:

The History and Culture of Iroquois Diplomacy: An Interdisciplinary Guide to the Treaties of the Six Nations and Their League

Iroquois Indians: A Documentary History (microfilm)

3 1235 00453 0114 WCL

EMPIRE OF FORTUNE

Crowns, colonies, and tribes in the Seven Years War in America

by FRANCIS JENNINGS

W · W · NORTON & COMPANY · New York · London

973.26
J 443
1988

I am grateful to the Public Record Office of Great Britain for permission to use crown copyright materials; and to the following institutions that have granted permission to reproduce and have provided photographs of materials in their possession or under their copyright: the Albany Institute of History and Art; the British Library; the John Carter Brown Library; the Colonial Williamsburg Foundation; the Guildhall Art Gallery, City of London; Illinois State Historical Library; the National Museums of Canada; the National Portrait Gallery of Great Britain; the Newberry Library; the Newport News *Daily Press;* Pennsylvania Department of Internal Affairs; University of Oklahoma Press.

Copyright © 1988 by Francis Jennings

All rights reserved.

Published simultaneously in Canada by Penguin Books Canada Ltd., 2801 John Street, Markham, Ontario L3R 1B4.
Printed in the United States of America.

The text of this book is composed in Janson, with display type set in Janson. Composition and manufacturing by The Maple-Vail Book Manufacturing Group.

First Edition

Library of Congress Cataloging-in-Publication Data
Jennings, Francis, 1918–
Empire of fortune: crowns, colonies, and tribes in the Seven Years War in America / by Francis Jennings.
p. cm.
Bibliography: p.
Includes index.
1. United States—History—French and Indian war. 1755–1763.
2. Indians of North America—Wars—1750–1815. I. Title.
E199.J54 1988
973.2'6—dc19 87–18746

ISBN 0-393-02537-3

W. W. Norton & Company, Inc., 500 Fifth Avenue, New York, N.Y. 10110
W. W. Norton & Company Ltd., 37 Great Russell Street, London WC1B 3NU

1 2 3 4 5 6 7 8 9 0

To the memory of
Marie Bloede Woollcott
Great Lady

Such is the empire of Fortune . . . that it is almost equally difficult to foresee the events of war or to explain their various consequences.

Edward Gibbon, *The Decline and Fall of the Roman Empire*

CONTENTS

ILLUSTRATIONS

MAPS

OVERVIEW ❧

About 1975, when celebrations were being planned for the coming Bicentennial of the American Revolution, I appeared before the Pennsylvania planning commission with a proposal to compile and publish a volume of articles of recent research as part of the celebration. The commission had been spending hundreds of thousands of dollars on pageants, showboats, and so on, so I anticipated little difficulty over my small request, made in behalf of a state historical society. My naiveté was quickly dispelled. The commission's treasurer leaned back in his chair and asked, "Mr. Jennings, why do we need another book on the Revolution? We already have a book on it over there in the library."

Utterly broken in spirit, I gave up.

Nevertheless, in retrospect there seems to be some point to his question. A reader may well be justified in asking, at least, why do we need *this* book? Professional historians may find sufficient reason in the correction of a record that has been badly botched in previous accounts by "authoritative" colleagues. Lay readers will want to know why that record is worth the bother.

Harmful myths

One good reason is that the lessons drawn from that erroneous history include myths harmful to people living today—myths of authoritarianism, racism, and militarism. To itemize:

- The traditional name for the hostilities between France and England in America between 1754 and 1763 is "The French and Indian War," with a plain implication that Indians fought only as allies of the French. Contemporary statesmen understood well that, if that had been true, France would have won; and the English spent much time and trouble on the difficult diplomacy of tribal alliance. (A Canadian colleague once remarked, tongue in cheek, "Up here we call it the *English* and Indian War.") English management of Indian affairs culminated in the Royal Proclamation of 1763, which drew a boundary line between Indians and colonial settlements. The Proclamation is still regarded as a precedent to be interpreted by the law courts of Canada and Australia, and its legal boundary between human communities led Frederick Jackson Turner to imagine a frontier line between "savagery" and "civilization"—two abstractions defined in terms of race. The great harm in Turner's concept lies in its assumption that peoples of different genetic stocks ("races") must ever be irreconcilable to each other. The record shows a contrary picture of negotiation and cooperation. The Seven Years War was not a war between races; in America it was a war of Frenchmen, French Canadians, and Indians against Englishmen, Irishmen, Scots, British colonials, and Indians.

- Lawrence Henry Gipson has remarked that "in its beginnings the war had nothing to do with the old animosities of Europe," yet he called it The Great War for the Empire. His reason for the strange comment was that a colonial struggle for possession of the Ohio Valley triggered the fighting. This is like saying that the old animosities of Europe had nothing to do with World War I because the war was started by an assassination at Sarajevo. In fact, France and England had been engaged in an on-again, off-again struggle for the North American interior since late in the seventeenth century. Gipson quoted England's prime minister, the duke of Newcastle, as saying "Let Americans fight Americans."[1] That would be quite in keeping with the duke's thrifty outlook, but it has no bearing on the objective he wanted those Americans to fight for, which was the dominion of the English crown in North America.[2]

This was recognized by the Americans, who regarded the war as so much the concern of the empires that provincial assemblies balked at supplying men, money, and equipment for the war. They have been attacked for insane greed in refusing to help Britain protect their own peoples, and their "treason," when seen in this light, becomes an argument that authoritarian, militaristic government is necessary for a country's safety. In fact, the assemblies were self-consciously following the example set by the English House of Commons when it refused support for the crown's dynastic wars until the crown conceded certain "liberties" accumulating to substantial power. Without a plan, provincial assemblies were inching toward independence in

1. Lawrence Henry Gipson, *The British Empire Before the American Revolution* (New York: Alfred A. Knopf, 1958–70), 6:10.

2. T. R. Clayton, "The Duke of Newcastle, the Earl of Halifax, and the American Origins of the Seven Years' War," *The Historical Journal* (Cambridge, Eng.), 24:3 (Sept. 1981), 579, 593; minutes of meeting at Newcastle House, 26 June 1754, mss., Newcastle Papers, Add. MSS. 32,029, f. 124, British Library.

fact while professing subjection in form.[3]

Francis Parkman saw clearly these "premonitions of the movement towards independence which ended in the war of Revolution," but spent much effort denouncing provincial assemblies for choosing to obstruct action when their aid to the crown was most needed.[4] His thesis that democracy must be suppressed in order to achieve liberty is echoed today in the rhetoric of self-identified libertarians. It is surely relevant to the validity of that argument, then as now, that Parkman had to mangle his sources to give credibility to his point.[5] Max Savelle could follow the evidence more faithfully to find that "Liberty," for the colonists, "meant the right to govern themselves."[6]

- To Charles and Mary Beard, the war "taught the colonies, so diverse in their interests and so hostile to one another in religion and politics, the art of cooperation. . . . The Albany conference [of 1754] failed, but the French and Indian war that broke out three years later drove the colonies into cooperation on a continental scale." About the only accurate statement in this remarkable effusion is the failure of the Albany conference. Only persons who wrote "without fear and without research" could have dated the outbreak of war "three years later" while identifying George Washington's capitulation at Fort Necessity as "the first shot" of the war; news of it arrived at Albany during the conference.[7]

Undeterred by factuality, the Beards discovered, in the three pages they devoted to the Seven Years War, that "America was fused by the fierce heat of the conflict at her very doors." Their preachment is the virtue and value of the nationalist melting pot. To reconcile such a notion with the political and cultural pluralism that prevailed in mid-eighteenth century British America is impossible.

In what the publishers called "the first major reinterpretation of American history since Turner, Parrington, and Beard," Daniel J. Boorstin

3. Leonard Woods Labaree, *Royal Government in America: A Study of the British Colonial System before 1783* (New Haven, Conn.: Yale University Press, 1930), 35, 448; Jack P. Greene, "The Role of the Lower Houses of Assembly in Eighteenth-Century Politics," in *The Reinterpretation of the American Revolution, 1763–1789* (New York: Harper and Row, 1968), 86–109; Edmund S. Morgan and Helen M. Morgan, *The Stamp Act Crisis: Prologue to Revolution*, rev. ed. (New York: Collier Books, 1963), 17; Max Savelle, *Seeds of Liberty: The Genesis of the American Mind* (New York: Alfred A. Knopf, 1948), 283–84.

4. Francis Parkman, *Montcalm and Wolfe* (1884), New Library ed., 2 vols. (Boston: Little, Brown and Co., 1909) 1:37–38.

5. See Francis Jennings, "Francis Parkman: A Brahmin among Untouchables," *William and Mary Quarterly*, 3d ser., 42 (July 1985), 305–28.

6. Savelle, *Seeds of Liberty*, 351.

7. Charles A. Beard and Mary R. Beard, *The Rise of American Civilization* (1927), rev. ed. (New York: Macmillan, 1939) 1:119–20.

devoted six chapters to a sustained attack upon Quaker pacifism and opposition to militarism, the centerpiece of which was the chapter on "How Quakers Misjudged the Indians." A sample sentence: "the minority of diehard Quakers which controlled the [Pennsylvania] Assembly would not budge from its traditional pacifism, though the whole border might burn for it."[8] This is unqualifiedly false. In Boorstin's pages bigotry and racism are very thinly veiled, and militarism is naked. Perhaps more to the point, his research into the sources has been so trivial as to make the Beards seem like Teutonic scholars. Lack of knowledge, however, has not deterred him from issuing a series of didactic pronouncements, the malice of which is equalled only by their factual error.

The Quakers understood very well what they were doing and as the result of their strenuous effort and sacrifice the scourge of raid and massacre was lifted from the backwoods of Pennsylvania. More, and rather to my surprise, I have discovered that the Scottish general who succeeded in taking French Fort Duquesne did so with the indispensable political and logistic help of the "King of the Quakers" with whom the general collaborated.[9] The Friends won by the simple device of establishing direct contact with Indians who themselves wanted peace, but the simplicity of the device is hidden behind the enormous complexity of getting it to work in the circumstances of the time.

Those circumstances were unique, and perhaps total pacifism is not a lesson to be drawn from them. For the record, I am neither a Quaker nor a pacifist. Further comment can best be reserved until after description of the events.

Though historians now usually identify the beginnings of the American Revolution in events following the British conquest of New France, the colonists' resistance that became the Revolution is clearly visible all during the Seven Years War. Regardless of forms, *effective* independence was the unspoken goal of the resisters who eventually avowed it openly as revolutionaries. What the Revolution was all about is therefore relevant here. Bernard Bailyn has correctly identified the colonials' concern with power, and has commented on the many pamphlets in which they argued themselves into rebelling against the crown's power. The American Revolution, he comments, "was to a remarkable extent an affair of the mind." True enough, but his sequel bears further examination: "Its dominant goals were not the overthrow of the existing order but the establishment in principle of existing matters of fact, and its means were the communication of understanding."

8. See Daniel Boorstin, *The Americans: The Colonial Experience* (New York: Random House, 1958), chs. 8, 9. Quotation on p. 55.

9. Ch. 17, below.

Two distinct assertions are contained in that sentence, one of which is much too comprehensive. For the Loyalists to whom understanding was communicated by tar and feathers, arson of homes and businesses, confiscation of goods, and deportation into permanent exile, it might have seemed a little odd that all this was intended to preserve the existing order, even in principle. In one sense, however, Bailyn is right, though he has not mentioned it explicitly; to wit, the colonials' acceptance of the principle of empire. The men who led the Revolution had more on their minds than freedom from Britain. They wanted that freedom in order to make American territory into their own empire rather than Britain's, and their success is evident in any historical atlas.

I differ also with Professor Bailyn over his apparent acceptance, in deed, of the "transit of civilization" theory of the formation of American culture—a theory I had thought conclusively discredited long ago. Yet he has remarked that his large project, which he calls *The Peopling of British North America*, does not "involve to any significant extent the movements of either of the two non-Caucasian peoples—the Native Americans and the Africans."[10] He acknowledges *pro forma* that the histories of these two peoples "are so vital a part of the story," but in practice he has avoided notice of their experiences in all of his publications. To acknowledge formally the existence and contributions of the many peoples of "British" North America is not enough. Apart from moral considerations, simple attention to validity demands their inclusion in a history heavily influenced by their activities and sheer numbers.

Issues are always enacted by individual persons. Our period was rich with strong and colorful men: George Washington; William Pitt; Mingo chief Tanaghrisson; rogue George Croghan; interpreter Conrad Weiser; Benjamin Franklin; Provost William Smith; Superintendent of Indian Affairs Sir William Johnson; the Delaware Indian chiefs Pisquetomen, Shingas, and Tamaqua (Beaver); Thomas Pelham-Holles, duke of Newcastle; George Montagu Dunk, earl of Halifax; Louis Joseph de Montcalm, marquis de Montcalm; William Augustus, duke of Cumberland; Pierre de Vaudreuil de Cavagnial, marquis de Vaudreuil; Ange Duquesne de Manneville, marquis Duquesne; Major General Edward Braddock; "king of the Quakers" Israel Pemberton, Jr.; Brigadier John Forbes; Major General James Wolfe; John Campbell, earl of Loudoun; Mohawk chief Hendrick; Proprietary Thomas Penn; Governors Robert Hunter Morris, William Shirley, and Thomas Pownall—these will do for a random sampling; the list properly should be much longer as will become evident. Records of these

10. Bernard Bailyn, *The Ideological Origins of the American Revolution* (Cambridge, Mass.: Belknap Press, 1967), 17; idem in *Perspectives in American History* 2 (1985), 15 and n15.

men's actions and utterances are voluminous and fascinating. Narrative of their actions defines the issues.

Reorientation

This conflict has long been seen in romantic terms that pit the forces of Good (England, civilization, progress) against the powers of Evil (France, savagery, perpetual wilderness). In such a perspective, Our Side performs heroic deeds to overcome the dastardy of the Other Side, and we are so ennobled in the conflict that we finally turn our faces against the nasty Old World to build a gloriously independent future in God's Country. The proper word for this is familiar to military men and farmers, but not permissible in professional discourse.

A different perspective appears herein, one in which grand historic forces, whatever they may have been, were determined by the cumulative actions of individual persons, often with unintended and unpredictable outcomes. In this perspective, nobility of purpose and behavior appears in unexpected places. So, too, with its opposite. It is astonishing to find that the weapon of deliberate, calculated terror was used extensively by powerful men on Our Side as well as theirs, and that such men on both sides used terror against their own people as well as the enemy's. Such discoveries must not be permitted to drown explication in moral outrage, though reportage of them is necessary to a valid picture of events. Atrocities are presented as straightforwardly as I have been able to manage after consigning much splutter to the wastebasket.

Two cautions are necessary. The first was given by that great "imperialist" historian Charles M. Andrews who warned that colonial history must be recognized "not merely as a phase preliminary to our own career as a nation, but also as an integral part of English and Continental history in an era of colonization and commercial and maritime aggrandizement."[11] The war must be considered in its own right, not merely as a precursor. Our second caution stands out from the subject matter: the Seven Years War was as immense, as complex, and in its own way as earth-shaking as the Revolution. When France and England dropped pretense in 1756 and declared formally the "covert" war that they had already been fighting in America for two years, their combat encircled the globe. It has often been called the first world war. Their troops and navies engaged in Europe, Asia, the Mediterranean, the Caribbean, the Atlantic and Pacific oceans, and on the continent of North America; and they drew into the fray Aus-

11. Charles M. Andrews, *The Colonial Period of American History* (1934–38), 4 vols., reprinted (New Haven, Conn.: Yale University Press, 1964) 1:xvi.

tria, Russia, Prussia, and Spain, not to speak of the native peoples in their colonial possessions. Yet the thing began in the backwoods of Pennsylvania, and it was in America that Britain committed the bulk of her troops.

Lawrence Henry Gipson devoted a long life and fifteen large volumes to the war, which include a distressing amount of misinformation. I have neither the time nor the ability to review the entire field of his labors; my discussion is limited to North America and the United Kingdom, and is confined between the covers of this one volume. Gipson called it The Great War for the Empire, leaving no doubt as to which empire he loved. He resolved all knotty issues not only in favor of Britain, but more particularly to the credit of the British crown and its military forces. Gipson's passion for war and gore showed its reverse side as an antipathy toward Quakers and other pacifists so strong that his massive volumes show little consultation of source materials written by Quakers in Quaker Pennsylvania. Instead he followed a pattern set long before by writing Pennsylvania's history almost exclusively from sources generated by enemies of the Quakers and their political allies. As such sources, when analyzed closely, show much propagandist distortion and fabrication, Gipson's account has required strong correction. His treatment of the great political struggles in Pennsylvania (and that of the writers who have depended on him) is so far wrong that validity is more at stake than fairness.

Gipson's Indians also are set in traditional molds. The immense research that went into his volumes was badly lopsided. He bypassed masses of treaty documents and manuscripts of private correspondence that explain the Indians' predicaments and quote their attitudes, though most of these papers were available to him in nearby repositories. Such sources have been given much attention herein.[12] Indians here have been restored to central roles in what once was called the French and Indian War, but they no longer appear as "stage" Indians, homogeneously ferocious and treacherous. Nor are they cast as noble savages. Within these pages distinctions are made between tribes and persons classed overall as Indian but varying in interests, policies, and behavior as much as the Frenchmen and Englishmen who were classed together as Europeans.

Such differences in approach resulted in a history greatly at variance from standard versions, but no revision has been introduced simply for the sake of sensation or novelty. Corrections have been dictated by cited

12. More than 9,000 documents have now been compiled in the Iroquois diplomatic history archive at the Newberry Library, Chicago. These are available in microfilm with a printed calendar and partial index entitled *Iroquois Indians: A Documentary History of the Diplomacy of the Six Nations and Their League*, eds. Francis Jennings, William N. Fenton, Mary A. Druke, and David R. Miller (Woodbridge, Conn.: Research Publications, 1985). Interpretive Essays and reference data are in *The History and Culture of Iroquois Diplomacy: An Interdisciplinary Guide to the Treaties of the Six Nations and Their League*, same eds. (Syracuse, N.Y.: Syracuse University Press, 1985).

and verifiable source evidence. It may be proper to mention that this book was researched and written primarily as a means of teaching myself rather than to instruct readers in my previously held understanding of its subject. The findings often deviate widely from what I had anticipated. New conceptualization imposed a heavy labor of reorganized presentation. The book's shape and presentation might have been simpler if I had known what to expect.

Approach

Although this book is complete in itself, it is the third in a trilogy on the Covenant Chain. The first volume—*The Invasion of America*[13]—after exploring the cultural consequences of contact between Europeans and American Indians, described the conquest strategies of Virginia and Puritan New England. The second volume—*The Ambiguous Iroquois Empire*[14]—traced the origins and development of the Covenant Chain as an institution of political and economic accommodation under the joint direction of the Iroquois League and the province of New York, with attention to changes impelled by the founding of Pennsylvania. The present volume describes how the Chain became a casualty of imperial war.

My approach has been an individual variant of ethnohistory. As this sort of history is relatively new and diversely practiced, some distinctions are in order. Along with other ethnohistorians, I reject the concept of race as fallacious and vicious. Instead, I follow the example of modern anthropologists by using the culture concept as my basic tool of analysis—though cultural fetters make me dependent on written documents. Unlike most anthropologists and some historians, my basic concern in this trilogy has been relations *between* peoples rather than the detailed delineations of culture-change within a particular entity.

In this volume as in its predecessors I had no thought of writing a definitive history, and have certainly not done so. My goal is to open the field rather than to close it. I have not viewed any of the actors in this history as other than human, with human faults and graces, but I have felt no need to lavish praise, nor have I tried to balance villainous acts with exculpatory comment that the villain loved dogs and children. *All* histories are interpretations made by writers predisposed by personal experience and cultural imperatives, and prone to human error. In my view, objectivity requires honesty in the citation and reportage of evidence, recognition of

13. Published for the Institute of Early American History and Culture (Chapel Hill: University of North Carolina Press, 1975), reprinted paperback (New York: W. W. Norton and Co., 1976).

14. New York: W. W. Norton and Co., 1984.

differing interpretations, and fairness of presentation; but "fairness," especially, is a category sometimes indistinguishable from "taste."

As to that, the semantics of criticism deserve a sidelong glance. Critics use *controversial* as a term of disapproval when they lack evidence to be specific. They forget that both sides of a controversy are controversial. Bertrand Russell's "declension of the adjective" is pertinent: "*I* am firm, *you* are stubborn, *he* is pigheaded." Controversy aside, I shall be very glad to acknowledge error when it is demonstrated, but I can be pretty firm when error is only asserted.

Acknowledgments

A number of my many debts have been noticed at particular places in the books comprising this series. More general acknowledgments and gratitude are due to the following institutions and persons. I request forbearance for inadvertent oversights.

FINANCIAL GRANTS AND RESEARCH ASSISTANCE

Grants from the National Endowment for the Humanities administered at the Henry E. Huntington Library and the Institute of Early American History and Culture; sabbatical salary from Cedar Crest College; other fellowships from the American Philosophical Society; John Carter Brown Library; Lawrence Henry Gipson Institute for Eighteenth-Century Studies; the Newberry Library; the Philadelphia Center for Early American Studies; the Rockefeller Foundation.

HOSPITALITY AND FACILITIES

The British Library; Brown University; Bucks County (Pa.) Historical Society; College of William and Mary; Dukes County (Mass.) Historical Society; Friends Historical Library at Swarthmore College; Friends Record Department; Haverford College Library; Henry E. Huntington Library; the Historical Institute (London); the Historical Society of Pennsylvania; Lehigh University Library; Public Archives of Canada; Public Record Office of Great Britain; University of London's Institute of United States Studies, and its Department of History; William Penn Library of Pennsylvania Historical and Museum Commission.

PERSONS

I owe deep gratitude to Richard S. Dunn for taking me under his wing at a hard time; my admiration for his superb qualities as scholar, gentleman, and humanitarian is unsurpassed.

Thanks to the late Henry Pommer, dean of Cedar Crest College, for unflagging encouragement while we were colleagues.

To Richard H. Brown, "dean" of Research and Education at the Newberry Library, for congenial partnership in my finest career experience, and to Lawrence W. Towner for presiding benevolently over it.

To James Axtell for enthusiastic companionship in voyages of discovery.

To William N. Fenton, "dean of Iroquois studies," for guidance and counsel.

To John Mohawk and Brian Deer for reviewing the book in typescript.

To Wilcomb E. Washburn for his good example and generous support.

To Norman Fiering and James L. Mairs, editors whose comments have deserved to be heeded.

To my students and colleagues, and to the fellows at the D'Arcy McNickle Center for the History of the American Indian, for battering new ideas into my stubborn head, and for their good company. Four names must represent them all: Mary Ann Druke, Jacqueline Peterson, William R. Swagerty, and Helen Hornbeck Tanner.

Special thanks to those utterly indispensable colleagues, the librarians who have coped with my demands and struggles at Cedar Crest College, Glassboro State College, Princeton University, the University of Pennsylvania, and Chilmark Public Library. To represent them all, let me name John Aubrey and Michael Kaplan at the Newberry Library, and old friend Peter J. Parker at the Historical Society of Pennsylvania.

And utmost gratitude to Joan Woollcott Jennings—patient, generous, sagacious, cheerful—my beloved partner in this enterprise as in all others.

March 1987 *Chilmark, Massachusetts*

Part One ❧ *THE ANVIL STRIKES the HAMMER*

Chapter 1 ❧ *THE BUTCHER*

Those [retreating highlanders] unable to keep up with the main body, and who fell into Cumberland's hands, were sent to jail, because, as he explained to Newcastle, "as they have so many of our prisoners in their hands I did not care to put them to death. But," he continued grimly, "I have encouraged the country people to do it as they may fall into their way. . . ." . . . The process of dehumanising the rebels by calling them "animals" and vermin," which started when their pursuit through England was compared with a chase, continued as Cumberland pursued them to the North of Scotland, which Sir John Ligonier called "the disagreeable hunting of those wild beasts." The chase culminated at Culloden. . . . And like a pack of wild beasts they were hunted down and killed as they fled from the field.

W. A. Speck

Chronology

5 August 1745. Prince Charles Edward Stuart lands in Scotland to arouse rebellion in the cause of his exiled father's claim to be rightful king of Great Britain.

16 April 1746. The rebellious Highlanders are decisively defeated in the battle of Culloden. Afterwards, by order of the duke of Cumberland, British troops lay waste to the countryside.

It can never be forgotten that when the United States of America were colonies of Great Britain they were part of an empire and responsive to happenings in other parts of the empire. When Great Britain went to war with France, British colonies automatically faced against neighboring French colonies and prepared defenses against the depredations of the French navy. So much is accepted without demur by historians.

Sometimes the train of influence *within* the empire is less plain to see than the direct effects of imperial war. One event that had diffuse, far-reaching influence was the Jacobite rising by Highland Scottish clans in 1745.[1] They rose in behalf of Charles Edward Stuart, the Young Pretender grandson of exiled King James II. Celebrated in song and story, the romance of the uprising disappears beneath its squalid reality, but it

1. For background in Britain's political situation see W. A. Speck, *The Butcher: The Duke of Cumberland and the Suppression of the 45* (Oxford, Eng.: Basil Blackwell, 1981).

will not be retold here. For present purposes it is enough to notice that the rebellious Highlanders were regarded by ruling aristocrats as savages and were suppressed with a ruthlessness—"the product of deliberate policy"—that would have appalled any American Indian tribe.[2] After the battle of Culloden destroyed the rebel army, the British commander suggested "no quarter" for the already beaten survivors, and his hint was acted on with frenzy.[3]

More explicitly he ordered devastation of the homes and flocks of known and suspected rebels and everyone who lived near them. The whole countryside was razed and burned to the ground.[4] To quote an eighteenth-century writer, "Detachments were sent off on every side, and they butchered, plundered, burned and destroyed every man and beast, hut and house: even the women were violated, and afterwards either assassinated or turned out with their children to starve on the barren heaths. In a word, the most shocking barbarities and ravages were committed that ever disgraced humanity. . . . In a little time, for the space of fifty miles, nothing was to be seen but silence, ruin and desolation."[5] Some persons fortunate enough to escape shooting and hanging were transported to America, taking their memories along.[6]

The man directly responsible for the terror was William Augustus, duke of Cumberland and younger son of King George II. At first he was idolized, for the uprising had occurred in the midst of one of Britain's perennial wars with France and it seemed to open the gates to French invasion. But the French never came, the war ended, and stories came down from the north of the merciless devastation by Cumberland's troops on Cumberland's orders. In revulsion the populace turned their hero into "the butcher," and Butcher Cumberland he has remained to the present day—with reason.[7]

About such matters as the welfare of Scottish peasants, the government's ministers were wholly unconcerned. What mattered to them was Cumberland's success in destroying the perpetually rebellious clans. This he accomplished; the clans never rose again. Soon, however, the Whig aristocracy began to worry about Cumberland's rocketing influence and power.

2. Bruce Lenman, *The Jacobite Risings in Britain, 1689–1746* (London: Eyre Methuen, 1980), 261–63.

3. E. M. Lloyd, "William Augustus, Duke of Cumberland," *Dictionary of National Biography* 61:341.

4. John Prebble, *Culloden* (1961), reprinted (Harmondsworth, Eng.: Penguin Books, 1967); James Browne, *A History of the Highlands and of the Highland Clans*, 4 vols. (Glasgow: A. Fullerton and Co., 1840), 3:255–57, 268–73; Speck, *Butcher*, pp. 148–56.

5. [John Almon], *A Review of the Reign of George II*, 2d ed. (London: J. Wilkie, 1762), 91.

6. Lenman, *Jacobite Risings*, 272; Speck, *Butcher*, 156–62, ch. 7.

7. Lloyd, "William Augustus," 61:342.

Like the shots subsequently fired at Concord Bridge, the cannon of Culloden resounded over great distances in space and time. Cumberland's associates there became the officers he trusted to head Britain's armies in America. The Scottish members of Parliament eliminated all possibility of charges against their loyalty by voting uniformly to support every measure of the crown. They made a formidable bloc for any "loyal opposition" to deal with.

Cumberland gathered a circle of supporters dedicated to preserving and enlarging the king's prerogative to govern without interference, especially in the military sphere. King George II openly openly avowed Cumberland as his favorite son (to the distress of the Prince of Wales) and appointed him captain general of the armies; that is, commander in chief. Whereupon Cumberland commissioned and appointed officers without consulting civil ministers, thus seizing from them an immense field of the patronage on which their power depended. Cumberland's own power increased with the same patronage, especially in the House of Commons where many of his colonels held seats.[8]

Then, in 1754, a "brush fire" war broke out between Britain and France in the Ohio Valley of North America. Undeclared, and temporarily confined to the backwoods region of its origin, its hostilities drew serious attention from the highest officials of Britain and France. How long could they be localized? Had the time come for another showdown between the empires? Could the expenses of a war be contained? Hawks and doves strove with each other in London and Paris as much as their diplomats struggled between the capitals.

Cumberland was a hawk. His was not the only voice for all-out war, but his commanding military position became a commanding position in politics also. He and his associates forced the issue whenever the temporizers seemed about to effect a compromise with France. In the meantime Cumberland controlled British policy in America. One of the casualties of his control was the former Whig policy of "salutary neglect." Cumberland's officers in the colonies were charged with political functions. They were to enlarge the crown's prerogatives and repress the powers of colonial assemblies. But the American colonists were more numerous and more distant than the Scots, and they were not to be beaten down as easily as the poverty-stricken, half-naked Highlanders. Cumberland's proconsuls

8. Ibid., 342, 344; *Military Affairs in North America, 1748–1765: Selected Documents from the Cumberland Papers in Windsor Castle*, ed. Stanley Pargellis (1936), reprinted (Hamden, Conn.: Archon Books, 1969), ix–x.

Bibliographic note: Pargellis was a scrupulous scholar, a committed militarist, and an American royalist. He thought Parliament's fears of a standing army to be "exaggerated" and that Cumberland's "ruthlessness in Scotland . . . was born neither of cruelty nor of abstract justice, but of calculated expediency" (p. ix). It did not occur to him that cruelty may be one of the calculations entering into expedience.

encountered suspicion that quickly turned to resistance—political resistance manifested as evasion and foot-dragging. Colonials wondered whether the servants of their own king were a more dangerous enemy than France. Cumberland's commanders fed that wonder by never winning a battle except against the colonial assemblies.

Cumberland was as inept as his commanders. He had been lucky enough at Culloden to have cannon against Highlanders armed only with broadswords, but Culloden was his last as well as his first victory. From 1748 to 1754, Cumberland engaged only in political combat, but when the American wilderness war heated up to what has been called the first world war, Cumberland took command of troops in Europe amid great pomp. Not long after, he marched and countermarched his men into a situation so impossible that he surrendered an entire army without a fight. That was the end of his domination of politics. (See chapter 16, below.)

His downfall was the colonies' boon for it gave power to William Pitt, whose colonial policies reversed Cumberland's. Pitt dissolved colonial resistance and won active cooperation by recalling Cumberland's commander from America (a colleague from the Scottish repression). Pitt restored prewar political relations, abandoning the effort to rule by royal prerogative. A series of victories followed almost at once, and France was driven out of North America.

The "great" men could drive lesser men to war or rebellion by control of institutional power, but such power was far from absolute. It had to contend with powers wielded by less famous men who achieved strength by banding together in diverse ways. During the Seven Years War, colonial assemblymen, tribal counselors, merchant associates, brethren in religion, and even lowly servants and slaves devoted energies to their own varied and often opposing interests. In that confusion the "great" men had to adapt to pressures from below, as well as those from each other, or miss their great goals. The Seven Years War in America cannot be seen correctly from only the vantage points of imperial metropoles. Nor from the colonies. Nor from the tribes. Effectual decisions were made by thinking persons in all those places, and all must be considered.

It seems safe to say that the American colonists would have been content to stay within the British Empire if they had been permitted to govern themselves as the crown's faithful subjects. Their Declaration of Independence protests that they were driven to secession by a long train of abuses and usurpations, and its identifications of such are confirmable. The Declaration also states that these abuses were deliberately destructive of government by consent of the governed, and this statement is also confirmable.

A dominant party in British aristocratic politics watched the increasing autonomy of the colonies fearful of its outcome, and determined to reduce the colonies to submission. Ironically, this party's repressive measures precipitated the event they dreaded. Their "cold" political war against the colonies began in the Seven Years War. So did the resistance.

Chapter 2 ❧ *THE OHIO COMPANY of VIRGINIA*

I incline to think that all these affairs of the French have taken their Rise from the Imprudent and high Talk of the Virginians, as if they would immediately build Forts and settle the Ohio Lands. This they should have done and not talked on it so long beforehand, because it has allarmed the French too soon.

Richard Peters, 9 July 1753

Chronology

15 March 1744.	Britain and France declare war.
16 June–7 July 1744.	Treaty at Lancaster, Pennsylvania, between Iroquois nations of Oneida, Onondaga, Cayuga, and Seneca, on the one side, and British colonies of Virginia, Maryland, and Pennsylvania on the other.
18 October 1748.	Peace between Britain and France at the treaty of Aix-la-Chapelle.
24 October 1747.	Formation of the Ohio Company of Virginia.
11 August–29 September 1748.	Pennsylvania's Conrad Weiser journeys to the Ohio country to treat with region's Indians.
11 January 1749.	Partner John Hanbury presents to the king in council the Ohio Company's petition for a grant of lands.
16 March 1749.	King George II orders grant to the Ohio Company.
15 June–9 November 1749.	Captain Céloron de Blainville leads an expedition to the Ohio country to restore New France's authority.
11 September 1750–29 March 1752.	Christopher Gist journeys twice, in behalf of the Ohio Company and the province of Virginia, to arrange for a treaty at Logstown.

In the middle of the eighteenth century two North American frontier regions dominated the strategic thinking of French and English statesmen. Between French Louisiana in the south and the English colonies of Georgia and the Carolinas lay a mostly mountainous region inhabited by the Indian nations of the Cherokees, Catawbas, Creeks, Choctaws, and Chickasaws—numerous peoples whose trade in pelts and Indian captive slaves excited French and English entrepreneurs to wage direct and vicarious war throughout the region.[1]

In the north, between the French colonies of Canada and Acadia and the English provinces of New England and New York, was another frontier region, also inhabited by Indians. Not so numerous as the southern tribes, the Abenakis, Mahicans, and Iroquois produced wealth through trade in animal skins and took sides in combat between the French and English. Abenakis generally allied themselves to France and often harassed the interior settlements of New England. The Iroquois League generally allied with the English though their status was formally neutral; the Iroquois had accepted the role of buffer between the empires[2] after losing prolonged war with the French in the seventeenth century.

Regardless of periods of peace between the sovereigns in Europe, on-again, off-again hostilities were endemic in the frontier regions. Colonials looked outward from their towns toward the frontiers with a mixture of anxiety and speculation. Attacks might come from those directions, but the potential for great wealth lay there also. The two frontiers drew English colonials in opposite directions, pulling their economic and psychological interests away from each other and creating sectional consciousness portentous for the future.[3] England's largest colony, Virginia, was considered to be southern, but its expansion into the southern frontier region was hampered by a specific charter boundary and obstructed by the energetic activity of Carolinians; in a different direction Virginians were frustrated by the giant estate of Lord Fairfax, which the crown confirmed against all challenge.[4] After some experiment, one group of the gentlemen expan-

1. See Verner W. Crane, *The Southern Frontier, 1670–1732* (Ann Arbor: University of Michigan Press, 1929); J. Leitch Wright, Jr., *The Only Land They Knew: The Tragic Story of the American Indians in the Old South* (New York: The Free Press, 1981), ch. 5; Theda Perdue, *Slavery and the Evolution of Cherokee Society, 1540–1866* (Knoxville: University of Tennessee Press, 1979), chs. 1, 2; James Howlett O'Donnell III, *Southeastern Frontiers: Europeans, Africans, and American Indians, 1513–1840, A Critical Bibliography*, The Newberry Library Center for the History of the American Indian Bibliographical Series (Bloomington: Indiana University Press, 1982).

2. See the essays in *Northeast*, ed. Bruce G. Trigger, vol. 15 of *Handbook of North American Indians*, gen. ed. William C. Sturtevant. For Iroquois history see Jennings, *The Ambiguous Iroquois Empire: The Covenant Chain Confederation of Indian Tribes with English Colonies* (New York: W. W. Norton and Co., 1984).

3. Although the traditional view divides the sections according to disparate economic development in the nineteenth century, they were already self-consciously distinct by the seventeenth. In the eighteenth century, their complementary economies were a unifying factor in trade.

4. Conflict with N.C.: Wright, *Tragic Story*, 91; Thomas Perkins Abernethy, *Western Lands and the American Revolution* (1937), reprinted (New York: Russell and Russell, 1959) 60–61, 227–28. Fairfax estate: *George Mercer Papers Relating to the Ohio Company of Virginia*, comp. and ed. Lois Mulkearn (Pittsburgh: University of Pittsburgh Press, 1954) 403–4; Arthur Procter James, *The Ohio Company: Its Inner History* (Pittsburgh: University of Pittsburgh Press, 1959), 6.

sionists of Virginia turned toward the northern frontier beyond the Fairfax lands.[5] Here their chartered boundary allowed as much as they could desire, for its lines extended westward from the Atlantic to the Pacific and in their vague outreach included even unknown Alaska.[6] When Virginia speculators organized to take advantage of that ample sanction, they became the greatest concern of the governors of New France.

Expansion by Virginians

Virginia's interest in what has come to be known as the Old Northwest manifested itself indirectly in June and July 1744 at the famed Lancaster treaty between the Iroquois League and the provinces of Virginia, Maryland, and Pennsylvania. In the deed of cession emerging from that treaty, the Iroquois were made to renounce and disclaim all their right, and to recognize the right and title of "our sovereign the King of Great Britain to all the lands within the said colony [of Virginia] as it is now or hereafter may be peopled and bounded by his said Majesty . . . his heirs and successors."[7]

Nobody told the Iroquois that Virginia's charter gave boundaries extending from sea to sea which could be argued to contain half of North America, and this bit of enlightenment was postponed by the outbreak of "King George's War" between Britain and France. Formally declared in March 1744, the war created conditions too hazardous for new settlements in the backwoods. (Coincidentally, the Jacobite rising in Scotland aroused English fears of French invasion of their home island.)

The war ended formally in October 1748. Anticipating peace, Virginia's Thomas Lee and eleven associates petitioned the governor and council in 1747 for a grant of 200,000 acres on the Ohio River. They met with obstruction, so they adopted a different tactic. Lee organized the Ohio Company of Virginia, petitioned for a grant of half a million acres directly from the crown, and offered a share in the Company to London's Quaker

5. Gipson, *British Empire*, rev. ed. 2:4–5; *Mercer Papers* facsimile "Case of the Ohio Company," 24; Abernethy, *Western Lands*, 3–5.

6. In 1750, Thomas Lee declared that "Virginia is Bounded by the Great Atlantic Ocean to the East, by North Carolina to the South, by Maryland and Pennsylvania to the North, and by the South Sea [Pacific Ocean] to the West including California." Gipson, *British Empire*, rev. ed., 2:3.

7. Deed, 2 July 1744, Colonial Papers, Folder 41, Item 10, mss., Va. State Library, Richmond, facsimile in Iroquois diplomatic history archive, Newberry Library; printed in *Virginia Magazine of History and Biography* 13 (1905–6) 141–42. Of Virginia's gold, £200 was compensation for the deed and £100 a special present. See Jennings, *Ambiguous Iroquois Empire*, 355–62.

merchant John Hanbury in consideration of Hanbury's great influence with officialdom.[8]

As a merchant and business agent Hanbury had long been involved in colonial affairs. His overseas "interests" extended from Hudson Bay to the Baltic Sea and included heavy involvement in the tobacco trade of England's southern colonies in America. In a society where money talked, Hanbury's great wealth was listened to with respectful attention by men in high places.[9] He accepted the Ohio Company partnership and presented the Company's petition to the king in council, 11 January 1749.[10]

8. Gooch to lords of trade, 16 June 1748, mss. Colonial Office 5, vol. 1327, ff. 7–8, Public Record Office, Kew, England. (Short citation: PRO / CO 5, 1327 / 7–8.); "Case," *Mercer Papers*, 2.

9. Because of neglect, and to avoid blocking the narrative, John Hanbury (1700–1758) requires a long note: he was a very important and almost forgotten man. Known as the greatest tobacco merchant in the world, he dealt with such great planters as the Byrds and the Custis estate that George Washington acquired by marriage, and he was the London agent for the College of William and Mary and an agent for the loan office of Maryland. His cousin Capel was M.P. for Monmouthshire and another cousin, Sir Charles Hanbury-Williams, was one of the crown's most important diplomats. John stood high in London's merchant circles. He became governor of the Hamburg Company of merchants and adventurers and was consulted by Parliament for advice about policy toward the Hudson's Bay Company. In politics he was a Whig with access to the duke of Newcastle, whose electoral interests in Bristol he served. In 1754 and 1755 he was Parliament's agent to forward £10,000 annually to Virginia, and in 1756 he was joined by John Thomlinson (agent for New Hampshire) to buy and forward specie for the expenses of the British troops in the campaign against Fort Niagara; they sent £14,800 to Connecticut. Hanbury's descendants married among the founders of Lloyd's and Barclay's banks and the Trueman brewing firm. Robert Hunter Morris remarked of Hanbury and Thomlinson, "I know of no two Merchants in London that have such personal weight and interest with the Ministry." Yet Hanbury is entirely missing from the *Dict. Nat. Biog.* and almost entirely from the Quaker archives in Friends House, London. In the first instance, snobbery seems the reason; in the second, embarrassment over Hanbury's profitable cooperation with the government's military measures.

I owe thanks to professor Jacob Price for help in compiling these data. Sources follow.

Va. Mag. of Hist. and Biog. 9(1901–2), 230–32; *Proceedings and Debates of the British Parliaments Respecting North America*, ed. Leo Francis Stock, 5 vols. (Washington, D.C.: Carnegie Institution of Washington, 1924–41) 5:353–54, 433n; *Procs. and Debates* continuation, eds. R. C. Simmons and P. D. G. Thomas (Millwood, N.Y.: Kraus International Publications, 1982) 1:44, 126; Theodore Thayer, "The Army Contractors for the Niagara Campaign, 1755–56," *Wm. and Mary Qtly*, 3d ser., 14 (1957), 42, 44; A. Audrey Locke, *The Hanbury Family*, 2 vols. (London: Arthur L. Humphreys, 1916); Arthur Raistrick, *Quakers in Science and Industry: Being an Account of the Quaker Contributions to Science and Industry During the 17th and 18th Centuries* (London: The Bannisdale Press, 1950), 69, 146–48; Sir Lewis Namier, *The Structure of Politics at the Accession of George III*, 2d ed. (London: Macmillan and Co., 1957) 203n4; Hardwicke Papers, Add. MSS. 35, 592, f. 323, Brit. Lib.; *The Public Records of the Colony of Connecticut*, ed. J. Hammond Trumbull, 15 vols. (Hartford, 1850–90) 10:547, 568; notes, *Wm. and Mary Qtly*. 1st ser., 17:103n, 2d ser., 1:16, 17, 23, 24; R. H. Morris's Diary printed as "An American in London, 1735–1736," ed. Beverly McAnear, *Pennsylvania Magazine of History and Biography* 64:358, 383; death notice, *Va. Mag. of Hist. and Biog.* 16:208.

10. *Acts of the Privy Council of England. Colonial Series, 1613–1783*, eds. W. L. Grant and James Munro, 6 vols. (Hereford, Eng., 1908–12), 4:55; *Mercer Papers*, 2.

FIGURE 1. George Montagu Dunk, second earl of Halifax *(on right)* and associates. Portrait attributed to H. D. Hamilton. This portrait was painted late in Halifax's career after he had won the much-coveted Order of the Red Garter. REPRODUCED BY COURTESY OF THE NATIONAL PORTRAIT GALLERY, LONDON.

It might have been approved there even without Hanbury's influence, for power was in the hands of aggressively expansionist ministers. When routinely passed for recommendation by the board of trade, the petition was welcomed by the board's president, George Montagu Dunk, earl of Halifax, who wanted to revive the anti-French policies pursued earlier by the board in the 1720s. Halifax was hot for empire and prerogative (and for Halifax); his name will recur frequently in this narrative.[11] He liked the Company's plan precisely because it "would be a proper step towards

11. Halifax belonged to the old and privileged family of Montagu, but when he was presented with the opportunity to marry a rich heiress on condition that he take her family's name, he chose to become George Montagu Dunk. He seems to have genuinely loved her as well as her fortune. In all his official activities, he was a "hawk" and an authoritarian, constantly urging the government to greater belligerence toward France and stronger restrictions on the colonies. His life in *Dict. Nat. Biog.* is under "Dunk." To my knowledge, no full biography has been published, but there are two doctoral dissertations. Robert Alan Blackey, "The Political Career of George Montagu Dunk, 2nd Earl of Halifax, 1748–1771: A Study of an Eighteenth Century English Minister," Ph.D. diss., New York University, 1968; Steven G. Greiert, "The Earl of Halifax and British Colonial Policy: 1748–1756," Ph.D. diss., Duke University, 1976.

disappointing the views and checking the incroachments of the French, by interrupting part of the communication, from their lodgements upon the great lakes to the river Mississippi."[12] He shared this understanding with French statesmen, who feared the plan for the same reason.

The petition was approved. On 16 March 1749, George II ordered a grant to be issued by Virginia's governor Gooch. But the grant was to contain certain conditions of a nature to arouse a hornet's nest. Its provisions required the Company to plant a settlement of 100 families in the Ohio Valley within seven years, and to build a fort for their protection. As Lawrence Henry Gipson remarks, the settlement provision implied erection "not only of a fort . . . but of a town as well."[13] The Company labored to fulfill these conditions, but as Governor Gooch had foreseen, they did "give umbrage" to the French. And not only the French. The Indians of the Ohio region regarded the Appalachian mountain range as their barrier against further European encroachment; Pennsylvania's traders in the region wanted no new competition from Virginia; proprietary lord Thomas Penn believed that the Company's settlement would violate his chartered boundaries; and in Virginia itself, where the Company's projectors were regarded with something less than veneration, a new host of claimants to western lands clamored for grants before the Company should get all the best.[14] In the event, it is not strange that the Company failed ultimately to achieve its goal. What must be contemplated seriously, however, is that the heedless greed of these few headstrong men lit a fire in the wilderness that spread to become a conflagration throughout the world. That they lost money in the process is only a crowning irony.[15]

Competition from Pennsylvania

Coincidentally, developments elsewhere determined the government of Pennsylvania to hold a treaty in 1748 with the tribes of the Ohio region,

12. *Acts of the Privy Council* 4:57. For the board of trade's policies in the 1720s, see Jennings, *Ambiguous Iroquois Empire*, ch. 14.

13. Gipson, *British Empire* 4:229.

14. Nicholas B. Wainwright, *George Croghan: Wilderness Diplomat*, published for the Institute of Early American History and Culture (Chapel Hill: University of North Carolina Press, 1959), 23–4; Abernethy, *Western Lands*, 7.

15. The Virginia Partners never got back their investment, but John Hanbury may have. He was considered as "one of our Company" and required to contribute equally with the other partners to purchases of goods, but following the custom of the day he would have charged a commission on the purchases he made in behalf of the Company, and probably charged interest also when he bought on credit. *Mercer Papers*, 3, 140–41, 143, 149, 235. It seems likely that Hanbury also obtained a commission as the agent for purchasing and forwarding the crown's Indian presents. However, editor Mulkearn misread a pronoun reference and thus erred by sending him to Virginia to take up 130,000 acres for himself. He never left England, *Mercer Papers*, 526, 226.

at Logstown (near Ambridge, Pa.), and it invited the governments of Maryland and Virginia to contribute presents for the Indians. Maryland declined. Virginia offered £200, entrusting the money to Conrad Weiser, the veteran Pennsylvania interpreter to the Iroquois Indians. Virginia's Thomas Lee had been trying for years to woo Weiser to the service of the Ohio Company. In February 1748 Lee sent him a letter informing that Virginia was "extending our Frontier by large grants of land as farr as Ohio, and I am concerned in one, which when we begin to settle I shall hope for your help to make it agreeable to the Indians." Weiser never wavered from his attachment and service to the Penn family.[16] His whole purpose in journeying to Logstown was to attach the Indians there more firmly to Pennsylvania. Though his official report of the treaty mentions giving one of the five "heaps" of presents in Virginia's name, the Indians later denied having heard any mention of Virginia.[17]

For clarity of narrative, the details of this significant treaty are deferred to chapter 3 below, but we may note the reaction of Pennsylvania's provincial secretary Richard Peters. In his capacity as Thomas Penn's most reliable informant, Peters told his master privately that Weiser was "in Raptures about the Soil and Waters" west of the mountains. "Surely then you will give Orders that the Virginians or Marylanders be prevented from selling any Lands within this province. What measures ought to be taken for this purpose you will best judge of." Deferentially as always, Peters suggested that perhaps some "men of Weight and Authority, to counter ballance the great men of the other Colonies" might be "employed imediately in the Indian Trade."[18] He intended to include himself.

On reflection, Thomas Penn saw the possible utility of expanded trade in the familiar imperial strategy of clandestine struggle through proxies, and he advanced £500 with instructions to his deputy governor at Philadelphia "to give the greatest as well as the most speedy encouragement, to Trade you can, that we may not be long after the Ohio Company."[19]

Intrigue was everywhere. Richard Peters had specific information as

16. Paul A. W. Wallace, *Conrad Weiser, 1696–1760, Friend of Colonist and Mohawk* (Philadelphia: University of Pennsylvania Press, 1945), 260–62; Lee to Weiser, 14 May 1748, mss., Peters Papers 2:102, Historical Society of Pennsylvania, Philadelphia, Pa. (HSP).

17. Entry of 17 Sept. 1748, Weiser's mss. journal, "copied from the original by Hiester Muhlenberg," photostat at HSP; a slightly variant copy is printed in *Minutes of the Provincial Council of Pennsylvania* ed. Samuel Hazard, 16 vols. (Harrisburg and Philadelphia, 1838–53) 5:348–58 *(Pa. Council Minutes);* speech of "Half-King" Tanaghrisson at Logstown, 1 June 1752, in "The Treaty of Logg's Town, 1752: Commission, Instructions, &c., Journal of Virginia Commissioners, and Text of Treaty," *Va. Mag. of Hist. and Biog.* 13(1905–6): 170.

18. Peters to Penn, 24 Oct. 1748, in P. Wallace, *Weiser,* 269–70.

19. Wainwright, *George Croghan,* 23–26; Penn to Hamilton, 31 July 1749, quoted in *Mercer Papers,* 531. As of 30 May 1750, Penn hoped that "the Governor will take all prudent Methods to secure the Trade at Ohio . . . that if possible we may make Settlement there before the Virginians," quoted in Gipson, *British Empire* 4:236.

well as general logic to justify his confidence in the trade. He knew the double game being played by interpreter Conrad Weiser from whom Peters picked up most of his knowledge about Indian affairs. "Conrad," wrote Peters to Penn, "having the Conduct of the Virginians affairs . . . and having it likewise in charge from your Governor to propose another Purchase [of land] and to make it appear for the Interest of the Indians that there be some Pennsylvania Settlements in the Western parts of this Province, it cannot be thought but if he succeeds for one Colony he will for the other. And as we shall know the Minds of the Indians the first, it will be our own fault if we dont make a proper use of it. . . . after all, the Province that can furnish the best Presents and the cheapest Goods will in the End carry all before them.—At present our Traders from their superior Skill and knowledge will have greatly the advantage of the Virginians, and it will be some time before those new Traders can get into the Knowledge of the Trade and the Confidence of the Indians."[20] Weiser confirmed Peters's strategic analysis with the suggestion that a Pennsylvania settlement be made "Some where on the East Side of Alleginy Hill to which Hill a Wagon road may be made for the Easy Carriage of the goods [which] would farr outdo virginia. Several other advantages not to be mentioned here."[21] Against such experts the Ohio Company never achieved much success in the Indian trade although it made elaborate preparations.[22]

What appears very clearly from all this is that Virginia's initiative stirred up competition and accelerated Pennsylvania's rate of expansion westward into Indian territory. It is also evident that Pennsylvania's traders performed as desired by Peters and Weiser. Thomas Lee, newly promoted as president of the Virginia council, and acting in that capacity as the province's chief executive, protested against the traders' slanders that his Company's fort would be a "bridle" on the Indians, and that its roads would let in their enemies to "destroy" them. All the animadversions used by the French against the English generally were used by the Pennsylvania traders against the Virginians. Governor Hamilton in Philadelphia assured Lee virtuously that he would "endeavour by all possible methods to put an end to so vile a Practice," but at the moment, unfortunately, none of the traders was "in the City."[23]

So much activity could not escape the notice of the French in Canada.

20. Peters to Penn, mss., Penn Papers, Official Correspondence 6:107, HSP. This is misdated 1753, which events make impossible. Internal evidence dates it before the treaty purchase of 7 Aug. 1750.

21. Weiser to Peters, 8 Dec. 1749, mss., Correspondence of Conrad Weiser 1:19, HSP.

22. The Company did set up a storehouse at Wills Creek (Cumberland, Md.) and hired the veteran traders Thomas Cresap and Hugh Parker to operate it. Both were also partners in the Company. *Mercer Papers*, 507.

23. *Pa. Council Minutes* 5:422–25.

Clearly some sort of response would have to be made, but what? The French were not sure how far they wanted to go. Unlike the English colonies, Canada had been a perpetual drain on the crown's finances, and because of recent unrest among the tribes French Indian policy was confused and ineffectual. Supposing confrontation should provoke war, did the French government want that? It did not. But if nothing should be done, the Ohio Valley would fall to the English by default.[24] Lacking better alternatives, the French tried bluff. New France's commandant general, the marquis La Galissonière, sent an expedition down the Ohio River to lay formal claim to the surrounding region and reduce its recalcitrant Indians to obedience.

Céloron de Blainville

On 15 June 1749, Captain Céloron de Blainville set out from Montreal with a company of 213 men on a round trip of about 3,000 miles. At intervals he buried lead plates inscribed with the French claim to sovereignty. He made formal addresses en route to those Indians who did not run away from his party, demanding the ouster of English traders and threatening dire retribution for disobedience while discreetly avoiding the subject of French sovereignty. This was not the best way to win friends among Indian nations proud of their independence, and the sovereignty claim was embarrassingly disclosed when some Indians acquired one of the lead plates and had it read to them. Céloron precipitated at least one tense situation that required utmost vigilance to leave with his skin intact. In Logstown, where English traders were much in evidence, the Indians "gave the French to understand that the land was theirs and that while there were any Indians in those Parts they would trade with their Brothers the English."[25]

When Céloron arrived back in Montreal, 9 November 1749, his report was grim. He wrote that the Indians' personal interests made them favor the English, "who give them their merchandise at one-fourth the price." Possibly the French could win the Indians over "by furnishing them merchandise at the same price as the English," but "the difficulty is to find out the means." Céloron knew, as every Montreal merchant knew, that

24. Memoir of La Galissonière in *Documents Relative to the Colonial History of the State of New York [N.Y. Col. Docs.]*, eds. E. B. O'Callaghan and Berthold Fernow, 15 vols. (Albany, N.Y.: Weed, Parsons and Co., 1856–87), 10:222–24.

25. W. J. Eccles, "Céloron de Blainville, Pierre-Joseph," in *Dictionary of Canadian Biography*, eds. George W. Brown, et al. (Toronto: University of Toronto Press, 1966–), 3:100 *(Dict. Can. Biog.)*; Donald H. Kent, *The French Invasion of Western Pennsylvania, 1753* (Harrisburg: Pennsylvania Historical and Museum Commission, 1954), 6–10; Gipson, *British Empire* 4:191–202; *N.Y. Col. Docs.* 6:533.

the English had developed an industrial and commercial system capable of underselling the French almost everywhere.[26] He concluded despairingly, "All I can say is, that the nations of these localities are very badly disposed towards the French, and are entirely devoted to the English. I do not know in what way they could be brought back."[27]

La Galissonière's strategy

Lacking ability to compete with the British economically, the French turned to military means. By the time that Céloron returned to Montreal, Commandant La Galissonière had been recalled to France. There he strongly influenced official policy with a comprehensive memoir. Admitting that Canada had "always been a burthen to France," La Galissonière insisted that it was nevertheless "the strongest barrier that can be opposed to the ambition of the English," and he declaimed that "motives of honor, glory, and religion" forbade its "abandonment." From that premise he argued that "no means must be neglected to increase and strengthen Canada and Louisiana; to settle permanently the neighborhood of Fort St. Frédéric, and the posts of Niagara, Detroit, and the Illinois."[28] The French court accepted his premises and implemented his conclusions.

The mission of Christopher Gist

French prospects grew more grim as the Ohio Company forced the pace of British expansion. Thomas Lee pushed ahead. Disregarding legal formalities and French menaces, he and his partners sent out an agent to reconnoiter the promised land. Their man, Christopher Gist, set out 11 September 1750.[29] Luckily for Gist, they arranged also to make him an official envoy of the province of Virginia.[30] As provincial agent, Gist was

26. Massive smuggling trades existed between Montreal and Detroit on the French side, and Albany and Philadelphia on the British side, because the French merchants acquired great amounts of fur and peltry from western Indians and they needed British trade goods to exchange for the peltry. If French-made goods had been as plentiful and cheap as the British kind, French merchants would not have smuggled to British dealers. Cadwallader Colden, "A memorial concerning the fur trade," (10 Nov. 1724), *N.Y. Col. Docs.* 5:726–33; Yves Zoltvany, "New France and the West, 1701–1713," *Canadian Historical Review* 46:4 (Dec. 1965), 301–22; Francis Jennings, "Bisaillon (Bezellon, Bizaillon), Peter," in *Dict. Can. Biog.* 3:65–66.

27. Kent, *French Invasion*, 9–10.

28. Etienne Taillemite, "Barrin de La Galissonière, Roland-Michel, Marquis de La Galissonière," in *Dict. Can. Biog.* 3:26–32; Memoire, Dec. 1750, *N.Y. Col. Docs.* 10:220–32.

29. *Mercer Papers*, 7–8.

30. Lieutenant Governor Robert Dinwiddie was admitted to Company partnership, along with Capel Hanbury (John's merchant cousin who was also a member of Parliament), 27

paid £20 to invite the Ohio Indians to come to Virginia for a treaty. As Company agent, he was paid £150 to search and discover the territory. The relative importance of his official and private functions is plain. In the light of what he was later to tell the Indians, it is noteworthy that "he engaged to Settle 150 or more Families on the Company's Lands contiguous one to the other, within two years."[31]

Though he received such a relatively small cash reward for his official provincial business, Gist became grateful for the camouflage it gave him. At Logstown the Indians showed the same toughness to Gist that they had displayed to Céloron: "they began to suspect me, and said, I was come to settle the Indians' Land, and they knew I should never go Home again safe. I found this Discourse was like to be of ill Consequence to me." Gist promptly took refuge in his official status. He told the Indians he had a message "from the King, by Order of the President of Virginia . . . This made them all pretty easy (being afraid to interrupt the King's Message) and obtained me Quiet and Respect among them, otherwise I doubt not they would have contrived some Evil against me."[32]

It was not so easy to deceive Pennsylvania trader George Croghan, but Croghan played along and introduced Gist formally to the Indians. As desired, Croghan mentioned Virginia's "large Present of Goods" to be given at the forthcoming treaty. This went down well, and Gist traveled under Corghan's very effective protection for several months, observing carefully the "fine, rich level land, well timbered . . . well watered . . . and full of beautiful natural Meadows" which wanted "nothing but Cultivation to make it a most delightfull Country."[33] Not till after his return home did Gist learn that Croghan was being helpful in a special sort of way. Virginia had wanted the Indians to come south for their large present. There they would have been under no influence but Virginia's. But Croghan held a conference with the chiefs of the Six Nations, the Delawares, the Shawnees, and the Wyandots which resulted in a message to the governor of Virginia that "our Brothers of Pennsylvania have kindled a Council Fire *here* [at Logstown], and we expect you will send our Father's

Mar. 1750. Dinwiddie's commission as lieutenant governor was dated 4 July 1751, and he did not appear in Virginia to take office until November. The sequence suggests that Company influence, exerted through the Hanburys, secured Dinwiddie's appointment. He never deviated from supporting the Company's interests. His biographer remarks that "he had gained the friendship of John Hanbury" as well as of John Carteret (Earl Granville and president of the privy council) and of George Dunk (Earl Halifax and president of the board of trade). *Mercer Papers*, 5; Gipson, *British Empire* 2:16–17; John Richard Alden, *Robert Dinwiddie: Servant of the the Crown*, Williamsburg in America series 9 (Williamsburg, Va.: Colonial Williamsburg Foundation, 1973), 14.

31. *Mercer Papers*, 5.

32. Gist's journal, 25 Nov. 1750, *Mercer Papers*, 9–10. Also printed in *Christopher Gist's Journals*, ed. William M. Darlington (Cleveland: Arthur H. Clark Co., 1893).

33. *Mercer Papers*, 14, 17, 18.

Speeches to us *here*, for we long to hear what our great Father the King of Great Britain has to say to us his poor children."[34]

It could not be helped, but the Company could at least have its messages delivered by its own men. Gist was sent back in the winter of 1751–52 to tell the Ohio Indians that Logstown had been accepted as the site of their grand treaty. This was his official mission from the government. For the Company he was to continue his task of observing and mapping the land.[35]

Once more he encountered the deep Indian uneasiness about European intentions regarding the land. "While I was at Mohongaly in my Return Home an Indian who spoke good English, came to Me and said—That their Great Men the Beaver and Captain Oppamylucah (these are two chiefs of the Delawares) desired to know where the Indian's Land lay, for that the French claimed all the Land on one Side the River Ohio and the English on the other Side; . . . after some Consideration, 'My Friend,' said I, 'We are all the King's People and the different Colour of our Skins makes no Difference in the King's Subjects: You are his People as well as We, if you will take Land and pay the Kings Rights You will have the same Privileges as the White People have.' "[36]

It was the same message that William Penn had once proclaimed, but with the difference that Penn meant it. A messenger brought Gist the pleased comment of the chiefs "that I had answered Them very true for We were all one Kings People sure enough."[37] All made ready for the great treaty at Logstown.

Multiple parties and purposes

The Ohio Indians' good fortune was also their misfortune. Their land was too rich and beautiful, and too strategically located, for them to be left alone by powers stronger than themselves. Moral rationalizations and legal fictions aside, the Indians lived on land that British and French governments and people wanted for themselves, each empire regarding the other as its greatest obstacle. In the resultant melee each empire's agents tried to make Indians into instruments to serve imperial desires, and the Indians had become so dependent on European trade goods that they could not stand aloof from imperial conflict, try as they might. In one way or

34. *Pa. Council Minutes* 5:537.
35. Company instructions, 16 July 1751, *Mercer Papers*, 31–32, and editor's comment, 411.
36. Journal, 12 Mar. 1752, *Mercer Papers*, 39.
37. Loc. cit.

another they had to take sides. They did so in varied ways, for *the* Indians were many tribes, far from united and often discordant.

As the empires recruited Indians for imperial purposes, so the tribes chose sides for their own purposes and changed sides when that seemed advantageous. So long as Britain and France were locked in combat and British colonies competed against each other as well as against the French, the tribes could maneuver among them.

To reduce all these struggling parties and clashing motives to a simple contest of abstractions such as race or nationality simply will not do. There are indeed patterns in the variety, but the pieces must be identified before the patterns can be seen. They began to fit together during the treaty at Logstown.

Chapter 3 ❧ *LOGSTOWN*

The view of American history from the Native American side of the frontier offers a curiously reversed image of the rise and fall of nations. Commonly, historians of the United States describe the period 1607 to 1776 as the "colonial period." For most Indian tribes, this same stretch of years represents a period of relative independence and equality between red nations and white colonies.

Mary E. Young

"The Indians tell so many Stories and the Traders are so senseless and credulous, and hate one another so heartily, that no confidence can be placed any where."

Richard Peters, 5 July 1753

Chronology

1702–29.	Dispossessed Brandywine Delawares migrate to Susquehanna and Ohio valleys.
1724.	Most Tulpehocken Delawares migrate to Ohio Valley.
1727.	A Shawnee band migrates from the upper Delaware Valley to the Ohio country.
1736.	Alliance between Pennsylvania and the Iroquois grand council.
1737.	William Penn's sons dispossess the Delawares of the "forks of Delaware" by the Walking Purchase.
1740s.	Many Senecas and Cayugas migrate to southern shores of Lake Erie and become known as Mingos.
1742.	Onondaga chief Canasatego subdues the eastern Delawares and declares them "women" without land. They scatter, but a few remain in the east.
1744.	Irishman George Croghan establishes trading post at Mingo town of Cuyahoga. His enterprises multiply, and he becomes a political power among the Ohio Indians.
15 March 1744.	Britain and France declare war.
June 1747.	New York's William Johnson instigates a Mohawk raid against Montreal in defiance of Iroquois grand council's neutrality policy. The raiders are ambushed with great losses.
July 1748.	Shawnees and Twightwees (Miamis) ask for alliance at Lancaster, Pennsylvania. Admitted to Pennsylvania's Chain of Friendship.
ca. 1748.	Iroquois grand council appoints Tanaghrisson as "Half King" over the Ohio Indians and gives Scarouady supervision over the Shawnees.

11 August–29 September 1748.	Conrad Weiser journeys to the Ohio country to treat with all the region's Indians. He takes the Wyandots into Pennsylvania's Chain of Friendship (distinct from the more extensive Covenant Chain of the Iroquois grand council). Shawnees draw close to Delawares.
18 October 1748.	Peace between Britain and France at the treaty of Aix-la-Chapelle.
1 June 1749.	The Sulpician mission of La Présentation founded by Abbé François Piquet at Oswegatchie (Ogdensburg, N.Y.). It draws many Iroquois to the French.
15 June–9 November 1749.	Céloron de Blainville fails to restore French authority in the Ohio region.
1750.	French raid against recalcitrant Shawnees fails to subdue them.
1750–52.	Christopher Gist reconnoiters the Ohio region for Virginians.
28 May–21 June 1752.	Virginians treat with Ohio Indians at Logstown. Virginians get confirmation from Mingos of land grant made at Lancaster in 1744.
21 June 1752.	Led by Charles Langlade, a party of Chippewas, Potawatomis, and Ottawas fall upon the Twightwee town of Pickawillany, destroy Croghan's trading post, and ruin the Twightwee alliance with Pennsylvania.

*In the first half of the seventeenth century, Indian tribes pur-*sued their own goals and the colonials adapted to tribal purposes in order to advance their own. In Virginia and New England this situation changed after colonial conquest of neighboring tribes, so that by 1677 the tribes were required to adapt their own activities to the wishes of their stronger European neighbors. The peculiar situation of the "middle colonies" of New York and Pennsylvania delayed the changeover there: in New York because of a slow buildup of colonial population, in Pennsylvania because of Quaker aversion to militarism, and in both because of reliance on trade with the Indians to provide profitable exports to Europe.

Though delayed, the change did come in the middle colonies also, and it came also because of conquest; but the conquering power in this instance was New France, and the conquest was remotely indirect. The strongest Indians of the British "middle" were those allied in the Iroquois League. They achieved great renown and arrived at the pinnacle of their power after they destroyed the polities of Hurons, Neutrals, Petuns, and Eries in the Iroquoian Beaver Wars from 1649 to 1655; and thereafter they raided widely in all directions. But they were turned back by Potawatomis, Mississaugas, and Illinois in the west, by Mahicans, Abenakis, and Sokokis in the east, and by Susquehannocks in the south. Curiously, some of these tribes later turned to the Iroquois for refuge from colonial aggression. At the end of the seventeenth century the Iroquois were decisively beaten by French regular troops and a coalition of Indian allies of the French. After

1700 the Iroquois adapted their policies to the wishes of British colonials and within the limits set by the French. They continued to press toward their distinct goals, but they no longer could impose their own purposes on either their British allies or their French foes.

During the first half of the eighteenth century, the Iroquois turned to diplomacy to recover some of their former stature. Through covert and overt arrangements with New York's and Pennsylvania's governments, they created hospitable refuge for tribes broken in war with Virginia, Maryland, Connecticut, Massachusetts, and New Plymouth, and they negotiated incessantly with western tribes to win them from the French. Their successes were negated, however, by several developments beyond their control. Chief among these was French management of Indian affairs. From outposts at Michilimackinac, Detroit, Louisiana, and along the Mississippi, the French maintained a degree of control over their Indian allies that the Iroquois never could penetrate for long; and in strong counterthrusts the French set up mission towns that drained Iroquois strength by attracting significant numbers of members from the Five Nations. Even the Pennsylvania alliance failed the Iroquois. When large numbers of European immigrants came to Pennsylvania after 1720, they crowded the Indians so oppressively that the province's eastern valleys ceased to be a refuge for even the indigenous tribes. No crashing conquests followed, as in New England and the southern colonies, but most of Pennsylvania's Indians migrated over the Appalachian Mountains to the "Ohio country" that included the valley of the Allegheny tributary of the Ohio River. There the immigrant tribes became too strong for the Iroquois to manage by dictation.[1]

Whoever controlled the junction of the Monongahela and Allegheny rivers at the head of the Ohio River proper would be in position to control the entire Ohio Valley all the way to the Mississippi River. The resident Indians were therefore aggressively wooed by competing crowns and colonies for alliance; but because so many of them had migrated from the east under pressure of colonial population buildup, they were wary of European entanglements. What they wanted more than anything else was security of habitation, which they saw being threatened especially by the big populations of the British colonies; and they maneuvered frantically to avoid being crushed between the expanding powers.

1. For the foregoing see Francis Jennings, *The Invasion of America: Indians, Colonialism, and the Cant of Conquest*, published for the Institute of Early American History and Culture (Chapel Hill: University of North Carolina Press, 1975) reprinted (New York: W. W. Norton and Co., 1976); and idem, *The Ambiguous Iroquois Empire* (New York: W. W. Norton and Co., 1984). The early paragraphs of this chapter have been researched intensively for some of my previous studies. These are cited here to avoid repeating the heavy documentation.

"Ohio country" Indians

At some vaguely known time in the seventeenth century, the Iroquois Five Nations had driven indigenous Shawnee people away from the Ohio country,[2] depopulating a large territory comprising roughly the present state of Ohio and the region of transmontane Pennsylvania. For perhaps a century this land remained open as hunting territory for tribes around its periphery. In the second quarter of the eighteenth century, Indian immigrants converged upon this Ohio country from both east and west—the easterners because they had been dispossessed of their homelands, the westerners because they wanted to get closer to centers of trade. Coincidentally with the rising competition between Britain and France for sovereignty over the Ohio country, Indian population in the region increased significantly.

The easterners' vanguard came from Pennsylvania, but they were joined by many "Mingo" Iroquois from present-day New York. Hospitality for Indians had ceased to be consistent in Pennsylvania immediately after William Penn's final return to England in 1701. Thereafter, particular communities or bands were pushed back from certain places while other bands were welcomed in other places. The first to be pushed were the Brandywine Delawares, whose reserved territory was sold out from under them in a prolonged process lasting from 1702 to 1729. They scattered. Some can be traced to the Susquehanna Valley.[3]

They were soon disturbed again there, along with their hosts, despite the refuge offered at the Susquehanna for Indians fleeing from oppression in the southern colonies. Governor Sir William Keith was obliged to report in 1718 that "in Referrance to the Surveys of Lands . . . [the Indians] had Expressed a willingness to Retire from Conestogoe; Yet the Government here had perswaded them to continue near us."[4]

Provincial officials were caught in a dilemma. The regular substantial income from trade with Indian residents and immigrants had to be weighed against high instant profit from sale of Susquehanna lands to new immigrants from Europe. Also in the balance was the need to locate the increasingly numerous Europeans somewhere, and this need tilted the scale toward quick profit for land speculators. The Indians were pushed out gradually until only a handful were still left along the lower Susquehanna by the 1750s.

2. James H. Howard, *Shawnee!: The Ceremonialism of a Native Indian Tribe and Its Cultural Background* (Athens: Ohio University Press, 1981), pp. 1–7; Charles Callender, "Shawnee," in *Northeast*, p. 622, and map, 623.

3. Jennings, "Miquon's Passing: Indian-European Relations in Colonial Pennsylvania, 1674–1755," Ph.D. diss., University of Pennsylvania, 1965, pp. 109–290, passim.

4. *Pa. Council Minutes*, 16 June 1718, 3:48–9.

In 1724 a sudden influx of Palatine German immigrants prompted most of the Delawares of the Tulpehocken Valley (today's Lebanon Valley) to depart for the west.[5] In 1727 a band of Shawnees became dissatisfied with domination by the Iroquois Six Nations (abetted by the province), and they too headed westward; neither entreaties nor commands persuaded them to return.[6]

The Walking Purchase

After 1735 the proprietary Penn family began to sell off unceded Indian lands in the upper Delaware Valley, and to make these transactions seem legal they contrived the notorious Walking Purchase. As this was to become a powerful issue when it re-emerged in the 1750s, it requires a brief description. Including preliminaries and cover-up, it extended from 1734 to 1742. The Penn brothers needed to sell much land in order to escape their creditors, but they lacked assets with which to purchase Delaware land for resale. With James Logan and other associates, they falsely represented to the Delawares that an old, incomplete, unsigned draft of a deed was a legally binding contract. They exhibited to the unlettered Indians a falsely labeled representation of the lands supposed to be conveyed by the spurious deed. Vaguely, the deed stipulated that the ceded lands were to be bounded by a walk of a day and a half from a stipulated starting point, but did not specify the direction of the walk. The Penns hired a walker to go in the direction most favorable to their desires. He covered sixty-four miles in his day and a half, from the end of which the Penns drew a line, the direction of which was also unspecified in the "deed." Promptly thereafter the so-called deed disappeared, leaving only in its wake what the Penns called a copy. When the Delawares protested, James Logan arranged for a delegation from the Iroquois Six Nations in 1742 to menace and dispossess the Delawares with a fabricated claim of former conquest.[7]

The Penns' henchmen involved in the proceedings kept the secret well. All of them depended on proprietary favor, and some of them would lose valid title to property in the disputed territory if the fraud were disclosed. The Delawares understood how they had been swindled, but they had no recourse in law because an Indian could not bear testimony in colonial courts against an Englishman, much less against a proprietary lord. Some

5. Jennings, "Incident at Tulpehocken," *Pennsylvania History* 35:4 (Oct. 1968), 335–55, esp. pp. 338–40. Delaware community movements are traced in C. A. Weslager, *The Delaware Indian Westward Migration* (Wallingford, Pa.: Middle Atlantic Press, 1978), ch. 1.

6. Jennings, *Ambiguous Empire*, ch. 15.

7. Ibid., chs. 16, 17, app. B.

of the Delawares settled sullenly, as ordered by the Iroquois, along the Wyoming Valley (the north branch of the Susquehanna). Others joined their brethren on the Ohio region. All preserved a rankling resentment that became one of the motives for lifting the hatchet in 1755 and led to one of the most famous and most misunderstood political controversies in the colonial history of the United States.

That story will be told in part III below. Here we must notice that as Indians migrated westward, the merchants who had traded with them were obliged to reorganize their system of commerce. Formerly the trade had centered on posts on the Schuylkill, Delaware, and Susquehanna rivers, where Indians and traders brought furs and deerskins from the interior to exchange for the merchants' goods. Since the prosperity of these trading posts depended entirely on Indians living nearby, when the Indians went west, the traders had no option but to follow after them.[8] Seventeenth-century man-carried and canoe-borne traffic gave way to the eighteenth century's pack horses. Ethnicity changed also. The Indian and French go-betweens of earlier times were largely supplanted by men from Ireland and Scotland. At the Ohio the trade grew rapidly. Indians drew the traders, and the traders drew more Indians.[9] Numbers of Seneca and Cayuga tribesmen from the Iroquois League migrated there as individuals, concentrating around the village of Cuyahoga (on the site of present-day Cleveland). They became known as Mingos and acquired an identity distinct from their parent tribes.[10] This development alarmed the grand council of the Iroquois because it implied loss of control by the council over those distant Mingos, a process that aggravated the weakening caused by continuing loss from Iroquoia to French mission villages.[11]

The traders drew Indians from the west also; but that was not a simple

8. Jennings, "The Indian Trade of the Susquehanna Valley," *Proceedings of the American Philosophical Society* 110:6 (Dec. 1966), 406–24. Traders were venturing "above 300 miles back" as early as 1728. James Logan to John Askew, 4 Oct. 1728, mss., Logan Parchment Letter Book, HSP.

9. The most complete compilation is Charles A. Hanna, *The Wilderness Trail; or, The Ventures and Adventures of the Pennsylvania Traders on the Allegheny Path, With Some New Annals of the Old West, and the Records of Some Strong Men and Some Bad Ones*, 2 vols., (New York: G. P. Putnam's Sons, 1911). Chaotic in organization, and nastily racist, it is useful for its sheer mass of data and detailed index. Its topography has been updated and corrected by Paul A. W. Wallace, *Indian Paths of Pennsylvania* (Harrisburg: Pennsylvania Historical and Museum Commission, 1965). Wallace's book is a model of clarity.

10. William A. Hunter, "Mingos," in *Dict. Can. Biog.* 3:xxxvii; James Mooney, "Mingo," in *Handbook of American Indians North of Mexico*, ed. Frederick Webb Hodge, 2 vols. (Washington, D.C.: Government Printing Office, 1907), 1:867–68 (*Handbook*, ed. Hodge.)

11. For example, see Robert Lahaise, "Picquet, François," in *Dict. Can. Biog.* 4:636–37. A concise summary of French mission history is in J. H. Kennedy, *Jesuit and Savage in New France* (1950), reprinted (Hamden, Conn.: Archon Books, 1971), ch. 3. See also the editors' Introduction to Father Joseph François Lafitau, *Customs of the American Indians Compared with the Customs of Primitive Times*, ed. and trans. William N. Fenton and Elizabeth L. Moore, 2 vols., Publications of the Champlain Society 48–49 (Toronto, 1974, 1977), 1:xxxi–xxxii.

process of personal decision by individual Indians, because those western Twightwees and Wyandots had been allied to New France, and the French forbade secession. It was axiomatic in Indian affairs that commerce and politics were linked.[12] Trade could not be conducted in the absence of minimum diplomatic relations; and, as trade increased a nonaggression pact was likely to develop into full alliance. The French understood this perfectly. For them, the expansion of Pennsylvania's trade into the Ohio country meant more than loss of profit for French traders; it implied the seduction away from French alliance of the Indians needed to substantiate French claims to sovereignty in the west.

The traders also understood that commerce required political relationships. Hundreds of miles distant from officialdom, with the single objective of profit, they assumed powers to treat with the Indians independently of the wishes of governors and assemblies and without sense of responsibility for the consequences. As a group they became a distinct power in the frontier region; indeed, for a number of years they exerted more power, more effectively than colony or crown. Such a situation could not long be tolerated by either French or English authorities.

Among the traders an Irishman named George Croghan rose to leadership by force of personality and ability to command large resources. Croghan must have kissed the Blarney stone before he fled from Ireland's potato famine in 1741. So far as is known, he had little, if anything, more than his native wit when he arrived in Pennsylvania, but within two years he had learned the Indian trade well enough to become a large-scale operator—on credit, we may be sure.[13] Croghan had a devil's knack for wheedling large loans out of otherwise hardheaded businessmen on no security but his often violated promise of profit. He had the same sort of knack with Indians.

In the autumn of 1744, Croghan established a trading post at the Mingo town of Cuyahoga (Cleveland). Not only was this a direct challenge to the French, whose traders had frequented Cuyahoga from their headquarters at Detroit; it was done in time of war between Britain and France. At Cuyahoga Croghan enjoyed the political advantage of association with the Mingo Iroquois who, though distant from League headquarters at Onondaga, yet assumed a derivative authority over the other Ohio tribes; and with their apparent sponsorship he expanded his trade to the Delawares

12. Editor's Introduction to Peter Wraxall, *An Abridgment of the Indian Affairs Contained in Four Folio Volumes, Transacted in the Colony of New York, from the Year 1678 to the Year 1751*, ed. Charles Howard McIlwain (1915), reprinted (New York: Benjamin Blom, 1968), xl. *(Wraxall's Abridgment.)*

13. Croghan's most recent biography is Wainwright's *George Croghan: Wilderness Diplomat*. Hanna devoted two long chapters to Croghan in *Wilderness Trail* 2, chs. 1, 2. A creditable life, somewhat supplementary to Wainwright's, is Albert T. Volwiler, *George Croghan and the Westward Movement, 1741–1782* (Cleveland: Arthur H. Clark Co., 1926).

and Shawnees at Logstown (Ambridge, Pa.) who still maintained a tradition of friendship with the English. That was the least of his irritations to the French. Against their threats to put him out of business, he took the offensive by sending his employees almost to the gates of the western French headquarters at Detroit. Worse, he conspired with the Twightwees and Wyandots in a plot to involve all the western tribes in a general revolt.[14]

There was some foundation for French apprehensions. In November 1747 a delegation of Ohio warriors came to Philadelphia to ask for arms to fight the French. They were defying the Iroquois grand council as well as New France. "The old men at the Fire at Onondago," they said, were "unwilling to come into the War," so "the Young Indians, the Warriors, and Captains consulted together and resolved to take up the English Hatchet against the will of their old People, and to lay their old People aside as of no use but in time of Peace. This the Young Warriors have done—provoked to it by the repeated Applications of our Brethren the English."[15] It is an interesting speech. Quaker Pennsylvania had certainly not made any such "applications." Governor Clinton of New York was inviting Indians to war, but his reach did not extend to the Ohio country.[16] The "English" at the Ohio were Croghan and his traders, among whom he had become a "meer Idol." The warriors at Philadelphia were given presents—as to what kind, the minutes are a little vague—and sent home with a promise of more to come. Trusted Conrad Weiser, the provincial interpreter, volunteered to deliver the rest himself, old as he was.

The Covenant Chain

The political framework for these negotiations was the bisocietal confederation called the Covenant Chain—an interlinked set of alliances of British colonies and Indian tribes. In this confederation, New York and the Iroquois League acted as a sort of steering committee with New York supervising colonial negotiators while the Iroquois spoke in behalf of most of the tribes; but after an important treaty in 1736 Pennsylvania acquired a special status in the Chain. This new arrangement's designers, with the approval of Proprietary Thomas Penn, were the provincial secretary James Logan, interpreter Conrad Weiser, and the Oneida chief Shickellamy who had been delegated by the Iroquois League to supervise Pennsylvania's

14. Wainwright, *Croghan*, ch. 1.
15. *Pa. Council Minutes*, 13 Nov. 1747, 5:146–7.
16. George Clinton to William Johnson, Instructions, 26 Aug. 1746, in *The Papers of Sir William Johnson*, eds. James Sullivan, et al., 14 vols. (Albany: University of the State of New York, 1921–65), 1:60–61; P. Wallace, *Weiser*, p. 248.

Indians from a headquarters at Shamokin (Sunbury, Pa.) at the great forks of the Susquehanna River. These men contrived an alliance so strong that Pennsylvania recognized the Iroquois as exclusive spokesmen for all the province's allied Indians.[17] In fact, the alliance constituted a joint conquest of the indigenous Delaware Indians in 1742, who were then assigned the status of "women" excluded from treaty negotiations and denied the right to sell or bargain for their own land. These eastern Delawares were further denied the right, after their great chief Sassoonan / Olumapies died, to choose a successor by customary processes; and Shickellamy kept them under watch from his post at Shamokin.[18]

In 1747, Shickellamy died. By that time most of Pennsylvania's Indians had migrated to the Ohio country. The handful of Delaware and Shawnee villages remaining in the east were close enough to Iroquoia for direct supervision, so there seemed no pressing need for the Iroquois grand council to appoint a new resident agent at Shamokin.[19] Instead, the Ohio country very clearly had emerged as the center of urgent necessity, so the grand council concentrated its attention there. Shickellamy's watchdog functions were transferred to Logstown on the Ohio, and the grand council appointed two men to perform them, but the precise date of this action is not clear. As their general spokesman who was to be also the spokesman for all the Ohio Indians allied to the English, they named as "Half King" the Seneca chief Tanaghrisson, and as special supervisor of the Ohio Shawnees they named Scarouady, who was an Oneida living at the Ohio. These two chiefs first come to view in 1748.[20]

Scarouady had an especially ticklish task because the Shawnees were a fractious lot who took dictation from nobody. They had gone to the Ohio against the express "commands" of the Iroquois, had rejected orders to return to Pennsylvania, and had actually entered into treaty relations with New France.[21] Now they wanted to return to the English fold, most likely

17. The Chain is discussed at length in Jennings, *Ambiguous Iroquois Empire.*

18. Jennings, "The Delaware Interregnum," *Pa. Mag. of Hist. and Biog.* 89:2 (Apr. 1965), 174–98.

19. However, the fragmented eastern Delawares were still independent enough to reject an Iroquois League "invitation" to remove their villages still closer to Iroquoia "at the heads of Susquehana." Weiser to Thomas Lee, 5 July 1746, mss., Correspondence of Conrad Weiser 1:15, HSP.

20. William A. Hunter, "Tanaghrisson," in *Dict. Can. Biog.* 3:613–14. Scarouady (Monacatootha) lacks a biography. He appeared at Lancaster, July 1748, as spokesman for an Ohio delegation. *Pa. Council Minutes* 5:307. His function as Shawnees' supervisor is mentioned by William A. Hunter, "History of the Ohio Valley," in *Northeast*, p. 592. He has many entries in the index to Hanna, *Wilderness Trail*, and the index to the *Johnson Papers*, vol. 14.

21. Abstracts of dispatches from Beauharnois and Hocquart, 1 Oct. 1728 and 25 Oct. 1729, *N.Y. Col. Docs.* 9:1013–14, 1016. Beauharnois to the minister, 15 Oct. 1732, in *Wilderness Chronicles of Northwestern Pennsylvania*, eds. Sylvester K. Stevens and Donald H. Kent (Harrisburg: Pa. Historical and Museum Commission, 1941), 5–6. Treaty minutes, 1732, in ibid., pp. 6–11; especially interesting is a Seneca chief's speech in this French treaty that his

because of the trade, and Scarouady had the delicate job of presenting himself as an authority over people who really made their own decisions. This was simultaneously more necessary and more difficult because the Shawnees had negotiated a great prize for Pennsylvania's Chain of Friendship. They brought with them to Lancaster, in July 1748, delegates of the Twightwee (Miami) nation, who were the Shawnees' next neighbors to westward; and the Twightwees, too, wanted to forsake their French alliance to join the English.[22]

Miamis/Twightwees join the Chain

Alliance to the English meant alliance also to the Iroquois League. Regardless of how independently the Twightwees and Shawnees made their decisions, it was vital to Iroquois pretensions of superiority that the independence of those decisions should be masked behind their presentation to the English through an Iroquois spokesman; and this was done. As "intercessors," the Iroquois requested Pennsylvania to forgive the Shawnees and receive them once again into friendship along with those attractive Twightwees.[23]

The request mandated its answer. One might say rather that the certainty of the answer mandated the request. Pennsylvania's government had long desired those Shawnees, and no English statesman could disregard the chance to win an important tribe from the French. The provincial commissioners waxed eloquent—more so, indeed, than their subsequent performance would justify.

At the Intercession of our good Friends and Allies the Six Nations [of the Iroquois League] we have granted you a Council Road, whereby you have free access to any of His Majestie's Provinces; we admit you into our Friendship and Alliance, and, therefore, now call you Brethren, an appellation which we hold sacred, and in which is included everything that is dear. It obliges us to give you assistance on

nation welcomed the Shawnees on its land, "especially that which belonged to me rather than to all the Iroquois." He thus contradicted the "order" by the Onondaga council for the Shawnees to return to Pennsylvania. *Pa. Council Minutes*, 26 Aug. 1732, 3:442. See also Howard, *Shawnee!*, 8–11.

Ethnologists, and perhaps some lawyers also, will want to note the Seneca's distinction between tribally owned lands and League-owned lands. I would speculate that the latter had been acquired by joint conquest or diplomatic action.

22. Andrew Montour, as Iroquois spokesman, mentioned the Shawnee role casually while taking credit for the League, but the Twightwee message to the Shawnees was specific: "as *You* [Shawnees] are the next to Us of the Indians in their [the English] Alliance, we entreat *You* to signify this our Desire to the other Indians, and that You and they will open us a Council Road to the English Governments." (My italics.) *Pa. Council Minutes*, 20 July 1748, 5:308.

23. Ibid., p. 310.

all occasions, to exercise unfeigned affection towards you, to take you into our Bosoms, to use our Eyes and Ears and Hands as well for you as for ourselves. Nothing is put in competition by an Englishman with the Faith and Honour due to those whom our Gracious King pleases to take into his Protection, admit into his Chain of Friendship, and make them our Fellow Subjects. From that Moment they become our own Flesh and Blood, and what hurts them will equally hurt us. Do you on your parts look upon this Important Name of Brethren in the same Light; You must no more think of Onontio [the French governor] and his Children, all that sort of Relationship now ceases—His Majesty's Friends are your Friends, and his Majesty's Enemies are your Enemies. On these Conditions we accept your Calumet Pipe . . . [and] we present you with this Double Belt of Wampum as an Emblem of Union.[24]

Having obtained a map of the Twightwee country, the commissioners observed among themselves that the Twightwees and their allies lived in twenty towns with a thousand fighting men, "whereby it is Manifest that if these Indians and their Allies prove faithful to the English, the French will be deprived of the most convenient and nearest communication with their Forts on the Mississippi, the ready Road lying thro' their Nations, and that there will be nothing to interrupt an Intercourse between this Province and that great River."[25]

This was heady stuff, and it left no doubt of the need for Pennsylvania to send an official emissary to Logstown to confirm and solidify the province's ties with the Ohio Indians generally. The French recognized its importance also, but for the moment they were impotent. Pennsylvania seemed to have a clear path all the way to the Mississippi. The darkest cloud on its horizon was the stirring of the Ohio Company of Virginia; but the Company's agent among the Indians at this time was Conrad Weiser, and Weiser was loyal to Pennsylvania.

Iroquois loss of control

When Conrad Weiser arrived among the Ohio Indians in 1748, his typically careful first move was to find out what he was dealing with. It was a good example that we may follow with profit. The Indians counted their own peoples in response to Weiser's request and gave him bundles of sticks as tallies. (The British Exchequer was still using the same method early in the nineteenth century.)[26] The census counted only warriors and came out as follows. Iroquois Mingos: 163 Senecas, 74 Mohawks (27 of whom

24. 22 July 1748, ibid., 5:313.
25. Ibid., p. 315.
26. "Tally" in *Encyclopaedia Britannica*, 11th ed.

were "French" Mohawks), 35 Onondagas, 20 Cayugas, and 15 Oneidas, totaling 307. Other Iroquoian speakers: 100 Wyandots (merged Hurons and Petuns). Algonquian speakers: 165 Delawares, 162 Shawnees, 40 Mississaugas (Tisagechroanu), and 15 Mahicans, totaling 382. The 789 warriors implied a total population of somewhere between 2,367 and 3,945, probably tending toward the smaller figure as many of the warriors were young men whose families would have been small.[27]

By way of comparison, the nearest figures available for the Iroquois Six Nations at home in Iroquoia are those of 1736, which give 1,100 warriors, implying total population of 3,300 to 5,500; but these are somewhat deceptive because during the twelve years from 1736 to 1748 many of those Iroquois left their homeland to become Mingos. It seems likely that the total Ohio population in 1748, not counting more distant Twightwees, was roughly equivalent to the total contemporary Six Nations' population in Iroquoia. If the Twightwees were to be added to the Ohio total they would heavily overbalance the scales.[28]

This sort of information meant much to Weiser, who shared the general assumption that tribal power was to be reckoned in terms of numbers of warriors. Having assured himself that such power now resided at the Ohio, he ignored the Onondaga grand council and took the Wyandots into Pennsylvania's Chain of Friendship after consulting informally with the Mingo Senecas and Onondagas.[29] It was a clear derogation of the grand council's presumed authority. When something similar had been done by New York's

27. Weiser's journal in *Pa. Council Minutes*, 15 Oct. 1748, 5:351. The "French Mohawk" remark is in the mss. journal at HSP, a photostat of the copy of the original made by Hiester Muhlenberg in 1830.

28. This is the enumeration of Philippe-Thomas Chabert de Joncaire, a French agent adopted by, and living among, the Senecas. *The Documentary History of the State of New-York (Doc. Hist. N.Y.)*, comp. and ed. E. B. O'Callaghan, 4 vols. (Albany: Weed, Parsons and Co., 1849–51), 1:15–26, identification at 23n; Malcolm MacLeod, "Chabert de Joncaire," in *Dict. Can. Biog.* 3:101–2.

Bibliographic note: Joncaire's and Weiser's figures are the best I can do. There are many reasons for not taking them too literally, including much movement and migration characteristic of Indians at this time and place. I wonder, also, about how motives of the estimators may have caused adjustments to suit purposes. Weiser wrote a series of articles for Christopher Saur's German-language newspaper, 1746–49. His mss. at HSP, entitled "Description of the Indians: Iroquois and Delaware," gives the Delawares "in Pennsylvania and Ohio" a total of 200 warriors and lists the Shawnees also at 200. The Iroquois come out at a total of 1850, but with qualifiers like "about," "perhaps as many," "at home or not far from home." Indian Records Collection, Item 310, HSP. (I have used the English translation.) Consider that after all the battering of the Seven Years War, the Delawares show up with 600(!) warriors in Sir William Johnson's figures for 1763. *Doc. Hist. N.Y.* 1:28. It seems legitimate, however, to accept the figures that Weiser submitted to officialdom as the basis for determination of official policy. However much the figures lack precision, there can be no doubt that a population buildup was occurring at the Ohio; and events show clearly that the Iroquois, whatever their claims, were powerless to command the peoples there.

29. Weiser's journal in *Pa. Council Minutes*, 15 Oct. 1748, 5:353.

governor Fletcher with Shawnees in the seventeenth century, the Iroquois had thundered and lightened, and Fletcher had bowed to their demand that the Shawnees must be sent to the grand council for admission to the Chain.[30] Now, however, the grand council was silent. Weiser had correctly gauged the difference between ostensible power and the reality.

Weiser analyzed the population figures in detail also. He could see that the Delawares and Shawnees outnumbered the Mingo Iroquois, and he concluded that the form of Iroquois ascendancy over these related Algonquians could not be maintained against the substance of manpower. (Weiser did not believe in the myth that other Indians shivered cravenly in the presence of the Iroquois.) When he returned to Philadelphia he recommended that Pennsylvania should "persuade the 6 nation to take off the petticoat from the delewares and give them a Breech Cloath to wear."[31] What this meant in practice was recognition of the Delawares as formally capable of speaking for themselves in treaty negotiations, a status of equality with the Iroquois in Pennsylvania's diplomatic system, and one that would enhance Delaware prestige among all the other Ohio Indians. When Pennsylvania accepted Weiser's advice, the new policy became especially galling to the Iroquois because they had claimed control over the Shawnees since 1714, and in future the Shawnees would choose the Delawares as their spokesmen.[32]

But this was a secondary consideration. Weiser's new policy amounted to unilateral revocation of the agreement made by James Logan and Weiser in 1736 when they had offered to recognize the Iroquois as sole spokesmen for all the Indians in alliance with Pennsylvania. The "absolute authority" of the Iroquois over other Indians that Provincial Secretary James Logan pumped into his minutes was at an end. It had never existed except in those minutes as an instrument of Logan's policy. Now Logan's closest associate in the formulation of that policy found it no longer useful to the province and initiated its termination. Richard Peters expressed the reason succinctly: "The Old Six Nations lose their Influence every day and grow contemptible."[33]

It must not be thought that either the Iroquois League or the French

30. Jennings, *Ambiguous Empire*, ch. 10.

31. P. Wallace, *Conrad Weiser*, p. 271.

32. Jennings, *Ambiguous Empire*, chs. 13, 15. A hint of the future closeness between Shawnees and Delawares is in the Delawares' speech at Logstown on 15 Sept. 1748 that "after the Death of our Chief Man, Olomipies, our Grand Children the Shawnese came to our own Town to condole with us over the loss of our good King, your Brother, and they wiped off our Tears and comforted our Minds," and they gave a present to confirm sincerity. Weiser's journal in *Pa. Council Minutes*, 15 Oct. 1748, 5:354. The relationship became very plain, despite Scarouady's efforts to keep control, in the treaty conference at Winchester in 1753, discussed in ch. 4, below.

33. Penn Mss., Off. Corr. 5:59, HSP, quoted in P. Wallace, *Conrad Weiser*, p. 285.

were idle spectators. By 1748, when Weiser went to Logstown, the Anglo-French war had ended, so Weiser was saved from the embarrassment of trying to get arms for the Indians from the Pennsylvania assembly dominated by Quakers. If he did give weapons, he concealed the fact. But while the war continued, New York's governor George Clinton had not hesitated to arm Indians and urge them to combat. Clinton had tried to recruit Indians for an invasion of Canada, and his close political ally William Johnson succeeded in mounting a Mohawk raid against Montreal. Unfortunately for British prestige, Johnson's raiders sustained serious casualties and were repulsed by the French.[34] The other Iroquois nations, striving to maintain neutrality, negotiated French pardon instead of retaliation for the Mohawks,[35] which they achieved by acceding to French desires that will be discussed in context further on. What is relevant here is the evidence of Iroquois League loss of control over its constituent nations.

The League tried to maintain neutrality by a policy of balance. When the Mingo council at the Ohio, and William Johnson's Mohawks in the east, tilted toward the British, the League council at Onondaga compensated by moving closer to the French. Thus, when peripatetic Conrad Weiser undertook still another journey in 1750, this time to Onondaga, some Mohawk friends told him "of the bad circumstances with the Six Nations, and that the Onondagers, Cayugers, and Senecas were turned Frenchmen . . . and that the Mohawks themselves who had fought against the French with the loss of much blood received no thanks for their good service."[36] By 1750, "half of the Onondagers had actually begun to live" at the new French mission at Oswegatchie (Ogdensburg, N.Y.). (This mission, called La Présentation by the French, had been founded in 1748.)[37] Weiser found that the Onondaga chief Canasatego, who was Pennsylvania's warmest advocate, had died under suspect circumstances and had been buried contemptuously. Weiser inferred a political execution. Canasatego's successor as leading chief of the Iroquois was the Roman Catholic convert Tohaswuchdioony, also known as The Belt of Wampum.[38]

It is not surprising that by mid-century the loyalty of the Iroquois League had become a matter of great concern to British officials. By treaty with France, the Indians of the Six Iroquois Nations were "subjects" of Great

34. Rouillé to La Jonquière, 4 May 1749, in *Collections of the State Historical Society of Wisconsin* 18, ed. Reuben Gold Thwaites (Madison, 1908), 24; conference minutes, Albany, July 16, 1747, *N.Y. Col. Docs.* 6:383; C. J. Russ, "La Corne, Louis de," in *Dict. Can. Biog.* 3:331.

35. Rouillé to La Jonquière, 4 May 1749, in *Colls. of Wisconsin* 18:23–24.

36. *Pa. Council Minutes*, 11 Oct. 1750, 5:471.

37. Weiser, on authority of Philip Livingston and Wm. Johnson, *Pa. Council Minutes*, 11 Oct. 1750, 5:475; Gipson, *British Empire* 5:103.

38. *Pa. Council Minutes*, 5: 474, 480; P. Wallace, *Conrad Weiser*, 311, 314.

Britain, which formality the British maintained for leverage against France; but everyone knew, and the Iroquois stoutly maintained, that they were a free people under their own government that negotiated treaties independently with Britain or France for their own advantage. They professed neutrality between the empires, but the conditions of their culture denied control over individual warriors who often disregarded the grand council's policies. Since passive neutrality could not be enforced or maintained, the grand council substituted as an equivalent the policy of balancing, as we have seen.

French officials understood and took advantage of this policy, but it was unacceptable to the British. The Iroquois League's importance to them, and to the British crown, had always been as an offset to French influence over the western and northern Indians, and as a means of penetrating the French protectorate in the west. If the League would not function as desired, the English must either abandon their expansionist policies or turn to other tribal instruments of implementation. Drawing back could not be considered as either desirable or possible. The crown's controls over colonial expansionists were too weak to compel speculators and traders in Virginia, Pennsylvania, and New York to sit on their hands and leave the field to the French or each other. While the crown's ministers struggled with the problem, colonials improvised policies on the spot. As New York's alternative to the Indian League's balancing, William Johnson persuaded the Mohawks separately to champion British causes. For Pennsylvania and Virginia the alternatives were the Ohio tribes whose fire burned at Logstown where, not by coincidence, the Pennsylvania traders established a headquarters. The colonies maintained formal relations with the Iroquois League's grand council, but they ceased to recognize it as exclusive spokesman for other tribes. Means were adapted to circumstance, but the expansionist thrust continued.

New France on the defensive

French response was complicated by several factors, one of which was English domination at sea during the 1744–48 war. The French ministry watched movement of individual tribes and bands much more closely than did ministers of the British crown, and the French minister of marine was acutely aware of the importance of trade goods in Indian diplomacy. He was equally aware of the difficulty of supplying those goods. Minister Rouillé, comte de Joüy, understood that "the lack of goods" had caused Shawnee bands to drift beyond French influence, and he worried that one of those bands might "do something evil." It ought to be brought back closer to authority, he wrote, "but in order to bring it back, it must be placed in a position to have its needs supplied."[39] Since the Pennsylvania traders were already doing just that, New France's Shawnee problem remained acute.

Another handicap was the uncertainty of government in New France. The marquis de La Jonquière had been appointed governor-general in 1746, but the English captured him in a sea battle. So the marquis de La Galissonière was sent from France to fill in until La Jonquière should be exchanged at war's end.[40] La Galissonière found the western protectorate in extreme disarray, and his resources just as extremely limited. A band of Wyandots under chief Memeskia (Nicholas La Demoiselle) migrated from the French base at Detroit to Sandusky (Ohio) where they not only welcomed Pennsylvania traders but plotted with other tribes to overthrow the French regime entirely. Omnipresent French agents among the Indians foiled the plot, but trouble continued to simmer.[41] In 1749, as we have seen (chapter 2), La Galissonière sent Céloron de Blainville to warn the western Indians back into the fold, but Céloron's escort was altogether too small. (A larger one would have been too expensive.) Céloron had intended to pick up a contingent of warriors from Detroit to overawe the recalcitrant tribes, but when the Detroit Indians learned how few Frenchmen were accompanying Céloron they refused to participate.[42] What had been intended as a show of force became apparent as hollow bluster that amused the Indians instead of intimidating them.

When La Jonquière arrived in August 1749 to take over the government of New France, he was faced by the same uncertainty, the same lack of resource, and the same short tenure as La Galissonière. His motions continued, like his predecessor's, to be defensive. Historians Pease and Jenison, who compiled source materials on French policy, have written that "from 1748 to 1754 the rulers of Canada were striving to maintain a French ascendancy in which in their hearts they appear to have had no faith."[43] But La Jonquière dutifully did what he could. He built Fort Rouillé (Toronto) to try to intercept Indians from north of the Great Lakes taking goods to New York's Oswego on Lake Ontario's south shore. He reinforced Detroit. He suppressed a smuggling trade to Albany that centered

39. Rouillé to La Jonquière, 4 May 1749, in *Colls. of Wisconsin* 18: 21.

40. Étienne Taillemite, "Taffanel de La Jonquière, Jacques-Pierre de, Marquis de La Jonquière," in *Dict. Can. Biog.* 3:610.

41. Idem, "Barrin de La Galissonière, Roland-Michel, Marquis de La Galissonière," in *Dict. Can. Biog.* 3:27–28.

42. George F. G. Stanley, *New France: The Last Phase, 1744–1760*, Canadian Centenary Series (Toronto: McClelland and Stuart, 1968), p. 44.

43. *Illinois on the Eve of the Seven Years' War, 1747–1755*, eds. Theodore Calvin Pease and Ernestine Jenison, *Collections of the Illinois State Historical Library* 29, French Series 3 (Springfield, 1940), p. xi.

among the mission Caughnawagas ("French Mohawks") at Sault Saint-Louis.[44] But among the critically important Ohio Indians the French succeeded only in antagonizing Shawnees by a futile raid in 1750. Meantime La Jonquière's venal intendant François Bigot drained exorbitant profits from Canadians and Indians alike; his activities were not calculated to win friends among Indians being cheated. Bigot's biographers comment that "the military and naval situations, which he thoroughly understood, made him pessimistic and ultimately cynical, as well they might."[45]

Issues and motives

In sum, when commissioners of Virginia and the Ohio Company approached Logstown in May 1752, the tribes were in ferment, Pennsylvania's traders occupied the ground, the Ohio Company intended to seize and settle the territory, and the Canadian French were desperately on the defensive. Nor was this all. The Iroquois League was temporizing with New France while it had completely lost control in the west and was rapidly losing authority in the east. Virginia and Pennsylvania negotiated separately with the Ohio Indians without a by-your-leave from Onondaga. Only Yorkers and the crown continued to keep up the facade of Iroquois pretensions to ascendancy over other tribes, the reason for which will appear in the next chapter. To this muddle, add that the individual participants at Logstown intended to serve themselves at least as well as their masters. With that in the background, we are ready to consider what happened at the treaty.

The treaty was conducted in a welter of cross-purposes and intrigue that almost baffles comprehension; it seems to have had more conspiracies present than people. Virginia's governor Robert Dinwiddie sent three provincial commissioners, but, though he commissioned all of them, two had been chosen by independent powers in the provincial House of Burgesses; and they not only were not working in the Ohio Company's interest but were engaged in speculations competing with the Company's. Rather than depend on such doubtful characters, the Company sent its own agent with its own instructions.

At first the Virginians were seriously handicapped by lack of their own interpreter because Conrad Weiser declined their invitation to work for

44. Taillemite, "Taffanel de La Jonquière," in *Dict. Can. Biog.* 3:611.

45. J. F. Bosher and J.-C. Dubé, "Bigot, François, in *Dict. Can. Biog.* 4:63. They note: "the fraud of which Bigot was accused was not based upon mere forgery or a surreptitious misuse of funds; it was a system of private enterprise on a grand scale with the collaboration of most of the other colonial officials and many army officers and merchants . . . This sort of corruption was a part of the political culture in Bourbon France" (p. 65).

them.[46] To eliminate this defect they turned to Andrew Montour,[47] a synethnic descendant of Iroquois and French parents who was supposed to be working for Pennsylvania but who willingly accepted a large bribe from the Virginians to advance their interests. No official delegation from Pennsylvania was present—this was Virginia's treaty—but Governor James Hamilton sent a goodwill message that he entrusted to Montour who passed it on to George Croghan who delivered it in Pennsylvania's name and thus inveigled himself into the proceedings.[48] Croghan also had distinct personal objectives. Though he was obliged to refrain from visiting Philadelphia for fear of debtors' prison, he owned much real estate in Pennsylvania, and the Logstown treaty presented certain opportunities to improve his situation.

Despite so many competing motives, one purpose united all the colonial parties and their hangers-on: to get an Indian quitclaim to the Ohio lands. When this primary requirement had been secured, they could contest with each other for shares of the prize. Three major difficulties were foreseeable: (1) French claims to the land; (2) the Iroquois grand council's claims to the same land;[49] (3) the claim to the same land still by resident Delawares and Shawnees. French claims were ignored. The grand council's claim and that of the regional inhabitants had to be handled with more finesse.

The commissioners made their way to Logstown after loading £1,000 worth of presents from the king on board "four large Canoes lashed together.[50] They paused en route for ceremonial courtesies and a little propaganda at several Indian towns, and arrived at Logstown on the thirty-first of May 1752. It had been anticipated in Williamsburg that the commissioners might have hard going, so they were instructed to "use all con-

46. Weiser's reason for declining is a little mysterious. Several possibilities are in P. Wallace, *Weiser*, 335–36. An alternative was given by Chief Tanaghrisson during the Logstown treaty when he said that Weiser had never given presents from the king or Virginia. As Virginia had entrusted goods to him in 1748 to be given in the names of the king and that province, it appears that Weiser had double-crossed the Virginians for the advantage of Pennsylvania. Knowing that this would come to light in 1752, he stayed away. "The Treaty of Logg's Town, 1752: Commission, Instructions, &c., Journal of Virginia Commissioners, and Text of Treaty." *Va. Mag. of Hist. and Biog.* 13 (1905–6), 170.

47. Montour's mother was "Madame Montour," a highly colorful Canadian French woman who lived at ease among the Indians, but still was regarded by Pennsylvanians in her later years as French. Wm. A. Hunter, "Couc, Elizabeth?" in *Dict. Can. Biog.* 3:147. Andrew has a chapter of biography in Hanna, *Wilderness Trail* 1:ch. 8.

48. Governor James Hamilton's memorandum to Montour, 18 April 1752, in *Pa. Council Minutes*, 5:568; "The Treaty of Logg's Town, 1752," *Va. Mag. of Hist. and Biog.* 13 (1905–6), 158–59.

49. Weiser's journal of conference at Onondaga, Sept. 1750, in *Pa. Council Minutes*, 11 Oct. 1750, 5:478, 479. The grand council members "repeated over and over that the Indians on Ohio had no right to sell any Land about Pennsylvania, Maryland, Virginia, or Ohio."

50. "Treaty of Logg's Town," 154–58.

venient Opportunities to enlarge upon" the royal present and to begin singing its praise at the very beginning of the treaty council instead of waiting until the end as was customary. Having thus established a mellow mood among the Indians, "your next Business will be (as some Doubts have arisen about the Treaty of Lancaster [of 1744], and Surmises have been spread as if the six Nations thought themselves imposed upon by it) to have that Treaty explained, and his Majesty's Title to all the Lands express'd and intended by the said Treaty to be fully confirmed."[51]

On its face the instruction required an impossibility, as the "pen and ink work" at Lancaster had tricked the Iroquois into signing a conveyance of half the continent when they thought they were ceding no farther "to the Sun setting than the Hill on the other Side of the Allegany Hill."[52] Even with all those presents spread out before the Indians' yearning eyes, how could the commissioners convert the Ohio Indians to Virginia's own interpretation of the provisions of the deed signed by League chiefs at Lancaster? Some agility would be required.

George Croghan thrust himself into the commissioners' notice at once. On the day after their arrival he presented himself "by Direction of the Governor of Pennsylvania" (untrue) to say that the Indians "shou'd receive their Brethren of Virginia kindly" (Governor Hamilton's true sentiments).[53] Serious business still had to wait until the Iroquois "Half King" Tanaghrisson, "with a Sachim deputed by the Onondago Council, and others, came down the River with English Colours flying."[54] The presence of the Onondaga sachem makes it seem that the grand council, with reason, did not wholly trust Tanaghrisson. There was more delay while the Indians conferred privately.

When formal business began on the tenth of July, the Virginia commissioners carefully displayed the king's present "before the Door where they lodged, Arbours being made for the Council to sit round about."[55] Then, while the Indians eyed the treasure, the commissioners fueled "the Council Fire already kindled here, by our Brethren of Pennsylvania" and brightened the Chain of Friendship. After this brief introduction the commissioners proceeded briskly to explain the Lancaster deed as it had been written, and to declare the purpose of "the King, our Father" to make a settlement "on the South East Side of Ohio," and thus provide the Indians with goods "much Cheaper than can at this Time be afforded." The Indians should welcome the new settlers: "Brethren, be assur'd that the King, our Father, by purchasing your Lands, had never any Intention of *takeing*

51. Ibid., 147–48.
52. Ibid., 168.
53. Ibid., 158–59.
54. Ibid., 160.
55. Loc. cit.

them from you, but that we might live together as one People, and *keep them from the French*, who wou'd be bad Neighbours."[56] And so on to other matters that need not concern us here.

The speech created many problems for Tanaghrisson. Formally, his authority derived from the grand council, and the grand council's representative was on hand to safeguard its interests. However Tanaghrisson responded, he would have to permit ultimate decision to be made in Onondaga.

There was also a difficulty of geography. Tanaghrisson's Mingos lived in a region centered on Cuyahoga (Cleveland), but the lands intended by Virginia for new settlement were near the source of the Ohio River (Pittsburgh) and occupied by a mixture of Indian immigrants, mostly Delawares. These were hotly opposed to any intrusion by colonials. What Virginia wanted could be tolerated by the Mingos from their safe distance, but it was an instant threat to the Delawares who had already experienced dispossession in the east. They could not possibly be persuaded to agree to Virginia's proposal. Tanaghrisson saw great possibilities in those rich Virginians; but, like them, he too faced a task that was impossible on its face.

Recognition of Delaware treaty status

The presence and developing status of the Delawares added to Tanaghrisson's difficulties, as those Ohio Delawares, in distinction from their eastern brethren, had been recognized by Pennsylvania as having the right to speak for themselves in council without Iroquois intervention; and now Virginia's commissioners were also talking directly to the Delawares. Tanaghrisson decided to dispose of the intertribal problem before going on to questions of land. Knowing that the Iroquois could not maintain power *against* Pennsylvania or Virginia, he resorted to the politician's ancient device: "if you can't lick 'em, join 'em."

The Virginians had complained about some backwoods affrays. Tanaghrisson turned to the Delawares to "take the hatchet" from them, thus asserting ties with the greater power. "You belong to me [the Iroquois], and I think you are to be ruled by me, and I, *joining with your Brethren of Virginia*, order you to go to war no more."[57] It was neatly put. To defy that "order" could get the Delawares in trouble with Virginia. They remained quiet.

Next day, Tanaghrisson dealt with Pennsylvania's previous offer to rec-

56. Ibid., 160–61. Italics in source.
57. Ibid., 166.

ognize the Delawares. "Nephews," he said, from the outset using a term of condescension, "you receiv'd a Speech last Year from your Brother, the Governor of Pennsylvania, and from us [the Iroquois], desiring you to choose one of your wisest counsellors and present him to us, for a King. *As you have done it*, we let you know that it is our Right to give you a King." The Delawares did not care to quarrel about so abstract a "right" as long as they made their own choices. "We think proper," continued Tanaghrisson, "to give you Shingas for your King, whom you must look upon as your Chief, and with whom all publick Business must be transacted between you and your Brethren, the English." The minutes picture the event: "On which the half King put a laced Hat on the head of the Beaver, who stood Proxy for his Brother Shingas, and presented him also with a rich Jacket and a suit of English Colours, *which had been delivered to the Half King, by the Commissioners for that Purpose*."[58]

One must remember that until then the Iroquois had insisted that they alone should speak for the Delawares in business with the English. Now at Logstown, Tanaghrisson, in a manner much used by the Iroquois, had managed to abdicate the substance of control under pressure while maintaining its form for possible future reassertion. Chief Shingas, who now assumed the role of spokesman for the Delawares, did so by the choice of his own people rather than the imposition of overweening kingmakers, and he did so by proper hereditary right for he was of the lineage of the Delaware "royal family" and a nephew of the deceased paramount chief Sassoonan.[59] Shingas would soon prove irrefutably that he was far from being a lickspittle client of the Iroquois or of the English.

Tanaghrisson's artifice

At the moment, however, Shingas was present only by proxy for the purpose of investiture, and Tanaghrisson dominated the proceedings. He turned to Virginia's commissioners to deal with their huge demands. "We are willing to confirm any Thing our [Onondaga] Council has done in Regard to the Land." This could not be faulted by Onondaga's observing representative, and it seemed like an auspicious response to Virginia, but it really begged the question of just what the grand council at Onondaga thought they had done. Tanaghrisson pled ignorance of the facts "so that we can't give you a further Answer now."[60] Consternation among the Virginians. Their whole purpose was to get a "confirmation" *now*.

58. Ibid., 167. Italics added.
59. "Account of the Captivity of Hugh Gibson," in *Collections of the Massachusetts Historical Society*, 3d ser., 6 (1837), 142–43, 148.
60. "Treaty of Logg's Town, 168.

Worse, Tanaghrisson made demands of his own. While the treaty was in session, a French party had raided and demolished the Twightwee / Miami town of Pickawillany, and the Indians at Logstown were sure that "the French design nothing else but Mischief," so Virginia ought to build a "strong House, at the Fork of the Mohongalio [the junction of the Monongahela with the Allegheny], to keep such Goods, Powder, Lead and necessaries as shall be wanting, and as soon as you please."[61]

This put the Virginians in a quandary because the Ohio Company had already promised the crown to build such a fort, but was trying to wriggle out of doing so because of the expense.[62] Still, the cost might be worthwhile if a quid pro quo could be arranged. The commissioners held a private meeting with Tanaghrisson and asked if his expression about a strong house implied "a Settlement of People, as well as an House." Unhappily, "He answered in the Negative."[63] As the issue of fort building was to become hot in Pennsylvania as well as Virginia, it is well to note that what the Indians wanted was definitely *not* a huge military structure with garrison supported by outlying settlements. They wanted something on the order of what Croghan and other traders had already built in other places: a stockaded trading post and arsenal. This distinction must be carefully made because the word *fort* used indiscriminately has led to much confusion in our histories.

Up to this point, Tanaghrisson was representing his varied constituencies blamelessly, but he suddenly let drop a hint that he was personally amenable to persuasion. An unedited draft of the minutes of that private session with the Virginians adds his comment that "he always spoke the sentiments of others and not his own."[64] Perhaps more was said that did not get into even the unedited draft. The commissioners caught Tanaghrisson's hint and acted on it. They drew up "an Instrument of writing for confirming the Deed made at Lancaster, and containing a Promise that the Indians wou'd not molest our Settlements on the South East Side of Ohio," and they "desired Mr. Montour to confer with his Brethren, the other Sachems, in private, on the subject, to urge the Necessity of such a Settlement and the great Advantage it wou'd be to them, as to their Trade or their Security.

On which they retir'd for half an Hour, and then return'd, and Mr. Montour said they were satisfied in the Matter and were willing to sign and seal the Writing which was done."[65]

61. Loc. cit.

62. Dinwiddie's instructions, ibid., 148–49; Company minutes, 25 Sept. 1749, *Mercer Papers*, 171.

63. "Treaty of Logg's Town," 169.

64. Loc. cit.; *Mercer Papers*, 63. Other discrepancies between the draft and the official minutes suggest careful editing for purposes other than accuracy.

65. "Treaty of Logg's Town," 171–72; *Mercer Papers*, 63.

The boys in the back room

There can be little doubt of the arguments used during Montour's half-hour of private conversation with the other Iroquois chiefs. Sufficient illumination is provided by the Ohio Company's payment to him of thirty pistoles plus Virginia's grant of 80,000 acres. Conrad Weiser later learned that Montour aimed at having "a large piece of ground over the hills and a good Number of Setlers on it to pay Contribution to him."[66] I assume that Tanaghrisson was satisfied in one manner or another also.[67]

The "writing" signed by Iroquois chiefs after they emerged from their private meeting reversed everything said in public. In it they "do hereby signify our Consent and Confirmation" of the 1744 Lancaster deed "in as full and ample a Manner as if the same was here recited." Further, "We in Council . . . do give our consent" to "a Settlement or Settlements of British Subjects on the southern or eastern Parts of the River Ohio . . . and do further promise that the said Settlement or Settlements shall be unmolested by us, and that we will, as far as our power, assist and Protect the British Subjects there inhabiting."[68] The Virginians could hardly ask for more.

What had happened to make the Onondaga sachem and the Delawares compliant in this contradiction of their wishes? As to the Onondaga, the answer is in the public minutes. Tanaghrisson had said in open council that "we have not the full Power in our Hands here on Ohio" either to confirm the Lancaster deed or to approve settlement. Such matters would have to be referred to the grand council at Onondaga for final decision. So far as the Mingo chiefs were concerned, what they agreed to could be reversed later by higher authority.

But how did the conspirators manage to sell the ground out from under the Delawares while the Delawares were right there, looking on? The answer to that is, they were not right there when the "writing" was written or when the Iroquois chiefs discussed it in the back room. Private consultations "in the bushes" were common in treaty councils and would not have excited undue notice. When the Mingo chiefs came out from the back room with their paper, it is pretty clear that its contents were not read aloud before or after they signed it. (There are no Delaware signatures on this paper.)[69] When we remember that the Indians could not

66. *Mercer Papers*, 143, 290; Weiser to Peters, Feb. 1753, mss., Corr. of Weiser 1:17, HSP.

67. Colonial officials considered bribery of influential Indians to be essential in negotiations, but what they called bribery functioned differently among Indians and Europeans. For Europeans it was a process of amassing personal wealth. For Indians, however, it was a process of amassing personal prestige through what feudal times called largesse to their followers.

68. "Treaty of Logg's Town," 173–74.

69. The signatures are in the appendix to the facsimile "Case of the Ohio Company," p. 22, which is inserted in *Mercer Papers* between pages 326 and 391.

read, the discrepancy between what that paper actually said and what the Delawares seem to have thought it said is explained, though the official reports do not concern themselves with Delaware reactions.

Pennsylvanians would have been much interested in the outcome of this treaty because the settlements approved by it were in territory claimed by Pennsylvania charter right. Unlike the Delawares they could have read the "writing," of course, but they did not get a sight of Virginia's prize document, and it is clear from Montour's reports back to the Pennsylvania government that he was less than candid. Secretary Richard Peters wrote, "It is certain by Andrews Accounts that the Ohio Indians want the Virginians to build a Fort, but not to settle any Lands about the Fort, or to take away that Country from them: and that they have referred all to the Six Nations" [at Onondaga]. Peters was puzzled by the sequel. He could not understand why, "notwithstanding this Disposition of the Indians, the Virginians are attempting to settle the Mohongialo [Monongahela] Lands tho' against the Inclination of the Indians."[70]

It remains to clarify why George Croghan cooperated in these interesting proceedings when he could have gained much credit in Philadelphia by exposing them. Once more the explanation is land. Croghan had been sent by Pennsylvania to Logstown in 1749 to counter the effect of Céloron de Blainville's expedition. To support his other powers of persuasion he had been given a large present to convey to the Indians. With his customary legerdemain in handling valuables, he obtained from the Mingo chiefs Tanaghrisson, Scarouady, and Cosswantinicea a "grant" of 200,000 acres. They had no power to dispose of such lands claimed by the Onondaga council, and the purchase was illegal under Pennsylvania law because the land had not yet been ceded to the province. Besides which, it appears highly likely that Croghan had used part or all of the provincial present as his purchase price. He tucked the "grant" away quietly until it could be made usable. Its lands just happened to lie next to where the Ohio Company proposed to settle. After Virginia's "confirmation" in 1752, all that

70. Peters to Weiser, 6 Feb. 1753, mss., Corr. of Conrad Weiser 1:38; Peters to Honoured Sir, 7 Feb. 1753, mss., Penn Mss., Off. Corr., 4:7, both HSP. This is another example of how the vague phrase "the Indians" obscures the distinct and often clashing interests of different entities. "The Indians" of Peters's comment were those of the Onondaga Six Nations who, as Peters noticed, "took it very ill in the Virginia Government to treat with any Indians independent of and without first consulting them. They have . . . a notion that the Present was sent to them, in Consequence of Coll. Lee's promises at Lancaster [in 1744], and that the Virginians have taken it from them, and given it to the Ohio Indians." Peters to T. Penn, 3 May 1753, mss., Penn Mss., Off. Corr., 6:47, HSP.

On the other hand, the Mingos had complained in 1750 that the Onondaga councillors "sell Lands and give us no account of the Value; therefore we are sent by the Ohio Council to desire . . . that when any Lands shall be sold we may have part of the Value." These chiefs, who included Andrew Montour, asserted that they had "become a great Body, and desire to be taken notice of as such." Conference at Croghan's plantation, 7 June 1750, in *Pa. Council Minutes*, 31 July 1750, 5:438–39.

Croghan had to do was to sit tight and wait for the right moment to show his old "deed."[71] The fox had been quiet at Logstown, but not asleep.

Provincial alarm

The Logstown treaty added new impetus to British expansion westward, but it occurred at just the historical moment when French statesmen recovered from their indecision and launched strong countermeasures. These did not deter the British expansionists, but they alarmed all the Indians, who realized that they would be the first to suffer, and it aroused fears among colonials who stood appalled by the prospect of renewed war in which they could see no advantage for themselves. Especially in Pennsylvania, the Quaker-controlled assembly put up resistance on principle as well as a matter of interest, and the issue became yet another factor in a developing conflict over the prerogative of the proprietary Penn family. For various reasons the New York and Virginia assemblies also heightened their resistance to royal prerogative as it was exerted by their belligerent governors. From this time forward, the imperial expansionism of the crown would clash head-on with the local interests of all colonials except the great speculators in western lands. The pretensions of crown and proprietary prerogatives met with struggle from popularly elected assemblies trying to achieve power for themselves in opposition to prerogative. And the empires ground on inexorably toward war.

71. Wainwright, *George Croghan*, 28; Volwiler, *Croghan*, 254, 256–57, with map; indentures for sale of parts of tracts, mss., Etting Collection, Ohio Papers, 1:92; 2:7, HSP. With his usual dexterity, Croghan converted his grant from the Mingos into a grant by the Onondaga council; and in 1768, after they had ceded all territory south of the Ohio, the Onondaga council did him a favor by "confirming" his grant among the lands they had already ceded. Fort Stanwix treaty minutes, 1 Nov. 1768, *N.Y. Col. Docs.* 8:128.

Croghan's business partner and brother-in-law William Trent worked behind the scenes at Logstown in 1752. Virginia compensated him with a grant of 200,000 acres. *Mercer Papers*, 290.

Chapter 4 ☙ *THE ROUNDABOUT ROAD to GREAT MEADOWS*

Fathers, Both you and the English are white, we live in a Country between; therefore the Land belongs to neither one nor t'other: But the Great Being above allow'd it to be a Place of Residence for us; so Fathers, I desire you [French] to withdraw, as I have done our Brothers the English; for I will keep you at Arms length: I lay this down as a Trial for both, to see which will have the greatest Regard to it, and that Side we will stand by, and make equal Sharers with us.

Tanaghrisson to Captain Marin

Chronology

1 July 1752.	Marquis Duquesne lands at Quebec to be governor-general of New France.
1752–53.	Hardship among Ohio Indians.
1753.	French drive British traders out of Ohio region.
1 February 1753.	First French party leaves Montreal to fulfill Duquesne's plan for building a chain of forts to hold the British east of the Appalachian Mountains.
June 1753.	Iroquois matrons treat with Captain Marin at Presque Isle. They proclaim Iroquois neutrality. Marin builds a fort there.
July 1753.	Marin builds a fort at Rivière aux Boeufs (French Creek).
September 1753.	Tanaghrisson leads a delegation of Mingo warriors to Presque Isle to demand that the French turn back. Marin rejects. Shawnees welcome French, disclaim Tanaghrisson.
September 1753.	Scarouady leads a delegation of Delawares and Shawnees to ask Virginians at Winchester treaty for help against French. Much dissension among Indians.
September–October 1753.	Scarouady's party goes on to treat with Pennsylvanians at Carlisle. Croghan intrigues.
November–December 1753.	George Washington carries Virginia's ultimatum to Captain Legardeur de Saint-Pierre at Rivière aux Boeufs, who rejects it. On the way, Washington tries futilely to enlist a large escort of Ohio Indians, but only Tanaghrisson and three Mingos accompany him.

1753–54.	A very hard, punishing winter in the Ohio region.
January 1754.	Captain Trent starts to build Virginia's fort at the point where the Monongahela and Allegheny rivers join to make the Ohio. Ensign Ward is left in charge.
April 1754.	Ensign Ward surrenders to Captain Contrecoeur, who completes building Fort Duquesne.
28 May 1754.	Lieutenant Colonel Washington leads a party of Virginians and Mingos to attack a French party under Ensign Coulon de Jumonville, who is killed under circumstances called "assassination" by the French.
4 July 1754.	Washington surrenders encampment called Fort Necessity at Great Meadows after Tanaghrisson's Mingos desert in contempt of Washington's leadership. Captain Robert Stobo is given as hostage.
28–29 July 1754.	Captain Stobo smuggles plans of Fort Duquesne to Philadelphia through Delaware chiefs Shingas and Delaware George.

In the disputation between France and Britain, tribal allegiances were critical to their diplomatic negotiations in Europe as well as to military strength on the frontier. English colonies held charter claims to territories extending from the Atlantic to the Pacific, but had no settled communities west of the Appalachian range of mountains. In contrast, French trading posts, missions, and stockaded forts extended in a wide arc along the Great Lakes and down the Mississippi Valley to New Orleans. From these strong points the tiny French minority effectively administered vast territories and peoples in the time-proven strategy of castle domination inherited from the Middle Ages. (It should not be forgotten that most of William the Conqueror's castles in England were wooden palisades; the stone monsters came later.)[1] Eighteenth-century diplomats conceived that charter rights required the backing of more basic rights of discovery, possession, or conquest. Sir William Johnson was explicit, though private, on this matter: "in a political Sense our Claims . . . in several Colonies include lands we never saw, and over which we could not Exercise full Dominion with 10,000 of the best Troops in Europe, but these Claims are kept up by European powers to prevent the Encroachments or pretensions of each other."[2] Johnson did not interfere with British diplomacy by going public with this understanding, but the French were as sophisticated as he, and they enjoyed demonstrating their prior discovery and effective possession of the Mississippi basin. British diplomats could resort only to rights of conquest, which would have been absurd if they had claimed those rights by their own conquest. Patently, no such conquest could possibly have occurred. However, the diplomatic imagination

1. David C. Douglas, *William the Conqueror: The Norman Impact upon England* (Berkeley: University of California Press, 1964), 216.
2. Johnson to John Tabor Kempe, 7 Sept. 1765, *Johnson Papers* 11:925.

was equal to the challenge. The British crown asserted that extensive, if somewhat vague, conquests had been made by its subject members of the Iroquois League, and it took the high moral tone of protecting its subjects' rights. This, too, was an absurdity, as the French well knew, but the mysteries of tribal history were hidden from most Europeans, including most Englishmen, and a carefully devised propaganda campaign gave color of justification to claims of British sovereignty based on Iroquois conquests.[3]

To be effective, such propaganda required Iroquois cooperation. This was given, but equivocally. The League's chiefs were willing, in treaties with British officials, to announce themselves as subjects, just as they accepted much the same status *pro forma* under France by addressing Canada's governor as "father." For the Iroquois, such terms in negotiations with Europeans became merely part of the rituals. They were proudly independent and did not hesitate to say so, even in the same speeches in which they acknowledged they were subjects. But the British diplomats had acquired the potent word *subjects* to use as a sort of incantation; and the Iroquois collaborated in practical situations when their own interests coincided with those of the British.

Following their disastrous defeats in the wars of the seventeenth century, Iroquois collaboration manifested itself chiefly by constant efforts to penetrate the French protectorate so as to divert trade from Montreal to Albany. They calculated that tribes so diverted would come under their influence, and perhaps even pay tolls for passage through Iroquois territory; certainly no western tribesmen could pass through until satisfactory treaty terms had been arranged. For this purpose the Iroquois perpetually intrigued among the western tribes, and the French maintained a perpetual alert against them.

Intertribal rivalries guaranteed that the Iroquois would acquire the enemies of new friends as their own new enemies, and they made the strategic mistake of allying closely to the belligerent Fox nation which was detested by all its neighbors. In 1730 a French-instigated massacre eliminated the Foxes as an independent force. Some fled to the Iroquois, whom they joined in anti-French intrigues, but the major French base among the Potawatomis of present-day Michigan, Chicago, and Green Bay, Wisconsin, remained faithful as a stabilizing force throughout France's protectorate.[4] The Potawatomis would talk to the Iroquois, but they remained the Iroquois League's most formidable opponents in the west. This situation did not faze English diplomats. With the effrontery of their kind, they

3. See Jennings, *Ambiguous Iroquois Empire*, ch. 2.

4. R. David Edmunds, *The Potawatomis: Keepers of the Fire* (Norman: University of Oklahoma Press, 1978), ch. 2; report of Le Porc Epic, 15 Mar. 1750, in *Illinois on the Eve of the Seven Years' War*, 166.

insisted that the territories occupied by the Potawatomis belonged to the Iroquois "by right of conquest," and therefore came under the sovereignty of the king of Great Britain.

Pickawillany and sequels

Some western tribes flirted occasionally with the Iroquois, but they were always quickly disciplined by French frontier commanders with the help of loyal allies. The unrest created by intrusion of Pennsylvania's traders in the 1740s appeared on a larger scale than formerly, but it was not unprecedented, and the means for dealing with it were well understood. While high officials waffled in uncertainty about intertribal and international repercussions, a Frenchman on the scene took action. Thus it came about that the Twightwees/Miamis treating with the British at Logstown heard in the midst of negotiations that their capital had been attacked and destroyed. On 21 June 1752, Pickawillany was struck by a large party of Ottawas, Chippewas, and some Potawatomis led by the synethnic French Indian agent Charles Langlade. They killed the chief Memeskia (known to the English as Old-Briton and to the French as La Demoiselle) and feasted ritually on his corpse to transfer his "power" to themselves. They also killed a British trader and took others prisoner back to Detroit.[5] In response the British did nothing, so the raid was wholly successful. Most Miamis returned to the French fold, other tribes abandoned all thought of revolt, and British traders abandoned the territory. What Céloron's expedition had failed to accomplish was achieved by Langlade's force. The Ohio Valley became again reliably French.[6] Among other consequences, British diplomats could no longer support sovereignty claims with either occupation by traders or treaty alliance with resident tribes. In the absence of these supports, their dependence on the myth of previous Iroquois conquests became total.

More immediately important was a different kind of dependence. As French policy firmed up, French-led raiding parties harried British traders into precipitate retreat back over the mountains, and the effect on the

5. Gipson, *British Empire* 4:219–23; Paul Trap, "Mouet de Langlade, Charles-Michel," in *Dict. Can. Biog.* 4:563; James A. Clifton, *The Prairie People: Continuity and Change in Potawatomi Indian Culture, 1665–1965* (Lawrence: Regents Press of Kansas, 1977), 96. The fullest description of Pickawillany's importance and the details of its destruction are in Hanna, *Wilderness Trail* 2:ch. 8. Maddeningly without citation, Hanna quotes Duquesne's letter of 25 Oct. 1752 with its praise of Langlade as having "much bravery, much influence on the minds of the savages, and much zeal when ordered to act," but it deprecatingly observes that he had "married a squaw" so Duquesne would "limit my demands on you, My Lord, to an annual pension of 200 francs, with which he will be exceedingly flattered." Ibid. 2:290.

6. Edmunds, *Potawatomis*, 47.

resident Indians was traumatic.[7] However much they might assert political independence, they had long since departed from the aboriginal culture that provided full independent subsistence. Enmeshed in the market economy of intersocietal trade, these Indians had lost the ability to live without the equipment and goods supplied through trade. Their independence had become a mere formality—a facade for dependent clientism so complete that whatever power supplied their trade goods dictated their politics. Hedges and qualifications must be allowed. If another source of supply appeared to become possible, the tribes might take the initiative to make it feasible; and their suppliers could never dare to push them to the point of desperation. French statesmen understood both the means and the limits of control, and were careful to observe the limits. When British traders were forced out of the Ohio country, French traders moved in and the Ohio tribes accommodated to their presence. Some did so reluctantly, but they were more reluctant to adopt any of the available alternatives of starvation, migration, or repeated long journeys eastward to trade at British colonial bases.

These were the options permitted by explicit and determined French policy.[8] Though Charles Langlade had attacked Pickawillany in ignorance of a new policy, the French crown had already resolved to put an end to British infiltration of the west. On 1 July 1752 a new governor-general landed at Quebec with strong instructions. Ange Duquesne de Menneville, Marquis Duquesne, took charge of the colony with firm intentions to restore French sovereignty in the Ohio valley.[9] It was by his order that France's protectorate was swept clean of British traders, and he had a clear directive to ignore Iroquois claims.

Minister Rouillé explained clearly:

> The river Ohio and the rivers which fall into it unquestionably belong to France. It was discovered by M. de la Salle; since then we have always had trading posts there, and our possession of it has been all the more continuous since it is the most used communication between Canada and Louisiana. It is only for a few years past that the English have undertaken to trade there; and today they wish to exclude us from it.
>
> However, up to now they have not claimed that these rivers belong to them. Their claim is that the Iroquois are lords over them and that being sovereign of those Indians, they can exercise these rights. But it is certain that the Iroquois have no claim there and that moreover this pretended sovereignty of the English over them is a myth . . .

7. Wainwright, *Croghan*, 50–52.
8. Rouillé to Duquesne, 15 May 1752, in *Illinois on the Eve*, 633; Marin's speech quoted in Kent, *French Invasion*, 50.
9. Pierre-L. Côté, "Duquesne de Menneville, Ange, Marquis Duquesne," in *Dict. Can. Biog.* 4:256.

However, it is of the greatest importance to check the progress of the claims and enterprises of the English on that side. Were they to succeed there, they would cut the communication of the two colonies of Canada and Louisiana.[10]

It is obvious today that the French "right of discovery" was as flimsy as the British "right" of vicarious conquest through the agency of the Iroquois. The Ohio and its inhabitants had been discovered by Indians long before either Frenchmen or Englishmen arrived in America, and the Iroquois had been chased out of the lower Ohio Valley though they maintained presence at the river's Allegheny headwaters. But "rights" were the cards played with by diplomats when they lacked secure possessions, and these diplomatic fictions haunt our histories.

Duquesne planned to stabilize French control by building and garrisoning a new line of forts whose functions would differ somewhat from the palisades in the remote wilderness. The new forts would be as useful as the older ones for regional administration of Indian affairs, but they would act primarily to guard the lifeline between Montreal and New Orleans, and most significantly to restrain British expansion within a frontier cordon. It was Duquesne's intention to keep British settlement and activity east of the Appalachian range, which was understood in Paris to be the proper boundary between New France and the British colonies. He did not delay. Within months after arriving in Quebec, Duquesne organized an expeditionary force, huge for the time and place, to fortify the French side of the boundary. Unlike Céloron's expedition, this one was to be manned almost exclusively by Canadians as the Indians were no longer trusted for such business. But the Indians had been cheaper. Duquesne's expedition was so large and expensive that it seriously strained Canada's resources and aroused much local resentment. Even the minister in France whose broad purpose was being served by Duquesne expressed some concern at the cost, but he did not forbid the enterprise; and Duquesne forged ahead in a rigid determination that brought all simmering issues to a boil.[11]

Perhaps, after all, there is reason for preferring the myths invented by diplomats to the dreadful realities created by militarists. While Duquesne cranked up his machinery, British and French diplomats had been seriously discussing compromises that might maintain peace between the empires. In these discussions, the expedient of a demilitarized buffer region between the empires became so prominent that eventually maps were exchanged with variant proposals for bounding such a region;[12] but Duquesne's line of forts invalidated all the comfortable discussions in the

10. *Illinois on the Eve*, ed. Pease, 631. Cf. Pennsylvanians' agreement about cutting communication. *Pa. Council Minutes* 5:315.

11. *Dict. Can. Biog.* 4:256.

12. The maps are reproduced in *Ill. State. Hist. Colls.* 27, between 150–51 and 190–91.

luxury of European palaces. The same forts, however, stirred up frantic and highly uncomfortable efforts at diplomacy on the frontier.

Iroquois east and west

As the vanguard of Duquesne's expedition assembled at Fort Niagara, it attracted the wary attention of the Iroquois who were usually employed there to portage goods past the falls. To clarify his purpose, Duquesne ordered the fort's commandant to hand them a wampum belt with the message that "I am going to settle on the Belle Rivière as on land that belongs to me without question."[13] Inasmuch as the Iroquois had been claiming since 1701 that the said lands belonged to them by conquest, also without question, and with vociferous English backing, there seem to have been more questions about that ownership than either side would concede. At the moment, however—it was April 1753—the Iroquois were not disposed to challenge New France's mobilized force. For them it was tremendous. At 2,200 men with cannon and equipment, it was of a size wholly unprecedented in that part of the world.[14] In June, after counciling in Onondaga, the Iroquois cautiously sought further clarification. Were the French marching "with hatchets uplifted, or to establish tranquillity?" Lending added significance, the question was asked by a delegation of Iroquois matrons rather than chiefs or warriors. Captain Marin, the expedition's commander, could assume confidently that the Iroquois would let him alone if he let them alone. He blustered with arrogance appropriate to his power and pretensions; but, stripped of its pomposity, his message was that the Iroquois were not his objective. Rather relieved, the Onondagas decided not to "meddle."[15] Perhaps the League elders may be forgiven for temporarily setting aside their frequently asserted responsibility for supervision and protection of the Ohio Indians.

The Delawares of Venango (called "Rivière aux Boeufs" by the French and now marked "French Creek" on maps) inquired about the expedition's purpose, but made no attempt to obstruct it.[16] Life had been hard for them in the winter of 1752–53, and the expedition's need for labor to transport its massive baggage offered rare opportunity to make a living. Donald H. Kent's comment stands in startling contrast to the rhetoric of savagery.

13. Kent, *French Invasion*, 44.

14. Ibid., 18.

15. Duquesne to the minister (20 Aug. 1753), in *Wilderness Chronicles of Northwestern Pennsylvania*, eds. Sylvester K. Stevens and Donald H. Kent (Harrisburg: Pennsylvania Historical Commission, 1941), 50–51.

16. William A. Hunter, *Forts on the Pennsylvania Frontier, 1753–1758* (Harrisburg: Pennsylvania Historical and Museum Commission, 1960), 66.

Many of the Indians thought only of making what profit they could from the expedition, coming to get presents in their accustomed manner. Many of them earned trade goods, food, and ammunition by carrying on the portages or by hiring out their horses. They sold the Frenchmen corn, and went hunting to get them fresh meat. The Niagara portage had long been a regular source of income to the Indians of that locality, and now the Presque Isle portage offered another golden opportunity to the Belle Rivière Indians, who came from Venango and from far down the Allegheny in search of work.[17]

At first all went well. A fort was built at Presque Isle (Erie, Pa.) and another at the headwaters of the Allegheny's tributary Rivière aux Boeufs / Venango / French Creek. Scarouady led a delegation of Delawares, Shawnees, and Mingo Senecas to the expedition's first new fort at Presque Isle; but Duquesne heard that, far from hindering progress, "they are very zealously assisting with their horses that they have brought along with them."[18] At Fort LeBoeuf (Waterford, Pa.), however, the advance bogged down and troubles mounted. Supplies were found to be short-weighted—an obvious indication of profiteering at the rear where Intendant Bigot was notorious for such venality.[19] Sickness broke out. Drought so lowered the waterways that passage downstream became impossible, while at the same time the route chosen for portage from Presque Isle to LeBoeuf churned into muck under the weight of men and horses. Morale plummeted, and Captain Marin proved under pressure to be as inept as he was bombastic.[20]

Meanwhile a strong contradiction appeared between the policies of the chiefs of the Iroquois League and those of the Ohio Mingos. Without overt sanction from the carefully quiescent Iroquois League chiefs, a delegation of Mingo warriors led by Tanaghrisson came to Fort Presque Isle early in September; and added one more party to the list of those claiming to own the Ohio Valley. "The river where we are," said Tanaghrisson, "belongs to us warriors. The chiefs who look after affairs [i.e., the Onondaga council] are not its masters." He forbade farther advance. "With this belt we detain you and ask you to have them cease setting up the establishments you want to make. All the tribes have always called upon us not to allow it. . . . I shall strike at whoever does not listen to us. . . . We ask you only to send there what we need, but not to build any forts there."

17. Kent, *French Invasion*, 46. Like firearms, horses did not exist in aboriginal America, but Indians had become adept with both. Usually, however, eastern Indians moved on foot or by canoe.

18. Hunter, *Forts*, 66–67.

19. Kent, *French Invasion*, 34–36; W. J. Eccles, *The Canadian Frontier, 1534–1760*, Histories of the American Frontier series (New York: Holt, Rinehart and Winston, 1969), 162. An especially illuminating article is J. F. Bosher and J.-C. Dubé, "Bigot, François," in *Dict. Can. Biog.* 4:59–70.

20. Kent, *French Invasion*, 36–40.

Marin ridiculed them. They were "like people who have lost their minds." Unyieldingly he asserted that the Ohio Valley "belongs incontestably to the King." As we shall see, Marin and the British general Braddock were stamped from the same mold—or, better, carved from the same block. "I despise all the stupid things you said," Marin continued, "I shall continue on my way, and if there are any persons bold enough to set up barriers to hinder my march, I shall knock them over so vigorously that they may crush those who made them." Tanaghrisson and his Mingos withdrew.[21]

Tanaghrisson had put up a front so bold as to be in reality a bluff. The tribes for whom he professed to speak were far from being unified under his leadership. On the very next day after Tanaghrisson's speech, Captain Marin was delighted to receive a delegation of Shawnees who repudiated Tanaghrisson's declaration. "We shall be as glad to see you in our village as you seem to be to hear us speak," they said. Donald H. Kent remarks shrewdly that they may have hoped to use the French to get rid of Iroquois domination. That seems likely. It would not have been the first time that Shawnees had resorted to French protection for the same purpose.[22]

Winchester and Carlisle

Tanaghrisson was not so naive as to think that he could turn back the French with words only. He confronted Captain Marin in order to fulfill the Iroquois ritual that required three warnings before the opening of formal war.[23] To provide substance for the gesture he had sent another delegation in a different direction. His partner Scarouady led ninety-eight assorted Ohio Indians eastward to Virginia and Pennsylvania to solicit help. They came first to Winchester where they began meeting with Virginia's commissioner and a bevy of gentlemen on Tuesday, 11 September, slightly more than a week after Marin rebuffed Tanaghrisson.[24] To my knowledge the minutes of this important conference have never been published, nor its transactions adequately reported. Some attention must be given to it here.

Composition as well as size lent importance to Scarouady's party. Besides Mingos it included chiefs of the Shawnees, Wyandots, and Twightwees, and four brothers of the "royal family" of the Delawares: "king" Shingas,

21. Ibid., 46–50.

22. Ibid., 51.

23. Ibid., 50; Arthur C. Parker, *The Constitution of the Five Nations, or The Iroquois Book of the Great Law* (1916), article 88, reprinted in *Parker on the Iroquois*, ed. William N. Fenton (Syracuse, N.Y.: Syracuse University Press, 1968), separately paged, p. 54. Fenton's introduction is mandatory reading.

24. P.R.O., C.O.5 / 1328, f. 22v. I have worked with a photocopy.

Beaver (Tamaqua), Pisquetomen, and Delaware George (Nenatchehan).[25] Pisquetomen was already well known in Pennsylvania, where colonial authorities had connived with the Iroquois to prevent his accession to paramount chieftainship of the eastern Delawares.[26] All four brothers soon became prominent in the making of war and peace.

The same mixed party treated first with Virginians at Winchester, then went on to treat with Pennsylvanians at Carlisle, and became involved at both places in the same sort of intrigue and manipulation that had occurred at Logstown. Mingo chief Scarouady, in a ruthless effort to maintain his leadership, dealt behind doors and behind the backs of resentful Delawares and Shawnees. Though the Delawares had won the right to speak for themselves, it was as yet only a formality for public meetings. As at Logstown, the issues of substance were settled privately without their participation.

To make sense of the backroom shenanigans it is necessary to compare the treaty documents of the Winchester and Carlisle meetings almost as if they were one event. The disposition of issues was what counted, rather than sequence of incident, so issues will be taken up in order.

Commissioner William Fairfax blundered at Winchester with what he intended as encouragement to resist the French. He recalled a message from the Six Nations council at Onondaga, "that They were now determin'd to secure *their* Lands on the Ohio, that Their Warriors were now to take those Lands under their imediate Care, and were resolv'd that if the French did not leave the Ohio: They had Orders to make War on them."[27]

Scarouady retorted sharply: "Brother, I let you know that our Kings [at Onondaga] have nothing to do with *Our* Lands; for We, the Warriors, fought for the Lands, and so the Right belongs to Us, and we will take Care of them."[28] Embarrassed Fairfax had to report afterwards that "the Indians did not positively, in Answer to my Speeches, give a Concession to the Lands on Ohio, agreeable to the Grant given last Year [at Logstown] . . . They were apprehensive His Majesty had given His Grant to several of His Subjects." Then a touch of discretion: "I did not Care to touch upon that Subject."[29] So the Logstown "writing" remained a secret. Per-

25. "Account of the Captivity of Hugh Gibson," in *Collections of the Massachusetts Historical Society*, 3d ser., 6(1837), 141–53. The royal family phrase is at p. 142.

26. Jennings, "The Delaware Interregnum," *Pa. Mag. of Hist. and Biog.* 89:2(April 1965), 174–98.

27. C.O.5 / 1328, f. 23r. Italics added.

28. PRO. CO5 / 1328, f. 24r.

29. Fairfax's memorandum, ibid., f. 31v. Samuel Wharton interpreted it later as follows: "On the back of the journal of this treaty is inserted a memorandum signed by Mr. Commissioner Fairfax, to this effect: That he did not dare to mention the affair of the lands over the Great Mountain, or the Lancaster deed, as the Indians were in a very bad humour on account of that transaction." [Samuel Wharton], *Plain Facts: Being An Examination into the Rights of the Indian Nations Of America, to their respective Countries; and a Vindication of the Grant,*

haps even Scarouady was ignorant of its contents; he had not signed it at Logstown.[30]

The Indians wanted arms. The colonials wanted to build forts. Their desires did not coincide, though Commissioner Fairfax tried to give that impression. He promised to build "a strong house at the Mouth of Mongahela [Pittsburgh] where a Quantity of Powder, Lead, et cetera, might be lodged;" in short, a blockhouse arsenal, fully supplied, where Indian women and children could be given protection. Scarouady forbade it publicly: "You told Us, You wou'd build a Strong House at the Forks [of Ohio] after bidding us take Care of Our Lands; We now request You may not build that Strong-House, for we intend to keep Our Country clear of Settlements during these troublesome Times."[31]

But later minutes seem to reverse the Indians' position about a fort. Scarouady is quoted in them as saying, abruptly without introduction or explanation, "And as to the Strong House that is to be built. We have considered and make Choice of Mr. Montour, Mr. Trent, and Mr. Gist to transact Business between You and Us."[32] This was "pen and ink work." Its falsity is exposed by (of all people!) George Croghan and Andrew Montour, both of whom had been on the scene at Winchester; they remarked privately to Pennsylvania's commissioners at Carlisle that a fort had been banned by the Indians at Winchester.[33] Historian Nicholas Wainwright has remarked that Scarouady consented to a fort "doubtless after some private meeting with Croghan."[34] Considering the pattern of Mingo dealings behind the backs of their allied tribes, *doubtless* seems like the right word. We can imagine hearing the Winchester minutes read aloud to the open meeting of the treaty council with simple omission of "the Strong House that is to be built." Phrasing would move smoothly from the Ohioans' request for trade goods to the appointment of Montour, Trent, and Grist "to transact Business."

It was necessary at Winchester to fiddle with the minutes because the decision to build a fort had already been made. The Ohio Company was

from the Six United Nations of Indians, to the Proprietors of Indiana, against the Decision of the Legislature of Virginia (Philadelphia, 1781), 44. Wharton's interest is clear from his title; he was one of the partners in the Indiana Company. I have used the copy in the rare book room of the University of Pennsylvania's Van Pelt Library.

30. "Case of the Ohio Co." appendix, *George Mercer Papers*, 22.

31. PRO. CO 5 / 1328, ff. 23r, 24r.

32. Ibid., f. 28r. The "strong house" phrase occurs abruptly in the midst of requests for trade goods to be sent. Montour, Trent, and Gist were in the pay of Virginia or the Ohio Company.

33. *The Papers of Benjamin Franklin*, eds. Leonard W. Labaree, et al. (New Haven, Conn.: Yale University Press, 1959–) 5:65. (Hereinafter *Franklin Papers.)* To avoid Indian hostility, the Pennsylvanians decided to lodge presents of arms in "a place of Security," p. 59.

34. Wainwright, *George Croghan*, 54. L. H. Gipson, who used the Winchester mss., accepted it at face value without questioning its contradictions. *British Empire* 4:284–85.

obliged to live up to its bargain with the crown and was not to be dissuaded by Indians. Indeed its decision had been made before Scarouady's party started from the Ohio on its treaty mission. The Company's agent, Captain William Trent, had taken Virginia's invitation for the Ohioans to treat at Winchester; on the same journey he examined the site for the intended fort, for which funds and cannons had already been provided.[35]

One cannot merely pass over such trickery with amusement at "politics as usual." The Delawares and their allies returned to the Ohio with the understanding that Virginia had agreed to their request not to build a fort, but they soon saw Virginia's men building "a strong Store House" at the mouth of Redstone Creek, followed by a train of horses loaded, as Major George Washington observed, "with Materials and Stores for a Fort at the Forks of Ohio."[36] It appeared that the British were no better than the French, worse in fact. From the Indians' point of view, the big difference between French forts and British forts was that the British immediately surrounded their forts with settlements that grew and grew. This, indeed, was Virginia's intention as subsequently demonstrated. The Indians well understood how forts would be used to control themselves. The Mingos continued to breathe fire against the French, but among the other Ohio tribes zeal for resistance evaporated to nothing. Put very simply, they felt betrayed, and they had reason.

We must return to Winchester. Commissioner Fairfax proudly informed the assembled Indians that Virginia had arranged for the southern Cherokees, Catawbas, and Chickasaws to march against the French whenever the Ohioans should request it. This announcement did not meet with the anticipated joyous reception. Scarouady expressed polite gratitude, but pointed out that the southern tribes were enemies of the Iroquois. A peace would have to be negotiated, and Virginia would have to bring it about.[37]

The treaty was partially redeemed by professions of undying alliance, but it ended on a very sour note. The issue, once more, was those fractious Shawnees. Scarouady's determination to flout Onondaga's presumptions did not extend to giving up Mingo authority over the other Ohio tribes. He was distressed when Delaware chief Beaver interceded independently and publicly to request that Virginia obtain the release of two Shawnee warriors held prisoner in South Carolina. (It will be remembered that at Logstown the Delawares had gained formal recognition of the right to treat for themselves; now they already were beginning to speak also in behalf of others.) Scarouady was incensed further when the Shawnee chiefs at Winchester met privately with Fairfax to hint that they, too,

35. Hunter, *Forts*, 43.
36. Ibid., 40; *The Journal of Major George Washington* (1754), reprinted facsimile (Williamsburg: Colonial Williamsburg Foundation, 1959), entry for 1 Jan. 1754, p. 22.
37. PRO. CO5 / 1328, f. 24r.

would like formal recognition. Scarouady understood where backroom deals could lead. He followed the Shawnees in a private meeting of his own with Fairfax on the same day, and he vetoed (!) release of the Shawnee prisoners in South Carolina. If Fairfax was startled by this display of antagonisms, his minutes do not show it. They report routinely that Scarouady desired "that an Express might be sent to the Governor of South Carolina, to enquire if any Shawnesse were detain'd Prisoners in Charles Town, if so, that *no Application may be made for their Releasement*, till said Monacatoocha [Scarouady] shall have Notice, intending to take his own Method, for that the Chiefs of the Shawnesse had no Power, without consulting and having Leave from the Six Nations, to transact any publick Business."[38] It was, no doubt, intended to bring the Shawnees to heel. When discovered, it was not likely to inspire undying affection.

The issue was exacerbated later at Carlisle where George Croghan and Andrew Montour gave it a different aspect in private talk with Pennsylvania's commissioners. As these schemers told the story, Scarouady "did at Winchester, in public Council, undertake to go to Carolina to sollicit the Release of Some Warriors of the Shawnesse Nation." As we have seen, Scarouady had done no such thing, but the Pennsylvanians were so concerned at possibly losing his services while the French were marching that they pleaded with him to return west to the Ohio. Otherwise "all may be irrecoverably lost at Allegheny, and the Loss with Justice be laid at your Door."[39]

Consternation among the Shawnees, rendered in the minutes as "Dissatisfaction." The Pennsylvanians offered to write jointly with the governor of Virginia to ask the release of the Shawnee prisoners in South Carolina, but it is clear that the Shawnee chiefs at Carlisle felt abused and conspired against. It also seems highly likely that they would have been far from heartbroken to get Scarouady off their backs, and now the incubus was being fastened on tighter than ever by the power whose help they needed. Just how clearly they understood the Pennsylvanians, and vice versa, is doubtful, because the messages were translated between the two languages by Montour. The commissioners had "some Trouble to satisfy" the Shawnees, "but at last it was effected." This is to be expected. One of the general characteristics of treaty minutes is that the Indians in them always end up "satisfied." Subsequent hostility thus becomes explicable only in terms of base ingratitude or treachery—qualities of savages.

Scarouady understood the situation, and he was indeed satisfied. "With a great deal of Pleasure," he responded, "I must acquaint you, that we

38. Ibid., ff. 28v. 29v.

39. *Franklin Papers* 5:105–6. Pennsylvania did intercede, without action by Scarouady, and won the release and return of the Shawnee prisoners. *Pa. Council Minutes* 5:696–98, 699–700, 733.

have set a Horn on Andrew Montour's Head [i.e., made him a chief], and that you may believe what he says to be true." The suppressed chiefs are not quoted.

There was another, very important reason for the Ohioans to be dissatisfied with the outcome of the Carlisle treaty. Toward its conclusion, on 4 October 1753, Pennsylvania's commissioners decided to withhold the presents provided by the assembly—£800 worth. This was because there was "too great a Risque" for the Indians to take those presents home with them. This was absolute nonsense. French policy at the time, explicitly announced, was that all western Indians were at liberty to travel east to the English for whatever they could get. This was unknown to the Pennsylvanians who got their information about the "Risque" from traders Michael Taafe and Robert Callender. It happened that these traders were associates of George Croghan; and, by no coincidence, Pennsylvania's commissioners were persuaded to put all the withheld presents into the keeping of Croghan "who is to transmit to the Governor, by Express, a true and faithful Account how your Matters are likely to turn out; and on the Governor's Order, and not otherwise, to put you into the Possession of them."[40] Between them, Montour and Croghan had not only maintained their ally Scarouady in charge of the Ohioans, but had acquired control of the goods the Indians needed for subsistence and defense. Croghan's dexterity at manipulation can only be admired. The consequences were another matter.

What happened to the goods entrusted to Croghan is anybody's guess.[41] The presents had been left in his care despite Commissioner Richard Peters's private opinion that Croghan was not a fit man "nor any Indian trader" to be trusted to give presents to Indians.[42]

As the Indians returned despairingly to the Ohio, Peters returned to Philadelphia to act as secretary of the province and to report events to Thomas Penn in his more private capacity as one of Penn's confidential informants. Within the limits of his knowledge and biases, Peters was an accurate reporter whose shrewd observations deserve close attention. He told Penn scathingly of Tanaghrisson's journey to the French commandant: "This Chief who went like a Lyon roaring out Destruction, came back like a Sheep with Tears in his Eyes, and desired the English to go away, for that the French who were coming down the River Ohio in two

40. *Franklin Papers* 5:105 and n.

41. Croghan stated that he and Montour passed the goods on to the Ohioans at a meeting on 28 Jan. 1754. There is no independent confirmation. Croghan's journal, *Pa. Council Minutes* 5:733. Wainwright notices that Croghan sent out £500 worth of provisions in May, on his own credit. *Croghan*, 61–62. But he was very deeply in debt at the time, and much distrusted. It would have been perfectly in character for him to have taken a large unreported commission out of Pennsylvania's presents which were worth £800.

42. Peters to T. Penn, 5 July 1753, ms., Penn Mss., Off. Corr. 6:73, HSP.

hundred Canoes, woud hurt them and make Spoil of their Goods." It did not occur to Peters—or he did not care—that the Ohio Indians were facing a military machine huger than anything in their experience. To him they were "a debauched People, and several of them will go over to the French notwithstanding their warm Professions." Yet, without sensing the connection, he told of the betrayal of faith that had much to do with the Indians' "debauchery." Settlers from Virginia, he wrote, "go in Companies, and that Country fills with a mighty bad Crew, rejected by Lord Fairfax, the very Scum of the Earth as every body says."[43]

Washington runs an errand

Military preparations advanced hand in hand with provincial diplomacy. Governor Dinwiddie, having received authorization from the crown, commissioned young George Washington to journey to Fort LeBoeuf and tell the French to go away. Diplomats are not normally so young—Washington was only twenty-one years old—but diplomats do not normally have to journey through swamp and forest in raw, wet weather.[44] If, on the one hand, Washington had no experience in negotiating, on the other hand he actually completed his mission. Little finesse was required. He was to deliver what amounted to an ultimatum, and he got the expected rejection.

Washington set out from Williamsburg on 31 October 1753; picked up a guide, interpreter, and a small escort on his way through Fredericksburg, Alexandria, Winchester, and Wills Creek; and arrived late in November at the village of Delaware chief Shingas, "where the Ohio Company intended to erect a Fort." Shingas accompanied him to Logstown where Washington was delayed for nearly a week by the intricacies of tribal diplomacy. It is clear from his account that the Mingos had lost control of their supposedly subordinate allies though they continued to insist that they spoke in behalf of all. Washington dealt directly with the "Half King" Tanaghrisson, who became very busy issuing orders to the Delawares and Shawnees to collect all the wampum belts they had received from the French so that Tanaghrisson could return them to the new French commandant at Fort LeBoeuf (Captain Marin having died). The Delaware and Shawnee chiefs had only recently returned from Winchester and Carlisle, and their enthusiasm for doing British chores had distinctly cooled, so Tanaghrisson's chore of collecting their French wampum belts proved to be a little like a search for a left-handed monkey wrench. The Shawnee

43. Peters to Honoured Proprietaries, 6 Nov. 1753, ms., Penn Mss., Off. Corr. 6:113, 115, HSP.

44. Kent, *French Invasion*, 70; Gipson, *British Empire* 4:296.

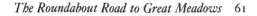

MAP 1. George Washington's journey from Williamsburg to Fort LeBoeuf. REPRODUCED BY COURTESY OF THE COLONIAL WILLIAMSBURG FOUNDATION FROM ITS FACSIMILE PUBLICATION *The Journal of George Washington* (1959).

chiefs could not be found. Shingas declared that the Delaware belts were in custody of Chief Custaloga at Venango and issued an "order" to Custaloga to deliver them, but Custaloga paid no attention to it. As for attendance upon Washington, Shingas excused himself on grounds that his wife was sick.[45] Only the Mingo chiefs showed any sign of cooperation.

45. *Journal of Washington*, 3–12.

Even Tanaghrisson and Scarouady were uncomfortably curious about Washington's business. On the twenty-eighth of November, as Washington recorded, they "begged, (as they had complied with his Honour the Governor's Request, in providing Men, &c.) to know on what Business we were going to the French? this was a Question I all along expected, and provided as satisfactory Answers to, as I could, and which allayed their Curiosity a little." But not much. Notably, Washington did not itemize just what he told those Indians. Washington's recorded speech says only that he had been sent to "deliver a Letter to the French Commandant, of very great Importance to your Brothers the English, and I dare say, to you their Friends and Allies." Tanaghrisson apparently wanted to know the letter's contents. He would have been much interested in its first sentence's declaration that "The lands upon the river Ohio, in the Western Parts of the Colony of Virginia are . . . notoriously known to be the property of the Crown of Great-Britain."[46]

It is to be feared that the future Father of his Country was no more candid with Indians than any other British colonial agent. The bullheaded French captain Marin had been far more straightforward. According to Tanaghrisson, Marin had told him bluntly, "Child, you talk foolish; you say this Land belongs to you, but there is not the Black of my Nail yours . . . If People will be rul'd by me, they may expect Kindness, but not else."[47] Whatever else may be said about such bluster, it was plainer speaking than anything the Ohioans had yet encountered from the British. It is not argued here that the French were incapable of duplicity; rather, the distinctions at this time are to be explained by the circumstances. Marin had spoken with a great armament at his command; Edward Braddock would be similarly forthright when similarly situated. Washington was armed with a letter. Nonetheless, Washington knew when he set forth on his journey what he was to do, and he showed no qualms about doing it. All through his life—even after his marriage to rich widow Martha Custis made him reputedly one of the wealthiest men in Virginia—Washington held single-minded determination to acquire vast western estates. It was sufficient eventually to turn him against the crown he was serving in 1753; and what is more revealing, it would be sufficient to motivate him to cheat his comrades in arms out of their war service bonus lands.[48] In due course,

46. Ibid., 11, 9, 25.

47. Ibid., 8.

48. In 1767, Washington suggested to his agent William Crawford that Crawford "evade" Pennsylvania's law by a device of registering an illicitly large tract of land in small parcels; this to be done with the connivance of "an Acquaintance of mine" in the land office. Bernhard Knollenberg has found that Washington also "infringed" Virginia law; seizing lands to which he was not entitled, surveying them illicitly through a man unqualified by law who laid them out in violation of legal stipulations as to size and location, and all to the detriment of Washington's Virginia comrades in arms for whom these lands had been intended "The

Washington would denounce Indians as "having nothing human except the shape." What compunctions could a man with such attitudes have about the rights of Indian tribes or the welfare of Indian persons? By personality or purpose, he seems to have stirred instant dislike among the Ohioans. When he resumed his march toward Fort LeBoeuf, only four Mingos accompanied him. Not a single representative of any other tribe went along, despite Tanaghrisson's previously declared intention of providing a guard of Mingos, Shawnees, and Delawares "that our Brothers may see the Love and Loyalty we bear them."[49]

Washington met with Marin's successor as commandant on the twelfth of December. Captain Jacques Legardeur de Saint-Pierre was thirty years Washington's senior, enough to make Washington call him "an elderly Gentleman." The interview between them was most unequal. A truly professional soldier, Legardeur was vastly experienced in Indian and military affairs. He had served at frontier posts in Acadia, Wisconsin, the Lake of the Woods region, and down the Mississippi to backwoods fighting in Alabama.[50] Washington amused him. He received the green youth with great urbanity and freely flowing hospitality (and Washington has never been noted as a teetotaller).[51] In response to the letter Washington

more he got of the allotted 200,000 acres, the less was available for the enlisted men to whom it was promised." Washington to Wm. Crawford, 21 Sept. 1767, in *The Writings of George Washington*, ed. John C. Fitzpatrick, 39 vols. (Washington, D.C., 1931–44) 2:468; Bernhard Knollenberg, *George Washington: The Virginia Period, 1732–1775* (Durham, N.C., 1964), 93–100, quotation at p. 99.

In 1769, Washington tried again to get larger shares of the bounty lands by arguing with Governor Botetourt that only men who had served under Washington (as well as Washington himself) were entitled to bounty lands under Dinwiddie's earlier proclamation, excluding Virginians who had served under other officers at other times. *Writings*, ed. Fitzpatrick, 2:528–32.

Dinwiddie's proclamation of bounty lands, dated 19 Feb. 1754, became the key document of a partnership between Washington and Colonel George Mercer. "We will leave no Stone unturned to secure to ourselves this land," wrote Mercer to Washington, 16 Sept. 1759. To prove it, he changed the wording of Dinwiddie's proclamation from granting land "For Encouraging Men to *enlist*" to "For Encouraging Persons to *Enter* into his Majesty's Service," which had the effect of squeezing officers into eligibility for grants. And Mercer made the proclamation say that lands would be proportioned according to recommendations of "their superior officers," which meant Washington above all. Washington won official approval of this in 1769, and lands were parceled out in 1773. Washington's "proportion" was 20,147 acres, Mercer's 13,532 acres.

The unique copy of Dinwiddie's proclamation as changed by Mercer is in the collection of Mr. and Mrs. Paul Mellon. It was printed with an explanatory introduction by Willis Van Devanter in *The Virginia Soldiers' Claim to Western Lands Adjacent to Fort Pitt* (New York: Privately printed at Spiral Press, 1966), short, unpaged.

49. *Journal of Washington*, 13, 10. Identification of Mingos in Hunter, *Forts*, 27n.

50. Donald Chaput in *Dict. Can. Biog.* 3:374–76.

51. *Journal of Washington*, 16–19. For Washington's drinking habits, see the hilarious and fully documented analysis in Marvin Kitman, *George Washington's Expense Account* (New York: Ballantine Books, 1970). As my trade's custom is to deplore such irreverence, let it be noted that the book includes a facsimile of the account in question.

carried, Legardeur declared that he had "made it my particular Care to receive Mr. Washington with a Distinction suitable to your Dignity, and his Quality and great Merit." And said no.[52]

While Washington was being regaled in the officers' mess, his Mingo aides swizzled quantities of brandy in less exalted quarters. They washed down much French enticement along with the brandy, and Washington began to worry that even the Mingos would be lost from his cause.[53] Tanaghrisson made excuses to stay behind as Washington started home. "I hoped," wrote Washington, that he would "let no fine Speeches influence him in their Favour." Tanaghrisson assured him that he knew the French too well. It would seem that he also knew French brandy well, but he did stay loyal.

Indian hardships

Nature gained time for the British. Disease crippled the French army and provisions for it became so difficult that most of the men were ordered back to Montreal until spring should make campaigning possible once more. With supplies falling short for even the soldiers, not much was left for Indians. Those who had become dependent on employment by the army were harshly afflicted. Custaloga's band of Delawares at Venango were reduced to the same starving state that the withdrawal of English traders had forced upon the Indians farther downstream. "I even believe that they have boiled the casks to smell the odor," wrote agent Joncaire. "Sometimes it is a sick man who sends to ask for a piece of bread, sometimes for a drink of wine. One is going to die, another cannot go hunting for lack of gunpowder. One has neither a shirt nor leggings; another's dead parents torment him continually in his sleep, reproaching him for not taking pity on them and for not feasting them with brandy; finally the devil sends others to ask for blankets, recalling all the promises made to them last summer, at the same time taking great pains to have it understood that, when the English were there, they did not suffer so much." Neither the French nor the British made many friends among the Ohio Indians that winter. Through the depths of winter, the Indians starved in despair, seeking consolation in almost perpetual drunkenness. Somehow, when the traders could get nothing else through, they managed still to deliver exceptionally profitable rum.[54]

52. *Journal of Washington*, 27–28.
53. Ibid., 19–20.
54. Kent, *French Invasion*, 65–66.

Materials for Fort Duquesne

Meanwhile Captain Trent finished the strong house at Redstone Creek and started work on a more substantial fort at the forks of the Ohio. Washington saw the building supplies as he returned to Virginia in January 1754, "and the Day after some Families going out to settle."[55] Tanaghrisson laid the first log of the new fort and declared that the Indians would make war against anyone who tried to prevent its construction. The Delawares, however, "being the only Indians who lived adjoining, to the place where the Fort was building," as Ensign Ward recollected, "could not be prevailed upon to hunt, tho' often applied to and offered great prices for any kind of meat they could bring in, even seven shillings and sixpence for a Turkey. At this time the Indians were much inclined to the French, but were afraid to declare in their favour."[56]

French spies observed all. As still another new commandant had taken charge at Fort LeBoeuf, they reported to Captain Claude-Pierre Pécaudy de Contrecoeur, who responded immediately by marching with 600 men to the forks of the Ohio. They found 41 Englishmen under Ensign Edward Ward. Contrecoeur issued an ultimatum. Ward tried to stall. Contrecoeur would have none of that. Ward counted the odds and capitulated. It was all done in gentlemanly fashion. Ward's men were to be permitted to march off with all their possessions at noon, 18 April. Meanwhile Ward was Contrecoeur's guest at dinner on the seventeenth. We may presume that no French dinner would be complete without liquid refreshment. True or not, the two gentlemen got along so well that Ward sold Contrecoeur his carpentry tools, with which the French resumed the building of the fort under their own auspices.[57] Thus came Fort Duquesne into being, expedited rather than hindered by British opposition.

Washington's first campaign

While this was happening on the frontier, Governor Dinwiddie prevailed on the reluctant Virginia Assembly "with great Persuasions, many Argum'ts and much difficulty" to appropriate £10,000. He raised troops, promoted George Washington to lieutenant colonel, and sent them all back

55. *Journal of Washington*, 22.

56. Hunter, *Forts*, 47–48. Ensign Edward Ward was Croghan's half-brother. Wainwright, *Croghan*, 61.

57. Deposition of Ensign Edward Ward, 30 June 1756, mss., Etting Coll., Ohio Co., 1:10, HSP; Fernand Grenier, "Pécaudy de Contrecoeur, Claude-Pierre," in *Dict. Can. Biog.* 4:617.

to the Ohio.[58] What happened then has been told so often that it may be summarized here briefly.

Washington's new commission gave him greater authority, but no one could commission for him a greater maturity than he had acquired in only twenty-two years. He was both hotheaded and vacillating, taking no advice from the Indians and ordering them about in authentic Virginia style. Tanaghrisson gave him the benefit of the doubt, saying later to Conrad Weiser that Washington was "a good-natured man but had no experience."[59] Tanaghrisson scouted a French party stalking Washington and showed him how to surprise the French at sunrise. In the ensuing engagement, the French commander Jumonville was killed.[60]

All knew that the French would retaliate promptly. Washington asked Tanaghrisson to summon the Delawares for help. A mixed group of forty men responded, but they were more curious than enthusiastic. A Mingo remarked that they had heard the English would destroy all the Indians who did not join them. Washington denounced the false story, and offered another in its place. "The only motive of our conduct," he assured the Indians was "to put you again in possession of your lands, and to take care of your wives and children, to dispossess the French, to maintain your rights and to secure the whole country for you; for these very ends are the English arms now employed."[61] Parson Weems might have swallowed that, but the Delawares had seen the incoming settlers.

A day later they once again raised their question about the Virginians' purpose. Washington was stuck with his feeble yarn, and he doggedly repeated that "we were come at their reiterated requests to aid them with sword in hand; that we intended to put them in possession of those lands which the French had taken from them." The skeptical Delawares, instead of applauding this heartwarming sentiment, obliquely criticized Washington's methods of dealing with them through Tanaghrisson. They reminded Washington that Virginia had given them a king at Logstown, "and told us he should transact all public business between you and us." They added that the Onondaga council had given them notice "that the English and French were upon the point of coming to an engagement on the Ohio

58. In view of the way Pennsylvania's Quaker-dominated assembly is often singled out for condemnation, the resistance of the militant Virginians is notable. Their assembly's bill, according to Dinwiddie, was "so clogg'd with unreasonable regulat's and encroachm'ts on the Prerogative that I, by no means w'd have given my Assent to it if His Maj's service had not immediately call'd for a Supply to support the Expedt." Gipson, *British Empire* 4:301–2, 304–6.

59. Weiser's journal, *Pa. Council Minutes* 6:151.

60. *The Diaries of George Washington, 1748–1794*, ed. John C. Fitzpatrick, 4 vols. (Boston: Houghton Mifflin Co., 1925), 1:87–88.

61. Ibid., entries of 12 June, 18–19 June, pp. 93–95.

river, and exhorted us to do nothing in that matter, but what was reasonable." And they reasonably avoided getting involved.[62]

Washington tried to retreat, but he had delayed too long. When his exhausted troops arrived at a place called Great Meadows, despite their knowledge of the hotly pursuing French, they could go no farther. He hastily threw up a stockade so obviously useless that even Tanaghrisson left in disgust. Tanaghrisson was not at all embarrassed in telling why. Washington "would by no means take Advice from the Indians . . . he lay at one Place from one full Moon to the other and made no Fortifications at all, but that little thing upon the Meadow, where he thought the French would come up to him in open Field; . . . had he taken the Half King's advice and made such Fortifications as the Half King advised him to make he would certainly have beat the French off; . . . the French had acted as great Cowards, and the English as Fools in that Engagement; . . . he (the Half King) had carried off his Wife and Children, so did other Indians before the Battle begun, because Col. Washington would never listen to them, but was always driving them on to fight by his Directions." Surrounded, abandoned, and overwhelmingly outnumbered, Washington capitulated about midnight and evacuated Fort Necessity at sunrise on the Fourth of July.[63]

Washington had killed the brother of the man who now defeated him, and the French would later make that episode into an atrocity story,[64] but at the moment the brother had sufficient revenge in his victory. He was magnanimous in the style of the professional soldier of the eighteenth century, so strange to war in the twentieth. Washington and all his men, with the exception of only two held as hostages, were allowed to march off.[65]

It was a rational decision. Virginia could not return to the field alone. The provinces and their desires receded to second rank as the empires moved to confront each other directly. And France had kept possession of the Ohio in greater strength than ever before. Magnanimity could be afforded.

The French became so confident that they let their guard slip. They politely gave the run of Fort Duquesne to their hostages. One of these, Captain Robert Stobo, was the stuff of which heroes are made. At the risk of his life, he smuggled valuable intelligence out of the yet-incomplete Fort Duquesne. Interestingly, the smuggling was carried out by Delaware visitors, one of whom was Chief Shingas. Another was Delaware George

62. Ibid., 97, 99–100.

63. Ibid., ed.n., 1:102; Tanaghrisson's speech is in Weiser's journal, *Pa. Council Minutes* 6:151–52.

64. Kent, *French Invasion*, 83; Hunter, *Forts*, 59. See also the annex following this chapter.

65. Hunter, *Forts*, 58–59.

who carried Stobo's letter past the French to George Croghan.[66]

Both Shingas and Delaware George had been present at the Winchester treaty and at Carlisle. Neither had lifted a finger to help Washington. The English were wrong about their being pro-French. They were pro-Delaware.

Chapter annex: How did Jumonville die?

It is perhaps impossible to get at the full truth of this affair now. The official French version was as follows:

> That deputy [Jumonville] set out with an escort of thirty men, and the next morning found himself surrounded by a number of English and Indians: The English quickly fired two vollies which killed some soldiers. M. de Jumonville made a sign that he had a letter from his commander; hereupon the fire ceased, and they surrounded the French officer, in order to hear it. He immediately ordered the summons to be read, and as it was reading the second time, the English assassinated him. The rest of the French that escorted him, were, upon the spot made prisoners of war.
>
> The only one who escaped, and who gave M. de Contrecoeur a circumstantial account of that affair, assured him, that the Indians who were with the English, had not fired a gun; and that at the instant M. de Jumonville was assassinated, they threw themselves in between the French and their enemies.[1]

W. J. Eccles gives much the same account from different sources, though he uses "struck down" instead of "assassinated."[2]

L. H. Gipson's account varies considerably: in this, Washington hoped to encircle the French "and attack them on all sides unexpectedly, but he was discovered. An engagement ensued. *In the fighting* the French commanding officer, Ensign Coulon de Jumonville, and nine other Frenchmen were slain."[3] This, like so much of Gipson's work, follows the account of Francis Parkman.[4] Parkman said that the original of the *Mémoire Contenant le Précis des Faits* had disappeared.[5]

66. Stobo's letter, 28 and 29 July 1754, *Pa. Council Minutes* 6:141–42, 161–63; Robert C. Alberts, *The Most Extraordinary Adventures of Major Robert Stobo* (Boston: Houghton Mifflin Co., 1965), chs. 8, 9.

1. *Mémoire Contenant le Précis des Faits* quoted in Charles H. Ambler, *George Washington and the West* (1936), repr. (N.Y.: Russell and Russell, 1971), 65.

2. "Coulon de Villiers de Jumonville, Joseph," in *Dict. Can. Biog.* 3:150–51.

3. *British Empire* 6:31. Italics added.

4. *Montcalm and Wolfe*, 2 vols. (1884), New Library ed. (Boston: Little, Brown and Co., 1909), 1:152–54.

5. P. 152n. Since writing the above, I have seen a printed copy, and an English translation, at the John Carter Brown Library, Providence, Rhode Island.

There is reason to believe that both sides smudged the facts for political and propaganda purposes. An affidavit was mentioned by Beverley McAnear from which I give a large extract below. It gives a picture different from all the others. It must be called hearsay because the deponent John Shaw was not with Washington's particular detachment in the engagement with the French (though he was in another detachment of Washington's forces), but it has a disquieting ring of circumstantial authenticity especially because Shaw had no axe to grind and it was reported not long after the event.

As this Deponent has heard, one of them [The French] fired a Gun upon which Col. Washington gave the Word for all his Men to fire. Several of them being killed, the Rest betook themselves to flight, but our Indians haveing gone round, the French when they saw them immediately fled back to the English and delivered up their Arms desireing Quarter which was accordingly promised them.

Some Time after the Indians came up the Half King [Tanaghrisson] took his Tomahawk and split the Head of the French Captain haveing first asked if he was an Englishman and haveing been told he was a French Man. He then took out his Brains and washed his Hands with them and then scalped him. All this he [Shaw] has heard and never heard it contradicted but knows nothing of it from his own Knowledge only he has seen the Bones of the frenchmen who were killed in Number about 13 or 14 and the Head of one stuck upon a Stick for none of them were buried.[6]

Tanaghrisson's role in Shaw's account is confirmed by a news account that first appeared in the *Pennsylvania Gazette*, 27 June 1754, and was reprinted in other English colonial newspapers. It is obviously slanted toward the official British line that Jumonville was a skulking spy (which may have been true), but it remarks: "One of those Five [Frenchmen] which were killed and scalped by the Indians, was Monsieur Jumonville, an Ensign, whom the Half King himself dispatched with his Tomahawk."[7]

This information is confirmed by a very careful reading of the French official version of assassination, making allowance for propagandist slanting. Governor Duquesne did not actually accuse Washington of killing Jumonville. Duquesne said only that Washington "authorized" the murder, and that he was silly enough to avow this in his capitulation at Fort Necessity.

The capitulation refers only to "the assassination" without identifying

6. Sworn affidavit of John Shaw before South Carolina governor James Glen, 21 August 1754, in *Documents Relating to Indian Affairs, 1754–1765*, ed. Wm. L. McDowell, Jr., published for the South Carolina Department of Archives and History (Columbia: University of South Carolina Press, 1970), 4–5. Beverly McAnear, "Personal Accounts," 742–59.

7. Quoted in Ambler, *George Washington*, 67–68.

its perpetrator. The single French witness who escaped said that the Indians had thrown themselves between the English and Jumonville and had not fired a shot. This, it appears, was an effective half-truth; assuming the factuality of John Shaw's account, Jumonville died under the hatchet, not by gunshot. The French officer and later historian Pierre Pouchot (who was not a witness) seems to have recognized how the Indians' maneuver might expose the weakness of the official atrocity story, so he threw in a touch of his own, writing that the Indians closed in "to protect" Jumonville from Washington's men. This is preposterous.[8]

8. *Papiers Contrecoeur et autres Documents concernant le Conflit Anglo-Francais sur l'Ohio de 1755 a 1756*, ed. Fernand Grenier (Quebec: Les Presses Universitaires Laval, 1952), 250; [Jacob Nicolas Moreau], *Memoire contenant le Precis des Faits avec leurs Pieces Justificatives* (Paris: De L'Imprimerie Royale, 1756), 126, 155; translated as *The conduct of the late Ministry, or, A Memorial Containing A Summary of Facts with their Vouchers, in Answer to the Observations, sent by the English Ministry, to the Courts of Europe* (London: W. Bizet, 1757), 70, 137, 173; [Pierre] Pouchet, *Memoir upon the Late War in North America, Between the French and English, 1755–60* (1781), trans. and ed. Franklin B. Hough, 2 vols. (Roxbury, Mass.: W. Elliott Woodward, 1866), 1:24n2.

Chapter 5 ❧ *THE LAST CONGRESS AT ALBANY*

Each colony sought to attain its own specific objective, to meet its own needs, which might be identical with those of its sister colonies but which were never merged with them. Thus it came about that neighbouring provinces could institute, each for its own part, Indian policies not only different, but contrary, and even hostile, to one another in stubborn competition. In such conditions it was only natural that their mutual distrust should result in disputes, or prevent them from taking effective action.

Guy Frégault

Chronology

ca. 1738.	William Johnson arrives in New York from Ireland in order to take charge of uncle Sir Peter Warren's New York estates.
1746.	Thomas Penn begins campaign against Pennsylvania assembly.
1747.	William Johnson sends the Mohawks against Montreal, but they are ambushed with heavy loss.
1747.	Benjamin Franklin organizes a military association for Pennsylvania's defense.
1748.	Franklin retires from management of his printing business, but retains clerkship of Pennsylvania assembly.
1749.	The Ohio Company petitions the crown for lands in the Ohio region, and proposes to build a fort there.
1750.	The Pennsylvania assembly rejects Thomas Penn's proposal for it to build a fort in the Ohio region.
September 1750.	William Johnson tries to prevent Conrad Weiser from treating with the Iroquois grand council.
July 1751.	Johnson resigns post as New York's agent in charge of Indian affairs.
1751.	Franklin elected a member of Pennsylvania assembly.
1751.	Thomas Penn and brother Richard refuse the assembly's unanimous request to contribute to expense of Indian affairs "or any other public expense."
1753.	Franklin: (1) is one of the commissioners treating at Carlisle with the Ohio Indians; (2) is awarded the Copley gold medal of the Royal Society for his experiments with electricity; (3) is appointed by the crown as deputy postmaster general of the British colonies in North America, serving simultaneously with membership in the assembly.

16 June 1753.	Mohawk chief Hendrick declares at Albany that the Covenant Chain has broken.
18 September 1753.	Board of trade orders a multi-provincial treaty with the Iroquois to redress complaints and renew the Covenant Chain under royal auspices.
1754.	Franklin journeys to the Albany Congress with a scheme for inter-provincial union. It is not authorized by the assembly.
14 June–11 July 1754.	Interprovincial Congress at Albany renews the Covenant Chain and approves Franklin's plan of union. Outside the formal sessions Conrad Weiser and John Lydius obtain land cessions from individual Iroquois chiefs.
July 1755.	In treaty with William Johnson, the Iroquois grand council criticizes and reduces Weiser's Pennsylvania deed, and repudiates Lydius's Connecticut deed.

As the Ohio Company could not make progress without securing its base in Williamsburg, so the expansionists in other colonies were enmeshed in the politics of the provinces as well as of the tribes. Imperial interests took them forward into confrontation in the Ohio Valley, but the local interests represented in the assemblies required protection of existing arrangements and aroused deep antipathy toward the impending conflict whose disturbances would threaten those arrangements. If there was to be aggression, each assembly wanted it to be in favor of its own province and its own members. Only too plainly the adventurism at the Ohio entailed great risk and expense for the benefit of other parties.

Though the British crown sent out governors and lieutenant governors to exert the crown's prerogative, the assemblies had encroached on that prerogative over the years. They had become accustomed to make the basic legislative decisions in their provinces, and a good many executive decisions as well—powers that they were determined to guard and use—and as the struggle with France caused governors to make greater demands, the assemblies dug in their heels to resist encroachment on their hard-won powers of decision. They understood well the kinds of demands that the crown's agents had made during the imperial war of the 1740s (known in the colonies as King George's War, in Europe as the War of the Austrian Succession). Now, as a new war heated up, the board of trade in London adopted policies that were simultaneously expansionist and autocratic. In resisting the one, the assemblies were forced into resisting the other as well, and this in time of impending war. Thrust into an awkward situation, they could not possibly come into overt opposition. Instead, they danced in guerilla politics around the crown's great power; they equivocated, stalled, quibbled, wrangled, complained, obstructed, encumbered, and held back funds and men as long as they could. The resistance was general, even in the usually militant provinces of Virginia and Massachusetts.[1]

In this chapter, we shall consider the linked politics and struggles of New York and Pennsylvania. Their linkage was that of the opposed poles of the same magnet which, in this case, was the Indian tribes of the Iroquois League and the Ohio Valley. New York and Pennsylvania had competed for the trade and allegiance of those tribes since William Penn's founding of his colony. For clarity let us consider them in turn, New York first.

Shifting channels of trade

New York was a colony directly under the British crown. Its politics were dominated by great merchants and plantation owners aligned in family factions. When a faction succeeded in winning the favor and patronage of the crown's governor or lieutenant governor, the other main faction went into opposition, so that much of the province's political life revolved around the person of the governor.[2] There was another durable and fundamental cleavage, however, that split the faction aiming at western expansion from the Albany merchants engaged in a lucrative smuggling trade with French counterparts at Montreal. This had been a going concern since the administration of Governor Thomas Dongan in the 1680s, and had survived strong efforts by the crown in the 1720s to suppress it. Because of its strong influence on public affairs, the operation of this trade demands a brief explanation.

Canadians nearly always had a surplus of peltry collected by the vast network of French traders among the tribes, but trade goods were often in short supply at Montreal, sometimes because of wartime interception by British ships, sometimes because of the long winter freeze over the St. Lawrence River, sometimes because of monopolies and high prices. Albany's merchants, on the other hand, had no trouble getting trade goods at almost any time of year at prices far below Montreal's, and Albany was always

1. For detailed discussion, see Jack P. Greene, *The Quest for Power: The Lower Houses of Assembly in the Southern Royal Colonies, 1689–1776*, published for the Institute of Early American History and Culture (1963), reprinted (New York: W. W. Norton and Co., 1972); and Alan Rogers, *Empire and Liberty: American Resistance to British Authority, 1755–1763* (Berkeley: University of California Press, 1974).

2. Stanley Nider Katz, *Newcastle's New York: Anglo-American Politics, 1732–1753* (Cambridge, Mass.: Harvard University Press, 1968), ch. 3; [Thomas Pownall], "Notes on Indian Affairs [1754], mss., Loudoun Papers, LO 460, Henry E. Huntington Library, San Marino, Calif. (HEH.)

Bibliographic note: Pownall's mss. is a broken-off, rough draft in two columns with marginal notes, insertions, and strikeovers. I have integrated these components for quotations that follow hereunder.

in the market for furs. Each side had what the other wanted, and the Jesuit mission Indians at Caughnawaga were only too happy to earn a safe living by transporting cargoes back and forth along the natural waterway between the two towns. From Montreal they paddled a few miles downstream to the mouth of the Richelieu River. Thence up the Richelieu, through Lake Champlain and Lake George, from the head of which a short portage took them to the Hudson River and down it to Albany. The route has been called "the warpath of nations" because of its frequent use by armies invading back and forth. (I have dubbed it "the Mahican Channel" in commemoration of the tribe whose territory bordered it.) The heavy commercial traffic along this channel was a very welcome accommodation for all involved.[3]

But it was indeed a smuggling operation, illegal at both ends, condemned by the agents of both French and British crowns, and bitterly opposed in Canada and New York by imperialists who regarded such "trading with the enemy" as a severe obstruction to their own plans for expansion in other directions. Because the British crown's expansionist plans identified the crown with New York's faction opposed to the Albany smugglers, the smuggling faction necessarily hampered the crown's governor Clinton by every available means.

The Iroquois Six Nations also became involved in the opposition to the smuggling trade because they wanted trade with western tribes to be transported through Iroquoia to Albany. Commerce over this route would give them a degree of control over access to Albany, and through that control a certain amount of leverage in diplomacy with the western tribes.[4] It was a kind of influence that the Iroquois had sought ever since their seventeenth-century defeats had forced them out of Ontario and the Illinois country. But the interests of the Iroquois League coincided with the interests of New York's expansionists only on the issue of the Albany-Montreal smuggling trade; some Mohawks flouted League policy by collaborating with their Caughnawaga kinsmen among the smugglers.

Adding to League injuries, even the expansionist Yorkers dealt a blow to the Iroquois in 1722 when they founded Oswego on the southern shore of Lake Ontario. The function of this new post was to intercept western Indians on their way to Montreal. It added another grievance to the lengthy

3. Cadwallader Colden, "A Memorial concerning the Fur Trade of the Province of New York," 10 Nov. 1724, *N.Y. Col. Docs.* 5:732–33; William Johnson to George Clinton, 12 Mar. 1754, *The Papers of Sir William Johnson*, eds. James Sullivan, et al., 14 vols. (Albany: University of the State of New York, 1921–65), 9:127–28; Thomas Elliott Norton, *The Fur Trade in Colonial New York, 1686–1776* (Madison: University of Wisconsin Press, 1974), ch. 8. Norton attempts to put the trade in perspective, unlike the source writers who were open partisans hostile to the Albany merchants.

4. Thomas Pownall to [earl of Halifax?], 23 July 1754, in "Personal Accounts of the Albany Congress of 1754," ed. Beverly McAnear, *Mississippi Valley Historical Review* 39:4 (Mar. 1953), 742–43; Norton, *Fur Trade*, 134.

list already held by the Iroquois because it also intercepted the western Indians before they got to Iroquoia. Squeezed out of the trade at one end by Oswego, and at the other end by the smuggling to Montreal, the Iroquois lost affection for their allies in New York.[5] Under pressure, the League began to dissolve in fact though it maintained a facade of unity. Seneca individuals went to work as employees of the French at Fort Niagara and of the English at Oswego. Though Mohawks joined British forces in the war of the 1740s, no other Iroquois chiefs could be persuaded to accompany them. Many Mohawks and others abandoned Iroquoia entirely to join Jesuit missions in Canada. The Canadian Caughnawaga mission became predominately "French Mohawks," and the Oswegatchie mission Indians, who numbered nearly 3,000 by 1751, consisted mainly of Onondagas and Cayugas.[6] Many Senecas and some others went off to the Ohio country as Mingos flaunting their independence of the League.[7]

We have seen that when Virginia and Pennsylvania lit a new treaty fire for the Mingos and took presents to Ohio that the Onondaga chiefs thought should have come to themselves, the elders' disillusion with their allies was complete. Their resentment appeared overtly at Albany in 1753 when it led the British crown to reorganize its machinery for Indian affairs.[8]

The rise of William Johnson

That restructuring was foreshadowed by the appearance on the scene of a young Irishman named William Johnson. Irishmen in those days were not well thought of by Englishmen, but Johnson was very well connected. His uncle was Sir Peter Warren, Britain's foremost admiral, and when Johnson appeared in New York about 1738 he was Warren's protégé and steward in charge of Warren's plantation in the Mohawk country.[9] John-

5. See the editor's note in Peter Wraxall, *An Abridgment of the Indian Affairs*, ed. Charles Howard McIlwain, Harvard Historical Studies 21 (1915), facsimile reprint (New York: Benjamin Blom, 1968), lxxiiin. McIlwain is particularly good at distinguishing economic interests from political ones.

6. J. N. B. Hewitt, "Caughnawaga," in *Handbook of American Indians North of Mexico*, ed. Frederick Webb Hodge, 2 vols. (Washington, D.C.: Government Printing Office, 1907), 1:220–21; idem., "Oswegatchie," in ibid., 2:162.

7. Charles A. Hanna, *The Wilderness Trail*, ch. 12. *Atlas of Great Lakes Indian History*, eds. Helen Hornbeck Tanner, Adele Hast, Jacqueline Peterson, and Robert J. Surtees, published for the Newberry Library (Norman: University of Oklahoma Press, 1987), 44.

8. Jack Stagg, *Anglo-American Relations in North America to 1763, and An Analysis of The Royal Proclamation of 7 October 1763* (Ottawa: Research Branch, Indian and Northern Affairs Canada, 1981), 93.

9. Daniel Claus, "Memorandum," in *The Papers of Sir William Johnson [Johnson Papers]*, eds. James Sullivan et al., 14 vols. (Albany: University of the State of New York, 1921–65), 13: 723–25.

Bibliographic note: The most recent biography of Johnson is Milton W. Hamilton, *Sir*

son quickly showed aptitude for getting along with the Indians. He learned the trade, started his own business and acquired his own land; and he became the Indian expert for Governor George Clinton who had been, like Johnson's uncle, an admiral. As Clinton was an obedient, if inept, servant to the crown, Johnson was immediately thrown by the rules of New York's politics into opposition against Clinton's enemies. The antagonism was almost inevitable because Clinton's enemies were heavily based among the Albany-Montreal smuggling group while Johnson traded directly with the Indians instead of through French middlemen, and oriented his trade westward instead of northward. As he gained favor with the Iroquois and Clinton, he became more heavily embroiled in provincial politics; for, as Stanley Nider Katz remarks, Governor Clinton's regime "witnessed an attempt on the part of the royal government to reassert its full prerogative in New York, an attempt that was thwarted by the assembly and smuggler James De Lancey, abetted by the helplessness of Governor Clinton."[10] There was much historical irony in the situation. The Iroquois hated the Albany crowd because Albany's merchants and commissioners of Indian affairs had cheated and abused the Indians in a thousand ways; but the same smugglers and "traders with the enemy" were the most steadfast defenders of liberty of the subject against the encroachments of royal prerogative. The situation makes no sense in terms of highflown rhetorical principles; behind them all were struggles for power, privilege, and wealth.

Johnson knew immediately which side he was on, and never wavered. He was the king's man, as well he may have been in a family sprinkled with knights and boasting as his first cousins the earl of Abingdon and Baron Southampton.[11] William himself aimed at nobility, and he would find a way to get the coveted title. The fact reveals a side of his character that sometimes passes unnoticed when attention is fastened on his congeniality with the Mohawks. When it suited his purpose or his humor, Johnson played at being Indian; he never became one. True, he joined the tribal dances, he distributed largesse in time of need, and he sat through endless wearisome hours of tribal counciling. He also took a Mohawk mistress and set her up as his "housekeeper" along with his official wife of German ancestry. (In the Indians' eyes, his Mohawk "housekeeper" was a second wife, but his will would distinguish very carefully the legitimate children of his German wife.)[12] All this was good for business and politics.

William Johnson: Colonial American, 1715–1763 (Port Washington, N.Y.: Kennikat Press, 1976). This awaits completion and it suffers from extreme hero worship, but it is superior to the others by being reliable at least in statements of factual data.

10. Katz, *Newcastle's New York*, 179–80, 182.

11. Ibid., 253.

12. *Johnson Papers*, 12:1062–75.

Marrying into a chiefly family was an old strategy for traders. Sitting in on councils showed that Johnson took them seriously, unlike Albany's commissioners of Indian affairs who would not spare time to do likewise.

What Johnson aimed at, and he achieved it in his own lifetime, was lordship over those Iroquois in the pattern of medieval lords who led tribesmen to battle, acquired title to their lands, and did not disdain the privilege to be free with their maidens. Johnson's sexual athletics have attracted much attention. Extreme rumors have him sleeping with every pretty Indian girl who caught his eye. (If all those rumors were true, he would have had no time or strength for anything else.)[13]

The pattern of feudal lordship over clans was still faintly visible in Johnson's native Ireland, even clearer among the Highland Scots, and he fitted himself to it as naturally as a pike in a pond. He acquired vast estates during his lifetime—over a million acres—by Iroquois donation, and he built strong stone mansions that served as castles in wartime. This Johnson served his king as a lord of woodland legions whom he alone could summon to the royal standard, and he gained the respect and patronage normal to such service.

But let us understand what this meant for the Indians. Johnson championed them exactly as the medieval lord looked after his peasant manpower—because it was the foundation of his own power. Altruism was foreign to his nature. When Johnson's interests or the needs of the crown required deceiving or betraying the Indians, he acted without hesitation or compunction. He could do this because of his consciously adopted strategy of divide-and-conquer applied skilfully to the Iroquois League and its Covenant Chain confederation. All he had to do was to exploit divisions that existed before he came along.[14] On the one side, as we have seen, he aligned himself in New York with the king's men. On the other side, he cultivated strong leaders among the Mohawks and their "younger brothers," the Oneidas, and helped them grow stronger. With his money, connections, and active leadership, he was able to restore the fading prestige of the Mohawks within the League. This took some years to accomplish, as will be apparent, but when achieved it gave him leverage for a measure of control over even the competing Onondagas and the distant,

13. Allen W. Eckert put Johnson to bed with a thousand Iroquois women. Since Conrad Weiser estimated Iroquois warriors at 2,000, Eckert's sustained orgy would have made Johnson the father of his country in real truth; the rest of Eckert's book is the same sort of slop. Paul A. W. Wallace, who was a real scholar, summoned tradition to attribute "something like a hundred" offspring to Johnson's wandering ways. Less incredible, this still sounds extreme. Not every romp makes spawn, and Indian women understood means of contraception. Eckert, *Wilderness Empire: A Narrative* [should be called *A Fiction*], (Boston: Little, Brown and Co., 1969); Wallace, *Conrad Weiser*, 247.

14. See Richard Aquila, *The Iroquois Restoration: Iroquois Diplomacy on the Colonial Frontier, 1701–1754* (Detroit: Wayne State University Press, 1983), 124.

independently minded Senecas. As intended lord of the Iroquois League and as New York's colonel, he aimed to restore the supremacy of the League council at Onondaga over the fragmented and scattered tribes of the Covenant Chain confederacy, especially those who had settled on the Ohio to trade with Pennsylvania's men and to negotiate independently with Virginia and Pennsylvania. Within the permitted limits of intercolonial political combat, Johnson set his face against Pennsylvania. But he was the crown's man (and his own) rather than New York's, so time would show some change in that regard.

As we pick him up in the late 1740s he was still struggling for status in New York and for domination of the Iroquois, and not making much headway in either direction. His position as mediator between Indians and colonials would one day win him great strength, but at first it simply exposed him to crossfire. The Mohawk parties he sent against Canada in 1747 went without aid from the other Iroquois, and the Mohawks returned in defeat. What was worse, the Albany smugglers who controlled New York's assembly turned a deaf ear to Johnson's pleas for support as transmitted through his ally and their enemy, the governor.[15] "I don't know whether I am right or wrong in calling down and sending out so many as I do," wrote Johnson in May 1747.[16] Events proved him both wrong and right. Wrong because the French won, and their busy agents among the Iroquois kept their victory unforgotten. But the Indians respected a fighter, and they saw that Johnson spent more time with them, and distributed more of his own provisions and goods among them, than any other Englishman. Johnson could still report with satisfaction in 1750 the remarks of a Cayuga chief "who untill last Summer was intirely in the French Interest . . . and the reason he gave me was, that the French he thought were a more warlike people than we, and being the Head Warriour of the five Nations Himself, Said he had a veneration for all those of his own disposition. Besides they always used him better by farr than our People, untill such time as he got acquainted with me, whence commenced his friendship for us, which I have been at a great deal of pains and Expence to Cultivate."[17]

Nevertheless, Johnson tired of the difficulties under which he had to labor as New York's agent handicapped by the antagonism of New York's assembly. In December 1750 he announced his intention to resign which he effected within six months though the Iroquios League chiefs protested strongly. He had not labored for love alone. By November 1748 he had

15. *Johnson Papers*, 1:314–24.

16. Johnson to Clinton, *N.Y. Col. Docs.* 6:361.

17. Johnson to Clinton, 20 Dec. 1750, *Johnson Papers* 1:315. Some skepticism should be preserved when reading Johnson's accounts of his dealings with, and status among, Indians. He never minimized himself.

been able to pay in advance over £7,000 for wartime expenses "of his private Fortune." Nearly £4,000 of that remained unreimbursed in July 1751 when he resigned, besides further outlays of almost £600.[18] He probably padded the figures heavily in the customary procedure for tapping the public purse, and he certainly took a businessman's profit on buying and selling, but the amount still looms very large for that era. Few merchants had resources on such a scale. By comparison, a modern scholar mentions that "such provinces as Pennsylvania and New York spent no more than £5,000 a year apart from war expenses."[19]

The sheer magnitude of Johnson's bills goes far to explain the reluctance of New York's assembly to rush forward with reimbursement, for he was demanding almost a year and a half's worth of normal provincial expense. New taxes would be required to pay that bill. But Johnson would make no allowance for such considerations. He refused to continue in office because "from what is past he has no reason to depend on any thing from the Assembly for that purpose."[20] However, retirement did not imply abandonment of private business. He stayed active in that wonderfully profitable Indian trade and continued to cultivate Iroquois leaders until the time came when he would emerge again as an official agent among the Six Nations by royal appointment, free thereafter of the assembly's financial constraints.

Competition from Conrad Weiser

During his term as New York's agent, Johnson had striven for influence with the Iroquois against the omnipresent French, but not only against them. He also contended against Pennsylvania's ambassador to the Indians, Conrad Weiser. The two were polite to each other; but, committed to opposing interests, they tried to move the Six Nations in different directions. Weiser wanted them to oppose the French at the Ohio. Johnson wanted them to attack the French at Montreal. Weiser had only contempt for Johnson's recruiting of Mohawks in 1747: "I dislike it," he wrote; more significantly, "the Six Nations are offended."[21] Yet Weiser could see

18. N.Y. council minutes, 5 July 1751, *Johnson Papers* 1:342–44. It should be noted that one source of Johnson's wealth was the contract to supply the garrison at Oswego. He complained that the assembly had reimbursed only five-sevenths of his outlays in that respect, but if he had followed standard eighteenth-century procedures in marking up costs, the assembly's fraction was probably about right for a fair price with a good profit. See also William Smith, Jr., *A History of the Province of New York* (1757, 1826), ed. Michael Kammen, 2 vols. (Cambridge, Mass.: Belknap Press, 1972) 2:90, 101, 105, 181.

19. E. James Ferguson, "Currency Finance: An Interpretation of Colonial Monetary Practices," *Wm. and Mary Qtly.*, 3d. ser. 10 (1953), 171.

20. *Johnson Papers* 1:344.

21. P. Wallace, *Conrad Weiser*, 248–49.

that the Iroquois League was coming apart, with Mohawks following Johnson while the Ohio Mingos went their own way and Onondaga sat tight. When Weiser lit a new treaty fire at Logstown, he was responding to the Ohio Company's thrust into the west, but now it must be noticed that he was simultaneously making an end run around New York's position. *Nothing* was simple in frontier politics.

In 1750, almost as Johnson's last official act for the province of New York, he intercepted Weiser on the older man's journey to Onondaga with a new mission to seek peace between the Iroquois and their southern Catawba enemies. Johnson said that he was already handling that, and the League should not be confused by several approaches. (He failed, by the way.) Weiser went on to Onondaga anyway to invite the League chiefs to a treaty with Virginia at Fredericksburg, but he failed also. The chiefs thought that Virginia should send an embassy to Albany. The net result was no treaty at all.[22]

Whatever was going on, the complications and expense became too much at that time for young William Johnson. After his resignation, French influence became dominant in Onondaga. As we have seen, Virginia and Pennsylvania treated at Logstown with the Mingos and other Ohio tribes. As the Seven Years War loomed on the horizon, the League at Onondaga seemed to have become a nullity.

Mohawk independence alarms the lords of trade

It was all too much for the Mohawks. Relying on Johnson's promises, they had warred against the French in 1747 without League support—and had been defeated with serious losses. Now the French were in the saddle at Onondaga; Virginia and Pennsylvania were ignoring the League; Johnson, their source of influence in New York, had resigned; and the people with whom they were to deal in future were the hated Albanians. To top off everything else, partners in a scheme called the Kayaderosseras patent were trying to swindle the Mohawks out of 800,000 acres of their territory.[23]

Though the Mohawks had been New York's most faithful allies since the colony's foundation—they had even stayed away from the League's treaties with Pennsylvania—their friendship dwindled with their territory. On 16 June 1753, Chief Hendrick stood up in conference with the provincial council of New York, faced Governor George Clinton squarely, and poured out his bitter anger.

22. Ibid., ch. 38.

23. Georgiana C. Nammack, *Fraud, Politics, and the Dispossession of the Indians: The Iroquois Land Frontier in the Colonial Period* (Norman: Unversity of Oklahoma Press, 1969), 53–57.

Brother when we came here to relate our Grievances about our Lands, we expected to have something done for us, and we have told you that the Covenant Chain of our Forefathers was like to be broken, and brother you tell us that we shall be redressed at Albany, but we know them so well, we will not trust to them, for they [the Albany merchants] are no people but Devils, so we rather desire that you'll say, Nothing shall be done for us; Brother By and By you'll expect to see the Nations [of Iroquois] down [here in New York City] which you shall not see, for as soon as we come home we will send up a Belt of Wampum to our Brothers, the [other] 5 Nations to acquaint them the Covenant Chain is broken between you and us. So brother you are not to expect to hear of me any more, and Brother we desire to hear no more of you.[24]

Suddenly the Mohawks got some attention. It was mid-1753. In the west the French had a strong fort at Niagara and were building more. North of Albany they held Fort St. Frédéric at the narrows of Lake Champlain; it was solidly built of stone, and it pointed like the tip of a spear down the valley toward Albany.[25] Quite perceptibly the long history of wars with France was entering a new chapter. Perhaps the quarreling Yorkers would not have composed their differences even then; but, like Weiser, the experienced members of the crown's board of trade in London immediately recognized the Mohawk declaration as a diplomatic event "of a very serious nature." The board saw that "the Indians . . . considered the alliance and friendship between them and the Province of New York to be dissolved;"[26] and this was most alarming because "the steady adherence of these Indians to the British interest" had been vital to secure Britain's colonies "from the fatal effects of the encroachments of a foreign power"—that is, France. Without the Indians, "all our efforts to check and disappoint the present view of this power may prove ineffectual."[27] It was curious language from a government that claimed to hold a protectorate over the Iroquois. At the very moment, British diplomats negotiating with the French claimed sovereignty over the Mississippi Valley by virtue of "conquest" there by Iroquois "dependents." Besides the military value of Iroquois warriors (which had been somewhat in decline as British colonial population rose), the diplomatic argument of Iroquois dependency was essential.

With what was lightning speed for that sluggish body, the board of trade moved to remedy the situation. It instructed the colonial governors

24. Conference minutes, New York, 16 June 1753, *N.Y. Col. Docs.* 6:788. Conrad Weiser thought that Hendrick "in a manner proclaimed Warr." P. Wallace, *Conrad Weiser*, 350.

25. Guy Omeron Coolidge, *The French Occupation of the Champlain Valley from 1609 to 1759* (1938), reprinted (Harrison, N.Y.: Harbor Hill Books, 1979), 115–28.

26. Lords of trade to earl of Holderness, 18 Sept. 1753, *N.Y. Col. Docs.* 6:799.

27. Lords of trade to Sir Danvers Osborne, 18 Sept. 1753, ibid. 6:800–801; same to De Lancey, 5 July 1754, ibid., 6:845–46.

to assemble the most impressive joint treaty with the Indians of the Covenant Chain that had yet been held, and to treat in the king's own name rather than in behalf of the individual colonial governments that the Indians so distrusted. Thus was born the famous Albany Congress of 1754.

Anticipating what the Congress did, we must notice here what the board of trade wanted it to do. There was little likeness. The lords commissioners of the board let their displeasure be known to Yorkers for that province's having let the Mohawks depart "without any measures taken to bring them to temper, or to redress their Complaints." They tactfully omitted this passage from their circular letter to governors of other colonies in which they described their limited objective concisely: "His Majesty having been pleased to order a Sum of Money to be issued for Presents to the Six Nations of Indians, and to direct his Governor of New York to hold an Interview with them for delivering these Presents, for burying the Hatchet, and for renewing the Covenant Chain with them, We think it our Duty to acquaint you therewith." It was left up to New York's governor to issue invitations and set the time and place of meeting.[28] In so ordering, the board of trade had begun to implement in one field a decision by the ministry that was also circulated to the colonial governors. This was an order from the crown for the provinces to be "aiding and assisting each other, in case of any invasion." Secretary of State Holderness reminded them emphatically of "the necessity of a mutual assistance."[29] As we shall see, the message from Holderness caught some colonial imaginations and formed a rationale for diverting the board of trade's congress from the board's objective. The board confined its own instruction to a joint proceeding in the king's name for reconciling disgruntled Indians, perhaps because its members understood only too well the difficulty of achieving collaboration between colonials who were almost rabidly competitive. Colonial gentlemen were willing to go blandly through the forms of cooperation only so far as those procedures did not interfere with their individual purposes.

Perhaps also the lords of trade had no inclination to see provinces come together on their own terms, thus magnifying their power vis à vis the crown. The independence from the crown that the colonies declared openly in 1776 showed itself in practice long before that year through various maneuvers and dodges. In 1753, however, the lords had no need to fear

28. Circular ltr., 18 Sept. 1753, ibid., 6:802. The board's instructions to New York's governor included an admonition "to take care that all the Provinces be (if practicable) comprized in one general Treaty to be made in his Majesty's name, it appearing to us that the practice of each Province making a separate Treaty for itself in its own name is very improper and may be attended with great inconveniency to His Majesty's service." *N.Y. Col. Docs.* 6:800–2; *Pa. Council Minutes* 5:711–12; 717–18.

29. *N.Y. Col. Docs.* 6:794–95.

genuine colonial unity. In that year, the gentlemen of Virginia had their own notions of how to deal with that foreign power at the Ohio, and they did not intend to be hindered by "cooperation" from Pennsylvania or New York or the crown itself. (Resistance to the crown was already an old story in Virginia.)[30] Virginia "excused" itself from attendance at Albany and the possible restrictions that attendance might have entailed, and Virginia continued its rash, calamitous adventuring.[31] Its logic was at the same time clear and insane: clear because Virginia's troops in occupation of the Ohio territory would be more than sufficient argument against charter claims by Thomas Penn or Iroquois dependency claims by New York; insane because Virginia flung a few hundred raw militiamen against the thousands of seasoned Canadian troops already on the scene. The news of Washington's capitulation at Fort Necessity would arrive at Albany to greet the Congress's participants.[32]

Pennsylvania proprietary versus assembly

But now we must backtrack once more to see what conditions brought Pennsylvania's delegates to the Congress. Unlike New York, Pennsylvania was a proprietary province, the fief of the Penn family; but very much like New York, its assembly was constantly embroiled with the province's deputy governors. We must recognize at once that Thomas Penn, who acted as the family executive, had inherited none of his father William's altruism. Thomas had every perquisite but one of a great lord of the British empire, with the greatest landed estate of them all. He lacked membership in the House of Lords, but he had a title, and it gave him more prerogative and estate than a duke's. He was True and Absolute Proprietary of the province of Pennsylvania, and in the 1740s he and his family owned outright (except for the Indian right called an "incumbrance") more than two-thirds of its land.[33] As the family's manager, he appointed deputy governors with the crown's consent. They, in turn, appointed all pro-

30. See Stephen Saunders Webb, *1676: The End of American Independence* (New York: Alfred A. Knopf, 1984), bk. 1.

Bibliographic note: Webb's passionate rhetoric must be read with care. He seems to me to be quite wrong in several important particulars. E.g., Nathaniel Bacon was certainly not a champion of the people, and the Covenant Chain was equally certainly not founded by a partnership of Edmund Andros and Onondaga sachem Garakontié. None of Webb's cited evidence supports the latter assertion even indirectly. For the discriminating reader, the book has much interesting material.

31. Gipson, *British Empire* 5:112n191, 113n1. The lords of trade expressed "surprize and concern" at the absenteeism. They were "at a loss to guess at the motives." *N.Y. Col. Docs.* 6:845–46.

32. Smith, *History of New York* 2:161.

33. The fraction is my own guesstimate based on map inspection.

vincial judges and magistrates, and picked the county sheriffs from a choice of men nominated by popular vote. The governor's advisory council was also appointed, and so were the other executive officers, including those of the Land Office that issued (or withheld) warrants to survey land and patents for title.[34] Penn had many places to dispose of, and much discretion about distribution of wealth-producing land. He and his officers also had complete control of the province's Indian affairs, and a law provided that no individual's purchase of land directly from Indians could be valid until the Penns had first acquired cession of that land to themselves. Further, the purchaser must then pay the Penns their price in order to get a valid patent, and forever after pay annual quitrent.[35]

That was the theory, and for many people it was the fact—for enough people, in fact, to make the Penns rich in money as well as lands.[36] But Thomas Penn was a skinflint who never got enough, and he resented his assembly's chartered controls over public money. In the words of James H. Hutson, when Thomas Penn became principal proprietary in 1746, he "silently declared war" on the Quaker-controlled assembly.[37] One reason

34. *The Charters of the Province of Pensilvania and City of Philadelphia* (Philadelphia: B. Franklin, 1742), sections IV, V, X, XVII; "Charter of Privileges Granted by William Penn," section III.

35. *A Collection of all the Laws of the Province of Pennsylvania Now in Force*, published by order of the assembly (Philadelphia: B. Franklin, 1742), ch. XX, p. 7; Charles Huston, *An Essay on the History and Nature of Original Titles to Land in the Province and State of Pennsylvania* (Philadelphia: T. and J. W. Johnson, 1849). For description of ways in which the laws were administered see Jennings, "Incident at Tulpehocken," *Pennsylvania History* 35:4(Oct. 1968), 335–55.

36. In 1759, Benjamin Franklin came into possession, "by accident," of Thomas Penn's own "estimate of the Province." This computed to lands worth about £10,000,000 sterling of which £1,000,000 sterling had been improved and settled. According to these calculations the whole value of all the property of all Pennsylvania inhabitants did not amount to more than £6,000,000 additional. Cf. John Penn's estimates of Penn property after the American Revolution. [Richard Jackson], *An Historical Review of the Constitution and Government of Pennsylvania* (1759), reprinted (New York: Arno Press, 1972), appendix; A. D. Chidsey, Jr., *The Penn Patents in the Forks of the Delaware*, Publications of the Northampton County Historical and Genealogical Society 2 (Easton, Pa., 1937), 18.

37. James H. Hutson, "Benjamin Franklin and Pennsylvania Politics, 1751–1755: A Reappraisal," *Pa. Mag. of Hist. and Biog.* 93:3 (July 1969), 321.

Bibliographic note: Hutson's writings depict a sincere and reasonable Thomas Penn who simply misunderstood and distrusted his province's assemblymen, but Hutson had trouble fitting that notion into the facts he uncovered. His solution was an "ambivalent" Penn. "Although he paid intellectual fealty to the concept of representative government he had difficulty accepting it when he confronted it in a robust incarnation like the Pennsylvania Assembly." With considerable respect to Hutson's scholarship, which I have found valuable, I cannot understand why he was so strongly influenced by the slanted trash of William S. Hanna, *Benjamin Franklin and Pennsylvania Politics* (Stanford, Calif.: Stanford University Press, 1964). For me, Thomas Penn's ostensible devotion to honor and integrity was entirely cover-up for a very clever, very avaricious, and entirely unprincipled man. See Jennings, *Ambiguous Iroquois Empire*, ch 5. 16, 17, and app. B. Hutson quotation above is at James H. Hutson, *Pennsylvania Politics, 1746–1770: The Movement for Royal Government and Its Consequences* (Princeton, N.J.: Princeton University Press, 1972), 6–7.

was the assembly's insistence on issuing paper currency on its own terms, which included receipt and management by the assembly of interest accruing from lending the paper to businessmen. The assembly gained a degree of executive power by this device, which Penn believed should rightfully be in his own hands. Penn also opposed the issuance of paper money on terms that threatened his quitrent income through inflation. He wanted sterling or its full equivalent on the exchange at London. It made no difference to Penn that the currency was regulated to the benefit of the colony, and that it "was esteemed by all classes and regarded as having contributed to the growth and prosperity of the colony." (Even Adam Smith would praise it in his *Wealth of Nations.*)[38] Penn wanted his pound of flesh from nearest the heart. The terms that he would accept were not satisfactory to the people in a rapidly expanding provincial economy drained of specie and needing a medium of exchange to maintain business activity.

A critical scholar has acknowledged that the assembly's "strength and dynamism stemmed from its embodiment and articulation of the attitudes and aspirations of its constituents, the people of Pennsylvania."[39] Antagonist Thomas Penn embodied only the aspirations of his family and a coterie of placemen, but Penn's legal powers and his skill as a courtier gave him great advantage against the popular will. Assembly after assembly locked horns with Penn's governors, with the full support of the electorate. With the support of the crown, whose prerogative he linked to his own, Penn issued legally binding instructions to each governor in minute detail, and required a personal bond of £5,000, to be forfeited if the governor deviated from the instructions.[40] In this respect he exceeded even the most prerogative-minded of the king's ministers: although the crown also issued instructions to governors of royal provinces, it required no bond so that royal governors were able to use some discretion in dealing with assemblies.[41] On matters important to Thomas Penn, which were also the matters most important to assemblymen, his governors had no latitude at all. They had to find ways of cajoling or coercing assemblies into doing what Penn wanted although those assemblies had all power over taxation and appropriation. And were very, very tough.

The most vulnerable side of Pennsylvania's assemblies until 1756 was

38. Ferguson, "Currency Finance," 159, 163.

39. Hutson, "Benjamin Franklin and Pennsylvania Politics," 320–23; Instructions of Thomas and Richard Penn to Governor Hamilton, 17 Mar. 1747, mss., clause 10, Pa. Misc. Papers: Penn and Baltimore; Penn Family, 1740–56, p. 79, HSP.

40. Ibid.; instructions to Robert Hunter Morris, 14 and 16 May 1754, Penn Mss., Assembly and Provincial Council of Pa., 64; Pa. Misc. Papers, Penn and Baltimore, Penn Family, 1740–56, 162; Cadwalader Collection, Thomas Cadwalader, Box 6a, folder Documents (Penn), all HSP. Hutson, *Pennsylvania Politics*, 29–33.

41. Many examples of discretion by royal governors are itemized in Greene, *Quest for Power;* see index entry "instructions."

their domination by Quakers. Assemblies in other provinces acted in much the same way as Pennsylvania's, and stubbornly held on until they got their way, but the pacifist Quakers in time of war lived under the threat of disfranchisement or disablement from holding office. (They had been so punished in England in William Penn's time, and they would be so punished again in Pennsylvania during the American Revolution.) Though the majority of Pennsylvania's voters elected them repeatedly against the strongest candidates the proprietary party could find, it was easy for Penn and his cohorts to stir up hostile sentiment in England. As example, Governor George Thomas, in 1741, remarked (for the benefit of ministers to whom his speech would be transmitted), "If your principles will not allow you to raise men for his Majestie's service for distressing an insolent enemy,—is it calumny to say your principles are inconsistent with the ends of government?"[42] "Treason" whispered between the lines.

It *was* calumny, however, because the Quakers did vote funds "for the King's use" when the crown made a direct demand; but the assemblymen would not authorize a provincial militia, and pacifism was only one of their reasons. They were willing enough to support volunteer soldiers who were not principled against military service, but they feared the power that a militia would put in the hands of Penn's governor. Perhaps a power to impress men into service against their will. Certainly a new engine of patronage through the selection and appointment of officers. Possibly use of the militia to win elections by forceful means.[43] (Proprietary partisans had hired a gang of seamen in 1742 to rough up the opposition.)[44] The Quakers did not fear attack on Philadelphia from the sea because the city stood hundreds of miles inland on the Delaware River, the treacherous shoals and currents of which required experienced local pilots for navigation. On the land side the whole province relied, like New York, on Indians as its first line of defense; and the Quaker assemblymen showed the fine distinctions in their principles by appropriating large sums of money for presents to Indian warriors.[45] This was more than Thomas Penn did, regardless of his high patriotic rhetoric and the immense estate protected

42. Theodore Thayer, *Israel Pemberton, King of the Quakers* (Philadelphia: Historical Society of Pennsylvania, 1943), 47. Thayer is a great rarity among professional historians because he paid serious attention to Quaker sources as well as the writings of their enemies.

43. [William Smith], *A Brief State of the Province of Pennsylvania* (London: R. Griffiths, 1755), 15–16.

44. Richard Peters is authority for this flat statement. He told Thomas Penn that the great merchant and proprietary supporter Joseph Turner, who was also partner to William Allen, had hired the seamen. Almost all historical accountes denigrate Quaker reporting of the event as propaganda, but Peters cannot be suspected of a Quaker bias. See William T. Parsons, "The Bloody Election of 1742," *Pennsylvania History* 36:3 (July 1969), 290–306, Peters quotation at p. 303. This article is by far the best discussion of the subject.

45. Theodore Thayer, *Pennsylvania Politics and the Growth of Democracy, 1740–1776* (Harrisburg: Pennsylvania Historical and Museum Commission, 1953), 31.

by those Indians. Indeed, Penn had embittered many of the Ohio Indians by his land swindles, but this was a well-kept secret until exposed in 1756.

Benjamin Franklin goes into politics

From the midst of this turmoil emerges the protean figure of Benjamin Franklin, a printer-bookseller-writer-scribe and amateur scientist who tried in the 1740s to mediate between the contending parties. To set up a militia despite assembly opposition, he organized a volunteer military association in 1747 and financed it by a lottery. For this he won no thanks from either side although the association was highly successful. What Franklin called the "stiffrump" Quakers (as distinguished from more flexible types) opposed the association on principle, and Penn's men feared it in practice because it created an independent political force out of their control.[46] Nonetheless, Franklin's busyness in community good works kept him on terms with all sides. As biographer Carl van Doren remarks, "In all this Franklin seems to have made the fewest enemies."[47] He had acquired enough wealth from business to be able to turn his enterprises over to managing partner David Hall; he retired with substantial income in 1748, and acquired leisure for politics.[48]

For a decade after 1755, Franklin would wage grim battle against Thomas Penn on every front, not least through exposure of Penn's corrupt management of Indian affairs, but the Franklin of 1751 had not yet come to that commitment. When elected to the assembly in 1751, Franklin was familiar with its business from fifteen years of service as its clerk.[49] Nevertheless he had refrained from aspersing proprietary party leaders; he had, in fact, positively sought out their friendship.

In Franklin's youth he had been befriended by proprietary wheel horse James Logan who was the very architect of Pennsylvania's Indian policy (and who reputedly owned the finest library in the colonies). Logan remained a "good old friend" until his death in 1749.[50] Rich William Allen, who had studied for law at the Inns of Court in London, liked Franklin enough to exert influence for his appointment in August 1753 as deputy postmaster general of the British colonies, and Allen was provincial chief justice by Penn appointment, and leader of the proprietary forces in electoral

46. Ibid., 20–23. Amusingly, Thayer converts Franklin's *stiffrump* into *stiff-necked*.
47. Carl Van Doren, *Benjamin Franklin* (New York: Viking Press, 1938), 188.
48. *Franklin Papers*, 317–20.
49. Van Doren, *Benjamin Franklin*, 198–99. Modern students might note that Franklin's flowing, legible script was an important reason for his appointment as assembly clerk.
50. *Franklin Papers* 3:483.

politics.[51] Provincial Secretary Richard Peters—Thomas Penn's most trusted informant—was on congenial terms with Franklin who liked to chide Peters humorously about the secretary's illegible scrawl.[52]

Though Franklin sympathized with the Quaker party in most of their political positions (always excluding the military), he cultivated prominent proprietary men, among others, for perhaps a variety of reasons. Such contacts were good for business, of course, but it appears that he enjoyed the company and conversation of well-educated, well-read men. He also wanted their support in the many community projects he initiated or took part in: his youthful Junto, the Philadelphia lodge of Freemasons, the Library Company, the Union Fire Company, the reorganization of the city watch, the Philadelphia Academy (ancestor of the University of Pennsylvania), the Pennsylvania Hospital, the first American fire insurance company, the lottery to finance a steeple and bells for Christ Church, and the founding of the American Philosophical Society. It is astonishing to consider how many of these institutions are still functioning robustly today.

In 1751, Indian affairs came under Franklin's scrutiny. By invitation, he read a manuscript copy of Archibald Kennedy's influential pamphlet, *The Importance of Gaining and Preserving the Friendship of the Indians to the British Interest*, and Franklin's comments stimulated correspondence on the subject between Kennedy and the recognized "authority" on the subject, Cadwallader Colden. Much impressed, Kennedy printed Franklin's comments in his published book.[53] As always, Franklin linked virtue with practicality. "Securing the Friendship of the Indians is of the greatest Consequence to these Colonies," he wrote, and "the surest Means of doing it, are, to regulate the Indian Trade, so as to convince them, by Experience, that they may have the best and cheapest Goods, and the fairest Dealing from the English." This much was old doctrine that had often been expressed by persons concerned about the unconscionable methods

51. Franklin to Peter Collinson, 31 May 1751, in *Franklin Papers* 4:134–36; Van Doren, *Benjamin Franklin*, 210–11. Franklin included Allen's recommendation in his 1751 letter. Allen wrote separately to David Barclay and Sons, 5 Nov. 1753, to offer whatever security might be needed for Franklin; as this would be "giving the finishing Stroke to an affair I have had much at heart." But security had already been found. *The Burd Papers: Extracts from Chief Justice William Allen's Letter Book . . . Together with an Appendix Containing Pamphlets in the Controversy with Franklin*, ed. Lewis Burd Walker (Pottsville, Pa., 1897), 10–11.

Bibliographic note: Allen's letter book contained copies of 187 letters dated 1753–70, from 87 of which this book printed extracts or copies. I have not been able to find the original letter book.

52. Franklin to Richard Peters, 17 Sept. 1754, *Franklin Papers* 5:431–32.

53. Franklin's letter was printed anonymously, like Kennedy's book. [Archibald Kennedy], *The Importance of Gaining and Preserving the Friendship of the Indians to the British Interest, Considered* (New York: James Parker, 1751). Reprinted in England, 1752. I have used the American copy at the Huntington Library. More convenient for the letter is *Franklin Papers* 4:117–21.

of the free enterprisers in Indian country. Franklin carried the logic a step further: "and to unite the several [colonial] Governments, so as to form a Strength that the Indians may depend on for Protection, in case of a Rupture with the french; or apprehend great danger from, if they should break with us." For Franklin, justice would be made to serve the ends of empire.[54]

It is of record also that Franklin purchased Colden's *History of the Five Indian Nations* in 1751, and there is nothing in his correspondence with Colden to suggest that he dissented from its imperialist theses. It seems to have fired his imagination to produce a famous passage that has been much quoted for varied reasons. "It would be a very strange Thing, if six Nations of ignorant Savages should be capable of forming a Scheme for such an Union [the Iroquois League], and be able to execute it in such a Manner, as that it has subsisted Ages, and appears indissoluble; and yet that a like Union should be impracticable for ten or a Dozen English Colonies, to whom it is more necessary, and must be more advantageous; and who cannot be supposed to want an equal Understanding of their Interests."[55] However else this remark may be interpreted, it notably lacks warmth of affection for those "ignorant Savages."

In that same year of 1751, during his first term in Pennsylvania's assembly, Franklin served on the committee to review expenses for Indian affairs, and the practical businessman seems to have gone into mild shock, about which more will be said a little further on. In 1753, Governor James Hamilton made him one of the commissioners to meet the Ohio Indians at Carlisle where he pumped Conrad Weiser, George Croghan, and Andrew Montour, and observed astutely the procedures of Iroquois treaties. Characteristically he made a little profit out of the affair by printing and selling its minutes.[56]

As a politician, Franklin became a personal force to be reckoned with. His booster activity won him many friends, and his service as deputy postmaster general would gain recognition and respect throughout the colonies (as well as free circulation for his newspaper). In 1753 he leaped to international fame when his experiments in electricity won him the Copley gold medal of the Royal Society of London for Improving Natural Knowledge.[57] Harvard and Yale bestowed honorary degrees on him.[58] He became

54. Ibid., 4:117.

55. Ibid., 4:76, 118–19. Cf. the argument by Mary E. Fleming Mathur, "Savages Are Heroes, Too, Whiteman" in *The American Indian and the American Revolution*, ed. Francis Jennings, Newberry Library Center for the History of the American Indian Occasional Papers 6 (Chicago, 1983), 34–41.

56. *Franklin Papers* 5:231n8.

57. The fame becomes visible in the earl of Macclesfield's speech of award. The earl seemed astonished that such talent could have shown itself in the resident of "a remote Country." Ibid., 5:126–34.

58. Benjamin Franklin, *Autobiography*, eds. Leonard W. Labaree et al., (New Haven: Conn., Yale University Press, 1964), 208–9.

more than a successful businessman and benevolent philanthropist. He was transformed into a *philosopher*, renowned in England and Europe, and a glorious ornament to his province. His fame helped win support for his attempts to compromise in the assembly between the Quaker majority and the proprietary party, but compromise was not in the lexicon of Thomas Penn. The more that Franklin tried to mediate, the more rigid and suspicious Penn became. Penn did not want independent great men in his estate. He put a secret spy on Franklin, and waited.[59]

It was impossible for Franklin to join any party but his own. If he lacked sympathy with Quaker pacifism, he was contemptuous of Penn's meanness in money matters—which he knew from personal experience as well as observation in the assembly.[60] But Franklin dreamed of empire in the west, and Penn seemed to be cautiously supporting expansion while the Quakers resisted it. Franklin used practical expedients, but he was not a mere opportunist. He was an imperialist Whig, believing in the simultaneous expansion of empire and liberty.[61] He had yet to learn of a contradiction between the two principles. Management of Indian affairs became his touchstone. As it was the key to western empire, so Penn's and the Quakers' contrasting approaches to it enlightened Franklin about his proprietary lord.

Indian affairs and expense

Disillusion commenced in 1750 when Penn became alarmed about the Ohio Company's plans to colonize. Though the Ohio region had not been surveyed, Penn believed, rightly, that the Company aimed at territory within his chartered boundaries. He responded to the Company's plan to build a fort there with a suggestion to preempt the place by having Pennsylvania build one first. He offered £400 toward construction and £100 annually toward maintenance. It was a typical Penn ploy. Nothing prevented Penn from building such a fort himself at his own expense (as the Ohio Company soon started to do), and Penn's proposed fort would ben-

59. Discussed in ch. 11, below.

60. While in the province, Thomas Penn ran up a bill for printing and subscriptions over the period from 1734 to 1745. Franklin billed without response. In 1757 he billed once again, and in 1759 he finally received his money. The editors of the *Franklin Papers* comment: "Thus two years and four months after Franklin submitted this bill and twenty-five years after the first charges were incurred, Thomas Penn's agent finally paid what was due." 7:157–58.

61. James H. Hutson is rightly concerned to rescue Franklin from opportunism, but in doing so he turns the man so Whiggish as to make it "imprudent to call him an independent during his early years in the Pennsylvania Assembly." "Benjamin Franklin and Pennsylvania Politics," 316–17. This goes too far. 1754 was only the fourth year of Franklin's membership in the assembly, and he was then working with or against the Quakers as he pleased.

efit only the Pennsylvania traders and Mr. Penn's claims against Virginia and New France. As Penn remarked, it would "in some measure protect the trade and be a mark of possession."[62] He did not add that it was his own possession to be marked and that the fort would cost many times more than what he proposed to advance.

The assembly refused, but, as an alternative it laid out £1,250 for presents to the Indians in 1750, and £1,260 in 1751, "besides several Accounts not yet adjusted," to which Thomas Penn contributed nothing. As a member of the assembly's committee reviewing accounts, Franklin tried to reason with Governor James Hamilton. "We have seriously considered the Offer made by our Proprietaries, of contributing towards building such a [strong] House; but as we have always found that sincere, upright Dealing with the Indians, a friendly Treatment of them on all Occasions, and particularly in relieving their Necessities at proper Times by suitable Presents, have been the best Means of securing their Friendship, we could wish our Proprietaries had rather thought fit to join with us in the Expence of those Presents, the Effects of which have at all Times so manifestly advanced their Interest with the Security of our Frontier Settlements."[63]

On this issue Franklin joined the Quakers with a whole heart. He saw that assembly outlays on Indian affairs had been negligible before Thomas Penn came to the province in 1732, and moneys appropriated for the purpose had been considered as the public's "free Gift" toward a responsibility that properly lay with the proprietaries, whose wealth derived from land ceded by the Indians. Especially during wartime, however, the pacifist-dominated assembly had "thought it proper to demonstrate, that they were not induced by mercenary Motives, to refuse joining in the making any Military Preparations," and had therefore laid out large sums. Altogether, between 1733 and 1751, it had spent £8,366 for the purpose. A unanimous assembly resolved "to request the Proprietaries in the most reasonable and in the most respectful Manner, to agree upon a proportionable Part of all such Charges on Account of Indian Treaties, as may hereafter accrue, to be paid by the Proprietaries and Province, respectively." It was a compromise offer to forget past accounts and start out fresh, and probably Franklin had helped to persuade the assemblymen to soften the principle that all Indian expenses should be borne by the Penns. But the response of Thomas and Richard Penn was "That they do not conceive themselves under any Obligation to contribute to Indian *or any other pub-*

62. Wainwright, *George Croghan*, 35. The Ohio Company in Virginia tried to be excused from its commitment to build a fort at the Ohio "as it is impracticable for them to do it out of their private fortunes the thing being of a Public Nature," but went ahead anyway. It later secured reimbursement for the expense. My source does not indicate who paid the reimbursement. *Mercer Papers*, 171, 622–23n573.

63. *Franklin Papers* 4:183.

lick Expences."[64] Though the Penns identified their own prerogative with the crown's, they did not accept the crown's responsibilities. When the crown's ministers sent royal presents to the Indians, the Penns locked up their pockets. Their utmost contribution was a recommendation to the assembly to lay out public money. Thomas Penn argued that his salary for Conrad Weiser was his contribution to the expense of Indian affairs, but the assembly always paid Weiser's expenses as well as the cost of presents.

The assembly tried reasonableness once more. It pointed out that the Penns paid no land taxes anywhere because "their great Estate not lying in Britain, is happily exempt from the Burthens borne by their Fellow Subjects there," and was not taxed in Pennsylvania either. Further, that the Penns had a monopoly by law for Indian land purchases so that they "reap the whole Benefit" of "Land they sell again to vast Advantage." Indian friendship "more particularly advances the Interest and Value of the Proprietary Estate than that of any other Estate in the Province," and therefore "tho' they may conceive themselves under no Obligation by Law, they are under the much stronger Obligations of natural Equity and Justice;" and the compromise was offered again, with equal futility.[65] When Franklin went to the Carlisle treaty in 1753, the £800 worth of presents taken along by the commissioners were paid for entirely by the assembly.[66]

Still Franklin temporized, and still the proprietary's men hoped to win him completely to their side. They had substantial grounds to hope. Franklin was cooperating with them in efforts to reduce the solid bloc of German support for the Quakers at elections.[67] He agreed with the imperialists on the issue of intercolonial union, and split from the Quakers on it, as will be shown.

Muddled issues

Thus, when Governor Hamilton in 1753 joined the issue of joint colonial reconciliation of the Indians to the rather different issue of intercolonial union, Franklin went along. He may indeed have suggested the device. It should be remembered that Secretary Holderness had desired "mutual assistance" among the colonies; and Lord Halifax at the board of trade ordered only a joint treaty with the Indians as had been "usual upon for-

64. Ibid., 4:186–89. My italics. Cf. the New York assembly's withholding of reimbursement to William Johnson for his outlays on Indian presents. See p. 79, above.

65. Ibid., 4:190–91.

66. *Franklin Papers* 4:183.

67. Ibid., 203–6; Thayer, *Pennsylvania Politics*, 35–36.

mer occasions."[68] Hamilton combined and transformed these communications. Watch how he finessed "acting in concert" into "a general union."

> Several Letters have passed between me and the Governor of New York, Virginia, and the Massachusetts, in which they make this Province the Tender of their Assistance, express an hearty Desire of acting in Concert with Us against his Majestie's Enemies, concur in Sentiment with His Majestie's Ministers of the Necessity of a general Union of all the Provinces both in Councils and Forces . . . I most earnestly recommend it to You [the assemblymen], and hope what is so well and justly said on this and other Matters by Lord Holdernesse, the Lords of Trade, and the neighbouring Governors, will have their full Force and Weight with You in your Deliberations."[69]

The assembly was not impressed. It refused to be diverted from the major business on its agenda, which was the issuance of paper money of a kind that Hamilton was under instruction to veto. On this issue, Franklin joined the assembly's response to Hamilton.[70]

But the French did not go away, and the issue of what to do about them remained alive. The assemblymen inspected Lord Holderness's letter closely and did not find in it what Hamilton said was there. "We cannot but observe some Differences between the Royal Orders, signified by the Earl of Holdernesse's Letter as well as the Letter from the Lords of Trade . . . and the Light in which the Governor is pleased to represent them."[71] Hamilton hotly and verbosely responded that his words were "very agreeable in their Sense and Meaning" to Holderness's letter "tho' not a bare Repetition."[72] A new wrangle commenced in which the assembly erroneously doubted that the province's boundaries extended so far as where the French were marching, and therefore withheld consent to build forts. Distinguishing carefully the order from the lords of trade, the assemblymen offered to comply with it by appropriating funds for delegates to the treaty conference at Albany despite being already in debt "about Fourteen Hundred Pounds" for the recent treaty at Carlisle.[73]

68. Holderness to Hamilton, 28 Aug. 1753, in *Pa. Council Minutes* 5:689–90; Halifax et al. to Hamilton, 18 Sept. 1753, in ibid., 5:711–12.

69. Ibid., 5:721.

70. Ibid., 5:723–29.

71. Ibid., 5:747.

72. Ibid., 5:753.

73. Ibid., 5:748–49. There is revelation in this remark about the size of contingent expenses at a treaty. The present at Carlisle cost £800, and contingencies including commissioners' travel expense cost £600. Carlisle is about 120 miles from Philadelphia. Compare with Sir William Johnson's journey in 1761 from his estate in New York to Detroit, a journey of not less than 500 miles, for which total expenses, including assistants, wampum, and presents, came to £305. The Pennsylvanians, among others, demonstrate that the businessman's "swindle sheet" was not invented in the twentieth century. *Johnson Papers* 3:503; Wilbur R. Jacobs, *Diplomacy and Indian Gifts* (Stanford, Calif.: Stanford University Press, 1950), 182.

To follow all those wrangles would be extraneous to present concerns. It is enough to note here that Hamilton tried once more to extract from the assembly an authorization to participate in intercolonial union. He modified it to a union "in Indian affairs" and asked for authority to instruct the delegates to Albany to concur in "a reasonable Plan" for that purpose.[74] He got nowhere. The assembly responded with a strong rejection through a committee report that did not bear Franklin's name. It declared that "no Propositions for an Union of the Colonies, in Indian Affairs, can effectually answer the good Purposes, or be binding, farther than are confirmed by Laws, enacted under the several Government's comprized in that Union." Which was to say that the assemblymen did not intend to abdicate in favor of a superpower.[75] It happened, however, that in disregarding Hamilton's urgings for union, the assemblymen confined themselves, as he did not, to what had been desired by the board of trade. Once more they dipped into the treasury to pay the expenses of commissioners and provide a present for the Indians worth £500. And once more Thomas Penn gave nothing, though his nephew John Penn was one of the commissioners, and his confidante, Secretary Richard Peters, was another. It must not be thought, however, that Thomas neglected the Albany Congress. He had personal plans for it, as will be seen.

It would seem that Governor Hamilton saw opportunity in the sharp division that appeared in the assembly on the issue of union. He appointed Franklin as one of the commissioners representing the assembly, and Speaker Isaac Norris, Jr., one of the more flexible Quakers, as the other.[76] In a letter to New York's governor, Hamilton hoped that a way could be found around the assembly's obstruction. Perhaps "something of a general Utility may be agreed upon," at the Congress, "or that a candid Representation of our Condition may be made to his Majesty, and his Interposition implored for our Protection."[77] Franklin went further. On his way to the Congress he discussed with several Yorkers a scheme for uniting the northern colonies to be established by act of Parliament. At its head would be "a Military man" appointed by the king and "to have a Salary from the Crown."[78] Nothing could have been more destructive to the power and principles of Pennsylvania's Quaker assemblymen. It is quite clear that B. Franklin at that moment was very angry with them. It is equally clear that he had been given full notice that they would not approve his schemes for intercolonial union, so he hoped to override them by the power of

74. *Pa. Council Minutes* 6:38.
75. *Franklin Papers* 5:277.
76. *Pa. Council Minutes* 6:47–48.
77. Ibid., 6:48–49.
78. *Franklin Papers* 5:335–38.

Parliament. It is hard to see resemblance between this Franklin and the man who became a leader of the American Revolution.

Albany Congress participants

When all the commissioners convened at Albany, intrigue and clashing interests abounded. Albany's merchants in the Montreal trade were determined to prevent interference with their system: and to that end, Lieutenant Governor James De Lancey, who was one of those merchants, seized control of the Congress by a legal trick. He circumvented his assembly by simply ignoring it. Although instructed by the board of trade only to summon the Congress, which would then normally have elected its own officers and set its own procedure, De Lancey put himself on a higher plane from the commissioners by appearing as governor rather than commissioner. As no other governor was present, he outranked everyone else, and he took charge, bringing along with him members of his council who were likewise without credentials as commissioners.[79] He tried to prevent the Congress from inquiring into Iroquois complaints about land swindles and the Montreal trade by meeting separately with the Indians for two days before the Congress was permitted to treat with them. In this respect, the Yorkers held firmly to their traditional doctrine that the Iroquois were *their* Indians, and De Lancey wanted no part of any outside intervention under the guise of intercolonial unity. De Lancey was equally antagonistic to the Oswego traders' party in his own province, represented by William Johnson, who came to Albany by request of the Iroquois.[80]

In direct conflict was the policy long maintained by successive governments of Massachusetts Bay for direct treaty relationships with the Iroquois unencumbered by New York's chaperonage. Massachusetts's

79. Gipson, *British Empire* 5:116–17.

80. Thomas Pownall's descriptions clarify these matters: memo, "Notes on Indian Affairs," [1754], mss., Loudoun Papers (LO 460), Huntington Library; ltr. to "My Lord" [apparently Halifax], in "Personal Accounts of the Albany Congress of 1754," ed. Beverly McAnear, *Mississippi Valley Historical Review* 39:4 (Mar. 1953), 740, 742–43.

Bibliographic note: Pownall's many, scattered reports deserve very close attention and respect if for no better reason (and there are better ones) than that he acted as eyes and ears for the board of trade whose secretary was his brother John. "What he had really had for the three years since he first came out with Sir Danvers Osborn was a roving commission to make himself useful and collect information for the home government wherever he might be." Charles A. W. Pownall, *Thomas Pownall* (London: Henry Stevens, Son and Stiles, 1908), 67. Leonard W. Labaree thought that Pownall "deserves more than any other Englishman of his time to be called a student of colonial administration." "Pownall, Thomas," *Dict. Amer. Biog.*, 15:16. For Indian affairs Pownall relied heavily on information from William Johnson. For John Pownall's importance, see Franklin B. Wickwire, *British Subministers and Colonial America, 1763–1783* (Princeton, N.J.: Princeton University Press, 1966).

commissioners came to Albany with full instructions to seek colonial union, and the Yorkers suspected a plot to make Massachusetts's governor Shirley the head of the proposed union. Yorkers could not accept such an exaltation of Shirley; among other reasons, because of a simmering dispute over their boundary line with Massachusetts.[81]

As noted, Virginia stayed away. So did New Jersey, on grounds that its government had no treaty relationships with the Iroquois League, and the unspoken corollary that its assembly did not want the expense of commissioners and Indian presents.[82]

Connecticut's men had their own goal. They came with the intention of buying territory from the Iroquois for a western colony of their own, and they got a deed for land in Pennsylvania's Wyoming Valley along the north branch of the Susquehanna River. (Wilkes-Barre is there now.) Pennsylvania sent Conrad Weiser along as interpreter with an extra mission to block Connecticut. Weiser wangled a deed also. The two colonies bought from many of the same individual Indians and their deeds overlapped. A decades-long struggle ensued, sometimes becoming violent to the shedding of blood, until the Revolution's Continental Congress settled it.[83]

The Indians also had differences. Mohawks faced off against all the other Iroquois nations, especially against Onondaga, for primacy in their League. A strong pro-French party existed in the League. The Ohio Indians were absent. The mixed peoples at Schaghticoke on the upper Hudson were not on speaking terms with the "river Indians" of Stockbridge; the two groups had to be dealt with separately. De Lancey grew indignant when Stockbridge mission Indians showed up without an invitation, expecting provisions and presents; Stockbridge was in Massachusetts, and these Indians had been drawn from New York by what the Yorkers thought was "refined kidnapping."[84] Perhaps most important of all was the general disillusion among the Iroquois. Observer Thomas Pownall summed it shrewdly.

He reported that the Iroquois were "conscious on one hand that their League and Alliance with the English" might oblige them to declare war on the French "and on the other being really and in good earnest afraid of the French, and having no confidence or trust in any measures or promises we enter into, and finding that by our measures we are neither able nor

81. "Personal Accounts of the Albany Congress," ed. McAnear, 727–28.

82. Gipson, *British Empire* 5:113n1.

83. Wallace, *Conrad Weiser*, ch. 41; Philip S. Klein and Ari Hoogenboom, *A History of Pennsylvania* (New York: McGraw-Hill Book Co., 1973), 171–72.

84. Thomas Atkinson's memo book in "Personal Accounts of the Albany Congress," ed. McAnear, 736, 738; Congress minutes in *N.Y. Col. Docs.* 6:864–65. It looks as though the Mohawks regarded the Stockbridges as renegades, not much different in that respect from the Mohawks who had gone off to the French.

willing to defend them, they were sensible that such a declaration (drawing the french upon them) must be the ruin of them. Their Resolution therefore was to observe a neutrality and, if they were press'd by the English (who themselves took no real and Actual Step) to declare, I am told they would have spoke, according as they express it, *from the Mouth and not from the Heart*. . . . all Sincerity and Reality is sunk into Political Farce and Compliment (In which for the address and management of it These People, tho we are apt to think them savages and so on, do actually exceed the Europeans)."[85]

To gain their distinct goals the commissioners intrigued and jockeyed for position inside and outside of the Congress's formal sessions. In itself this sort of maneuvering should not cause surprise as it is normal procedure when politicians with diverse interests come together. At Albany, however, the participants carried the process so far that their meeting had little resemblance to what the board of trade had instructed them to do.

The board wanted the Congress to act in the name of the king, and so it did in sessions with the Indians, but the formality bore a dual appearance to the delegates; for, while they acted *in behalf* of the crown, they did so *by authority* of their provincial governments. New Hampshire's commissioner Theodore Atkinson read their documents with a raised eyebrow: "I observed that most of them began with the Stile of the Governors, not the King, Philadelphia and ours only with the regal Stile." Because the Yorkers had no commission at all, the others concluded that governor De Lancey must be present "at every Consultation."[86]

The Yorkers struggled, as always, to keep the Iroquois under their own domination. They were "very disgustfull" about "Commissioners from other Provinces making inquisition into" their conduct, according to Thomas Pownall, and Governor De Lancey negotiated separately with the Iroquois in New York's name rather than the king's. The commissioners did not object—they had other fish to fry—but what went on in those separate meetings was just what the board of trade had intended to be transacted by the Congress as a whole. The Iroquois spoke their grievances and De Lancey made promises that he hoped would forestall repetition of such complaints before the assembled commissioners from other colonies.[87] He failed, but not for lack of effort.

85. Pownall to My Lord, in "Personal Accounts of the Albany Congress," ed. McAnear, 740–41.

86. Atkinson's memo book in ibid., 731.

87. Pownall in ibid., 745; N.Y. council minutes, 27, 28 June 1754, in *N.Y. Col. Docs.* 6:865–68. These minutes say that the Indians requested the meetings. If so, they requested through an interpreter who was employed by New York. Pownall remarked on how "extream bad" the interpreting was at the general treaty, "And a Standerby may observe that at times there are things which do not alway on the face of the Treaty appear in their true meaning." He got this judgment from a gentleman fluent in the Mohawk language with whom he was

Renewal of the Covenant Chain

In New York's separate sessions, Mohawks did all the recorded talking. Canadagara, speaking for their "lower castle," raised the issue of encroachment: "this is the place where we are to expect a redress of our grievances, and we hope all things will be so settled that we may part good friends"; and he named the Kayaderosseras patent as the chief grievance of his people. "We understand that there are writings for all our lands, so that we shall have none left but the very spot we live upon and hardly that." De Lancey promised to look into the problem. "I will do you all the Justice in my power."[88] It would seem that Canadagara had not been told that he was supposed to get redress from the whole Congress in the king's name.

On the following day, sachems representing all six nations of the Iroquois League spoke with De Lancey and his council members. Again, the accredited commissioners were not present. Chief Hendrick of the Canajohary Mohawks spoke for all in phrases that disclosed some division within the League. His Canajoharies had deliberately arrived late at the treaty, he said, because the other Iroquois were accusing them of being "Coll. Johnson's Councellors . . . if we had come first, the other Nations would have said, that we made the Govrs. speech . . . we are looked upon to be a proud Nation, and therefore staid behind. Tis true, and known we are so, and that we the Mohawks are the head of all the other Nations; here they are, and they must own it."[89] Nobody denied it. For public consumption, at least, the other nation's silence implied consent. In their actions, however, they had long been following policies distinct from the Mohawks'.

Now a strange thing happens in those minutes. The entry for 2 July 1754 reports the answer of the Six Nations "to the general speech made to them on Saturday last by His Honour the Lieut. Govr. of New York, in His Majty's name, and in the presence and behalf of the several Governts on the continent therein named."[90] That speech had been worked over by all the commissioners until every phrase was accepted by all, but the minutes for Saturday, 29 June, say only that the commissioners "attended his Honour while he delivered the speech." Nothing is noted of the circumstances attending the occasion.[91] We know the contents of the speech from its approval on 27 June, however, and we can reconstruct what happened at its delivery from the account sent by Thomas Pownall, probably to the

"intimately acquainted." "Personal Accounts," 742. The gentleman in question seems to have been William Johnson. Pownall could not have been disparaging Conrad Weiser as translator; Weiser was certainly not "extream stupid, ignorant and illeterate," though his spelling leaves something to be desired.

88. Minutes, *N.Y. Col. Docs.* 6:865–66.
89. Ibid., 6:867–68.
90. *N.Y. Col. Docs.* 6:868.
91. Ibid., 6:864.

earl of Halifax. In brief, the speech renewed and brightened the ancient Covenant Chain of alliance; it exhorted the Iroquois to recall their scattered persons to live compactly and thus gain strength; and it denounced French measures that "must necessarily soon interrupt and destroy all Trade and intercourse between the English and the several Indian Nations." Finally, had those measures been taken "with your consent or approbation?"[92] Pownall watched the Iroquois response and saw something that "occurrd in the course of the Treaty which does not appear upon the Face of it. When the Great Chain or Covenant Belt was deliver'd to and receiv'd by the Indians, the whole Five Nations, according to the usual Custom, every Nation singly after one another, shou'd have sounded the Yoheigh-igh. (This is the Form by which in Treaty they express their solemn acceptance of the Belt deliver'd and approbation of the proposition made. . . . Instead of that they sounded but one great Indiscriminate Yo-heigh-eigh till, being reminded that the other was expected of them, they afterward gave the Yo-heigh-eigh according to the usual Custom. Some say this was from mere forgetfullness; but that is very unlikely from them who are such strict observers of These forms. Therefore others say it was they had a mind to disguise that all the Nations did not universally give their hearty assent to the Covenant 'till they saw what redress they were likely to find and upon what terms they were likely to be for the future."[93] Something definitely was amiss. "Never were so few Indians seen at a conference," according to Johnson's secretary Peter Wraxall.[94]

The formal reply of the Six Nations to De Lancey's general speech in behalf of the whole Congress "was read" at the Congress session of 2 July. The odd phrasing raises questions because the nonliterate Iroquois did not *read* their speeches. These minutes are not straightforward. According to them, Mohawk chief Hendrick spoke first: "We do now solemnly renew and brighten the Covenant Chain with our Brethren here present, and all our other absent Brethren on the Continent," he began. That sounded agreeably to the commissioners, but Hendrick had not come just to spout platitudes. "You have asked us the reason of our living in this dispersed manner. The reason is, your neglecting us for these three years past." He was just warming up. As to the French encroachments, no Iroquois had given permission or approval, *but* "The Govr. of Virginia, and the Govr. of Canada are both quarrelling about lands which belong to us . . . [and] the Govrs. of Virginia and Pennsylvania have made paths thro' our Country to Trade, and built houses without acquainting us with it. They should first have asked our consent to build there, as was done when Oswego was

92. Ibid., 6:861–63.

93. "Personal Accounts," ed. McAnear, 741.

94. Wraxall, "Some Thoughts upon the British Indian Interest in North America," [Jan. 1756], *N.Y. Col. Docs.* 7:20.

built." (Virginia and Pennsylvania had treated instead with the Ohio Mingos.) It seems that the Iroquois resented the condescension implied in De Lancey's general speech to them. Hendrick went on to the offensive: "Brethren. You desire us to speak from the bottom of our hearts, and we shall do it. Look about you and see all these houses full of Beaver, and the money is all gone to Canada, likewise powder, lead and guns, which the French now make use of at Ohio." It was a direct challenge to De Lancey, who was one of the merchants in the trade with Montreal.

When Hendrick finished, his brother Abraham rose to remind the commissioners that the Iroquois had desired William Johnson to have the management of Indian affairs. Three years earlier, former governor Clinton had been supposed to carry that request to the king. It seemed that the request had been "drowned in the sea." Nevertheless, so far as the Iroquois were concerned "the fire here is burnt out." Which, translated, meant that they would no longer have any dealings with the provincial agents at Albany. "Turning his face to the New York Commissrs of Indian Affairs at Albany who were there present [he] desired them to take notice of what he said."[95]

Promises and mollification followed, and large presents were delivered which had an effect. But Pownall was dubious. "Their Satisfaction rests in a Confidence of the English being in Earnest in the Promises they have made them. If after this Solemn treaty they find themselves deceiv'd, They will be more alienated than ever."[96] As the board of trade and the crown were quite intent on deceiving the Indians about their intentions toward the Ohio country, a dilemma appeared. How was it going to be possible to induce the Indians to fight against the French in order to gain British access to the Ohio when the Indians wanted them both out of the region? William Johnson suggested a way (which will be mentioned in chapter 6), as a result of which he emerged from the Albany Congress as the only indisputable winner among the English though he was there as a mere observer. But this is to go too far ahead of events.

Revision of the Covenant Chain

We may skim over the details of the Congress during which the commissioners played with moonshine schemes for a superpower over united colonies. The essential fact is that not one colonial assembly approved the Congress's final plan, and the lords of trade did not bother considering it.[97] Yet that scheme has acquired a mythical quality by virtue of much

95. *N.Y. Col. Docs.* 6:868–71.
96. "Personal Accounts," ed. McAnear, 743.
97. Gipson, *British Empire* 5, ch. 5.

rhetoric from writers who wanted it to be something noble. Listen to Frederick Jackson Turner: "The effect of the Indian frontier as a consolidating agent in our history is important. . . . This frontier stretched along the western border like a cord of union. The Indian was a common danger, demanding united action. Most celebrated of these conferences was the Albany congress of 1754 . . . It is evident that the unifying tendencies of the Revolutionary period were facilitated by the previous cooperation in the regulation of the frontier."[98]

If Turner had swum out of his intoxicating phrases just long enough to look at the sequence of Iroquois treaties at Albany, he would have seen that the 1754 Congress represented the very opposite of unifying tendencies. Meetings had been held at Albany and its predecessor Dutch settlement for a century before the "most celebrated" Congress, and they had involved delegates from a number of northern British colonies since 1677 when Sir Edmund Andros presided over the formation of the "silver chain" confederation of the Covenant Chain. These multilateral negotiations of the Covenant Chain had constituted genuine, though erratic, cooperation in the regulation of the frontier.[99] What the Congress of 1754 showed very clearly to the board of trade in London was that the Covenant Chain system had ceased to be viable as previously operated. The unity that emerged from Albany was like the peace that passeth understanding. The board quickly took Indian affairs out of the hands of the colonies, as completely as it could contrive at so great a distance, and put all such affairs in charge of agents directly responsible to the crown. Albany was the *end* of a system. The Congress of 1754 was the last multicolonial treaty with the Iroquois to be held there.[100]

Land frauds at the Congress

Though the public transactions revealed only failure to achieve substantive results, dealings "in the bushes"—actually in gentlemen's lodgings—made the situation even worse. In the acerb language of William Brewster, "Two private land grabs, consummated at Albany at the time, were more

98. Frederick Jackson Turner, "The Significance of the Frontier in American History" (1893), in Turner, *The Frontier in American History* (New York: Holt, Rinehart and Winston, 1920), 15.

99. I have traced the system in my preceding books: *Invasion of America*, ch. 18, and *Ambiguous Iroquois Empire*, throughout. See also *The History and Culture of Iroquois Diplomacy: An Interdisciplinary Guide to the Treaties of the Six Nations and Their League*, eds. Francis Jennings, William N. Fenton, Mary A. Druke, and David R. Miller (Syracuse, N.Y.: Syracuse University Press, 1984).

100. See John R. Alden, "The Albany Congress and the Creation of the Indian Superintendencies," *Miss. Valley Hist. Review* 27:2 (Sept. 1940), 193–210.

important in future results than all the doings of the congress. They were engineered by two men, renowned for their piety, the Rev. Richard Peters, an Episcopal clergyman, and Timothy Woodbridge, a Puritan deacon."[101]

The land grabs in question concerned western Pennsylvania and the Wyoming Valley of the Susquehanna River's north branch, and they were so important because they created still another grievance for Indians already defending against French and Virginian encroachment at the Ohio and against seizure of Mohawk lands by the partners of the Kayaderosseras patent. As if these were not enough, now Connecticut and Pennsylvania began to struggle for a territory overlapped by the charters of both colonies and occupied in 1753 only by Indians. Wyoming is a wide, fertile valley between forbiddingly high ranges of mountains that nevertheless were good hunting lands. Its residents in 1753 were Delaware and Mahican converts to Moravianism, though not all were equally strong in their new faith. They were also "nephews" of the Iroquois League, which claimed Wyoming as a part of its territory.[102] In 1753 they were alarmed by intrusion of several "gentlemen like" persons from Connecticut who had been sent by the newly organized Susquehannah Company to spy out the land in preparation for a new colony to be sent out by that company. This news was quickly reported to Philadelphia and Onondaga, causing much concern in both places.[103]

Pennsylvania's governor Hamilton wrote a letter of protest to Connecticut's governor Wolcott. Note well that he was indignant at the efforts of Connecticut men "to treat with the Mohocks about these Lands . . . as it may create a Difference between the Mohocks and the Rest of the Six Nations, between whom there is an Agreement that *the Mohocks shall have nothing to do with the Lands in Pennsylvania*, nor take any Part of the Presents receivd for them . . . therefore the Mohocks never come here in Treaties for Land."[104] Hamilton's first thought was to send Conrad Weiser to

101. William Brewster, *The Pennsylvania and New York Frontier, 1700–1763* (Philadelphia: George S. McManus Co., 1954), 36, 47n. Timothy Woodbridge was the missionary to the Stockbridge Indians. Julian Boyd remarks that he was "an Indian interpreter at the Albany Congress of 1754, where he attended to his political, missionary, and economic enterprises with a mental dexterity that one finds mildly surprising in a religious man." Introduction to *The Susquehannah Company Papers*, eds. Julian P. Boyd and Robert J. Taylor, 11 vols. (Wilkes-Barre, Pa., and Ithaca, N.Y., 1930–71) 1:lxxi.

102. Anthony F. C. Wallace, *King of the Delawares: Teedyuscung, 1700–1763* (Philadelphia: University of Pennsylvania Press, 1949), 47–50.

103. Wm. Parsons to Hamilton, 8 Feb. 1754, in *Pa. Council Minutes* 5:736; A. Wallace, *King of the Delawares*, 50–55.

104. *Pa. Council Minutes* 5:769. Wolcott's reply evaded the boundary issue and treated the dispute as a matter of no importance. He concluded with the eighteenth-century equivalent of a "Rastus" joke. "This brings to mind a story a Gentleman told me that he went in to see his Negroe Man then dying, and seeing him just gone said to him, 'Cuffee, you are just going, are you not sorry?' 'No,' says the Fellow, 'Master, the Loss won't be mine.' " It gave simultaneously the measure of the man Wolcott and the attention he would pay to Pennsylvania's protests. Ibid., 5:771–73.

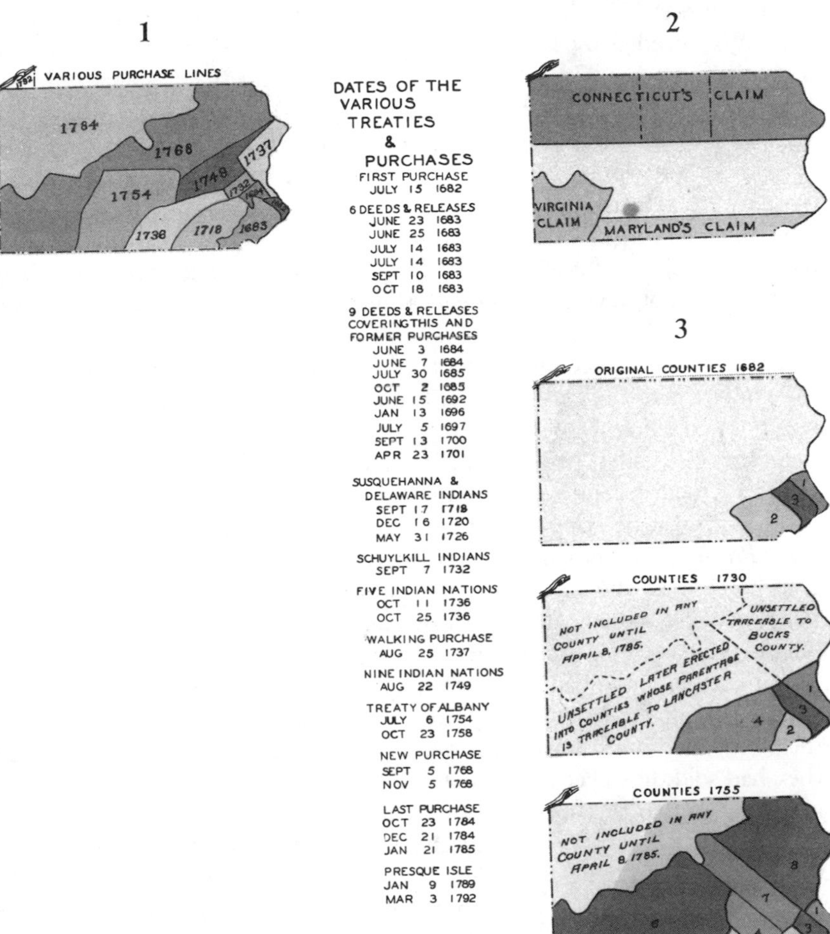

MAP 2. (1) Expansion of Pennsylvania within its chartered boundaries. (2) Conflicting colonial claims. ADAPTED FROM THE GENEOLOGICAL MAP OF THE COUNTIES, COMPILED AND PREPARED IN THE BUREAU OF LAND RECORDS, DEPARTMENT OF INTERNAL AFFAIRS, COMMONWEALTH OF PENNSYLVANIA. (3) Establishment of jurisdictions.

Onondaga to forestall Connecticut's people, but Weiser had become too old to tramp through the mountains in the soggy ground and bone-chilling air of early spring. So it was settled that he would accompany Pennsylvania's commissioners to Albany where he might "perhaps fall in with some greedy fellows for Money, that will undertake to bring things about to Our wishes."[105] He did, and the Penns got a deed for almost all the land still unceded by Indians within their province's bounds. (Interestingly the deed was witnessed by Assembly Speaker Isaac Norris and Benjamin and William Franklin as well as Weiser.) Although the Mohawks, according to Governor Hamilton, had no right in Pennsylvania, this deed of cession was signed by five Mohawk chiefs, but only one Onondaga. There were also five Tuscarora signers, who could not possibly have had any legitimate right under Iroquois rules because the Tuscaroras were (and still are) "on the cradleboard" of the League, allowed to speak in council, but not to vote. This deed, though publicly made, was clearly off color.[106]

There was also deception in its text. When Weiser later began to survey the boundary of the cession, "the Indians stopt, and said that the Course was not according to the Bargain, because it was expressly said and stipulated by the Chiefs of the Six Nations, and the Commissioners of Pensilvania" that the line should not touch the lands on Juniata River, "otherways the Purchase must only include the Land *then settled by the white People*." The Indians protested because the deed's text made the purchase extend all the way to the present state of Ohio, far beyond any of Pennsylvania's settlements. It also overlapped and conflicted with the deed obtained by the Virginians at Lancaster in 1744. Weiser had no loyalty to Virginia, though he had been hired by that province in 1744; but he was worried about the Iroquois League's reaction to the discrepancy between the words of Pennsylvania's new deed and what the Iroquois chiefs thought they had sold, however illegitimately. "You know, Sir," he wrote to Richard Peters, "that the Indians actually said so, and we took Lewis Evans's map before us, and we assured the Indians that that Line would never touch the River Zinachsa [Juniata] below the Big-Island, and so the Indians consented, but I saw plain that that course would cross Zinachsa river . . . I should be sorry if their Honours the Proprietors should insist upon that Line to be run, against the Indians Mind."[107]

But Thomas Penn expressed "great satisfaction" with the deed. He gave thanks, and 2,000 acres each to Peters and Weiser; and ordered the Juniata lands settled "as fast as possible."[108]

105. Weiser to Peters, 15 Mar. 1754, mss., Correspondence of Conrad Weiser 1:44, HSP.

106. Deed, 6 July 1754, in *Pa. Council Minutes* 6:119–23. The "Henry Peters" first among the Indian signatories was Chief Hendrick. The one Onondaga signed "in behalf of himself and all the Chiefs of the Onondagoes, there being none others present of that Nation" (p. 122).

107. Weiser to Peters, 12 Oct. 1754, mss., Corr. of Weiser 1:47, HSP.

108. T. Penn to Peters, 17 Oct. 1754, mss., Penn Ltr. Bks. 4:4–11, HSP. This seems to contradict the oft-noticed eviction by Pennsylvania of colonial settlers on Juniata lands, but the contradiction was only superficial. The dispossessed settlers were squatters who had paid no purchase money or quitrent. Penn wanted settlers who paid.

In the minds of Englishmen dealing with Indians, the tribesmen had become contemptible. Already in 1747, William Johnson saw them as "a blood thirsty revengefull sett of people to any whom they have a regard for, should they be mislead or deceived by them," and wailed that "it is impossible to do any thing with them while there is such a plenty of liquor to be had all round the neighborhood, being for ever drunk."[109] Conrad Weiser moaned that "they are apostates to their Old Natural principle of Honesty, and become Drunkards, Rogues, Thieves and Liars."[110] The double standard of morality is nowhere more clearly demonstrated than in this comment of Weiser's, which he wrote in the same letter that described how he was deceiving the Indians about the survey of their ceded land. Thomas Pownall also remarked that the Iroquois "are no longer that plain simple People they were once, but are become wily and covetous and encrease in Jealousy and suspicion as they encrease in Guile and Avarice." As he observed, the sachems carefully refrained in public from touching "the least share of the public Presents . . . But they must be all closetted privately and experience very palpable and solid marks of our freindship for them, or all the Rest we do is doing nothing." Pownall saw clearly how the frauds practiced upon the Indians had led to their demoralization, but he was no bleeding heart. He understood that there was no unity among the Indians. "In the point of trade . . . it is said that they use all the Arts of trade under which they have sufferrd, towards the farr off Indians who trade with them." And after long and acute description of the land swindles that had been practiced upon them, he noted that they had picked up a trick or two themselves. "In the point of Land Jobbing it is said that they will sell the same lott twenty times over if they can or make the Purchaser pay over and over again for it if they can, that they will treat with a purchaser for a certain lott that they describe: receve his money and then not lett him take up above half that lott." Much to our present interest: "private Indians will gett money out of Purchasers who, when they come to take up their purchase, shall be prevented by the Castles [tribal councils]."[111]

In Pownall's manuscript is the explanation for the backdoor deals at

109. *N.Y. Col. Docs.* 6:360–62. After his appointment in 1756 as royal superintendent of Indian affairs, Johnson spelled out a policy of systematic bribery. With supreme effrontery, this merchant and lord on the make remarked, "The Indians are naturally a mercenary people," and advised a rule of corruption: "I apprehend it is best to make a sure Bargain and give to those Indians only who will act with us and for us, which is the method I propose for the future . . . I conceive giving Presents in the old general [customary] way, would be imprudent and an ineffectual Profusion." Johnson to lords of trade, 10 Sept. 1756, in *The Documentary History of the State of New-York*, ed. E. B. O'Callaghan, 4 vols. (Albany, N.Y.: Weed, Parsons and Co., 1849–51), 2:735.

110. Weiser to Peters, 15 Mar. 1754, mss., Corr. of Weiser 1:44, HSP.

111. T. Pownall, "Notes on Indian Affairs," mss., Loudoun Papers (LO 460), Henry E. Huntington Library (HEH).

Albany. Pennsylvania and Connecticut both set out to get crooked deeds from Indians who were not properly entitled to make such transactions in such circumstances, and the Indians obliged because they knew that the legitimate councils of the Iroquois nations and League would refuse to countenance the transactions. Thus it came about that five of the same chiefs signed cession of some of the same territory to both provinces, and that others sold land to which they had no right.[112] Chief Hendrick, who had declared secession from Albany, stayed clear of Connecticut though a note claims he was "party" to it; but he signed Pennsylvania's deed. As Pownall sized him up, Hendrick was "a bold, artfull, intriguing Fellow and has learnt no small share of European Politics." He "obstructs and opposes all businesses where he has not been talk'd with first and retain'd too."[113] When we consider that Conrad Weiser was on the lookout for "some greedy fellows for Money," it becomes easy to understand why Mohawk chief Hendrick was willing to sell land in a province where the Mohawks had no claim recognized by the other Iroquois nations.

Connecticut intrudes

Weiser saw to it that Pennsylvania's transactions preserved the appearance of legitimacy. His colleague Richard Peters even requested that the minutes of Pennsylvania's proceedings should be incorporated with the minutes of the Albany Congress, but Governor De Lancey objected to that. On the other hand, Connecticut's John Henry Lydius ignored all the proprieties. He picked up chiefs one by one, got them drunk, gave them some money, shoved a paper under their noses, and said sign here. What did they care about disputes between two English colonies? Yet it is hard to excuse Hendrick, who signed for Pennsylvania after he had stipulated firmly that "As to Wyomink and Shamokin and the Land contiguous thereto on Sasquehannah, We reserve them for our hunting Ground." Neither Pennsylvanians nor New Englanders were to settle there. "No body shall have this Land."[114] Perhaps he drew a distinction between selling title to the land and selling permission to settle. Certainly the lands he itemized were embraced in the deed he signed.

It took a little while for the grand council of the League to sort out all

112. Cf. signatures on Pennsylvania deed (n106, above) with those on the Susquehannah Company deed, 11 July 1754, in *Susquehannah Company Papers*, eds. Boyd and Taylor, 1:101–21. The deeds' overlap is shown on the map in *Franklin Papers* 5:225.

113. Pownall, "Notes on Indian Affairs," mss., Loudoun Papers (LO 460), HEH. The remark about Hendrick is toward the end of this long and informative document. It is in rough draft in two columns with marginal notes and insertions and strikeovers.

114. *Pa. Council Minutes*, 6 July 1754, 6:119.

this intrigue. They got it straight by July 1755 when they met with William Johnson at his mansion, Mount Johnson. It was a big and important affair that will require more attention further on. Here we need note only the speech made by one of Johnson's most favored chiefs, the Oneida sachem Conochquiesie: "Brother. You promised us that you would keep this fire place clean from all filth and that no snake should come into this Council Room. That Man sitting there (pointing to Coll: Lyddius) is a Devil and has stole our Lands. He takes Indians slyly by the Blanket one at a time, and when they are drunk, puts some money in their Bosoms, and perswades them to sign deeds for our lands upon the Susquehanna which we will not ratify nor suffer to be settled by any means."[115]

Pennsylvania was dealt with more gently, but it is clear that its deed had become suspect. "The Govr of Pennsylvania bought a whole Tract and only paid for the half, and we desire you will let him know, that we will not part with the other half but keep it." And he "gave a very large Belt of Wampum" to signify that this was very important business. Johnson cozened the Indians into saying that they would go along with Pennsylvania's deed, but subsequent events showed that they spoke only "from the mouth, and not from the heart."[116]

Connecticut's Susquehannah Company ignored all protests, whether from Indians or from officials of other colonies. The company continued to prepare for colonization of Wyoming; and, as predicted, blood was shed.[117]

There is much irony in the whole situation. Lydius's associate in getting the company's deed was Timothy Woodbridge, the superintendent of the Puritan mission village of Stockbridge. At Wyoming in the "purchased" tract, the Delaware Indian residents were Moravian converts. The pious gentlemen of Connecticut would in time show one aspect of their religion by assassinating the chief of those Delaware converts in a religious effort that brought down upon them a retaliatory massacre when the time became propitious. (See chapter 19, below.)

The beginnings of all this conflict are directly traceable to the Congress called at Albany, which has been hailed as the great foreshadowing of

115. Treaty minutes, 3 July 1755, in *N.Y. Col. Docs.* 6:984. Conochquiesie had signed Lydius's deed; presumably he knew what he was talking about.

116. Loc. cit. and p. 987. But Johnson later advised a "voluntary and open Surrender of that Deed of Sale" on grounds of policy. Ltr. to lords of trade, 10 Sept. 1756, in *Doc. Hist. N.Y.* 2:737.

117. Paul A. W. Wallace, *Indians in Pennsylvania* (Harrisburg: Pennsylvania Historical and Museum Commission, 1964), 153–57. Besides the conflict between Indians and colonials, there was a series of "Yankee-Pennamite Wars" between settlers from Connecticut and others from Pennsylvania.

American national unity.[118] The Congress did indeed exemplify the growing colonial attitude of disobedience to royal command. Ordered by the ministry to satisfy Indian grievances, the participants not only turned their attention to business of their own devising, but actually added to the already existing Indian grievances. Yet the Congress was not engaged in preserving or enlarging the privileges of colonial assemblies. Quite to the contrary, the assemblies unanimously rejected the Congress's proposals to erect an intermediate lordship between the colonies and the crown. The ferment working at Albany was something new and suspect. It was not, however, the beginning of frontier unity against an Indian menace.

118. Cf. "This plan showed far-sighted statesmanship, in advance of its time." Samuel Eliot Morison, Henry Steele Commager, and William E. Leuchtenburg, *The Growth of the American Republic*, 6th ed., 2 vols. (New York: Oxford University Press, 1969), 1:115.

Chapter 6 ❧ *THE BIRDS of LONDON*

The governing authorities may have been acting immorally; but they were playing the diplomatic game according to the rules. *Raisons d'etat* are always more important than mere truthfulness.

George F. G. Stanley

All governments lie.

I. F. Stone

Truth is the first casualty of war.

U. Thant

Chronology

1701. Britain obtains an Iroquois "deed" to western lands purportedly conquered by the Iroquois though later abandoned by them under pressure from enemies.

1713. The treaty of Utrecht recognizes Iroquois as British subjects.

1724. Thomas Pelham-Holles, duke of Newcastle, is appointed secretary of state for the British ministry's southern department, with responsibility to supervise the American colonies. His policy is known as "salutary neglect."

1744. Britain and France declare war (King George's War).

1745. George Montagu Dunk, second earl of Halifax, is appointed president of the lords commissioners for trade and plantations (board of trade).

1745. Massachusetts governor William Shirley directs campaign that captures Louisbourg, but the fort is returned to the French by the peace treaty.

1746. William Augustus, duke of Cumberland, suppresses the Jacobite rising in Scotland and is made captain general of the British army.

1746. Newcastle appointed to the northern department of the ministry.

1746. Halifax persuades the ministry to strengthen Nova Scotia. The town of Halifax founded.

1748. Treaty of Aix-la-Chapelle restores peace between Britain and France.

1749. Céloron's expedition.

1750.	Commissioners appointed to negotiate American territory disputed by Britain and France.
1750.	British build Fort Lawrence and French counter with Fort Beauséjour at disputed border between Nova Scotia and Acadia.
1750.	The Ohio Company obtains a grant to western lands.
1750–51.	La Galissonière, governor-general of New France, repeatedly warns the French ministry of two necessities: (1) to preserve the loyalty of the Indian tribes; (2) to preserve the lifeline between Canada and Louisiana from British interception.
1752.	Commissioner William Shirley recalled from futile negotiations in Paris.
1752–54.	Skirmishing and fort building in the Ohio region.
1753.	French harry Pennsylvania traders out of Ohio region.
1753.	Halifax revives Britain's claim to the Ohio country through "right of conquest" by "subject" Iroquois.
October 1753.	Thomas Pownall arrives in New York as informant for board of trade.
March 1754.	Newcastle becomes head of the ministry as first lord of the Treasury.
14 June–11 July 1754.	The intercolonial Albany Congress.
26 June 1754.	Newcastle's inner cabinet resolves to defend Britain's northern colonies from French "invasion."
4 July 1754.	Washington surrenders Fort Necessity at Great Meadows.
August–September 1754.	Board of trade and ministry discuss need for unified action by colonies. Ministry decides upon a military commander in chief to be financed by colonies. Cumberland nominates Edward Braddock.
8 September 1754.	News of Washington's surrender reaches London and stimulates Newcastle to appeal for help from Cumberland.
December 1754.	British ministry authorizes Massachusetts governor Shirley to raise troops.
January 1755.	Britain sends two regiments to Virginia.
February 1755.	France sends seventy-eight companies to Canada.
13 February 1755.	John Mitchell's inflammatory map of North America published under patronage of Halifax and the board of trade.
17 February 1755.	French ministry authorizes instigation of Indians against British colonies.
23 February 1755.	General Braddock arrives in Williamsburg, Virginia.
10 April 1755.	British ministry orders a fleet to intercept French troops and seize French ships of war.
14 April 1755.	Braddock convenes a council of war at Alexandria, Virginia. He outlines strategy for campaigns against French, authorizes attack on Acadian forts, and presents expectation of colonial financing. He commissions William Johnson as superintendent of Indian affairs.
23 April 1755.	Admiral Boscawen's fleet sails with orders to strike a blow against French naval forces.
3 May 1755.	A French fleet sails with transports of troops for Canada.
19 May 1755.	Rangers sail from Boston to attack Acadian forts.

8 June 1755. Boscawen's fleet seizes two French ships and one-tenth of troops being transported. Remainder get safely to Quebec.

16–17 June 1755. Forts Beauséjour and Gaspereau fall to the attacking New Englanders.

Colonial unity was not a new thought in England. Officials understood well that unity or coordination would generate strength, but they vacillated between desiring that strength for use against the French and fearing the possibility of its use against government by the English.[1] The Albany Plan of Union had only superficial likeness to unity proposals arising from time to time in the board of trade. At Albany, on Franklin's insistence especially, the conferees had decided to submit their plan to all colonial assemblies for approval before asking Parliament to enact confirmation. They thus recognized, and their plan would have had Parliament legitimize, the powers gained by assemblies for home rule. Such a devolution of power could not have been farther from ministers' intentions. As conceived in England, unity was to be achieved by exertion of the royal prerogative, and was to be fashioned to strengthen the prerogative. In the mind of the earl of Halifax, president of the board of trade, unity entailed reducing the colonial assemblies to a subordination that would conform their real powers to what they were supposed to be in legal theory and imperial formality. Even the duke of Newcastle could not accept the Albany plan. His long tenure in the office responsible for the colonies had been marked by the "salutary neglect" that allowed the rise of assembly powers; but, to introduce an anachronistic term, Newcastle was no "liberationist." He feared "the ill Consequence to be apprehended from uniting too closely the Northern Colonies with Each other; An independency upon this Country being to be apprehended from Such an Union."[2] The Albany

1. James A. Henretta, *"Salutary Neglect": Colonial Administration under the Duke of Newcastle* (Princeton, N.J.: Princeton University Press, 1972), 332ff.; Alison Gilbert Olson, "The British Government and Colonial Union, 1754," *Wm. and Mary Qtly.*, 3d series, 17 (1960), 22–34.

2. Greene, *Quest for Power*, 8.

Bibliographic note: Though confined to the southern colonies, Greene's detailed and informative study fairly represents them all in what Leonard W. Labaree called a century-long movement to substitute government "by the consent of the governed" for government "by royal grace and favor." Viewing from a different standpoint, James H. Kettner sees a transition from medieval to modern ideas: "The medieval notion of 'allegiance' reflected the feudal sense that personal bonds between man and lord were the primary ligaments of the body politic; the modern notion of 'nationality' assumed a legal tie binding individuals to a territorial state and rendering them subject to its jurisdiction. The 'community of allegiance' was in essence personal, the 'national state' primarily territorial." It may be noted that the magistrates of Massachusetts were talking about their *nation* as early as the 1630s. Leonard

plan had no chance of being adopted by men of such persuasions. They reverted instead to the installation of a commander in chief of all armed forces in the colonies, appointed by, and solely responsible to, the king; and they provided him with troops to enforce his commands, regardless of the wishes of colonials and their assemblies. Almost necessarily these troops had to become an army of occupation, and they did. The same soldiers whose primary mission was to conquer Canada became the instrument of royal authority for disciplining the colonies.

These events will be described in their turn. Here it is necessary to notice the circumstances that brought them about. In all the colonies, from Quaker-pacifist Pennsylvania through degrees of militarism to Calvinist-belligerent Massachusetts, the assemblies had long struggled against the powers used and abused by royal officials invoking the crown's prerogative. As long as those officials lacked a military establishment to enforce their demands, the assemblies had been able to extort or bribe concessions that in the long run amounted to substantial privilege for themselves. Despite differences in formal status, Parliament and the assemblies functioned similarly in their respective spheres as buffers between the monarch and his subjects. No matter how much the elected representatives on both sides of the Atlantic declaimed about the most excellent king ever known, they fought vigilantly against the encroachments of that king's servants on their liberties and interests. And, as ever, there were plenty of colonials aiming to enhance their own wealth and privilege regardless of duty, morality, or other abstract principles.

"Salutary neglect"

In 1724, Thomas Pelham-Holles, the duke of Newcastle, was appointed secretary of state for the crown's southern department, a bureaucratic classification that included executive responsibility for the American colonies.[3] Newcastle rose to power in the government by his exceptional

W. Labaree, *Royal Government in America: A Study of the British Colonial System before 1783*, Yale Historical Publications Studies 6 (New Haven, Conn.: Yale University Press, 1930), 428, 448; James H. Kettner, *The Development of American Citizenship, 1608–1870*, published for the Institute of Early American History and Culture (Chapel Hill: University of North Carolina Press, 1978), 3.

3. Bibliographic note: Although Newcastle was prominent in high office nearly fifty years, and his papers form one of the largest collections in the British Library, no book-length biography was published until 1974. Then two Americans published within a year of each other: Ray A. Kelch, *Newcastle, A Duke without Money: Thomas Pelham-Holles, 1693–1768* (Berkeley: University of California Press, 1974); Reed Browning, *The Duke of Newcastle* (New Haven, Conn.: Yale University Press, 1975). Neither is fully satisfactory. Kelch attends only to Newcastle's financial affairs. Browning paints a larger portrait of public and private aspects

ability to find and distribute patronage. Although his policy toward the colonies has often been called "salutary neglect," the phrase misleads. He "neglected" only to exert stringent measures to enforce centralized authority which, in the circumstances, meant royal prerogative. He paid very close attention to colonial opportunities for patronage appointments, which he used to lure and to reward supporters of his interest in Parliament.

This process did not always work to support the authority of the crown, because the royal theory of empire included an assumption that colonials must pay for their government by royal officials. As most appointees to royal office in the colonies aimed primarily to reward themselves and only secondarily to advance the larger ends of the crown, they were highly susceptible to pressures from the colonial assemblies that granted salaries and fees at discretion. Assemblies everywhere used their power to withhold a governor's "support" until, like Pooh-Bah, he mortified his family pride with a discreet bargain to the assembly's advantage. Newcastle paid little attention to this dangerous development. By the time he left the southern department in 1746, some assemblies had pushed their power, as Jack P. Greene has noted, "even beyond that of the British House of Commons" by acquiring a share in handling executive affairs.[4]

While the assemblies were enjoying themselves so, some developments in ministerial politics produced a gradually hardening attitude toward the colonies. Newcastle was promoted to the northern department (responsible for European affairs) and was replaced in the southern department by John Russell, duke of Bedford, who soon aligned himself with the duke of Cumberland—"the butcher"—fresh from his triumph at Culloden. Cumberland's rise to power correlated precisely with a reduction of the patronage power of Newcastle's whigs. This reorientation was soon complicated further by the appointment in 1748 of a new president of the board of trade (lords commissioners of trade and plantations) responsible for oversight of the colonies. This was George Montagu Dunk, second

of the man, but lacks adequate analysis of the issues of the day. Though differing in detail, these writers agree in certain highly important matters of substance that set them against the stereotype created originally by Horace Walpole and repeated by Sir Lewis Namier. They acknowledge Newcastle's dithering eccentricities, which were picturesque, but do not find him incompetent in public affairs. In their view, Newcastle was a professional in politics and diplomacy who discharged his responsibilities with credit if not heroically, à la William Pitt. This seems self-evident from Newcastle's sheer duration in high office; even eighteenth-century England put limits to toleration of incompetence at the top. Kelch and Browning agree also that Newcastle dissipated his vast inherited wealth by squandering it on luxury and ostentation rather than by using it for political corruption as so often charged. His "corruption" was the management of official patronage and bribery with Secret Service funds. By these means he built a Whig "machine" that sometimes controlled Parliament and always had to be reckoned with. Such processes were not new in Newcastle's day, and have not disappeared since.

4. Greene, *Quest for Power*, 8.

earl of Halifax, who sympathized wtih Cumberland's party though Newcastle was his cousin and patron.[5]

On the surface these changes bear the appearance of a simple shuffling of personalities, but they involved an issue fundamental to political power in England as well as America. This key question was the crown's prerogative to govern independently of Parliament. In England, Whig lords conceived the issue as a struggle for the preservation of Great Britain's "constitution," by which they meant the power of the Whig aristocracy, against royalist subversion. A biographer scion of one of the great Whig families notes that suspicions of the duke of Cumberland's "good faith and intentions made the ministers unwilling to increase the military forces in England."[6]

In America the assemblies marched under the banner of "the rights of Englishmen." When Bedford and Halifax associated with Cumberland, they showed themselves as champions of the royal prerogative on both sides of the Atlantic, and Cumberland's rise became an issue for colonials in two distinct but interlocked processes. One of these was the defense of assembly powers, whether conceived as rights or usurpations, against Halifax's attempts to cut them down. Linked with this was the aggressive bellicosity of Cumberland's party, which manifested itself in special hostility to France. Cumberland personally was primarily interested in overpowering France in Europe. Halifax aimed at driving France out of America. With their clients and supporters they formed a war faction that repeatedly forced the hand of the Whigs led by Newcastle and his half-brother Henry Pelham.[7] As is common enough, the party of war was also the party of authoritarianism. This is not to say, however, that its opponents were democrats; they were not.[8]

Wars generate more wars. Cumberland's party began to form in the midst of the 1740–48 War of the Austrian Succession (King George's War in the colonies). His decisive triumph in the battle of Culloden was an event to inspire thought in Whigs, whose domination had begun with the Glorious Revolution of 1688. As the son of George II, and as newly appointed captain general (i.e., general in chief) of the British army, Cumberland was a natural center of attraction for ambitious politicians in an

5. For Halifax, see ch. 2 above, n11.

6. Philip C. Yorke, *The Life and Correspondence of Philip Yorke, Earl of Hardwicke, Lord High Chancellor of Great Britain*, 3 vols. (Cambridge, Eng.: Cambridge University Press, 1913), 2:199, 44–45.

Bibliographic note: Yorke's large work is based primarily upon the Hardwicke Papers at the British Library. It prints a selection of the political papers from that collection and is especially valuable for expression of the Old Whig outlook on events as they happened.

7. Henretta, *Salutary Neglect*, 292; Yorke, *Life of Hardwicke* 2:256–58.

8. See J. R. Pole, *Political Representation in England and the Origins of the American Republic* (London: Macmillan, and Co. 1966), 386.

era when factions formed around personalities. As Stanley Pargellis has remarked, "Cumberland's faction tried to rely not only on the parliamentary interest its adherents had, but on the votes of army officers who had seats in parliament and knew the value of Cumberland's favor."[9] The memory of Cromwell's military dictatorship lingered even more powerfully in England than in America; Whig lords knew as well as colonial assemblymen the political uses of standing armies, and for them the threat of Cumberland's power was clear and present. Quoting Pargellis again, "One cannot understand the circumstances of [William] Pitt's rise to power without realizing that Cumberland was the great rival whom he had to destroy."[10] Ironically, Pitt would have to win the war that Cumberland's men botched after they had brought it on.[11]

The foregoing analysis rests in part on the excellent study by James A. Henretta of Newcastle's policies. As Henretta summarized, statesmen in England divided into two opposed theories of empire. "The first system was based on the primacy of the colonial assembly; it sought in fact, if not always in theory to involve the settlers in their own governance." This was the theory of the Old Whigs. Opposed to it was the theory held by the prerogative men: "In their view the basic institution of colonial administration was not the local assembly, but the imperial bureaucracy;" the colonies were to be administered by "bureaucrats financially and politically immune from the control of those they ruled."[12] To put this another way, the colonies were to be reduced to colonial*ism*.

Royal reorganization

The Albany Plan of Union was set aside in England because the duke of Newcastle had decided against any scheme for colonial union more than a month before the plan arrived in his office. When the plan did come, Halifax and his board of trade sneered it to oblivion. In a representation to the king in October 1754, they noted that the Albany commissioners had considered "1. The management and direction of Indian Affairs. 2. The strengthening the Frontiers: and 3. The providing for these services by a general plan of Union . . . they have delayed making any provisions for, or pointing out any measures of carrying the two first of these points into execution, till the Plan of union agreed upon by them shall have been considered by their respective Assemblies and afterwards offered to the consideration of Parliament, and . . . such delay may prove not

9. *Military Affairs in North America*, ed. Pargellis, x.
10. Ibid., xi; cf. Yorke, *Life of Hardwicke* 2:44–49, 256.
11. Ibid., 2:199, 256.
12. Henretta, "*Salutary Neglect*," 317–18.

only prejudicial but fatal to Your Majesty's interest and the security of the Colonies, if Indian Affairs should continue to be mismanaged." Though the board formally omitted to "make any observations upon" the Albany plan, but merely transmitted it "simply for Your Majesty's consideration," the burden of its representation was in substance a devastating attack and a reiteration of the board's alternative plan submitted previously in August.[13]

In the board's plan, the colonial assemblies were allowed to raise and pay for troops and to defray the costs of maintaining frontier forts, but "*the command* of all the Forts and Garrisons and of all Forces raised upon emergencies and the sole direction of Indian Affairs [were to] be placed in the hands of some one single person, Commander in Chief, to be appointed by Your Majesty, who is to be authorized to draw upon the Treasurer or other proper Officer of each Colony for such sums of money as shall be necessary, as well for the ordinary as extraordinary service, according to the Quota settled for each Colony."[14]

Influence of Lord Halifax

Thomas Pownall's report on New York and Indian affairs indicted the province for mismanagement that was not likely to change. Having observed the same mismanagement in other colonies, Halifax decided that the crown had to assume direct management through agents directly appointed by and directly responsible to itself. For all practical purposes, this policy would mean direction of Indian affairs by Halifax supervising his own appointees and bypassing governors and assemblies. It was another slashing attack on colonial powers (though they certainly deserved it in this case), and it was made more cutting by the recommendation of William Johnson to exert the royal authority in the northern colonies.

Johnson's own remarks presented a clear and cogent plan for dealing with the Iroquois independently from colonial governments.[15] From the circumstances it may be assumed that John Pownall went along, and perhaps added his own voice to his brother's. Whereupon, the board of trade enlarged its August plan in its October "representation" to the king, by adding more recommendations on Indian affairs. It "humbly submitted" that "Colonel Johnson should be appointed Colonel over the Six [Iroquois]

13. *N. Y. Col. Docs.* 6:901–3, 916–20. Gipson interpreted these documents as meaning that the board had "a real desire to see the colonies evolve their own plan of union rather than have one formulated for them in England." Gipson, *British Empire* 5:165. See Alison Gilbert Olson, "The British Government and Colonial Union, 1754," *Wm. and Mary Qtly.*, 3d series, 17:1 (Jan. 1960), 22–34.

14. The mss. is Halifax to Newcastle, 15 Aug. 1754, Add. MSS. 32, 736, f. 243, BL.

15. *N. Y. Col. Docs.* 6:897–99.

Nations . . . The reasons of our taking the liberty to recommend this Gentleman to Your Majesty are the representations which have been made to us of the great service he did during the late war, in preserving the friendship of the Indians and engaging them to take up the hatchet against the French; the connexions he has formed by living amongst them, and habituating himself to their manners and customs; the publick testimony they have given at the last meeting of their friendship for, and confidence in, him; and above all the request they make that the sole management of their affairs may be intrusted to him."[16] As we have seen in chapter 5, Johnson was at bitter odds with New York's assemblymen, but there was nothing they could do about it when the crown set him in a place of authority superior in many ways to their own, and definitely independent of them.

One word neatly distinguishes the board of trade's plan from the Albany plan: the board called for a *concert* of the colonies rather than a *union*.[17] Under the board's plan the colonies were not to be consulted except to determine how money was to be raised from their own peoples after the commander in chief had decided how much each was to be assessed. The appointment and power of the commander in chief "depends singly upon Your Majesty; who may, as we humbly apprehend, legally and by virtue of your own authority, invest any person your Majesty shall think proper, with such power." The colonial assemblies were to be permitted to agree to the commander's power to draw money from them, but not to disagree; for, if they refused to cooperate, "We can see no other method that can be taken, but that of an application for an interposition of the Authority of Parliament."[18] More than a decade before the Stamp Act, Parliament was already being considered by imperialists on both sides of the Atlantic as the ultimate power to bring the colonies to heel. Lord Halifax gauged its potential well; there was no possibility that Parliament would authorize intercolonial *union* because, in the view of Commons's speaker, "an Independency upon this country [was] to be feared from such an union."[19]

Although the ministry ignored the Albany plan, Halifax paid close attention to the descriptions of Indian affairs forwarded by observers Thomas Pownall and William Johnson. Pownall was the board of trade's own man, brother to its secretary, and an employee in its office for eight years until he was sent to America as its unofficial inspector general.[20]

Indian affairs were intensely interesting to the board's activist presi-

16. Ibid., 6:919.
17. Add. MSS. 32,736, ff. 247–252, BL; *N. Y. Col. Docs.* 6:901–6.
18. Ibid., 6:902.
19. Olson, "British Government and Colonial Union," 31.
20. W. P. Courtney, "Pownall, Thomas (1722–1805)." in *Dict. Nat. Biog.* 46:264–65; Greiert, "Earl of Halifax," 203.

dent, Lord Halifax, because the Indians—especially the Iroquois—seemed to be indispensable instruments to evict the French from America.[21] Influence among the tribes made it possible for the French colonial population, one-twentieth the size of British colonials, to hold off the British juggernaut. For Halifax the logic was very simple: win the Indians to his side, and the French were lost.

As a specialist in American colonies, Halifax was also a "notoriously hawkish" British minister.[22] He used American issues as instruments with which to push the government into ever more belligerent policies toward France. After only a year in the board of trade, Halifax persuaded the ministry to strengthen Nova Scotia by founding the town called Halifax with Protestant settlers as an offset to the French Catholic Acadian *habitants*, and to create a military threat to the French naval base at Louisbourg on Cape Breton. This buildup of Nova Scotia was an expensive enterprise that cost £336,700 within three years before the start of the Seven Years War.[23] Naturally the apprehensive French resorted to countermeasures.

Virginia's expansionist lieutenant governor Dinwiddie was a close friend of Halifax[24] (which may explain Dinwiddie's appointment). While Dinwiddie and the Ohio Company challenged French occupation of the Ohio country, Halifax revived the British crown's claim to own the west by virtue of sovereignty over the Iroquois League and its "conquests." In 1701 the Iroquois had given a deed to Britain for territory in Ontario and the Ohio and Illinois countries, from which they had been driven by the French and French tribal allies.[25] Halifax chose to regard the Iroquois ownership of the abandoned lands as still valid, and to claim derivative British sovereignty over them because the French had acknowledged in the 1713 treaty of Utrecht that the Iroquois were British "subjects." So what belonged to the Iroquois belonged to Britain. In August 1853, Halifax revived this dormant claim and pushed it at the duke of Newcastle, who was then secretary of state for the northern department. Halifax immediately followed up with a representation from his board of trade to the privy council claiming that the Ohio River ran through Virginia. The French were *invading* Virginia, asserted the board, by driving out British subjects "not more than 200 or 250 miles from the Sea Coast."[26] (A mod-

21. Lords debates, 10 Dec. 1755, *Proceedings and Debates of the British Parliaments Respecting North America, 1754–1783*, eds. R. C. Simmons and P. D. G. Thomas (Millwood, N.Y.: Kraus International Publications, 1982–), 1:115.

22. Greiert, "Earl of Halifax," 378.

23. Ibid., 28–31.; Blackey, "Political Career of George Montagu Dunk," 409.

24. Greiert, "Earl of Halifax," 224.

25. See Jennings, *Ambiguous Iroquois Empire*, ch. 2, 210–13.

26. Greiert, "Earl of Halifax," 294–95; Halifax to Newcastle, 15 Aug. 1753, Newcastle Papers, Add. MSS. 32, 029, f. 96. Newcastle thought this paper important enough to have

ern road map puts Pittsburgh 379 miles from New York City, 421 miles from Norfolk, Va.)

The reluctant cabinet, obviously uncomfortable with these hawkish pressures, abstained from direct action by dumping on colonial governors the responsibility for resisting French encroachments.[27] We have seen how Governor Dinwiddie precipitated crises that gave Halifax materials for further demands on the ministry. He was soon joined by a greater power, the duke of Cumberland, whose aggressiveness exceeded even that of Halifax.

(I do not mean by imply by these remarks that Johnson, Pownall, Halifax, Dinwiddie, Cumberland, et al., had a conspiratorial plan outlined in detail. Rather, they were like-minded men in certain respects, who cooperated as circumstances permitted.)

1754 was the year of decision. Henry Pelham died, 4 March 1754, upon which his half-brother the duke of Newcastle became first lord of the Treasury and head of the ministry.[28] Newcastle opposed the most extreme demands of the hawks; but he thought that only the threat of a general war could prevent French encroachments in America.[29] The French must be made to understand that an aroused Britain would defend its territory by all necessary means. Newcastle learned too late that he had opened a door to the warmongers by providing opportunity for them to redefine British territory. Halifax saw that opening and walked right through.

Two months after Newcastle assumed leadership, he convened a meeting of a select group of ministers, including Halifax, to consider the French "invasion" of the king's dominions. This inner cabinet determined that measures must be taken to defend the northern colonies and prevent the Indians from being "cut off." £10,000 in specie was to be sent immediately to Virginia's aggressive governor Dinwiddie for Indian affairs, including any "gratuity that he may think necessary." A credit for £10,000 more was supplied to Dinwiddie to be drawn from Mr. Hanbury.[30]

it copied for Sir Thomas Robinson, secretary of state for the southern department. Ibid., f. 113. T. R. Clayton has drawn attention to the influence of Halifax's aggressiveness on Newcastle. T. R. Clayton, "The Duke of Newcastle, the Earl of Halifax, and the American Origins of the Seven Years' War," *The Historical Journal* (Cambridge, Eng.), 24:3 (Sept. 1981), 576–78, 591.

27. Greiert, "Earl of Halifax," 295.

28. Basil Williams, *The Whig Supremacy, 1714–1760*, 2d ed. rev. by C. H. Stuart, *Oxford History of England* (Oxford: Clarendon Press, 1962), 345.

29. Clayton, "The Duke of Newcastle," 585.

30. Minutes of meeting at Newcastle House, 26 June 1754, Newcastle Papers, Add. MSS, 32,029, f. 124, BL. The reference to Hanbury is significant in several ways: besides being a partner in the Ohio Company and its agent in London, he was also very active in Whig politics, especially supporting Newcastle's interest at Bristol. As a Quaker he was far from orthodox in pacifism; during 1754 and 1755 he served as Parliament's agent in forwarding £10,000 each year to Virginia "towards the payment and provision of the Forces employed, or to be employed, in the Defence of his Majesty's Colonies on the River Ohio." John and

Propaganda battle

Obviously these decisions edged beyond previous policy, and in the direction demanded by Halifax. Significantly, this meeting occurred before George Washington's fourth of July capitulation at Great Meadows. It was a time of uncertainty among Englishmen with political interests. The backwoods struggle was viewed ambivalently, if one may judge from *The Gentleman's Magazine*, which became a propaganda battleground for varied interests. In its July number it carried an account of the Ohio Valley contest up to the point where Washington had defeated Jumonville. This was accompanied by a map by Emanuel Bowen, "Geographer to His Majesty"; both the account and the map are notable for what they do not say. Though they invoke the treaty of Utrecht to claim the Iroquois as British subjects, neither asserts an Iroquois empire. The map confines the Six Nations to their own tribal territory, and the text refers to their Indian *allies*.[31] Neither supports Halifax's imperial vision.

The September issue reported Washington's surrender, with the ominous comment that "there have been frequent councils lately held here upon this subject; and we have good authority [i.e., a leak] to say, that our interest in America will in a very short time be effectually supported." The writer hastened to reassure his public that "the disputes there [would be] decided without producing a declaration of war."[32]

A strong rejoinder, copied from the *Evening Advertiser*, appeared in the November issue. Its author was every bit as imperialist as Lord Halifax,

Capel Hanbury to The Lord Chancellor, 13 Apr. 1754, Hardwicke Papers, Add. MSS. 35,592, BL; Sir Lewis Namier, *The Structure of Politics at the Accession of George III*, 2d ed. (London: Macmillan and Co., 1957), 203, 232; *Proceedings and Debates of the British Parliaments*, eds. Simmons and Thomas, 1:44, 126. See Jacob M. Price, "The Great Quaker Business Families of Eighteenth-Century London: The Rise and Fall of a Sectarian Patriciate," in *The World of William Penn*, eds. Richard S. Dunn and Mary Maples Dunn (Philadelphia: University of Pennsylvania Press, 1986), 363–99. Professor Price remarks that the Hanburys' "consultation by the government during the formulation of the strategy that led to Braddock's expedition enabled a prominent anti-government pamphleteer to describe that campaign as a Quaker plot to get others to fight for them to protect the Hanburys' interests in the Ohio lands and to win transport and supply contracts for their firm" (p. 379). The cited pamphlet: [John Shebbeare], *A Letter to the People of England on the Present Situation and Conduct of National Affairs, Letter I* (London, 1755), 33–43. Thomas Penn claimed that he and Hanbury solicited "Succours from hence" for Virginia's struggle at the Ohio, and Hanbury was so anxious about the ministry's deliberations on that score that he asked Newcastle to delay the sailing of a man-of-war so that no time should be lost in getting news of the ministry's decision to America. Hanbury earned the trust of his partners in the Ohio Company. T. Penn to R. Peters, London, 17 Oct. 1754, mss., Penn Ltr. Bks. 4:4–11, HSP; Hanbury to Newcastle, 14 June 1754, Newcastle Papers, Add. MSS. 32,735, f. 462.

31. "Some Account of the Encroachments made by the French on the British Settlements in America," *The Gentleman's Magazine* 24 (July 1754), 320–23. Bowen inserted the Iroquois claims in the later edition of "An Accurate Map of North America" (London: Robert Sayer, 1763).

32. "Account of Our Affairs in America," *Gentleman's Magazine* 24 (Sept. 1754), 399–400.

but he believed that Britain's interest lay elsewhere than at the Ohio. Since he summarized a large body of opinion that I have given little attention to so far, he may be quoted at length. He thought that if war with France should become necessary, "it would be infinitely better" to secure Hudson Bay

> than to send forces to the banks of the Ohio. For, supposing we should prove victorious, what could we gain by settling colonies in that part of the world [the Ohio]? Colonies so greatly distant from the sea, that we could never have any intercourse with them in the way of commerce? Colonies, which would be a continual expence, and could be of no advantage,—whose very situation would put them under a necessity, and the fruitfulness of whose country would afford them the means of rivalling Great Britain in every article of its manufactures; so that new Bradfords, new Birminghams, new Manchesters, and new Norwiches would inevitably rise up on the banks of the Ohio, and between the lakes, to the destruction of the mother country?—the interest of the mother country plainly consists in this;—to people those regions well, whose vicinity to the sea, and to navigable rivers, shall enable them to transport the peculiar produce and raw materials of their country into Great Britain, at an easy and moderate expence, and to receive our manufactures in return. This is a beneficial trade, because it is reciprocally advantageous; this would cause a colony to flourish without any jarring of interests with the mother country. . . .
>
> As to the Apalatean mountains in America, the only point in which Great Britain can be concerned, is to see, that the passes of these mountains are in the possession of her own subjects . . . The English possess already more lands in America, than will be sufficiently peopled in five hundred years. . . . Particularly let us not imitate the French in this part of their conduct; for their distant, inland settlements on the continent of America, are in fact and reality, whatever may be pretended, a consuming expence and a dead weight to old France: and the blunders and mistakes of one nation should be a caution to another.[33]

Thus spoke the merchant, dissenting from the land speculator and the militarist. Curiously, coming from different directions and with wholly different objectives, the merchants shared the colonial assemblies' objections to imperial aggression at the Ohio. It contradicts the concept of mercantilism as "an effort to combine 'war after the war' with that other principle, of 'business as usual.' "[34] Although it is questionable whether any European power could have held off the surge of emigration into the Ohio Valley, it is clear enough at the present day that the merchant spokesman in *The Gentleman's Magazine* had foresight greater than that of the statesmen who insisted on confrontation with France.

33. "Certain objects particularly worthy the attention of a British Parliament at the present juncture," ibid. (Nov. 1754), 502–5.

34. Herbert L. Osgood, *The American Colonies in the Eighteenth Century* (1924), 4 vols. reprinted (Gloucester, Mass.: Peter Smith, 1958), 2:309–10.

The issues debated in 1754 seem to me to indicate the very opposite of L. H. Gipson's contention that "new conceptions of colonialism" prevailing over the older mercantilism supported "interests that Americans had greatly at heart." Land speculators are not to be equated with "Americans." Gipson put a halo over his beneficent new imperialist colonialism: "Little as it would mean in material benefits to the average Englishman or Scot in his lifetime to see the right of Virginia to control the forks of the Ohio vindicated, that right was to be upheld whatever the cost to Englishmen and Scots in wealth as well as in lives."[35] This is mere propaganda in outrageous flouting of observable facts. The experience of British armies in America demonstrated beyond doubt that few Englishmen or Scots went willingly to the slaughter, and certainly colonial assemblies resisted as strongly as they could the oppression associated with it. The overruled merchants shrugged and took war profits.

Cumberland takes over

From the moment that news of Washington's capitulation at Great Meadows reached Britain, the merchants lost their case. Newcastle determined that "something must be resolv'd and that something must be (if possible) Effectual."[36] This was the precise turning point of British policy and politics signaling the end of the era of "salutary neglect" under the oligarchic rule of the Old Whigs. Intercolonial union was already a casualty in its Albany manifestation; now it was dropped as a project under royal prerogative, and Newcastle would not consider it as an offspring of Parliamentary law.[37] As an alternative, Newcastle turned to military force, still hoping to contain hostilities short of full-scale general war with France. But King George had an "utter aversion" to sending troops to America, so Newcastle appealed to the duke of Cumberland because only Cumberland could overcome the king's aversion.[38] The decision was fatal to control by Newcastle and his Old Whigs of the developing situation. Cumberland's foot was no sooner in the door than he shoved his way in completely. Stanley Pargellis notes that Cumberland thereafter "sat in cabinets when American policy was discussed, and from exercising the command over the army itself he came to have more weight than any other individual in determining where and how the army was to function abroad."[39]

35. Gipson, *British Empire* 6:56.
36. Henretta, *"Salutary Neglect,"* 338. Newcastle got the news of the Great Meadows affair from John Hanbury. Newcastle Papers, Add. MSS. 32,029, f. 30, BL.
37. Wickwire, *British Subministers*, 340–44.
38. Gipson, *British Empire* 6:55; *Military Affairs*, ed. Paragellis, xi.
39. Ibid., xi.

Newcastle had not realized how Cumberland's intentions made his own plan impossible. According to Sir Charles Grant Robertson, Cumberland wanted "to expel the French neck and crop";[40] and, of course, the French would not give up their whole American empire after only a bit of localized scuffling. Newcastle awoke too late to the implications of Cumberland's dispositions. He had agreed to send two regiments to America for the purpose of taking Fort Duquesne and expelling the French from the Ohio Valley. That was his original reason for appealing to Cumberland. And Newcastle approved of an attack on Fort St. Frédéric at Crown Point to eliminate the French threat to Albany; but when Cumberland proposed to raise two New England regiments for a simultaneous attack on the French in Acadia / Nova Scotia, Newcastle drew back because that would press the French toward a general war. Cumberland outmaneuvered him. Newcastle's cabinet included Cumberland's ally Henry Fox as secretary at war, and Fox simply did what Cumberland wanted before Newcastle could stop it.[41] Soon Newcastle wailed that he had become a mere "butt," loaded with all responsibility, but lacking power to direct or govern.[42]

War made inevitable

The brawling at the forks of the Ohio was not the cause of the Seven Years War; rather it served as an excuse for powerful Englishmen who wanted to fight France. The "bush war" could have been contained and settled somehow by negotiation as other conflicts at the periphery of empire had previously been eased. This was what George II and Louis XV wanted, and it was what their chief ministers wanted, but the English belligerents demanded what the French moderates could not concede, and the French hard-liners forced responses that the English moderates could not accept. Each side maneuvered for positions of strength that could not be abandoned. Having achieved strength, each side had to use it. The "doves" lost control when they conceded the "hawks" fundamental premise that the two countries' "natural" enmity could end only by conquest.[43]

40. Sir Charles Grant Robertson, *England Under the Hanoverians* (1911) reprinted (London: Methuen and Co., 1958), 123–24.

41. Clayton, "The Duke of Newcastle," 594–95.

42. Gipson, *British Empire* 6:57n48.

43. See T. R. Clayton, "The Duke of Newcastle . . . ," 571–603; Patrice Louis-René Higonnet, "The Origins of the Seven Years' War," *Jounal of Modern History* 40 (Mar. 1968), 57–90.

Bibliographic note: These two studies cover much the same ground, but there are serious problems with Higonnet's documentation, including one reference that I have been unable to find in the Public Record Office. Clayton wrote to correct misstatements by Higonnet. I thank Dr. John Hemphill of Colonial Williamsburg for showing me Clayton's article.

Cumberland and Fox forced the issue irrevocably by advertising the troop movements in the court *Gazette*, thus blasting Newcastle's hopes for secrecy. As he had feared, the French crown responded by preparing troop movements of its own. Under Cumberland's pressure, the British forces expanded to 10,000 men in seven regiments and several independent companies. They were assigned to take Fort Duquesne, Fort St. Frédéric, Fort Niagara, and Fort Beauséjour on the Chignecto isthmus connecting the peninsula of Nova Scotia to the mainland.[44] These forts were scattered over regions larger than the United Kingdom. The French ministry did not delude itself that such wide-ranging attacks constituted a local conflict.

The colonies were informed of their role rather than consulted about it. Secretary Robinson told the governors to expect troops from Britain, to recruit more, and to feed them all "at the expence of your Government," besides quartering the troops as directed by the commander in chief, and providing for their transportation. The colonies were also to contribute to a "common fund" for the general service of North America, but it was common only for contributions; it was to be spent solely by the said commander. All this was politely "recommended to you," but "the King will not therefore imagine that either you or the rest of his Governors will suffer the least neglect or delay in the performance of the present service." What it came down to, as the lords of trade had earlier proposed, was a levy on the colonies to finance the crown's war for increased empire. At this stage, Robinson did not even pretend otherwise. He said nothing of protecting the king's good subjects against a foreign foe, and it became quickly clear that those loyal subjects did not feel the need of such protection. Robinson's sole justification for burdening the colonies with the maintenance of the king's troops was only "the defence of His Majesty's just rights and dominions in those parts."[45]

Left unsaid, but clearly plain, was the inclusion among those "just rights" of his majesty's prerogative to order tribute from his subjects. This became plainer yet from the appointment of Major General Edward Braddock as commander in chief, for Braddock was the choice of the duke of Cumberland. By this appointment, Cumberland gained another advance in his campaign to enlarge the royal prerogative in Britain as well as America. An alarmed Whig lord reasoned that "One great political reason for avoiding a war, by all means that were safe and decent, was the enormous power which was likely to be thrown by it into the Duke [of Cumberland]'s hands": this from Lord Royston, Hardwicke's son. Lord Shelburne judged that "The war was contrived by the Duke of Cumberland under-

44. Clayton, "The Duke of Newcastle," 595–96.
45. Robinson to the governors, 26 Oct. 1754, *N.Y. Col. Docs.* 6:915.

hand. . . . The Duke of Newcastle was frightened, bullied and betrayed into it." Braddock was seen as a political appointee without military ability, "the last man in the army . . . for that command." But Cumberland had gained his point, and the ministry let him seize more and more power rather than resign to avoid responsibility for what they could not control.[46] As so often is true, the authoritarians in Britain were able to seize power at home by leverage from power permitted abroad.

Futile commissioners

In one aspect the Seven Years War may be seen as a resumption of the War of the Austrian Succession (King George's War) that ended in 1748. Many issues, left unresolved in the exhaustion that ended that war at the treaty of Aix-la-Chapelle, had been turned over to a joint Franco-British commission for diplomatic resolution. American problems were not the only issues before the commissioners, but positions in America were central to their discussions—or, rather, to their debates because few compromises emerged. Gipson remarks that, "by the summer of 1752, the disputes between the two Crowns, instead of tapering off, as it were, by reason of the endeavours of the diplomats, were unhappily becoming intensified and broadened."[47]

The kings wanted peace. George II worried nervously about what might happen to his patrimonial duchy of Hanover where he felt more at home than in England. If war broke out again, France's great armies would almost certainly swarm over Hanover. George's fears affected British diplomacy to the point that Britain became "an insurance office for Hanover."[48] On the other side, Louis XV was "perhaps the greatest pacifist in his court, personally brave, but distressed beyond measure at human suf-

46. Yorke, *Life of Hardwicke* 2:256–57. The French court dated British decision to invade Canada "so early as the month of November 1754, and very probably several months before," basing this judgment on papers captured from Edward Braddock. [Moreau], *Conduct of the Late Ministry*, 28. Using the same sources, the French commander-in-chief in Canada, baron de Dieskau, identified Cumberland as "the prime mover of the whole." Dieskau to Doreil, Montreal, 16 Aug. 1755, *N.Y. Col. Docs.* 10:311–12.

47. Gipson, *British Empire* 5:318. Though Gipson's adulation of the British empire was flaunted to the point where it embarrasses even an anglophile, he did not share the bloodthirst of Francis Parkman. Gipson wrote, as Parkman never would, that "the importance of this international commission should not be obscured by its failure to accomplish any of its objectives; to the end it remained the symbol that peaceful solution of vexed questions was the civilized way for peoples involved in dispute." It was wishful thinking contrary to fact but creditable as a wish. *British Empire* 5:304.

48. Ibid., 6:349–51, 369; W. F. Reddaway, "The Seven Years' War," in *The Old Empire*, vol. 1 of *The Cambridge History of the British Empire*, gen. eds. J. Holland Rose et al. (New York: Macmillan, 1929), 463.

fering on the battlefield."[49] Certainly the European balance of power was constantly in the minds of all diplomats, and certainly European territorial contentions were part of the tinder that flamed up after war began, but what brought Britain and France to blows was their failure to reconcile their claims in America.

In the simmering dispute over the Ohio Valley, the British ministry and its commissioners tenaciously based their claim on the deeds given by Iroquois chiefs in 1701 and 1726, which, as we have seen, Lord Halifax thrust forward. Thus, declaimed the British, the territories of Iroquois "conquests" had rightfully come under British sovereignty. Frenchmen knew what nonsense this was, and refused, literally, to give ground.[50]

In hindsight, the doom of this joint commission appeared at its beginning. Among its early members were two tough hard-liners: La Galissonière on the French side and William Shirley on the British. Apparently they had been appointed to make sure on each side that no soft negotiator should give away an "essential interest." As governor of Canada, La Galissonière had conceived the strategy that led to France's aggressive fort building in the Ohio Valley. His mind was dominated by conceptions of military strategy, and he was certain that France could not retreat an inch without losing all. Shirley, as governor of Massachusetts, had conceived and organized the campaign that captured Fort Louisbourg in 1745. Though he was a civilian, he envisioned a political prospect of British empire over all of North America. Both men thought of the joint commission as a means to win their objectives; neither intended to compromise.

After a shuffling start, Shirley insisted that proposals be exchanged in writing, and he set about preparing massive legal briefs that were doubtless brilliant as argument but irrelevant to negotiation. The French side countered with another brief so huge that it could not even be copied; the original had to be chivvied back and forth between London and Paris.

49. *Anglo-French Boundary Disputes in the West, 1749–1763*, ed. Theodore Calvin Pease, Collections of the Illinois State Historical Library 27, French Series 2 (Springfield, 1936), xxvi. Bibliographic note: There is no substance whatever to the stupidly vicious allegation of Francis Parkman that "it was the fatuity of Louis XV and his Pompadour that made the conquest of Canada possible." Nor to Parkman's misogynist libels that France's "infatuation . . . had turned her from her own true interest to serve the passions of the two empresses and the Czarina Elizabeth," repeated as "the rage of the two empresses and the spite of the concubine." Parkman, *Montcalm and Wolfe*, 2 vols. (1884), New Library ed. (Boston: Little Brown and Co., 1909), 1:4; 2:407, 424. For a cooler and more sensible discussion of the "continental system," see Gipson, *British Empire* 6: chs. 11–12, 14. Among other matters, Gipson's treatment of Prussia's Frederick II is strongly opposed to Parkman's adoration of that royal butcher. Less anglophilia will be found in shorter treatments by George F. G. Stanley, *New France: The Last Phase, 1740–1760*, Canadian Centenary series (Toronto: McClelland and Stewart, 1968), ch. 9; and a good pro-French account is in Guy Frégault, *Canada: The War of the Conquest*, trans. Margaret M. Cameron (Toronto: Oxford University Press, 1969), 74–88.

50. See La Galissonière's memoir, Dec. 1750, *N.Y. Col. Docs.* 10:228.

Shirley's method served only to produce justification for what each side wanted; it allowed no latitude for give and take. His colleague Mildmay complained bitterly to patrons in London about Shirley's high-handed ways, and Shirley was recalled in 1752, having accomplished nothing except the reduction of his own reputation.[51]

Not only the Ohio country was at stake in America. The colonists whom Lord Halifax sent to Nova Scotia encountered hostility from Micmac Indians and French peasants which resulted in death and destruction, but the crown's commissioners in far-off Paris neither smelled the smoke of burning villages nor heard the screams of victims of guerilla raids and retaliatory punitive expeditions. Paris was comfortable and amusing. The commissioners haggled politely about procedures, prepared enormous historical reviews, referred trivia as well as important issues back to their respective ministries, and killed more time pleasantly while waiting for sometimes exasperated responses. They so impressed both governments with their futility that the ministries reverted to normal diplomatic channels through their ambassadors. From 1750 to 1755 the commissioners exercised their talents for sophistry until preparations for war became too overt for either crown to bother continuing the charade. By June of 1754 Newcastle sputtered, "I am quite sick of Commissaries, Tho' I don't well know how to get rid of Them. I am sure, They will do no Good; and Therefore hope, We shall not be so far amus'd by Their Conferences, as To suspend or delay, taking The Proper Measures to defend Ourselves, or recover our Lost Possessions."[52]

We have seen the military measures then decided upon by the British ministry, but cosmetic diplomacy continued. In January 1755, Britain dispatched two regiments from Cork, Ireland, to Virginia; in the same month, Sir Thomas Robinson proposed vaguely to the French ambassador Mirepoix that "possessions in North America be restored to the same state in which they were at the time of the conclusion of the . . . Treaty of Utrecht" [in 1713]. As all the wrangling up to that time had been precisely centered on just where those pre-Utrecht boundaries should be drawn, French response was predictable: Minister Rouillé observed that the territory of the Ohio River "belongs incontestably to the King [of France] and has always been regarded as a part of his American possessions." In a demonstration that the British had no monopoly on double talk, the French sent seventy-eight companies of well-trained troops to Canada under command of the baron de Dieskau.[53]

51. John A. Schutz, *William Shirley, King's Governor of Massachusetts*, published for the Institute of Early American History and Culture (Chapel Hill: University of North Carolina Press, 1961), ch. 8; Stanley, *New France*, 126–27.

52. Loc. cit.

53. Memoir, 22 Jan. 1755, and Rouillé's instruction, 3 Feb. 1755, in *Anglo-French Boundary Disputes*, ed. Pease, 100, 107; Gipson, *British Empire*, 6:100.

Maps as weapons

Then began the diplomatic battle of the maps. In March the British proposed to set up a buffer zone in America, and they drew lines on a map. The French countered with their own lines. On the British map, the buffer zone spread between the French possessions at the Wabash River to the British lands west of the Appalachian mountain range; this map gave to Britain, outside the buffer zone, the forks of the Ohio where Fort Duquesne was on the scene. On the French map the buffer zone moved bodily eastward so as to put Fort Duquesne into the neutral zone, and British Fort Oswego as well. Even Niagara would have been neutral; it looks as though the French ministry had decided to make a genuine effort at negotiation, but Britain's hard-liners were not having any of that.[54]

Lord Halifax argued in the cabinet against even the idea of a buffer zone.[55] Halifax was well prepared to argue geography because he was "on intimate terms" with cartographer John Mitchell, whom he had employed since 1750 to prepare a new map of the North American colonies.[56] Mitchell's biographers remark that "his foremost interest" in preparing his map "was to point up the growing threat to British ambitions of French expansion."[57] And Mitchell "was determined to give the Mother Country the benefit of every doubtful point when it came to delineating English boundaries in relation to those of the French."[58]

In the reading of another scholar, Mitchell conceded no rights to France except the city of Quebec and the trading post of Tadoussac.[59] A topographically more accurate map was published, also in 1755, under the patronage of the Pennsylvania assembly, and perhaps printed by Franklin. Its author Lewis Evans relied as much as Mitchell on the Iroquois deeds to Britain, but insisted that only lands itemized in the deeds had been properly conveyed.[60] Mitchell, on the other hand, extrapolated from

54. Maps in *Anglo-French Boundary Disputes*, ed. Pease, between pp. 150–51 and 190–91.

55. Greiert, "Earl of Halifax," 383; Clayton, "Duke of Newcastle," 600.

56. Edmund Berkeley and Dorothy Smith Berkeley, *Dr. John Mitchell: The Man Who Made the Map of North America* (Chapel Hill: University of North Carolina Press, 1974), 176.

57. Ibid., 175.

58. Ibid., 61.

59. Walter Klinefelter, *Lewis Evans and His Maps*, Transactions of the American Philosophical Society, new series 61:7 (July 1971), 49.

60. Evans had the friendship of Thomas Pownall, but embroiled himself in fierce political war with Governors Shirley and Morris, escaping trial only by dying. Colonel Henry Bouquet found his map highly accurate in Bouquet's subsequent campaigns in the Ohio country, and Thomas Pownall reprinted it with a tribute. See Klinefelter, *Lewis Evans*, 46–57; Lawrence Henry Gipson, *Lewis Evans, to which is added Evans' A Brief Account of Pennsylvania, Together with Facsimiles of His Geographical, Historical, Political, Philosophical, and Mechanical Essays, Numbers I and II* . . . (Philadelphia: Historical Society of Pennsylvania, 1939); Thomas Pownall, *A Topographical Description of Such Parts of North America as are Contained in The (Annexed) Map of the Middle British Colonies, &c. in North America* (1776), reprinted as *A Topo-*

the Iroquois deeds language to convey everything the Iroquois had ever looked at, which he called conquest. Mitchell relied heavily on those Iroquois "rights of conquest" and their donation to the British crown by deeds of 1701 and 1726.[61]

Appropriately dedicated to "The Earl of Halifax And the other Right Honourable The Lords Commissioners for Trade and Plantations," Mitchell's map was a political device intended to outflank Britain's "doves" and was instantly recognized as such by Lord Chancellor Hardwicke. He tried futilely to stop publication because the map extended "the Limits of the British Colonies as far or farther than any other I have seen. . . . it may fill people's heads with so strong an opinion of our strict Rights as may tend to obstruct an Accommodation, if attainable."[62] Hardwicke understood the situation perfectly.

The map was published 13 February 1755[63] and aroused the French ministry to total rejection. In May the French submitted a memoir remarking, with the virtue of accuracy, that "The Indians in question are free and independent and none of them can be termed subjects of either crown. The statement of the Treaty of Utrecht is faulty in that respect and cannot change the nature of things. It is certain that no Englishman would dare, without running the risk of being murdered, to tell the Iroquois they were English subjects."[64] The British side responded with what amounted to an ultimatum, and military preparations increased.[65]

Acadian battleground

Besides the Ohio country, the hot spots in America included Acadia/Nova Scotia and the great French fortress of Louisbourg on Cape Breton. The 1713 treaty of Utrecht, confirmed by the treaty of Aix-la-Chapelle, had ceded "all Nova Scotia or Acadia" to Britain "with its ancient boundaries."[66] As Andrew Hill Clark observes, the consequence was "a good

graphical Description of the Dominions of The United States of America, ed. Lois Mulkearn (Pittsburgh: University of Pittsburgh Press, 1949).

61. My inspection of the copy at the Newberry Library discloses a number of downright lies on it, such as that the Iroquois had "been in Possession" of southern Ontario for "about 100 Years," and that the Mississauga Indians had been "Subdued by the Iroquois and [were] now united with them making the 8th Nation in that League." Mitchell's Iroquois comments are politically motivated fabrications.

62. Clayton, "Duke of Newcastle," 600.

63. Berkeley and Berkeley, *Dr. John Mitchell*, 202. Title: *A Map of the British and French Dominions in North America . . .*

64. *Anglo-French Boundary Disputes*, ed. Pease, 223–24. See also the instructions to Vaudreuil, 1 Apr. 1755, in *N.Y. Col. Docs.* 10:290–94.

65. English answer, 7 June 1755, In *Anglo-French Boundary Disputes*, ed. Pease, 234–43.

66. Gipson, *British Empire* 5:307.

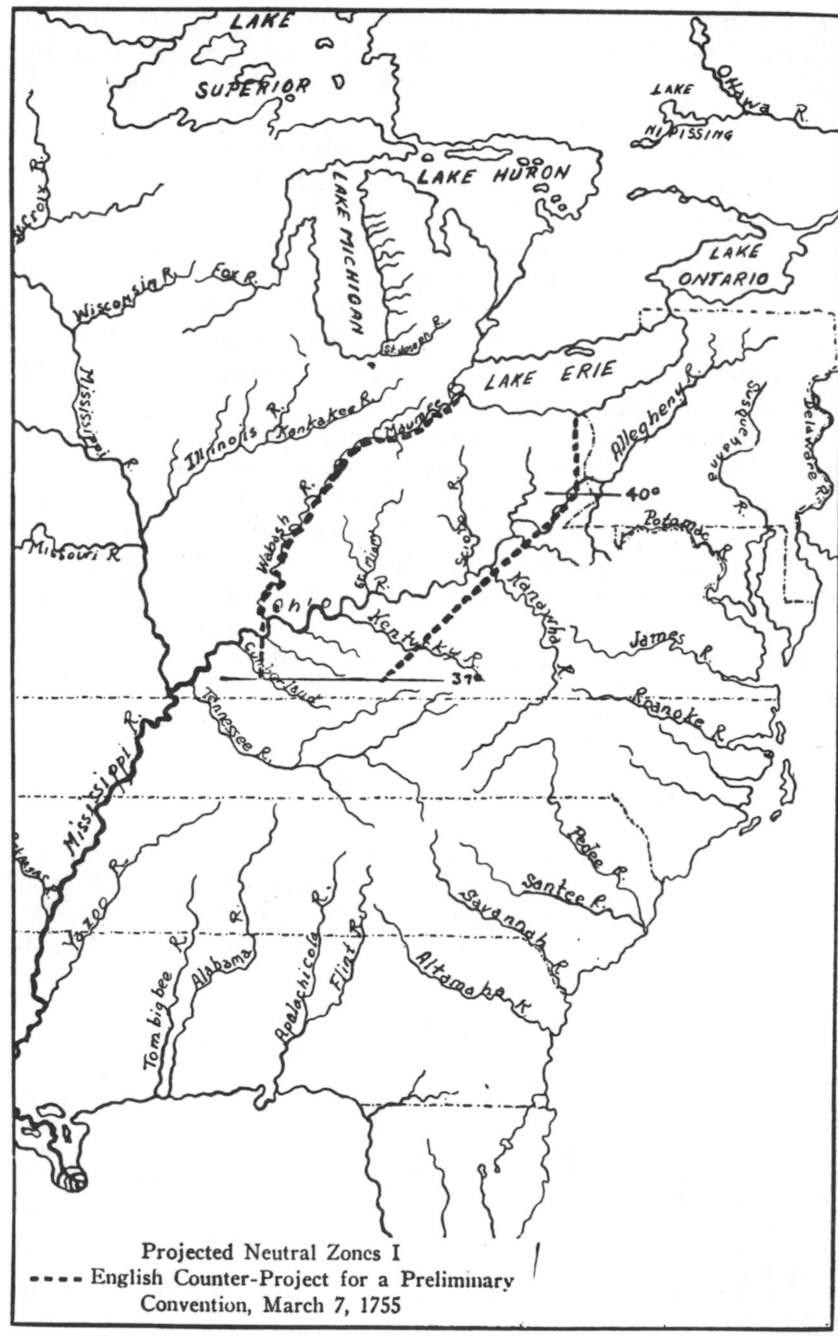

MAP 3. Neutral zone proposed by British *(above)* and French *(facing page)* diplomats. REPRODUCED FROM *Anglo-French Boundary Disputes in the West, 1749–1763* BY PERMISSION OF THE ILLINOIS STATE HISTORICAL LIBRARY.

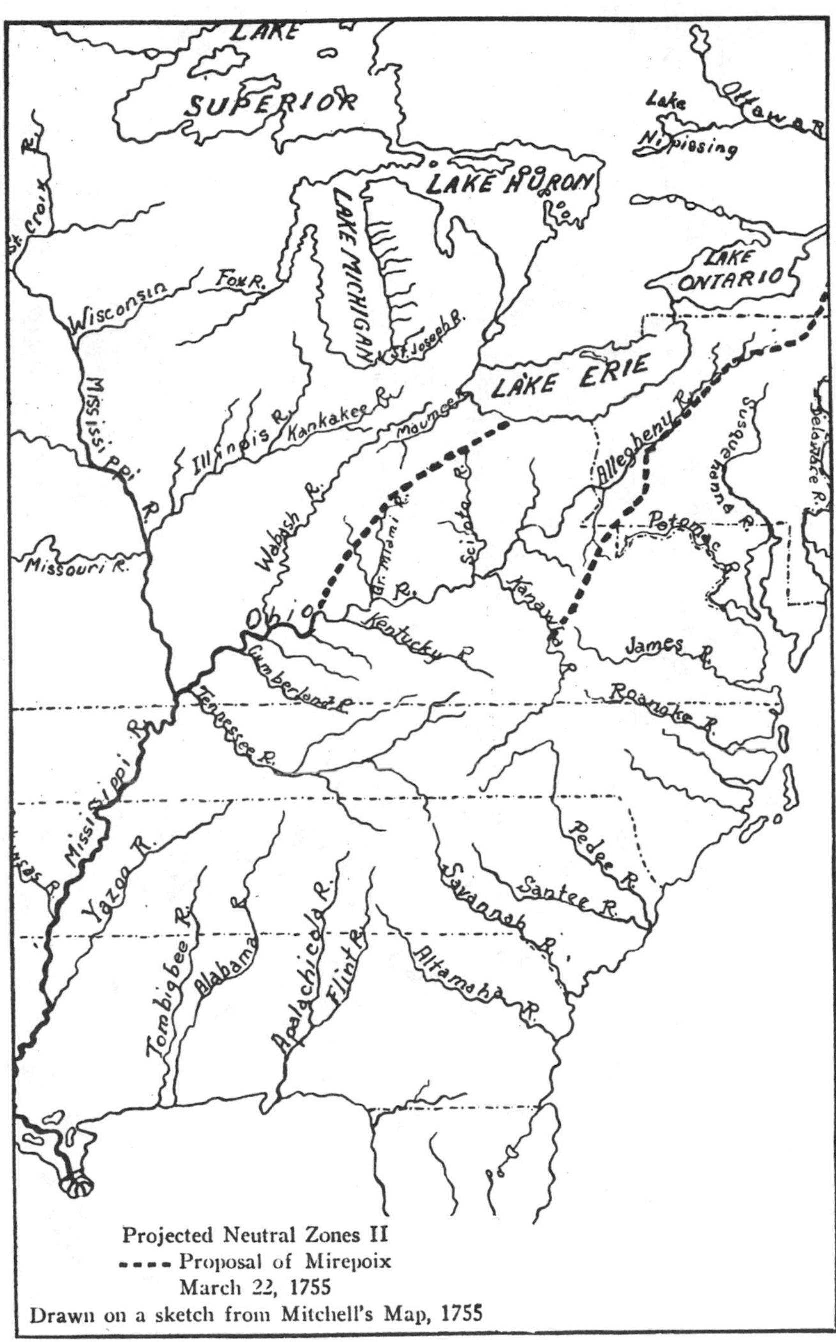

Projected Neutral Zones II
---- Proposal of Mirepoix
March 22, 1755
Drawn on a sketch from Mitchell's Map, 1755

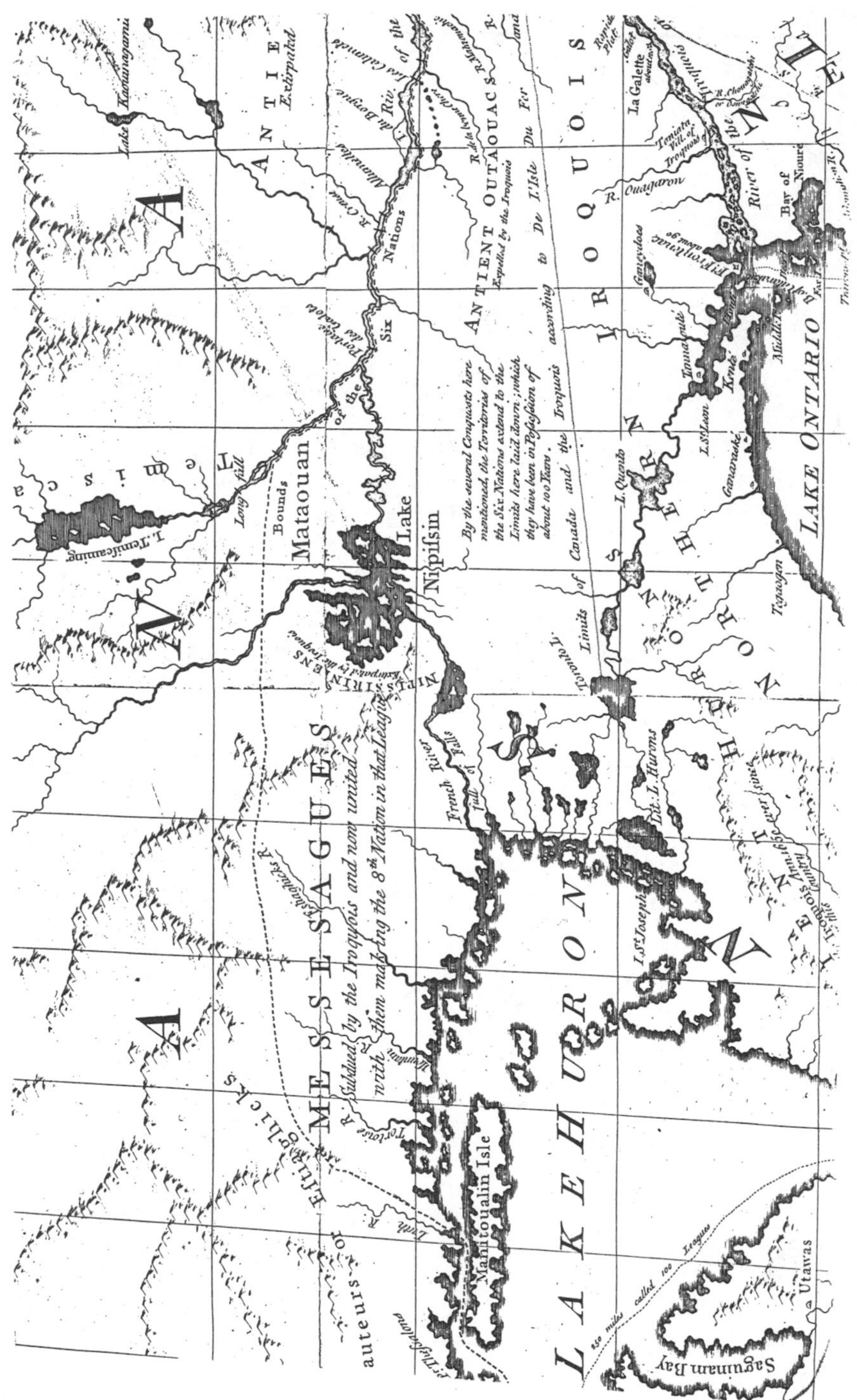

MAP 4. Extract from John Mitchell's map. The essential feature of this map for diplomatic purposes was the dashed line north of Lake Huron and running along

A MAP of the
British and French Dominions in
North America
WITH THE
Roads, Distances, Limits, and Extent of the
SETTLEMENTS,
Humbly Inscribed to the Right Honourable
The Earl of Halifax,
And the other Right Honourable
The Lords Commissioners for Trade & Plantations,
By their Lordships
Most Obliged,
and very humble servant
Jno. Mitchell.

the Ottawa River identified as the "Bounds of the Six Nations." This extract asserts falsely that "By the several Conquests here mentioned, the Territories of the Six Nations extend to the Limits here laid down; which they have been in Possession of about 100 Years." At another point it claims that the "Messesagues" had been "Subdued by the Iroquois and [were] now united with them making the 8th Nation in that League." In fact, the Mississagas had defeated the Iroquois and driven them out of the Ontario territory more than fifty years before Mitchell's map was published. REPRODUCED WITH PERMISSION FROM THE COPY IN THE NEWBERRY LIBRARY. (Title cartouche of John Mitchell's map REPRODUCED WITH PERMISSION FROM THE ORIGINAL IN THE NEWBERRY LIBRARY.)

deal of diplomatic double-talk" and "obvious special pleading" about those ancient boundaries among the commissioners in Paris.[67] While the commissioners chatted, each side sought to gain advantage from positions of strength on the scene. The French built Fort Beauséjour on Chignecto, the neck of land joining Nova Scotia to the mainland at the head of the Bay of Fundy's Cumberland Basin. The British countered with Fort Lawrence on an opposing ridge. From Beauséjour, French agents instigated Micmac convert Indians to raid British settlers in Nova Scotia, and they put heavy pressure on French Acadians to refuse an oath of allegiance to the British crown. Abbé Le Loutre, a Spiritan missionary, led the resistance. He explained his strategy in a letter to the minister of Marine: "As we cannot openly oppose the English ventures, I think that we cannot do better than to incite the Indians to continue warring on the English; my plan is to persuade the Indians to send word to the English that they will not permit new settlements to be made in Acadia . . . I shall do my best to make it look to the English as if this plan comes from the Indians and that I have no part in it." But nobody was fooled; the British put a price on Le Loutre's head. Nor was Le Loutre much kinder to the Acadians who did not want to abandon farms and homes created by lives of labor. In an era of the most devout religious conviction, he "threatened to abandon the Acadians, withdraw their priests, have their wives and children taken from them, and if necessary have their property laid waste by the Indians."[68] As events were to demonstrate, it was not an idle threat. Le Loutre's Indians prevented the British from seizing the strategically placed village of Beaubassin by burning the inhabitants' buildings, after which the neutral Acadians of that locality had no choice but to go over to the French forces.[69] It can be conceived as a devastating form of impressment.

In all of this, Le Loutre was heartily supported and urged on by French officialdom on both sides of the Atlantic,so much that it is hard to say how much was performed on his own initiative and how much was done under orders. There is no doubt that he acted like a bishop of the Crusades. The British retaliated with oppressive measures of their own against the suspect Acadians under their control; and, as those Acadians lived on large tracts of good land that they had rescued from the wild by hard labor, British officials and settlers came to think that the lands of the Acadians were worth more than their allegiance. Temporarily they were preserved on their farms because their produce was as essential to feed the

67. Andrew Hill Clark, *Acadia: The Geography of Early Nova Scotia to 1760* (Madison: University of Wisconsin Press, 1968), 72. Clark's precisely detailed maps are clear and valuable.

68. Gérard Finn, "Le Loutre, Jean-Louis," in *Dict. Can. Biog.* 4:453–58; John Clarence Webster, *The Career of the Abbe Le Loutre in Nova Scotia with a Translation of His Autobiography* (Shediac, N.B.: Privately printed, 1933).

69. Stanley, *New France*, 73.

soldiers of Britain as those of France. Harassed on all sides, the Acadians could do nothing right. Out of deep loyalty to their fatherland and religion, they would not swear oaths of allegiance to Britain's king nor adopt his Protestant state religion. All they wanted was to be left alone, but this was not permitted by either of the great powers. Those Acadians who succumbed to Le Loutre and fled to the vicinity of Fort Beauséjour experienced miserable living conditions and near starvation. Those who defied Le Loutre to cling to their farms were harassed by hostile British governors.[70] It is an open question whether at this stage they were treated worse by the British or the French.

Conquest of Forts Beauséjour and Gaspereau

Early in 1755, Newcastle learned of French intentions to reinforce Canada. In response his full cabinet council decided, 10 April, to outfit a naval squadron to "cruise off Louisbourg, with instruction to fall upon any French ships of war that shall be attempting to land troops in Nova Scotia or to go to Cape Breton, or through the St. Lawrence to Quebec."[71] Though diplomatic talks were still progressing (if that is the right word), France's minister of Marine had anticipated British escalation of force. He advised Governor Duquesne in Canada that 3,000 reinforcements were on their way "To protect that Colony from any attacks to which it might be exposed;" and "if, to assure that defensive on your part, you should judge necessary to make the Indians act offensively against the English, his Majesty will approve of your having recourse to that expedient."[72]

Both sides had talked much of defending essential interests, but both sides were now defending by offensives. In Nova Scotia/Acadia, a British offensive against French fortifications had been preparing since the closing months of 1754. It was initiated by Governor Lawrence of Nova Scotia and Governor Shirley of Massachusetts (returned from his tour of duty in diplomacy).[73] These gentlemen saw an irresistible opportunity presented by a turncoat spy in Fort Beauséjour who had been feeding information

70. Ibid., ch. 5; Frégault, *Canada: The War of the Conquest*, 167–68; Gipson, *British Empire* 6: ch. 9; L. F. S. Upton, *Micmacs and Colonists: Indian-White Relations in the Maritimes, 1713–1867* (Vancouver: University of British Columbia Press, 1979). ch. 4. Details of populations and economic activity are in Clark, *Acadia*, ch. 8. Frégault (pp. 167–68) observes that the Indians were ordered to "include in their parties a few Acadians dressed and painted like Indians, in order to compromise the white populations still more deeply and thus provoke violent repression by the English. This, in La Jonquière's opinion, would help considerably 'to attract Acadian families to our territory.'"

71. Gipson, *British Empire* 6:103.

72. De Machault to Duquesne, 17 Feb. 1755, in *N.Y. Col. Docs.* 10:275–78.

73. W. S. MacNutt, *The Atlantic Provinces: The Emergence of Colonial Society, 1712–1857* Canadian Centenary series (Toronto: McClelland and Stewart, 1965), 41.

to the British military at least since September 1754.[74] In August 1754, Shirley and Lawrence wrote separately to Lord Halifax to suggest a campaign against the Acadian forts, but what happened next is a bit murky.[75] Cumberland proposed the campaign, but Newcastle thought it too aggressively likely to bring on a general war with France.[76] Nonetheless, Shirley was authorized in December to reactivate two regiments of colonial troops, and by mid-February Shirley had raised 2,000 men.[77] His activities had been kept secret from the French, and seem not to have been clearly understood in London. Halifax and Newcastle's "considerations" about military strategy in America put Acadia at the end of a series of other campaigns against Forts Duquesne, St. Frédéric, and Niagara, and the same priorities appeared in the instructions given to General Braddock when he sailed to take command of the forces in America.[78] But when Braddock arrived and convened a council of war, Shirley laid before him, "the Measures concerted between him and Govr. Lawrence for repelling the French from their new Encroachments on the Bay of Fundi, which I [Braddock] approv'd of, and immediately sent orders to Lt. Colonel Monckton to take upon him that Command and carry it into execution."[79] Once again, Newcastle's carefully laid plans for gradual escalation, with pauses for possible negotiation, were circumvented by the hard-liners playing back and forth across the Atlantic into each others' hands.

Unaware of how he had lost control of the priorities on which his policy depended, Newcastle still hoped to prevent a general war by a restrained show of force. Thus, as Professor T. R. Clayton remarks, "the fleet which sailed to America under the command of Admiral Boscawen on 23 April 1755 was designed to deter France from a declaration of war, not to precipitate one. Newcastle believed that if Boscawen could achieve 'a great Blow to their naval Force, *that* may discourage them, and I hope from making War at all, and dispose them to reasonable and proper conditions of Peace in America.'"[80] But Boscawen's instructions were to intercept a French fleet that sailed on the third of May with its transports full of troops, and on the nineteenth of May the rangers from New England sailed from Boston to their destination at the head of the Bay of Fundy.[81] Such convergence could only result in clash.

74. A full account is "The Treason of Thomas Pichon," in Gipson, *British Empire* 6: ch. 8. See also T. A. Crowley, "Pichon, Thomas," in *Dict. Can. Biog.* 4:630–32.

75. *Military Affairs*, ed. Pargellis, 22–30.

76. Clayton, "Duke of Newcastle," 594.

77. Schutz, *William Shirley*, 187–89; Stanley, *New France*, 109–10.

78. *Military Affairs*, ed. Pargellis, 36–39, 45–48; *N.Y. Col. Docs.* 6:920–22. Pargellis's document echoes Halifax to Newcastle, 7 Nov. 1754, Newcastle Papers, Add. MSS. 32,029, f. 138; BL.

79. *Military Affairs*, ed. Pargellis, 181.

80. Clayton, "Duke of Newcastle," 601.

81. Gipson 6:103–6; I. K. Steele, "Monckton, Robert," in *Dict. Can. Biog.* 4:540–42.

Bad weather hindered Boscawen from performing his task fully, He was able to seize two French ships and a tenth of the troops being transported, but the rest got safely into the Gulf of St. Lawrence past his blockade, and arrived eventually at Quebec. Newcastle fretted, "we have done either too little or too much."[82] But so far as New England's enterprise was concerned, Boscawen performed brilliantly because his harassment forestalled aid to the garrison of beleaguered Fort Beauséjour from either Louisbourg or the new troops from France.

What happened at Beauséjour can scarcely be called a French defense. The fort's physical structure was sound enough, but its garrison's morale was rotten. Apart from bellicose Abbé Le Loutre, nobody in the fort really wanted to fight. The place was staffed mostly by Acadians who later declared that they had been threatened with death if they failed to muster. Regardless of the validity of this excuse, their lack of military fervor is indisputable. The fort was commanded by a creature of the corrupt Intendant Bigot, who placed him there with advice that fell somewhat short of do-or-die: "Profit by your place, my dear Vergor; clip and cut—you are free to do what you please—so that you can come soon to join me in France and buy an estate near me."[83] Commandant Vergor was a rational man who saw much sense in this advice. Another rational man on the scene was Thomas Pichon, the British "mole," who found ready ears for his counsels to surrender. As for the officers, they followed their commandant's example; when the British summons to surrender arrived, they busied themselves energetically in plundering the king's stores in anticipation of being allowed to keep their "personal" possessions at the end.[84]

Fort Beauséjour capitulated after a "velvet siege" of four days.[85] Its surrender inspired the garrison of Fort Gaspereau across the Chignecto isthmus to capitulate without a shot, and the British were in full possession of Nova Scotia by the end of June, with ominous implications for the Acadians. General Braddock had only just begun his march to Fort Duquesne on the Ohio. As the easy conquest of Beauséjour and Gaspereau deprived fortress Louisbourg of its hinterland and increased its vulnerability, Britain seemed to have turned the tables in America.

Nevertheless, Newcastle's fears were well grounded. Despite British superiority at sea, almost all of France's reinforcements had gotten through

82. Gipson, *British Empire* 6:107–17.

83. Ibid., 6:233; Parkman, *Montcalm and Wolfe* 1:251; Bernard Pothier, "Du Pont du Chambon de Vergor, Louis," in *Dict. Can. Biog.* 4:249–51.

84. Gipson, *British Empire* 6:233.

85. Stanley, *New France*, 111–17, presents a rugged, should-have-fought-on description that seems a little silly in the circumstances, but has detail. Frégault, *Canada*, 178–79, has a contrary judgment. See also Gustave Lanctot, *A History of Canada*, tr. Josephine Hambleton and Margaret M. Cameron, 3 vols. (Cambridge, Mass.: Harvard University Press, 1963–1965) 3:95.

to Quebec. Besides these regular troops the French had in their Canadian habitants a tough militia that was, man for man, more than a match for any colonial force the British could field. And the Indians who were willing to fight were almost entirely with the French. These facts were known by the British ministry, which was also not permitted to forget that their king's beloved Hanover still lay hostage to French arms in Europe though the French West Indies were as vulnerable to British sea power as Hanover was to French armies. Fully aware of the increasingly tense confrontation in America, the governments of Britain and France feared the consequences of open war in their other imperial possessions. The diplomats continued to smile in front while their military establishments stabbed in the back. All eyes watched Edward Braddock as his cumbrous expedition labored toward the Ohio.

The Seven Years War started as a war for more American possessions and more efficient control over them. It aroused resistance among the British colonies as well as hostilities by the French and their allies. It resulted in the gain of Canada, but the eventual loss to Britain of the thirteen continental colonies whose concordant resistance to occupation forces and imperial authority moved them to precisely the kind of colonial unity that Newcastle had seen and dreaded. The American Revolution began with the Seven Years War.[86]

86. Alan Rogers, *Empire and Liberty: American Resistance to British Authority, 1755–1763* (Berkeley: University of California Press, 1974), 132; Jack P. Green "'A Posture of Hostility': A Reconsideration of Some Aspects of the Origins of the American Revolution," *Proceedings of the American Antiquarian Society* 87 (Apr.–Oct. 1977), 27–68.

Bibliographic note: Green's article followed, by eight years, an exchange between him and Bernard Bailyn in which Bailyn insisted that the reign of George II was "benign" toward the colonies. Jack P. Green, "Political Mimesis: A Consideration of the Historical and Cultural Roots of Legislative Behavior in the British Colonies in the Eighteenth Century," with "A Comment [rejoinder] by Bernard Bailyn, and Greene's 'Reply,'" *American Historical Review* 75:2 (Dec. 1969), 337–60, 361–63, 364–67.

Chapter 7 ❧ *UNDECLARED WAR*

We are as well acquainted as themselves with all their treacheries, from General Braddock's papers, which have been found on the field of battle near Fort Duquesne. There are some from this General to the British Minister, Mr. Robinson; copy of the latter's answer; also one from the Duke of Newcastle and the Secretary of the Duke of Cumberland. It appears that this last is the prime mover of the whole. Their plan was concluded two years ago, since which time they have not ceased their preparations for its execution this year.

Baron de Dieskau, 16 August 1755

Chronology

29 July 1754.	Captain Robert Stobo smuggles plan of Fort Duquesne to Pennsylvanians, with help of Delaware chiefs. It is eventually delivered to General Braddock.
November 1754.	Thomas Penn indoctrinates Braddock against Pennsylvania assembly and Quakers.
February 1755.	Pennsylvania deputy governor R. H. Morris tells Quartermaster General St. Clair that assembly will not help the army.
28 February 1755.	Braddock threatens to quarter troops on Pennsylvanians.
March 1755.	Benjamin Franklin steers the assembly to provide help to Massachusetts troops and Braddock's army, circumventing Morris's veto.
14 April 1755.	Braddock convenes council of war at Alexandria, Virginia.
26 April 1755.	Franklin advertises for wagons for Braddock and gets the army going.
6 May 1755.	Pennsylvania begins building a military road for Braddock's use.
May 1755.	George Croghan leads fifty Mingo warriors and families to Braddock's camp at Fort Cumberland.
20 May 1755.	Braddock orders Croghan's Indians out of camp. Eight remain as scouts.
ca. May 1755.	Braddock rebuffs offer of help by Shingas and other Delaware chiefs.
June–July 1755.	William Johnson and William Shirley compete antagonistically to recruit Iroquois warriors. None go to help Braddock.
9 July 1755.	Braddock routed by French and Indians in the Battle of the Wilderness. Survivors retreat to Albany by way of Philadelphia, leaving the backwoods undefended.
16–22 August 1755.	Scarouady presents offers by Wyandots and Delawares to ally with Pennsylvania against French, but Governor Morris only refers them to the Iroquois grand council.

21 August 1755.	Assembly puts £1,000 in hands of a committee to buy and distribute arms to back settlers.
21 August 1755.	Morris demands that assembly provide a militia under his command. No response.
8 September 1755.	Johnson's troops and Indians halt Commandant Dieskau's offensive from Crown Point and capture Dieskau.
ca. 17 October 1755.	Beginning of hostilities against Pennsylvania by French-led Delawares.
5 November 1755.	Pennsylvania assembly inquires about injustice motivating Indians to hostilities.
1756.	French government publishes memoir based on Braddock's papers, using it to justify a declaration of war.

When Virginia's governor Dinwiddie appealed to other provinces for aid in 1754, he was obliged to reveal that his own assembly had voted only £10,000 "for supporting the British Interest against the Invasions of the French, &ca."[1]

Pennsylvania's governor James Hamilton was surprised and displeased at the smallness of the sum. Hamilton had been laboring with his own assembly for five weeks to get money to resist the French incursions. He knew his Quakers well enough to understand that they would never appropriate funds in explicit terms for war, but he also knew that their pacifism was a variable factor, and not always a controlling one. Though some members were inflexible, a substantial number of Quakers were willing, in extremity, to compromise conscience with circumstance. Hamilton "thought they might have been brought to make a handsome Grant to the King's Use, and have left the Disposition of it to me, as they have done upon other Occasions of the like Nature." Had Pennsylvania known of Virginia's measures, Hamilton told Dinwiddie, the money very likely would have been forthcoming. (Dinwiddie's request for help arrived one day after Pennsylvania's assembly had adjourned.) Hamilton took a dim view of expectations of any material help from other (non-Quaker) provinces; and he was himself by no means convinced of the advisability of Virginia's measures though his messages to his assembly were confident and assertive. Virginia's appropriation, he estimated, would not equip and maintain more than 400 men for as much as seven months. If a larger force could not be launched at once, he hinted, there was a grave question whether military action should be taken at all, "for unless we are able to make a good and secure Lodgment against the Enemy this Summer it is clear that the whole Expence of the Armament will be thrown away and perhaps

1. Dinwiddie to Hamilton, 23 Feb. 1754, *Pa. Council Minutes* 5:765.

the lives of many of his Majestye's Subjects sacrificed to little or no Purpose."[2]

As Hamilton had foreseen, the Pennsylvania assembly later responded to Virginia's call for assistance with an appropriation "for the King's use." By the euphemism, some Quakers rendered Caesar's due, the theory being that if the king's agents were sinful warriors, the Quakers were not morally responsible. A group of less flexible Friends refused the compromise, which they rightly regarded as a semantic dodge, but enough votes were garnered to vote an appropriation equal to Virginia's; that is, £10,000. The fact that a wrangle immediately ensued over the method of raising the money so that the grant finally died is not evidence of a triumph of pacifist dogma. Once the assembly had decided to make the military grant, the question of pacifism became moot. The appropriation died in a dispute over power; in disputing types of taxes and methods of levying them, as distinct from the purpose to which they were to be put, the assembly's motive was antiauthoritarian, not antimilitarist. Narrowly split in its decision to grant the funds, the assembly was unanimous in its decision "to judge, and determine, not only of the Sum to be raised for the Use of the Crown, but of the Manner of raising it." The frontier representatives and the militarists subscribed to this as well as the easterners and pacifists. Anglicans and Presbyterians supported it as well as Quakers. Neither pacifism nor religious affiliation had anything to do with it.[3] The same sort of issues arose in Maryland, New York, and New Jersey, with the same net result. Only North Carolina voted help finally, in the amount of £12,000—a larger appropriation than Virginia's own.[4]

Thomas Penn's personal war

Why, then, have Pennsylvania's assembly and Quakers been singled out for special condemnation? One must look for reasons in the mass of source materials created as propaganda in the province's political struggles. A prime source was the campaign waged by Thomas Penn to gain control over the assembly. Until 1756, a "Quaker Party" dominated the assembly's resistance, so Penn's strategy aimed at discrediting the assembly by attacks on the Quakers. Penn was clever, competent, and wholly without scruple. He had many agents at command, and he was skilful at manipulating the levers of power in royal government.

2. Hamilton to Dinwiddie, 13 Mar. 1754, ibid., 6:1–3.
3. *Votes and Proceedings of the House of Representatives of the Province of Pennsylvania, Pennsylvania Archives*, 8th ser., 8 vols. paged continuously (Harrisburg, 1931–35) 5:3701–02, 3706. (Hereinafter *Pa. Assembly Votes.*)
4. Osgood, *Eighteenth Century* 4:336–37.

In November 1754, Thomas Penn wrote to Secretary Richard Peters that he intended to see General Braddock before Braddock left England for America. Penn intended to give Braddock "informations and advices, as I think he cannot meet elsewhere, and which will be for the good of the Cause."[5] It was not the crown's cause; Penn was much more intent on winning his own battles than the crown's. When he approached Braddock, his purpose was to add the general's power to his own. His method was to poison Braddock's mind against the Pennsylvania assembly and its then-Quaker leaders.

Penn was always careful to guard against mischance carrying his letters into the wrong hands, so this letter to Peters establishes only his intent to interview Braddock. What doubt might remain is dissipated by events in America. Braddock arrived in Virginia on the nineteenth of February 1755. He had absorbed Penn's indoctrination well, and it was reinforced by the skilful lying of Penn's new deputy governor Robert Hunter Morris to Braddock's quartermaster general, Sir John St. Clair. In response to St. Clair's request for help, Morris told him that the Pennsylvania assembly would not give money "upon any Terms but such as were directly contrary to his Majesty's Instructions and inconsistent with their own dependence upon the Crown."[6] This was how Morris explained his repeated vetoes of assembly grants, which he had made under instructions from Penn; and we have Penn's own word that royal instructions had nothing to do with them. After Braddock, two succeeding commanders in chief would break the deadlock between Pennsylvania's governors and assemblies by instructing the *governors* to accept the assemblies' terms.

Braddock, however, had information from only one side, and Morris's deceptions heaped fuel on Penn's fire. Braddock erupted with a denunciation of the "pusillanimous and improper Behaviour in your Assembly." He ranted on about the assembly's "absolute Refusal to supply either Men, Money, or Provisions for their own Defence while they furnish the Enemy with Provision," and he threatened to "repair by unpleasant Methods," including the quartering of troops, "what for the character and Honour of the Assemblies I should be much happier to see chearfully supplied."[7]

5. Penn to Peters, 7 Nov. 1754, mss., Gratz Coll., Case 2, Box 33a, HSP.

6. St. Clair to Morris, 14 Jan. 1755, and Morris to St. Clair, 10 Feb. 1755, in *Pa. Council Minutes* 6:298–300.

7. Braddock to Morris, 28 Feb. 1755, in *Pa. Council Minutes* 6:307–8. Braddock's reference to smuggling of provisions to the French takes on special interest from a letter of Penn's not overly bright receiver of rents, Richard Hockley, 26 Oct. 1755. Hockley reported that Philadelphia's mayor Plumsted, a strong proprietary supporter, "though he bears a Commission under You is deeply concern'd in the French trade which is a very great shame." Penn Mss., Off. Corr. 7:133, HSP. A pamphleteer named Cross averred that during King George's War, "six or eight particular persons of the Governors party claimed an exclusive right to that trade [with the French and Spaniards in the West Indies] and . . . if any body else

About two weeks later, Braddock returned to the charge with a denunciation of the assembly's "endeavouring to take advantage of the common Danger in order to encroach upon his Majesty's Prerogative in the Administration of His Government"—a faithful echo of what Thomas Penn was saying in London. Braddock did not see a distinction between the king's prerogative and the proprietary's. If the Pennsylvania assembly would not supply the money he demanded, he menaced that "the Government at Home will take some Method to oblige 'em to act for the future as becomes the Duty of His Majesty's Subjects."[8]

Braddock's "high stile" suited Governor Morris's purposes precisely. He replied provocatively, denouncing the assembly again and exaggerating the wealth and population of the province to make its efforts seem proportionately meaner.

In his letter the population of the province became "upward of Three hundred Thousand," which would have made it a quarter of all the people in the British colonies. Pennsylvania is disappointingly lacking in reliable statistics, but after a quarter-century more of rapid growth, Governor John Penn in 1775 estimated its population at only 302,000. Demonstrating the adage about lies, damn lies, and statistics, Morris asserted that his province could support an army of 100,000 men, which would have been quite a feat for even his exaggerated population and certainly would have surprised George Washington during the American Revolution. Resorting to yet another statistic, Morris produced "five hundred vessels" clearing annually from Philadelphia, "mostly owned by the Merchants of this Town." To obtain his figure he took the number given in a fiercely anti-Quaker pamphlet, and added 100 to it.[9]

At this time the basic issue between the proprietary party and the assembly was control of the funds to be raised by the assembly. By obstinately vetoing grants made on other terms than his own, Morris (under Penn's direction) hoped to force the assembly to capitulate to the exigen-

attempted the same, their vessels were sure to be seized." *An Answer to an invidious Pamphlet, intitled, A Brief State of the Province of Pennsylvania* (London: S. Bladon, 1755).

Bibliographic note: Theodore Thayer, on the authority of William Franklin, attributed this pamphlet to Joseph Galloway, but Dr. John Fothergill lent money to Cross to pay the printer. Was Cross an agent for Galloway? Thayer, *Pennsylvania Politics*, 40; [John Fothergill], *Chain of Friendship: Selected Letters of Dr. John Fothergill of London, 1735–1780*, eds. Betsy C. Corner and Christopher C. Booth (Cambridge, Mass.: Belknap Press, 1971), 219–20.

8. Braddock to Morris, 9 Mar. 1755, mss., Loudoun Papers (LO 558), Henry E. Huntington Library, San Marino, Calif. (HEH). This is dated 10 Mar. in *Pa. Council Minutes* 6:332–33. For Penn on the relative prerogatives of the crown and himself, see Penn to Morris, 26 Feb. 1755, mss., Gratz Coll., Papers of the Governors, Case 2, Box 33-a, HSP.

9. Morris to Braddock, 12 Mar. 1755, in *Pa. Council Minutes* 6:335–38; Robert V. Wells, *The Population of the British Colonies in America before 1776: A Survey of Census Data* (Princeton, N.J.: Princeton University Press), 143. The pamphlet referred to was [William Smith], *A Brief State of the Province of Pennsylvania* . . . (London, 1755). See p. 4.

cies of the war which were denounced in such strong terms by Braddock. Put simply, Morris wanted to spend the money that the assembly raised. When he recalled the assembly into session on 17 March 1755, he laid Braddock's furious letter before them with the complacent expectation that it "would have some influence upon their conduct."[10] It did, but not as Morris had expected. Benjamin Franklin was back in the assembly now, and a new sinuosity became manifest in the body's proceedings.

Franklin outwits Morris

Franklin was an imperialist, and certainly not a pacifist, so Morris had thought that Franklin would side with him against the Quakers. He saw that Franklin was "labouring hard" with them to assure a grant of £40,000.[11] But when the assembly compromised for £25,000, all to be given in one manner or another to the necessities of the moment, Franklin was willing to call it a bargain. And when Morris vetoed once again, Franklin refused to play along with the proprietary men's strategy. Perhaps he was impelled to special exertions because of a special appeal from the man whose influence he had been cultivating; namely, Massachusetts's governor William Shirley. The assembly had before it not only Braddock's demands, but also a request from Shirley by his representative Josiah Quincy, for assistance to the campaign against the French at Crown Point. The Quaker assemblymen offered a gift of £10,000 for Shirley's use. Whereupon militarist Morris vetoed again on the astonishing pretext, believed by nobody, that approval would be a "breach of duty to the crown." Quincy, in desperation, appealed to Franklin who dictated a new letter for Quincy's signature, deprecating the governor's veto, praising the assembly, and renewing the appeal. This was the first kind word given to the assembly by an official during the entire crisis.[12]

Had the Quakers been left to their own devices, Quincy might have been given words of solemn advice about the sinfulness of the governor and allowed to return to Massachusetts penniless. But with Franklin present, the assembly performed some financial sleight of hand. From the provincial Loan Office under the assembly's direct jurisdiction, it borrowed £15,000, which the Loan Office did not in fact have, by issuing bills of credit against future payments by debtors to the Loan Office. The effect was to issue paper money without going through the formal process legally required for such an issue. By this technicality the assembly cir-

10. Morris to Penn, 9 Apr. 1755, in *Pa. Archives* (1)2:286–88.

11. Morris to Shirley, 25 Mar. 1755, *Pa. Council Minutes* 6:334–35.

12. Josiah Quincy to Morris, 21 Mar. 1755, ibid., 6:329–30; 31 Mar., 6:340; 1 Apr., 6:352–53; Quincy to the assembly, 1 Apr. 1755, *Franklin Papers* 6:4–5.

cumvented the requirement for the governor's approval, and Massachusetts got its £10,000 in an act passed in spite of the determined opposition of Governor Morris. While at this pleasant occupation, the assembly issued enough of its bills of credit to have a surplus of £5,000 for General Braddock's immediate expenses, and thereby disarmed the threat from that quarter. Taken all in all, it had accomplished a masterpiece of maneuver, and everyone knew that Franklin was the man who perfected the scheme. His friend, Shirley, wrote to thank him for it. Shirley wrote also to Governor Morris to acknowledge Pennsylvania's "repeated Instances of their contributing towards the Defence of his Majesty's just Rights and Dominions in the Expedition against Crown Point." Morris suppressed this letter from the council minutes, where it would have given the lie to his continual assertions that the assembly refused to support the war effort, but assemblymen got hold of it and printed it, together with an address of thanks to Shirley.[13]

Morris wrote off in a fury to the secretary of state in England, hotly denouncing "such Powers in the Hands of any Assembly, and especially of one annually chosen by a People, a great Part, if not a Majority of whom are Foreigners, unattached to an English Government, either by Birth or Education."[14] But Shirley was grateful, and Braddock was mollified.

Assemblymen were concerned to find out what was eating Braddock. They knew only that they had repeatedly passed bills to appropriate money for support of the army's needs, and that the governor had just as repeatedly vetoed their efforts. Surely Braddock should have understood who was obstructing his support. The assemblymen knew nothing of Penn's "informations and advices" or of Morris's misinformation; Morris recorded his letters to Braddock in the council minutes which were closed to assembly inspection, and he was highly selective about what he made public. However, it was evident on the face of Braddock's letters that he was getting information somewhere, and the assembly wanted badly to set the record straight. An opportunity was offered by Braddock himself in his request for a postal service to be set up between his camp and the provincial capitals.[15] Who would be better qualified to arrange such a service than the crown's servant, the deputy postmaster general? The assembly promised to pay the costs of the whole service; and with this extra present to appease the general, Benjamin Franklin went traveling again.[16] His

13. Ibid., 6:3–7, 390–92; *Pa. Assembly Votes* 5:3877, 4278–79, 4283–84; I. Pemberton to John Fothergill, 19 May 1755, mss., Etting Coll., Pemberton Papers 2:2, HSP.

14. Morris to Sir Thomas Robinson, 9 Apr. 1755, quoted in Gipson, *British Empire* 6:69–70. Gipson deplored the assembly's "unconstitutional" action.

15. Braddock to Morris, 28 Feb. 1755, *Pa. Council Minutes* 6:307.

16. *Pa. Assembly Votes* 5:3858, 3866.

traveling companions for part of the way included Governor Morris as well as Shirley of Massachusetts and De Lancey of New York, all of whom were on their way to an interprovincial strategy conference with Braddock at Alexandria, Virginia.[17] We must temporarily take leave of Franklin, as they did, in order to consider the business of that conference.

Braddock's council of war

On the fourteenth of April 1755, Braddock convened a council consisting of his colleague Augustus Keppel, commander in chief of British naval forces in North America, and the provincial governors of Massachusetts, Virginia, New York, Maryland, and Pennsylvania.[18] South Carolina's governor James Glen had not been invited, about which something will be said a little further on.

Braddock did not consult the governors about strategy. That had been settled by higher authority before he left England. What he wanted from them, before anything else, was money. The terse minutes of the council list, "1st. That a fund be established conformable to his Instructions . . . and to sir Thomas Robinsons Letter to the several Governors dated October 26, 1754."[19] The minutes politely call this a "proposal," but neither Braddock's instructions nor Robinson's mentioned letter had suggested the fund as a matter to be decided by democratic discussion.

At this point began in earnest the colonial resistance to imperial rule that would culminate eventually in its overthrow. The resistance was not the choice of the governors, imperialists to a man; rather, they were obliged reluctantly to confess themselves powerless to fulfill the crown's demand because of their awareness of the resistance among their peoples. "The Governors present acquainted his Excellency that they had severally made application to their respective Assemblies for the establishment of the common fund proposed, but had not been able to prevail upon 'em to agree to it, and gave it as their unanimous opinion that such a Fund can never be established in the Colonies without the aid of Parliament." Here was another clash with Newcastle's Old Whigs, who had determined to avoid appealing to Parliament.

Nor could the colonial governors get their assemblies to accept the quo-

17. Morris memo, 8 Apr. 1755, *Pa. Council Minutes* 6:358; Franklin to Shirley, 22 May 1755, *Franklin Papers* 6:59.

18. The minutes were kept by Shirley. Mss. copies are in Newcastle Papers, Add. MSS. 32,029, ff. 174, 178, BL. Printed *Pa. Council Minutes* 6:365–68; *Doc. Hist. N.Y.* 2:648–51. The news of the council apparently was transmitted to Newcastle by John Hanbury. Add. MSS. 32,854, f. 378.

19. *Pa. Council Minutes* 6:200–202.

tas assigned in London for each of the colonies individually to provide support. A way would have to be found for "compelling them to do it." The governors would "use their utmost endeavours to raise all possible supplies," but they agreed unanimously that "the present Expedition must be at a stand unless the General shall think proper to make use of his credit upon the Government at Home to defray the expence of all the Operations under his direction."

It was a shocking, though not wholly unanticipated, message for the general at the very beginning of his operations, but it did not mean that he would get no support at all. The provincial assemblies met and raised money. What they rejected were commands to raise specific amounts and to turn them over to Braddock to spend as he saw fit. The moneys granted by the assemblies were limited to what the assemblies determined, and were laid out in the same way. Quaker Pennsylvania was only one of the provinces involved, undistinguished from all the rest except in the obstacles raised by its Anglican governor. Dinwiddie's Virginia had begun the war with its adventuring at the Ohio, and Shirley's Massachusetts was preparing to campaign in Nova Scotia on its own account (and for the profit of some of its leading citizens),[20] but the governors of these colonies were as certain as Pennsylvania's Morris that the assemblies could not be commanded by ministerial decree.

Curiously the only money raised by the provinces "which ever passed through the General's hands," according to his aide-de-camp, was an appropriation of £6,000 from South Carolina whose Governor Glen had been excluded from the Alexandria conference.[21] At first glance this is the more strange because Braddock's further "proposals" at Alexandria centered on measures to win the help of Indians, and Glen is now generally reputed to have been an outstanding governor.[22] At the time, however, this was not his reputation in London. One must distinguish chronologically. Glen was certainly one of the most active governors in Indian affairs, but his activity's success was another matter. He had badly botched an aggressive attempt to win the Choctaw nation away from French alliance, an effort condemned in Edmond Atkin's manuscript history for having provoked the Choctaws to an uprising supported with no weapons except

20. Schutz, *William Shirley*, 198–99; Stanley, *New France*, 121–22.

21. Gipson, *British Empire* 6:71–72.

22. See *The Appalachian Indian Frontier: The Edmond Atkin Report and Plan of 1755*, ed. Wilbur R. Jacobs (1954), reprinted (Lincoln: University of Nebraska Press, 1967), which cites (xxi,n27) Mary F. Carter, "James Glen, Governor of South Carolina," Ph.D. diss., University of California, Los Angeles, 1951. Gipson thought that the exclusion of Glen constituted "the Achilles heel" of attempts to eject the French from Ohio. *British Empire* 6:65.

glass beads to be used as bullets.[23] Glen's personal intrusion into the Indian trade had aroused the highly vocal enmity of traders already established, and he had not endeared himself to Dinwiddie by threatening to seize, fine, and confiscate the goods of Virginians trading among the Cherokees.[24] Glen's exclusion from Braddock's council may have been due partly to squabbles between him and Dinwiddie, but he was seen as unreliable in precisely the sort of Indian management that Braddock needed.

The one colonial who had deeply impressed the lords of trade with his skill in Indian affairs was William Johnson. Braddock's second "proposal" to the governors at Alexandria was to secure the Iroquois nations "and their Allies" to the British interest, and that Colonel Johnson, "the fittest person for that purpose," should be employed in it.[25] The governors agreed, and Johnson was duly commissioned.

Money and Indian affairs aside, Braddock's other proposals concerned assignment of troops and commands. As shown in Chapter 6, Braddock approved an immediate campaign in Acadia / Nova Scotia, and he now assigned Brigadier General Robert Monckton to command. Braddock reserved for himself the campaign against Fort Duquesne and a possible march on Fort Niagara afterwards if Duquesne should fall quickly enough. Shirley was given "the direction of the affair" of strengthening and reinforcing Fort Oswego, and a campaign from there to Fort Niagara if Braddock should be delayed. Johnson was entrusted with the attack on Fort St. Frédéric at Crown Point. The governors left Alexandria with confidence in Britain's military might and apprehensions about their assemblies; and Braddock turned to his task of moving men and equipment through dense woods and over trackless high mountains toward the Ohio.

23. Introduction, *Appalachian Indian Frontier*, ed. Jacobs (xxi) with citation of Atkin's mss., "Historical Account of the Revolt of the Chactaw Indians," London, 2 Jan. 1755, British Library Lansdowne MSS. 809. Richard White ascribed the Choctaw rebellion to the intrigues of Chief Red Shoes, allowing Glen only to "claim credit" for Red Shoes's revolt. White holds that "Glen's greed" and the "incompetence" of his agent "would deprive the Choctaws of trade goods, alienate the bulk of the nation, and condemn their remaining adherents to destruction." White "Red Shoes: Warrior and Diplomat," in *Struggle and Survival in Colonial America*, eds. David G. Sweet and Gary B. Nash (Berkeley: University of California Press, 1981), 65.

24. James Adair, *History of the American Indians* (1755), reprinted as *Adair's History of the American Indians*, ed. Samuel Cole Williams (New York: Promontory Press [1973]), x–xii; David H. Corkran, *The Cherokee Frontier: Conflict and Survival, 1740–62* (Norman: University of Oklahoma Press, 1962), 30–31; *Colonial Records of South Carolina: Documents Relating to Indian Affairs, 1750–54*, ed. William L. McDowell, Jr. (Columbia: South Carolina Archives Dept., 1958), 134, 524–32; Gipson, *British Empire* 6:25–26, 49. Glen's internal struggle to control the Indian trade is noticed in Greene, *Quest for Power*, 313–15. John Phillip Reid notes that Glen "*in time* became the most knowledgeable of Indian experts." *A Law of Blood: The Primitive Law of the Cherokee Nation* (New York: New York University Press, 1970), 58–59 (my italics).

25. *Doc. Hist. N.Y.* 2:648.

Franklin converts Braddock

Physical obstructions were the least of his difficulties. With the proper equipment they could be surmounted, but Braddock despaired of "the difficulties and Disappointments I have met with from the want of Honesty and Inclination to forward the Service in all Orders of people in these Colonies."[26] His deputy quartermaster general Sir John St. Clair used stronger language. Writing in June from the vanguard camp, he fumed that "no Magistrate in Virginia or I believe in Maryland gave themselves the least trouble to assist in collecting the Country People to work upon the Roads, and to provide us with Carriages: But on the Contrary every body laid themselves out to put what money they cou'd in their Pocketts, without forwarding our Expedition." In the light of previous experience, the absence of Pennsylvania's name from the list of colonies denounced is notable. St. Clair even added a tribute to "the People in Pennsylvania . . . by their Assistance we are in motion."[27] And Braddock added his own carefully stinted approval: Pennsylvania's people "tho' they will contribute very little to the Expedition are exact in their Dealings, and much more industrious than the others."[28]

For the explanation of this remarkable about-face, we must rejoin the ubiquitous Mr. Franklin. The postmaster stayed with the general at Fredericktown (Md.) for several days while they arranged postal services for the army. At that time, Braddock was so prejudiced against Pennsylvania that Franklin thought he "seemed more intent on an Expedition against us than against the French. They had been told that we refused to supply them with Provisions and Carriages, tho the pay for it had been offered us, and would not agree to open a Road from this Camp to our Settlements, and it was very constantly insinuated that we were at the same time supplying the French with Provisions." This according to the indignant report of Quaker assemblyman Israel Pemberton, Jr., who learned it from Franklin after the event.[29]

Happily, however, the circumstances of Franklin's stay with Braddock conduced to sociability rather than confrontation. They dined together daily, and Franklin "had full opportunity of removing all his prejudices, by the information of what the assembly had actually done before his arrival, and were still willing to do, to facilitate his operations."[30] Franklin told what Governor Morris had suppressed: "that the Assembly had voted

26. Braddock to Adjutant General Robert Napier, 8 June 1755, in *Military Affairs*, ed. Pargellis, 84–85.

27. St. Clair to Napier, 13 June 1755, ibid., 93–94.

28. Ibid., 85.

29. Pemberton to Fothergill, cited n13.

30. *The Autobiography of Benjamin Franklin*, eds. Leonard W. Labaree et al. (New Haven, Conn.: Yale University Press, 1964), 217.

£5,000 to be laid out in Provisions and made ready for their arrival, that no Notice had ever been given of their wanting any more Carriages than the Virginians and Marylanders had undertaken to furnish, and that a Committee was then surveying the Ground in order to lay out the Road."[31]

For the army, as Braddock acknowledged, Franklin performed the indispensable task of getting it on the road.[32] When Braddock despairingly declared that there could be no expedition without the horses and wagons that Maryland and Virginia would not or could not deliver, Franklin "happen'd to say" that he thought the needed vehicles might be obtained in Pennsylvania. He was commissioned on the spot. He rushed off to Wright's Ferry (now Columbia), Pennsylvania, where he consulted with Quaker assemblyman James Wright and his sister Susanna. Miss Wright suggested calling the population together. Franklin seized on the idea and passed it on to Chief Justice William Allen who was at Lancaster, riding circuit. Allen cooperated to the utmost; he presented a strong appeal from the bench, and ordered the constables to call in the people.[33] Franklin publicized the whole proceeding with a famous broadside that nicely combined appeals to cupidity, fear, and patriotism, and the wagons rolled in. But the Germans who brought them had no faith in the promises of generals. Franklin was obliged to give his personal bond to indemnify those whose horses or wagons should be lost.[34]

For once there had been genuine cooperation among all the contending political factions in the province. Except, of course, Penn and his governor. But Franklin alone deserves credit for an additional device that won the hearts of Braddock's command. While with the army, Franklin "com-

31. Pemberton to Fothergill, cited n13. Actual work on the new road began on 6 May 1755; see John Armstrong to [Morris], Carlisle, 18 May, mss. interleaved between pages 242 and 243 of vol. 1 of Washington Irving, *Life of George Washington*, 14 vols. (New York: "privately illustrated," 1898) in Olin Library Rare Book Room, Cornell University. *Pa. Council Minutes*, "Road" in index. For its heavy cost see *Franklin Papers* 6:199–201.

32. The assembly's help to Braddock is summarized in ibid., 6:206–9.

33. William Allen, though a pillar of the proprietary party, differed from Thomas Penn and Governor Morris on the issue of defense. Because of his great wealth and special status as leader of the "Old Light" Presbyterians, Allen could afford independence; Penn needed him more than he needed Penn. Biography: Ruth Moses Kistler, *William Allen*, rev. ed., Proceedings of the Lehigh County Historical Society 24 (Allentown, Pa., 1962). Warmly sympathetic notices of Allen appear in Melvin H. Buxbaum, *Benjamin Franklin and the Zealous Presbyterians* (University Park: Pennsylvania State University Press, 1975). This book pleads the Presbyterian cause against "bigoted" Franklin.

34. Franklin, *Autobiography*, ed. Labaree, 217–21. For the full story, other documents must be consulted as the vain old man who wrote the autobiography omitted mention of the Wrights and William Allen. See *Franklin Papers* 6:19–27 and notes. William Smith had political reasons for omitting the Quaker Wrights from his account, and he made much of William Allen's role for the same reasons. [William Smith], *A Brief View of the conduct of Pennsylvania For the Year 1755* London: R. Griffiths, 1756), 32–33. See also Whitfield J. Bell, Jr., and Leonard W. Labaree, "Franklin and the 'Wagon Affair,' " *Proceedings of the American Philosophical Society* 101 (1957), 551–58.

miserated" the poverty of the junior officers, and quietly suggested to an assembly committee with available funds that a gift of little luxuries would be well received. Typically, he enclosed a list. Nothing in Quaker principles forbade benevolence toward men enduring privations, and the assembly responded without argument to Franklin's list. Twenty horses appeared in Braddock's camp from Philadelphia, well laden with old Madeira wine, Jamaica rum, hams, cheeses, chocolate, tea, coffee, and so on. Each horse, with its welcome burden, was presented to one officer; and there were no more slurs on Pennsylvania's assembly in the officers' mess.

However, this success lasted only as long as Braddock's march. Though Thomas Penn was set back in one of his maneuvers, he was by no means defeated, as will be seen. Present concerns, however, are to follow Edward Braddock and his army. Perhaps, if they had been gifted to foresee their doom, they would have been less grateful to the Pennsylvanians who expedited them toward it.

Braddock and Indian allies

Braddock's masters in London had anticipated and provided against colonial resistance to paying for the crown's war. While he thundered that the penuriousness of assemblies played into the hands of the French, he was secretly confident of the ministry's assurance of crown funds to make up shortfalls.[35] Except for the transportation crisis overcome by Franklin's ingenuity, Braddock brought, bought, or had given to him all the provision and equipment he needed. According to William Allen, he had £25,000 sterling in a chest at the time of his defeat.[36] He did not fail for lack of any material necessity.

In one respect, however, he was deficient. His instructions stressed the need for Indian help in wilderness combat, and he was thorough and systematic enough to follow instructions to the limit of his ability, but the limit was short and strong. He commissioned William Johnson as colonel of the Iroquois, and Johnson promptly sent an order to George Croghan to join Braddock with the Mingo warriors who had fled from the Ohio to Croghan's plantation at Aughwick (near Carlisle, Pa.).[37] Croghan brought

35. Private instructions in *Military Affairs*, ed. Pargellis, 53–54.

36. William Allen to D. Barclay and Sons, 21 July 1755, in *The Burd Papers: Extracts from Chief Justice William Allen's Letter Book . . . Together with an Appendix Containing Pamphlets in the Controversy with Franklin*, ed. Lewis Burd Walker (Pottsville, Pa., 1897), 22. This very rare book contains extracts of 87 of the 187 manuscript letter book, dated between 1753 and 1770. I have not found the original manuscript book.

37. Braddock's commission for Johnson, 15 Apr. 1755, *Johnson Papers* 1:465–66. Johnson also received commissions as major general in command of provincial forces for the Fort St. Frédéric / Crown Point campaign; given by Governors De Lancey and Shirley: ibid., 1:468–71; *Doc. Hist. N.Y.* 2:651–53. Johnson to Croghan, 23 Apr. 1755, *Johnson Papers* 1:475–76.

fifty warriors to Braddock's headquarters at Fort Cumberland, Maryland. That was well and good, but the warriors brought their families, and that was not so good. Officers and men quickly demonstrated that sex-starved males lose race prejudice. Romance, of a sort, bloomed, and turmoil ensued. Braddock stopped it in the decisive military way by sending the women home. The warriors, however, went with them. What they had seen of Braddock disinclined them to serve under him in any circumstances.[38] Braddock was full of "pride and ignorance," according to Scarouady later. "He was a bad man when he was alive; he looked upon us as dogs, and would never hear anything what was said to him. We often endeavoured to advise him of the danger he was in with his Soldiers; but he never appeared pleased with us and that was the reason that a great many of our Warriors left him and would not be under his Command."[39] Braddock was left with eight Indians, an altogether insufficient number.

Scarouady's judgment on Braddock was not just the sulking of an insulted Indian. It is confirmed by two provincials of widely differing politics: Assemblyman B. Franklin and Thomas Penn's cohort, Chief Justice William Allen, both of whom wished Braddock and his army all success. Franklin remembered in his *Autobiography* how he had cautioned Braddock against Indian "ambuscades," whereupon Braddock "smil'd at my Ignorance, and reply'd 'These Savages may indeed be a formidable Enemy to your raw American Militia; but upon the King's regular and disciplin'd Troops, Sir, it is impossible they should make any Impression.'" Franklin "said no more."[40] Allen wrote that Braddock was "an improper man, of a mean Capacity, obstinate and self-sufficient, above taking advice, and laughed to scorn all such as represented to him that in our Wood Country, war was to be carried on in a different manner from that in Europe."[41]

These were the men whose help he had found indispensable. Perhaps they might be criticised on grounds of retroactive disappointment, but there is other testimony, from William Shirley, Jr., Braddock's secretary, who was destined to die in battle side by side with Braddock. "We have a General," wrote the younger Shirley, "most Judiciously chosen for being disqualified for the Service he is employed in, in almost every Respect."[42] Another subordinate, Colonel Joseph Yorke, remarked confidentially, "I have known him these 14 years and I never knew him do anything but swear . . . he is not of my recommendation."[43]

38. Wainwright, *George Croghan*, 86–89.
39. *Pa. Council Minutes* 6:589.
40. Franklin, *Autobiography*, ed. Labaree, 224.
41. Allen to Barclays, 21 July 1755, *The Burd Papers*, 23.
42. Shirley to Morris, Ft. Cumberland, 23 May 1755, mss., Indian and Military Affairs of Pa., 309, APS.
43. Yorke, *Life of Hardwicke* 2:357.

Governor Dinwiddie had promised Braddock a contingent of 400 warriors from the populous southern tribes, but Dinwiddie's feud with South Carolina's governor Glen erupted in such diplomatic struggles among the tribes that they, too, stayed home.[44] Johnson treated auspiciously with the Iroquois, and got their promise to support the campaign; but Johnson was undone by Shirley's jealousy of his rising authority. Shirley sent an agent to recruit Iroquois warriors for *his* campaign in defiance of Johnson's appointment to "the sole management and superintendency of all affairs" relating to the Iroquois. The Iroquois denounced Shirley's agent, Colonel Lydius, as the "snake" and "devil" who "stole our Lands" for Connecticut's Susquehannah Company, and, regardless of Johnson's mollifying, the damage was done.[45] Irritated and suspicious, when the Iroquois learned that the southern Indians, their ancient enemies, were to march with Braddock (and failed to learn that the southerners had changed minds) they refused to cooperate.[46] Perhaps Johnson was not too eager to send *his* Indians to Braddock. By inability or design, he failed to start his big treaty with the Iroquois until 21 June 1755. He presented Braddock's speech requesting help on the twenty-fifth. The treaty concluded on 4 July.[47] As Braddock joined battle, 9 July, hundreds of miles away over rough terrain, it obviously would have been impossible for the Iroquois to get help to him before the battle began. The upshot was that after Croghan's Mingos left Braddock, neither Dinwiddie's southerners nor Johnson's Iroquois reported to the general.

Delawares learn Braddock's purpose

He had one more chance. The Delawares and Shawnees of the Ohio country, despite being suspected of French sympathies, had not committed finally to either empire. Fearful of the designs of Britons and Frenchmen alike, these displaced Indians wanted only to preserve their living space.[48] This had been understood by the lords of trade when they nom-

44. Gipson, *British Empire* 6:70–71; Corkran, *Cherokee Frontier*, 54–61.

45. *Johnson Papers* 1:644–45, 665, 771–72, 733–39; treaty minutes, June–July 1755, *N.Y. Col. Docs.* 6:984. Johnson insisted that the only "fire" for Iroquois treaties must be at this place, and that the chiefs must "totally to extinguish all other deceitful and unnatural fires," which put him on a direct collision course with Shirley's recruiting agent as well as with the old commissioners of Indian affairs at Albany. He summarized the struggle with Shirley's man in a letter to the lords of trade, 3 Sept. 1755, ibid., 6:965, 993–97.

46. Peter Wraxall, "Some Thoughts upon the British Indian Interest in North America," Jan. 1756, *N.Y. Col. Docs.* 7:22–23. Cf. ibid., 6:978–79.

47. *N.Y. Col. Docs.* 6:964, 974–75, 989.

48. Hunter, *Forts on the Pa. Frontier*, 129. For a detailed analysis of Delaware attitudes see William A. Hunter, "Documented Subdivisions of the Delaware Indians," *Bulletin of the Archaeological Society of New Jersey* 20(1978), 33.

inated Johnson for the superintendency of Indian affairs, and it was certainly clear to Johnson, who had carefully baited his hook for the Iroquois with a promise to recover *their* lands from the French. Had Braddock been that clever or hypocritical—Johnson was certainly not truthful—the general could have gained Delaware and Shawnee warriors to fight on his side in the critical battle for Fort Duquesne. But Braddock's arrogant and disastrous candor in his interviews with the Ohioans can hardly be called negotiations.

He asked George Croghan to bring him some Delaware chiefs. Croghan knew how to make contact, and soon there appeared a delegation that included Delaware "king" Shingas. We have on record only the account given by Shingas to a captive Pennsylvanian. Neither Braddock nor any of his men bothered to memorialize the occasion beyond mentioning casually that it had happened, a fact which in itself adds credence to the substance of Shingas's report.[49] Shingas gave his account at the mixed Delaware-Shawnee village of Kickenapawling (near Stoyestown, Pa.) on 8 November 1755, about seven or eight months after the interview with Braddock, and also after the outbreak of hostilities between the Delawares and the English.[50]

> Riseing up From his seat with Appearance of Deep Concern on his Countenance he addressed his Prisoners with Great Solemnity Telling them that he was sorry For what had happened Between them and the English But that the English and not the Indians were the Cause of the Present War—he then Proceeded to give Account of those Causes and said—That he with 5 other Chiefs of the Delaware, Shawnee, and Mingo Nations (Being 2 from Each Nation) had applied to Genl Braddock and Enquired what he intended to do with the Land if he Could drive the French and their Indians away. To which Genl Braddock replied that the English Shoud Inhabit and Inherit the Land, on which Shingas askd Genl Braddock whether the Indians that were Friends to the English might not be Permitted to Live and Trade Among the English and have Hunting Ground sufficient To Support themselves and Familys as they had no where to Flee Too But into the Hands of the French and their Indians who were their Enemies (that is Shingas' Enemies). On which Genl Braddock said that No Savage Should Inherit the Land.

49. The references to Shingas's visit are vague and inconsistent in detail, but they severally testify to the fact. "Mr. George Croghan's Account of Indian Affairs . . . ," mss., Penn Mss., Indian Affairs 1:52, seemingly contradicted by "A Journal of Indian Transactions by George Croghan, Esq.," 14 Mar. 1757, mss., HSP transcripts of Board of Trade Papers, Plantations General (Bundle P, 2–20), unpaged volumes arranged by date. Introductory memoir, Seaman's Journal, and Orme's journal in *The History of an Expedition Against Fort DuQuesne in 1755; Under Major-General Braddock*, ed. Winthrop Sargent, Memoirs of the Historical Society of Pennsylvania 5 (Philadelphia, 1855), 174–75, 312–14, 380. Croghan's inconsistencies may be explained by his habit of adjusting his writings to his purposes at different times.

50. "The Captivity of Charles Stuart, 1755–57," ed. Beverley W. Bond, Jr., *Mississippi Valley Historical Review* 13(1926–27), 58–81.

On receiving which answer Shingas and the other Chiefs went that night to their own People—To whom they Communicated Genl Braddock's Answer And the Next Morning Returnd to Genl Braddock again in hopes he might have Changed his Sentiments, and then repeated their Former Questions to Genl Braddock again and Genl Braddock made the same reply as Formerly, On which Shingas and the other Chiefs answered That if they might not have Liberty To Live on the Land they would not Fight for it, To which Genl Braddock answered that he did not need their Help and had no doubt of driveing the French and their Indians away.

On which Shingas with the other Chiefs went away from Genl Braddock To their People To whom they Communicated what had Passd between them and Braddock, at which they were very much Enraged and a Party of them went Immediately upon it and Join'd the French But the Greater Part remained neuter till they saw How Things wou'd go Between Braddock and the French in their Engagement, And they made it their Business to draw nigh the Place where the Engagement Happened that they might see what Passd at it and were still in hopes that the English wou'd be Victorious.[51]

Thus bluntly the Ohio Indians learned from the horse's mouth (as the expression goes) what the English colonials had understood from the beginning: that, in truth, this was The Great War for the Empire so far as the empire's rulers were concerned. Braddock gave the lie to the plea by Johnson and the lords of trade that the war was to recover the Indians' lands for themselves, and the Indians drew much the same conclusion as the colonials: let the imperialists fight their own war.

In what amounts almost to a cottage industry, much armchair generalship has been devoted to showing how Braddock *ought* to have won his fateful battle before Fort Duquesne. It is repeated almost as an article of faith that he did everything according to the tested maxims of military strategy, and that the weakness of Fort Duquesne and its garrison guaranteed victory except for an accident puzzlingly close to an Act of God. This argument achieves frail tenability only by the assumption that the Indians would not, or could not be trusted to, play a decisive role. It won't wash. When Braddock turned away the Ohio Indians, he had in his possession intelligence from a Scottish captive in Fort Duquesne that had been smuggled out months earlier by those selfsame Indians and forwarded by George Croghan to Philadelphia. The source was Captain Robert Stobo, who had been left behind as a hostage by Washington after the capitulation at Fort Necessity in Great Meadows. Stobo improved his captivity by pacing off the measurements of Fort Duquesne where he had the freedom of an officer held by parole of honor. He drew a detailed plan of the fort, complete with locations of walls, ditches, and batteries. In unchaperoned conversations with Indian visitors, he turned the map over

51. Ibid., 63–64.

to the Mingo, Moses the Song, brother-in-law of Scarouady, who was helped by Delaware chief Shingas and his brother, Delaware George (Nenatchehunt). Along with the map, these Indians brought Stobo's specific information to Croghan, revealing the weakness of the fort's garrison. Such invaluable information establishes beyond doubt the validity of the offer made later by the Ohio Indians to help Braddock.

Indeed they may have offered to take the fort for him. Stobo suggested as much. "The Indians have great liberty here; they go in and out when they please without notice. If 100 trusty Shanoes, Mingoes and Dillaways were picked out, they might surprise the Fort, lodging themselves under the platform behind the palisades by day, and at night secure the guard with the Tomhawks. The guard consists of 40 men only and five officers." (These documents were among Braddock's papers captured later by the French, and they nearly lost Stobo his head.)[52]

Braddock had not come all that way to see the glory of his triumph usurped by a lot of savages. With Stobo's information in hand, he was sure that he did not need more help from Indians. The assurance of victory became so certain and easy that he violated one of the basic maxims in the books on strategy. He divided his army in two and rushed forward with the smaller vanguard detachment.

Fort Duquesne's commandant Claude-Pierre Pécaudy de Contrecoeur watched Braddock advance through the eyes of Indian scouts. These Indians were different from those who had approached Braddock. These were "Far Indian" Potawatomis and Ottawas from the west, who were reliably in the French interest because the territory being fought over was not their homeland; they were more concerned about French favor for themselves than conscious of a racial desire to save "Indian" land for "Indians."[53]

52. Robert C. Alberts, *The Most Extraordinary Adventures of Major Robert Stobo* (Boston: Houghton Mifflin Co., 1965), ch. 8 and p. 169; Stobo's ltr., 29 July 1754, in *Pa. Council Minutes* 6:141–43.

Bibliographic note: The fact of Stobo's information is noted without the information about the Indians in Lee McCardell, *Ill-Starred General: Braddock of the Coldstream Guards* (1958), reprinted (Pittsburgh: University of Pittsburgh Press, 1986), 141.

Bibliographic note: McCardell's heavily documented book is full of gossip and "colorful" writing. It misses entirely the issue of the prerogative, and its Indians are stereotypical savages. Its Quakers are also stereotypes. Though sympathetic to Braddock, its information confirms, rather than refutes, his arrogance.

53. Edmunds, *The Potawatomis*, 50–51. George Stanley erroneously names only Shawnees and Delawares in the "mixed bag of Indians." He thus misinterprets tribal politics and objectives, though apparently by negligence rather than design. His book shows little concern for such issues. Rather curiously after all these years, Stanley's book leaves small doubt that he is a military man with the same turn of mind as Braddock's. Stanley, *New France*, 98. Frégault, in *Canada: The War of the Conquest*, 95, does not distinguish his homogenized "Indians" by tribe. Commandant Contrecoeur had to make such distinctions; he mentioned "the Indians from Detroit and Michilimakinak," in Paul E. Kopperman, *Braddock at the Monongahela* (Pittsburgh: University of Pittsburgh Press, 1977), 250.

They were joined at the last minute by a party of the Ohio Indians angered by Braddock's rejection of their offer to aid *him*.

Braddock's defeat

Under Contrecoeur's orders, Indians harassed Braddock's advance, inflicting a few casualties without serious effect. They raided the back settlements of Maryland and Virginia, but Braddock refused to be deflected from his objective. Contrecoeur knew that his fort could not withstand pounding from Braddock's artillery; his garrison of Frenchmen and Canadians was pitifully small, and Indians were not temperamentally suited to fight long behind walls. In desperation, he tried a sally to stop the English before they could get within range and bring their big guns into play. On the morning of 9 July he sent out his available force: 72 regulars of the marine, 146 Canadian militiamen, and 637 assorted tribesmen, under command of Liénard de Beaujeu. When they encountered Braddock's advance troops, both sides were surprised. Beaujeu impetuously ordered a charge. Volley after volley from the disciplined British troops halted the charge and killed Beaujeu. His second-in-command, Jean-Daniel Dumas, improvised new tactics. Holding the narrow road with his regular troops, he deployed his Indians in the trees lining the road on both sides, and on the height of land overlooking it.[54]

It was then that Braddock learned that Indian warriors were to be feared in pitched battle as well as in harassment along a line of march. From the trees the Indians poured forth a devastating fire while the British fired back aimlessly at targets they could not see. Some of Braddock's subordinates suggested dispersing the men to take cover and fight back in frontier style, but he would have none of that—he still fought by the wrong book—and when his desperate men began to break ranks on their own initiative he charged into them and forced them back into line with the flat of his saber.[55] Lawrence Henry Gipson's mild observation takes a prize for

54. This much is generally agreed by the historians except for some small differences over numbers of men. I have followed Frégault, *Canada: The War of the Conquest*, 95–6.

55. Kopperman, *Braddock*, 78–79. Kopperman's statement is the more impressive because he systematically tries to excuse or rationalize Braddock's faults. The weight of evidence which he conscientiously and thoroughly compiled is strengthened against his interpretation by a document he overlooked. John Campbell, who had participated in the battle, told Charles Swaine later that "Croghan, Montour, and Washington applied to have the command and let the men spread, but he would not consent." Swaine to Morris, Shippensburg, 19 July 1755, mss., Penn Mss., Off. Corr., 7:85, HSP. See also John Armstrong to Richard Peters, Carlisle, 21 July 1755, mss., ibid., 7:93, and Washington's statements in Kopperman, pp. 247–48. It looks as though Braddock thought that his men had been so rigidly drilled to fight in formation that they would run away if released from it. Possibly that thought might have been correct; the whole purpose of rigid drill is to repress individual initiative. But the officers' charges of cowardice among the troops are disproved by the length of time they held out in a hopeless situation. The officers had to prove that *they* were not at fault.

understatement: "the British need of adequate Indian support became painfully apparent."[56]

The wonder is not that the British finally panicked and fled, but how they held out longer than two hours during which their casualties were so heavy that Guy Frégault calls it "a massacre rather than a battle."[57] Two thirds of the enlisted men were killed or wounded, nearly three quarters of their officers. Statements made afterwards raise a question of how many of those officers may have been killed by their own men who had reached the limit of tolerance for commands to stand and die.[58] From an unknown source, a bullet struck Braddock, wounding him mortally. He lingered long enough to direct retreat, and died on 13 July 1755. He was buried under the trail so that the marching army would efface the evidence of his grave.

His reputation is another matter. Its most admirable feature is his bravery under fire, but rationalizations and alibis notwithstanding, the disaster was Braddock's fault from beginning to end. Regardless of should-have-beens, it is certain that Braddock lost; that he commanded an army twice the size of his opponents'; that he had overwhelming superiority in artillery (which he never got to use) and equipment; that he rejected the help of Indians who could have prepared him for the French surprise attack; that most of the forces opposing his "regular and disciplin'd troops" were irregular Indians with a different style of discipline;[59] that they fought in their own way; and that, in the face of such novelty, Braddock was ragingly helpless. There is absolutely no valid reason to condone this stupid brute of a man whose prime qualification for command was the political favor of the party of royal prerogative.

The tattered remnants of Braddock's army, though they still outnumbered the French with a reserve of 1,000 men who had not taken part in

56. Gipson, *British Empire* 6:93.

57. Frégault, *Canada: The War of the Conquest*, 96.

58. Kopperman, *Braddock*, disparages such statements as he reports them with logic not always impeccable. Pp. 97–98, 137–40, 238–39, 240.

Casualties (versions vary slightly). British side: 456 killed, 421 wounded, not counting women and servants. 538 soldiers emerged from the battle safely. French side: 28 killed, "about" same number wounded; 11 Indians killed, 29 wounded. Figures for deaths do not take into account men who have died of wounds after the battle. [Pierre] Pouchot, *Memoir upon the Late War in North America, Between the French and English, 1755–70* (1781), trans. and ed. Franklin B. Hough, 2 vols. (Roxbury, Mass.: W. Elliott Woodward, 1866), 39–43. (Consulted at the Newberry Library.) Variants appear in *Relations Diverses sur La Bataille du Malangueule* [Monongahela] *Gagné le 9 Juillet 1755 . . .* , Recueillies par Jean Marie Shea, Shea's Cramoisy Press series 14 (Nouvelle York: De La Presse Cramoisy, 1860). (Consulted at John Carter Brown Library.)

59. Contrary to myth, Indian strategy and tactics were founded in specific principles, and warriors were trained to conform to them. See Leroy V. Eid, " 'National' War Among Indians of Northeastern North America," *Canadian Review of American Studies* 16:2 (Summer 1985), 125–54.

the battle, were in such shock that they could not be relied on to fight again. Colonel Thomas Dunbar assumed command and ordered an ignominious retreat all the way to the coast, abandoning the heavy guns that had been dragged over mountains with such great labor.[60] Astounded Philadelphians read Dunbar's request for winter quarters for the army—in July!—but when the army arrived in the city it marched miserably through, to settle finally in Albany.[61] Such privations as it had endured on its advance to the Ohio were nothing compared to those of its precipitate retreat after abandoning its baggage. The Pennsylvanians who had briefly united to support the campaign contemplated the pitiable spectacle and united once more in condemnation, and in a contempt that opened minds to previously unthinkable notions that the military might of Britain could be challenged successfully. In Franklin's mild words, "This whole Transaction gave us Americans the first Suspicion that our exalted Ideas of the Prowess of British Regulars had not been well founded."[62] The Ohio Indians picked up the same "suspicion."

The jubilant French had never dared even to hope for so complete a rout of so massive a foe. Their victory seemed uncertain at first when their Far Indians decided that one good battle was enough for that season, picked up their plunder, and vanished westward, so that Fort Duquesne lay exposed with a tiny garrison to face the remaining British strength which included those thousand fresh men. When Dunbar retreated instead of returning to the attack, the French could hardly believe their luck. They gathered up the abandoned British cannon and used them later in a campaign against British Fort Oswego.[63]

Braddock's chest of money and papers was also abandoned, and also picked up; the papers disclosed to fascinated French eyes all the strategic military plans for campaigns against Niagara and St. Frédéric, a clutch of political letters from ministers of the crown, and—woefully for Captain Stobo—his letters and sketch of the fort that had been smuggled out of Duquesne. Canada's governor Vaudreuil inferred that the papers supplied "most authentic proof of extensive plans, for long the principal occupation of the court of Great Britain, to surprise this colony and invade it at a time when, on the faith of the most respectable treaties of peace, it should be

60. Dunbar to Napier, Ft. Cumberland, 24 July 1755, in *Military Affairs*, ed. Pargellis, 109–11. The captured artillery apparently consisted of six cannon, four howitzers, three mortars, and much munitions. Slight variants in *Relations Diverses*, ed. Shea, 13–14, 21–25. Fifty-seven smaller howitzers in *N.Y. Col. Docs.* 10:311. In a revealing anonymous letter, 25 July 1755, an officer charges mismanagement at every stage of the campaign. *Military Affairs*, 112–24.

61. Gipson, *British Empire* 6:128, 133.

62. Franklin, *Autobiography*, ed. Labaree, 226.

63. Contrecoeur in Kopperman, *Braddock*, 250; Edmunds, *Potawatomis*, 51; Stanley, *New France*, 143.

safe from any insult." Vaudreuil leaped to a further conclusion with less justification, that George Washington had "assassinated" Jumonville in 1754 with the knowledge and consent of British ministers. (See chapter 4 annex.) Vaudreuil juxtaposed the British attacks in Acadia, their naval assaults on the French fleet, and the Braddock fiasco, and sent his strong denunciation to Paris along with Braddock's papers. The *Mercure de France* published his outcry with the observation that events and Braddock's documents proved a British "design to take possession of Canada."[64] This was precisely what British diplomats had been denying, insisting rather that they wanted only to recover Britain's rightful possessions on which the French had encroached. Relations between the British and French courts strained further, but not yet quite to the breaking point. There were still those other parts of the world to be considered. Hostilities in America still held the status of a bush war, not yet worth the empires' total commitment.

Vaudreuil's plan

Before the news of Braddock's disaster reached newly arrived Governor Vaudreuil in Quebec, he surveyed his situation and found it bad. He "dreaded" to hear what was happening at Fort Duquesne, and as to Fort Niagara, he was "certain that should the English once attack it, 'tis theirs."[65] The British had more people, more fighting men, more money, and more goods, not to speak of supremacy at sea. But Vaudreuil was a Canadian-born soldier with an attachment to the country, unlike the visiting French officers for whom Canada was an unpleasant assignment best to be done with as soon as possible. Though his resources were severely inadequate, Vaudreuil determined to make the best fight possible.

On the principle that the best defense is offensive, he coordinated forces for an attack on Oswego on the south shore of Lake Ontario. Possession of Oswego would disrupt all British plans to campaign against Niagara because Oswego was the staging area. It was also the greatest Indian trading center of New York, overwhelmingly important to the Iroquois, and it could serve in French hands as a reversed staging center for campaigns into the Mohawk Valley.[66] Braddock's defeat, when the news arrived, forced a change in strategy.[67]

64. Frégault, *Canada*, 97. Braddock's papers became the source for the French government's diplomatic accusations of British duplicity and bellicosity. [Jacob Nicolas Moreau], *Memoire contenant le Precis des Faits avec leurs Pieces Justificatives* (Paris: De L'Imprimerie Royale, 1756). This was translated in London as *The Conduct of the Late Ministry*.

65. Vaudreuil to Machault, 24 July 1755, *N.Y. Col. Docs.* 10:306–7.

66. Ibid., 10:308–9.

67. Dieskau to Doreil, 16 Aug. 1755, ibid., 10:311–12.

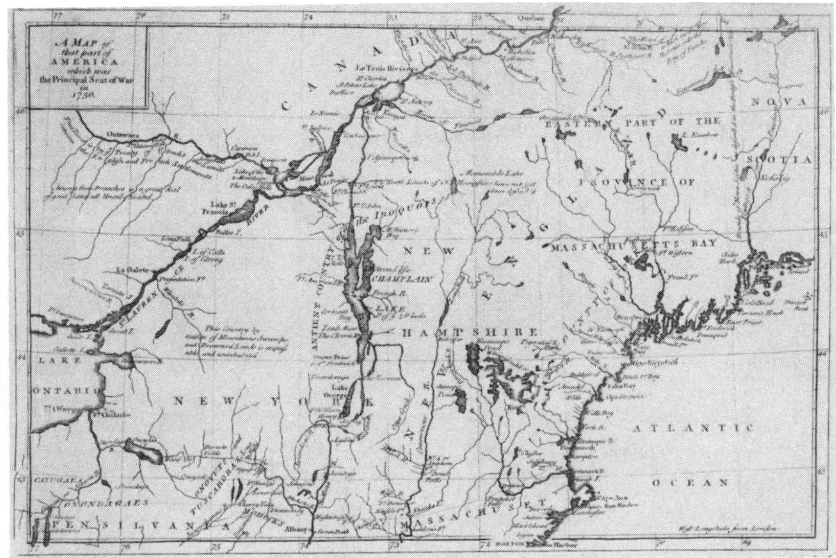

MAP 5. "The Principal Seat of the War." REPRODUCED BY PERMISSION FROM THE COPY OF *The Gentleman's Magazine* IN THE JOHN CARTER BROWN LIBRARY, BROWN UNIVERSITY.

A large force could not be maintained at distant Duquesne through a wilderness winter, and there was no longer any danger there, so Vaudreuil withdrew most of Duquesne's men to Niagara, taking Braddock's cannon along with them, and thus strengthened Niagara immeasurably.[68] Informed by Braddock's papers as well as Indian intelligence of the British campaign against Fort St. Frédéric (Crown Point) at the southernmost tip of Lake Champlain, Vaudreuil postponed his offensive against Oswego in order to rush reinforcements to Fort St. Frédéric. He put them in charge of Jean-Armand Dieskau, baron de Dieskau, an officer with a great reputation, newly arrived from France, and he gave Dieskau precise instructions.[69] Buoyed up by the triumph at Fort Duquesne, Vaudreuil prepared to go on the offensive.

Johnson versus Shirley

At the center of British difficulties was an ancient feud between Massachusetts and New York—so old, indeed, that it had begun before English

68. Vaudreuil to Machault, 25 Sept. 1755, ibid., 10:325–26; Osgood, *Eighteenth Century* 4:367.

69. Dieskau's biography by J. R. Turnbull is in *Dict. Can. Biog.* 3:185–86.

conquest made New York out of Dutch New Amsterdam.[70] By 1755 the antagonism continued in a context over the boundary between the two provinces, relations with the Iroquois, and more heatedly in controversies over the ambitions of several powerful men.[71] The highest of these in position was Massachusetts's governor William Shirley. An ardent expansionist, Shirley coveted the governorship of New York, the key post to direct and control movement west.[72] The crown never granted this wish, but it commissioned Shirley as second in command to Braddock with responsibility for a campaign against Fort Niagara; and after Braddock's death, Shirley became commander in chief of all land forces in British America.

He dispatched his associate of Louisbourg days, Captain John Bradstreet, to build a fleet at Oswego for launching when troops should be assembled. Bradstreet encroached on the jealously guarded preserve of William Johnson by conferring and negotiating with all sorts of Indians, and Shirley aggravated the wound to Yorker sensibilities by trying overtly to draw the Iroquois Six Nations from Johnson's authority to his own. He was not subtle. Johnson, he told the Iroquois, "was but an upstart of yesterday. . . . he has his Commission and all the monies for carrying on your affairs from me and when I please, I can take all his power from him . . . I am Ruler and Master here."[73]

Shirley outraged the powerful De Lancey family by attempting to cut off the smuggling trade between Albany and Montreal on which De Lancey fortunes were founded.[74] Johnson and the De Lanceys (who were related by marriage) retaliated in their various ways. Johnson persuaded most of the Iroquois to have nothing to do with Shirley's campaign—which was not hard to do as they already regarded Shirley's agent Lydius as a "snake."[75] The De Lanceys denied support to Shirley's campaign, knowing very well that if Shirley and his Massachusetts crowd should

70. See Jennings, *Ambiguous Empire*, 125–26; *Invasion of America*, 313–26.

71. George Arthur Wood, *William Shirley, Governor of Massachusetts, 1741–1756*, Studies in History, Economics and Public Law 92 (New York: Columbia University, 1920), 370; William Smith, Jr., *The History of the Province of New-York From the First Discovery to the Year 1732*, (1757) ed. Michael Kammen, 2 vols. (Cambridge, Mass.: Belknap Press, 1972), 2:184.

72. Stanley Nider Katz, *Newcastle's New York: Anglo-American Politics, 1732–1753* (Cambridge, Mass.: Belknap Press, 1968), 228, 233.

73. William G. Godfrey, *Pursuit of Profit and Preferment in Colonial North America: John Bradstreet's Quest* (Waterloo, Ont.: Wilfred Laurier University Press, 1982), 57–63; Chief Hendrick's speech, 4 Sept. 1755, *N.Y. Col. Docs.* 6:998.

74. Osgood, *Eighteenth Century* 4:369; Gipson, *British Empire* 6:144.

75. Treaty minutes, 3 July 1755, *N.Y. Col. Docs.* 6:984. The situation is described colorfully in James Thomas Flexner, *Mohawk Baronet: Sir William Johnson of New York* (New York: Harper and Brothers, 1959), ch. 9. Like most books about Johnson, this one gushes romance, but it is useful for some purposes. Note that Lydius, the chief Indian agent of Governor Shirley, and the "snake" denounced by Iroquois chiefs, was also the agent of Connecticut's Susquehannah Company invading the Wyoming Valley of Pennsylvania.

master the Iroquois and conquer Niagara it would be no easy task to pry them loose.[76] Shirley faced the task of mounting his campaign through territory almost as hostile as his French enemy. Not surprisingly, he got nowhere. By the time he assembled his troops at Oswego—half as many as he had judged necessary—the season had become too cold for campaigning. Shirley had to content himself with more plans for the following year.[77] Meantime he had another sort of battle proceeding hotly in London where ministers wanted to see more results than plans and where the De Lancey and Johnson connections ganged up to destroy him.[78] Against Shirley the French had to do nothing more than sit tight and watch the show.

Johnson becomes a certified hero

Johnson got farther on the march with his campaign against Fort St. Frédéric at Crown Point, though he never came within sight of the fort. Distracted by his struggles with Shirley, he stayed in Albany until the eighth of August. On the twenty-second he called a council of his officers in camp at the Great Carrying Place between the Hudson River and Wood Creek. Suddenly it became clear that the British would be defending instead of attacking as the French were "all in motion in Canada towards Crown Point." Erroneous available intelligence gave the French "8,000 men besides Indians" to fling against Johnson's 3,000 provincials besides an unrecorded number of Indians. In actuality the two sides were about even in numbers.[79]

We need not go into detail about the ensuing engagement on 8 September. Baron Dieskau, who subscribed to the French military tradition of audacity, raced ahead with part of his troops to attack Johnson's camp. The maneuver failed, the French were repulsed, and Dieskau was wounded and captured. He held to tradition further by blaming somebody else for what went wrong, in this case the Indians. Dieskau complained of their "treachery" that had spoiled his carefully laid ambush when some of the Canadian Iroquois showed themselves prematurely to warn their Mohawk kinsmen.[80] Such a warning seems entirely possible, but Dieskau apparently felt that it would carry little weight if he tried to explain to Governor

76. Patricia U. Bonomi, *A Factious People: Politics and Society in Colonial New York* (New York: Columbia University Press, 1971), 175–76.

77. Gipson, *British Empire* 6:147–61.

78. Ibid., 6:186–89.

79. Council of war minutes, 22 Aug. 1755, *N.Y. Col. Docs.* 6:1001; Wraxall to De Lancey, 10 Sept. 1755, ibid., 6:1003.

80. Dieskau to d'Argenson, 14 Sept. 1755, *N.Y. Col. Docs.* 10:317; same to Vaudreuil, 15 Sept., ibid., 10:318; "Dialogue" with Marshal Saxe, n.d., ibid., 10:342.

Vaudreuil why he had disregarded Vaudreuil's orders. He could hardly say that as a French professional, he had no intention of obeying a mere Canadian. It would seem that the wounded baron anticipated better treatment from Johnson than from Vaudreuil for he refused to be carried back to his men.[81] (Vaudreuil furiously denounced Dieskau when he learned of the fiasco.)[82]

The affair is usually dismissed as a standoff, because losses were about equal on both sides and neither gained any territory, but other consequences ensued from it. Johnson emerged from the battle as a hero of the empire for capturing Dieskau, who had been second in command in New France with no superior except Governor Vaudreuil. After Braddock's debacle and Shirley's shilly-shallying, the British home and colonial publics were hungry for anything that could be interpreted as victory. Parliament voted Johnson a reward of £5,000 (a sum that would require a contemporary college professor a hundred years to earn).[83]

Indian war

The real victory was hidden from all the celebrators, but Vaudreuil knew that his whole strategy must be revised because he became so concerned for the safety of Fort St. Frédéric that he had to send reinforcements, and the diversion so weakened the army intended against Oswego that that campaign had to be postponed until another year.[84] More ominously, it became evident from Dieskau's failure that the French would not be able to penetrate the British front. The loss of momentum by their massed armies implied resort to a different kind of warfare in order to keep the British off balance. Vaudreuil knew what that had to be from the example set by his governor father who had kept New England at bay with Indian raids.[85] "I apply myself particularly," wrote the son, "to sending parties of Indians into the English Colonies. . . . Nothing is more calculated to disgust the people of those Colonies and to make them desire

81. Montreuil to d'Argenson, 10 Oct. 1755, *N.Y. Col. Docs.* 10:353–54.

82. Vaudreuil to Machault, 25 Sept. 1755, ibid., 10:318–23: the third article of Vaudreuil's instructions explicitly ordered Dieskau to march "with the entire of his army without ever dividing his forces." Ibid., 10:328.

83. Gipson, *British Empire* 6:190; T. W., *Two Letters to a Friend on the Present Critical Conjuncture of Affairs in North America* (Boston, 1755) reprinted (London: T. Jeffreys, 1755), 27. For comparison with Parliament's £5,000 grant, a professor in the College of Philadelphia received annual salary of £50.

84. Vaudreuil, *N.Y. Col. Docs.* 10:324–27.

85. See Yves F. Zoltvany, *Phillippe de Rigaud de Vaudreuil, Governor of New France, 1703–25*, Carleton Library 80 (Toronto: McClelland and Stewart, 1974), ch. 4, p. 201.

the return of peace. . . . the English have lost one hundred men for our one."[86]

In the absence of countervailing British power, the Ohio Indians had become dependent on French trade goods, and they faced the fear-inspiring possibility of destruction by Far West Indians under French direction. Dependency produced subordination. Let Shingas tell what happened.

Shingas explains

After the French had ruined Braddocks Army they immediately compelld the Indians To join them and let them know that if they refused they wou'd Immediately cut them off, On which the Indians Joind the French for their Own Safety—They However sent [Delaware] Capt Jacobs with some other Indians to Philadelphia to hold a Treaty with the Government.[87]

Shingas's narrative can be interrupted here by a description of what happened in Philadelphia. Once more, the Delawares let Scarouady speak for them. "Brethren, the English," he addressed Governor Robert Hunter Morris, "We let you know that our Cousins the Delawares, as well as our Brethren the Nanticokes, have assured me that they were never asked to go to war against the French in the late Expedition, but promised in the strongest Terms that if their Brethren the English (especially those of Pennsylvania) will give them their Hatchett they would make use of it, and would join with their Uncles [the Iroquois] against the French. So we assure you by this belt of Wampum that we will gather all our Allies to assist the English in another Expedition. One word of Yours will bring the Delawares to join You; . . . any Message you have to send, or answer you have to give to them, I will deliver to them."

Morris's reply simply referred the matter to the Onondaga council of the Iroquois: "Brother: Return our hearty thanks to the Delawares and Nanticokes for their generous offer of engaging in another Expedition if this Government will put the Hatchet into their hands; We take this as a high proof of their particular attachment to us, and we hope they will always continue their Friendship to us and wait the Determination of the Six Nations, which they may expect to receive very soon from themselves."[88] In short, Morris passed the buck, but the Delawares were in no situation to stall.

86. Vaudreuil to Machault, 8 June 1756, *N.Y. Col. Docs.* 10:413.
87. "Captivity of Charles Stuart," 64.
88. *Pa. Council Minutes*, 22 Aug. 1755, 6:588–91.

Raids in Pennsylvania

We may pick up Shingas's narrative again.

> On their returning home From Philadelphia without meeting with the necessary Encouragement [which would necessarily have required a supply of weapons] the Indians agreed To Come out with the French and their Indians in Parties To Destroy the English Settlements. The French haveing appointed 1400 French and Indians to come out in Small Parties for that Purpose—the First Breach was made on the South Branch of Patowmack near Fort Cumberland from which they carried a number of Captives and Scalps with Considerable Plunder, Immediately on the return of this Party to Fort Du Quesne Capt Jacobs, King Shingas, Capt John Peter and Capt Will a Delaware Chief were sent out by the French Commander at Fort Du Quesne against Pennsylvania and accordingly they went out, Divideing themselves into two Parties, one of which under Capt Jacobs went against the Canallaway, and the other Party under Shingas with the two other Chiefs, Capt John Peter and Capt Will Fell upon the Great Cove—Thus begun the War between the English and the Indians and Such have Been the Consequences thus far.[89]

Perhaps this is one time when Governor Morris may be acknowledged to have been caught in a bind not made by himself, for Braddock's defeat precipitated uncontrollable situations. When the Delawares asked Morris to given them the hatchet, Morris knew that he would have to get funds for arms from his assembly. That the Quakers would give arms to Indians to fight Frenchmen and other Indians did not seem likely. Morris may even be seen to have acted responsibly in this instance by not promising what he could not deliver. But Morris was no more willing than the assembly to surrender political positions already taken.

Political battle

When the reports arrived in Philadelphia of Delaware attacks on the outlying settlements—reports of slaughter, captivities, and total destruction by fire—Morris scented certain opportunities to exploit the excitement caused by them. He immediately called upon the assembly to grant money for him to spend on relief, and to authorize a "regular" militia. He would exempt pacifists from service, but *regular* meant that the officers were to be appointed by himself and the appropriations were to be at his disposal, with the result that a new patronage machine would be created and put under his control. As for raising money, he would not pass "any Bill of the same or a like Tenor of those I have heretofore refused." From

89. "Captivity of Charles Stuart," 64.

that dug-in position, he "earnestly" recommended to the assembly "to afford in Time that assistance which your bleeding Country stands so much in need of."[90] In short, he tried to stampede the assembly into giving him what he had demanded all along.

The assembly responded curiously. Its predecessor assembly had appropriated £1,000 "for the King's use," a phrase that rendered to Caesar while narrowly preserving the pacifist conscience, and the money was entrusted to a committee consisting of unchurched Benjamin Franklin and anglican Evan Morgan. These were men who had no scruples against buying and distributing arms, and they quickly spent the whole sum for munitions sent to the afflicted back country inhabitants. This action has escaped the notice of historians who see only the assembly's denial of money for the governor to spend.[91]

There was more on the Quaker conscience than casuistry about arms. *Why* had the Indians lifted the hatchet? Months earlier, Israel Pemberton, Jr., the "king of the Quakers," complained to his English correspondent that "no proper Care" had been taken to solicit the Indians' friendship and assistance, "when it is said little more than an Invitation was necessary to engage a large Number of them into the Publick Service."[92] Regardless of Pemberton's compulsion for euphemism, he was on the right track, and he was not to be diverted from it by gubernatorial blusterings. When the assembly responded to Morris, it repeated Pemberton's concerns. Left unsaid was what lay behind them. The Quakers were troubled by events that violated all the assumptions of the Friendly creed which postulated that if people are treated kindly they will respond with kindness—certainly not with torture and massacre. Surely Pennsylvania had always dealt fairly with the Indians; therefore the horrors in the back settlements were incomprehensible without further explanation. But what if there had been dealings, hidden from public view, that had not been fair? Indian affairs were in the hands of the proprietary and his agents, and the assemblymen were ready by this time to believe any wickedness by Thomas Penn. "It seems absolutely necessary," wrote Speaker Isaac Norris, Jr., by order of the house, "to request the Governor would be pleased to inform us whether he knows of any disgust or Injury the Delawares or Shawanese have ever received from this Province, and by what means their affections can be so alienated . . . we are resolved to do everything in our power to redress them if they shall appear to have received any wrong or Injury at

90. *Pa. Council Minutes*, 3 Nov. 1755, 6:670–72.

91. The excellent editors of the *Franklin Papers* consulted the sources instead of the propaganda. See 6:165, 170–71, 229n3. See also Peters to Penn, 13 Nov. 1755, mss., Gratz Coll., Ltrs. of R. Peters to Proprietaries, p. 13, HSP; Peters to Penn, 25 Nov. 1755, mss., Peters Letterbook, 1755–57, p. 19.

92. Pemberton to Fothergill, 19 May 1755, mss., cited n14, above.

our hands, tho' nothing of that kind hath come to our knowledge, and if possible to regain their affections, rather than by any neglect or refusal of that Justice we owe to them and all our Indian allies, entail upon ourselves and our posterity the Calamities of a Cruel Indian War."[93]

It was an expression of high-minded principle under stress, and its philosophical assumptions and factual suspicions were sound—the Indians had indeed been abused and mistreated—but its evasion of direct formal response to Morris's demands left the assembly vulnerable to charges of callous indifference to calamities of persons who had seen their families killed and homes burned. For victims and onlookers, "a cruel Indian war" was not a prospective possibility; the atrocities were real and present, and neighbors feared their own victimization. It was true, however, that the assembly had raised an extraordinarily sensitive issue because Thomas Penn and his henchmen had, in grim fact, swindled and cheated the Delawares without scruple or mercy. So also, as the scandalized Quaker assemblymen were to woefully discover, had some of their respected Quaker ancestors.[94] When they raised the issue of abuse of the Indians, whether they knew it or not, they were aiming at Thomas Penn's jugular; other colonies had lost their charters for mismanagement of Indians that brought on war. Penn knew this, and he fought back with every weapon at his command.[95] Governor Morris saw in the assembly's evasions a prime opportunity to inflame public opinion. As governor and assembly locked horns once more, a new era of contention began in Philadelphia, fiercer than anything that had gone before; and the Indian raids made the issues for many people a matter of life or death.

93. *Pa. Council Minutes*, 5 Nov. 1755, 6:677–78.
94. Details in Jennings, *Ambiguous Iroquois Empire*, chs. 16, 17, app. B.
95. See chs. 11–17, below.

Part Two ☙ *VARIOUS VICTIMS*

INTRODUCTION

The introduction of barbarians and savages into the contests of civilized nations is a measure pregnant with shame and mischief; which the interest of the moment may compel, but which is reprobated by the best principles of humanity and reason. It is the practice of both sides to accuse their enemies of the guilt of the first alliances; and those who fail in their negotiations are loudest in their censure of the example which they envy and would gladly imitate.

Edward Gibbon

Americans tend to think of the Seven Years War in terms of glamour and romance. Hazily we deplore Braddock's foolishness before Fort Duquesne, but Washington emerges as a hero, and the provincial troops teach those foolish Britons how to fight in the wilderness, Robert Rogers and his rangers reinforce the impression by their gloriously reported exploits deep behind the French lines. Wolfe and Montcalm have inspired generations with their gallantry. And so on. True, there were those dreadful raids in the backwoods by the savages, but these were overcome, and civilization and progress triumphed to march irresistibly westward in the conquest of a vast empire. The war's myth blends with the general myth of the Frontier, and thus serves to ennoble and democratize the heroic colonials who became Americans. Samuel Eliot Morison thanked "the brave redskins" for making us "pay dear for the mastery of a continent."[1] The blood spilled by the war was bitter but replenishable, and it was strong medicine.

We owe this myth in the first place to the novels, miscalled histories, of Francis Parkman, who provided nearly all its ingredients. It is a nineteenth-century saga of the ancestors' great and valorous deeds. As such it has explained, to the gratification of generations of Americans, why we are a Chosen people, the Elect of God and / or the supreme race, because of which endowment we have become the world's mightiest, wealthiest nation.

1. Samuel Eliot Morison, *The Oxford History of the American People* (New York: Oxford University Press, 1965), 15–16.

The myth is false. The war was brought on and directed by some very ugly, powerful men motivated by greed, self-aggrandizement, and the desire for yet more power. It was conducted in the usual bloody, dirty way of wars by officers who relied heavily on the strategy of massacre and terror over troops and civilians alike, by methods that had become integral to European culture. Such impulse as can be seen toward greater democracy arose from British colonials' resistance to British autocrats and oppression. The "war-loving Indian savages" most earnestly desired to keep out of the war and let the empires' own troops fight it out; only intense pressure, deception, and bribery drew them in. The undeniable cruelty of their kind of fighting was matched in every respect, and more, by what Parkman called "the gallant noblesse" of Europe. And, just incidentally, the frontiersmen of Canada were incomparably superior to the "American" colonials in their adaptation to wilderness campaigning.

The myth's harmful preachment is the glory of conquest by armed force. Falsehood is an absolute necessity because conquest is a dirty, nasty business that cannot be glorified in its nakedness. To this general rule, the Seven Years War was no exception. In it, the scourges of violence, hate, and ruthless policy victimized an assortment of people whose dearest wish was to live and let live. Many were destroyed, others mutilated in body or possessions. Still others managed by luck or resolution to outwit their pursuing demons and almost miraculously emerged from the horrors, enriched in experience though rarely in goods. Neither colonials nor Indians were spared.

More subtly, the war reached out to hurt people across the Atlantic. I have not examined its effect in France, but British troops shipped from Scotland, Ireland, and England suffered almost incredible casualties; and young men were swept up from public places for impressment into virtual slavery in the royal navy. Many of them died for purposes not their own, and all were "disciplined" under the lash. Civilians were taxed to the screaming point. Their civil liberties eroded so rapidly under authoritarian abrasion that even the elite of war profiteers regretted the war's ascension to power of the authoritarians.

The loss of civil liberties must be reserved to part V. Part II will consider four victimizing processes: (1) the punishment of French Acadians and their Micmac allies by the conquering British; (2) the atrocities committed by Indians under French and British direction upon backwoods colonials and other Indians; (3) the privations and casualties of the armed forces; and (4) a trans-Atlantic conspiracy to deprive Pennsylvania's pietists and Roman Catholics of the rights of freemen.

These were not all. The war inspired royal efforts to achieve rule by prerogative in the British colonies; profiteers in New France as well as the British colonies seized every opportunity for warring upon their own peoples in their own ways; and, most terribly, British troops invading Canada wrought deliberate "total war" devastation of the kind previously practiced in Ireland and Scotland. Parts III and IV will demonstrate.

The victimizers in each case were gentlemen who prided themselves on their honor and their devotion to Christian virtue. Ostensibly, the advancement of civilization and the public good was defined by a particular national or religious devotion. In ways familiar to those who read history in the sources, the public good coincided more often than not with the private benefit of a select few exploiting the misery and travail of the rest.

Chapter 8 ❧ *ACADIA / NOVA SCOTIA*

Though their struggle with the colonial administration was couched in political terms, the French Neutrals were actually fighting to preserve their way of life, a unique blend of French and Indian folkways forged on the seventeenth-century Acadian frontier.

Carl A. Brasseaux

Chronology

1726.	Nova Scotia governor Lawrence Armstrong demands oath of allegiance from Acadians and pretends to allow them neutrality in wars between Britain and France.
1730.	Governor Richard Philipps makes an unwritten promise of neutrality.
1751.	New France's governor-general the marquis de La Jonquière orders Acadians under French jurisdiction to swear allegiance and enroll in his militia.
4 March 1754.	Board of trade says Acadians' land tenure depends on unqualified oath of allegiance.
16–17 June 1755.	Forts Beausèjour and Gaspereau fall to attacking New Englanders.
3–4 July 1755.	Representatives of Acadians refuse oath. Council decides on deportation of recusants. Some then offer to swear allegiance but are refused permission after their earlier denial, and are ordered into confinement.
28 July 1755.	After consultation with military officers, council orders deportation and dispersal of Acadian recusants.
13 October 1755.	Transports with 1,100 Acadians take them into exile.
November 1755.	Arrival of Acadian contingents in British colonies.
June 1761.	Micmac treaty of peace with Nova Scotia after which the Indians are dispossessed of property but remain in the country.

The triumph in Acadia secured British Nova Scotia, isolated French Louisbourg, and doomed the so-called French Neutrals who had refused the oath of allegiance to King George II.*

*Since this book went to press, a commendable study on the subject of the Acadians and their diaspora has appeared. I wish it had been available earlier for enrichment of this chapter. Carl A. Brasseaux, *The Founding of New Acadia: The Beginnings of Acadian Life in Louisiana*,

A few words are in order about what sort of people these Acadians were. They were peasants, deeply devoted to their own collective homeland and family farms. Their greatest ambition was to increase families, herds, and acres under cultivation, at which they labored incessantly, multiplying and prospering. Ardently Roman Catholic, they were monarchist in political theory though localist in practice. Unfortunately, they were loyal to the wrong monarch; France's Louis XV neither could nor would interfere with British rule over subjects who had been ceded to the British crown.[1]

In matters closer to their experience, the Acadians made shrewder arrangements. Many of their skilled fishermen had become acquainted with Protestant fishermen from New England, and it appears that differences of religion had not prevented interregional and interfaith smuggling from thriving out at sea.[2] (In some quarters it is darkly suspected that smuggling between Nova Scotians and Yankees continues to the present day.)

Though intensely ethnocentric, the Acadians' outlook was regional rather than racist. Of all European colonials in North America, they seem to have accommodated most wholeheartedly with the Indians of their vicinity. They intermarried so freely with neighboring Micmac and Abenaki Indians that the British board of trade despaired of breaking their allegiance without setting a similar pattern in Nova Scotia. For reasons of high strategy, the board repeatedly issued instructions (which were not obeyed) for the encouragement of similar intermarriage between British Nova Scotians and Indians.[3] In this respect the calamity that befell the Acadians holds significance transcending themselves, for it aborted a promising experiment in ethnic reconciliation.

The Acadians' misfortune was to be in the wrong place at the wrong time. On the map they seem to be remote and isolated, but that is because the map does not show traffic at sea. Off the coasts of Nova Scotia and Newfoundland were, and still are, the richest fisheries in the world. "A thousand miles of misty sea," remarked James T. Shotwell, yielded "a harvest which for a long time rivalled in importance the produce of our opening wilderness."[4] All the nations of western Europe fished in those

1765–1803 (Baton Rouge: Louisiana State University Press, 1987). Despite the subtitle's dates, the study includes attention also to the 1750s.

1. Gipson, *British Empire* 6:263.

2. Clark, *Acadia*, 230–32, 254–55.

3. Ibid., 89, 361; J. S. Brebner, "Subsidized Intermarriage with the Indians," *Canadian Historical Review* 6:1(1925), 33–36; Alfred Goldsworthy Bailey, *The Conflict of European and Eastern Algonkian Cultures, 1504–1700* (1937), 2d ed. (Toronto: University of Toronto Press, 1969), 18, 112.

4. J. T. Shotwell, "Foreword," in Harold A. Innis, *The Cod Fisheries: The History of an International Economy*, published for the Carnegie Endowment for International Peace (New Haven, Conn.: Yale University Press, 1940), vii.

waters for a catch that in its mass formed a substantial proportion of Europe's diet and commerce; and statesmen paid close attention to this great industry as "a nursery of seamen" for royal navies.[5] French Louisbourg and British Halifax were founded to guard and control the fisheries as much as for any other reason, and Acadian farmers fed the garrisons of both bases.[6] As the two empires ground ever closer to overt war, each laid claim to the Acadians' exclusive loyalty, and each side implemented its claim with force.

For a century, New England competed with Acadia in trade with the Indians, and often in war; but the Acadians had managed to hold their own until 1713 when their uncertainly bounded country was ceded by the French crown to Britain in the treaty of Utrecht. The peninsular part became Nova Scotia, but it was not immediately repopulated. Nothing much changed except the substitution of British military rule for French government. British immigration did not begin significantly until 1749, when the seaport town of Halifax was founded.[7] British officials contented themselves with superficial formalities of Acadian loyalty because the rulers lacked power to enforce the real thing. They left the Acadians in possession of their lands and permitted Catholic priests to officiate in their parishes, but the issue of allegiance did rise repeatedly.

The illusion of neutrality

In 1726, Nova Scotia's governor Lawrence Armstrong demanded an oath of submission to the British crown. The Acadian *habitants*, through their spokesmen, made a counterdemand to be exempted from bearing arms because they wanted to be neutral in wars between Britain and France. Faced with their obduracy, Armstrong seemingly accepted their amendment, but not really. He ordered it "written upon the Margent of the

5. *An Accurate Description of Cape Breton* (London: M. Cooper, 1755), 54, 70; Innis, *Cod Fisheries*, x; J. S. McLennan, *Louisbourg from Its Foundation to Its Fall, 1713–1758* (London: Macmillan and Co., 1918), 3; Basil Williams, *The Life of William Pitt, Earl of Chatham* (1913), 2 vols., reprinted (New York: Octagon Books, 1966) 2:83.

6. Halifax: Innis, *Cod Fisheries*, 185. Louisbourg: Clark, *Acadia*, 270–71, 287, 293–94. Provisions: ibid., 254–57, 357. Because of remarks in the literature that Louisbourg guarded the entrance to the St. Lawrence River, it must be stressed that the fort did no such thing. Its guns could not possibly reach out to block shipping in the vast Gulf of St. Lawrence though it might harbor a fleet with the capacity to blockade. It was a naval base functioning primarily to protect the fisheries, and Halifax performed the same function for the British. When British naval forces were superior they bottled up the French ships in Louisbourg harbor and sailed in and out of the St. Lawrence at will as they did during the campaign against Forts Beauséjour and Gaspereau while the French at Louisbourg could give no help to their besieged compatriots. Thanks to Professor Russell Weigley for help with this matter.

7. Clark, *Acadia*, 334–39; Maxwell Sutherland, "Mascarene, Paul," in *Dict. Can. Biog.* 3:435–39; J. Murray Beck, "Cornwallis, Edward," ibid., 4:168–69.

french translation in order to gett them over by degrees." J. B. Brebner, who reported this from council minutes, observed that the marginal amendment "did not appear on the version sent to England, and I have been unable to discover it elsewhere."[8] Thus the Acadians thought they had a legal agreement, but the crown's records showed an unqualified submission.

Something similar happened again in 1730. Governor Richard Philipps, after less than a year in office, sent to England the unqualified allegiance of the whole Acadian population. This would have been "in the nature of a miracle," according to Brebner, who believed that Philipps "almost certainly" made a "solemn verbal promise" that the *habitants* would never be called to military service and avoided a written contract by "verbal adroitness and calculated hauteur"—which translates, I think, to bluff and bluster.[9] It is clear from the Acadians' subsequent behavior that they thought they had been granted a right to neutrality which they adhered to unyieldingly.

This became the more critical when some were persuaded or coerced to cross into French jurisdiction, where they were ordered by the governor of Canada in 1751 to take *his* oath of allegiance and enroll in the French militia.[10] If the British made neutrality difficult, the French made it impossible.

Crisis came in 1754 when Nova Scotia's lieutenant governor Charles Lawrence determined that military conquest was the only solution to the guerilla warfare being instigated by the French from beyond his disputed borders. Massachusetts rallied to this plan, as shown in chapter 6. Forts Beauséjour and Gaspereau capitulated, and Lawrence suddenly acquired power to deal with the Acadians on his own terms.

Mass dispossession and exile

Lawrence's terms were also the terms of the board of trade, though perhaps he executed policy more precipitously than the board had anticipated. In its letter of 4 March 1754, the board told Lawrence that the Acadians had no right to their lands "but upon condition of taking the Oath of Allegiance absolute and unqualified with any Reservation what-

8. John Bartlet Brebner, *New England's outpost: Acadia Before the Conquest of Canada*, Studies in History, Economics and Public Law 293 (New York: Columbia University Press, 1927), 88–89.

9. Ibid., 94–97.

10. Ibid., 177–78, 205; Gérard Finn, "Le Loutre, Jean-Louis," in *Dict. Can. Biog.* 4:455–57.

ever."[11] In October the board waffled a bit. It again raised the issue of title to lands, but threw responsibility upon Nova Scotia's chief justice Jonathan Belcher, Jr., to give an "opinion" that became in effect a decree. This seems to have been merely a tactical device, for Lord Halifax at the board was much too well informed about officials in America to be in doubt about how Belcher would rule. What emerged from the justice's pen simply served, as intended, to put a face of legality on the fact of confiscation and forceful expatriation.[12]

John Bartlet Brebner's doctoral dissertation concludes that "the expanding energies of New England" were responsible for the event; it notes that the decision to deport was made by Governor Lawrence's council, "men who were either New Englanders or who, without exception, had been saturated with that policy [of New England's expansion] for years." Calling Lawrence the "agent" of that policy, Brebner charged that Lawrence "disobeyed express and oft-repeated orders" from the crown. In a cursory search, I have not found such orders. It seems likely that Brebner misinterpreted the crown's desire *to prevent Acadians from going over to the French* as meaning that they must be *kept on their lands*. But the board of trade was explicit and emphatic about the oath of allegiance being essential to validation of land title, and after the fact of Acadian dispossession the board praised Lawrence and secured his promotion from lieutenant governor to governor. However that may be, the Acadians were first ordered to take the oath of submission. When they once again refused on grounds of what they believed to be their guaranteed right of neutrality, the council declared that refusers should be removed from the province as "Papist Recusants." In a sudden panic, an Acadian delegation then offered to take the unconditional oath. They were told that this was no longer possible after it had once been rejected, and "they were thereupon ordered into Confinement."[13] Thus, on 4 July 1755, began a process of deportation and devastation in America that paralleled what the duke of Cumberland's men had done ten years earlier in the Scottish Highlands.[14]

Considered exclusively as a military measure, the expulsion strategy was successful. Other considerations require qualification of that judgment. Economically the crown lost thousands of industrious productive subjects who instantly became costly charges on its other subjects, and on the crown treasury. Not content with deporting the Acadians, the British

11. *Selections from the Public Documents of the Province of Nova Scotia*, ed. Thomas B. Akins (Halifax, N.S.: Charles Annand, Publisher, 1869), 207. *(Nova Scotia Docs.)*

12. Ibid., 235–37; Brebner, *New England's Outpost*, 223–24; Gipson, *British Empire* 6:252n.

13. Brebner, *New England's Outpost*, 222, 229, 233; *Nova Scotia Docs.*, 207–8, 235–37. Cf. Dominick Graham, "Lawrence, Charles," in *Dict. Can. Biog.* 3:361–67, and L. H. Gipson, *British Empire* 6:250–53.

14. Cf. Prebble, *Culloden*.

destroyed their homes and all the improvements so laboriously made upon their lands. Among the improvements so destroyed were the dikes with which the Acadians had prevented the high tides of the Bay of Fundy from drowning farms in salt water. When the dikes were wrecked, the tides rolled in and the lands became useless for cultivation until the salt could be leached out of the soil after many years of lying fallow. Ironically, to restore the dikes years later, the helpless British had to summon help from experienced Acadians who had escaped the great dispersion.[15]

In both Highland Scotland and Nova Scotia, the only persons to benefit from victimization of the resident peasantry were those who moved in later to take over the victims' herds and lands. In Nova Scotia, resettlement was delayed by war's complications. When the newcomers began to arrive in significant numbers in 1760, most came from New England.[16]

Diaspora

The success in purely military terms of the expulsion strategy bears a different countenance as treatment of human beings. The officials who ordered deportation of the Acadians had no plan beyond getting rid of them, destroying their buildings, and confiscating all their land and movable stock. As the crown had not ordered such action specifically, no financing for it could be expected from England. The province itself would pay only for transportation, funds for which came largely out of the confiscated possessions of the Acadians. Officialdom would not permit the Acadians to travel to French possessions for fear that they would return as enemies. (Some managed to do so anyhow.) They were not sent directly to Britain for fear, it seems, of irritating ministers who would resent the costs thus thrust upon *them* for looking after the deportees. Transport after transport sailed instead to Britain's seaboard colonies to surprise governments from Georgia to New York. (New England's governments had advance notice.) All in all, some six or seven thousand persons were exiled during the last four months of 1755—one of the largest mass migrations of the era.[17] Other exiles followed.

15. Clark, *Acadia*, 238–42, 365.

16. John Bartlet Brebner, *The Neutral Yankees of Nova Scotia: A Marginal Colony during the Revolutionary Years* (New York: Columbia University Press, 1937), ch. 2.

17. Gipson, *British Empire* 6:263–85. As always, Gipson is useful for discrete facts; and, as always, tilts heavily in interpretation toward denying every sin and fault of the British. Cf. Clark, *Acadia*, 360–64. But Gipson is the essence of objectivity compared to J. A. Doyle, who remarked that "the eviction of those Acadians who at the bidding of their priests withheld allegiance from the British Government, has no important place in the history of the war looked at from a colonial point of view." This, with four more sentences, constitutes Doyle's entire treatment of the conquest of Acadia. *The Colonies under the House of Hanover* (London: Longmans, Green and Co., 1907), 589.

They were dispersed into all the seaboard colonies and the West Indies. They suffered much from privation and disease, the hostility of officials and rabid anti-Catholics, and their own stubbornness. (They would not burn that pinch of incense.) A few philanthropic individuals rallied to their relief, sometimes at great personal cost, but the Acadians refused to accept arrangements for them to work, on the grounds that they were prisoners of war and that their captors were therefore obliged by the laws of war to support them.[18] This argument did not impress the British colonials, but they were not quite so brutal as to deny all succor.

Until some of the Acadians were dumped in France, the French crown kept studiously unconcerned. Forced by the arrival of refugees to do something, French ministers ordered provision for Acadian subsistence and allotments of land for the refugees to farm. But the soil of the allotments in France was so infertile that those redoubtable Acadians refused to be stuck with it. In consequence, most of them remained on a dole until, in 1785, 1,600 emigrated to Louisiana by arrangements with the government of that colony (Spanish at the time), which wanted tough frontiersmen as security against the encroaching English. (The embarrassed French prohibited further emigration when they discovered how willing the Acadians were to go.)[19]

Other Acadians had earlier found circuitous ways to Louisiana, where they again became difficult to deal with. Many joined the 1768 insurrection against Governor Ulloa, but in Louisiana they were finally beaten down. Ulloa was replaced by Alexandro O'Reilly who "had the insurgent leaders arrested and eventually punished with imprisonment and death" whereupon the Acadians yielded and in 1769 took the oath of loyalty to Spain that O'Reilly demanded. We are told that they later "comported themselves well as militiamen . . . and served the colony and the Spanish well." They salvaged their sense of unique identity and community and became the distinctive, colorful "Cajuns" of modern Louisiana. At least one Acadian, a man named Brusar, escaped by land to the Mississippi and traveled "1,400 leagues [3,500 miles] to recover his native country.[20]

The historical lessons that seem to be taught by their experience are not

18. Gipson, *British Empire* 6: ch. 10.

19. Oscar William Winzerling, *Acadian Odyssey* (Baton Rouge: Louisiana State University Press, 1955), ix–x, 60–63, 85–86, 88, 90–91, 152, 155.

20. R. E. Chandler, "The St. Gabriel Acadians: the First Five Months," *Louisiana History* 21 (1980), 287–96; Jacqueline K. Vorhies, "The Acadians: The Search for the Promised Land," in *The Cajuns: Essays on Their History and Culture*, ed. Glenn R. Conrad, 2d ed. (Lafayette, La.: Center for Louisiana Studies, University of Southwestern Louisiana, 1978), 109. This volume has several useful essays, including Glenn R. Conrad, "The Acadians: Myths and Realities," 1–20; Gamaliel Smethurst, *A Narrative of an Extraordinary Escape out of the Hands of the Indians* . . . (1774), reprinted facsimile in *The Garland Library of Narratives of North American Indian Captivities*, comp. Wilcomb E. Washburn, vol. 10 (New York: Garland Publishing, 1977), separately paged, 16–17.

pleasant. They paid a terrible price for their devotion to king, church, and each other. They lost all their property, so tediously accumulated by lives of rigorous toil. Incalculably large numbers lost their lives from hardship and epidemic. And in the end the survivors had to take such oaths of allegiance as would have saved them in the first place. Nor is it comforting to realize that what finally broke their wills in Louisiana was the terror imposed by Governor O'Reilly. As we shall see (in chapter 11) their intransigence brought distress even to persons who treated them benevolently.

Reception in New England

Connecticut and Massachusetts Bay had advance notice that they were to receive quotas of Acadians. Massachusetts's former governor Phips had reason enough to know as he had proposed the exiling before it was decided. But when the first contingent of Acadians arrived at Boston on 12 November, it was Counselor Thomas Hutchinson, rather than Phips, who befriended them. Massachusetts's provincial council provided temporarily for food and shelter "in the Country Towns," but wrote stiffly to Nova Scotia of its "expectation of being indemnified from all charges." Nova Scotia's council took this demand under consideration and filed it. In December, Massachusetts's assembly enacted a law "to employ, bind out or support" the Acadians which, in practice, resulted in the separation of many children from their families as indentured "bond" servants.[21]

A question arises as to possible differences in culture, as binding out of children was common among the English, but the Acadians protested strongly. Possibly what was seen as atrocity by them was regarded by Englishmen as routine practice, but it is fairly clear in Maryland and Pennsylvania that binding out of Acadian children was seen in a punitive light.[22]

Gipson reports that Massachusetts paid out in relief for support of the exiles the sum of £9,563 sterling which he regards as a respectable sum, but that was for the period from the fall of 1755 to summer of 1763. When averaged out over eight years, it comes to about £1,200 per annum. As more than 2,000 exiles were in Massachusetts already by 19 November 1755, the province's outlay for Acadian charity looks to have been less than one pound per person per year, or about two-thirds of a penny per day. Even in those days, that was not enough to live on. The average may

21. Gipson, *British Empire* 6:325–27.

22. For New England's indenturing of children see Edmund S. Morgan, *The Puritan Family: Religious and Domestic Relations in Seventeenth-Century New England* (1944), rev. ed. (New York: Harper and Row, 1966), 76–77.

have been increased slightly by the flight of many Acadians back to the region still under French jurisdiction along the St. John River.[23]

Forewarned, Connecticut dispersed its Acadians to the towns and, except for provincial assumption of subsistence for incapables, made the towns responsible for management of the exiles quartered among them. The town of Guilford's "doubtless rather typical" solution was "to put out to service so many of the French family, which is amongst us, as they can dispose of, without expense to the town, to free it from charge."[24]

Reception in the southern colonies

The southern colonies, except underpopulated North Carolina, refused to accept responsibility for this sudden imposition upon them, which would involve heavy drains on their finances. Their dilemma had more than two horns. They feared possible Acadian contact with the French instigators of Indian attacks on their back settlers, as well as possible subversion of the Black slaves who outnumbered their masters (a spectre that never ceased to haunt); while, on the other hand, the southerners did not want to incur the crown's displeasure, and Nova Scotia's governor Lawrence averred that he was following crown policy. But the southern colonies also faced the likelihood of special tensions between the rigidly Catholic Acadians and the intensely Protestant Huguenots who had settled in their midst after fleeing from persecution in Catholic France.

The classic solution to a dilemma is to evade the issues. Georgia and South Carolina achieved it by passing those Acadians along. With governmental connivance or assistance, hundreds of them became "boat people" coasting northward in the hope of reaching their homeland again. Some did, and promptly joined the French forces at St. John's (in today's New Brunswick). Most, however, died of epidemic smallpox or "disappeared." Disappearance from Georgia seems to have translated sometimes as escape to Louisiana or the French West Indies. Georgia's officials did not try to find out.[25]

South Carolina's governor Glen tried to dump fifty Acadians on Virginia, perhaps still pursuing his feud with Virginia's Dinwiddie; but Dinwiddie rejected them and sent the hapless Acadians along northward. He had reasons. Dinwiddie could have no Frenchmen in his province, which had launched the war and was under heavy attack on its frontiers by French-directed Indians. When Virginia's quota of exiles arrived from Nova Sco-

23. Gipson, *British Empire* 6:324–32.
24. Ibid., 6:323n160.
25. Ibid., 6:288–91.

tia, Dinwiddie spent £5,000 to redeport them to England where they became a charge on the royal treasury. L. H. Gipson remarked that "this did not awaken any sentiments of gratitude on the part of His Majesty's government."[26]

In November and December 1755, 913 Acadians were debarked at Maryland's Annapolis and promptly dispersed among the eastern plantations; but no public provision was made for them except a ban on their reception by any of the province's numerous Catholics. Some humane Protestants and the "skeptic" (i.e., freethinker) Henry Callister came charitably to their aid and placed many in good homes through the winter, but Gipson remarks that the exiles "remained a dead weight upon the generosity of a few people." And Callister was not reimbursed.[27]

This sampling has been given to vivify abstractions concerning the Acadians' uprooting. It stimulates comparison with Indian treatment of captives taken in war. Those condemned to death died horribly under torture, no doubt about that, but if a captive fared well enough to be spared, he was adopted into a family and treated thereafter equally with other kinsmen. Our equivocal terminology would make the "savage" custom more "civilized" than the behavior of pious Christians.[28]

To pursue the poor refugees through all their scattered wanderings would require still another book added to the many already written about them, but our concern is only to see them as part of the scene of war. No attention has been given here to those who were transported to Pennsylvania: they became an additional issue in the great political battles between the provincial assembly and the province's proprietary party, and they will be noticed in that context further on.

Dispossession of the Micmacs

It is requisite, however, to spare some attention for the Indian allies and kinsmen of the Acadians who were equally intent on preserving identity and polity. In their case, identity was tribal. Though the Micmacs and Abenakis had become Catholics, their religion may have been more polit-

26. Ibid., 6:292–97; 302–3.

27. Ibid., 6:304–5 and n87.

28. See James Axtell, *The European and the Indian: Essays in the Ethnohistory of Colonial North America* (New York: Oxford University Press, 1981), ch. 7; idem, *The Invasion Within: The Contest of Cultures in Colonial North America* (New York: Oxford University Press, 1985), ch. 13. See also J. Norman Heard, *White into Red: A Study of the Assimilation of White Persons Captured by Indians* (Metuchen, N.J.: Scarecrow Press, 1973).

Bibliographic note: James Axtell is a foremost historian of cultural interaction in colonial North America. *The Invasion Within* is the first volume in a projected trilogy of great importance.

ical than ideological.[29] Certainly they did not cherish deep-rooted illusions about his sovereign majesty in Versailles. The Indians had their own distinct objectives in warring against Britain, parallel to rather than identical with the French war.[30] As L. F. S. Upton has remarked, "The Micmac war of resistance was a response to the extension of English settlement, not an expression of high strategic concerns."[31] The Eastern Abenakis were split; some of them tried to remain neutral, but were forced by both the French and English to take a side which, in the circumstances, had to be French. Looking ahead, we can see that the Indians' resistance ended when the fall of Louisbourg, in 1758, deprived them of a source of ammunition.[32]

In June 1761, Chief Joseph Shabecholou signed a peace treaty for his Miramichi Micmacs, promising friendship to the British, but making no mention of territorial cession.[33] A division then emerged between the concerns of the British crown and the objectives of its colonists. In December 1761 lord Halifax's hope of wooing Indians to firm alliance with Britain expressed itself in a board of trade instruction to all colonial governors to prevent Indian lands from being seized in violation of treaties. As it might seem that this instruction forestalled encroachment on the Micmacs who had so recently made peace, it posed certain problems to Nova Scotia's governor Jonathan Belcher, Jr., who had no intention of letting *his* Indians keep their lands. He resorted to a device that had precedent in the province. Obediently he issued a proclamation in accordance with the board's instruction, but he did not issue it "at large," which means, I think, that he kept it secret in Nova Scotia while reporting it ostensibly dutifully to London. Privately he argued with the board of trade that treaties with the Indians were irrelevant "since the French derived their Title from the Indians, and the French ceded their Title to the English under the Treaty of Utrecht."[34]

Of intrigue and maneuver there was a surfeit, but one fact emerges clearly from the murk: whatever the board of trade intended, the Indians lost their land. Upton remarked that "the dispossession of the Micmacs was a very rapid process," and "the spread of settlement showed that the

29. Clark, *Acadia*, 89.

30. See the discussion in Kenneth M. Morrison, *The Embattled Northeast: The Elusive Ideal of Alliance in Abenaki-Euramerican Relations* (Berkeley: University of California Press, 1984), ch. 5.

31. L. F. S. Upton, *Micmacs and Colonists: Indian-White Relations in the Maritimes, 1713–1867* (Vancouver: University of British Columbia Press, 1979), 53. It is curious that Upton, who was highly sympathetic to the Indians, should think that protection of homeland was not an expression of high strategic concerns. Cross-cultural semantics are treacherous.

32. Dean R. Snow, "Eastern Abenaki," in *Northeast*, 137–47; Upton, *Micmacs and Colonists*, 57.

33. Nova Scotia Docs., 699–700.

34. Upton, *Micmacs and Colonists*, 59–60.

Indians were accorded no overall rights to the land, and that any specific grants they claimed were more a matter of oral tradition than anything else."[35]

Nevertheless the Indians were not scattered to the far corners of the earth like the Acadians. In this situation, reliance upon the tribe proved sounder than reliance upon church or state. The tribes could not hope to defeat the overwhelming power of Britain, but they beat a retreat in as orderly a manner as the situation would permit, and they are still there.

35. L. F. S. Upton, "Indian Policy in Colonial Nova Scotia, 1783–1871," *Acadiensis* 5:1 (Autumn 1975), 4, 5.

Chapter 9 ❧ *THE BACKWOODS*

> *Necessity* will make us all forsworne
> Three thousand times within this three yeares space:
> For every man with his affects is borne,
> Not by might mastred, but by special grace.
> If I break faith, this word shall breake for me,
> I am forsworne on meere *necessitie*.
>
> *Love's Labour's Lost*, Act 1, Scene 1

It is difficult to identify with certainty the first victims of the backwoods war. A foreshadowing might be seen as early as 1745 when Peter Chartier's Shawnees plundered British traders and fled down the Ohio.[1] As noted in chapter 4, more blood was shed (Twightwee/Miami and trader blood) in 1752 when Charles Michel Langlade led Chippewas and Ottawas in their destructive attack on Pickawillany.[2] Besides forcing the Twightwees back into the French protectorate, this raid was followed by the forced flight of Pennsylvania traders over the Appalachians to refuge in the east. (Ever after, they appealed under the common name of the "Suffering Traders" for compensation from the crown, and their accounts of loss multiplied with the years.)[3]

We have seen how Washington's Virginians attacked and killed some Frenchmen in 1753, and how the French retaliated in 1754.[4] All this, however, was skirmishing. Apart from hostilities in Acadia, serious fighting started with Braddock's approach to Fort Duquesne. How were the French to respond?

1. Paul A. W. Wallace, *Indians in Pennsylvania* (Harrisburg: Pa. Historical and Museum Commission, 1961), 172.

2. Charles A. Hanna, *The Wilderness Trail* 2:289–92.

3. Abernethy, *Western Lands and the American Revolution*, see index. A number of the "Suffering Traders' " manuscript accounts are in the Etting Collection, Ohio Company, vol. 1, HSP. Trader Thomas Mitchell remarked confidentially that his accounts "will answer my own (as well as my Creditors) most Sanguine Expectations," 1:42.

4. Chap. 4, above.

"Beaucoup de ravages"

No matter how brilliantly the French fought, and allowing for the almost incredible incompetence of British commanders, the sheer mass of British resources was bound to prevail in the long run. Frenchmen in high places understood this. Some, like Intendant Bigot, piled up war profits against the day when they should return to France; for them the nation might lose, but they, individually, intended to win. Other Frenchmen, especially the Canadians who had nowhere else to go, fought doggedly on against the odds, in the desperate hope that if they held on long enough salvation would come from somewhere else. Given the circumstances, strategy could not envision the possibility of decisive battles forcing the British to give up. Complete triumphs could be no more than great forays, after which the victors must retire back to their defensive lines. The objective of such battles, besides the booty to be had, was to stall the British by throwing them into confusion, exhausting their supplies, and demoralizing their men. The French managed by such means to prevent British advance everywhere except in lost Acadia until 1758.

Because of insistence by the ministry, the set battles were fought under command of professional officers sent from France, but there was another kind of fighting, despised by the French professionals, which the Canadians had perfected for a century; and this was at least as effective as the set battles in upsetting and intimidating the British. This was Indian war, about which atrocity stories are rife and cool analyses hard to find. This chapter will present a sampling of the atrocities as germane to the general horrors of war, but it will also notice the direction and organization of Indian attacks. They did not occur at random. They were not motivated by simple bloodlust, though certainly powerful emotions were aroused by them. The raids were calculated to hit particular targets for particular reasons, and they were initiated and organized by political agreements made for rational if often delusive ends. The Indians fought for French objectives so long as they thought those were tribal objectives. When the British took the trouble to negotiate seriously with the tribes, the raids stopped, but only the beginning of that process can be noticed here; later chapters will pick up the story.

One of the highest ranking "visiting" officers was Louis Antoine de Bougainville, comte de Bougainville and aide to the marquis de Montcalm. Bougainville confided to his journal, "The cruelties and the insolence of these barbarians is horrible, their souls are as black as pitch. It is an abominable way to make war; the retaliation is frightening, and the air one breathes here is contagious of making one accustomed to callousness." A year later, his abstract sensitivity remained, but that predicted callousness had joined it in practice: "What a scourge! Humanity shudders at being obliged to make use of such monsters. But without them the match would be too much against us."[5]

To Canadian-born Governor Vaudreuil, Indian warfare was an old story. He accepted the necessity without any evident twinges of conscience. "The parties I have sent out this winter [1755–56] to harass the enemy have not been as considerable as I wished," he reported to the minister of war: "I could not do entirely as I wanted in this matter, because no fort was sufficiently supplied with provisions, and the roads have not been passable, as the season has been one of the most unsettled. Nevertheless, I calculate that, without exaggeration, the English have, since my arrival, lost one hundred men for our one." He did not bother to explain that most of the British casualties were civilians, nor did the minister of Europe's most self-consciously superior *civilisation* press him on the point. But Vaudreuil had one regret: "all those movements cannot be made without immense expense, and this is what causes me most uneasiness."[6]

At Paris there was boasting of how Vaudreuil had kept parties of Canadians and "savages" continually on campaign during the winter of 1756–57, and how they had given alarm to the British colonies by making "*beaucoup de ravages.*"[7]

Varied tribal purposes

Indian warriors rallied to the French cause and submitted to French or Canadian officers for a variety of reasons. One has been widely noticed; to wit, that the land hunger of Britain's multiplying colonials frightened Indians in general and convinced them to resist while they could. To the more remote Indians this fear was an abstraction; it was felt most keenly by the eastern tribes who had been dispossessed and displaced from their homelands, among whom the large Delaware tribe held much influence and was supported consistently by Shawnees of the Ohio region. The New England region contained remnants of formerly populous Indian nations ruined by the aggressive wars of Massachusetts and Connecticut; Catholic Abenakis had long been accustomed to taking up the French hatchet at the bidding of their missionary.[8] The Ojibwa, Ottawa, and Potawatomi

5. [L. A. de Bougainville], *Adventure in the Wilderness; The American Journals of Louis Antoine de Bougainville, 1756–1760*, tr. and ed. Edward P. Hamilton (Norman: University of Oklahoma Press, 1964), 41, 191.

6. *N.Y. Col. Docs.* 10:410–12.

7. *Relation De la Prise du Fort Georges, or Guillaume-Henry, situé sur le Lac Saint-Sacrement, et de ce qui s'est passé cette année en Canada* (Paris: Bureau d'Adresse aux Galleries du Louvre, 18 Oct. 1757), 1. (JCB.)

8. See Gordon M. Day, *The Identity of the Saint Francis Indians*, National Museum of Man Mercury series, Canadian Ethnology Service Paper 71 (Ottawa, 1981), 24–45; Cornelius J.

nations of the west—"Far Indians" to the British, "Upper Nations" to the French—were closely linked to New France by ties of trade and alliance cemented by residence and intermarriage among them by ethnic Frenchmen who often were adopted as tribal members. These Indians constituted the "Three Fires" and were regarded by the French as reliable allies.[9] Close to Quebec and Montreal were the "domiciliated" Indians of the Jesuit mission reserves, many of whom engaged in the Montreal-Albany trade; these generally followed French direction except in matters involving the Iroquois Six Nations. A large proportion of the mission Indians had migrated from Iroquoia and still felt strongly the ties of kinship, and they kept up constant communication with pro-French factions among the Iroquois. All these Indian nations, impelled by varied motives, were more or less susceptible to French coordination, but certain reservations must be made.

Chiefly these reservations or qualifications concern the Iroquois, who presented, as always, a special case. Their Covenant Chain confederation with the British and allied Indians had already become a shadow of its former self before the war broke out, (as has been shown in chapters 3 to 5 above). After Braddock's downfall the Ohio Indians joined the French, and so did many Iroquois. The Covenant Chain disintegrated completely, and the core League of the Iroquois seemed in a fair way to fall apart also, under French pressure that was real and strong.

Governor Vaudreuil left few options to the Iroquois. In October 1755, while the Delaware and Shawnee terror was launched, Vaudreuil resolved, "should any of the Five Nations be found next spring among the English, I will let loose all our Upper [western] and domiciliated Nations on them; cause their villages to be laid waste and never pardon them," and he sent this message to the Senecas and Cayugas.[10]

For the next three years, very few Iroquois (except Mohawks) aided the British, as even William Johnson was obliged to admit, while on the other hand the French records are full of notices of Iroquois warriors among French raiding parties. I cannot tell how much of this situation came about because of Vaudreuil's menace. However, two results come into view. One was a split in the League. Bougainville observed in 1757 that the Onondagas "held first place" in the League and noted as a fact "the defection of the Mohawks."[11] Obviously the split, however it was manifested, was not permanent, and it may have been a device to insure the League's survival by keeping a foot in each camp. It is also clear from Bougainville's

Jaenen, *The French Relationship with the Native Peoples of New France and Acadia* (Ottawa: Research Branch, Indian and Northern Affairs Canada, 1984), 185–90.

9. Edmunds, *Potawatomis*, chs. 1, 2; Robert E. Ritzenthaler, "Southwestern Chippewa," in *Northeast*, 743.

10. *N.Y. Col. Docs.* 10:378, 392; [Bougainville], *Adventure in the Wilderness*, 30.

11. Ibid., 102.

invaluable journal that the Iroquois were influencing French policy almost as much as the French directed the Iroquois. The great goal of all the Iroquois was to eliminate European forts and garrisons from Iroquoia. To this end, some Iroquois helped the French drive out English troops; others helped the English drive out the French. Details of these actions follow in chapters 13, 16, and 18.

Finally, the French knew better than to try to exert rigid controls over even the most willing of their allies. Persuasion and presents were essential to gain cooperation rather than obedience. "One is a slave to Indians in this country," wailed Bougainville, and in various ways he repeated the message, "in this sort of warfare it is necessary to adjust to their ways."[12] Adjustment required endless counciling and much distribution of scarce food and drink, an expense that seems to have galled Bougainville and even Vaudreuil though it certainly came to a smaller cost than paying wages to troops and their officers.

Although western Indians were used by the French as components of their major armies, and as menaces to keep the eastern tribes in line, the bands of guerilla raiders seem to have been composed in each region of Indians native to or familiar with that territory. In Acadia, the Micmacs harried British settlers. In New England, it was the Abenakis. In New York, however, the native Iroquois were outnumbered by Indians brought in from more distant tribes; but several factors made New York a special case, among them the equivocal role of the Iroquois League and the great concentration of British soldiery from Lake George through Albany along the Mohawk Valley to Oswego.

Most of the guerilla raids were launched from the Ohio region, and we need to remind ourselves yet once more that the French presence there was a military occupation of territory inhabited by Indians. The Ohio Indians had two simple options before them: they could accommodate to French rule and accept French management, or they could get along without French trade goods. In the latter case, since English traders had been driven away, the abstaining Indians would nobly starve. The nobility of such starvation was not very clear to them, so they accommodated and fought French battles. Raiding parties were organized with a Frenchman or two at the head of each, and they brought fire and slaughter to the inhabitants of Pennsylvania, Maryland, and Virginia. Motives of the Ohio Indians were mixed. They had no illusions about the significance for their own future of the massive bulk of Fort Duquesne, and it is quite evident that they would have preferred to sit out a war between Britain and France. Yet, though they were under French compulsion, they moved under a pull as well as a push. Every Delaware and Shawnee at the Ohio had

12. Ibid., 170, 37.

earlier tasted the bitterness of encroachment and dispossession by British colonials, and all had been humiliated by Iroquois arrogance backed up by the colonials. When the French organized raids after Braddock's defeat, unprecedented opportunity beckoned for revenge, and it is notable that the Germans of the Tulpehocken Valley who had driven out the "royal family" of the Delawares were among the first targets for revenge.[13] In the classic manner of imperial conquest, one victimized people set upon another and, in doing so, served the purposes of the masters. Following the same rule, the crown of England sent troops that were mostly recruited from Scotland, Ireland, and the colonies to fight the empire's battles—then called them cowards when their officers bungled.

Devastation in the backwoods

The Indian raids fanned out in all directions from the interior position of the French. From Fort Duquesne, parties of Delawares, Shawnees, and "more than sixty Indians of the Five Iroquois Nations" marched into Pennsylvania, Maryland, and "as far even as Virginia" and "committed frightful ravages."[14] Virginians looked on appalled as Braddock's successor at the Ohio, Colonel Dunbar, not only ran away with his own troops, but summoned off even the three independent companies of regulars who had been assigned to Governor Dinwiddie's command. A "general Desertion among the Provincial Troops" followed, and Virginia's back country lay exposed. Braddock had created his shambles in July of 1755; by the end of October, Dinwiddie reported that enemy Indians "had murdered and taken off about eighty of our frontier Settlers, burning and destroying their Houses, and etc."[15]

By spring of 1756, George Washington told Dinwiddie that "the Bleu-Ridge is now our Frontier," and that if the devastation were continued, "there will not be a living creature left in Frederick-County: and how soon Fairfax, and Prince William may share its fate, is easily conceived."[16] By June the settlers had withdrawn 150 miles and were still in retreat.[17]

Abandoned by their royal protector, Virginians knew where to turn.

13. *Pa. Council Minutes* 6:703–5; "Lists of Pennsylvania Settlers Murdered, Scalped and Taken Prisoners by Indians, 1755–1756," *Pa. Mag. of Hist. and Biog.* 32(1908): 309–19.

14. *N.Y. Col. Docs.* 10:408, 423.

15. Dinwiddie to R. H. Morris, 31 Oct. 1755, mss., BR Box 257(4), Brock Collection, HEH.

16. Winchester, 27 Apr. 1756, *The Papers of George Washington, Colonial Series*, eds. W. W. Abbot et al. (Charlottesville: University Press of Virginia, 1983–) 3:58–62.

17. Rev. James Maury quoted in Richard L. Morton, *Colonial Virginia*, 2 vols. published for the Virginia Historical Society (Chapel Hill: University of North Carolina Press, 1960) 2:680–81.

Washington urged that "there should be neither trouble nor expence omitted to bring the few [Indians] who are still inclined into our Service, and that too with the greatest care and expedition."[18] The government shared his desire, and anticipated it by treaties with the Catawba and Cherokee tribes to "wage war with all their Power against the French King, and all his Indian Allies."[19] These attitudes and actions by one of the most belligerent colonies become especially significant in comparison with what happened in Pennsylvania when Quakers proposed Indian treaties to pacify that province's frontiers. (Compare chapters 15 and 17 below.)

Virginia's provincial troops suffered as much, it seems, as the civilians. Besides the casualties of combat, the First Virginia Regiment was exposed (in 1758) to "such bitter winter cold that some of them froze to death." They served more than two years without a complete change of clothing. Many had to be hospitalized after returning to Virginia.[20] These veterans, by the way, were explicit in their understanding of war goals. Their officers remonstrated to Governor Dinwiddie, "The idle argument which is often used, namely, you are defending your Country and property; is justly look'd upon as inapplicable and absurd. We are defending part of the Domain of Great Britain."[21]

The strategy's effectiveness

Three small forts in Pennsylvania were destroyed. An abstract of despatches from Canada for the winter of 1755–56 boasted that "the French and Indians have, since Admiral Braddock's defeat, disposed of more than 700 people in the Provinces of Pennsylvania, Virginia and Carolina, including those killed and those taken prisoners."[22]

In New York, a party of unidentified Indians took twenty scalps and five prisoners "at the gates" of Oswego, and a surprise attack overwhelmed the defenders of Fort Bull along the supply line to Oswego.[23] At Fort Bull the assailants "put every one to the sword they could lay hands on. One woman and a few soldiers only were fortunate enough to escape the fury of our troops." And a rather embarrassed admission: "Some pretend that only one prisoner was made during this action."[24]

18. *Washington Papers, Col. Ser.*, ed. Abbot, 3:59.
19. 21 Feb. 1756 and 7 Mar. 1756, "A Treaty Between Virginia and the Catawbas and Cherokees, 1756," *Va. Mag. of Hist. and Biog.* 13:3(Jan. 1906): 225–64.
20. Gipson, *British Empire* 7:295.
21. [16 Apr.?] 1757, *Writings of Washington*, ed. Fitzpatrick 2:26.
22. *N.Y. Col. Docs.* 10:423.
23. Ibid., 10:416, 403.
24. Ibid., 404.

New England seems to have suffered less, perhaps because of better preparations for defense, but the outlying settlers were so intimidated that they had not yet begun sowing their fields as late as June 1756.[25]

The foregoing information, including many expressions of satisfaction, comes from French reports. They also include perfunctory pious remarks about how the French officers tried to persuade the "savages" to minimize "murder," but it is hard to take such comment seriously. The policy and strategy motivating such conduct was deliberate state terrorism. However much it might be excused by arguments of military necessity, no amount of rhetorical hypocrisy can mask its cruelty—or, to use a term often employed in another direction, its *savagery*.[26]

The policy was highly effective in several ways. As intended, it staggered the British advance, and as a side effect, it dealt a heavy blow at the economy. Allowing for probable exaggeration in Vaudreuil's report of 700 British colonials "disposed of," the quality of such casualties multiplied their impact far beyond comparable losses in set battles. Men lost in combat were, almost by definition, nonessential to the economy: they had become soldiers because they could be spared from production. But the destruction of whole families and their working farms eliminated a substantial component of British production besides providing plunder to alleviate Canadian scarcity. Pennsylvania's John Harris summarized tersely: "should but a company of Indians come and Murder but a few Families hereabouts, which is daily expected, the situation we are in would oblige numbers to abandon their Places, and our Cattle and Provisions, which we have plenty of, must then fall a prey to the Enemy." He added that large numbers of families fleeing from attacks at the headwaters of the Potomac River were already passing by his community of Paxton on the Susquehanna.[27]

Rage of the refugees

Such flight weakened the steadfastness of the few Indians remaining loyal to the British. At the first news of the ravages in Pennsylvania's backwoods, the mixed Indians at Shamokin (Sunbury) at the forks of the Sus-

25. Ibid., 427.

26. An apocryphal French document boasts in detail of an attack by Vaudreuil on an island called "Manton," identified as "the capital of Canada, belonging to the English," 18 July 1756. This is a fabrication apparently based on the French capture of Port Mahon in Minorca, but it has some significance as expression of an attitude; according to this paper, Vaudreuil personally ordered the garrison of "Manton" "put to the sword" and all the inhabitants "slaughtered and burned." *N.Y. Col. Docs.* 10:429–30 and n. The paper's tone is boastful.

27. *Pa. Council Minutes* 6:645–46.

quehanna told Conrad Weiser that they wanted to fight, but needed arms and colonial reinforcements; they were "extremely concerned for the white people's running away, and said they could not stand the French alone."[28]

The refugees rushed to the safety of towns, where they became consuming liabilities instead of producing assets. Their flight created panic and demoralization, and their natural fury created new political situations that troubled government and handicapped efforts to cope with the raids. The atrocities roused undiscriminating race hatred that played into the French hand by frightening off the remaining Indian allies capable of resisting guerilla war. Even before the raids began in Pennsylvania, Conrad Weiser reported, "our People are very malicious against *Our* Indians; they curse and damn 'em to their Faces and say, 'must we feed You [wives and children] and your Husbands fight in the meantime for the French,' &ca."[29] Moravian bishop Spangenberg was obliged to defend his Indian converts against malicious charges of coming and going among the French. Certainly some had come to Bethlehem and left later, but it was "mistaken" to think they aided the French. They had put themselves under English protection in Bethlehem and "afterwards had their Houses at Gnadenhütten [mission] burnt, their Provisions destroyed, and their Horses carried away . . . For these very same Indians were, as well as all other Men in Bethlehem, continually employed in the Time of War, in keeping Watch, &c., and kept about Bethlehem for fear of being hurted by others, or of frightening them. And when Peace was a making they were our Watchmen in the Harvest-Time, or they set themselves to work, Which is so notorious, than on Occasion one could bring One Hundred Evidences to prove it."[30]

Through speaker Isaac Norris, the assembly observed that "the Indians who are still inclined to preserve their alliance with us, seem equally terrified lest the remote Inhabitants and the English generally, should revenge upon them the barbarities committed by parties of the Delawares and Shawanese Indians."[31]

Refugees perceived the enemy as the demons who had tomahawked their kin and neighbors, and devastated their homes. In this perception the French instigators faded off behind the screen of monsters of a race other than human. Refugees did not want to hear of proposals to solve problems or negotiate agreements with the Indians whose land many of the refugees had been occupying. Reasoned discussion became irrelevant to the emotions of people who had fled from the storm. Government

28. Ibid., 6:649–50.
29. Ibid., 6:494–95.
30. "Joseph" Spangenberg to R. Peters, Bethlehem, Pa., 31 July 1758, in *Pa. Archives* (1)3:500–501.
31. *Pa. Council Minutes* 6:677–78.

understood the necessity of negotiation to win tribes away from French alliance, but refugees wanted hot revenge.

Not all powerful men were disturbed by this obstruction to a steady course. In heavily afflicted Pennsylvania the proprietary's men seized upon the grief and rage of the refugees as a club for beating the assembly, but this phenomenon must be postponed to a following chapter. Another consequence must also be set aside for the moment; that is, how the war changed meaning in the minds of persons who had previously been far from enthusiastic about what they saw as the crown's war for the crown's empire, and no pressing concern of their own. The firestorm in the backwoods sent that conception up in smoke.

Captives of Indians

Here, however, we consider another class of backwoods victims—the survivors who did not escape to refuge—the captives.

Let me stress that the sources consulted for this section are a random sample rather than a comprehensive survey of types. Yet certain specific data reported in them can be accepted confidently for the purpose of this book—at minimum in their demonstration of the variety of captivity experiences and individual responses. A certain number of prisoners from every raid were taken back to their captors' villages for torture and conspicuous murder.[32] If taken by western tribesmen, some of the captives might be killed and eaten.[33] They were probably luckier than the unfortunates reserved for slow torture, which was always as cruel as the captors' imaginations could devise.

Reliable statistics are impossible to compile, but captivity narratives

32. E.g., see "Thomas Gist's Indian Captivity, 1758–1759," ed. Howard H. Peckham, *Pa. Mag. of Hist. and Biog.* 80:3 (July 1956): 285–311.

33. The ritual of cannibalism requires careful distinctions. It was not "Indian" because many tribes did not practice it at any recorded time, the Delawares among them. Indeed the contemptuous Delaware name for Mohawks was *Maqua* meaning "man-eaters." By mid-eighteenth century, eastern tribes generally had abandoned the practice if ever they had indulged in it. But the fact of cannibalism among some tribes is indisputable. See the many index references in *The Jesuit Relations and Allied Documents: Travels and Explorations of the Jesuit Missionaries in New France, 1610–1791* 1896–1901), ed. Reuben Gold Thwaites, 73 vols. reprinted facsimile in 36 vols. (New York: Pageant Book Co., 1959). A 1757 example is in 70:125–29. Other examples of the period are in *The Siege of Detroit in 1763: The Journal of Pontiac's Conspiracy and John Rutherfurd's Narrative of a Captivity*, ed. Milo Milton Quaife, Lakeside Classics (Chicago: R. R. Donnelley and Sons, 1958), 135–36, 143, 229, 234–35. Incidentally, cannibalism was not unknown among colonial captives starving in the woods after escape, but this was a matter of desperation rather than ritual. Isaac Hollister, *A Brief Narration of the Captivity of Isaac Hollister, Who was taken by the Indians, Anno Domini, 1763* (1767), reprinted facsimile in *The Garland Library*, comp. Wilcomb E. Washburn, 10: separately paged 3–6.

generally give the impression that most prisoners were kept alive after ritual hazing that ranged from mere formality to severe brutality. The material motive of ransom saved many a life. Others were preserved by an odd mix, peculiar to Indian cultures, of humanity and acquisitiveness. These captives were preserved for adoption into Indian families to replace dead kin. The warrior who had taken a prisoner might keep him as personal property or accept him as a brother. Or he might offer the prisoner to the village, in which case any woman had undisputed right to claim the captive for adoption.[34]

Adoptees were not selected wholly at random. Old and infirm prisoners were rejected at sight; their chances of survival were small, and it is easy to understand why. The Indian family was an all-purpose institution for economic production and mutual support; few families welcomed the burden of complete strangers incapable of supporting themselves. The additional factor of psychological malleability told in favor of the young who might be expected to acculturate more readily than mature adults already set in their ways. In general, it appears also that women were more likely than men to be made captive and adopted, on the same assumption that they would be more docile than men. Though not always correct, these assumptions seem to have been well grounded. What a prospective Indian adopter preferred most of all was a male or female adolescent, strong enough to work, young enough to be molded into tribal ways, and attractive in person (but not necessarily according to European notions of beauty). Indentured servants were great prizes because so many of them gladly adopted Indian freedom in lieu of their hard work and punishments as servants. Young women accustomed to male domination at home were likely to respond favorably to their higher status in Indian societies.

Despite the fixed notion common among colonials that Indians were uniformly hideous, many young women found Indian men attractive enough to make good husbands, sometimes several in succession.[35] Others were grateful for not being sexually molested; Marie Le Roy and Barbara Leininger preferred to go off with their Indian captors rather than remain at the mercy of the French garrison at Fort Duquesne.[36]

Young male captives were not all averse to the charms of Indian women.

34. Titus King, *Narrative of Titus King of Northampton, Mass.: A Prisoner of the Indians in Canada, 1755–1758* (1938), reprinted facsimile in *Garland Library* 109, separately paged; [Hugh Gibson], "An Account of the Captivity," 141–53; Examination of John Baker, 31 Mar. 1756, mss., Penn Mss., Indian Affairs 2:78, HSP; Deposition of John Craig, 30 Mar. 1756, loc. cit.

35. James E. Seaver, *A Narrative of the Life of Mrs. Mary Jemison, Who was taken by the Indians in the year 1755 when only about twelve years of age, and has continued to reside amongst them to the present time* (1824), reprinted (New York: American Scenic and Historic Preservation Society, 1950).

36. "The Narrative of Marie Le Roy and Barbara Leininger, for Three Years Captives among the Indians," (1759) tr. Edmund de Schweinitz, *Pa. Mag. of His. and Biog.* 29 (1905):411.

In old age, one former captive remembered with a twinkle what had happened when the Shawnee braves of his community marched east for a new campaign; he left his Indian family "in the country" for a sojourn in the village so suddenly bereft of young men, and he returned to the country, in discretion or exhaustion, just before the warriors came back. It was the very stuff of adolescent daydreams.[37]

Yet the pull of his nativity drew him eventually to escape. His casual remark demands thought: "I was determined to be what I really was."[38] Indians understood that pull, and watched their new kin carefully. Captives overtly resisting acculturation were threatened and punished as well as cajoled and caressed. Despite all care, a certain number managed to elude guards and make their way back to what they still saw as their own people, sometimes hundreds of miles through woods and swamps, evading pursuit, enduring semi-starvation and the hazards of a nature that was not benign.[39]

For others, however, the moment of return came when the war ended and peace treaties were concluded. There are enigmatic features in these treaties for, as a rule, they speak only of *return* of captives among the Indians. Only rarely does a phrase mention *exchange* of Indians held by the colonials. Were the Indians so agile that none was caught, even when seriously wounded? Or did the spirit of Culloden dictate treatment of captured warriors? Or what?

"*White Indians*"

It is observable that the behavior of neither captives nor captors was uniformly racial, regardless of the participants' perceptions in terms of race. Explanation by race is refuted first by the indisputable fact of assimilation of many captives into the culture and society of their captors; still more plainly by the refusal of so many to return to their families and communities of origin at the end of hostilities. These facts shocked and bewildered many contemporary Euramericans—"Whites" in self-conception—precisely because such a process could not be reconciled to conceptions of inherent "racial" constitutions and attitudes. Unable to forsake dogma, the "Whites" invented the term "White Indians" as though such scandalous persons were freak mutations. We know better now. Given certain conditions, their behavior was predictably normal. Children reared in colonial families by the rule of the rod can surely be forgiven for preferring to grow under the Indian regimen of persuasion and exclusively

37. "Thomas Gist's Indian Captivity," 301.
38. Ibid., 302.
39. See the narratives of Hugh Gibson and Marie Le Roy and Barbara Leininger.

verbal correction. Adolescents driven by sex urges were allowed in Indian villages to experiment with each other instead of being punished by whip and pillory for the same sort of conduct in colonial towns. Indian women did not have to endure beatings from their men, nor to obey their husbands' orders. And work, for all Indians, did not imply grinding exhaustion after long hours of monotonous toil. When the horror and trauma of initial capture had faded into memory, many captives perceived life among their Indian families and friends to be better *for them*—never mind theology and ideology—than the life left behind in the colonies, and they opted rationally for a change of cultures in their own self-interest. Those who made that judgment tried to evade compulsory return. When forced "home," many escaped back to their Indian families.

Some poor souls remained torn between the two cultures their whole lives long, identified with both, yet alienated from both. For them, no treaty could bring peace.[40]

Atrocity by the British

The British founded strategy on their advantage in resources, aiming to go beyond harassment to ultimate seizure of the enemy's citadels, but British brass was as indifferent as the French to principles of humanity. True, British officers fumed in outrage against the atrocities committed under French direction, but the same officers organized "rangers," including a company of Stockbridge warriors, to commit the same sort of atrocities; in this respect, the difference between the two high commands showed chiefly in that the French were better at it and had more Indians on their side. As early as 1755, General Shirley instructed the commander of "Roberts' Rangers" to "distress the French and their allies, by sacking, burning, and destroying their houses, barns, barracks, canoes, battoes, &c. and by killing their cattle of every kind; and at all times to endeavour to way-lay, attack, and destroy their convoys of provisions by land and water, in any part of the country."[41] Obviously such instructions could

40. E.g., *History of the Capture and Captivity of David Boyd from Cumberland County, Pennsylvania* (1931), ed. Marion Morse, in *The Garland Library* 109, separately paged, esp. 38–39; John Ingles, Sr., *The Story of Mary Draper Ingles and Son Thomas Ingles*, eds. Roberta Ingles Steele and Andrew Lewis Ingles (Radford, Va.: Commonwealth Press, 1969). Bibliographic note: Because a profitable market has existed for captivity narratives, the reader must guard against the sensational fictionalized variety. Two examples will serve: Peter Williamson, *French and Indian Cruelty; Exemplified in the Life and various Vicissitudes of Fortune of Peter Williamson, A Disbanded Soldier* (1757), in *The Garland Library* 9, separately paged; "Affecting History of the Dreadful Distresses of Frederic Manheim's Family . . ." in *Held Captive by Indians: Selected Narratives, 1642–1836*, ed. Richard Van Der Beets (Knoxville: University of Tennessee Press, 1973), 202–42. Editor comments on unreliability (203).

41. Robert Rogers, *Journals of Major Robert Rogers* (1765), reprinted facsimile (Readex Microprint, 1966), 15.

not be carried out without eliminating the obstructive persons attached to houses, barns, convoys, and so on.

As for the Indian enemy, New England had long been in the business of buying Indian scalps. In this war, even Pennsylvania's governor Morris proclaimed scalp bounties. Retaliating for Indian attacks on backwoods homesteads, Pennsylvania's John Armstrong surprised the Delaware village of Kittanning and burned residents in their own houses;[42] and Robert Rogers massacred the families of the Abenaki Catholic mission village of St. Francis.[43] Though the dimensions of this counter-terror do not begin to match the massive French operations that served as its excuse, it was the same thing in principle, and we may note that the depraved Rogers was lionized in London when he published his boasting *Journals* there.[44]

A question may also be raised about the smallpox epidemics that took great toll of Indians during the war, naturally without discriminating warriors from noncombatants. It cannot be disputed that epidemics often accompany war as the natural consequence of demographic turmoil, but a remnant of suspicion remains as to the origins of the disease at this time. There is on record a fully documented case of deliberate British infection of enemy Indians with smallpox at Fort Pitt in 1763, several years later than the period now under discussion but involving many of the same combatants. (See chapter 20, below.) My point is that the deed then, though ordered from above, was actually performed before the orders arrived, on the initiative of someone in the besieged fort. It seems that germ warfare was not unthinkable to soldiers of that era.[45] I can add nothing definite to that finding except that smallpox made many casualties in the backwoods, possibly more than deaths in battle, but quantification is impossible. Nobody counted the victims. We have only general reports of epidemics, begin-

42. John Armstrong, "Scheme of expedition to Kittanning," 1756, Miscellaneous Manuscripts, APS; Armstrong's report, 14 Sept. 1756, in *Pa. Council Minutes* 7:257–63. The report acknowledges heavy loss without numbering; the Delawares reported 40 of Armstrong's men killed compared to 14 of their own, but Kittanning was burned to the ground. "Captivity of Hugh Gibson," 143; "Narrative of Marie Le Roy and Barbara Leininger," 410.

43. Roberts Rogers, *Journals*, 146–47. Perhaps it would be better to say that Rogers *tried* to massacre, though there seems no doubt that he killed indiscriminately. He gave the figure of 200 Indians killed, but French sources allowed only 20. See Day, *Identity of the Saint Francis Indians*, 43–45; and Gordon M. Day, "Rogers' Raid in Indian Tradition," *Historical New Hampshire* 17 (1962), 3–17. Thanks to Colin Calloway for this.

On the other hand, Rogers's own casualties were dreadful. An admiring romantic writer acknowledges that 200 men marched out with Rogers, of whom 41 were lost in less than six days. Another 49 succumbed on the return from St. Francis amid sufferings so terrible that they cannibalized corpses. John R. Cuneo, *Robert Rogers of the Rangers* (New York: Oxford University Press, 1959), ch. 9.

44. Editor's foreword, Rogers, *Journals*.

45. Details in ch. 20, below. I have been surprised by an account of the Iroquois practicing bacteriological warfare by corrupting with animal carcasses the drinking water of British troops. Jaenen, *French Relationship*, 168, quoting from Charlevoix.

ning among the Canadian Indians in 1756, spreading to the Iroquois in 1757, and to the "Farr Indians" after the fall of Fort William Henry in 1757, and reported from forts in western Maryland and Pennsylvania in 1758.[46] These appeared while I searched for other types of information. It seems likely by the nature of the disease that more data could be compiled by directed research.

Massacre of friendly Indians

It is difficult also to get a true understanding of Indian losses from what may be called lynching parties. The raids by hostile Indians so inflamed emotions among the back settlers that they were ready to kill any Indian, foe or friend, and this fury had political implications. At least one example of a lynching, and another of an intended massacre, were recorded in Pennsylvania. (I have not searched for others elsewhere. Perhaps there were none, though that seems unlikely.)

On 14 December 1763, fifty-seven Scotch-Irish Presbyterian men from Paxton on the Susquehanna River rode to Conestoga where they shot and hacked six peaceful Indians to death. These were remnants of the Susquehanna-Conestoga tribe, one of whom still held the tribe's 1701 treaty with William Penn. Ostensibly the "Paxton Boys" were revenging Indian raids of Pontiac's War—an Indian war that flared up after the Seven Years War and was a continuation of it—but Pontiac's War had claimed no victims in eastern Pennsylvania.

Provincial Governor John Penn (great nephew of William Penn) issued a proclamation for the arrest and punishment of the lynchers, which was ignored although their identity was no secret. The magistrates of Lancaster collected the remaining Conestogas into the public workhouse in order to protect them. Their act merely made the next slaughter easier by bringing all its intended victims together, and the Paxton Boys struck again, 27 December, sparing no one. Notably, the protection promised to the Indians failed to appear.

Meantime, some converted Delawares of the Moravian mission were killed, and the rest lived under threat from surrounding colonials of the

46. *Johnson Papers* 2:503, 727; 9:412, 800, 813, 820; [Henry Bouquet]. *The Papers of Henry Bouquet*, eds. S. K. Stevens, et al. (Harrisburg: Pennsylvania Historical and Museum Commission, 1951–) 2:61, 89, 96; Laura E. Conkey, Ethel Boissevain, and Ives Goddard, "Indians of Southern New England and Long Island, Late Period," *Northeast*, 185; Thomas Hutchinson, *The History of the colony and Province of Massachusetts-Bay* 1764–1828), ed. Lawrence Shaw Mayo, 3 vols. Cambridge, Mass.: Harvard University Press, 1936) 3:38–39. See also Map 32, "Epidemics," and accompanying text in Helen Tanner, Adele Hast, and Jacqueline Peterson, *Atlas of Great Lakes Indian History* (Norman: University of Oklahoma Press, 1986).

"Irish Settlement" in the Delaware Valley. For protection the converts were withdrawn to Province Island at Philadelphia. These Indians, by the way, had incurred the contempt of other Delawares by becoming pacifists. It is not necessary to detail how they were chivvied about; the essential point is that the Paxton Boys recruited many new followers and rode under arms to Philadelphia.

Moravian missionary John Heckewelder remarked their political purpose:

> Although at first it was believed, that the only object of the rioters was the destruction of all the Indians, under the idea that they were descendants of the Canaanites, who, by God's commandment, were to be cut off from the face of the earth; it soon became evident that they aimed at nothing short of overturning the whole form of government. Their design appearing now to be; first to cause a general consternation, thereby spreading devastation and misery over the country, and then to take the reins of government into their own hands.

A great many young men of Philadelphia rallied to defend the Indians and the city (including Quakers who hardly knew one end of a gun from the other). Fortunately Mr. Franklin persuaded the Paxton Boys that the odds were against them, so these heroes returned home. But they claimed victims nevertheless. In the Moravian converts' close confinement, fifty-six sickened and died. After peace returned, they journeyed back to Bethlehem, saw the destruction of their villages, and traveled on to seek refuge in the Ohio country. Instead, however, these Christian pacifists met martyrdom there in a massacre by frontiersmen who professed a "higher Christianity."[47]

Bloodshed, "civilized" and "savage"

In trying to picture a war, it is always difficult to penetrate beyond the atrocity stories to what actually happened. In the Seven Years War, atroc-

47. Franklin wrote an unusually impassioned account of the Paxton Boys in *A Narrative of the Late Massacres, in Lancaster County* . . . (1764), reprinted with notes in *Franklin Papers* 11:42–69. Readers with a taste for alibis will find a smarmy assortment in *The Paxton Papers*, ed. John R. Dunbar (The Hague: Martinus Nijhoff, 1957). The coolest, most straightforward description is in John Heckewelder's *Narrative of the Mission* . . . (1820), extracted in *Thirty Thousand Miles with John Heckewelder*, ed. Paul A. W. Wallace (Pittsburgh: University of Pittsburgh Press, 1958), chs. 6, 12; quotation at p. 80. For Pontiac's war, see ch. 20 below.

Bibliographic note: John Heckewelder's writings are among the most authentic sources for Indian history and culture during his lifetime. Parkman denounced them because Heckewelder's facts exposed Parkman's falsehoods. Paul Wallace deserves historians' gratitude for making Heckewelder easily available again, and Pittsburgh University Press has reissued Wallace's compilation in paperback as *The Travels of John Heckewelder in Frontier America* (1985).

ity was as rife and as real as in any other war, but the glare of its accounts tends to throw other facts into shade. When the casualties are totted up, imperfect as the statistics are, it is evident that the greatest losses were suffered by the men recruited or impressed to fight. Exceptions ought perhaps to be allowed for the Indian villages smitten by smallpox, and the civilians of Quebec pounded under incessant cannon fire; but otherwise the casualties in the successive battles fought at Lake George, not to speak of the men who succumbed to hardship and disease in camp and on the march, seem to have outnumbered greatly the horrors in the backwoods. These military casualties, with certain exceptions, have not carried the emotional impact of the Indian raids reported in sensational (and sometimes exaggerated) detail; but the men who perished in "civilized" war (and the women and children of Quebec) became just as dead and often just as painfully as the backwoods settlers who went down under Indian hatchets. A kind of horrific glamour casts the backwoods casualties in the mold of savagery while Wolfe and Montcalm, who devastated and destroyed on the grand scale, have become martyrs instead of blackguards. Because they were "civilized."

Chapter 10 ❧ *IGNORANT ARMIES*

War, which is much more than the sum total of battles on land and sea, may well be described as a ravaging disease in the body of human society . . .

Douglas Edward Leach, *Arms for Empire*

And we are here as on a darkling plain
Swept with confused alarms of struggle and flight,
Where ignorant armies clash by night.

Matthew Arnold, *Dover Beach*

*It seems almost miraculous that so tremendous a historical phe-*nomenon as the Seven Years War could even come into existence when so many discrete and discordant forces were at work.* Perhaps this is true of all large-scale events. A natural response by the historian is to simplify them as abstract trends and tendencies, but that would be an evasion of empirical fact. People, in the aggregate, make trends and tendencies; and abstractions are exactly what the term itself says—concepts abstracted from phenomena. Abstractions act upon people only within their minds. However much an abstract idea may contribute to motivation, the decision to act, and to act in a particular way, is a person's decision, not an abstraction's; and it is always jumbled together with all the rest of what is going on in that person's head to make the logic of a life. When decisions are concerned with what one *ought* to do, or refrain from doing, we call them moral, but the abstractions of moral preachment cannot be relied upon for understanding moral culture. What people do is infinitely more revealing of their true beliefs than what they say.

It is therefore wholly inadequate to study the generals' expressions of horror at Indian-style warfare. It is necessary to examine what those generals did and ordered done. We have seen already how French commanders used Indians as instruments of terroristic strategy against civilians.

*Research for this chapter was done to prepare the paper, "Militarism and the Puritans," for the Symposium on Military History at Texas A & M University, 22 Apr. 1985. The chapter is not the same as that essay.

British generals were equally devoted to the strategy of terror, but they had fewer Indian allies so they used other means.

One of their cruelest commanders was General James Wolfe who had trained at Culloden and on "police duty" in the Scottish Highlands.[1] Wolfe's glamorous aura in the schoolbooks dims greatly when exposed to the facts of his commands. In 1758, while General Amherst laid siege to Louisbourg on Cape Breton Island, Brigadier Wolfe ranged over the Gaspé peninsula, destroying whatever he reached, and when he acquired independent command of the siege of Quebec he ordered scouting parties "to burn and lay waste the country."[2] The artillery officer who offhandedly reported these data was with Wolfe at Quebec; looking upon the city for the first time, he saw "a very fair object," but it was fair "for our artillery."[3] He observed later that "the British batteries wrought more destruction than the French because they were directed against the buildings of the town"—that is, civilians—and he observed later that "the havoc is not to be conceived . . . its streets are almost impassible."[4] Because the citadel was on Quebec's heights above the reach of British artillery, the cannon were aimed where they could hit. This was done with full knowledge that the targets were not "military," and of course it was done by Wolfe's order.[5]

Terrorism by authority was the order of the day. When the inhabitants of Quebec wanted to capitulate to escape the terrible bombardment, Montcalm and Vaudreuil, who were secure in their citadel, threatened to turn Indians upon the hapless civilians.[6] Quebec's people knew that the military and clergy had done just that in Acadia. In 1759, General Amherst informed the French commanders that he would kill two French prisoners for every British woman or child scalped by the French or their allies.[7]

Other examples may be deferred for consideration in chronological context. Our subject in this chapter is not so much what the armies did as

1. Gipson, *British Empire* 7:373; Prebble, *Culloden*, 101.

2. Captain John Knox, *An Historical Journal of the Campaigns in North America For the Years 1757, 1758, 1759, and 1760* (London, 1769), reprint ed. Arthur G. Doughty, 3 vols., Publications of the Champlain Society 8, 9, 10 (Toronto, 1914–16) 1:274, 438.

3. Ibid., 1:411.

4. Ibid., 2:133n3, 135. "It would be impossible to describe the miserable state of the city; near one third of the houses were reduced to ashes, and what remained were so shattered by the cannon during our besieging it, that very few were fit to be inhabited." "Letter from an Officer of the Royal American Regiment," Quebec, 24 May 1760, *Gentleman's Magazine* 30 (July 1760) 311–15. Frégault, *Canada*, 251–52.

5. Wolfe reported to Pitt that the lower town had been "entirely destroyed," although "the business of an assault would be little advanced by that." 2 Sept. 1759, in *Gentleman's Magazine* 29 (Oct. 1759) 467, 469.

6. Knox, *Historical Journal* 1:441; 2:251.

7. Thomas Mante, *The History of the Late War in North-America, and the Islands of the West-Indies, including the Campaigns of 1763 and 1764 against his Majesty's Indian Enemies* (London: W. Strahan and T. Codell, 1772), 207. (JCB.)

what they were, for which purpose Stephen Saunders Webb is concise: "The essential element in the definition of empire is the imposition of state control on dependent peoples by force. The instrument of that imposition is the army. There are no empires without armies."[8] But despite drill and regimentation, the human material composing armies never reduces quite to homogeneity. The men of the armies of the Seven Years War were an especially motley lot who behaved in very different ways according to their different origins and cultural assumptions.

British regulars

The basic instrument of British imperialists was the *regular* army sent from the British isles and controlled directly by the crown's officers. From the time of their arrival, the regulars annoyed, exasperated, and finally enraged the colonials. Benjamin Franklin said it succinctly: imperialist though he was, he could not stomach the precipitate retreat of Braddock's defeated army which prompted the remark in his *Autobiography* that the retreating commander "was requested to afford some protection to the inhabitants; but he continu'd his hasty march thro' all the country, not thinking himself safe till he arriv'd at Philadelphia, where the inhabitants could protect him."[9] Even before the disaster, Braddock had treated the Virginia regiment so arrogantly that " 'no person of any property, family or worth' had since enlisted in it," so Dinwiddie had been obliged to fill up new companies with Scots.[10]

Franklin was far from enamored with those British regulars even at their pre-battle bravest and showiest. "In their first march, too, from their landing till they got beyond the settlements, they had plundered and stripped the inhabitants, totally ruining some poor families, besides insulting, abusing, and confining the people if they remonstrated. This was enough to put us out of conceit of such defenders if we had really wanted any."[11] Such conduct was not permitted to troops in Britain except when putting down rebellion. Franklin's remark reveals that Braddock's regulars conceived themselves to be in an alien land, officers and men alike. The inhabitants saw in such troops a confirmation of their tradi-

8. Stephen Saunders Webb, *The Governors-General: The English Army and the Definition of the Empire*, published for the Institute of Early American History and Culture (Chapel Hill: University of North Carolina Press, 1979), xvii.

9. Franklin, *Autobiography*, 225–26.

10. Richard L. Morton, *Colonial Virginia*, 2 vols., published for the Virginia Historical Society (Chapel Hill: University of North Carolina Press, 1960) 2:687–88.

11. Franklin, *Autobiography*, 226.

tional fear of standing armies.[12] So early did Americans vaguely begin to perceive the crown's forces as an army of occupation—corrupt police rather than liberating heroes.

British provincials

Antagonisms prevailed not only between the regulars and civilians, but also between provincial troops and regular men in arms. The regulars were contemptuous of provincial slovenliness, and the provincials were aghast at the cruelty of disciplinary measures among the regulars. Undeniably the provincials lacked discipline. Equally without doubt, the lack was harmful to themselves. Men pitched their tents any which way and wherever they pleased. They located latrines for convenience rather than sanitation, right in the midst of camp, and they dug wells close by. Nature did not suspend her laws in deference to democracy, so the casualty lists were frightful before ever an enemy came in sight. Many more men sickened and died in the midst of their own filth in camp than were struck down in battle. The casualty lists were the strongest imaginable argument against military democracy. "At its worst," writes Fred Anderson, "life during the late campaigns was routinely riskier than it had been during the worst epidemics in New England's history."[13]

The same lack of discipline prevailed on the march and in combat. Although highest commanders were appointed by assemblies (much to the chagrin of royal governors) the troops elected their company officers who were never allowed to forget that another election could displace them. The consequence was that "orders" took on the qualities of persuasion and cajolery rather than command.[14] Disgusted British officers would not trust provincials with responsibility. As one lieutenant colonel explained, the Americans were "sufficient to work our Boats, drive our Waggons, to fell Trees, and do the Works that in inhabited Countrys are performed by peasants."[15] Such treatment did not contribute to cordiality between Britons and Americans.

The worst offenders against discipline were the glamorous rangers, the

12. John Shy, *Toward Lexington: The Role of the British Army in the Coming of the American Revolution* (Princeton, N.J.: Princeton University Press, 1965), 47; see John Phillip Reid, *In Defiance of the Law: The Standing Army Controversy, the Two Constitutions, and the Coming of the American Revolution* (Chapel Hill: University of North Carolina Press, 1981).

13. Fred Anderson, *A People's Army: Massachusetts Soldiers and Society in the Seven Years' War*, published for the Institute of Early American History and Culture (Chapel Hill: University of North Carolina Press, 1984), 90–107; quotation at p. 101.

14. Leach, *Arms for Empire*, 254, 360; Anderson, *People's Army*, 47–48, 125–27.

15. Shy, *Toward Lexington*, 100.

elite corps of scouts and guerillas whose services were so necessary that they did as they pleased without fear of retribution.[16] This situation contradicted British officers' expectations. The neat plans laid in England had assumed that American recruits generally would be good marksmen with experienced skill in woodland warfare, but the provincial recruits turned out to be mostly plowboys and drifters, younger sons and recent immigrants who had never spent a night in the woods. In an ambush they panicked disastrously.[17] To do the job for which they had proved incompetent, the rangers were recruited; but the rangers understood only too well how necessary they were, and they thumbed their noses at authority.[18]

Discipline by torture

In contrast, the regulars performed in orderly fashion according to the training manuals that British officers had to know, but the price of discipline was atrocious. The regulars were literally whipped into shape. For infractions of discipline, a common sentence was 300 lashes on the offender's bare back, laid on with a cat-o'-nine-tails. Punishments short of death for enlisted men (officers were exempt from corporal punishment) included such as 2,000 lashes for stealing from a sutler, 1,000 lashes for refusing to turn out with the guard, 1,000 lashes for being drunk and asleep on sentry duty, 1,000 lashes for stealing a greatcoat from an officer, 1,000 lashes for stealing twenty dollars from a dead man, 1,000 lashes for stealing a pound of butter, 1,000 lashes for stealing a shirt.[19] Punishments were inflicted as publicly as possible, always in front of a formation of the offender's own unit. Care was taken to keep him alive because of the expense of recruiting a replacement. A physician attended to resuscitate him if he fainted, and to postpone completion of the punishment if too much blood flowed. The whole performance was intentionally horrific, designed to make the common soldier fear his officers more than the enemy. It accomplished that end, but its unintended by-product was intense hatred of the whole British system by observing colonials.[20]

16. Stanley McCrory Pargellis, *Lord Loudoun in North America*, Yale Historical Publications, Studies 7 (New Haven, Conn.: Yale University Press, 1933), 303–4. Commander in chief, Lord Loudoun, reported to Secretary Holderness that the rangers were "a Species of Troops we cannot be without, now that I may venture to say we have no Indians, and the Enemy have so great a Body of them." mss., 16 Aug.–17 Oct. 1757, Loudoun Papers, LO 4239, HEH.

17. Shy, *Toward Lexington*, 129; Pargellis, Lord Loudoun, 98.

18. Gipson, *British Empire* 7:154–56.

19. Pargellis, *Lord Loudoun*, 331.

20. Anderson, *People's Army*, ch. 4.

A question arises: Why should the infliction of such pain have only the name of *punishment?* If done by Indians, it would be called *torture*, and rightly. In this respect, torture functioned in oddly distinct ways in the two cultures. Both regarded it as punishment, but Indians tortured only their enemies. To make the analogy complete, we should have to assume that British upper-class officers conceived lower-class enlisted men as enemies. In a society divided as rigidly as Britain's by social class, the assumption seems reasonable. It gains credibility from comparison with the provincials.

British and provincial forces were not only distinct, they were different, and their difference reflected the diversely evolving societies from which they came. Fred Anderson has observed that British regulars were "the product of a society and culture more different from New England than the New Englanders had ever suspected."[21] Class and caste existed in the new England as well as in the old, but there was "a divergence between England and the colonies," as Stanley M. Pargellis has observed, "in the ideas of a man's social and economic worth."[22]

(A remnant of the rigid British stratification could still be observed in World War II when off-duty noncoms in the service club associated only with others of the same rating: three-stripers with three-stripers, two with two, and one with one; and no noncom would be seen in company with a lowly private for fear of losing caste.)

Military effectiveness

In New England the concept of *covenant* dominated social relations. Wars in the region raged so frequently that every generation saw men summoned to the colors, and procedures had become fixed by custom as well as law.[23] Generally the wars were fought by volunteers; the militia were rarely called up though selective impressment from militia ranks sometimes occurred. Men would volunteer only for service under officers whom they respected and trusted. In true Puritan fashion, officers and men understood that a covenant existed between them, and officers knew that

21. Ibid., 141.

22. Financial compensation was a straightforward gauge: provincial soldiers were paid more than double the net wages for enlisted men among the regulars, but provincial officers received less pay than officers of the regulars. Pargellis, *Lord Loudoun*, 101.

23. The origins and early history of the militia are described in Darrett Bruce Rutman, "A Militant New World, 1607–40: America's First Generation, Its Martial Spirit, Its Tradition of Arms, Its Militia Organization, Its Wars," Ph.D. diss., University of Virginia, 1959. The pattern set by Massachusetts Bay for New England generally is detailed in Jack Sheldon Radabaugh, "The Military System of Colonial Massachusetts, 1690–1740," Ph.D. diss., University of Southern California, 1965.

they would lose community standing if they violated that covenant. They might, in fact, lose all their troops through desertion.[24] In contrast, British officers usually bought their commissions and were supplied with troops through an impersonal recruiting service. They could never comprehend the notion of covenant, and they felt no need to earn their men's respect; they wanted only the men's fear and unquestioning obedience.[25] The difference between the New England principle and the British regular principle was the difference between leadership and command.

However, there was also the difference between an army of amateurs and one of professionals. Provincials enlisted for a campaign, went home at the end of it, and perhaps re-enlisted for the next campaign; perhaps not. The regulars were in for the duration or for "life"—usually about twenty years. Essentially, provincials were civilians "just visiting" the army;[26] but for the regulars the army was home and community. It followed that the regulars could be used, in due course, as a royal police force in a manner not possible with the provincials, who were conscious of being part of the community being policed and whose first allegiance was to their provincial governments rather than the crown.[27]

The regulars trudged through the Seven Years War despite vainglorious bungling by some extremely stupid officers, of whom Braddock was only the first in a row. Casualties were frightful, and victories came late in the war. I cannot agree with John Shy that the regulars won the war except insofar as they triumphed in the final battles. Shy surveys recent military historians and finds a kinder judgment than mine of the British generals, particularly because of the difficulties of terrain that created great obstacles to logistics.[28] The difficulties cannot be denied, but the armies of New France fought on the same terrain.

It is said that the French had an advantage by fighting on "interior lines," but this comment must be qualified. Distance from Montreal to the forts at Lake George was and is greater than the distance from Albany. Supplies for Fort Duquesne were sent from Montreal via Forts Frontenac and Niagara on the French side, while the British could carry from Philadelphia through settlements on the Susquehanna or from Williamsburg via Winchester. French ships had to sail more than 400 miles up the St. Lawrence before they could unload at Quebec, and another 160 to supply Montreal; British ships dropped cargo at New York on the coast and transshipped it 156 miles to Albany. The French did move men and arms

24. Anderson, *People's Army*, ch. 6.
25. Pargellis, *Lord Loudoun*, ch. 4; Anderson, *People's Army*, 121.
26. Leach, *Arms for Empire*, 17–18.
27. Shy, *Toward Lexington*, 40, 67, 82–83; Anderson, *People's Army*, 172.
28. Shy, *Toward Lexington*, 19, 84–89.

swiftly from one front to another because they had to; but this was not easy and the British did not have a similar necessity.

Military historians have almost as many alibis as their heroes. It won't do to say, as some writers do, that the French "managed" to keep their troops supplied to the very end of the fighting; the point is that a large bulk of their arms and supplies came *from England* by courtesy of Generals Braddock, Shirley, and Webb. The fact is inescapable that until William Pitt reorganized political and military affairs the British *lost* every big battle except Johnson's and Bradstreet's, and those exceptions reflect no credit on the British high command; Bradstreet was an outsider from Nova Scotia whose troops were bateaumen auxiliaries, and Johnson's troops at Lake George were provincials and Indians. The British military system and its commanders were simply rotten. (Chapters further on present a bill of particulars.)

Yet there is a sense in which John Shy is right. The big armies and the set battles did decide final victory in the war. Guerillas harass and create panic. They do not—and they did not—overcome the power of densely settled communities organized for defense. The experience of modern revolutions demonstrates that none succeeds until its guerillas have been consolidated into a formal army capable of winning decisive battles. This was true also in the Seven Years War. Indian raids weakened, frightened, intimidated the British, but did not dislodge them. By maintaining massive armies in the field, however ineptly led, the British drained New France of men and resources, and eventually overwhelmed the French by sheer weight. When the breakthrough came, the regulars took Quebec and Montreal. In that sense they "won" the war.

Naval impressment

A word is in order about the royal navy. Though its quality at the time was inferior, ship for ship, to the French navy, British naval officers were more aggressive and British ships outnumbered French, two to one. Moreover Britain won great advantage by a "preemptive" seizure of 800 French merchant ships and 3,000 seamen before war was declared.[29] In the war's early years, Britain succeeded at sea better than on land, but militarism exacted the same heavy price in both arenas. By unrestricted impressment of men in seacoast towns, the royal navy came to be feared as much as the French enemy, for, as Jesse Lemisch has so concisely

29. W. J. Eccles, "The French forces in North America during the Seven Years' War," in *Dict. Can. Biog.* 3:xvi–xvii.

declared, "to be in the navy was in some sense to be a slave."[30]

Negatively, colonials feared the brutal discipline—more cruel, if possible, than in the regular army. Positively, they preferred the higher wages and potential plunder of merchant service and privateering. Unable to maintain crews by voluntary enlistment, frustrated naval officers resorted to press gangs with which they outraged colonial conceptions of liberty and incidentally disrupted the commerce of coastal towns.

Seaman labored in status little above that of chattel slaves, and their sufferings elicited little concern on humanitarian grounds from the elite ranks of provincial society, but their labor was essential for transportation of goods. To quote Lemisch's seminal article again, the effects of impressment "pervaded and disrupted all society, giving other classes and groups cause to share a common grievance with the press gang's more direct victims: just about everyone had a relative at sea. Whole cities were crippled. A night-time operation in New York in 1757 took in 800 men, the equivalent of more than one-quarter of the city's adult population."[31]

Incidentally, Britain's commander in chief in America boasted about that operation which consisted of surrounding the city with three battalions of troops who moved in to conduct a house-to-house search in the middle of the night. "The whole was finished by Six in the morning," bragged Lord Loudoun, who justified this despotic action by writing that "without this measure we could not have Sailed for want of Seamen."[32] Indisputably Loudoun could not launch his amphibious attack against French Fort Louisbourg without those seamen; if military exigency could be sufficient justification for his violation of the personal liberty of Englishmen to make them "in some sense" slaves, then Loudoun was an

30. Jesse Lemisch, "Jack Tar in the Streets: Merchant Seamen in the Politics of Revolutionary America," *Wm. and Mary Qtly.*, 3d ser., 25:3(1968):371–407; quotation at p. 383. This essay appears also as "The Radicalism of the Inarticulate: Merchant Seamen in the Politics of Revolutionary America," in *Dissent: Explorations in the History of American Radicalism*, ed. Alfred F. Young (DeKalb: Northern Illinois University Press, 1968), 37–82.

31. Loc. cit. Impressment usually has been noticed in histories only as a cause of the War of 1812. Cf. Richard W. Van Alstyne, "Impressment of seamen," in *Dictionary of American History*, ed. J. T. Adams, 5 vols. (New York: Charles Scribner's Sons, 1940) 3:80–81. But major riots against impressment broke out at Boston in 1745 and 1747, accompanied by formal protests from the town and provincial governments. William Pencak comments that "the *Independent Advertiser*, America's first anti-war and protest newspaper was founded one month after the great anti-impressment riot of 17–20 November 1747 by the twenty-five-year-old Samuel Adams, among others." Protests were made again during and after the Seven Years War. Colonial impressment of militiamen for the armies did not raise such hostility because it was conducted selectively by "leaders who knew a great deal about their townsmen's affairs" in contrast to naval impressment, "which amounted to the virtual abduction of merchant seamen." Lemisch, "Jack Tar," 387–93; William Pencak, "Warfare and Political Change in Mid-Eighteenth-Century Massachusetts," in *The British Atlantic Empire before the American Revolution*, eds. Peter Marshall and Glyn Williams (London: Frank Cass, 1980), 60; Anderson, *People's Army*, 41–42.

32. Loudoun to Pitt, New York, 30 May 1757, mss., Loudoun Papers, LO 3741, HEH.

efficient and proper servant of his royal master. It is doubtful that the impressed men or their kin thought in those terms.

Seamen learned to flee to the interior when a man-of-war appeared on the horizon. Enough made themselves scarce so that commerce became sluggish as merchants searched unavailingly for crews to ship their goods. Franklin remarked in 1759 that impressment often hurt trade "more than the Enemy hurts it."[33]

The "liberty of the subject," so much vaunted by Englishmen, stopped at the water's edge. Crown counsel Sir Michael Foster stated the rationale in *The King v. Alexander Broadfoot* (1743): "The right of impressing mariners for public service is a *prerogative inherent in the Crown*, founded upon common law, and recognized by many acts of Parliament."[34]

French armed services

Historians habitually remark that the disunity of British forces in America exposed them to defeat by the highly centralized command of New France. Plausible though this appears, in consideration of the early French victories with inferior numbers, the situation in Canada was not quite that simple. French forces, like the British, were a heterogeneous lot, and sweet harmony prevailed seldom.[35]

To the basic Canadian militia the French added regular troops under authority of the ministry of Marine, many of which had seen long service in Canada before 1754. They were regarded as regulars of New France. In contrast to Britain's arrangements, the officers of these Marine regulars were mostly native Canadians who had earned rank by service and conspicuous valor at New France's western outposts. They composed tough and skilled outfits, against which the British provincial troops and militia were "no match. Great mobility, deadly marksmanship, skilful use of surprise and forest cover, high morale, and . . . a tradition of victory, gave the colonial regulars their superiority."[36] So far, so good: the troops of the Marine fought the set battles, and the militia mustered for defense. No problem of disparity of pay arose there because the militia were paid nothing.[37]

But there were not enough troops of the Marine when tensions mounted

33. Franklin to Galloway, London, 7 Apr. 1759, *Franklin Papers* 8:315–16. Franklin was still imperialist enough to yearn in the same letter for Pennsylvania's government to become royal instead of proprietary.

34. "Impressment," *Encyclopaedia Americana* (1974), 14:829.

35. Eccles, "French forces," xv–xviii; Frégaut, *Canada*, 62–64. The antagonisms are prominent in the biographies of military men in *Dict. Can. Biog.*

36. Eccles, "French forces," xvii.

37. Ibid., xvii–xviii.

between the empires, so France sent out reinforcements from Europe. These *troupes de terre* came from the ministry of War, which had a history of antagonism to the ministry of Marine. Though they were put under the Marine to insure unity of command, they were a sadly inferior lot characterized by incompetence and corruption. Their officers' commissions were bought rather than earned. Their men frequently were the sweepings of the streets. To make things worse, they were officially distinguished from the colonial regulars by being regarded as Frenchmen serving outside their own country, and were therefore paid more than double what the troops of the Marine got. It was a recipe for heartburn, and the Frenchmen did not improve the situation by insulting and abusing their Canadian comrades in arms.[38]

The very qualities that made the rugged Canadians so formidable disgusted the Frenchmen. To march without baggage trains or field hospitals—to carry supplies and equipment on their own backs—no matter the swift and flexible operations thus made possible, was mere barbarity, not war as carried on by civilized people. W. J. Eccles dryly notes, "When rivers were encountered they had to wade or swim across. Resentful Canadians who were ordered to carry them across on their backs had an unfortunate habit of tripping in mid-stream."[39]

The only branch of service in which New France held undoubted numerical superiority in the early years of the war was the Indian component. Unpredictable and unreliable as the Indian tribes were, for their objectives were neither identical with those of New France nor with each other's, they were the only agency available to the French for tactical offensives. Their raids distracted the British, who were forced to deploy troops over a long military frontier for defense. In consequence, the British could never concentrate their overwhelming superiority in men and weapons for their own offensive.[40]

New France's centralized command may have given some advantage against Britain's superior numbers and equipment; but New France's Indians were a greater advantage. Braddock was defeated by Indians. Johnson at Crown Point was saved by his Indian contingent. As we shall see, Britain's forces triumphed only in battles where Indians abandoned the French, were opposed by Indians allied to Britain, or where they played a negligible role.

But this invaluable instrument of war—the allied Indians—horrified the Frenchmen even as they asserted its indispensability and negotiated for its use. Bougainville confided to his mother that "your child shudders at the

38. Ibid., xviii–xx.
39. Ibid., xix–xx.
40. Ibid., xviii; Eccles, "Rigaud de Vaudreuil de Cavagnial, Pierre de, Marquis de Vaudreuil," *Dict. Can. Biog.* 4:668.

horrors which he will be forced to witness" committed by "the most ferocious of all people, and great cannibals by trade"; and to his brother he commented that the "Far West" Indians had been "drawn from 500 leagues by the smell of fresh human flesh and the chance to teach their young men how one carves up a human being destined for the pot. . . . I shiver at the frightful spectacles which they are preparing for us."[41] Engineer officer Jean-Nicolas Desandrouins deplored "the horrors and cruelties of the Indians." He assured a correspondent that "the idea entertained thereof in France is very correct. It is a misfortune to make war with such people, especially when they are drunk—a condition in which nothing stays their fury."[42] General Montcalm regarded the Indians with contempt, "declaring that their only merit was to be a good thing not to have against one." But the contradictions inherent in French policy impelled him to claim that he had won so much "affection" from the Indians as to make Governor Vaudreuil jealous.[43]

It is, by the way, a reflection on the psychology of men in power. Nothing "obliged" the French to instigate Indian raids with all their attendant horrors—nothing, that is, except the desire to win, and a disinclination to stickle at the means. In law, the instigator of a crime is as guilty as the performer, sometimes more so. In history, however, the man in the ruffled shirt and gold-laced waistcoat somehow levitates above the blood he has ordered to be spilled by dirty-handed underlings. The raids of Bougainville's Indian monsters were not the Indians' idea. How revealing is his journal entry of 12–13 September 1756: "We now have six hundred Indians, and hold a council to send them off in detachments, but it is a long job to get them to make up their minds. It requires authority, brandy, equipment, food and such. The job never ends and is very irksome."[44] But this was all "a necessary evil,"[45] so the hand that bought the scalps did not feel the taint of the hand that lifted the hatchet.

For the French as for the English, America was foreign territory. Its colonial inhabitants stood somewhat higher in esteem than the native Indians, but not up to the level of full equality with civilized Europeans. Antagonism started at the very top where it was produced by the structure of command as well as clash of personalities. Under the ministry of Marine, supreme command was vested in the governor general of New France who happened to be a native Canadian, Pierre Rigaud de Vaudreuil de Cavagnial, marquis de Vaudreuil. He controlled strategy and

41. [Bougainville], *Adventure*, ed. Hamilton, 331.
42. 28 Aug. 1756, *N.Y. Col. Docs.* 10:466.
43. W. J. Eccles, "Montcalm, Louis-Joseph de, Marquis de Montcalm," in *Dict. Can. Biog.* 3:460.
44. [Bougainville], *Adventure*, ed. Hamilton, 12–13 Sep. 1756, p. 36.
45. Ibid., 20 Oct. 1756, p. 60.

gave orders to the army commander, who theoretically controlled tactics. The successive army commanders were from the ministry of War, both Europeans, both professional soldiers, and both chafing at the governor-general's bit. The first one, Jean-Armand Dieskau, baron de Dieskau, disobeyed orders and lost the battle of Lake George where he was taken captive in September 1755. He was replaced by Louis-Joseph de Montcalm, marquis de Montcalm, who lasted longer and had some impressive successes before losing Quebec and his life in 1759. Vaudreuil believed that he personally deserved credit for the strategy that produced those successes, and that Montcalm could and should have accomplished more.[46] Montcalm's simmering resentment appears in his aide's comment that Montcalm was "under the orders of a man, limited, without talent, perhaps free from vice, but having all the faults of a petty spirit, filled with Canadian prejudices, which are of all the most foolish, jealous, glorious, wishing to take all credit to themselves. He no more confides in M. de Montcalm than in the lowest lieutenant."[47] In retrospect it seems impossible that two men who despised each other so much could have accomplished anything at all. Their personal antipathy was compounded by precisely opposed notions concerning strategy. Montcalm wanted to sit tight in his fortifications and fight a strictly defensive war. Vaudreuil insisted on spoiling attacks intended to upset British plans and operations. Vaudreuil's authority prevailed, but Montcalm's defeatism and laggard action reduced the strategy's effectiveness.[48]

French mobility

In fact, what has been perceived as unified central command in the French forces should be seen more truly as an advantage of mobility. The French could transport by water along the St. Lawrence River and the "Mahican Channel"; that is, the Richelieu River–Lake Champlain–Lake George route. Though the British used the Hudson River, goods and men from New England had to come overland through mountainous territory. At Fort Duquesne on the Ohio, the French fought from an exterior position, but most of their supply line ran along waterways whereas the British had to trudge and haul through woods and over high mountains. The British had comparatively easy marching along the Mohawk Valley to reinforce their Fort Oswego or to mobilize against French Fort Niagara, but that was Iroquois territory, and the wise Iroquois were playing a dou-

46. Cf. Eccles, "Rigaud de Vaudreuil" and "Montcalm," ; J. R. Turnbull, "Dieskau, Jean-Armand (Johan Herman?), Baron de Dieskau," *Dict. Can. Biog.* 3:185–86.
47. [Bougainville], *Adventure*, ed. Hamilton, ltr. to Mme. Herault, 30 June 1757, p. 331.
48. Eccles, "Montcalm," 459–60.

ble game between the great powers. (See ch. 12). It is hard to think of a strategy by which they could have better served their own interest.

Edward Gibbon has observed that "the winds and waves are always on the side of the ablest navigators."[49] The British generals compounded their difficulties with nature by decisions fundamental to their style of warfare. Instead of training men to march swiftly with minimum equipment, the generals encumbered their armies with ponderous baggage trains that slowed marching to the rate of the heavy wagons. In contrast, the Canadians and, of course, the Indians, moved as fast as their feet could take them, disdaining heavy gear and accepting discomfort for the sake of speed. To the British they seemed like phantoms in the woods. Except for a few hundred rangers, the British stuck to roads, either well-established or newly cut. The ghost of Braddock haunted British soldiers; they feared the woods in which Canadians and Indians felt at home. British provincials for the most part shared the fear. When assigned to garrison duty in frontier forts, they clung to shelter within the walls.

British military strategy remained fundamentally the same from beginning to end, but their abundant resources remained inadequate until appropriate political arrangements temporarily harmonized the interests of empire, colonies, and tribes.

Decisive role of Indian allies

To speak of "Indians" is to oversimplify the diversity of tribal peoples and their goals, which must be taken into account as carefully as the dissensions and factions on the French and British sides. Only thus can we begin to understand why many Indians—not *the* Indians—served with the French forces in the war's early years only to desert them later or to take up arms against them, while other Indians—again, not *the* Indians—joined the British.

The most reliable "French" Indians were those of the Jesuit missions. They were called "domesticated" because they had become Catholic Christians and had separated from their tribes of origin to place themselves under missionary direction. In a roughly descending order, the French sources describe the "Far Indians"—Potawatomis, Ojibwas, Ottawas—as next most reliable because they would usually stay on the job after a raid or battle instead of running home immediately with their trophies. "Home" for them was too far away for jaunting back and forth. They contrasted with the traditional French allies among the Canadian Algonquins and

49. Edward Gibbon, *The History of the Decline and Fall of the Roman Empire* (1776–82), reprint ed. J. B. Bury, 7 vols. (London: Methuen and Co., 1909), 7:190.

Abenakis who served (like New England's militia) for a single campaign, not staying on so much as a day after the first battle. Then there were the new allies of the Ohio Valley, the Delawares, Shawnees, and Mingos who had been won over by persuasion or compulsion through Fort Duquesne's controls. These were the warriors who harassed the back country of Virginia, Maryland, and Pennsylvania with French or Canadian officers in the raiding parties.

Least reliable from the French point of view (and the British viewpoint also) were the Iroquois of the Six Nations, who must be distinguished sharply from the Iroquois of the missions. (Sources are often ambiguous.) The usual term for the Six Nations is "neutral," and it is convenient in the absence of a better, but they were not neutral in the sense of standing pat and avoiding both sides. Instead they cannily lined up on both sides at times and in ways carefully chosen to advance their own interests; and they intrigued incessantly to achieve leadership among the other tribes. They never wholly severed contacts with the mission Iroquois whose kinship was well recognized by both sides, and that consciousness of kin may have been a determinant in the outcomes of the battle of Lake George.[50]

French and British officialdom constantly bewailed the expense of Indian allies—the presents and bribes and equipment necessary to get a contingent in the field—but no one, then or since, has attempted to compare that cost with what was laid out on the regulars.[51] I hazard a guess that it was only a fraction.[52] It seems odd that Indians should have been expected to fight on the cheap when army officers had to be paid substantially and provided with perquisites that the naked eye does not readily distinguish from the bribes paid to Indian chiefs. Pennsylvania's secretary Richard Peters observed the Indian point of view: "Bribery, among the Indians no more than among the French, is not deemed a crime, but a mark of respect and a Proof that you know their Importance, and whoever neglects it is impolitick and will suffer."[53] Peters tactfully omitted Englishmen from

50. *N.Y. Col. Docs.* 10:317, 318, 342.

51. For example, Halifax's absurd wail that "if the [Mingo] Half King is for the future to be subsidized as European Princes are, I don't know what will become of us." Halifax to Loudoun, London, 11 Mar. 1757, mss., Loudoun Papers, LO 3018, HEH. The standard study of present giving is Wilbur R. Jacobs, *Diplomacy and Indian Gifts: Anglo-French Rivalry Along the Ohio and Northwest Frontiers, 1748–1763* (Stanford, Calif.: Stanford University Press, 1950).

52. We have some figures that show how utterly incommensurate the Indian presents were to European subsidies. For example, Sir William Johnson's accounts for Indian presents for the nineteen months from Mar. 1755 to Oct. 1756 added up to £19,619/9/1½ and to £17,072/2/10¼ for thirteen months from Nov. 1758 to Dec. 1759; and we may be sure that they were not understated. Cf. these sums to the £670,000 granted to Prussia's Frederick II for twelve months following Apr. 1758; and to the £1,191,894 granted to the Electorate of Hanover and the Margravate of Hesse-Cassel between 23 Jan. and 20 Apr. 1758. Jacobs, *Diplomacy and Indian gifts*, 66; Gipson, *British Empire* 7:129–30.

53. Peters to Shirley, 12 May 1755, mss., HEH.

his comparison. He might readily have included even the highest-ranking ministers of state. The meaning of bribery was and is "influencing the action of another by corrupt inducement." In the case of British officers, the inducement went under the name of *perquisites*, and it cost much more than the Indian chief's *bribery*. The semantic difference, however, conduces to contempt for the chief and honor for the general.

In a broad way, the tribes may be classified into those who were feeling British encroachment on their territories and those of the far west beyond that immediate pressure. In a very real sense, the Abenakis of Maine, the Micmacs of Nova Scotia, the Six Nations, and the Ohio Indians were trying to preserve their homelands whereas the westerners were more concerned about plunder and the preservation of their advantageous standing in the French trading system. The distinction was to have important consequences. Tribes fighting primarily against British encroachment were far from delighted by French military occupation. What seems as vacillation among them can be seen otherwise as the attempt to shake off first the one intruder, then the other, as occasion permitted.[54] That the Indians failed in the long run does not alter the nature of the effort. The westerners, whose turn to resist was still to come, simply went home when they saw no further gain for themselves, and the mission Indians stood by New France till the end. But the mission Indians were a small minority. When the French lost the bulk of their Indian allies, they effectively lost the war. How that happened must be a major theme in this history.

Persons of the present era have grown accustomed to bombings in which civilians suffer more casualties than the armed forces. By and large, this was not true of North America in mid-eighteenth century, though exceptions have been noted. The men who took up arms, voluntarily or otherwise, suffered and died from exposure, malnutrition, epidemics, and ill treatment directly caused by their conditions of service, including captivity, not to mention wounds and death in battle. As Douglas Edward Leach has observed, "The time is long past when armed conflict may be presented to serious, sensitive readers as a kind of glorious adventure."[55]

Desertion

The particulars of combat casualties can best be considered further on with accounts of sieges and battles. Here we may notice that one method for enlisted men to escape the hazards and hardships of service was to

54. In following chapters, compare Delaware conduct toward Fort Duquesne and afterward Fort Pitt; Oneida conduct toward Fort Bull; Seneca conduct toward Fort Niagara.

55. Leach, *Arms for Empire*, xi.

leave it. Every province had trouble drumming up enlistments in the first place, though they were for short terms; and re-enlistments were minimal. More seriously, many men disregarded the terms of enlistment after they had gotten a taste of the other side of glory; they simply took to their heels. There are so many laments about desertion in officers' reports that losses on that account often seem to have been greater than casualties in battle. Enhancing officers' dismay, the deserters were given refuge and hospitality by civilians. Records do not describe conversations between deserters and their hosts, but it is not hard to imagine aggrieved details of abuse and hardship that would scarcely conduce to arousing popular support for the war. The mere fact of deserters being harbored shines brilliant light on popular sentiment.[56]

Hostility between regulars and provincials

The contemptuous treatment of provincials by British officers could not fail to provoke resentment that spilled over into antagonism toward the crown that had sent them. This was inherent in the situation, for there was reason enough for the contempt. Colonel Henry Bouquet found that provincial *officers* "haven't an idea of service, and one cannot depend on them to carry out an order."[57] General James Wolfe, however, expressed extreme contempt for Americans that was simply a notch higher than his violent dislike of his own soldiery. Wolfe thought that "there never was people collected together so unfit for the business they were set upon [as the provincials]—dilatory, ignorant, irresolute and some grains of a very unmanly quality and very unsoldier-like or unsailor-like." To another correspondent he spluttered: "The Americans are in general the dirtiest, the most contemptible, cowardly dogs you can conceive. There is no depending on 'em in action. They fall down dead in their own dirt and desert by battalions, officers and all." (Perhaps Wolfe planned to clean the site on which he would fall dead.) He was not a charitable sort in any sense. His opinion of British soldiers almost matched the degradation of the Ameri-

56. Desertion is a constant theme in the generals' correspondence. See, for examples, Loudoun Papers, LO 4705, LO 5495, LO 2662; Abercromby Papers AB 495, AB 531, AB 948; and the orderly book of Lieutenant Joseph Bull, HM 687, all mss., HEH; *Bouquet Papers* 2:182, 183n16. The odd legalism of the process as shown by Bouquet's remark: "I do not think that they can be hung as they have not been paid," ibid., 2:50.

A graphically detailed description of the British technique of sentencing to death, then commuting the sentence to service abroad—combined with execution of three ringleaders of a mass desertion defined as mutiny, and the pathetic speech of penitence of one of the men executed is in John Prebble, *Mutiny: Highland Regiments in Revolt, 1743–1804* (New York: Penguin Books, 1977), 74–87. This regiment was later sent to America where it suffered terrible casualties. My thanks to Colin Calloway for showing me this.

57. *Bouquet Papers* 2:72.

cans: "I know their discipline to be bad and their valour precarious. They are easily put into disorder and hard to recover out of it. They frequently kill their officers through fear, and murder one another in confusion."[58] It seems impossible that such attitudes would not have been sensed and resented by their objects.

Historian John Shy distinguishes the slovenly, undisciplined provincials of the Seven Years War as persons outside the militia structure, unlike the tough fighters of the American Revolution. After some experiment, provincials were chiefly assigned to the inglorious dirty work of campaigning, set to labor to the point of exhaustion.[59] Brigadier John Stanwix followed the pattern, but allowed them some sympathy as he saw the effects: "there is such a surprizing falling off from the working men of these Battalions that from 5600 intended for the service this way that not 1500 left fit for duty and these I am sending down sick in Boat loads every day. I think all the Provincials whilest with me have behaved well but they are really worn out, work'd down, and fairly jaded with Fatigue, to which the Batteau Service and Caderaqui [Fort Frontenac] has not a little Contributed." Naturally enough, these men wanted to go home. Stanwix wrote on 22 October 1758, facing the demand of his Boston battalions to leave when their time would be up on 1 November, with the New Jersey regiment to follow two weeks later.[60]

Nevertheless, the provincials captured the forts of Acadia and held the French to a draw at Lake George, while the regulars, with all their vaunted skills and discipline, lost every engagement until 1758.[61] "Regular" armies are standing armies; and since before Cromwell, Englishmen had preserved a sensible fear of standing armies as instruments of oppression. Even the Puritan founders of Massachusetts Bay, Cromwell's co-religionists, had subscribed to that principle. When they set up their citizen-militia, as Darrett Rutman has noted, "Massachusetts created its military structure primarily as a response to the threat from England."[62] So early as the 1630s, colonials perceived that they were different peoples from Englishmen, despite their claims to the "rights of Englishmen," and they

58. Osgood, *Eighteenth Century* 4:450; J. H. Plumb, *England in the Eighteenth Century*, The Pelican History of England (Baltimore, Md.: Penguin Books, 1950), 128–29; Prebble. *Culloden*, 58.

59. John W. Shy, "A New Look at Colonial Militia," *Wm. and Mary Qtly.*, 3d ser., 20 (1963), 185; idem, *Toward Lexington*, 19.

60. Stanwix to Abercromby, 22 Oct. 1758, mss., Abercromby Papers AB 781, HEH. This followed by three weeks Stanwix's Sept. report of 2,750 men fit for duty. Stanwix supposed the sickness "owing to their living wholy upon salt pork without pease, roots, or greens." 29 Sept. 1758, AB 703, HEH.

61. Shy cites the greater battle casualties of the regulars as his reason for saying they won the war. These numbers seem to me only to demonstrate the regular officers' incompetence. Shy, *Toward Lexington*, 19.

62. Rutman, "A Militant New World," 574.

particularly resisted governance by Englishmen in illegal as well as legal ways. Sometimes they rioted, sometimes they revolted. Always they schemed to acquire more power to govern themselves, and their assemblies never forgot for a moment that control of the armed forces is essential to independence. When the alien troops from Britain landed in their tens of thousands, and immediately began to demand and command, the assemblymen dug in; and when provincial troops brought back tales of what life was like under British officers, the assemblymen knew they were right. No longer need they feel qualms of conscience about merely protecting local interests against "the best king on earth." They had become *morally* right.[63]

63. The importance of the moral issue appears in Richard L. Bushman, *King and People in Provincial Massachusetts*, published for the Institute of Early American History and Culture (Chapel Hill: University of North Carolina Press, 1985), see especially ch. 2.

Chapter 11 ❧ *WITCH HUNT*

We wonder not that we should be mistaken, misconstrued, and misrepresented in what we believe and do to salvation, since our betters have been so treated in the primitive times. Nor indeed is it only about doctrines of religion; for our practice in worship and discipline have had the same success.

William Penn, *Primitive Christianity Revived*

There was now a Flame rising in every Part of the Country, which the Assembly with all their Arts could not suppress. The People were daily suffering: They demanded Protection; and they would listen to no insinuating Stories about Privileges and Liberty, while the Sword of the Enemy was at their Throat, ready to deprive them of their Lives and their Privileges together. On this Occasion, there was the fairest Chance of ridding our Assembly of Quakers* for ever, if our constitution had not this Absurdity in it, that there is not a Power of Dissolution in the Governor . . .

*There was another way of getting rid of them, by cutting their Throats, which Expedient a great many sanguine People of the back Countries had resolved upon . . .

[Rev. William Smith], *A Brief View of the Conduct of Pennsylvania, For the Year 1755*

Chronology

1733.	St. Joseph's Roman Catholic Chapel is built in Philadelphia.
1734.	Governor Thomas Penn demands its suppression. The Quaker-dominated assembly protects it.
1751.	William Smith comes to New York as tutor to two boys. He immediately begins a campaign of anonymous letter writing to newspapers.
May–June 1753.	Smith visits Philadelphia and becomes friendly with Benjamin Franklin.
1753–54.	Smith returns to England, is ordained in the Church of England, and is hired as a secret political worker for Thomas Penn.
Spring 1754.	Smith is made rector of the Academy of Philadelphia.
December 1754.	Smith delivers the *Brief State* for publication. It demands exclusion of Quakers from office by means of a test oath.
March 1755.	College of Philadelphia is created with Smith as provost.
July 1755.	Braddock's defeat.
July 1755.	Conrad Weiser stirs up anti-Catholic hysteria. Assembly dampens it.
October 1755.	Quakers re-elected to assembly.
November 1755.	Responding to suggestion from Thomas Penn, Smith organizes a remonstrance to the crown petitioning for exclusion of Quakers from assembly.

November 1755.	Deported Acadians delivered to Philadelphia. Assembly provides food and shelter.
January 1756.	Thomas Penn promises to do all in his power to help Smith's remonstrance.
February 1756.	Thomas Penn meets with London Quakers and disavows hostility.
February 1756.	Smith publishes the *Brief View* in London. The "Filius Gallicae" letters are intercepted as apparently intended. All pretend an alliance between Quakers and Pennsylvania Catholics to aid the French enemy.
3 March 1756.	Board of trade recommends banning of Quakers from assembly.
March 1756.	John Hanbury and other weighty Quakers lobby against test oath. They promise that if it is dropped the pacifists in Pennsylvania assembly will withdraw for duration of the war. Oath bill dies.
June 1756.	Six Quaker pacifists withdraw from the assembly. Franklin takes leadership of anti-proprietary forces.
September 1756.	Pennsylvania Quakers set up a Meeting for Sufferings.

In provincial Pennsylvania, ethnic relations held as much latent power as relations of social class.* Issues between Indians in general and Europeans in general had none of the simplicity of Red versus White. Tribes opposed and struggled with each other. So did the varied colonials: Quakers, Anglicans, Germans of the sects, Germans of high Lutheran and Evangelical churches, Germans of the Catholic church, Moravians, "New Light" and "Old Light" Scotch-Irish Presbyterians, Catholic "mere" Irishmen, Afro-Americans free and slave, some Huguenot French, and after the conquest of Acadia a seasoning of Catholic French families. They mingled, especially in trade, but Pennsylvania was not a "melting pot." In that era, ethnic identities were jealously preserved in churches, communities, and tribes. In matters affecting the general welfare, groups and individuals formed alliances that shifted with circumstance. What held all together in reasonable, if somewhat bewildering, order was the policy of toleration inaugurated and preserved by the Quakers. The war imposed great strain on this policy. As usual in wartime, the Seven Years War was marked by political witch hunts. As usual also, particular persons initiated and sustained the witch hunts in Pennsylvania for their own gain. Two religious communities—Quakers and Roman Catholics—were the special objects of persecution.

By the 1750s, Quakers had become a minority in Pennsylvania, but large communities of German immigrants subscribed to the Friendly principles of pacifism and toleration. Other, nonpacifist Germans also gave their votes to Quaker candidates for the assembly because the Friends

*This chapter is adapted and expanded from Francis Jennings, "Thomas Penn's Loyalty Oath," *American Journal of Legal History* 8:4 (Oct. 1964), 303–13.

seemed to the Germans to be the caretakers of William Penn's pledge of spiritual and material liberties. So long as the Quakers ran the assembly, the Germans reasoned, worship would be free and property would be protected. Until the Germans had come to Pennsylvania, neither their faiths nor their possessions had been secure, and they were taking no chances of a return to the bad old days in Germany. They suspected the proprietaries and their supporters as "noblemen," a class to be feared.[1]

Besides the Germans, who formed a constituency estimated at one-third of the province's population but who preferred to keep a low profile, there were the Church of England people, who preferred a high profile. Despite many past political battles with the Friends, most Anglicans in mid-century collaborated with the Quakers. Assembly Speaker Isaac Norris, Jr., a "defense" Quaker, explained why.

> The Church of England are well Apprized that Their Interest is not sufficient Alone, and upon search they have found it Difficult to find men among Themselves, with whom they Could Confide Their Liberties. They dread the Presbyterians, and the Germans more, so that in the Nature of things upon a Political System only, the Church of England know, they must keep in with the Quakers to keep the others out. . . . And the Dutch [Germans] Joyn them in dread of an arbitrary Government.—So that it seems Absolutely Necessary to keep the Quakers as a Ballance here.[2]

It was natural, therefore, for Thomas Penn and his placemen to conclude that the anti-proprietary resistance could most readily be broken by destroying Quaker leadership. For Penn the Quaker faith of his father was a long past experience. He had left the Society of Friends and gained the more powerful patronage of the established Church of England shortly after returning to England from his stay in Pennsylvania. Having thus secured his home base, he set about building a political machine through agents in the province.[3] He kept them ignorant of each other's reports, permitting no one to achieve the status of commander that he reserved for himself with careful attention to the most minute details. Coordinating campaigns in Pennsylvania with lobbying in London, he ran about busily to ministers to make it seem that his goals should be the crown's, and his influence was enhanced by the great wealth gained from his colonial estate.

1. Dietmar Rothermund, "The German Problem of Colonial Pennsylvania," *Pa. Mag. of Hist. and Biog.* 84:1 (Jan. 1960), 5–7; see also idem, *The Layman's Progress: Religious and Political Experience in Colonial Pennsylvania, 1740–1770* (Philadelphia: University of Pennsylvania Press, 1961).

2. Norris to Charles, 29 Apr. 1756, mss., Norris Letter Book, 1719–56, 70–71, HSP. So-called defense Quakers were willing to vote appropriations for defense of the province. See Theodore Thayer, *Israel Pemberton: King of the Quakers* (Philadelphia: Hist. Soc. of Pa., 1943), 88–89.

3. To my knowledge, no one has surveyed and analyzed the workings of Penn's machine.

Secret agent William Smith

We have seen how Penn manipulated General Braddock, and how Benjamin Franklin's ingenuity turned back that attack. On a different front, however, Penn gained more success. He tried to get Quakers perpetually disqualified from holding office by the device of a requirement by Parliament for officials to swear an oath of allegiance contrary to Quaker religious principles. Though his conspiracy was thwarted, as will be shown, he aroused such popular feeling in England that the absolute pacifists among Quakers in Pennsylvania retired from the assembly to forestall Parliamentary action. For this achievement, Penn's primary agent was the Reverend William Smith, professor of "Logick, Rhetorick, Ethicks and Natural Philosophy" at the Academy of Philadelphia.

Smith had come to America in 1751, where he supported himself for two years as tutor of two boys on a Long Island estate. He attracted Franklin's notice by writing a treatise on education at the time when Franklin was organizing his academy.[4] They became friends; indeed Franklin became infatuated with the younger man and deluded himself into thinking that Smith was his "pupil."[5] Smith had larger plans and clearer perception. Almost instantly upon his arrival in New York, he began to send verses and articles to the newspapers. In the custom of the day, these were pseudonymous, but Smith appealed to principle as well as custom for refusing to sign his own name. For him secrecy was synonymous with liberty of the press. "Were Men to subscribe pieces written in Order to lash powerful Vice, or arrouse their Country to stop the Progress of growing Tyranny, they would frustrate the very End of their own Writings by exposing themselves to certain Destruction."[6]

Along with the assumption of righteousness, Smith had certain very clear objectives, one of which had probably firmed up during his youth as an Anglican in Aberdeen, Scotland, where the lord duke of Argyll had striven mightily to suppress the 1745 uprising in the Highlands. Smith was eighteen years old in 1745, an impressionable age. Apparently he did not take part in the repression personally, as he was a student from 1743 to 1747 at the University of Aberdeen (curiously without receiving a degree),[7] but the events of his life imply strongly that he approved whatever seemed necessary to support royal authority and "regular" religion. By the latter term he meant the Church of England.

When Smith came to America he was distressed by the absence of an

4. Albert Frank Gegenheimer, *William Smith, Educator and Churchman, 1727–1803* (Philadelphia: University of Pennsylvania Press, 1943), 5–6, 14–31.
5. Franklin to Smith, 18 Apr. 1754, *Franklin Papers* 5:263.
6. Gegenheimer, *William Smith*, 6–7.
7. Ibid., 1–3.

establishment of his church in New York and Pennsylvania. His reasons were at least as much political as theological. He stated them bluntly though, as always, anonymously, in the *New York Mercury*. "As to the Political Uses of national Establishments [of religion], he must indeed be a very shallow Politician who does not see them. . . . The Statesman has always found it necessary for the Purposes of Government, to raise some one Denomination of religions above the Rest to a certain Degree." The government "is thus enabled to turn the Balance and keep all in Subjection . . . [if] all Sects and Persuasions be equally favor'd . . . how shall they be influenc'd or how rul'd?"[8]

In plain language, Smith was an authoritarian bigot and poison penman, hostile to all the libertarian and tolerationist trends of the society to which he had emigrated. He hated Quakers especially because of their rejection of bigotry, and that hatred made him a perfect instrument for Thomas Penn's campaign against the Quakers of Pennsylvania.

Smith sailed to England early in 1753 to be ordained in the Church of England, to renew his considerable connections, and to hire on as Penn's spy on Franklin and general hatchet man. On returning to Pennsylvania in 1754, Smith was appointed to the faculty of the Academy and immediately began political work.[9] In December 1754 he delivered a manuscript to Lieutenant Governor Morris. Though the writing was Smith's, Morris knew that the persons concerned in it were "very much" Penn's friends. And Secretary Richard Peters (who was also an ordained minister of the Church of England) wrote separately in rapture: Mr. Smith was "ungracious" in delivery and accent, "but he speaks the Language of Angels and has the heart of a Saint." Apparently another copy had gone directly to the printer in London, but Morris thought that Penn ought to see "what was intended for the Press." Morris was warier than Peters: he found the

8. Quoted and attributed in Carl Bridenbaugh, *Mitre and Sceptre: Transatlantic Faiths, Ideas, Personalities, and Politics, 1689–1775* (New York: Oxford University Press, 1962), 152.

9. Gegenheimer, *William Smith*, 36–37; Smith to Peters and Franklin, (Feb. 1754), in *Franklin Papers* 5:202–18; T. Penn to Smith, 14 Aug. 1754, mss., William Smith Papers 2:3, HSP. (These are facsimiles, the originals having been withdrawn by owners.) Minutes of the Trustees, 25 May 1754, mss., University of Pennsylvania Archives. Ralph L. Ketcham, "Benjamin Franklin and William Smith: New Light on an Old Philadelphia Quarrel," *Pa. Mag. of Hist. and Biog.* 88:2 (Apr. 1964), 143–44, 146. Smith's contemporaries caught on to him, as shown by their satirical "autobiography," in ibid., 157. That later scholars missed Smith's conspirings and falsehoods is partly owing to bias, partly to the pattern set by Francis Parkman of using Smith as a reliable source, and partly to the suppression of political documents from the massive biography written by Smith's great grandson, who was filially and theologically pious without scruple for historical truth: Horace Wemyss Smith, *Life and Correspondence of the Rev. William Smith, D.D.*, 2 vols. (Philadelphia, 1879–80). Smith's retainer from Penn for what we now call covert operations is confirmed by ltr., T. Penn to R. Peters, 21 Feb. 1755, mss., Peters Mss., 4:4, HSP: £50 per year, Pennsylvania currency, were "my own private benefaction and therefore no address is to be made to the Proprietors for it." In the eternal pattern of such benefactions, Smith overdrew his account, and annoyed Penn could do nothing about it without betraying the secret; but it leaked somehow anyway.

book intended "to induce the Parliament to take measures for the future security of this Province by excluding the Quakers from the Legislature. Those who know the Affairs of the Country [i.e., Penn's friends] say it is well drawn up; but that you will judge of."[10]

The issues must be kept clear. Provincial security was the "good" reason professed in order to mask the real one. The book had been written in the latter months of 1754, well before any substantial number of Pennsylvanians felt exposed to danger. Governor Morris knew that royal forces were on their way—Braddock's army—and that all the money requested for their support had been offered already by the Quaker-dominated assembly; only his own signature was wanting.[11] The "clamours of the People," as Peters reported, were directed not against an oppressive oligarchy in the assembly, but against the proprietary and his few friends.[12] The effort to disqualify the Quakers was an act of desperation, an effort not to befriend the populace but to behead it.

Smith's Brief State

Smith's anonymous book, *A Brief State of the Province of Pennsylvania*, starts with falsehood on the title page and maintains character, with one exception, throughout. It professes to be by "a Gentleman who has resided many years in Pennsylvania." Actually, Smith, at its time of writing, had visited Philadelphia for several weeks in 1753, and had resided there less than eight months in 1754. Smith's candid exception to his rule of mendacity occurs near the book's beginning when he explains what is basically wrong with Pennsylvania's government: "the People, instead of being subjected to more Checks, are under fewer than at first; and their Power has been continually increasing with their Numbers and Riches, while the Power of their Governors, far from keeping Pace with theirs has rather been decreasing in the same Proportion ever since." He attributes this evil decline into the substance of "a *pure Republic*" to the influence of the Quakers and the electoral power of the Germans. The province has too much toleration. "Extraordinary Indulgence and privileges" are granted to papists. (This referred to public celebration of the Mass in St. Joseph's Church in Philadelphia.)[13] The Quakers conduct "political Intrigues, under the

10. Peters to Penn, 23 Dec. 1754, mss., and R. H. Morris to Penn, ca. 26 Dec. 1754, mss., Penn Mss., Official Correspondence 6:251–53, 257.

11. Morris informed the assembly on 19 Dec. 1754 that the forces were being sent. *Pa. Council Minutes* 6:202–3.

12. Peters to Penn, 21 Dec. 1754, mss., Penn Mss., Off. Corr. 6:247.

13. [William Smith], *A Brief State of the Province of Pennsylvania, . . . In a Letter from a Gentleman who has resided many Years in Pennsylvania to his Friend in London* (London: R. Griffiths, 1755), p. 8.

Mask of Religion." (As did the other churches also.) For their own ends the Quakers have taken "into their pay" a German printer named (Christopher) Sauer "who was once one of the *French* prophets in Germany, and is shrewdly suspected to be a *Popish* emissary." (Sauer was an Anabaptist doggedly independent of everyone, including Quakers.) The "worst Consequence" of the Quakers' "insidious practices" with the Germans is that the latter "are grown insolent, sullen and turbulent." They give out "that they are a Majority, and strong enough to make the Country their own," and indeed they would be able, "by Joining with the *French*, to eject all the *English* inhabitants. . . . [The French] know our *Germans* are extremely ignorant, and think a large Farm the greatest Blessing in Life. Therefore, by sending their *Jesuitical* Emissaries among them, to persuade them over to the *Popish* Religion, they will draw them from the English, in Multitudes, or perhaps lead them in a Body against us. This is plainly a Scheme laid by the *French* many Years ago, and uniformly pursued till this Time, with the greatest Address; being the true Cause of their continual Encroachments, and holding their Countries by *Forts*, without settling them." The Quakers oppose every effort to remedy this evil state of affairs, attacking all "regular [i.e., Anglican] Clergymen as Spies and Tools of State." The Quakers hindered these regular clergymen from "having Influence enough to set [the Germans] right at the annual Elections." (In fact, the Quakers were allied with Anglicans in the assembly.)[14]

The greatest German sect was the Mennonists—people like the Quakers. A quarter of the Germans were "supposed" to be Roman Catholics.[15] (Some were; the supposed percentage is wild exaggeration.)[16] In Smith's dark, gothic imagination even the Moravians at Bethlehem, whose break with the Vatican long antedated that of Smith's own church, became a "dangerous People" who held "some Tenets and Customs . . . very much a-kin to those of the Roman Catholics."[17] (But not nearly as much akin as Smith's Church of England.) The *Brief State* climaxes with an acknowledgment that "all our Misfortunes can be charged no where but upon our People themselves, and I have shewn that it would be plainly repugnant to their Interest to remedy Grievances. All Redress therefore, must, if it comes, come from his Majesty, and the British Parliament."[18] It proposes a five-point legislative program: (1) a test oath for members of the assembly (which would disqualify Quakers); (2) suspension of voting rights for Germans for "about twenty Years" because "What can be more absurd and impolitic, than to see a Body of ignorant, proud, stubborn Clowns

14. *Brief State,* 26–28, 30, 33–34.
15. Ibid., 35.
16. See pp. 243–47 below.
17. *Brief State,* 35–36.
18. Ibid., 44–45.

(who are unacquainted with our Language, our Manners, our Laws, and our Interests) indulged with the Privilege of Returning almost every Member of Assembly?" (3) introduction of Protestant ministers and schoolmasters among the Germans (the Germans were resisting efforts to herd them into indoctrination schools); (4) a requirement for all legal papers to be in the English language; (5) suppression of foreign language newspapers.[19]

It does not seem necessary to comment upon what such a law would do to Pennsylvania's "pure republic." Thomas Penn wished "all imaginable Success to the scheme to exclude Quakers from the Assembly by a test oath," but Penn was unconvinced of "the propriety and usefulness" of the *Brief State* because "Appeals to the public are not well looked upon by an Administration without whose consent nothing will be done."[20] To Governor Morris, Penn reported discouragingly little interest by British officials, but Penn had no intention of dropping the campaign. His end remained constant; only the means required improvement. It would be better, Penn suggested, "if such a thing was proposed in a representation from People of the Country." Then "some answer could be given to it."[21] The suggestion was taken seriously, as all Penn's "hints" were intended to be, but action was postponed until after the hard-fought elections in October 1755.

Meanwhile the *Brief State* smote Quakers on both sides of the Atlantic. The ministry paid no attention to it—Braddock was on his way to Fort Duquesne—and the Pennsylvania assembly treated it lightly; but a century of experience with persecution had taught Friends what could result from such propaganda. The book arrived in Philadelphia in April 1755 where it made a "prodigious Noise," as Smith boasted to Thomas Penn.[22] In May, the Friends Quarterly Meeting wrote to the London Meeting for

19. Ibid., 39–42. Smith touched a raw nerve with his remarks about the Germans. Much of what he wrote reflected the sentiments of Benjamin Franklin's overwrought letter to his Quaker correspondent Peter Collinson in London, 9 May 1753, with which Smith was familiar. Franklin's fear of a German takeover in Pennsylvania moved him to unusually crude expression: "Those who come hither are generally of the most ignorant Stupid Sort of their own Nation . . . they are under no restraint of Ecclesiastical Government . . . they come in droves, and carry all before them."

In the same letter, Franklin suggested that providing relief for the poor was "fighting against the order of God and Nature." With such attitudes he got along famously with young William Smith and was able to cooperate for a while with Thomas Penn. The temptation to speculate is strong: did Franklin's later break with these two cynics, and the association with more humane men accompanying the break, influence a change in his philosophy? *Franklin Papers* 4:477–86. See also Dietmar Rothermund, "The German Problem of Colonial Pennsylvania, *Pa. Mag. of Hist. and Biog.* 84:1 (Jan. 1960), 10–13.

20. Penn to Smith, 28 Feb. 1755, mss., William Smith Papers 2:4, HSP. Also copied into T. Penn Ltr. Bks., mss., 4:64–67, HSP.

21. Penn to Morris, 26 Feb. 1755, mss., Gratz Coll., Papers of the Governors, Case 2, Box 33-a, fol. Thomas Penn, HSP.

22. Smith to Penn, 1 May 1755, mss., Penn Mss., Off. Corr. 7:29–30, HSP.

Sufferings—their device for coping with persecution—appealing to the Friends in London for help.[23] A delegation of Londoners called on Thomas Penn, who blandly assured them that he had no intention of abridging the liberties of Friends in Pennsylvania. (Penn's public face was always different from his private, conspiring one.) But the news of Braddock's disaster had reached England by the time that London Friends reported their interview with Penn, and they had become aware of great hostility in its wake. With the *Brief State*'s demands in mind they urged Pennsylvania Friends to reconcile with the proprietary's men. Otherwise, they feared, the province's great charter, with its guarantee of liberties, might be revoked entirely. Friends in the assembly would have to realize that they must accept the responsibilities of their office—a veiled reference to support for measures to secure the province against invasion. English Quakers differed substantially from Pennsylvania's defenders of the faith; for example, by paying war taxes without scruple. They rendered unto Caesar what Caesar required, and what he did with his treasure was not their responsibility. Pennsylvania Quakers were in a more complex situation, with much more than pacifism at stake, but it took a while for the full gravity of their plight to register in London. Nevertheless, the London Meeting of Friends assured the Pennsylvanians: "Ye are our Brethren, Bone of our Bone and Flesh of our Flesh whose Welfare is dear to us as our own, and to whom we are united in the Bonds of Gospel Fellowship; whatever such an Union requires, that we hope to fulfil."[24] They were as good as their word.

Braddock went down in July, and the news of his defeat reached Philadelphia late in that month. Instantly all the old battles between governor and assembly resumed. These will be described further on. What is relevant here are some dates. The assembly adjourned, 30 September 1755, in an atmosphere of great acrimony. Braddock's routed army had already marched to and through Philadelphia on its way to winter quarters in Albany. Pennsylvanians were therefore very much aware of the need for security against the triumphant French and their Indians. If any part of the proprietary accusations against the assembly had been believed by the

23. Epistle, 5 May 1755, mss., Minutes of the [Pa.] Meeting for Sufferings 1:11–19. Haverford College. The efficiency of the Friends' means for acquiring information is shown by their having caught on quickly to Smith as the author of the *Brief State*. Isaac Norris was informed "I think, by one pretty much in the Secret" about the pamphlet, and passed the word to Robert Charles, the Assembly's agent in London, that "your friend Smith is the Tool to Propagate the Doctrine." Norris to Charles, 18 May 1755, mss., Norris Letter Book, 1719–1756, 72–73, HSP.

24. London Meeting for Sufferings to Philadelphia Quarterly Meeting, 3 Oct. 1755, mss., in Minutes of the [Pa.] Meeting for Sufferings 1:19–23, HC. See also Jack D. Marietta, "Conscience, the Quaker Community and the French and Indian War," *Pa. Mag. of Hist. and Biog.* 95:1 (Jan. 1971), 3–5, 19–21.

electorate, its members would have been rejected in the elections that took place immediately after its adjournment; but every member of the old, Quaker-dominated assembly who stood for office was re-elected. The frontier county of Lancaster chose an entirely Quaker delegation although, as Speaker Norris observed, there were "scarcely One Hundred of that Profession in The whole County." Norris reported to the province's agent in London that the people were "very Unanimous" and it was "Absurd to call the Opposition a Party."[25]

Penn's men could not manipulate Pennsylvania's electorate, either then or after subsequent horrors in the backwoods. With all the resources of patronage and institutional machinery at their command, they *never* won a majority of the assembly in elections. Their alternative, as already indicated by Smith's *Brief State,* was to manipulate power in London. Once again, Smith assumed leadership, and once again he hid that fact from public view. He had quickly become an important man. With Penn's patronage he was promoted in March 1755 to the newly created post of provost of the newly created College of Philadelphia, upgraded from the old Academy. (Clerk Charles Thomson, who was to become "the Sam Adams of Pennsylvania," resigned from the college faculty on the same day; Thomson knew his man.)[26]

A petition to disfranchise Quakers

Immediately after the proprietary defeat in the elections, Smith picked up Penn's earlier "hint" and wrote a petition appealing to the king for action to succor the Pennsylvanians from the dreadful consequences of self-government.[27] We have an account in manuscript of how the petition was circulated; it is the more interesting for having been written by a not very bright kinsman and retainer of Penn's; namely, Richard Hockley, whose job was to collect Penn's rents. Hockley obviously had not been let in on any secrets. He wrote indignantly to Penn of having been "call'd in by a Magistrate [all magistrates being Penn's appointees] and ask'd to Sign a Petition that is to be presented the King (which I refused) setting forth

25. Norris to R. Charles, 5 Oct. 1755, mss., Norris Letter Book, 1719–1756, 83, HSP.

26. Minutes of the Trustees, 17 Mar. 1755, mss., University of Pennsylvania Archives. Thomson's resignation is the more significant because he was a Presbyterian, and Smith was working closely with the Presbyterians in politics. Thomson, on the other hand, took a job in the Quaker school, and worked as a scribe for Quakers. (His tiny script is beautifully clear—and economical of paper.)

27. "You will see by the enclosed Representation, Remonstrance &c (which as well as the Petition to the King were drawn up by Me)." But "The Good I do depends upon my doing it silently without being seen." Smith to Penn, 27 Nov. 1755, mss., Penn Mss., Off Corr. 7:173, HSP.

the defenseless state of the Province . . . and the reason given is, because a sett of People whose religious principles disavow self defence . . . thrust themselves into the Legislative Power." The petition had been signed by twenty persons when Hockley saw it, with Chief Justice William Allen and Mayor William Plumsted leading the list. This was a scandalous thing, thought Hockley, for everyone knew that Plumsted "though he bears a Commission under You is deeply concern'd in the French trade."[28] That is, Plumsted was trading with the enemy. The information caused no concern to Thomas Penn.

Chief Justice William Allen, an Old Light Presbyterian and great dealer in lands, and reputed to be the richest man in the province, gave the petition the momentum needed to achieve results. He undertook to pay the costs of presenting Smith's petition to the privy council. He engaged Thomas Penn's personal solicitor, Ferdinando J. Paris, as counsel, and he urged Thomas Penn's cooperation![29] Apparently Penn's earlier commitment was guarded even from Allen. This would be wholly in keeping with the policy evident in Penn's correspondence with his various associates; he kept check on them by receiving their reports about each other and by rarely letting one know what he was scheming with another. Penn was especially cautious with Allen whose personal wealth put him in a class different from the hangers-on subsisting on the crumbs from Penn's table.

Much history has been made by bad communications. Ironically, as Penn's men were concocting their petition to disfranchise the Quakers, the intended victims were becoming disposed, Quaker-fashion, to seek some means of accommodation with Penn. The proprietary's most intransigent opponent was now that unpacifist independent Benjamin Franklin, and his aggressiveness troubled the strict Quakers. Israel Pemberton, Jr., who was officially known as clerk of the Annual Meeting and unofficially as "King of the Quakers," disliked Franklin's "Indecent and virulent Terms" in the assembly's messages to the governor; and he was afraid that things were tending to an "irreparable breach with the Proprietaries." He was urged by London Friends to make peace with Penn.[30] But making peace

28. Hockley to Penn, 25 Oct. 1755, mss., Penn Mss., Off. Corr. 7:133, HSP. Hockley thus confirms the scandalous account of proprietary men monopolizing the trade in provisions to the French and Spanish West Indies. *An Answer to an invidious Pamphlet, intituled, A Brief State of the Province of Pensylvania* (London: S. Bladon, 1755).

29. Allen to Penn, 25 Oct. 1755, and Allen to Paris, 25 Nov. 1755, mss., Penn Mss., Off. Corr. 7:135; Allen to Penn, 26 Oct. 1755, mss., ibid., 137; R. Peters to Penn, 8 Nov. 1755, mss., remarks that "The Governor thinks Mr. Allen will have his own Way or not assist," Gratz Coll., Case 2, Box 33-a, Ltrs. of Richard Peters to Proprietaries. All HSP.

30. Israel Pemberton, Jr., to Dr. John Fothergill, 27 Nov. 1755 and 17 Dec 1755; Fothergill to Pemberton, 8 July 1755 and 18 Aug. 1755, mss., Etting Coll., Pemberton Papers 2:7, 8, 3, 4. HSP. Fothergill's letters are printed, with itemized omissions, in [Fothergill],

is a two-way affair. Although we can see in hindsight that the moment was ripe for the proprietary partisans to woo the strict Quakers away from their as-yet halfhearted support of Franklin, it was just at this moment that Smith and Allen chose to strike at the Quaker jugular. With Penn's eager cooperation.

Penn wrote early in January 1756 to say that their petition had arrived in his solicitor's hands and that he, Penn, would do "every thing in my power" to help it along.[31] Diverse pressures were now coordinated from several directions. The Anglican hierarchy had been drawn in by a letter from William Smith to his friend, the archbishop of Canterbury, who was, by virtue of his office, a member of the privy council.[32] Solicitor Ferdinando Paris conferred with the leading Presbyterian clergyman, Dr. Samuel Chandler, who suggested the device of drafting the proposed oath bill to require the same qualifications for members of assemblies of proprietary colonies as already existed for assemblymen in royal colonies.[33] Paris drafted a bill, which he transmitted to Secretary Henry Fox, to require that no person should sit or vote in any assembly except such as had "duly and solemnly taken such Oaths, upon the Holy Evangelists as by the Laws and Statutes of this Kingdom, for the time being, are, or shall be, required to be taken, to qualify any person to sitt or vote in the House of Commons for this Kingdom."[34] By mid-February, Penn himself had lobbied with the highest dignitaries in the government, and he had the attorney general's promise to see that his desired bill would be "properly done."[35]

Meantime, Penn played the hypocrite with the London Quakers. He called upon his Quaker physician, Dr. John Fothergill, to discuss Penn's relationships with the Pennsylvania Friends, and both his and Fothergill's reports of the visit have survived. They do not agree. Penn virtuously wrote that he told Fothergill about the petition to require oaths, "and the part I should take, as I think it very unbecoming me to act any other than

Chain of Friendship, 158–161, 165–67. See also his two letters of 4 Oct. ibid., 167–70. Fothergill was eminent in his profession; among his other patients were Thomas Penn and the earl of Halifax.

31. Penn to Peters, 10 Jan. 1756, mss., Thomas Penn Letter Books 4:206, HSP.

32. Smith to Canterbury, 22 Oct. 1755, in H. W. Smith, *Life and Correspondence*, 1:118–20.

33. Chandler to Paris, and Paris to Chandler, both 23 Jan. 1756, mss., Penn Mss., Off. Corr. 8:21,23.

34. Ltrs. from Paris to Henry Fox, one undated, other 24 Jan. 1756, Pa. Misc. Papers, Penn and Baltimore (unnumbered vols.), mss. pp. 169, 175, 177. Paris noted in the margin of the bill's draft: "The whole Scheme is this: None shall sitt, but those who will *swear*." Emphasis in original.

35. Penn to William Allen, 14 Feb. 1756, mss., T. Penn Letr. Bks. 4:238–39.

a frank open part."[36] Fothergill wrote that Penn "desired me to let [the Pennsylvanians] know he kindly accepted their respectful remembrance of his family and himself, that he was desirous of maintaining a good correspondence with them, that if he differed with them in one particular point, meaning provision for defense, it was not through dislike to them but because it seemed to be both his duty and for their interest—or to this effect."[37]

The formal machinery of government began to move when the privy council referred the Smith-Allen petition to the board of trade, which considered it on February eighteenth and appointed a formal hearing for the twenty-sixth. From the text reposing in the board of trade's files we find who had signed this purported outcry of an anguished people, and our suspicions are confirmed. The 106 signatures are familiar as those of old wheel horses of the proprietary party—placemen and land speculators for the most part—with some recognizable names of Presbyterian sectarian leaders among them. Amusingly, Smith had not signed the petition he had written. The text averred that Pennsylvania was "the only One of Your majestys Colonyes in these Parts which has not armed a single Man." This was about par for Smith's veracity; it was given the lie, with a twist, by no less a person than Thomas Penn, who "inform'd his Royal Highness [Cumberland], my Lord President [Granville], and Mr. Fox [secretary of state] of the committee of Assembly's sending up Arms without your knowledge." Penn was not so carried away by a passion for truth that he passed this information to the board of trade; he expertly pushed the Smith-Allen petition through the cumbersome government machinery in record time. Even before the board reported, Secretary Fox delivered the petition into the House of Commons.[38]

Smith's complex fabrications

Something more than corridor intrigue was mixed into the plot. Smith's *Brief State* had set off a propaganda war of such importance that space must be permitted here for its consideration. An *Answer* in pamphlet form

36. Penn to W. Smith, 14 Feb. 1756, mss., Penn Papers, Thomas Penn, 1730–66 (Boxed), HSP.

Bibliographic note: To meet the sailing date of the packet boat, Penn wrote on the same date to Governor Morris, R. Peters, W. Allen, J. Hamilton, and R. Hockley; and he copied these letters into his Letter Book (4:224–43), but he did not copy the letter to Smith. A duplicate of the Smith letter appears, with a postscript dated 22 Mar. 1756, in William Smith Papers 2:7. Apparently it was sent in case the first should miscarry. All HSP.

37. [Fothergill], *Chain of Friendship*, 175.

38. Mss. transcripts: Board of Trade Papers, Proprietaries 19 (unpaged), indorsed V.152; Board of Trade Journals 64: 89–90, 97–98, HSP; Penn to Morris, 10 Jan. 1756, mss., T. Penn Ltr. Bks. 4:202, HSP.

appeared in London in 1755, clearly not by a Quaker because it recommended assumption of Pennsylvania's government by the crown. Smith sneered at it in another pamphlet of his own that arrived in London in time to be set in type early the following year. This book, *A Brief View of the Conduct of Pennsylvania, For the Year 1755* is even more bloodcurdling than the *Brief State*, and even more inventive. Smith had perfected a technique of planting letters in newspapers in order to quote them in subsequent publications as though he was thus drawing support from other writers in other places. He employed this technique in a complex way in the *Brief View*. As a "Vindicator" of the earlier *Brief State*, he published an anonymous letter in the *New York Mercury*, then quoted this at length in *Brief View* as though it was from a strong endorser of his opinions.[39]

He invented facts to give credence to his outrageous opinions. As "Vindicator," he quoted in turn two fabrications that had earlier appeared in Boston. These supposedly had been written by one "De Roche," an officer of the French high command identified as important enough to summon "all the commanding Officers in New France, to meet me within ten Days at Montreal." There was no such officer by that name, and the names given for the summoned commanders were likewise invented.[40]

39. *Franklin Papers* 6:53n; [William Smith], *A Brief View of the Conduct of Pennsylvania, For the Year 1755; . . . Interspers'd with several interesting Anecdotes and original Papers, relating to the Politics and Principles of the People called Quakers* . . . (London: R. Griffiths, 1756); supplement to the *New York Mercury* no. 168, 27 Oct. 1755. Identification of Smith as author of *New-York Mercury* piece is in [Joseph Galloway], *A True and Impartial State of the Province of Pennsylvania* (Philadelphia: W. Dunlap, 1759), 149. Galloway's authorship is in Lawrence C. Wroth, *An American Bookshelf, 1755* (Philadelphia: University of Pennsylvania Press, 1934), Appendix 5. Thanks to Norman Fiering for showing me Wroth.

Bibliographic note: Smith scribbled as compulsively as any hack writer with delusions of literary grandeur, and he was able to churn out so much because he made up so many of his "sources" out of his imagination. See [William Smith], *Some Account of the North-America Indians . . . To which are added, Indian Miscellanies . . . Collected by a learned and ingenious Gentleman in the Province of Pennsylvania* (London: R. Griffiths, 1754). In this one, Smith has "an Indian Maid of the Royal Line of the Mohawks" write a letter to the "Principal Ladies of New York" in their "high wigwams." This was safe; how many Englishmen would know that Mohawks did not live in wigwams, let alone the rest of this nonsense? Characteristically, when this was reprinted in *The Columbian Magazine* (June 1790), 367, Smith praised its author (himself) as "distinguished in the republic of letters in Pennsylvania" and "particularly eminent in rhetorical compositions." Smith identified in *Bibliotheca Americana: A Dictionary of Books Relating to America from Its Discovery*, eds. Joseph Sabin, Wilbeforce Eames, and Robert W. G. Vail, 29 vols. (New York, 1868–1936), no. 84673n, 21:155–56.

See also [William Smith], *A Letter from a Gentleman in London, to his Friend in Pensylvania; with a Satire; containing Some Characteristical Strokes upon the Manners and Principles of the Quakers* (London: J. Scott, 1756). Sabin 21:139. In this awful doggerel, Smith denounces the "scandalous Behaviour" of the Pennsylvania assembly as "very evidently proved by the ingenious Author of the *Brief State of Pennsylvania*", p. 3. Military men have an old trick of making a few men seem like a multitude by moving them about to shoot from different positions; Smith used the same trick with a pen instead of a gun.

40. [William Smith], *A Letter from Quebeck, in Canada, to M. L'Maine, a French Officer* (Boston: Thomas Fleet, 1754), 3. The supposed officers' names do not appear in *Dict. Can. Biog.*

The second "De Roche" letter appeared in the *Boston Evening Post* of 8 September 1755 and was republished as a broadside.[41] To this, "Vindicator" added still a third "De Roche" letter that was published in the *New York Gazette* of 22 September 1755.[42] Smith was so busy in his varied roles that he apparently failed to make copies of his effusions so that he quoted in *Brief View* from memory instead of the texts. Thus he dated one De Roche letter in the *Brief View* at June 1755 whereas the date on its published version was 10 April.[43] The contents of all these "letters" were so obviously from the same pen that I conflate them here, as indeed Smith did. Though phrases vary, their arguments are homogeneous. Uniformly they attacked Quakers, Moravians, Germans, and the Pennsylvania assembly. Uniformly they pretended a great Catholic plot in the back country to bring in French armies and overthrow British government. Frenchmen had been using the Quakers for a long time. When Louis XIV found that he could not conquer England by military means, a "faithful Jesuit" had infiltrated England and "was the Means of founding a Sect of Quietists or Non-resistants, who held it unlawful to spill Christian Blood." Unfortunately, Quakerism did not have the great success in England that the French had hoped for in order to make "an easy Conquest of the whole Island of Britain," but "the good Scheme seems still in a fair Way to take Effect at last" in Pennsylvania. There the "faithful Missionaries" of the French were reporting that "this meek and peaceable People are serving us most effectually."[44] They were so easy to manage: "These we shall indulge with many Privileges, for their not opposing our Measures, and quietly surrendering their Lands, and submitting to the godly Admonitions of our holy Fathers."[45] All these letters were conveniently written in breezy, colloquial English (from Frenchman to Frenchman), and generally they were pretty crude affairs; one had its supposedly French writer characterize his own people as hiding in burrows in "sculking Places."[46] But no anti-Catholic propaganda could be too crude for Boston, where two of the "letters" were published before Smith swept them up in his *Brief View* with some adaptations. (For example, he omitted the fake names of French commanders after the real identities of French generals became known.)

We cannot forget that the *Brief View* appeared while French forts and armies occupied Pennsylvania territory and organized massacre and pillage against Pennsylvania's people. Its accusations were calculated to arouse

41. The *Evening Post* letter is printed in "The Antipathy of New England Aroused . . ." in *The American Catholic Historical Researches* 17(1900): 68–72.

42. *Brief View*, 18.

43. Ibid., 16; "Antipathy of New England," 68.

44. *Brief View*, 16–17.

45. *Letter from Quebeck*, 6. Am I right in thinking that Roman Catholics do not use the term *godly?* I know it is much used by Anglicans.

46. "Antipathy of New England," 71.

hatred and hysteria, and its advice was to lynch Quakers—not just figuratively or politically, but in actual physical murder. Once again, the device was a "letter," this one supposedly from a righteously indignant "back inhabitant" of Pennsylvania. It calls the Quakers "the bloodiest People in our Land," "hard-hearted Wretches" who probably have entered into secret agreements with the French to preserve themselves while sacrificing the Scotch-Irish frontier people; and it attributes to a particular Quaker assemblyman, Nathaniel Grubb, the quoted remark that some of the Scotch-Irish, if killed, "could well enough be spared."[47] (Grubb indignantly affirmed an affidavit, when he saw the book, that this was a lie; but its anonymity forestalled a libel suit, and Smith did not surface to challenge Grubb's affidavit.)[48] The "back inhabitant's" letter concludes that "Such a Religion ought to be rejected, and if possible extirpated from the face of the whole Earth, by every good Patriot and good Christian." How was this to be done? Anonymous Smith comments as author of the book, abandoning the "back inhabitant" pose at this point, that one way of getting rid of the Quakers would be "by cutting their Throats." He observes that this certainly would have been done "by great many sanguine People of the back Countries . . . if great Pains had not been taken to prevent it."[49]

One would not very readily guess from this diatribe that the frontier county of Lancaster, three months before its writing, had elected four Quakers to its four assembly seats. Thomas Penn read the book with great satisfaction. It was "very judiciously wrote," he told Smith, "and published at a most proper time." Very judiciously also, Penn did not copy this remark into his record of outgoing correspondence.[50] "Equally void of truth and shame" was the restrained comment of Assembly Speaker Isaac Norris.[51]

Smith's authorship was guessed at in Pennsylvania, where his inventions and invective aroused hostility only against himself, but he made a strong impression on the English public. "Popular clamour was raised to a very great height," wrote London Friend John Hunt, "and the prejudices of people in general were such that they had no Ears to hear; therefore 'twas no time for Us to speak, but patiently to sustain all their Calumny."[52] The clamor was not directionless. Smith's *Brief View* arrived

47. *Brief View*, 58.

48. *Pennsylvania Journal and Weekly Advertiser* no. 705 (10 June 1756), repeated in no. 707 (17 June 1756).

49. *Brief View*, 61, 70n.

50. Penn to Smith, cited n36 above.

51. Norris to Fothergill, 16 June 1756, mss., Norris Ltr. Bk., 1719–1756, 98–100, HSP.

52. John Hunt to John Pemberton, 23 Mar. 1756, mss., Pemberton Papers 11:61. The effect in Pennsylvania was the reverse of that in England. Furious altercations raged in *The Pennsylvania Journal* from Mar. through June 1756, in which Smith was thrashed.

in London in time to be set in type by February 1756.[53] Thus it was circulating at just the time when it could have maximum effect, while the bill to exclude Quakers from Pennsylvania's assembly was under consideration.

"*Filius Gallicae*"

At about the same time that the *Brief View* arrived in London, the ministry intercepted a series of letters purportedly from one "Filius Gallicae" in Pennsylvania to the duc de Mirepoix, the French ambassador in England. These letters were written in English, "not doubting that your Grace is well acquainted with that Language" although the writer supposedly knows French well. They are in much the same rather breezy style as that of the spurious De Roche at Montreal, and they harp on the same themes—Smith's favorite themes. The writer is a treacherous Roman Catholic who asserts that other Catholics are only waiting for opportunity to rise in favor of French invaders; indeed this writer pretends to have recruited many thousands of disaffected persons to strike at the right moment. He is sure that the immigrant Germans are indifferent whether England or France rules, and he gloats that the Quakers would not "be prevailed upon to have a proper Militia Act." He professes to praise Acadian refugees in Pennsylvania who had "flocked" to him to help overthrow the British. As intense inquiry disclosed no person who conformed to the self-identifications given in the letters, it seems clear that they were written in order to be intercepted and to make an effect upon the ministry that could not be achieved by an open publication. Although it is obvious today that the letters were fabricated, they contained much information that could have been known only to a few highly-placed persons, including details of the deployment of British troops, and they were overtly, undeniably treasonous. The ministers were gravely concerned. Of the first letter, Lord Halifax wrote, "What inclines me to think more seriously of the anonymous Letter than I otherwise should do, is that almost every Fact mentioned in it is, either in the whole or in great part, true."[54]

The factual details were accessible to William Smith through his intimate association with Pennsylvania's executives, and the style of writing is much in the mode of *Brief State* and *Brief View*. The issues touched on to provoke ministers' alarm were precisely those that Smith had aimed at in his publications, and the letters appeared at just the right time to enhance

53. Printer's advertisement, *Brief View*, 88.

54. "Intercepted Letters, 1756" in *American Historical Association Annual Report of the Year 1896*, 2 vols. (Washington, D.C.: Government Printing Office, 1897) 1:662–85. Halifax quotation at 685.

the effect of the overt publications. I think these were as much productions of Smith as the equally anonymous books. He had reason to preserve special secrecy; these letters would have hanged him. Whether or not Smith was in fact the author, the letters achieved the effect desired by him of creating alarm, and this will be noticed again further on. Here we may recognize that the propaganda's linking of supposedly disloyal Catholics with assertedly fanatic and stupid Quakers created a climate of opinion highly favorable to Thomas Penn's lobbying.

The oath deflected

Ministers were almost stampeded. They took a grave view of avowed pacifists leading the legislature of a colony suffering the ravages of invasion and seemingly susceptible to insurrection. "You accept of a publick trust," they told Quaker lobbyists, "which at the same time you acknowledge you cannot discharge. You owe the people protection." It was no use for the Quakers to point out that the Pennsylvania assembly had in fact raised great sums of money for the war effort, euphemistically appropriated "to the King's use." Or that a voluntary militia had been established such as was acceptable to the majority of Pennsylvanians. Or that the assembly seemed to have done in one way or another all that any assembly could do. Or that, far from being unique, it was acting in the pattern of all the other colonial assemblies. Events had moved too far for such reasoning to take effect. On 3 March 1756, the board of trade made a strong report to the privy council on the Smith-Allen petition to bar Quakers from the assembly.[55]

What might be called the Quaker International saved the situation in the long term by a compromise demanding short-term sacrifice. There were many men of weight and substance among the London Quakers whose wealth and political connections commanded respect. We have seen how that greatest of merchants in the tobacco trade, John Hanbury, acted as London spokesman for the Ohio Company of Virginia. Hanbury had powerful friends. He had helped Lord Chancellor Hardwicke to electioneer for the Whigs.[56] Hanbury was well acquainted with Lord Granville, president of the privy council, possibly because of Granville's large estates

55. Board of Trade Journals, mss., 64:104; Fothergill to Israel Pemberton, 16 Mar. 1756, mss., Etting Coll., Pemberton Papers 2:10, all HSP.

56. John and Capel Hanbury to lord chancellor, 13 Apr. 1754, mss., Hardwicke Papers, Add. MSS. 35,592, BL. Capel Hanbury, John's cousin and partner, was a member of Parliament from 1741 until 1765, and his son John "inherited" his seat from 1765 until 1784. They had to qualify for membership by taking the same oath being resisted in behalf of Pennsylvania Friends. Locke, *Hanbury Family* 1:165.

in North Carolina. In his own right, Hanbury was a very important man,[57] and he remembered that he was united to Pennsylvania Friends "in the Bonds of Gospel Fellowship." As Dr. Fothergill reported, Hanbury "exerted himself with great zeal on this occasion with several people of the first rank."[58] Newcastle was one of them.

In the present situation, Hanbury's friendship with Lord Granville was critical. Thomas Penn was Granville's brother-in-law, and Penn counted heavily on his support. Indeed, when Penn presented Granville with a copy of the Smith-Allen petition, he observed complacently that Granville had received it "with a peculiar satisfaction."[59] It was peculiar enough, but not in the sense meant by Penn. Granville was a veteran politician who knew as well as his brother-in-law how to intrigue secretly. He got in touch with John Hanbury, and Hanbury waited upon him with a Quaker delegation that included Dr. Fothergill and Franklin's friend Peter Collinson among other prominent persons. Granville not only informed them of the progress of the Smith-Allen petition; he suggested a device to frustrate its objective. If the Pennsylvania Quaker assemblymen would withdraw voluntarily from the legislature for the duration of the military emergency, Granville thought he could stop passage of the oath bill to debar them permanently. The Pennsylvanians would be obliged to "cast about for proper, moderate people" who would administer military affairs without scruple. The bargain was accepted by the London Quakers, who pledged on their own honor that the "greater part" of Friends in the assembly would withdraw as desired.[60]

Thereupon Granville exerted himself strenuously with other officials, and apparently won Lord Halifax over to a grudging agreement to try his scheme. Halifax told one Quaker that everything depended on how the Pennsylvanians would fulfill the pledge made for them[61] It was a somewhat unnerving condition as earlier correspondence with their overseas brethren had made the Londoners far from free of doubt on the point. Several urgent letters to Pennsylvanians are still in existence, stressing the unavoidability of the bargain and the involvement of the Londoners' honor.[62] The London Meeting for Sufferings wrote a formal Epistle to the Yearly

57. See ch. 2, n9 above.

58. Fothergill to I. Pemberton, 16–19 Mar. 1756, mss., Etting Coll., Pemberton Papers 2:10, HSP, printed in *Chain of Friendship*, eds. Corner and Booth, with valuable notes, 173–78. But in print *zeal* becomes *zest* (?), some passages are noted as omitted, and there seem to be some editorial adjustments of the text. The editors use the mss. cited here.

59. Penn to William Allen, 14 Feb. 1756, mss., T. Penn Ltr. Bks. 4:238–39, HSP.

60. Fothergill to Pemberton, cited n58; Henton Brown to James Pemberton, 11 Mar. 1756, mss., Pemberton Papers 11:55, HSP.

61. Fothergill to I. Pemberton, 3 Apr. 1756, mss., Etting Coll., Pemberton Papers 2:11.

62. Besides Fothergill, Friend Henton Brown kept in touch. Brown to James Pemberton, 18 Feb. 1756; same to Israel Pemberton, 19 June 1756; same to James Pemberton 31 July 1756, mss., Pemberton Papers 11:50, 86, 102, HSP.

Meeting in Philadelphia, and underscored its concern by sending two emissaries to exert all possible powers of persuasion in person.[63] Pennsylvania Friends seem to have impressed even their brethren abroad as very firm types. But the honor of the Londoners was upheld. Ten strict Quakers withdrew from the assembly, and those who remained were of the "defense" persuasion that did not scruple against necessary military measures though they did not knuckle under to Thomas Penn either.[64]

Granville's skill at maneuver cleared the storm away even more quickly than it had blown up. Neither the privy council nor Parliament took any further action on the oath bill. Thomas Penn wrote disconsolately to Smith that "this affair is ended." But it was not entirely over. Certain of the ministers of government had been annoyed enough to turn on Penn. Not only in Pennsylvania, they pointed out, but in all the colonies, the assemblies had been giving trouble about money; and there was a "licentious spirit" in others besides Quakers. Would Penn guarantee, if the Quakers were to be disqualified from the assembly, that the succeeding non-Quaker assemblies would be any more tractable? He fumbled, "I could not positively engage for it." The general outcome was an attitude among the ministry that frightened Penn a bit. "It will be most prudent, and best approved here," he told Smith," for you to recommend it to every body to forbear any further controversy."[65] And the flood of anonymous malice stopped as if by the turn of a tap.

Penn had won a Pyrrhic victory. Though the strict Quakers were ousted from the assembly, they became active in private associations that were to bedevil Penn more than he ever had anticipated. And they found prudent and moderate men to replace them in the assembly from the ranks of certain "Old Churchmen," as Richard Peters called them. "They are meer Franklinists and will go which way he pleases to direct," Peters wrote to Penn. "They may prove even worse Enemys to the Proprietors than the

63. In September the Pennsylvania Yearly Meeting set up its own Meeting for Sufferings, and in December that Meeting responded to the Londoners' epistle, at which time the emissaries from London were present. (They were John Hunt and Christopher Wilson. Minutes of the Meeting for Sufferings for Pennsylvania and New Jersey, mss., 1:28, 32–33.) John Pemberton is listed as a member of the Meeting for Sufferings, and James Pemberton was chosen as Clerk (pp. 31, 44), but brother Israel is not listed, perhaps because of his heavy responsibilities in the Yearly Meeting.

64. Marietta, "Conscience," 18. Marietta describes other issues besides assembly membership, notably the strict Pennsylvanians' refusal to pay war taxes, a resolution which the Londoners thought jeopardized the whole Quaker community (18–22). Theodore Thayer's books do not discuss the London Friends' intervention.

65. Postscript dated 22 Mar. 1756, unique to ltr., Thomas Penn to William Smith, 14 Feb. 1756, mss., William Smith Papers 2:7; Penn to Gov. Morris, 13 Mar. 1756, mss., T. Penn Ltr. Bks. 4:245–46, HSP. The letter to Morris observes interestingly that several ministers disliked Penn's oath bill because "as the Quakers are a Body of People much respected here, were the chief Settlers of the Province, and as a considerable Body there they are not willing to make them Enemys by a permanent disqualification."

Quakers."[66] Himself an ordained minister of the Church of England, Peters despaired of winning support for the proprietary even in his own church, and he was right.

But the anti-Quaker propaganda had long-term victimizing effects. It undoubtedly contributed to the enactment of test oaths during the American Revolution that succeeded in even worse disfranchisement than Smith and Penn had failed to achieve.[67] And the propaganda is clearly visible in a multitude of histories.

Roman Catholicism in Pennsylvania

What was the reality behind the spectre of Catholic uprising countenanced by Quakers? There was, in fact, a Roman Catholic minority in Pennsylvania; equally factually, Quaker tolerance had extended to Catholics the same right to public worship that other faiths were allowed. In 1692, Maryland prohibited celebration of the Mass and arrested Jesuits, relenting in 1704 only to permit worship in private homes. Thereupon, as a Catholic historian remarks, "Pennsylvania was the only one of the British Provinces that did not except Roman Catholics from the operations of laws permitting Religious Toleration."[68] There were limits that must not be overlooked. By the terms of required oaths or affirmations, Catholics were excluded from holding office. So also were Jews, Unitarians, and unbelievers.[69] But worship was free.

66. Peters to Penn, 28 Apr. 1756 and 1 June 1756, mss., Gratz Coll., Peters Letter Book, 1755–57, 47, 54, HSP.

67. These test oaths and the victimization of the Quakers and other pacifist sects are usually swept under the rug in histories of the American Revolution. For a brief summary of their legislative history see Philip S. Klein and Ari Hoogenboom, *A History of Pennsylvania* (New York: McGraw-Hill Book Co., 1973), 94–98. The fullest and most valuable account that I have seen is Thompson Westcott, *Names of Persons Who Took the Oath of Allegiance to the State of Pennsylvania Between the Years 1777 and 1789, with a History of the Test Laws of Pennsylvania* (Philadelphia, 1865). Persons refusing to swear were "declared to be incapable of holding office, of serving on juries, of suing for debts, of electing or being elected, of buying, selling or transferring real estate . . . they were liable to be arrested as spies if they traveled out of the city or county of their residence" (p. xix). It was estimated in 1784 that "nearly one-half of the inhabitants of Pennsylvania were deprived of the privileges of citizens" (p.xxxvi). Such comment puts a different light on the oft-repeated remark that Revolutionary Pennsylvania adopted the most democratic constitution of all the states; in effect Pennsylvania came under the dictatorship of the presbyteriat. I consulted the copy of Westcott's rare book in the Stewart Collection at Glassboro State College, N.J.

68. Marvin I. J. Griffin, "Why Old St. Joseph's, Philadelphia, was not Founded until 1733," *The American Catholic Historical Researches* 9 (1892), 18. See also John D. Krugler, "Lord Baltimore, Roman Catholics, and Toleration: Religious Policy in Maryland During the Early Catholic Years, 1634–1649," *Catholic Historical Review* 65:1 (1979): 49–75; and Jay P. Dolan, *The American Catholic Experience: A History from Colonial Times to the Present* (Garden City, N.Y.: Doubleday and Co., 1985), 72–85.

69. John Tracy Ellis, *Catholics in Colonial America*, Benedictine Studies 8 (Baltimore, Md.: Helicon Press, 1965), 372.

In 1733, Jesuit Father Joseph Greaton built St. Joseph's Chapel next to the Quaker almshouse in Philadelphia. Of the thirty-seven parishioners, twenty-two were Irish and the rest Germans. When a Presbyterian mob advanced with axes in 1740 to destroy the chapel, a dozen Quakers intervened and saved the building.[70] A plaque on the wall of Old St. Joseph's Church memorializes its founding.

WHEN IN 1733
ST. JOSEPH'S ROMAN CATHOLIC CHURCH
WAS FOUNDED AND
DEDICATED TO THE GUARDIAN OF THE HOLY FAMILY
IT WAS THE ONLY PLACE
IN THE ENTIRE ENGLISH SPEAKING WORLD
WHERE PUBLIC CELEBRATION OF
THE HOLY SACRIFICE OF THE MASS
WAS PERMITTED BY LAW.

IN 1734
THE PROVINCIAL COUNCIL OF PENNSYLVANIA
DEFENDING THE LIBERTY OF WORSHIP
GRANTED BY WILLIAM PENN TO THIS COLONY
SUCCESSFULLY WITHSTOOD
THE DEMAND OF THE GOVERNOR OF THE PROVINCE
THAT THIS CHURCH BE OUTLAWED
AND SUCH LIBERTY BE SUPPRESSED.

THUS WAS ESTABLISHED PERMANENTLY
IN OUR NATION
THE PRINCIPLE OF RELIGIOUS FREEDOM
WHICH WAS LATER EMBODIED INTO
THE CONSTITUTION
OF
THE UNITED STATES OF AMERICA

The governor who had demanded the church's suppression in 1734 was Thomas Penn, then residing in the colony.[71] Penn apparently changed his mind later. Marylanders charged that they lost advantage in the Lancaster treaty with the Iroquois in 1744 because of connivance between Penn and Jesuits.[72]

Like most handicapped minorities susceptible to harassment, Pennsylvania's Roman Catholics made themselves inconspicuous, and not much in the way of substantial documentation for them has survived. What I have found in a brief search suggests that some came up the Susquehanna

70. Griffin, "Why Old St. Joseph's," 21.
71. *Pa. Council Minutes*, 25 and 31 July 1734, 3:546–47, 563–64.
72. Ed. n., *Amer. Cath. Hist. Researches* 9 (1892), 42; Ellis, *Catholics in Colonial America*, 354.

from their earliest lodgment in Maryland, in order to settle in Lancaster County. Reliable numbers seem impossible to get, but enough communicants were in the vicinity to warrant service by a succession of priests.[73] Conrad Weiser, who was one of Penn's trusted men and worked hand-in-glove with William Smith, stirred up an anti-Catholic scare in July 1755, and Governor Morris pressed the assembly about it. The Catholics had "bad Designs." Thirty well-armed Indians lurked about their "very magnificent" chapel, and their priest had given notice that he would be away for at least nine weeks, "whereupon some imagine they've gone to consult with our Enemies at Du Quesne." The Papists were armed "against which the Protestants are not prepared, who, therefore, are subject to a Massacre whenever the Papists are ready." The assembly responded by examining Weiser and another of the Berks County justices associated with him, and concluded that "there is very little foundation for that representation.[74]

Two facts seem relevant: the justices were all proprietary appointees, and their sensational representation came in the midst of Governor Morris's campaign to extract a "regular" militia from the assembly; that is, one whose officers would be appointed by himself.

What information exists, apart from rumor, suggests that at mid-eighteenth century about one percent of the population were Roman Catholics. In March 1757 the Catholic priest in Philadelphia responded to the governor's demand for information with a list of communicants in Philadelphia "and of those whom I visit in the Country." ("The country" for him was Chester County.) It appears that at least one other priest officiated in Berks and Lancaster counties. The Philadelphia priest listed 179 communicants. For those beyond his personal knowledge, primarily Germans, he reported a colleague's remark "that the whole Number of Roman Catholicks, English, Irish and Germans, including Men, Women and Children, does not exceed Two Thousand." This compares to an official estimate of 200,000 Pennsylvanians of all persuasions.[75]

It may very well be that the loyalty of some members of this minority was open to question. Catholic Irishmen had little enough reason to feel loyal to His Britannic Majesty. In Montreal, Bougainville reported that a family of Germans captured in Pennsylvania "assert that if the French should appear in Pennsylvania, this province would make itself an independent republic under the protection of France," but Governor Vaudreuil "did not believe me, or at least he acted as if he had not."[76] If the French plotted an uprising in Pennsylvania, their governor failed to know

73. S. M. Sener, "The Catholic Church at Lancaster, Penna.," *Records of the American Catholic Historical Society of Philadelphia* 5:1 (1894):307–38.

74. *Pa. Council Minutes* 6:503, 533–34.

75. Ibid., 7:447–48.

76. [Bougainville], *Adventure*, ed. Hamilton, 191.

of it; and I have seen no instance of an actual insurrection on even a small scale.

Acadian exiles in Pennsylvania

When 454 refugee Acadians in three sloops arrived in the Delaware River late in November 1755, they became very conspicuous immediately, and their situation provided much grist for William Smith's propaganda mill. Governor Robert Hunter Morris was so alarmed "at the thought of having a number of enemys scattered in the very bowels of the country" that he posted a guard to prevent the refugees from landing. The assembly, on the other hand, voted provisions and protection for the Acadians. Quaker Anthony Benezet (a descendant of Huguenots) visited the refugees, ascertained their needs, and obtained "at least £1,000 currency" to relieve them. "I am proud to say," wrote nineteenth-century chronicler William B. Reed, "that in their relations to those unfortunate fugitives, I find on the records of the popular representative body no trace of the malignant animosity and sectarian antipathy which actuated the Executive."[77] This is the more noteworthy as the province was then gripped by hysterical panic in the wake of Braddock's defeat and the subsequent Indian depredations that had become public knowledge only a month earlier.

Between 1755 and 1761, the assembly spent "upwards of £7,000" on the refugees "to which neither the Crown nor the Proprietaries, as far as I can discover, contributed a farthing."[78] This statement by our chronicler is not quite right because the crown did contribute substantially, though involuntarily, when the assembly reduced its own burden by defining alms for the Acadians as service to the crown that had deported them. Therefore, the assembly paid for this service out of the sums appropriated "for the King's use."[79]

But the exiles were as rigid in Pennsylvania as elsewhere. They refused to work in order to force recognition of their rights as prisoners of war and thus to be included in prisoner exchange; but the crown would not recognize them as such. They won no friends in that bustling colony by standing idle on public dole, and they got into trouble—more trouble—

77. William B. Reed, "The Acadian Exiles, or French Neutrals, in Pennsylvania," *Contributions to American History*, Memoirs of Hist. Soc. of Pa. 6 (Philadelphia: J. B. Lippincott, 1858), 292–97; *Pa. Council Minutes* 6:713, 729, 751.

78. Reed, "Acadian Exiles," 302.

79. Benjamin Franklin was one of the commissioners dispensing the funds, but he was silent concerning the Acadians. "The Acadians in Pennsylvania Ordered to Be Dispersed in 1756," *Recs. of Amer. Cath. Hist. Soc. of Phila.* 5 (1894), 353–56; *Franklin Papers* 6:393–95.

by begging and pilfering. The assembly enacted a law in 1757 to bind out their children, but in 1761 had still not administered it.[80]

The assembly's care is all the more striking in contrast to the callousness of officialdom. When John Campbell, Earl Loudoun, came to Philadelphia early in 1757 as British commander in chief in America, his only concern with the Acadians was to ferret out possible subversives—he had orders to discover "Filius Gallicae"—and to reduce the rest to submission.[81] Loudoun decided they were "mutinous," seized five leaders, and sent them off to England "to be disposed of as his Majesty's servants shall think proper." He suggested impressment in the royal navy.[82]

I lose track of them all after 1761. It seems likely that some went back to Acadia at the end of the war. It is certain, however, that Quaker benevolence and assembly humanitarianism gained no reward except censure, condemnation, and the risk of punishment by the crown. Few people at war admire generosity toward those identified as enemies, no matter how pitiful, and fear adds power to hate. William Smith understood how to make the victims seem able to summon demons from the vasty deeps of the wilderness. The hapless Acadians became a burden to the assembly heavier in propaganda effects than in money costs. The contrast could not be plainer: while Penn's men harassed the helpless victims and used them as a stick to beat Quakers and the assembly, the Friends gave humanitarian aid despite the brand they thus incurred as "friends of the enemy."

80. Reed, "Acadian Exiles," 301–2, 309.

81. Fox to Loudoun, 7 May 1756, *Annual Report of the Amer. Hist. Assn.* (1896), 1:662–63.

82. Loudoun to Pitt, 25 Apr. 1757, mss., Loudoun Papers LO 3467, HEH; *Pa. Council Minutes* 7:446.

Part Three ❧ *WAR FOR WHAT?*

INTRODUCTION ❧

In 1755, Edward Braddock's terrible defeat before Fort Duquesne was offset by British conquest in Acadia. In 1756 and 1757, however, the news from America was almost unmitigatedly disastrous for the British crown, and worse for its colonists. Immense armies marched like those in the nursery rhyme, up hill and down again. The crown's most trusted generals, hand-picked by the duke of Cumberland, proved to be as cowardly as they were inept. Far inferior French forces defeated the British in every engagement but one relatively minor affair, and often did so with captured British artillery and materiel. But the French victories carried little glory when understood, for they were marked by massacre and atrocity as much as by skill in combat.

The immense superiority of British forces on the continent and on the seas was canceled out by a sort of political civil war waged by the ministry against colonials whose resistance drew fiercer attack by the generals than was waged against the French. So long as the duke of Cumberland directed policy from England, the French had little to fear in America.

During these years the French retained Indian tribal allies almost without challenge, and the tribes provided expert manpower far superior in woodland warfare to anything the British could contrive. But the tribes were often at odds with each other. The Iroquois Six Nations carefully balanced negotiations and support on both sides in a remarkable effort to retain and expand Iroquois leadership among the tribes. This policy became entangled with provincial politics in Pennsylvania when leading Quakers sought to end the fighting by direct negotiation with hostile Indians, thus eliminating the Iroquois role as dominating spokesmen for tributary Indians. Thomas Penn's proprietary placemen fought bitterly against the Quaker activities in fear of exposure of ancient scandals, and the confusion was thrice confounded by much mutilation and fabrication of source records.

While all this was going on, backwoods refugees from hatchet and torch straggled in to comparative safety in the towns where they vented bitter wrath. Not privy to the maneuvers in distant capitals, these refugees knew only how they had been struck at their homes by fierce "savage" enemies.

In their understanding, the friends of their enemies could only be monstrous enemies of themselves.

The situation was ideal for manipulation by demagogues who were not slow to seize upon it, both at the time and subsequently.

Chapter 12 ☙ *ENTER TEEDYUSCUNG*

This very Ground that is under me . . . was my Land and Inheritance, and is taken from me by fraud.

Teedyuscung

Chronology

1737.	The fraudulent Walking Purchase of Delaware Indian lands.
1742.	At the instance of Pennsylvania's government, Iroquois chief Canasatego denounces the Delawares as "women" and orders them off their land.
ca. 1755.	Eastern Delawares unite and choose Teedyuscung as chief.
October 1755.	Ohio Indians begin raiding Pennsylvania. Assembly commissioners distribute £1,000 worth of arms and ammunition. Lieutenant Governor Morris denounces the act.
25 November 1755.	Assembly passes and Morris signs Franklin's militia bill. Franklin is then elected colonel of the militia.
27 November 1755.	Assembly passes Supply Act to finance construction and garrisoning of a chain of defensive forts.
December 1755.	William Pitt's bill for English county militias is defeated in the House of Lords.
20–23 February 1756.	William Johnson demands that the Iroquois exert control over Delawares.
28 February 1756.	William Smith stages a rally at the College of Philadelphia for his unofficial military association, which breaks up as Franklin parades the official militia toward it.
April 1756.	Iroquois chiefs meet with resistance from eastern Delawares, on which they recognize Teedyuscung as Delaware chief.
14 April 1756.	Against Quaker protest, Governor Morris proclaims war against enemy Indians and sets a rate schedule for scalp bounties.
19–23 April 1756.	Quakers meet with Scarouady and other allied Indians in Israel Pemberton's house.
25 April 1756.	Pemberton appeals to William Johnson "for assistance" in peace negotiations.
7 May 1756.	Penns appoint duke of Cumberland's nominee, Colonel William Denny, as lieutenant governor of Pennsylvania.

June 1756.	Teedyuscung visits Niagara to explore possibilities of French help, but is disappointed.
13 June–12 July 1756.	William Johnson holds a great treaty with the Iroquois at Onondaga. He takes the petticoat off the Delawares and recognizes Nutimus as their chief. Johnson's patent as a baronet arrives. The Delawares ignore him.
20 July 1756.	Pennsylvania council appoints Kanuksusy/Newcastle and Teedyuscung as the province's "agents" in Indian transactions.
21 July–7 August 1756.	Quakers and government of Pennsylvania treat with Teedyuscung at Easton. Agree on preliminaries toward formal peace.
20 August 1756.	Colonel William Denny relieves Robert Hunter Morris as lieutenant governor of Pennsylvania.
8 September 1756.	Sir William Johnson notifies Pennsylvania government that negotiations with Indians are his responsibility.
22 September 1756.	Commander in chief Lord Loudoun orders Pennsylvania to cease Indian negotiations. Government evades the order.
8–17 November 1756.	Pennsylvania treats with Teedyuscung at Easton. Responding to Denny's question, Teedyuscung denounces the Walking Purchase fraud. Secretary Peters refuses to record the speech, but Charles Thomson does.

When the Indians struck at Pennsylvania in October 1755, responses varied widely. Backwoods people who did not flee to safety demanded arms to defend themselves. Franklin and the other assembly commissioners responded immediately by buying and giving £1,000 worth of guns and ammunition, but they made the mistake of distributing through the province's "best men" who seized the opportunity to pass the arms on in ways that enriched themselves.[1] Governor Morris fumed, not at the profiteers, but at the commissioners who had dared to act in the emergency while he was away at Newcastle in his "other government" of the Three Lower Counties on Delaware. On the twenty-ninth of October, Morris offered only his "best advice and assistance" for the protection of the back inhabitants because he had "neither Arms nor Ammunition at my disposal."[2] Returning to Philadelphia, he learned that the assemblymen had already sent arms and ammunition "to several parts of the Province," an action that he thought "an infringement on the rights of Government."[3]

1. *Pa. Council Minutes* 6:679; Peters to Penn, 28 Feb. 1756, mss., Peters Ltr. Bk., 29–30. Peter's "best men," of course, were the proprietary's cohorts.

2. *Pa. Council Minutes*. 6:653.

3. Ibid., 6:663. Penn reported to Cumberland, Lord President Granville, and Secretary Henry Fox about the assembly's action in distributing arms without Morris's concurrence, "of which they did not like." Controls, authority, and power were the issue; the inhabitants were not to be protected except by controlled means. Penn to Morris, 10 Jan. 1756, mss., T. Penn Ltr. Bks. 4:202.

But in his public pronouncements, Morris accused the assembly of leaving the province defenseless.

Provincial militia

As Quakers still dominated the assembly, Morris (with the propaganda assistance of William Smith) made his argument credible by citing Quaker opposition to the creation of a provincial militia, but as usual he managed to twist the fact by semantic jugglery, since what he demanded was a "regular" militia; that is, one whose finances he would control, whose officers he would commission, and whose top command he would have. Nobody in Pennsylvania except the proprietary henchmen would agree to put that much power and patronage in the hands of Thomas Penn's creature. This was an issue of power, not of pacifism. Even that hardy militarist Benjamin Franklin, who had opposed the Quakers to form his own military association in 1747, would have nothing to do with Morris's scheme.

Under the terrible pressure of Indian raids, the assembly legislated a militia, but it violated all of Morris's demands by making the officers elective, giving command to the elected colonel (who was Franklin), and keeping control of finances in the assembly. This was in the pattern adopted by other provinces, including militarist Massachusetts, but Morris denounced it furiously, William Smith lied about it expertly, and Thomas Penn lobbied for its repeal by the crown.[4]

Meantime, as related in chapter 11, Penn, Smith, and their cohorts strove to get Parliament to disqualify Quakers from holding assembly posts. As we have seen, strict pacifists did withdraw from the assembly in order to fend off the oath legislation, but the newly constituted assembly under Franklin's lead became tougher than ever, and busier than ever. The assembly financed and garrisoned a ring of defensive forts at the "gap" passes through the mountains. Franklin inspected the forts and drilled his troops.[5]

This did not happen simply, because Morris still had a few tricks up his sleeve. Let Richard Peters report how the governor was forced to accede to popular clamor. "The Inhabitants of the several Wards of the City whilst the Governor was at New York formed themselves into Companies and chose their Officers under the present Law, and presented them to the Governor for his Approbation, but without Lists of the Names or a Return of the Poll of Election, and the Governor with Advice of Council desiring

4. Morris to Loudoun, 13 Aug. 1756, mss., Loudoun Papers (LO 1479), HEH; Smith *Brief View*, 16, 56–61, 72–81; Penn to Cumberland, 18 July 1757, in *Military Affairs*, ed. Pargellis, 384–85.

5. Hunter, *Forts on the Pennsylvania Frontier*, 185–93.

them to do this, or he could not accept the Choice, the Officers put it to the Vote of the Electors standing before the Governors Door whether they should do this or no, and they unanimously voted they would not give in their Names, and then voted that what they had done should be as nothing, and all this unanimously, and in a rude indecent manner." Up to this point, one might sympathize with Morris; how could he authorize troops whose very names were unknown? But Peters continued: "The Reason given by the Officers for this Treatment of the Governor was that in Conversation he told some of them, as soon as he had the Names of the Companies, he would incorporate them with the Regulars which were coming from New York, and then they would be subject to military Discipline"—the kind of terroristic discipline we have seen in chapter 10. Peters still: "This it seems the Governor denies he said with respect to the Militia, tho' he did mention some such thing with respect to the Guards posted on the Frontiers and in the Pay of the Province; but such Umbrage was taken at the very Thought, that the whole City was in an Uproar, and the Governor treated most rudely in their Discourse, and by Papers thrown into his House."[6] Peters must be credited with keeping Penn informed of the true state of affairs distinct from propaganda versions, and it is notable that Penn continued to rely on Peters as his major informant, year after year.

Franklin opposes Smith

William Smith continued to do battle. He conceived a Plan of Association "for promoting *Military Discipline* among the Freemen of Pennsylvania, who are not WILLING and DESIROUS to act under the present *Militia Law.*" The name and idea were lifted bodily from Franklin's old association of 1747; even his cannon were to be used for training. But the purpose now was to block Franklin from accomplishing anything with his new militia, which loomed as a Frankenstein before the proprietary's men. The denouement was colorful. Notice was given that a public meeting would be held at Smith's College of Philadelphia for the promotion of the anti-pacifist, anti-militia association. We may be sure that Provost Smith had a rousing oration ready, but he never delivered it because Colonel Franklin ordered the first review of the legal militia in State House Square,

6. Peters to Penn, 17 Feb. 1756, mss., Penn Pprs., Off. Corr. 8:29–32, HSP. Cf. Morris to Shirley, 22 Dec. 1755, mss., Loudoun Papers (LO 705), HEH. In it, Morris says that obedience to orders in the militia can only be enforced "by the Junction of Regulars with the Provincial Forces." The popular understanding of Morris's intentions is further reinforced by his request for authority from Shirley to hold courts-martial. Morris to Shirley (extract), 9 Feb. 1756, mss., Loudoun Papers (LO 811), HEH.

on the same date as the association's meeting at the College. Then Franklin ordered the troops, under arms, to parade the quarter-mile through the city streets to the College. The Associators, given warning, decamped hurriedly.[7]

It makes a strange and fascinating picture. A bespectacled and bald, middle-aged, fat philosopher astride a probably rather stately horse, and leading a wobbly column of untrained, ununiformed, enthusiastic, non-academic youth to besiege the college he had founded and of which he was still nominal president. Did ever town and gown confront each other in more dubious battle?

Several months later, Smith embroiled himself directly with the assembly, which jailed him for contempt. He escaped and fled to England where he had to remain until the slow processes of review rescinded his conviction—on a technicality.[8]

The militia in Britain

Disputation about militias was one of the more curious oddities of this politically complex war. Historians on each side of the Atlantic have paid attention to the issue as manifested on their own side without showing awareness of what was happening on the other side. Yet, while the colonial assemblies jealously guarded against the possibility of their governors gaining control of their militias' power and patronage, the same issue appeared in England where the Whig aristocrats struggled to prevent Tories and the king from creating an institution that would threaten Whig power.

William Pitt introduced a bill in the House of Commons in December 1755 purporting to reorganize the county militias. In reality he was trying to *revive* them as they had long fallen into disuse under the discouragement of successive Whig administrations. Pitt's bill passed Commons but was defeated by the Lords upon the urging of Lord Hardwicke that Pitt's bill was too democratic. Taking advantage of the fears aroused by military setbacks, Pitt reintroduced his bill, and it became law in June 1757, but its local administration faltered. The duke of Newcastle gloated to a correspondent: "I am sure you are not sorry to see that the militia goes down

7. *Franklin Papers* 6:415–18.

8. The best descriptions of this affair are in *Gentleman's Magazine* 28 (1758): pro-Smith, 194–95; pro-assembly, 275–77. Amusingly Smith's biographer portrays his subject's flight as "the only way to obtain action on his appeal," but has to acknowledge that the fugitive was one jump ahead of the assembly's sergeant at arms. Gegenheimer, *William Smith*, 145–47. Smith's crimes deserved punishment, but for the sake of civil liberties we may be grateful for his final victory in the case as it put some limits on the assembly's arbitrary powers to crush dissent.

in very few counties; so I hope we shall soon have an end of that chimera."[9]

Newcastle's motive went deeper than dislike of impracticality; he really feared the possibility that the militia might work. Its establishment, he thought, "would be, in time, the ruin of our Constitution and the immediate destruction of the Whig Party."[10] Newcastle had learned that the Tories were using militia musters to rally support for opposition candidates to Parliament.[11] In 1760, when Parliament considered a bill to establish a militia in Scotland, Newcastle summoned "all our friends from every part of the kingdom" to defeat it.[12]

Though Whig lords ostensibly feared too much democracy, while colonial assemblies feared too much prerogative, they mutually worried about a military power out of their own control.[13] Both were promptly abused as unpatriotic by the jingos. Invective aside, Newcastle's political instincts were generally correct. As will be shown in part V, the Whigs did lose power when militarism became dominant in Parliament, and the correlation was more than coincidental.

Beat the Indians or conciliate them?

In Pennsylvania, Governor Morris and Assemblyman Franklin tried to cope with Indian raids by military means, but pacifist Israel Pemberton could not accept this as the right way. While the militarists organized counterforce, Pemberton searched for reasons. Since Pennslyvanians had always treated the Indians fairly, why had the Indians taken up the hatchet? Or was it possible that the treatment had not always been fair? If that were so, the logical way to stop hostilities would be to remove the causes of grievance.

Underlying the distinct attitudes of Pemberton and Franklin (not to speak of Morris) lay contrasting assumptions about what Indians were. Franklin, despite his genius, conceived the human species in terms of race.[14]

9. O. A. Sherrard, *Lord Chatham: Pitt and the Seven Years' War* (London: The Bodley Head, 1955), 96–97, 109, 174, 276. *Gentleman's Magazine* 26 (1756) esp. 457–60, 509–10.

10. Sir Lewis Namier, *England in the Age of the American Revolution*, 2d ed. (London: Macmillan and Co., 1961), 118 and n6.

11. Reid, *In Defiance of the Law*, 108.

12. Sherrard, *Lord Chatham*, 360.

13. That power, rather than pacifism, was the issue in the colonies is demonstrated by Virginia's militia being organized in the same way as Pennsylvania's. The frontier people would serve only under their own elected officers. R. L. Morton, *Colonial Virginia* 2: ch. 22, esp. p. 687.

14. Cf. his remarks in "Observations concerning the Increase of Mankind, Peopling of Countries, &c.," par. 24, *Franklin Papers* 4:234.

For him the natural attribute of the "tawny" race was a state of savagery.[15] Ironically, Franklin can be seen as the more forward-looking of the two men, anticipating as he did the heavy emphasis that nineteenth-century scientists would put on race. Sometimes thought's progress forward is backward.

Though Pemberton convinced him eventually that the Delawares had real grievances, and Franklin then took practical steps to do justice, his instant response to the backwoods raids was management of the crisis, as we have seen. In short, if there had to be a war, Franklin wanted to win it. His desire is hard to fault.

Conceptually, Pemberton was the more conservative of the two, reasoning from assumptions of religion instead of race. He responded to war by trying to stop it, and his particular religion comprehended an understanding of Indians rather different from the concept of savagery. To the faithful followers of William Penn, Indians were fully human persons, lacking only the light of true religion. Thus, they were rational beings. Thus, they responded gratefully to kind treatment and resentfully to abuse. It followed that Indians on the warpath must have been abused.[16]

Pemberton was right. Almost from the day that William Penn returned to England in 1701, the Delaware Indians, and later the Conestoga and Shawnee bands in Pennsylvania, had been encroached on, swindled out of their lands, and generally pushed around. Their troubles have been recited in full, documented detail in this book's predecessor volume. Precisely because such conduct could be defended neither morally nor legally, it had been hidden from view in conspiracies and secrecy. (Critics of conspiracy theories of history deserve respect only after they attend to the evidence of conspiracy facts.)

Thomas Penn personally had managed the key conspiracy, the Walking Purchase of 1737 with its sequel, the Pennsylvania-Iroquois dispossession of the Delawares in 1742. Accordingly, when Pemberton searched for Delaware grievances, he necessarily uncovered evidence of Penn's wrongdoing. In doing so, he abruptly reversed the initiative in Pennsylvania's political struggles by throwing Penn onto the defensive. Both Franklin's short-range coping and Pemberton's long-range probing were required to

15. In a passage much quoted by Indians who assert that admiration for the League of the Iroquois influenced the writing of the U.S. Constitution, Franklin remarked, "It would be a very strange thing, if six Nations of ignorant Savages should be capable of forming a Scheme for such an Union . . . and yet that a like Union should be impracticable for ten or a Dozen English Colonies . . ." Attribution of this to the making of the Constitution is absurd. It was written, 20 Mar. 1751, advocating colonial union *against* those "ignorant savages." *Franklin Papers* 5:118–19.

16. For William Penn's conceptual distinctions, see Jennings, *Ambiguous Iroquois Empire*, 242–48.

frustrate Thomas Penn's schemes to break the assembly's power. Both set to work almost immediately after the raids began.

The enigmatic Iroquois

Though Israel Pemberton was not a member of assembly in 1755, his brother James belonged to the dominant Quaker group. Their attitude was plainly expressed in the assembly's first response to Governor Morris's demand to be supplied with arms and a militia. Having already distributed £1,000 worth of arms through its commissioners, and being utterly opposed to the creation of a provincial armed force, the assemblymen passed over Morris's demands in order to express their own concerns. As of 5 November 1755 they hoped to contain the damage: "we are resolved to do every thing in our power to redress them [the Indians] if they shall appear to have received any wrong or Injury at our hands, tho' nothing of that kind hath come to our knowledge, and if possible to regain their affections, rather than . . . entail upon ourselves and our posterity the Calamities of a Cruel Indian War." With that statement of policy they asked Morris to inform them of any "disgust or Injury" that might have alienated the Delawares and Shawnees.[17] He ignored the question.

Though this Quaker policy of the assembly was short-lived there and has suffered much condemnation in histories parrotting Morris and Penn, it was soundly conceived, for the Delawares were as divided in councils as the Pennsylvanians. At Kittanning, the Delaware "capital," though the marauding warriors led by Shingas and Captain Jacob had brought home a hundred prisoners, Shingas's brother Tamaqua (Beaver) refused to take up the hatchet offered by the French commandant of Fort Duquesne. This intelligence came to George Croghan from Delaware Jo, an eastern convert Indian, and Croghan passed it on to Morris and council. According to Delaware Jo's account, a party of Delawares had first been persuaded to strike Virginia "in April or May" of 1755 (while Braddock was still on his march), and this had happened through the intervention of a party of Iroquois warriors accompanied by Caughnawagas and Algonquins on their way to their perpetual war against the southern Indians. "Neither the Beaver nor several others of the Shawonese and Delawares approved of this measure nor had taken up the Hatchet, and the Beaver believed some of those who had were sorry for what they had done, and would be glad to make up Matters with the English."[18]

We may remember Stobo's account of how the Delawares had offered

17. *Pa. Council Minutes* 6:678.
18. Ibid., 6:781–82.

to take Fort Duquesne, only to be summarily rebuffed by Braddock.[19] One can sigh wistfully at the thought of what might have been if the peace parties among Delawares and Pennsylvanians had been able to communicate, but bellicosity prevailed. Morris must certainly take a share of the blame, but other Europeans and some other Indians were also involved. Morris and his council were much perplexed by Delaware Jo's additional information that he had traveled as far as Logstown, and "That there are more or less of the Six Nations living with the Shawonese and Delawares in their Towns, and these always accompanied them in their Incursions upon the English and took Part with them in the War." Croghan confirmed this by accounts from other Indians "that the Delawares and Shawonese acted in this hostile Manner by the Advice and with the concurrence of the Six Nations."[20] Yet the Pennsylvania government's official policy was to rely upon the Six Nations to summon the raiders off the warpath. How was the policy to be reconciled with such facts?

Tribal politics were as vigorous as the provincial variety. When Superintendent of Indian Affairs William Johnson demanded that the Iroquois Six Nations pacify the warring Delawares, the League chiefs agreed to do so.[21] Nevertheless, as we have seen, Iroquois warriors raided with the western Delawares; and, as will be shown in chapter 13, other Iroquois collaborated with the French in their home territory in the Mohawk Valley. We must pause to consider this anomalous situation. The concept of race war must be discarded as irrelevant to a conflict in which Indians could be found allied to Euramerican colonials on both sides. Geography provides a clue. The Iroquois raiders in the west were probably Senecas and Cayugas.[22] Iroquois collaborators with the French in New York (or, better, in Iroquoia) are identifiable as Oneidas and Onondagas. The only Iroquois who remained doggedly loyal to the British were the Mohawks, whose eroded territories had been consistently protected by William Johnson against further encroachment. Indeed, by the mid-1750s, the Mohawks had become practically feudal retainers of Johnson's. The territorial claims of the other distinct nations of the League coincided with the regions in which their warriors were fighting.

Iroquois did not attack British colonials in lands that acknowledgedly had been

19. See ch. 7 above.
20. *Pa. Council Minutes* 6:783.
21. Treaty minutes, 19 Feb. 1756, *N.Y. Col. Docs.* 7:57. Note the speaker's remark that the Iroquois had "already sent some of our people to take the Hatchet out of the hands of our Nephews the Delawares, and we should be glad that you would draw your Troops from the Frontiers." In his letter transmitting this to the lords of trade, 8 Mar. 1756, Johnson recommended that *more* forts be built in Iroquoia. Ibid., 7:41–43. The highly confused issue of fort building requires distinctions: when the Indians asked for forts, they wanted places of refuge for their women and children, but the British wanted them to control the Indians. Obviously these were different sorts of constructions subsumed under the same word.
22. *N.Y. Col. Docs.* 7:118.

ceded by treaty to Pennsylvania. When this pattern is seen, the seeming contradictions in Iroquois behavior make sense in terms of Iroquois interests and goals. The chiefs of the League were not naive. Their strategy was essentially the same as Governor Vaudreuil's; that is, to keep greater powers off balance and uncertain. The chiefs knew from long experience that British and French scribes wrote treaty agreements to suit British and French interests, so what the chiefs did was to speak "from the lips only" whatever their interlocutors wanted to hear. What they did was another matter, a distinction we must observe most carefully.

Besides their territorial objectives, the Iroquois aimed to restore the intertribal leadership they had exercised in the Covenant Chain confederation before the Chain shattered.[23] In this connection, also, distinctions must be noted. Obviously the chiefs at Onondaga were in no position to give orders to the Ohio Delawares backed by the fortified French and the Senecas and Cayugas. But the fragments of eastern Delawares were surrounded on three sides by British colonies and the Mohawks, Oneidas, and Onondagas. In case of a showdown, those eastern Delawares could be trounced. Besides that outstanding fact, the lands claimed by Delawares in Pennsylvania had been ostensibly ceded to Pennsylvania by the Walking Purchase deed, which the Iroquois had endorsed for reasons of their own. Iroquois credit was so much bound up with that swindle that the Delawares dared not even mention its fraudulence until the end of 1756.

All these factors added up to an activist Iroquois strategy—definitely not passive neutrality—aimed at recovering tribal lands and intertribal leadership. In eastern Pennsylvania the strategy produced Iroquois admonitions to the Delawares to get off the warpath and make peace with their Pennsylvania brothers. Though the Delawares did not scorn or reject the advice, the process of peacemaking became entangled with provincial politics and the ambitions of their rising "pine tree chief" called Teedyuscung.

Delawares in the east

We must distinguish very sharply between the eastern and western Delawares for, in the era under discussion, they acted quite independently of each other. For all practical purposes they had become separate political entities linked only by language and an awareness of kinship. Thus, when the eastern chiefs promised to stop marauding, the westerners paid no attention. From the confused reports of backwoods horrors, it seems likely

23. *N.Y. Col. Docs.* 7:42.

that some young eastern warriors joined the raiding parties in disregard of their chiefs' commitments.

Chief Teedyuscung became a key man in Delaware diplomacy until his death in 1763. He was imposing physically, tall and portly, vigorously middle-aged (about fifty-five). A native of the Delaware Valley on the New Jersey side, he had been a witness to the negotiations that led to the Walking Purchase of 1737, which dispossessed his family among many others. He refuged briefly as a convert in the Moravian mission of Gnadenhütten, but his pride rebelled against the mission's discipline. In 1754, when the Six Nations summoned Gnadenhütten's converts to leave the mission and take up residence in Wyoming Valley on the Susquehanna's north branch, Teedyuscung was among the sixty-five converts who responded.[24]

The Iroquois had two reasons for this maneuver: they wanted the eastern Delawares closer to themselves, away from the separatist and pacifist influence of the Moravians, and they wanted Delaware warriors at Wyoming to stop settlement by Connecticut's invading Susquehannah Company. It soon became evident that Teedyuscung was a warrior and a leader. Charles Thomson explained what happened next.

> The Indians on Susquehannah, about the beginning of the present Quarrel between England and France, considering their Situation and divided State, every Tribe being a distinct and independant Government, plainly saw that their Force could not be great, and that they might one by one be easily crushed, they, therefore, resolved to new-model their Government, and out of the several Tribes to form one Nation: Accordingly the Munseys, and two Tribes of the Delawares, viz. the Lenopi and Wanami, joined together in a League, and chose a Chief, Sachem or King, into whose Hands they put the Management of their Affairs. Those who had been Sachems before, now willingly, for the Sake of the public Good, resigned their Dignity, contenting themselves with a Place in the Council. Teedyuscung was the Person chosen King: He immediately appointed Captains, and regulated the Force of the Nation. Soon afterwards a Number of straggling Indians, who lived up and down without any Chief, joined in and strengthened the Alliance. By this Means, and the Junction of some of the Mohiccons, or [Hudson] River Indians and Shawanese, Teedyuscung soon saw himself at the Head of a very considerable Body. In this Manner he resolved to wait and see what Turn affairs would take, and, when it was determined to attack the English, he took his Measures so, that, at the same Time the Frontiers of Pensylvania, New-York, and New-Jerseys, were ravaged and destroyed.[25]

24. Anthony F. C. Wallace, *King of the Delawares: Teedyuscung, 1700–1763* (Philadelphia: University of Pennsylvania Press, 1949), chs. 3, 4, esp. p. 53.

25. Charles Thomson, *An Enquiry into the Causes of the Alienation of the Delaware and Shawanese Indians from the British Interest* (London, J. Wilkie, 1759). I have used a facsimile unidentified by publisher, place, or date.

Bibliographic note: Thomson was a Presbyterian employed as master of the Friends school

FIGURE 2. Conference at Johnson Hall. "Johnson Hall," BY E. L. HENRY. REPRODUCED BY COURTESY OF THE ALBANY INSTITUTE OF HISTORY AND ART.

This new confederation under Teedyuscung's strong leadership altered the terms of relationships between the Iroquois League and its eastern tributaries. In February 1756, William Johnson pressed the Iroquois to bring Teedyuscung's people under control.

He tried to frighten them. "I plainly foresee," he told them, "unless you the Six Nations, who have always maintained a superiority over the Indians, will now exert yourselves in this case, you will not only lose that

and used as a scribe on several occasions. He had strict standards of justice and religion, and was his own man—by no means a flunky for the Friends. He demonstrated his independence in later years by leading the Revolutionary cause in Pennsylvania and becoming clerk of Congress, in which capacity he served when Congress ordered his Quaker former employers into exile in western Virginia. As will be shown, he was chosen by Teedyuscung to take treaty minutes for the Delawares, and he had much opportunity to talk with them about the background of treaty events.

Thomas Penn's personal, marginally annotated copy of Thomson's *Enquiry* is in the John Carter Brown Library. Several of Penn's notes try to reverse earlier documents. E.g. (p. 22): "the Minisinks were never supposed owners of Land on the west side of Delaware;" but Thomas himself had obtained Minisink signatures for his 1737 quitclaim in the Walking Purchase. (25 Aug. 1737, Penn Papers, Indian Affairs, mss., 1:41, HSP.) And (p. 70): "The Six Nations always claimed a right to the Lands on Delaware;" contradicted by the privately acknowledged refusal by the Iroquois to lay claim until Penn and James Logan bribed them to do so. (Jennings, *Ambiguous Iroquois Empire*, 321–22.

Although Paul A. W. Wallace, relying on a document by Conrad Weiser, has decried Thomson's truthfulness, I have checked Weiser's assertions of fact and found them false. Thomson stands up well. Conrad Weiser, "Observations, made on the Pamphlet, intituled 'An Inquiry into the Cause of the Alienation of the Delaware and Shawano Indians from the British Interest," mss., Moravian Archives: P. A. W. Wallace, *Conrad Weiser*, 71–72; Jennings, "Miquon's Passing, 477–82.

authority which they have hitherto acknowledged, but will have them your enemies."[26] The scare tactic failed to take effect. Onondaga chief Ononwarogo (Red Head) responded evasively: "We always looked upon the Delawares as the more immediate care of Onas [Pennsylvania's governor], that they were within the Circle of his arms." Ononwarogo suggested that the Delawares had justification for their hostilities: Onas had "not taken that friendly care of them as he ought to do, and therefore our common Enemy hath taken the advantage of his neglect."[27]

This was not at all what Johnson wanted to hear, though he took careful note of its implications about abuses in Pennsylvania. His driving purpose was to get those Delawares away from the immediate care of Pennsylvania and into the circle of his own arms. He steered the conference away from considerations of justice to motives of power. "Retrieve your pristine Fame," he exhorted the Iroquois. "Endeavour to bring as many nations of Indians under your alliance as possibly you can . . . settle the minds of all such as are wavering, and those who are now ready to rebel against you." If they would cleave to the English, their brethren would protect and defend them, "and moreover can, and will supply you, and all your allies with the necessarys of life at a cheaper rate than the French can." And he gave "the largest Pipe in America made on purpose."[28]

The appeal to self-interest met a more favorable response than the scare tactic. Johnson made it quite clear that he was a big, important man whose favor could mean much to the Six Nations, and he gave presents with a lavish hand, which was not a trifle in time of war, when ordinary subsistence pursuits were often interrupted for long periods.

So the Six Nations made an effort to comply with Johnson's urging. They sent deputies to meet with the eastern Delawares. What happened at that unrecorded all-Indian council depends a little on which subsequent report is to be credited. According to Seneca captain Kanuksusy (Newcastle), in an account passed on by Conrad Weiser, the meeting was all sweetness and light. Said the Iroquois deputies to a silent congregation of Delawares, "You will remember that you are women," meaning that the Delawares were obliged to refrain from speaking in treaty councils. "Our forefathers made you so, and put a petticoat on you." Sad to say, the Delawares had prostituted themselves with the French and deserved to be chastised. Nevertheless, "we will still Esteem you . . . We now give you a little Prick and put it into your private Parts, and so let it grow there till you shall be a compleat man. . . . do as we bid you and you will become a noted man."[29]

26. Treaty minutes, 20 Feb. 1756, *N.Y. Col. Docs.* 7:59.
27. Ibid., 21 Feb. 1756, 7:61.
28. Ibid., 23 Feb. 1756, 7:63–64
29. *Pa. Council Minutes* 7:218.

Teedyuscung, via Charles Thomson, remembered the scene otherwise. According to him the Six Nations deputies opened the council haughtily with an order "to get sober, as they looked upon their Actions as the Actions of drunken Men." Ordinarily such an order would have settled the matter, but times had changed. "We are Men," responded the Delawares, "and are determined not to be ruled any longer by you as Women . . . so say no more to us on that Head, lest we make Women of you as you have done of us." Which, interpreted, was an upstart assertion that the Delawares would speak for themselves at treaties thereafter, and no longer accept Iroquois spokesmen—with a gratuitous insult that if the Iroquois made an issue of it, the Delawares would lick them. In other circumstances, the Iroquois probably would have accepted this challenge, but the League could not be proud at this time for reasons of *realpolitik*. A danger existed that the western Delawares would come to the help of their eastern kinsmen. Perhaps more importantly, the Senecas sided with the Delawares who in turn acknowledged Seneca pre-eminence separately, and the Senecas outnumbered all the other Iroquois combined. Recognizing that "nothing was to be done by Threats," the League deputies changed to "smoother Measures."[30]

Both accounts agree that the eastern Delawares would speak for themselves through their chief at future treaty councils. The situation appears to be a repetition of the tactic used by the Iroquois at Logstown four years earlier, when the Ohio Delawares chose Chief Shingas to negotiate with Virginia and Pennsylvania. In 1752, asserting pre-eminent right in principle, the Iroquois had "given" the Ohioans the chief they had already chosen.[31] Now, in 1756, Teedyuscung emerged as chief in the same way.

The disparities between the Newcastle / Weiser and the Teedyuscung / Thomson accounts were not negligible, and it is further significant that Conrad Weiser presented his to the governor's council officially, but Charles Thomson very unofficially wrote a book to be read in London as a defense of assembly policies. Much confusion and discrepancy in the records of negotiations yet to come were foreshadowed. Underlying the differences, the basic issue was the status of the eastern Delawares vis à vis the Iroquois League. Officialdom, including Pennsylvania's proprietary, his lieutenant governors, and his placemen, not to speak of Superintendent William Johnson, were determined to uphold and enhance the authority of the Six Nations, with which policy the Six Nations themselves cooperated warmly. Pemberton's Quakers, blocked from influence with the Six Nations, had to commit themselves to Delaware independence if they were to play any role at all in Indian affairs. As they correctly had no faith in officialdom

30. Thomson, *Enquiry*, 86–87.
31. See ch. 3 above.

and devoutly hoped to right great wrongs, they had no option but to become Teedyuscung's champions. Thus the struggle centered upon Teedyuscung's person and standing, which the proprietary side denigrated at every opportunity.

Unfortunately for his and the Quakers' cause, Teedyuscung had a great thirst for rum and an ability to stay on his feet, but not to keep his head, after swilling astounding quantities of it. With a little embroidery from proprietary scribes, his utterances when in his cups make him appear as a clown, the mere dupe of the Quakers for their own horrid schemes against Thomas Penn. There are good reasons, however, to believe that Teedyuscung used the Quakers more than they used him. This man was no fool. When sober, which was most of the time, he exhibited the qualities that had won Delaware leadership over the heads of men better qualified by birth. The sources must be read with this understanding.

Pennsylvania declares war

Harried Morris had to do something, anything, to recover at least an illusion of authority. General Shirley rejected his request for royal troops to be sent into the province.[32] The assembly withheld control over provincial troops and arms, and Morris's stonewalling defense of Penn's estate and prerogative led to dissension even among Penn's supporters.[33] There

32. Penn to Newcastle, 20 Jan. 1756, mss., Newcastle Papers, Add. MSS. 32,862, f. 159, BL. Penn wrote from premature information. Shirley apparently changed his mind and provided regulars that Morris posted at Reading and Easton. Morris to Shirley (extract), 9 Feb. 1756, mss., Loudoun Papers (LO 811), HEH.

33. See Peters to Penn, 13 Nov. 1755, mss., Gratz Coll., Ltrs. of R. Peters to Props., 12, 14; same to same, 8 Nov., 1755, mss. ibid., case 2, Box 33-a, HSP. For the popular hatred of the proprietaries, and their supporters' suspicions of each other, see Peters to Penn, 13 Nov. 1755, mss., ibid., 13; and same to same, 24 Oct. 1756, in *Pa. Mag. of Hist. and Biog.* 31 (1907), 247. One of Penn's strongest supporters, ex- and future governor James Hamilton, was so disgusted with Penn's ploy of a "free gift" of £5,000 of delinquent quitrents that he advanced £1,000 out of his own pocket and shamed Penn into paying him back, but not before Penn had protested that Hamilton's "goodness" was "not necessary, and will distress us beyond measure."

Penn's solution for the delinquent quitrents was to try to make the assembly collect them, a neat trick for foisting harsh dealing onto his adversaries. "This is the time," he wrote, "and this is the most popular pretence that ever can happen for our forcing the Arrears." Penn to Peters, 9 Oct. 1756, mss., and Penn to Hamilton, 8 Jan. 1757, mss., T. Penn Ltr. Bks. 5:24–25, 68, HSP.

A series of Penn's letters insists that not a farthing should be paid to the public service out of any other of his receipts than the delinquent quitrents, and urges his agents to seize properties from nonpaying owners. Notable in this sequence is his demand that a portion of even the delinquent rents, when collected, should be forwarded secretly to him instead of being used to defray his "free gift." This was done. It is plain that persons who had fled the Indian raids were most likely to be in arrears, and there is no indication in any of Penn's writings that such fugitives should be exempt from his extortions. His agents Richard Hock-

was plenty of dissent also among the opponents of the proprietary, who split into hostile factions of pacifists and belligerents.[34] Among the latter were the assembly's commissioners, a sort of executive committee for doing business between sessions of the full assembly. On 10 April 1756, while Franklin was away in Virginia, the remaining four commissioners proposed formally to Morris "that it is necessary for this Province immediately to declare War against the Delawares and all other Enemy Indians" and promised to supply funds for scalp bounties. They appended a neat schedule of prices, including one of 50 dollars "for the Scalp of every Indian Woman" and 130 dollars for "every Male Indian above Ten Years old."[35]

Some "Strict and reputable Quakers" promptly protested, but Morris and his council endorsed war, with the notable dissent of Quaker grandee William Logan; and Morris issued his proclamation on the fourteenth "in the Presence of the Council, Supream Judges, Magistrates, Officers, &ca., and a large Concourse of People."[36] It was the worst thing he could have done. Even Conrad Weiser opposed the scalp bounties on the grounds that the nearest and most likely scalps to be brought in would be those of friendly Indians.[37] The first practical effect of the declaration was to abort William Johnson's pacification of the eastern Delawares, and thus to add Johnson to the multitude of Morris's critics.[38]

Johnson's star was rising in London because he seemed there like the only colonial official capable of stopping the drain of Indian support to the French. Thomas Penn read the signs and hastened to offer friendship to Johnson, who coolly kept him waiting for a response. Penn instructed Peters to offer a bribe to Johnson.[39] Penn tried also to recover lost political advantage by offering the post of his province's lieutenant governor to Johnson's cohort Thomas Pownall, who was much consulted by the ministers about American affairs, and the mere rumor of the offer caused panic among the provincial placemen; but Pownall refused when he learned

ley and Edmund Physick threatened publicly to "distress" renters in arrears.

Thomas Penn Ltr. Bks. 4:191–92, 207, 211, 212, 215, 217, 222, 232, 234, 241–43, 256, 301, 346–47, 352–53; *Pa. Journal* 690 (27 Feb. 1756), p. 1; Hockley's broadside, 24 Jan. 1757, Penn Papers, Off. Corr. 8:223, HSP.

34. See Israel Pemberton to John Fothergill, 26 Apr. 1756, mss., Etting Coll., Pemberton Papers 2:12. For context see Ralph L. Ketcham, "Conscience, War, and Politics in Pennsylvania, 1755–1757," *Wm. and Mary Qtly.*, 3d ser., 20 (1963), 416–39.

35. *Pa. Council Minutes* 7:78.

36. Ibid., 7:88–90.

37. P. A. W. Wallace, *Conrad Weiser*, 434.

38. Johnson to Shirley, 24 Apr. 1756, *Johnson Papers* 2:447.

39. Penn to Johnson, 12 June 1756, mss.: "Whenever I can be of service to you or your Interests I shall always think myself most agreeably employed." T. Penn Ltr. Bks. 4:317, HSP. Printed, *Johnson Papers* 9:471–72. After months of silence from Johnson, Penn suggested to Peters that a "compensation" should be given to Johnson "for his trouble." Penn to Peters, 11 Dec. 1756, mss., T. Penn Ltr. Bks. 5:52.

how Penn intended to hobble him with instructions.[40] Worried Penn rushed to the duke of Cumberland again, and thereby compounded his problems. For what he gained by sycophancy he lost through Cumberland's nominee, who was Colonel William Denny.[41] Denny proved in a very short time to have the single talent of quarreling with everybody. Like many such quarrelsome persons who insist on the deference due to them, Denny was short on genuine self-esteem; he accepted Penn's ironbound instructions without demur, but lacked the backbone to keep his bargain.[42]

While the courtiers danced their rituals, the raids continued in the province. Quakers outside the assembly had been quiescent in politics while they attended to relief for the afflicted Moravians.[43] Israel Pemberton, for one, expressed great unease about the "indecency" of the assembly's rows with the governor[44]—but Morris's declaration of war could not be ignored by pacifists. They stormed at him and sent a protest to the crown without noticeable effect. Then they settled down to practical activity. Israel Pemberton determined that if the government refused to bring about a peace, the Friends would do it instead.

Friends campaign for peace

The first requirement for making peace was to make contact, which could only be done through the agency of friendly Indians. Several Iroquois Indians were in Philadelphia, the most important of whom was Scarouady, the "Half King" of the Mingos—but a Half King in prudent flight from his presumed subjects in the Ohio Valley, Pemberton held a

40. *Franklin Papers* 6:453n7; Fothergill to Pemberton, 8 May 1756, mss., Etting Coll., Pemberton Papers 2:13.

41. *Military Affairs*, ed. Pargellis, 367n; Ketcham, "Conscience, War, and Politics," 430–31.

42. Denny's commission, instructions, and £5,000 sterling bond cover 14 folio pages of tiny script. The bond was to be forfeit if he violated instructions given in minute, explicit detail. Penn insisted to Peters that it was "very plain" that governors were "obliged to conform to Instructions from their Proprietors, tho' they are not from the King." He repeated the thought: "tho' it may be natural to say the King has the greatest power, it is not reasonable to say, he can exert his power in every instance where the Proprietor may." Pa. Misc. Papers, Penn and Baltimore, Penn Family, 1756–1768, mss., 7, 9, 11, 13; Penn to Peters, 21 Feb. 1755, Peters Papers 4:4, HSP.

43. £267.15 was collected immediately by Quakers in response to Moravian bishop Spangenberg's request, Pemberton Papers 71:31, 35, HSP.

44. Pemberton to Fothergill, 27 Nov. 1755, mss., Etting Coll., Pemberton Papers 2:7, HSP. In the light of proprietary propaganda about the "Quaker-dominated" assembly (and its continuance in histories), Pemberton's antagonism is highly notable. He deplored "the Darling Scheme of gaining some Advantage over the Governor and Proprietor, for the sake of which every other Consideration seem'd to be little regarded." Same to same, 17 Dec. 1755, mss., ibid., 2:8.

series of conferences with Scarouady and the other Iroquois at his home, along with a group of substantial Friends.[45]

In the light of what was to happen later because of the Friends' intervention, it is interesting to see how careful they were at this time to do everything through proper channels. They first obtained Governor Morris's approval of their project—he seems to have become desperately willing to try anything—and they used Pennsylvania's official interpreters headed by Conrad Weiser.

Not surprisingly, Weiser suggested an appeal to the Six Nations. The others agreed, and Pemberton asked Scarouady to take the appeal to Onondaga. He offered in behalf of Friends "to restore that peace and Harmony . . . at our own expence and in our own persons." Undoubtedly altruistic and seemingly innocuous, the remark contained the seed of much future difficulty because, no matter what Morris might agree to, William Johnson had received a royal commission giving him exclusive charge of Indian affairs, and Johnson intended to enforce his jurisdiction. When Pemberton and his Quakers reached out to the Six Nations to "restrain" the Delawares, they were encroaching on Johnson's most jealously guarded privilege. It did not matter that Pemberton's intended objective conformed fully to Johnson's public strategy. The Quakers were setting themselves up as a distinct power in Indian affairs, a competitive power that Johnson would not suffer.

Pemberton was so intent on peace that considerations of personal interest probably did not enter his mind at the time, though they might not have deterred him in any case.

Naively, Pemberton turned to Johnson for help, writing that "our principal Reliance for Assistance . . . is on thee. The Interest thou hast both with your Governor and with the Indians will enable thee to do more than any or even many others can; and without the Interposition and concurrence of some, in whom the Indians can confide, there's no room to expect a permanent Peace will be made." He offered, in behalf of Friends, to pay Johnson's expenses in the peacemaking.[46] Pemberton was soon to discover how badly he had misplaced his principal reliance.

That was yet to come. Meanwhile, in one of the conferences at his home

45. A number of manuscripts report the meetings at Pemberton's on 19, 21, and 23 Apr. 1756. My version is based primarily on the Papers Relating to the Friendly Association, mss., 1:79, 103, 107, 123, Friends Historical Library, Haverford College. Two more copies, somewhat variant, are in Misc. Mss., 1756, 4mo. 31, same place. Weiser's signed report is in the Indians Coll., HSP (formerly Etting Coll., Misc. Mss. 1:84, 86).

46. Pemberton to Johnson, 25 Apr. 1756, Loudoun Papers, HEH, printed in *Johnson Papers* 9:441–43. Pemberton was so intent on getting past possible political obstruction that he sent this copy directly to Johnson while also sending another via New York governor Sir Charles Hardy. Pemberton to Hardy, 27 Apr., and Hardy to Pemberton, 29 Apr. 1756, mss., Loudoun Papers, HEH. I have not found any response from Johnson.

he told Scarouady that if the Six Nations would prevail upon the Delawares his Quakers would "stand between them and our Government for as we consider they have no King and their old Wisemen are gone we look on them as Children, who do not know what they are doing, therefore if they will repent, We will do all we can to have them forgiven." To emphasize sincerity, Pemberton repeated this message two days later and read it into a large white belt of wampum for Scarouady to carry. This Quaker whose religion banned ritual caught on to the forms of tribal ritual swiftly enough.

Scarouady gave a grateful tribute to the Quakers (which Conrad Weiser omitted from his report of the conferences) and undertook the mission. But Pemberton's "affectionate cousin," the provincial councilor William Logan, sounded a private warning. He had "Very Good Grounds," he wrote, to think that "whatever Measures may be proposed, however promising their Appearance may be, they will in the End Prove abortive and be thought by some too difficult, if not Impossible, to be put in Execution."[47] Logan withheld explanation of his enigmatic comment. Pemberton forged ahead.

Teedyuscung, Johnson, and the Iroquois

The confused eastern Delawares beheld great powers converging upon them from every direction. In the west, French troops at Fort Duquesne backed Delaware kinsmen and Shawnees. The French at Niagara maintained a force of allies in the northwest. Directly northward was the Iroquois grand council at Onondaga. William Johnson held court in the northeast. Directly east, Connecticut's Susquehannah Company threatened to move into Delaware territory at Wyoming. Southeast were the Moravians and their mission, and beyond them the hostile colonials of New Jersey; and directly south sprawled the towns and government of Pennsylvania. Such a situation should have crushed Delaware morale, but instead it inspired unprecedented aggressiveness. Seneca support and the mere fact of having raided colonial settlements and gotten away with it created a mood of exhilarated bellicosity so strong that Teedyuscung decided to do what no eastern Delaware had ever done previously. He would see what the French might do for his people. With French backing he could join his Ohio brethren and defy the pressures of William Johnson and the Six Nations.

He took a delegation of warriors to Niagara in June, 1756, but ardor cooled as they observed the garrison's straitened circumstances. Com-

47. Logan to Pemberton, 26 Apr. 1756, mss., Etting Coll., Pemberton papers 11:71, HSP.

mander Pouchot had scarcely enough provision and arms for his inadequate garrison; only promises could be spared for the Delawares.[48] Teedyuscung decided to shop in Pennsylvania. He sent notice that he would respond to the province's invitation to negotiate.[49]

This did not accord with William Johnson's plans to concentrate all Indian negotiations in his own bailiwick, where he was cooperating with the Iroquois rather than controlling them; and where he had a hard time trying to reconcile the divergent and competing interests of the individual nations of the League.

While Pemberton conferred with Scarouady in Philadelphia, Johnson met with a delegation of Onondagas at his home where Speaker Tiogwanta summoned him to a grand council at Onondaga in which to meet the Six Nations, the Delawares and Shawnees, "and our several Allies." Johnson agreed, but soon had to wonder what was happening within the League when a delegation of Mohawks arrived separately to oppose his attendance at the Onondaga council. Their real reason, as distinct from specious expressions of concern for Johnson's safety, appears to have been the ancient rivalry with Onondaga for League leadership. They reminded Johnson of his previous statement that the Mohawks "were the head or Masters of the Delaware and Shawanese Indians" and that it was Mohawk responsibility to "take the Hatchet out of their Hands." Fairly clearly, the Onondagas had outmaneuvered them, and Johnson apologetically had to keep his explicit agreement to meet the League at its central fire.[50]

The council took place in June. It confirmed Johnson's suspicions of "uneasiness and coldness to our Interest" amongst the Six Nations, "particularly the upper Nations;" that is, those west of the Mohawks. The council's many issues are beyond present concerns; we must concentrate on the Delaware connection.[51]

Johnson created a paper victory for himself, suitable for admiration in London, by compelling a Delaware "king" to agree to peace at the Onondaga negotiations; but the "king" whom Johnson recognized was doddering old Nutimus, who had long passed the age when he could lift a hatchet. Nutimus's leadership was hereditarily legitimate in one village of the several whose warriors were following Teedyuscung, and Teedyuscung stayed

48. *Johnson Papers* 2:510–11; A. F. C. Wallace, *King of the Delawares*, 96–97. Pouchot did not distinguish Teedyuscung's deputation from the miscellaneous "Indians of the upper country" coming to Niagara for food and equipment. He wailed that shortages were so serious that he would have to abandon the fort if supplies did not come. [Pierre] Pouchot, *Memoir* 1:61.

49. Teedyuscung kept all his options open. When Pennsylvania's behavior appeared unreliable, he went to Niagara again in 1757, but it was only a tentative gesture. A. F. C. Wallace, *King of the Delawares*, 152–55.

50. Johnson's minutes, *N.Y. Col. Docs.* 7:97, 98, 106–7, 108, 114, 115–16.

51. Johnson to lords of trade, 17 July 1756, *N.Y. Col. Docs.* 7:118.

away from the Onondaga meeting. This was one occasion in which the device of diplomatic recognition failed to have the desired effect; Nutimus did not displace Teedyuscung. The Iroquois kept quiet about their own previous recognition of Teedyuscung as eastern Delaware "king," or, if they said anything to reveal it, Johnson's minutes took no notice.[52]

Johnson was becoming more powerful among British colonials almost by the hour. His newly arrived royal commission as superintendent of Indian affairs put him outside the authority of provincial governors though it required him still to obey the "Commands and Directions" of Commander in Chief William Shirley. That requirement was more formal than substantial since Johnson communicated directly with the ministry where he enjoyed high favor with Lord Halifax.[53] As the Onondaga conference ended, Johnson announced jubilantly that he had been ennobled as a baronet; thenceforth he was to be *Sir* William Johnson.[54] Such things were not trivial in the rank-conscious colonial society, nor to the Iroquois who paid much attention to rank and titles in their own society; but Johnson was far from controlling the Iroquois. They knew the difference between

52. A. F. C. Wallace, *King of the Delawares*, 98–99; *N.Y. Col. Docs.* 7:119; minutes, ibid., 7:130–61.

This occasion illustrates once more why a student must read treaty documents with care. Colonials often recognized particular Indian authorities for the colonials' convenience; the chiefs so recognized were not always the authorities accepted by the Indians concerned. The device has a long history in diplomacy generally, and is still much practiced worldwide.

53. Board of trade secretary John Pounall to Johnson, 5 Mar. 1756, *N.Y. Col. Docs.* 7:40–41; commission, 17 Feb. 1756, *Johnson Papers* 2:434–35; ltr. transmitting, 13 Mar. 1756, *N.Y. Col. Docs.* 7:76–77. The letter informed Johnson of his Parliamentary grant of £5,000, his salary of £600 per year, and his baronet patent. No colonial official could match such marks of court favor.

Johnson's rise is often attributed to the Pownall brothers. They had influence, to be sure, but one must take account also of the recommendation made by Lord Loudoun before he became commander in chief. Loudoun (to Halifax, 1755), Remarks on affairs in North America, mss., Loudoun Papers (LO 722), HEH.

54. Treaty minutes, 11 July 1756, *N.Y. Col Docs.* 7:158. *On nobility:* I have been chided by my late friend Donald Kent for classing Johnson's baronetcy as a lordship, on grounds that it did not qualify him for the peerage. Insofar as nobility is identical with membership in the House of Lords, Mr. Kent's point is well taken, but my usage is broader. According to Edward Augustus Freeman, the British peerage "is an institution purely local"; he defined nobility generally as "a pre-eminence founded on hereditary succession, and on nothing else." (Which might explain old references to "nobles" among Indians.)

James I, who created the dignity of baronet for such a fee as William Johnson paid, stipulated that it should rank between barons and knights, should entitle its holder to be addressed as "Sir," and should entail knighthood for male heirs on their coming of age. See "Nobility" and "Baronet" in *Encyclopaedia Britannica*. 11th ed.

Actually the concept of lordship in England is as muddled as most English institutions regardless of heraldic dicta. Viscounts bear the "courtesy title" of "Lord" though not qualified to enter the House of Lords until their fathers die. And "life peers" cannot bequeath their titles, so that, by Professor Freeman's stress on heredity as the determining factor, they are not noble though they sit in the House of Lords. Can there be any doubt that Thomas Penn's proprietorship of Pennsylvania made him a great lord in fact, though not of the peerage?

Johnson's projection of authority onto Nutimus and Teedyuscung's exercise of real power. They preferred also to preserve all their options rather than become mere agents for Superintendent Johnson, so they continued recognition of Teedyuscung as the chief of the eastern Delawares.[55] Accordingly, when Teedyuscung rode into Easton in July, 1756, he could speak, as the diplomats like to say, from a position of strength. He found the Pennsylvanians in a state of wild disarray.

Preliminaries to peace in the east

Teedyuscung came first to Bethlehem, the Moravian town on the Lehigh, or Delaware West Branch, River.[56] It says much for the character and discipline of the Moravians that he chose to return among the people who had suffered much from the depredations of his followers. For security, the projected treaty was appointed to be held at Easton, a village on the fringe of colonial settlement where the Lehigh falls into the Delaware. The choice held much symbolism, for it was at Easton, in 1742, that the Iroquois had figuratively taken the Delawares by the hair of the head and thrown them out of their homeland.[57] From that time onward, the eastern Delawares had been compelled, as "women," to keep quiet at treaties—if indeed they were allowed to attend—while the Six Nations' chiefs spoke for them. Now, in 1756, Teedyuscung would speak for himself.[58]

55. Peters to Johnson, 3 Sept. 1756, *Johnson Papers* 2:556. Johnson's belated and grudging acknowledgment of Teedyuscung's status, and announcement of intention to reduce it, is in Johnson to Abercromby, 28 Apr. 1758, ibid., 2:824–30.

56. *Pa. Council Minutes* 7:198–99.

57. Jennings, *Ambiguous Iroquois Empire*, 342–46, 388–97.

58. The minutes of this first meeting, taken by Richard Peters with assistance from Conrad Weiser, show already the obfuscation that was to become the trademark of that team's records about Teedyuscung. Officially they quote him as saying, "I am here by the Appointment of ten nations among which are my Uncles the Six Nations authorized me to treat with you, and what I do they will all Confirm." (*Pa. Council Minutes* 7:208). A manuscript by another observer shows what the official version left out. In this one Teedyuscung says, "I have the Appointment of Ten Nations, among which are my Uncles the Six Nations *authorizing me to transact Business for my own Nation*, and what I do they will all confirm." (Council at Easton, July 1756, mss., (possibly by William Logan), APS, unpaged, quotation under 28 July.) It may be noticed that the editorial tampering with this speech for the official version transformed its grammar by substituting *authorized* for *authorizing*.

By the official version, Teedyuscung seems to claim rule over the Six Nations as well as the Delawares—a device that Conrad Weiser used to discredit Teedyuscung with the English and get him in trouble with the Six Nations. But the editing was spotty. Further on it permits him to say, in seeming contradiction, "I am but a messenger from the United Nations. Tho' I act as a Chief man among the Delawares, I must now hear what you have to say to my People . . . [and] deliver it faithfully to the United Nations, and let them, as they are my superiors, do as they see Cause." (*Pa. Council Minutes* 7:208–9). From this record, proprietary men could pick and choose according to whether at any given moment they wanted

The provincial assembly was embarrassed by a shortage of available funds because of its financial battles with Governor Morris, but it found £300, intending half for presents and half for Morris's expenses. Morris, however, spent three-quarters on his retinue. The Quakers came to the rescue with a collection among themselves which Morris had to accept, with a promise to deliver it in their name, because his present otherwise would have been so "trifling."[59] It was well that they provided, for otherwise, as Richard Peters told Thomas Penn, "we should have been ruined."[60] At the treaty, Teedyuscung mentioned the Delawares' "want and Distress," and asked Morris to "act the part of a Charitable and wise man." He promised, "I will do my Share. Whatever Kindness you do to me or my People, shall be published to ten Indian Nations; we won't hide any Presents you shall give us."[61]

If he had publicized only Morris's tiny remnant, the Indians would have seen it as a sign of contempt. Morris lumped the Quakers' large present in with his small one and mentioned casually that a "part" of the whole was from the Friends.

This was a sideshow, though not unimportant. The council's business was peace. "Wish Shiksy!" said Teedyuscung, which he translated as "do it Effectually and do it with all Possible Dispatch." But Morris would not conclude an agreement until he should see Teedyuscung's "whole People" and all their captives. "While you retain our Flesh and Blood in slavery It cannot be Expected we can be friends with you, or that a Peace can come

to flagellate Teedyuscung as a braggart claimant to powers he did not have, or whether they wanted to demean him as nothing more than an errand boy.

From other sources a more coherent picture appears. What Secretary Richard Peters wrote to Thomas Penn shows that the muddled state of the official minutes was deliberate. In Peters's private version, confirmed by other sources, Teedyuscung is clear and straightforward: he is quoted as saying that the Six Nations, "having now incorporated five other Nations, had appointed only two Kings to do their Business, and he was one of them, who was to preside over and do the Business for the Delaware and four other nations." (Peters to Penn, 4 Aug. 1756, mss., Penn Mss., Off. Corr. 8:135; see also Peters to Johnson, 3 Sept. 1756, HSP, *Johnson Papers* 2:556).

We have seen the phrasing of the APS manuscript above. Another, by a Moravian observer, noted that a Six Nations chief had been appointed to transact business other than Teedyuscung's (Treaty held at Easton, 28 July 1756, mss., Moravian Archives, Bethlehem, Pa.) This partner "king" appears to have been Seneca chief Newcastle (Kanuksusy) who made it quite clear that Teedyuscung had been authorized, in a council that took place about July 1755, to act under Iroquois patronage. (*Pa. Council Minutes*, 20 July 1756, 7:99). Thereupon, the Pennsylvania council accepted Newcastle and Teedyuscung as official intermediaries between Pennsylvania and the Indians. (They were appointed as Pennsylvania's "agents.") Teedyuscung's subsequent negotiations without Newcastle are explained by Newcastle's death from smallpox. (*Pa. Council Minutes* 7:307, 337).

59. *Pa. Council Minutes* 7:203–4; Pemberton to Fothergill, 26 July 1756, Etting Coll., Pemberton Papers 2:15

60. Thayer, *Israel Pemberton*, 110.

61. *Pa. Council Minutes* 7:208–9.

from our hearts." The captives' return was "a Necessary Condition of Peace."[62]

So the chief accomplishments of the council were to avoid further alienation and to agree upon another, more conclusive meeting. Even this minimal first step was threatened by Morris's secret launching of a raid upon the Ohio Delawares' town of Kittanning, news of which arrived in Philadelphia shortly after the conference with Teedyuscung.[63] We may be sure that he heard of it too. New Jersey jeopardized the peace still more by declaring war on the Delawares and attacking the easterners' abandoned village at Wyoming. (The Indians had retreated to Tioga.)[64]

Perhaps these actions were justified on practical grounds as well as retaliation for Indian attacks, for long experience had proven that colonials could win in woodland combat only by destroying the warriors' home bases. Morris had authorized the strike at Kittanning before meeting with Teedyuscung, and the Jerseyites were not privy to his negotiations. Nevertheless, the attacks could hardly have impressed Teedyuscung's people as compatible with peacemaking. There were more difficulties. Sir William Johnson wrote to advise tactfully that *he* would look after Pennsylvania's interest with Indians.[65] General Shirley's successor commander in chief, Lord Loudoun, peremptorily ordered a stop to the province's Indian proceedings.[66] Someone from Fort Johnson sent advice to Teedyuscung that the Pennsylvanians were plotting to kill his people "as soon as any considerable Number could be got together."[67]

Treaty at Easton

But the Quakers and the assembly persisted. A new governor, Colonel William Denny, had come to replace Morris, and Denny had been instructed by Lord Halifax in London to pay close attention to Indian affairs. Bewildered by Loudoun's contradictory order to leave them to Johnson, he consulted the assembly. There must have been lawyers in that body, for it managed to interpret Loudoun's order into a meaning precisely opposed to its language. Denny should avoid giving a "disgust" to the Indians, advised the assembly. To withdraw from an arranged treaty would have a bad effect. By semantic slight of tongue, the assembly advised an "inter-

62. Ibid., 7:209, 212.

63. Morris's orders to Lieutenant Colonel John Armstrong, 14 June 1756, *Pa. Council Minutes* 7:161, 230; Armstrong's report, 14 Sept. 1756, ibid., 7:257–63.

64. A. F. C. Wallace, *King of the Delawares*, 95–96.

65. Johnson to Denny, 8 Sept. 1756, *Pa. Council Minutes* 7:278–79.

66. Loudoun to Denny, 22 Sept. 1756, mss., Loudoun Papers (LO 1876), HEH. Printed in *Pa. Council Minutes* 7:269–70.

67. Thomson, *Enquiry*, 97–98.

view" in which Denny should make a firm peace for Pennsylvania but should refer the Delawares to Sir William Johnson "for a final Conclusion and Ratification." Whereupon the "interview" popped up again as a "treaty." To proceed thus, the assemblymen argued, would be "not inconsistent with the Intention of Lord Loudoun's Letter."[68]

Denny's council agreed with the assembly for once. Neither body wanted to have provincial powers diverted to other hands, no matter how royal—perhaps especially if royal. Richard Peters thought Loudoun's letter "of the most extraordinary nature that was ever wrote to a Governor." He complained to Thomas Penn that "if Indian affairs are taken out of the hands of this Government so as neither to suffer the Governor to confer or treat with Indians all our friendly Indians will soon turn against us and we shall have a most lamentable winter."[69] This sudden unanimity occurred, it should be noted, when the assembly was no longer under Quaker management, but was more hostile than ever to the proprietary Penns.

Grumblingly, Denny agreed, and the interview/treaty took place after all. A curious inversion occurred in the preparations. In July, Teedyuscung had ridden to Easton with a few followers while Governor Morris had gone in pomp with a large military guard. Now, in November, Teedyuscung was so worried about the hostilities and warnings intervening that he posted companies of warriors on the frontiers "to wait for Accounts how he was received, and to act accordingly."[70] But the provincial assembly refused to fund a military escort for Governor Denny on grounds that it was unnecessary—as indeed it was. Denny took six officers anyway.[71] He arrived at Easton, 8 November, with this honor guard, Secretary Peters, Councilor William Logan, four commissioners from the assembly (including Franklin) "and a Number of Citizens of the City of Philadelphia, chiefly of the People called Quakers."[72]

Teedyuscung did not bring all his people as he had promised in July, nor any of their captives. The campaign against the treaty had frightened him enough to leave all the Delaware women and children at home, and to post his warriors strategically, as we have seen. Precise numbers are on record: he was accompanied by four unidentified Indians from the Six Nations, not including Kanuksusy/Newcastle (who was dying of smallpox in Philadelphia), sixteen Delaware followers, two Shawnees, six Mahicans, and a Christian Delaware from New Jersey who acted as interpreter.

68. Ibid., 99; *Pa. Council Minutes* 7:307–08.

69. Peters to Penn, 2 Oct. 1756, mss., Gratz Coll., Peters Ltr. Bk., 93–94, HSP. Printed *Pa. Mag. of Hist. and Biog.* 31 (1907), 246–48. Curiously, Peters suspected Franklin and his friend Thomas Pownall of instigating Loudoun's order, but Franklin wrote the assembly's rationale for evading it. Rogers, *Empire and Liberty*, 31–32.

70. Thomson, *Enquiry*, 98.

71. Pemberton to Fothergill, 26 July 1756, mss., Etting Coll., Pemberton Papers 2:15.

72. *Pa Council Minutes* 7:313; Thomson, *Enquiry*, 99.

The omens were not propitious. Nevertheless, the parties got down to business.

Several reports of what happened at Easton still exist. Richard Peters wrote one, and if not for his deception and subterfuge, one could almost sympathize with Peters's plight. He was a gregarious fellow who wanted to be on good terms with gentlemen of all persuasions, but he was also absolutely dependent on Thomas Penn's favor; and, as keeper of the provincial records, he knew more about the handling of Indian affairs than comforted him in the present circumstances. If Morris had still been in the governor's chair, Peters would have happily sheltered behind Morris's stone wall, but Denny was out of control. During Denny's short tenure so far, his obstinacy and bad temper had so alienated proprietary men that they stayed away from Easton, and Peters faced the combined forces of Pemberton's Quakers and Franklin's assembly commissioners with only Conrad Weiser and Quaker councilor William Logan for support. Peters observed with less than pleasure that minutes were being taken by persons besides himself. The Moravian missionary David Zeisberger wrote industriously among the observers, Quaker Abel James also. Most disquietingly, the master of the Friends' school, Charles Thomson, had been brought along by Pemberton to make a record competing with Peters's for accuracy.[73]

The Walking Purchase exposed

Despite some hubbub, the council moved well enough toward its purpose. Teedyuscung "behaved exceeding well," according to Peters's private evaluation, and negotiations avoided "the two Rocks that might hurt"; namely, making a peace separate from the other colonies, and acting in conflict with Sir William Johnson. But there was one "unhappiness." The Indians "publickly complained of *Injustice* done them in their *Sales* of Lands, by the Proprietors . . . and the Quakers have by this Declaration, gained great Cause of Triumph, thinking they have fairly shifted off the Cause of the War and Bloodshed from themselves . . . upon the Proprietors."[74]

It was definitely not Peters's fault, and this can be believed. He and Weiser tried, with various specious excuses, to prevent Governor Denny from questioning the Indians about their grievances.[75] Peters tried to con-

73. Minutes of the Friendly Assn., mss., p. 21a. Indian Records Coll. (Am. 525), HSP; Peters to Penn, 22 Nov. 1756, mss., Penn Papers, Off. Corr. 8:201–5.

74. Ibid.

75. P. A. W. Wallace, *Conrad Weiser*, 461; Minutes of the Friendly Assn., mss., 19b–20a, HSP. Peters had been instructed by Penn, long before, that in any negotiations with the Delawares, "you must take care not to be imposed upon by Friends to throw any blame on us." Penn to Peters, 14 Feb. 1756, mss. T. Penn Ltr. Bks. 4:232–33, 237–38.

vince Denny that the Delawares had always attributed their hostility to French instigation and deceit, so why stir up new trouble? Weiser argued that this was the wrong situation for questions about grievances. But Denny was stubborn. As Peters reported to Penn, Denny had been told "by some principal men in the Ministry that the Indians had cause of complaint, and it was suspected that the Proprietaries had not dealt justly with them." He was determined therefore, "as much as the Quakers or Commissioners," to get a statement from them.[76] So Denny asked a fateful question in full, open session: "Have we, the governor or People of Pennsylvania, done you any kind of Injury?" The matter was so important that he adjourned sessions to allow preparation for an answer next day, which was Saturday, 13 November.[77]

The Indians responded jubilantly. Pemberton saw such joy in their faces as he could not express. They "hurried across the Benches to offer the Governor their hands. One of them cry'd out, Oh! he is a good Man, there is no Evil in his Heart."[78]

This was a curtain raiser. The drama came to climax next day when Denny repeated his question: Had the Indians received grievances from Pennsylvania's government or others? "I have not far to go for an Instance," responded Teedyuscung; "this very ground that is under me (striking it with his Foot) was my Land and Inheritance, and is taken from me by fraud."[79] Thus rose the long-haunting spectre of the Walking Purchase of 1737, and it so frightened Richard Peters that he put down his pen and declared himself unable to record its appearance.

As to this, it may as well be said plainly that Peters's feigned amazement had a purpose. He knew the background of Teedyuscung's charge as well as any man living. He understood very well that Thomas Penn had been guilty of criminal fraud and that he, Richard Peters, had been, and continued to be, Penn's accomplice. Richard Peters had been present on that occasion also. He knew everything that needed to be known about the Walking Purchase. When he threw down his pen in 1756, his purpose was simply to suppress Teedyuscung's charge from official records.[80]

But Charles Thomson among the observers continued to write, so Denny ruled that Thomson's notes should be adopted officially "as the most Perfect." Worse yet, from Peters's point of view, Denny invited some of the Quakers and Franklin to dinner, where addled Peters could only pretend to be glad that opportunity had risen to prove the groundlessness of the

76. Peters to Penn, 22 Nov. 1756, cited n73.
77. *Pa. Council Minutes* 7:320.
78. Minutes of the Friendly Assn., mss., 20a, HSP.
79. *Pa. Council Minutes* 7:324.
80. See Samuel Parrish, *Some Chapters in the History of the Friendly Association* . . . (Philadelphia: Friends' Historical Assn., 1877), 35–39.

Indians' complaint."[81] Ever-pragmatic Franklin suggested that the easiest way to remove the Delaware grievance would be to pay compensation on the spot. A payment of £500 could be arranged so as to remove the final obstacle to peace. Franklin was right; much grief and trouble, not to speak of expense, would have been avoided if his suggestion had been adopted, but star-crossed Teedyuscung declined. The land was not his personally. (His use of the first person singular was a convention of Indian rhetoric when referring to the speaker's tribe.) The particular owners of the land at issue were not present, and Teedyuscung would not act without their prior approval, so the meeting broke up with many expressions of good will, but yet some unfinished business.[82]

Thomas Penn's reaction

The peacemaking had begun, but only begun. Thomas Penn, the greatest landowner in the British empire, understood at once the implications for himself of the Delaware and Quaker exposé of the Walking Purchase fraud. Because the crown had revoked colonial charters when the chartered lordships brought on Indian wars, Penn knew that he must put the blame for Delaware hostilities entirely on French instigation if he was to save his own government. This required that he must clear himself of the charge that the Walking Purchase fraud had created Delaware hostility, which implied in turn that he must discredit Teedyuscung and block Pemberton. He exerted all his skills of lobbying and contrivance. Ironically this occurred at just the moment when orthodox Quakers were trying to separate themselves from assembly truculence in order to seek reconciliation with the Penns.

Penn had stated his strategy in Indian affairs succinctly: "we should

81. Minutes of the Friendly Assn., mss., 20b, HSP. On the day following Teedyuscung's statement, Presbyterian convert Moses Tatamy told Pemberton the Indians' version of the Walking Purchase. This was resurrected by A. F. C. Wallace in *King of the Delawares*, p. 21, after centuries of neglect. Moses Tatamy's Account, mss., Etting Coll., Misc. Mss. 1:94. See also Jennings, *Ambiguous Iroquois Empire*, 330–31. For Tatamy's standing see William A. Hunter, "Moses (Tunda) Tatamy, Delaware Indian Diplomat," in *A Delaware Indian Symposium*, ed. Herbert C. Kraft, anthropological series 4 (Harrisburg: Historical and Museum Commission, 1974), 71–88.

82. Peters to Penn, 22 Nov. 1756, mss., Penn Papers, Off. Corr. 8:203. Peters's private admission to Friends at Easton is notable. They told him that Teedyuscung was complaining specifically about the Walking Purchase. "He said that is true, that Walk cannot be vindicated. The Proprietaries always despised it, and that it was unworthy of any Government." Peters knew perfectly well that his remark about the proprietaries was untrue, that John and Thomas Penn had organized and supervised the Walking Purchase; but Peters desperately thrashed about for some rationale that would simultaneously save his face with the knowledgeable Quakers and save the rest of him from the Penns. Minutes of the Friendly Assn., mss., 21a, HSP; Jennings *Ambiguous Empire*, ch. 17, app. B.

learn to strengthen as much as possible the hands of the Six Nations, and enable them the better to be answerable for their Tributarys."[83] Translated, this meant that Penn meant to try to repeat the arrangement of 1742 when the Iroquois, at Pennsylvania's urging, had denounced the Delawares as "women" and ordered them out of their homeland. Given such patronage, the Iroquois League unsurprisingly watched the rise of Teedyuscung with wary eyes. As we have seen, when the League chiefs found that they could not prevent the ascension of Teedyuscung to lead the eastern Delawares, they formally recognized him as "king" of the tributary group and bided their time. Subsequent events make clear, however, that they did nothing to help the Quaker peace effort and probably a good deal to hinder it. They did not intend to let the Delawares, east or west, assume first place among Pennsylvania's Indian allies.

The Friendly Association

In an oddly pertinent phrase, the Quakers had only begun to fight. On 1 December 1756, a number of contributors to the Friends' peace fund met under Israel Pemberton's leadership to form the Friendly Association for Regaining and Preserving Peace with the Indians by Pacific Measures. The meeting chose sixteen "weighty Friends" as trustees of the new association and undertook responsibility for the peace fund, which had already collected £3,000 and was soliciting more among Schwenkfelders and Mennonites as well as Quakers.[84] This organization became the instrument by which the Quakers conducted their independent enquiry into Indian grievances and established independent negotiations with the tribes.

Against Iroquois as well as proprietary powers, Pemberton and the Friendly Association struggled for more than a year to complete peace in eastern Pennsylvania and reach out to the Ohio Indians. He could not get past all the obstructions to make the essential western contact until a most unlikely new power appeared in Pennsylvania in 1758. Chapter 17 will give details, but we must leave the Friends temporarily in order to give attention elsewhere.

83. Penn to Peters, 10 Jan. 1756, mss., T. Penn Ltr. Bks. 4:205, HSP.

84. Thayer, *Israel Pemberton,* 124–25; Minutes of the Friendly Association, Indian Records Collection, mss., 25, HSP.

Chapter 13 ❧ *VICEROY in QUICKSAND*

Between 1754 and 1758 . . . the New World became the graveyard of British military reputations.

Lawrence Henry Gibson

Chronology

1744.	"King George's War" begins between Britain and France.
1745.	Prince Charles Edward Stuart raises the Highlanders in rebellion. Royalist John Campbell, fourth earl Loudoun, loses his army to the rebels at Prestonpans.
1745.	Massachusetts governor William Shirley directs a campaign that captures Louisbourg.
1746.	Earl Loudoun flees from the "rout of Moy" to the safety of Skye, and sits out the rest of the Jacobite rising until Cumberland wins at Culloden.
1748.	"King George's War" ends. Louisbourg returns to France.
July 1755.	General Braddock routed.
ca. September 1755.	Iroquois declare neutrality to New France's governor-general Vaudreuil and permit him to attack Oswego without interference.
January 1756	Thomas Penn indoctrinates Earl Loudoun against Pennsylvania assembly and Quakers.
27 March 1756.	De Léry captures Fort Bull in Oneida territory.
17 May 1756.	England declares war on France. Lord Loudoun, the nominee of the duke of Cumberland, sails to America to supersede Shirley as commander in chief.
3 July 1756.	Bradstreet fights off French attack near Oswego.
23 July 1756.	Loudoun arrives at the city of New York with Thomas Pownall as his "secretary."
July–November 1756.	New England troops refuse to come under British officers and regulations. Loudoun denounces their "mutiny," abandons campaign against Crown Point, dismisses the troops, and discharges General John Winslow from service.
14 August 1756.	Montcalm takes Oswego.

1756–57.	Loudoun quarters regular troops on colonials against strong opposition.
1756–57.	Thomas Pownall in England briefs ministers on American affairs.
ca. May 1757.	Loudoun surrounds New York City for a nocturnal dragnet impressment of seamen.
June 1757.	Loudoun's fleet sails against Louisbourg.
4 August 1757.	Loudoun withdraws from Louisbourg without attacking.
9 August 1757.	Fort William Henry capitulates to Montcalm.

A pause is in order for consideration of the meteoric rise of Sir William Johnson.* Johnson's differences with Thomas Penn were those of two men on the same side, but competing for personal advantage. They were marchland lords in the crown's interest (as well as their own) and they set themselves consistently against the collective lordships of the assemblies that resisted the crown's demands.

March Lord Johnson

It is essential to recognize that Johnson, though his title was only baronet, had become a great lord in substance and was on his way to yet more greatness. Within a limited meaning of lordship, Johnson held one of the largest estates in New York, with hundreds of European tenants who were his dependents; the courthouse on his estate was his personal property. He settled over a hundred families during the Seven Years War.[1] In a broader sense, his office of superintendent of Indian affairs embraced the same function as that of an early medieval count with responsibility to recruit the peasants to fight the crown's battles.[2] Like many a march lord predecessor, Johnson moved to make his office a property by making it hereditary; his son did acquire it after Sir William's death, but the American Revolution interrupted the succession. It was a glamorous office. Thomas Penn was one among many courtiers in London, but Johnson lived in exotic splendor out among the "wild men," and seemed to be the

*Thanks to Michael McGiffert for his helpful reading of an early draft of this chapter.

1. See Edward Countryman, *A People in Revolution; The American Revolution and Political Society in New York, 1760–1790*, Studies in Historical and Political Science, 99th ser. (Baltimore: Johns Hopkins University Press, 1981), 16, 21, 23, 117–18. Sung Bok Kim has identified Johnson as "already the owner of more than a million acres by 1769." Kim, "A New Look at the Great Landlords of Eighteenth-Century New York," *Wm. and Mary Qtly.*, 3d ser., 27 (1970):586; Peter Marshall, "Imperial Regulation of American Indian Affairs, 1763–74, Ph.D. diss., Yale University, 1959, p. 81.

2. I follow the general argument in Marc Bloch, *Feudal Society* (1940), tr. L. A. Manyon, 2 vols. (Chicago: University of Chicago Press, 1964). My reasons for classing the Indians as tribal peasants are in Jennings, *Invasion of America*, ch. 5.

indispensable man to keep them in order. His own dispatches contributed greatly to that impression.[3]

Johnson had strong family connections among the British nobility and an independent "interest" at court developed through the Pownall brothers and Lord Halifax, and he never deviated from being the court's man among the colonials. By the magic of public relations, his drawn battle at Lake George became the greatest victory ever won by British forces in America. He acquired a fabulous fortune: besides his immense landed estates, he made money out of every function and office and kept a steady income from trade as well as the rents and produce of his estates. Though he never followed the medieval model to the point of making private war against other lords, he did not hesitate to set tribe against tribe for his own and the crown's advantage, and he was a furious infighter at court, as William Shirley learned disastrously. When Johnson and his friends brought Shirley down, they knowingly toppled the most powerful man in British America, governor of one of the richest colonies and commmander in chief over all. How heady!

Such a rise was bound to evoke opposition, and Shirley still had friends willing to speak up for him. One, William Livingston, hinted that Johnson's conduct at the battle of Lake George had been less than glorious. More seriously, he attacked "the grossest imposture" of Johnson's "so much magnified influence" over the Iroquois. "If ever any man obtained laurels without earning them, it was this fortunate general; who, by the splendid representations of his secretary, and the sovereign decree of his patron, is exalted into an eminent hero."[4]

But Johnson's grip on the imaginations of the ministers did not weaken. Knowing the source of power, he rushed to pay court to it when Shirley's replacement as commander in chief appeared on the scene.

Lord Loudoun assumes command

The British ministry never intended William Shirley to command in America for an extended time. Everyone knew that Shirley's profession

3. For instance, *An Account of Conferences held, and Treaties made, Between Major-general Sir William Johnson, Bart. and the chief Sachems and Warriours of the . . . Indian Nations in North America . . . in the Years 1755 and 1756. With a Letter from the Rev. Mr. Hawley to Sir William Johnson, written at the Desire of the Delaware Indians* . . . (London: A. Millar, 1756), reprinted facsimile (Lancaster, Pa.: Lancaster Press, 1930).

4. [William Livingston], *A Review of the Military operations in North America . . . to the Surrender of Oswego, on the 14th of August, 1756* (London: R. and J. Dodsley, 1757, internally dated 20 Sep 1756), 58–63, 70–71. Johnson's secretary Peter Wraxall had written *An Abridgment of the Indian Affairs contained in Four Folio Volumes . . . to the Year 1751* (1754), reprint ed. Charles Howard McIlwain, Harvard Historical Studies 21 (1915), facsimile (New York: Benjamin Blom, 1968); idem, "Some Thoughts upon the British Indian Interest in North America," *N.Y. Col. Docs.* 7:15–31.

was politics, and that he was only an amateur in matters military; and when the Filius Gallicae letters aroused suspicions the ministry lost trust even in his loyalty.[5] To replace Shirley, the duke of Cumberland considered the available field of trustworthy professional soldiers.[6]

He chose one who had demonstrated trustworthiness by helping Cumberland to suppress the Highland rising of 1745 and had demonstrated professionalism by marching undauntedly from one defeat to another. John Campbell, fourth earl of Loudoun, had lost nearly all the men of his regiment at the Battle of Prestonpans (20 September 1745). He had escaped the debacle to gather a new force, which lost Inverness to the rebels, though Loudoun was able to march off again, this time to Skye "to sit the war out there until after the Battle of Culloden." Unlike Cumberland, Loudoun had not even one victory to his credit.[7] But he was certainly trustworthy. A chief of Clan Campbell, he had fought that clan's traditional Highland foes as a committed royalist; and as one of Scotland's representative peers in the House of Lords he voted consistently with the ministry.[8] Loudoun believed firmly in royal rights and kingly prerogative. He also knew all the manuals on military methods. These qualifications fitted him, in Cumberland's estimation, to assume formal powers greater than were held by any other general in the empire.[9]

The powers were given him in "a positive attempt on the part of Great Britain to unite the colonies for military purposes"—that is, the conquest of New France.[10] The principle of unification was to be general obedience to the prerogative, which implied that colonial assemblies would have to give up powers they had wrested from royal governors; and that in turn

5. Stanley McCrory Pargellis, *Lord Loudoun in North America*, Yale Historical Publications, Studies 7 (New Haven, Conn.: Yale University Press, 1933), reprinted (Hamden, Conn.: Archon Books, 1968), 76–77.

Bibliographic note: My dependence on Pargellis's careful scholarship should be plain, but his field of research was so narrow that his interpretations of complex events are sometimes inadequately founded, and he was more apt than I to find excuses for the faults of the highly placed.

6. Gipson, *British Empire* 6:188.

7. Besides Prestonpans, Loudoun lost at Inverury and in the "rout of Moy." At Moy, Loudoun's troops were comically thrown into panic by the bluffing of "a blacksmith and other four." T. F. Henderson, "Campbell, John, fourth Earl of Loudoun," *Dict. Nat. Biog.* 8:376; David Daiches, *The Last Stuart: The Life and Times of Bonnie Prince Charlie* (New York: G. P. Putnam's Sons, 1973), 198–200; [John Daniel], "A True Account," in *Origins of the 'Forty-Five*, ed. Walter Biggar Blaikie, Publications of the Scottish History Society, 2d ser., 2 (Edinburgh: T. and A. Constble, 1916), 178–79; Robert Forbes, *The Lyon in Mourning*, ed. Henry Paton, 3 vols., Publications of the Scottish History Society 20–22 (Edinburgh: T. and A. Constable, 1895), 1:148–50; 2:134–38, 268–70.

Cumberland has been called victorious at Dettingen, but George II was in direct command there.

8. Pargellis, *Lord Loudoun*, 42.

9. Ibid., 79.

10. Ibid., 44.

meant that in some sense Loudoun was to conquer the assemblies on his way to conquering the French.[11] As long as Cumberland held sway over the ministry's American policies, Loudoun worked hard at his assignment. He did not conquer the assemblies. He did not conquer the French. His accomplishments were the systematization of military organization and supply,[12] and the negative inspiration for phrases in the Declaration of Independence.

The cabinet's method of replacing William Shirley led to absurdity. First they decided to sack him and immediately sent Major General Daniel Webb to break the news and assume temporary command. Two days later, Major General James Abercromby sailed to replace Webb as interim commander. (There appear to have been some well-founded worries about Webb's ability.) Then some time elapsed while the various departments of state wrapped each other and the supplies intended for troop reinforcements in red tape. Disorder was not a monopoly of the colonies.[13]

Cumberland chose Loudoun, and Loudoun had personal preparations to make. More than an army officer, he was a peer, and his dignity was not to be scanted. He was also appointed as absentee governor of Virginia, to increase his emoluments and prestige, and as "General and Commander in Chief of all and singular our Forces employed or to be employed in North America." Time was consumed just to get the legal wording straight in his commissions. There was also the matter of his entourage. Equipped with wines, dinner plate, and other essentials, it consisted of seventeen servants, four aides, "and two women, one of them, Jean Masson, his mistress."[14]

Britain formally declared war on France on 17 May 1756. On the same day, Loudoun set out from London. His ship sailed on the twenty-second, but calm winds slowed his voyage so that he did not arrive in New York until the twenty-third of July. He astonished the local dignitaries by landing from a pilot boat at three o'clock in the morning, spoiling the usual pomp of a reception by the city regiment. But some guns were fired, and a hasty assemblage of council, assembly, and corporation members, together with other "Gentlemen of Distinction," managed to present formal compliments by ten that morning. "And at Night the City was handsomely illuminated."[15] The scrambled proceedings foretold how Loudoun would fail perpetually to achieve coordination with the colonials.

The woes that befell him after this awkward commencement were inflicted by the French, by the colonials individually and in their assem-

11. Ibid., 360.
12. Ibid., 335.
13. Ibid., 76–79; Gipson, British Empire 6:192.
14. Pargellis, *Lord Loudoun*, 57–61, 81–82.
15. *New-York Mercury* no. 207, 26 July 1756.

blies, by his special aide Thomas Pownall, and by himself. He worked and traveled incessantly. He went everywhere and supervised everything. If sheer devotion to duty and attention to detail were enough to win a war, Loudoun would be among the world's great conquerors. Unfortunately, nagging, threatening, and fussbudgetry win few friend as a general rule, and Loudoun fell within the rule. It must be allowed that not every calamity should be blamed on him. He had to contend with conditions on the verge of chaos, and his assigned political duties guaranteed alienation of the provincials. In spite of these handicaps he did bring some system to the mess, but perhaps a better phrasing is that he made the mess systematic instead of chaotic.

Exit Shirley

The first task before Loudoun was to get rid of Shirley—not just to supersede him, but to get him out of the way entirely. Shirley refused to cooperate. As governor of Massachusetts Bay he took care to join the committee that welcomed Loudoun to New York City. However, this obvious effort to ingratiate himself with the new commander failed to soften Loudoun. Instead of exchanging the pleasantries and compliments usual on such occasions, Loudoun laid down a barrage of questions.[16] Plenty of evidence points to Loudoun's "Secretary Extraordinary" Thomas Pownall as animator for this inquisition. Much more evidence establishes good reason for it.

Shirley had managed his military functions as though they were more politics. He gave friends large contracts and averted his eyes from their fulfilment. He distributed commissions lavishly to supporters, and thereby won control of the Massachusetts legislature.[17] From time immemorial to the present day, this sort of patronage has been the quintessence of politics in every form of government known to history, certainly not excepting the England of Loudoun and Pownall; but Shirley pursued politics single-mindedly, and after the conquest of Acadia the battles he won in the political arena had no counterpart military victories.

He had not the wit to cover his tracks well; he kept accounts so clumsily that they revealed more than they concealed. Stanley Pargellis acknowledged, after making many excuses for Shirley, that the case against him was based not so much on "the prejudiced tales of his political enemies in Massachusetts and New York, but rather [on] the impartial and more damning indictment to be found in ledgers, returns, and accounts."[18] Any

16. Schutz, *William Shirley*, 238.
17. Shirley's methods appear in William Pencak, "Warfare and Political Change," 51–73.
18. Pargellis, *Lord Loudoun*, 165.

experienced army officer could deduce what had happened by reading between the confused lines. Loudoun, who was the very model of a modern major general, grew more and more irate as he inspected those accounts.

Though instructed repeatedly to return to England for an accounting there, Shirley continued to function in Boston as governor of Massachusetts. Among other things, he made fifty-nine new appointments to offices in civil government within two months. Such "lame duck" appointments are an ancient political device to deprive one's successor of patronage, and so they were seen by Loudoun. As Shirley hung on to what remained of his power base, Loudoun became "thoroughly convinc'd that no good can arise to the Civil Department of his Majesty's Service by your Endeavours to support and draw after you parties by misleading the People to expect that it is not certain that your political Connections with them will end." It is an even bet whether Loudoun's epistolary style resembles sludge more than wind, but he managed for once in this instance to say what he meant in so many words: "you are ordr'd to depart for England directly without Delay."[19] Finally Shirley went.

Thomas Pownall followed after, to make sure that Shirley would be finished off in London. Pownall bustled about to various high personages, and did his job so well that Shirley never again returned in office to Massachusetts. But Pownall did, as Shirley's successor in the office of governor.[20]

For the sake of tying up loose ends, it may be noticed that Shirley faced a court of enquiry in London, from which he emerged unscathed (but not vindicated) by persuading the duke of Newcastle to urge the Treasury to forgive Shirley's "muddled" accounts. In the words of his generally favorable biographer, Shirley had adopted "unusual methods" and "unprecedented procedures." He was no traitor, nevertheless, and he won favor again, via Halifax to Newcastle. He gained a commission as lieutenant general (kept safely away from an army) and was eased out of harm's way to the soft berth of governor of the Bahamas. After passing this post on to his son in 1767, he lived in retirement until 1771, when he returned to Massachusetts to die.[21]

19. [William Shirley], *Correspondence of William Shirley, Governor of Massachusetts and Military Commander in America, 1731–1760*, ed. Charles Henry Lincoln, 2 vols. (New York: The Macmillan Co., 1912), 2:547.

20. Schutz, *William Shirley*, 242; T. Pownall to Loudoun, London, 7 Dec. 1756, mss., Loudoun Papers LO 2321, HEH. Interestingly, Pownall remarked that "Mr. Hanbury and Thomlinson" were Loudoun's friends. This is odd because the great merchant John Thomlinson had been one of Shirley's staunchest supporters in London, and would praise him again in 1757. Schutz, *William Shirley*, 42, 56, 226, 245–46.

21. Ibid., ch. 13.

Bradstreet at Oswego

Three weeks after Loudoun landed at New York, one of the most important British bases in America fell to a sudden French raid. This was Oswego, with its companion Fort Ontario, located in Iroquoia where Oneida Lake discharges through Onondaga River into Lake Ontario. Founded in 1727 as part of the expansionist program of the then-dynamic board of trade, Oswego functioned as the most important post for Yorkers to trade with Indians. "Far Indians" canoed over Lake Ontario, sometimes bypassing French Fort Niagara, to trade at Oswego. William Johnson had accumulated a small fortune by placing his traders there.[22] The place dominated Iroquoia like a castle in Wales. It vexed the French, and events would show that it alienated the Iroquois, but the British viewed it as absolutely necessary to their own commercial and military strategy.

In his glory days as commander, Shirley planned to use Oswego as the launching point for his intended campaign against Niagara. To do so, however, required negotiations with the Iroquois that William Johnson resented as encroachments on his private preserve. Thus started the enmity between the two that ended in Shirley's downfall.[23] In the midst of their brawling, the garrison at Oswego suffered from neglect to the point of outright famine. Its men became so weak and diseased that they could not repair the fort's fabric, which had deteriorated so far that its cannon could not be fired for fear of collapsing the walls from shock.[24]

In March 1756, Oswego's weakness alarmed Shirley. He ordered troop reinforcements and hired 2,000 bateaumen to take provisions and supplies. This corps, armed with muskets and (significantly) hatchets, he put under the command of Lieutenant Colonel John Bradstreet, the Nova Scotian who had first proposed the 1745 campaign against Louisbourg.[25]

But Shirley had been too much preoccupied with political battles. When he got around to ordering Bradstreet, on 17 March 1756, to supply Oswego, the French were already in motion to cut off the supply line. A force of 360 Indians, Canadians, and French regulars under Lieutenant Gaspard-Joseph Chaussegros de Léry attacked British Fort Bull at the west end of the critical carrying place between the Mohawk River and Wood Creek

22. Johnson Gaylord Cooper, "Oswego in the French-English Struggle in North America, 1720–1760," D.S.S. diss., Syracuse University, 1961, ch. 4 and app. 7.

23. See ch. 7, above.

24. [Peter Williamson], *French and Indian Cruelty* (1757), reprinted facsimile, *Garland Library of . . . North American Indian Captivities* 9 (New York: Garland Publishing, 1978), 55–56, 58–60; *Military Affairs*, ed. Pargellis, 190.

25. Shirley to Bradstreet, Boston, 17 Mar. 1756, in [Shirley], *Correspondence*, ed. Lincoln, 2:418–22.

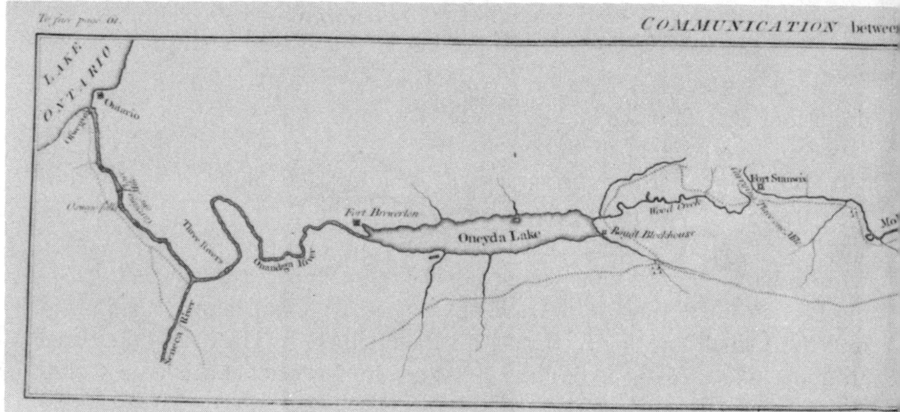

MAP 6. Communication between Albany and Oswego. FROM THOMAS MANTE, *The History of the Late War in North-America* (1772). REPRODUCED BY PERMISSION FROM THE COPY IN THE JOHN CARTER BROWN LIBRARY, BROWN UNIVERSITY.

that falls into Lake Oneida.[26] Significantly, no Indians warned the garrison about the French advance; indeed, the Oneidas "made us take Fort Bull," according to Bougainville.[27]

Léry stormed the fort on 27 March and destroyed great quantities of the munitions and provisions stored there for Oswego's relief. His men seem also to have committed a massacre although reports conflict as to its dimensions.[28]

There is no doubt at all, however, about the threat to Oswego posed by Fort Bull's loss; nor, more immediately, about the privation it implied for a garrison already down to starvation rations.

Still commander at the time, Shirley understood these implications, and so did his old colleague Bradstreet. With demonic energy, Bradstreet

26. F. J. Thorpe, "Chaussegros de Léry, Gaspard–Joseph," *Dict. Can. Biog.* 4:145–47. Date: *Johnson Papers* 2:692n.

27. [Bougainville], *Adventure*, ed. Hamilton, 89.

28. Léry's methods give credence to extreme reports. In what seems to have been his own report, he gets information from two captives by threatening to "have their brains knocked out by the Indians" if they misinformed or concealed, and they babbled. The same report has all his men rush into the fort "and put every one to the sword they could lay hands on. One woman and a few soldiers only were fortunate enough to escape the fury of our troops." Then, "Some pretend that only one prisoner was made during this action." *N.Y. Col. Docs.* 10:403–5. Montcalm wrote to his wife that the garrison "was put to the edge of the sword." Godfrey, *Pursuit*, 76. A letter from Quebec, 14 Apr. 1756, has the garrison killed "except about three," without mention of women. *N.Y. Col. Docs.* 10:396–97 Interpreter James Campbell lived to testify that he had been taken prisoner "when that Fort and garrison were destroyed," *Johnson Papers* 2:786. He gave no numbers. Another prisoner reported all the garrison but five put to the sword. Robert Eastburn, *A Faithful Narrative of . . . his late Captivity among the Indians* . . . (Philadelphia), reprinted (Boston: Green and Russell, 1758), 5–7.

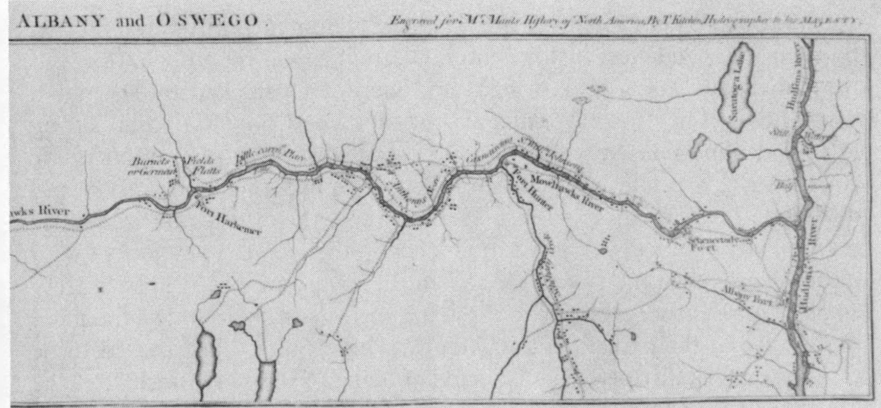

drove his men to build a hundred new boats. With 1,000 men and 350 boats he delivered a vast quantity of food and goods over the 160 miles from Albany to Oswego by the end of May.[29]

The French had been surprised by his speed, so they did not impede the delivery, but they ambushed him on the way back. Canadians and hostile Indians who infested the surrounding region attacked his advance division of about 300 men on the third of July, nine miles south of Oswego as they rowed upstream. Bradstreet was among the ambushed detachment, and he turned the surprise around. Rallying his outnumbered tough crew, he charged the 700-odd attackers in their own style of warfare. (Suddenly it became plain what the hatchets in his armament were for.) The French forces retreated through swamps to the riverbank, where they had no option but to fight or swim. They tried to cross the river, offering such easy targets in the open stream that more were shot than could be counted because their bodies were washed downstream.[30]

It was the last good news in Albany for two years to come when the same Bradstreet would triumph once more, and once again with bateau-

29. Godfrey, *Pursuit*, 77–78. For the munitions and provisions in Oswego when Montcalm captured it in Aug., see his report, *N.Y. Col. Docs.* 10:444. They included more than 100 pieces of artillery besides ample ammunition, and nearly 3,000 barrels of food.

30. Godfrey, *Pursuit*, 79–80. French and English sources conflict in propaganda effusions. French: *Relation de la prise des Forts de Choueguen ou Oswego; & de ce qui s'est passé cette année en Canada* (n.p., 1756) has Bradstreet's convoy being destroyed "in effect" with "more than 500" men killed or captured (p. 3). English: *New-York Mercury*, nos. 206, 207, 208, dated 19 and 26 July and 2 Aug. 1756. These extracted in *Doc. Hist. N.Y.* 1:482–87. The English version is far more circumstantial and, in the circumstances, more credible.

men who were not even classed as soldiers. These men infuriated officers by their independence, insubordination, and general rough behavior; but they obviously knew how to fight and were not panicked by an Indian war-whoop. They were working at jobs they knew how to do, not sitting idly or drilling nonsensically; and they were serving under an energetic commander, as tough as themselves, who excited their admiration and devotion. These men accomplished vastly more than the glamorized rangers who went on scalp-bounty hunts when in the mood. They fought with more success than the troops for whom they were supposed to be merely auxiliary provisioners. Honor to these unsung victors is overdue—the more so because of their treatment at Albany where Shirley had ceased to be commander. Bradstreet was suspected of being too close to Shirley, so the reward of his victory was to be excluded from the new military councils; of his men, who had shown themselves to be the best fighters yet employed by the British in any capacity, 400 were immediately discharged.[31]

French capture of Oswego

The new commanders paid scant heed to Bradstreet's alarm about the French threat to Oswego. He arrived in all haste on 12 July. On the sixteenth, General Abercromby convened a council of war without Bradstreet, which recommended reinforcement of Oswego by a regiment of regulars "forthwith."[32] After due consideration, Abercromby ordered General Webb to make his regiment ready to depart for Oswego, but nobody was in a hurry. On the twenty-eighth Lord Loudoun arrived in Albany and pried Webb loose, but only so far as Schenectady, about fifteen miles away, where Webb and his regiment were still to be found on 6 August while he squabbled about contracts for provisions.[33] On the fourteenth of August, Webb had crawled to the German Flatts (Herkimer, N.Y.), about seventy crowflight miles from Albany, with about a hundred more still between him and Oswego. On this date, Oswego surrendered to the besieging French.[34] Three weeks had passed since Loudoun's arrival in America.

31. Godfrey, *Pursuit*, 81–82; Cooper, "Oswego," 248n. Bradstreet had committed political error on his own account by condemning the "scandalous" manner in which Johnson's men traded at Oswego. Gipson, *British Empire* 6:154.

32. Minutes, *Johnson Papers* 9:485–87.

33. Pargellis, *Lord Loudoun*, 164; Shirley to Fox, 15 Sept. 1756, [Shirley]. *Correspondence*, ed. Lincoln, 2:575. Provisions were available for Webb. He refused to accept them from the "wrong" contractors. *The Conduct of Major Gen. Shirley* . . . (London: R. and J. Dodsley, 1758), 102–03. (Webb was a colonel in Britain, but a major general during his service in America.)

34. The whole sequence of these dates is clear in Cooper, "Oswego," 215–22.

Let us stay with Webb a few days longer. He received word of Oswego's fall and advanced to the great carrying place by the twentieth, where he observed the unfinished state of the rebuilt forts and the undisciplined state of Major Craven's troops.[35] Hearing frightful rumors of a French advance, Webb "was seized with panic, burned the forts [so laboriously rebuilt], had trees thrown into Wood's Creek in order to delay the enemy's advance, and without a moment's hesitation, made the rest of his way down the Mohawk [River] to the settlement of German Flats, fifty miles distant."[36] We can assume that Webb put himself bravely at the head of his troops during this expeditiously executed advance to the rear. This time, he did not dawdle.

Nobody on the British side came out of this episode with glory. Loudoun sent Webb in the right direction, but at a snail's pace. Whether Abercromby was doing much of anything is not clear. If Johnson had actually won Iroquois support, it did not go to Oswego. Webb was either a mental defective or a poltroon or both; he certainly showed no desire to get to a place where he would actually have to engage the enemy. The whole episode is a mind-boggling story of blundering asininity and worse. But the brass took care of its own; no sanctions were invoked against Webb.

Iroquois policy

With friends like these, the garrison at Oswego obviously needed no enemies, but the poor fellows inside the fort were doomed simply by having been put there because their presence was obnoxious to the Iroquois. In this perspective one can see and understand the otherwise strange behavior of the twelve Iroquois who had accompanied Bradstreet to deliver supplies to Oswego. Recruited for him by Sir William Johnson, eleven of the twelve immediately deserted when Bradstreet was attacked. It was neither cowardice nor "savage" instability; their behavior was the consequence of Iroquois League policy. The League had previously assured Governor Vaudreuil "that he should not carry the war to them, *that he could carry it to Oswego but not farther.*"[37]

Was this, then, just a case of "savage treachery"? Again, the explanation is more rational. Iroquois policy had been to balance the British at Oswego with the French at Niagara. While they competed for Indian trade, the Iroquois gained much advantage in two ways. The obvious one was com-

35. Craven to Pitt, 1 Feb. 1758, [William Pitt], *Correspondence of William Pitt, when Secretary of State, with Colonial Governors and Military and Naval Commissioners in America*, ed. Gertrude Selwyn Kimball, 2 vols. (New York: Macmillan, 1906), 1:173; Pargellis, *Lord Loudoun*, 164n58.

36. Ed intro., [Pitt], *Correspondence*, ed. Kimball, 1:xxviii.

37. [Bougainville], *Adventure*, ed. Hamilton, 30. My italics.

mercial: competition reduced prices. Less obvious, but perhaps more important to the chiefs of the Six Nations, was the prestige they acquired in intertribal diplomacy when "Far Indians" came to trade and could not avoid the Iroquois. If they traded with the French at Niagara they must be on terms with the Senecas in whose territory Niagara stood; if they went to the British at Oswego they had to deal politically with the Oneidas whose lands surrounded Oswego. The westerners had to conclude that access to the wealth and power of the Europeans could be had most easily via the Iroquois League, and the League in this situation manifested its "neutrality" by identifying itself with both Britain and France, using them both to enhance its own status.

France and Britain tacitly accepted this state of affairs until 1755, and the Iroquois policy protected both trading entrepôts.[38] But when France's Vaudreuil and Britain's Shirley decided to strike at each other's lifelines to the west, the Iroquois were compelled to reconsider policy; and when Shirley poured troops and supplies into Oswego to stage a campaign against Niagara, the Iroquois went into opposition. For them the governing fact was the distinction between the Europeans' strategies. If the British conquered Niagara, they would stay there, but French defensive strategy dictated that a strike against Oswego would be hit-and-run.[39] Of the available options, New France's was the lesser evil. The Iroquois League interpreted neutrality to mean aid for the French—certainly none for Oswego.

Negative as well as positive considerations motivated the Iroquois. Governor Vaudreuil had threatened to strike at them with his western allies if they aided the British, and Sir William Johnson heard that "if they sent their warriors to act with us, they suspected the French and the Indians in their Neighbourhood would fall upon their Towns and destroy the remainder of their People. Thus their proximity to the Enemy gave them all things to fear, and their Distance from us little hopes of our timely assistance."[40] That fear of the greater deliverable power of the French played a part can hardly be doubted, but it does not by itself explain all of Iroquois conduct; for example, why so little information about French movements was passed on to the British.

Massacre by agreement

With hindsight, it should not surprise us as much as it did Montcalm that Oswego capitulated easily under his attack. The garrison was demor-

38. Gipson, *British Empire* 6:154.
39. See *Johnson Papers* 2:707.
40. *Johnson Papers* 9:902.

alized from long neglect and maladministration. The fortifications were crumbling. The surrounding Indians were hostile. The supposedly centralized military command headquartered at Albany was riven by political vendetta, and its general in the field ran from shadows.

Unaware of all these British liabilities, Montcalm was reluctant to undertake the campaign against Oswego. To his mind the critical spot was Lake George, but Vaudreuil prodded him and almost physically shoved him toward Oswego. Defeatist Montcalm acceded, hoping that at least he would have made "a diversion."[41] We must note well one of his preparations discreetly omitted from his reports. A French officer observed that Montcalm "had the report spread throughout all the Indian nations that there would be plunder for those who would come and fight with us."[42] For Indians of that time and place, plunder meant scalps above all other trophies.

After a difficult and painful but otherwise uneventful march, Montcalm invested Oswego on 11 August 1756. The garrison made little resistance, and when its commander was killed by a cannon shot his successor hastened to capitulate, on the fourteenth of August. Two very discrepant copies of the articles of capitulation exist in print, both with Montcalm's signature, and the reason for discrepancy seems to have been his effort to cover up the atrocity committed under his patronage. This was a massacre of persons "included in the capitulation," according to the officer who disclosed Montcalm's offer of plunder for the Indians. He estimated more than a hundred killed thus "without our being able to prevent them or *having the right of remonstrating with them*."[43] What but a prior agreement with the Indians could deny such a right?

That there was substance to his report of massacre was conceded by the most authoritative French historian of the event. The Indians "hurled themselves on the English prisoners and killed a certain thirty (1) so many as in hospital (2) and at the place of embarkation."[44] Numbers and other details vary; the substantial fact is confirmed.

The cover-up began with suppression of the original articles of capitulation as signed by Oswego's commander Littlehales. In these he stipulated, and Montcalm countersigned, that "The Capitulation applies only to the Military. Besides, private merchants and hired men will be at liberty to retire whenever they please. *No injury will be done them*."[45] This stipulation vanished from the copy of the articles forwarded by Vau-

41. Montcalm to d'Argenson, 20 July 1756, *N.Y. Col. Docs.* 10:434.
42. Anon., "Camp at Chouaguen," 22 Aug. 1756, ibid., 10:454.
43. Ibid., 10:456. Italics added.
44. Richard Waddington, *La Guerre de Sept Ans: Histoire Diplomatique et Militaire*, 5 vols. (Paris: Firmin-Didot et Cie., 1899), 1:233–34.
45. *N.Y. Col. Docs.* 10:444.

dreuil, also signed by Montcalm, after having been edited to be suitable for publication, and Vaudreuil concocted the oldest alibi in police manuals to explain why only twelve British lives were lost "in action" of the forty-five he reported as the total killed: "the remainder were killed in the woods by our Indians *whilst trying to escape.*"[46] These would be military lives exclusively; no one counted civilians.

Given the state of these mangled sources, only speculation is possible. It appears to me that a number of the merchants and hired men whose liberty had been agreed upon attempted to use it, and that Montcalm let the Indians take their "plunder."

Montcalm hinted at the massacre but took great care to absolve himself. "No capitulation will ever be so difficult to enforce. The Indians wished to violate it. I have put an end to that affair. It will cost the King from eight to ten thousand livres, which will preserve to us the affection of the Indian Nationals more strongly than ever; and there is nothing I would not have done rather than commit an act contrary to French good faith."[47] It is not a denial. It seems to say that he let the killing go on for a while; then, perhaps in response to protests, he bought off the Indians. But the persons who "tried to escape" were beyond succor.

I have given so much attention to this incident because of Montcalm's reputation as a great gentleman, so sedulously cultivated and so uncritically sustained in the histories. "Gentlemen" in his day, as in our own, believed in a concept of "realism" that sanctioned massacre and worse. (The Englishmen at Culloden were gentlemen of the highest rank, and France had such precedents as St. Bartholomew's Day.) Whatever else he may have been, Montcalm was a professional soldier whose function was to amass power and win battles. Daintiness about the means was not part of his charge; indeed, the Indian weapon had been approved by the crown's supreme officers. Montcalm's chief aide, Bougainville, shuddered "at being obliged to make use of such monsters," but the governing word was *obliged*, for "without them the match would be too much against us."[48] The judgment of Herbert L. Osgood cannot be disputed: "From the beginning to the end of these conflicts [the French] systematically made use of the Indians, led their expeditions and encouraged them in the perpetration of the horrible massacres, burnings and plunderings by which the British frontier was laid waste. It was such events which largely gave character to that struggle."[49] Gentleman or not, Montcalm was in charge, and as he needed to keep his Indian allies he had to allow them the "plunder" he had promised. That he was ashamed enough to try to cover up is another matter.

46. Ibid., 10:474–75, 473.
47. Montcalm to d'Argenson, Montreal, 28 Aug. 1756, *N.Y. Col. Doc.* 10:464.
48. [Bougainville], *Adventure*, ed. Hamilton, 191.
49. Osgood, *Eighteenth Century* 4:399.

Effect of Oswego's conquest

Of his victory Montcalm wrote, "It is the first time that 3,000 men and inferior artillery [it was Braddock's] have besieged eighteen hundred who could promptly be reinforced by 2,000 and could oppose our landing, having a superior navy on Lake Ontario. The success has been beyond all expectation."[50] In material terms, Montcalm captured all the provisions and equipment that had been so painfully conveyed there. Among the booty were six vessels of varied sizes and more than a hundred pieces of artillery that were promptly hauled off to Lake George to defend against the British there. Strategically the fall of Oswego gave control of Lake Ontario to the French, and thereby strengthened their lines of communication to the western outposts, especially Fort Duquesne. It eliminated any thought of British attack on Niagara, as planned since Braddock's arrival in America. Instantly, Iroquois "neutrality" tilted toward Canada. Johnson Cooper notes that "their leaders no longer made Mount Johnson their rendezvous, nor did they invite [William] Johnson or his agents to the councils at the Onondaga fireside." Sir William summoned a meeting in November 1756, but had to cancel it because of embarrassingly poor attendance.[51] Cooper seems justified in concluding that this was "the most serious blow the English suffered during the Seven Years War" in America.[52]

Loudoun against provincials

British generals learned nothing from Oswego. They continued to be so intent on politics and protocol that they could not mount the long-planned campaign against the French at Crown Point. Loudoun outraged provincial officers by enforcing a rule that the highest of them was to be outranked by a regular captain and by ordering that provincial troops should be incorporated with the regulars. These orders were resisted. General Edward Winslow, in command of the provincials, tried to explain to Loudoun that the men had enlisted "on particular terms" specified by their assemblies and which would be breached by merger with the regulars. Rather than waste time waiting for more argument, Winslow moved his men to Lake George in position to attack Fort Ticonderoga. But Winslow erred badly in thinking that fighting the enemy was more important than army protocol. Loudoun denounced the New Englanders' protest about violation of covenant as mutinous behavior. In the midst of the dispute,

50. *N.Y. Col. Docs.* 10:462.
51. Cooper, "Oswego," 273 and n16.
52. Ibid., 283.

Loudoun learned of Oswego's fall. He recalled Winslow's troops to Albany, ostensibly to protect the place that the French did not dream of attacking, and when they arrived there Loudoun discharged them from service. Thus the grand campaigns of 1756 fizzled out with Webb running away from Oswego, Winslow withdrawing disconsolately from Lake George, and Loudoun fighting British colonials far more fiercely than he did the French.[53] It is a measure of that era's military standards (and of Loudoun's) that Winslow was retired from service thereafter while Webb became commander in New York during Loudoun's absence in 1757; as he had lost Oswego through evident cowardice, he would once again lose important Fort William Henry in the same manner, and once again he would suffer no personal privation in consequence. (See chapter 14, below.) After the damage was done, he was transferred to Europe, where seniority eventually bucked him up the ladder to lieutenant general.[54]

Quartering

The Crown Point fiasco ended Loudoun's 1756 effort at campaigning, whereupon he turned full attention to the political side of his commission. Politics emerged naturally and promptly when he started to arrange winter quarters for his troops. The provincial troops presented no problem because they had enlisted only for the campaign and could simply be discharged and sent home. Getting quarters for the regulars was another matter. Loudoun complained to William Pitt, "I have had disputes to Settle, all over this Continent, in settling the Winter Quarters for the Troops; from whence I find that the manner of Quartering in England as in time of Peace, on Publick Houses only, will in no shape answer the intent in this Country; for here, there are few Publick Houses, and the most of them . . . possess only one room . . . where Men cannot be Quartered."[55]

Loudoun had more in mind than winning the war. He looked forward to the problem that would arise after peace should eliminate the excuse of emergency necessity, and he concluded that "a new Regulation" should authorize quartering "on private Houses."[56] For townsmen, such a prospect was horrifying to contemplate, regardless of what compensation they

53. Gipson is succinct: *British Empire* 6:205–9.

54. S. M. Pargellis, "Winslow, John," and "Webb, Daniel," in *Dict. Amer. Biog.* 20:396–97; 19:573–74. Pargellis attributed Webb's dilatory tactics to the disease of palsy instead of cowardice. If so, the question is still pertinent: why was a palsied man entrusted with command? The answer is not merit. Like Loudoun, Webb had been chosen by the duke of Cumberland who thought him a "sensible, discreet man." This should be translated as "a strong prerogative man."

55. Loudoun to Pitt, 10 Mar. 1757, in *Corr. of Pitt.*, ed. Kimball, 1:20.

56. Loc. cit.

might receive. Everyone knew the reputation of British soldiers—lewd and vicious outcasts of society, many of them criminals discharged from jail on condition of serving long terms in the army. How could a respectable, churchgoing head of family expose his wife and daughters to depraved men in such intimacy that intercourse daily might become intercourse nightly? How could he suffer the indignities and insults (not to speak of profanity) of swaggering, coarse brutes? It was hardly necessary even to formulate the questions; everyone knew the answers. When Loudoun imperiously demanded quarters for his regulars, colonial officials prepared to do battle.

Though the quartering issue came to the point of soldiers invading private homes only twice, it was so charged with emotion that, as Stanley Pargellis has observed, it eventually reached "as violent a stage as in England under the Stuarts," it led to a clause in the Declaration of Independence, and it "began with Loudoun."[57] Resistance to arbitrary quartering was neither idiosyncratic nor peculiar to one province. It rested solidly on precedents long established as "a fundamental liberty of Englishmen,"[58] Loudoun had such insubstantial legal support that he resorted to moral argument, the "right" of royal prerogative, and, when all else failed, the military force at his command. Law or no law, with these weapons he could win, and did.[59] The colonials got a taste of what it was like to have an army in occupation.

Yet, even while deferring to his force, the assemblies managed to submit in such a manner as to preserve their own authority. They provided quarters according to Loudoun's fiat but by their own acts, in their own ways.[60] Slight as that distinction may seem, it had critical political implications. The technique had been honed to a sharp edge during more than a century of struggles with royal and proprietary governors. What it achieved was the assemblies' right to consider and discuss the demands of their overlords rather than simply perform as automatons. Discussion of *how* to obey led by rough stages to discussion of *whether* to obey and how to evade; ultimately to decisions to reject and defy. An American war for independence was yet inconceivable. The American colonies' struggle for independent management of their own affairs was well under way.

57. Pargellis, *Lord Loudoun*, 187.
58. Ibid., 195.
59. Bibliographic note: I do not understand why Pargellis attributed Loudoun's success to "Holding always in the background the threat of force." *Lord Loudoun*, 206. Loudoun frequently brought that threat explicitly and emphatically into the foreground by giving an ultimatum with a deadline, past which he said he would order troops into the place resisting his orders. Pargellis's soft language in this instance typifies his generally extenuating judgments of Loudoun's behavior that are so contradictory to his straightforward reports of facts.
60. Pargellis, *Lord Loudoun*, 206.

Quartering at Albany

To be effective, threats must be believable. Loudoun was compelled to establish credibility in Albany, his base of operations because of its strategic location on the direct route to Montreal. Thousands of troops inundated this town, whose people had little enthusiasm for campaigns against Canada. Experience in earlier wars taught that Canadians retaliated when forces started northward from Albany. More positively, Albanians could consider that, in earlier times, the neutrality of intermediate Iroquois Indians had bestowed peace on Albany while French-instigated Indians devastated New England. There was also the matter of the long-established smuggling trade by which Albany exchanged trade goods for Montreal's peltry. War's interruptions were Albany's loss. As Loudoun reported, the Albanians "have complained loudly, that since my arrival, I had stopped up every Path, so that the Trade was totally cut off."[61]

In the same letter, Loudoun mentioned mildly that he had had to threaten force to get quarters in Albany for his men. The colonial historian of New York gave a fuller picture of the scene.

> His Lordship insisted upon a speedy compliance . . . and to convince [the committee] that free quarters were every where usual, he would assert it upon his honor, "which," says he, "is the highest evidence you can require." The demand took air; the citizens raved, and the corporation, consisting generally of elective officers, were at their wit's end . . . A committee was appointed . . . to present a memorial to the Governor, imploring his mediation, and asserting that free quarters were against the common law, and the petition of rights, the Stat. 31. Car. II. and the mutiny and desertion act [They understood Loudoun's honor.]; and that the colonists were entitled to all the rights of Englishmen. The Governor escaped, for as soon as the Earl saw the opinion of the corporation, he replied to the Mayor, who alone was admitted to his presence, "G–d d—n my blood! if you do not billet my officers upon free quarters this day, I'll order here all the troops in North America under my command, and billet them myself upon this city." The magistrates, countenanced by the conscious dread and impotency of the citizens, promoted a subscription to defray the expense, and a calm ensued; but with a general abhorrence of the oppressor, who soon after proceeded through Connecticut to Boston.[62]

The drama of this little scene gains impact from knowledge that this secondary dispute over compensation occurred after the main issue had been settled by force. Loudoun had hardly arrived in Albany when he rejected the mayor's protest in order to billet troops by the dictation of his

61. Loudoun to Halifax, New York, 26 Dec. 1756, Loudoun Papers, mss., LO 2416, HEH.

62. William Smith, Jr., *The History of the Province of New-York*, 2:210–11.

own quartermaster. When an Albanian—a "Canadian trader" according to Loudoun—threw an officer's baggage into the street and barricaded his door, "I sent a file of men, and put the officer into Possession; my resolution is, if I find any more of this work, whenever I find a leading man shut out any of the people, to take the whole house for an hospital, or a storehouse, and let him shift for himself."[63] While Loudoun engaged in this kind of combat, Oswego fell to the French.

He had a room-to-room survey made of Albany's houses and decided that the town's 329 families could easily accommodate 146 officers *and* 1,443 enlisted men—in an emergency, 190 officers and 2,082 men—without compensation, as we have seen, though Pargellis says that the inhabitants eased that strain by organizing profitable trade with the soldiers.[64] Doubtless many did, but were there no Albanians too poor to have trading capital?

Loudoun tried to ease the "general abhorrence" of his oppression by building barracks at the crown's expense, but the work remained incomplete when new levies arrived for the campaign of 1757, so Loudoun slammed 1,300 men into private houses once more.[65] Pargellis extenuates again with the remark that Loudoun "took forceful measures . . . on two brief occasions only," but the brief occasions produced unwanted tenants for the full length of Albany's long winters.

After the example set at Albany, Loudoun did not again have to support his threats with action. He did threaten, almost compulsively, even when nothing was needed but negotiation. To Pennsylvania's governor Denny he threatened to quarter troops as had been done in Scotland during the Jacobite rising—that ghost still haunted—and "if the number of Troops now in Philadelphia are not sufficient, I will instantly march a number sufficient for that Purpose, and find Quarter to the whole they make necessary." (General Webb was to command.)[66]

Quartering in Philadelphia

Pennsylvania's assembly had already provided by law for quartering in public houses, in the belief that these had ample room, and this law, in due course, passed the crown's privy council without objection.[67] How-

63. Loudoun to Cumberland, Albany, 29 Aug. 1756, in *Military Affairs*, ed. Pargellis, 231; Loudoun to Halifax, New York, 26 Dec. 1756, Loudoun Papers, mss., LO 2416, HEH.
64. Pargellis, *Lord Loudoun*, 195–96.
65. Ibid., 197–98.
66. Loudoun to Denny, New York, 22 Dec. 1756, in *Pa. Council Minutes* 7:379. Erroneous dates are corrected in *Military Affairs*, ed. Pargellis, 273.
67. See the series of exchanges in *Pa. Council Minutes* 7:340–81, reprinted by Franklin without comment in *Pennsylvania Gazette* no. 1461, 23 Dec. 1756, p. 1.

ever, when the Royal Americans under Lieutenant Colonel Henry Bouquet arrived in Philadelphia, the public-house accommodations fell short of adequacy. Though there were 117 of them for the care of 500 enlisted men, too many were only drinking places rather than inns. Bouquet's quartermaster reported, on the day after Christmas, that all the men were under shelter but 94 of them slept on straw and 73 "had nothing to lay on and not Sufficient quantity of covering." The report noted that "the rest have good Beds and Accomodations," but there were "No Quarters fit for Officers."[68] These data show that two-thirds of the men were in satisfactory circumstances before Loudoun's letter arrived, and none had been compelled to sleep in the open.

That the remaining third had less than adequate accommodations was the fault of Governor Denny, another autocratic protégé of the duke of Cumberland, fully as competent as any of the rest. On 18 December, Bouquet had appealed to the governor for a warrant to quarter those men in private homes. Denny promptly issued a warrant, ignoring the law he had previously signed. The sheriff showed the warrant to assemblymen, who protested angrily to the governor that he should obey his own law. Though Denny's council advised him to discuss the matter, he rejected their advice and simply asserted his right, very much in the Loudoun mode. Their backs up, the assemblymen defied him; they created a commission empowered to act in their behalf, and adjourned without further action.[69]

It was this commission that heard Loudoun's letter on 26 December, and its members did not include a single pacifist Quaker in good standing. Their spokesman was Benjamin Franklin, still very much the imperialist.[70] They met with Colonel Bouquet for an hour or two and negotiated arrangements so satisfactory that when Bouquet later went to command in the southern colonies he tried to get quarters and hospitals "as we have it in Pennsylvania."[71] He "hinted" to Provincial Secretary Richard Peters that he should have applied to Franklin for those quarters in the first place, and not to the governor.[72]

Loudoun's threat was unnecessary to accomplish his announced objective. His other purpose, to assert overbearing power, was widely resented in Philadelphia as in New York.[73] He had a special grudge against Penn-

68. Lewis Ourry to ———, 26 Dec. 1756, in *Franklin Papers* 7:62–63.

69. Cited n67, above.

70. Besides Franklin, the commissioners were Assembly Speaker Isaac Norris, Jr., John Mifflin, Lynford Lardner, Joseph Fox, John Hughes, William Masters. *Pa. Council Minutes* 7:380.

71. [Bouquet], *Papers*, eds. Stevens et al., 1:72–73.

72. *Franklin Papers* 7:64n.

73. For the difficulties in South Carolina, Maryland, and New Jersey, see Pargellis, *Lord Loudoun*, 202–5.

sylvania,[74] to satisfy which he wanted an excuse for punitive action. The quartering flap provided the excuse, after which he refused to compensate Pennsylvania for the beds and firewood provided to the troops, thus excepting them from his rule in regard to other colonies. He hoped that "making a difference between those that comply willingly . . . and those that are refractory, will have a good Effect."[75] This sort of huffandpuff has become Holy Writ in the histories in total disregard of the actuality.

But in the same paragraph he wondered how much effect the "difference" might have in Boston, where he had "reason to apprehend" some indisposition to comply willingly with his demands. He was right about that. If anything could prove conclusively that resistance to quartering arose from more than Quaker principles, it would be what happened later in Massachusetts Bay.

Quartering in Boston

Under Shirley's management, Massachusetts had built barracks on Castle Island out in Boston's harbor, so there was no problem housing the troops in 1756. An unforeseen difficulty arose in the fall of 1757 when a party of royal recruiters descended on the town from Nova Scotia. Their methods differed widely from the provincial system by which leading men gathered followers in their own companies or regiments. Recruiters for royal regiments, after a manner of speaking, sold a pig in a poke. Enlistees had no choice of officers, and they enlisted for long terms, sometimes for the duration of their active lives. Ordinarily a man would want to think twice before making such a commitment, and the longer he thought the more likely he was to lose enthusiasm. The job of the recruiter was to sign him up before he had a chance to think. The recruiter had a technical advantage because law provided that a man who accepted a coin ("the King's bounty") was deemed to have signed on, whether or not he knew it. So recruiters were free with offers to buy men drinks, and when a young fellow had become a little fuzzy he might be grateful for a coin to buy another drink. Then he was in the army. Sometimes recruiters kidnapped men, after the fashion of naval impressment. They had an evil reputation among local authorities. Magistrates were known to imprison

74. Thomas Penn indoctrinated Loudoun as he had earlier denigrated Pennsylvania to Braddock, and Governor Robert Hunter Morris misinformed Loudoun as he had Braddock. Penn to Loudoun, Spring Garden, 21 Jan. 1756, Loudoun Papers, mss.; R. H. Morris to Loudoun, Philadelphia, 13 Aug. 1756, ibid., LO 1479; same to same, 15 Aug. 1756, ibid., LO 1493, HEH.

75. Loudoun to Cumberland, Albany and New York, 22 Nov.–26 Dec. 1756, *Military Affairs*, ed. Pargellis, 273–74.

prospective prey on false charges of indebtedness simply to keep them out of the recruiters' clutches.[76]

Boston quartered the recruiters from Nova Scotia in the barracks on Castle Island where they were effectively isolated and frustrated, at which they protested. Thus the quartering issue in Boston had nothing to do with adequacy or comfort of shelter; the question was whether recruiters were to be provided quarters where they insisted on them. Governor Thomas Pownall tried to negotiate with a very unsympathetic lot of magistrates only to be told that there was plenty of room in the barracks.[77] Pownall reported this to Loudoun, who reacted immediately with his habitual menacing pomposity. Climaxing a letter of twelve furious pages, Loudoun decreed that his messenger should wait no more than forty-eight hours for response. "If on his Return I find things not settled I will instantly order into Boston the Three Battalions from New York, Long Island, and Connecticut, if more are wanted, I have two in the Jerseys, at hand besides those in Pensilvania."[78]

Pownall laid the threat before his assembly for their "most Serious and immediate attention," but they did not scare.[79] What Loudoun wanted was immediate action by the magistrates under the authority of Parliament's law concerning quartering. The assembly held otherwise that "there being no Act of the Province for Quartering, that it lies with them to make Provision by Law."[80] Loudoun regarded this as wanting "to take away the King's undoubted Prerogative, and the Rights of the Mother Country; They attempt to take away an Act of the British Parliament."[81] What had started as a dispute over how to put up a few recruiters blew up into an issue of the fate of the British empire. "Endeavouring to set aside an Act of the British Parliament must at once throw the Whole Continent of North America into such Confusion as must be it's instant Ruin."[82] Suddenly Boston was a fiercer enemy than the French—Loudoun never referred to the French in such frenzied terms.

Loudoun's posturing was as stupid as it was silly. He seems almost to have been trying to alienate everybody, conceiving himself as some sort of drillmaster with the task of shaping up a continent full of raw youngsters. Utterly paranoid, he surrounded himself with visions of enemies (which he then created), among whom he eventually included even Pow-

76. Anderson, *People's Army*, 39–48; Pargellis, *Lord Loudoun*, 104–31.
77. Ibid., 207–9.
78. Loudoun to Pownall, Albany, 15 Nov. 1757, Loudoun Papers, mss., LO 4838, HEH.
79. Pownall to Council and House of Reps., Boston, 26 Nov. 1757, ibid., LO 4905, HEH.
80. Pownall to Pitt, 1 Dec. 1757, in *Corr. of Pitt*, ed. Kimball, 1:128.
81. Loudoun to Pownall, New York, 6 Dec. 1757, ibid., LO 4955, HEH.
82. Loudoun to Pownall, New York, 6 Dec. 1757, ibid., LO 4958, HEH.

nall, his closest associate.[83] Loudoun's careless way of ranting on in his letters almost destroyed Pownall's utility as royal governor, and drove him to the brink of a nervous breakdown when Massachusetts's politicians noticed Loudoun's reference to a "private" letter from Pownall. It aroused "strong, insurmountable Suspicions" of a plot between the two "to subvert the present constitution to a military Government and to putt the whole Service of this Country under the command of the Regulars under Military Discipline &c. and the Articles of Warr." Pownall wanted to resign, "since I am by this Fatality become embroil'd with the People here,"[84] but he was persuaded to hang on until Loudoun's recall, after which he managed to regain the province's confidence.

Perhaps Loudoun thought he had to have a victory over *someone* because he was still smarting from two more major military defeats (to be noticed below). It seems also that his fierce threats against Massachusetts were bluff, and that his bluff was called by those hard-nosed Yankees. The assembly saved his face by voting a conciliatory address sufficiently humble in form, but they kept their law. In the upshot, Loudoun canceled his orders to occupy Boston, and put "a total End" to the dispute.[85] It was indeed an end in a manner unforeseen. Within a week, Mr. Pitt signed the order for Loudoun's recall.[86] This was coincidence, of course—Pitt's motive was Loudoun's dismal record against the French—but Pitt's subsequent reversal of Loudoun's policies made it seem like an act of justice.

Louisbourg

At the outset of the war, the British ministry aimed "to *recover* the Territories belonging to His [Majesty's] Colonies there and to His subjects and allies, the Indians."[87] By the ministry's definitions it was not a small goal, but it would have permitted France to continue to hold the entire St. Lawrence Valley and the great fortress of Louisbourg on Cape Breton Island (renamed Isle Royale). This slightly limited objective fell short of

83. Loudoun to Cumberland, New York, 17 Oct. 1757, in *Military Affairs*, ed. Pargellis, 404–7.

84. "Private ltr.," Pownall to Loudoun, Boston, 15 Dec. 1757, Loudoun Papers, mss., LO 5014; same to same, 19 Dec. 1757, ibid., LO 5041, HEH.

85. Loudoun to Pownall, New York, 26 Dec. 1757, ibid., LO 5114, HEH.

86. Pitt to Loudoun, 30 Dec. 1757, in *Corr. of Pitt*, ed. Kimball, 1:133–34.

87. "Sketch for the Operations in North America," 16 Nov. 1754, in *Military Affairs*, ed., Pargellis, 45. The full extent of these claims was displayed in John Mitchell's map of 1755. Mitchell spelled them out in *The Contest in America between Great Britain and France . . . By an Impartial Hand* (London: A. Millar, 1757). Mitchell would have allowed France no North American territory except Tadoussac and Quebec (p. 198). He may be understood as representing Lord Halifax's position. I have used the copy of his book in HEH.

the demands of many Englishmen who perceived the strategic and commercial importance of Louisbourg. New Englanders had long itched to get their hands on the place, had actually captured it in 1745, and were angry at the diplomats who returned it to France in the treaty of Aix-la-Chapelle after King George's War. As early as 1746, a little book appeared in London arguing the advantage and even the necessity of seizing and keeping Louisbourg.[88] Early in 1757, Secretary Pitt and the earl of Loudoun independently concluded that Britain's former strategy of attempting to force passage through Lakes George and Champlain should be supplemented by a drive up the St. Lawrence to Quebec.[89] What had been officially only an effort to "recover" vast western territories and Acadia changed to a strike at New France's heart.

It appeared to the strategists that this would first require seizure of Louisbourg. Quite apart from its importance as a military base on the way to Quebec, Louisbourg was a great prize in its own right. Founded in 1713, the place was one of France's most valuable commercial possessions, functioning in several wealth-producing capacities. It was port for a large fleet that exploited the cod fisheries of the Grand Banks of Newfoundland, which are still today such a rich resource that Japan and the Soviet Union fish it on a large scale. In the mid-eighteenth century the French caught and sold three times as much fish there as Britain and its colonies combined.[90] Louisbourg served as a haven for French fisherman and as a base for raiders to harass the British. A Canadian writer avers that Louisbourg's "harvest from the sea—mainly codfish—was far more valuable to the economy of France than the fabled fur trade of the interior."[91]

In terms of money he probably is right, though politically the fur trade was essential to maintain tribal alliances.

Ships from France dropped cargoes at Louisbourg and picked up fish and other Canadian products for the return voyage. Smaller vessels from Quebec navigated down the river to this transshipment point, thus saving

88. [William Bollan], *The Importance and Advantage of Cape Breton* (London, 1746), reprinted (Toronto: S. R. Publications, 1966).

89. Loudoun to Pitt, 10 Mar. 1757, Loudoun Papers, mss., LO 3004, HEH.

90. J. S. McLennan, *Louisbourg*, 226; Bollan, *Importance of Cape Breton*, 88–91. McLennan remarks on how "surprising it is to find that Louisbourg "surpassed the colonies of England engaged in the same trade," p. 226.

91. John Fortier, *Fortress of Louisbourg* (Toronto: Oxford University Press, 1979), 3. I am reminded of Alison Quinn's observation to me that economic historians often overlook the importance of fish. Statesmen of the eighteenth century knew it. One pamphleteer rated North America's fisheries as "of more Value than the Mines of Peru and Mexico, or than any other Possession or Property that can be had in any Part of the World." *An Accurate Description of Cape Breton*, 70. For him, Louisbourg was "the Key and Protection" of the whole fishery (p. 54). A modern scholar observes that "the encouragement of the fishery as one part of navigation policy gave the Atlantic maritime regime of the New World a crucial position in the struggle between the mercantile systems of Europe." Shotwell, in Innis, *The Cod Fisheries*, x.

the ocean-going ships expense and hazard and creating employment for Canadian capital and labor.[92]

Smuggling throve between Louisbourg and New England; though outlawed by regulations on both sides, it was tacitly countenanced by authorities on both sides because of its mutual profitability. (Compare to the Albany-Montreal trade, chapter 5, above.) All in all, Louisbourg's commerce made it the third or fourth most active port on the Atlantic coast, surpassed only by Boston, Philadelphia, and sometimes New York.[93]

In point of military strategy, historian McLennan calls the fort "a sentinel in the gateway of the St. Lawrence" and identifies its value as "a naval base."[94] These carefully chosen phrases bear notice. It is foolish to speak of Louisbourg "blocking" entrance to the river, as some writers have done. The fort's guns could not reach across the vast Gulf of St. Lawrence—that would be impossible even for the cannon of the twentieth century.[95] But those eighteenth-century guns were powerful enough to protect French ships in Louisbourg harbor and keep British ships out; and when the British gave up and left, the Frenchmen could instantly emerge to resume their harassment of British commerce and fisheries.

To seize Louisbourg would be a great blow at France. Together with Britain's earlier-established control of Acadia, it would cut Canada off from Europe and provide Britain with a stage from which to mount invasion into the heart of the country. Therefore, when Loudoun prepared to attack the fortress, implacably anti-French New Englanders were willing to forgive him much. To their disgust, however, he held bumblingly true to form.

Loudoun did not monopolize fault. Pitt's hopes of sending troops from England before March were blasted by bureaucrats who did not hire transports until June 1757. Some brilliant soul ordered specialized cargoes: one vessel carried cannon; another, ammunition; and still another, powder. Had one vessel gone astray, the others would have sailed in vain. Someone bought gunpowder without testing it, and what he bought was useless. Loudoun had his American contingent of troops waiting in New York by the end of April for shipping to Halifax, but could not get them seaborne until late in June. Admiral Holburne's fleet, which was to join him for the attack, arrived in American waters on the ninth of July. Holburne and Loudoun dithered while the French concentrated a fleet at Louisbourg superior to theirs.

92. Bollan, *Importance of Cape Breton*, 67–68, 70–71; McLennan, *Louisbourg*, 75–76. McLennan adds that Louisbourg was "a clearing-house" especially important because its trade was "always on a specie basis," p. 228. On this account alone it was unique among both French and British colonies which were always short of coin.

93. Fortier, *Fortress of Louisbourg*, 3; McLennan, *Louisbourg*, 222–26.

94. Ibid., 2.

95. My thanks to Professor Russell Weigley for his expert help with this issue.

A contemporary chronicler of the war spluttered, "as if delay had been an essential part of their instructions, near a month was consumed at Halifax in exercising the troops . . . These steps were condemned by some as 'keeping the courage of his Majesty's soldiers at bay and expending the nation's wealth in making sham fights and planting cabbages when they ought to have been fighting the enemies of their king and country in reality.' " Two hundred troops died of disease at Halifax and five hundred more sickened enough to be hospitalized, all without seeing a Frenchman.[96]

One of the officers accompanying Holburne was major general lord Charles Hay, an intrepid, much-scarred veteran of wars on the European continent. Lord Charles had a reputation for being in front of his troops when they went into battle, and he was as little afraid of Loudoun as of the enemy in arms. What he saw at Halifax disgusted him, and he said so to anybody who would listen. When Hay rode out to where troops drilled for an attack on fortifications, he told them cynically "that was the only Attack that would be undertaken this Year."[97]

At a council of war, he propped his legs up on a window sill and jeered at his colleagues so that they dared not confess their qualms about combat. Loudoun solved the problem by holding three "private Meetings" on shipboard and in his own room, excluding Hay and taking some pains "in order to prevent Lord Charles from discovering, that the business was carried on without him." Loudoun did not want Hay on the scene while he interpreted Pitt's instruction. Pitt had allowed discretion only as to whether to attack Louisbourg or Quebec or both. Loudoun decided that he "could not reconcile myself to acting in that way, of following on Instructions" and thus "endanger the entire loss of my Masters Army."[98]

On 4 August, Holburne and Loudoun confirmed Lord Charles's prediction. They agreed that the season was too far advanced and the enemy too strong, so Loudoun picked up his troops—those that were able to

96. McLennan, *Louisbourg*, 202–4; Holburne to Pitt, various ltrs., 29 Sept.–15 Oct. 1757, *Corr. of Pitt*, ed. Kimball, 1:114–18; quotation from John Entick, *The General History of the Late War*, 5 vols. (London: Edward Dilly and John Millan, 1763–64), 2:392. Entick suspected that someone in or near the ministry had betrayed the Louisbourg plan to the French, noting that the first French reinforcements left Brest already on 30 Jan. 1757. He thought that unless the French had had early intelligence "it would have been impossible to have provided so expeditiously for its defence." Ibid., 2:168–69. I have used the copy of Entick's rare book at Swem Library, College of William and Mary.

97. Loudoun to Cumberland, Halifax, 6 Aug. 1757, in *Military Affairs*, ed. Pargellis, 392.

98. Ibid., 392–93. Hay was not the only skeptic. Loudoun reports in the same letter that Major General Hopson "started a difficulty" about Pitt's instructions, which Loudoun overrode. Notably, Loudoun explained all this to Cumberland, not to Pitt. Loudoun settled scores with Lord Charles Hay by hinting that Hay was insane and by bringing him before a court-martial in London. The baffled court referred decision to the king, and Hay died before George could make up his mind. James Rowley, "Hay, Lord Charles," in *Dict. Nat. Biog.* 25:253.

travel—and sailed back to New York. Considering the time of year, the decision seems rational. Bad weather comes early in the North Atlantic, and Holburne's fleet suffered great damage from a violent storm in late September while he waited around in hopes of luring the French fleet out for battle. But Loudoun won no friends in either America nor Britain by such enormous and costly preparations to no purpose.[99]

A contributor to the *Gentleman's Magazine* (possibly Shirley?) recalled how, in 1745, undisciplined New Englanders had "made a descent, erected batteries, vigorously continued a siege of 49 days, and at last succeeded in an attempt, which certain modern heroes on this side the water would, no doubt, have concluded to be impracticable, and with the assistance of a council of war would—have left the place as they found it." (He might have added also, had he known, that a Cape Cod Indian—apparently a Mashpee Wampanoag—made the 1745 triumph possible. This Indian remains anonymous in the way usual to lower ranks. He was hired "to crawl in at an embrasure and open the gate" of the fortress for the besieging men from Massachusetts to rush in and take the place.)[100] Not bothering to invoke history, another *Gentleman's Magazine* correspondent in 1757 observed tartly of Loudoun's futilities that "the more we are strengthened from Great Britain, the more ground we lose against the French, whose number of regular troops is much inferior to ours."[101]

Loudoun had angered a great many people by his own contributions to the preparations, including an embargo on all colonial shipping. This was supposed to accomplish two purposes—to prevent news getting to the French of his mobilization against Louisbourg and to cut off the smuggling trade that had become essential to Canada as British seapower intercepted shipments from France. It must be acknowledged that not all the opposition that developed to the embargo was high-minded. Smugglers as well as legitimate merchants howled in anguish at Loudoun's stoppage of their wartime profits. Governor after governor capitulated to their pressure by reopening his colony's ports on his own authority. To Loudoun's intense humiliation, Lieutenant Governor Dinwiddie of Virginia led the pack. Besides being commander in chief, Loudoun was governor of Vir-

99. "These disappointments gave great disgust. Lord Loudun had been selected by the Duke [of Cumberland] and [war secretary] Fox for this command, and our expectations had been raised high of what he would perform. Here was another summer lost! Pitt expressed himself with great vehemence against the Earl." Horace Walpole, *Memoirs of the Reign of King George the Second*, ed. Lord Holland, 2d ed., rev. 3 vols. (London: Henry Colburn, 1847), 3:39–40. "His Lordship had done nothing against Louisburgh, and was censured by his own army." W. Smith, *History of New-York*, ed. Kammen, 2:222.

100. *Gentleman's Magazine* 28 (Mar. 1758):103; the Indian role: Yasuhide Kawashima, *Puritan Justice and the Indian* (Middletown, Conn.: Wesleyan University Press, 1986), 120, quoting Shipton's *Harvard Graduates* 6:587.

101. *Gentleman's Magazine* 27 (Oct. 1757), 443.

ginia. Here was his personal government flouting the orders he gave as commander in chief. Appeals to the royal prerogative could have no effect because the governors, including Dinwiddie, were as much royal appointees as Loudoun himself. He salvaged some dignity by lifting the embargo everywhere when he took ship for Halifax.[102]

A more localized episode showed that, however much Loudoun failed to engage the French, he could attack English colonials with great success. This occurred when he learned of a shortage of sailors to man his transports from New York. As noticed in chapter 10, Loudoun surrounded the city with his troops, descended upon it in the dead of night, and kidnapped 800 men for his ships.[103] Through the intervening centuries, I seem to hear them saying, "And then the lousy blank blank blank didn't even fight!"

Training for revolution

More than fifty years ago, the deservedly respected historian Charles M. Andrews insisted that Britain's American colonies should have their history written in their own right and not merely as embryonic of the American Revolution. Much work since then has demonstrated the value and fruitfulness of that approach, but even when it is maintained most scrupulously the historian cannot avoid arriving eventually at the epic moment when these colonies appealed with a decent respect to the opinions of mankind to justify their course. When they published their Declaration of Independence in 1776, some of their grievances had arisen relatively recently, but others can be traced back to Earl Loudoun's mission and behavior.

Much has been written about the colonists' beginning to think about independence after removal of the French menace at the end of the Seven Years War, and there is often a hint of implied ingratitude for the great boon conferred on the colonies by Britain's sacrifices in that war. But that was not how the colonists considered the matter.

Bibliophile Lawrence C. Wroth observed that the leaders of the people "received a training in resistance to authority" through their struggles against the crown's agents in the Seven Years War, "which enabled the country

102. Pargellis, *Lord Loudoun*, 266–67. Loudoun lifted the embargo by direction from the crown because of crop failure in Great Britain and Ireland that created great need for American provisions. George Louis Beer, *British Colonial Policy, 1754–1765* (1907), reprinted (Gloucester, Mass.: Peter Smith, 1958), 85. The incident throws into sharp contrast the resources of the competing empires: New France imported food from Old France, but Old England imported food from its American colonies.

103. Lemisch, "Jack Tar in the Streets," 383. Pargellis's notice is brief, bland, and palliating: *Lord Loudoun*, 237.

in 1765 to oppose with success the operation of the Stamp Act, and from their printed literature the people themselves received instruction in the principles and theories of citizenship that prepared them for the test of 1776."[104] It is not necessary to ascribe special virtues to those colonists, or wisdom beyond the average of human capacity, to recognize how Thomas Jefferson spoke for them in his elegantly plain phrase: "He [the king] has affected to render the Military independent of and superior to the Civil power." That colonial resistance, with its consequences, is worth remembrance.

104. Lawrence C. Wroth, *An American Bookshelf, 1755* (Philadelphia: University of Pennsylvania Press, 1934), 27.

Chapter 14 ❧ *MASSACRE as POLICY*

The old Enlightenment idea of progress so central to French teaching lacked credibility "after the tragedies of the 20th century and our discovery of savagery in the heart of the civilized world."

French minister of education Alain Savary,
quoted in *The New York Times*, 24 April 1984

Chronology

June 1757.	Lord Loudoun sails against Louisbourg, leaving General Daniel Webb in command at Albany.
June 1757.	Vaudreuil prepares an attack against Fort William Henry and Fort Edward.
9–12 July 1757.	Montcalm promises plunder to Indian allies.
10 July 1757.	French prisoner informs Webb of impending French attack.
2 August 1757.	Webb learns of Montcalm's force sixteen miles distant from Fort William Henry.
3 August 1757.	Webb retreats to Fort Edward, leaving Lieutenant Colonel George Monro in command at Fort William Henry.
4 August 1757.	Webb refuses plea by Monro for reinforcements. He advises Monro to capitulate on terms.
4 August 1757.	Loudoun decides to abandon siege of Louisbourg.
9 August 1757.	Monro surrenders. Massacre follows.
Afterwards.	Smallpox spreads among Indians. Montcalm destroys Fort William Henry but retreats to Montreal without investing Fort Edward. Webb retreats to Albany. Excuses proliferate.

The most direct route between New York City and Montreal is the series of waterways that lie along what I have called the Mahican Channel (for lack of another comprehensive name). It is often known more colorfully as the Warpath of Nations. From the highlands near Albany, the Hudson River falls to the sea at New York. The same watershed drains northward through Lake George, Lake Champlain, and the Richelieu River to the St. Lawrence. Perhaps the most strategic spot for transit through the channel was the narrow link between Lakes George and Champlain. Recognizing it as such, the French built two forts there: Ticonderoga where the link is narrowest (a mere creek) and St. Frédéric on what the English called Crown Point, about fifteen miles farther north where Lake Champlain broadens. These forts effectively defended Canada against invasion from the south. They also threatened Albany and even distant New York City with possible French attack, and they could stage a campaign to the south and east through mountain passes against Massachusetts.

To fend against these threats the English built two forts of their own. At the southernmost end of Lake George they built Fort William Henry, about sixty miles south of Ticonderoga; and about seventeen more miles south of that, on Hudson headwaters, they built Fort Edward. During much of the war, the bulk of belligerent troops faced against each other across the interval between the two sets of forts.

The fall of Fort William Henry

For the most part, the French acted defensively, as became their inferior numbers and material. From the beginning, British strategy aimed at hammering a way past the French forts and through Lake Champlain. As noticed above, William Johnson fought a battle at Crown Point in 1755; and in 1756 Lord Loudoun marched up to it and prudently back again without fighting. Now, in 1757, Montcalm seized the opportunity presented by Loudoun's removal of the main British force to Louisbourg. He marched against Fort William Henry on 29 July.[1]

Major General Daniel Webb met this advance with utter consistency. Webb could never be made a character in fiction because the most accomplished novelist could not make him believable. He had had intelligence already in April of a concentration of troops and artillery amidst great activity at Ticonderoga. Beyond mentioning this in a letter to Loudoun, he did nothing. Early in July came more intelligence from captive Frenchmen, including information that Montcalm was expected to arrive "with the main body of the army."[2] Webb did nothing.

On 25 July he surveyed the situation at Fort William Henry. Gipson says he was accompanied by three officers. The Reverend John Entick wrote more informatively in 1763 that Webb had 4,000 men camped near

1. Gipson, *British Empire* 7:78.
2. Ibid., 7:79.

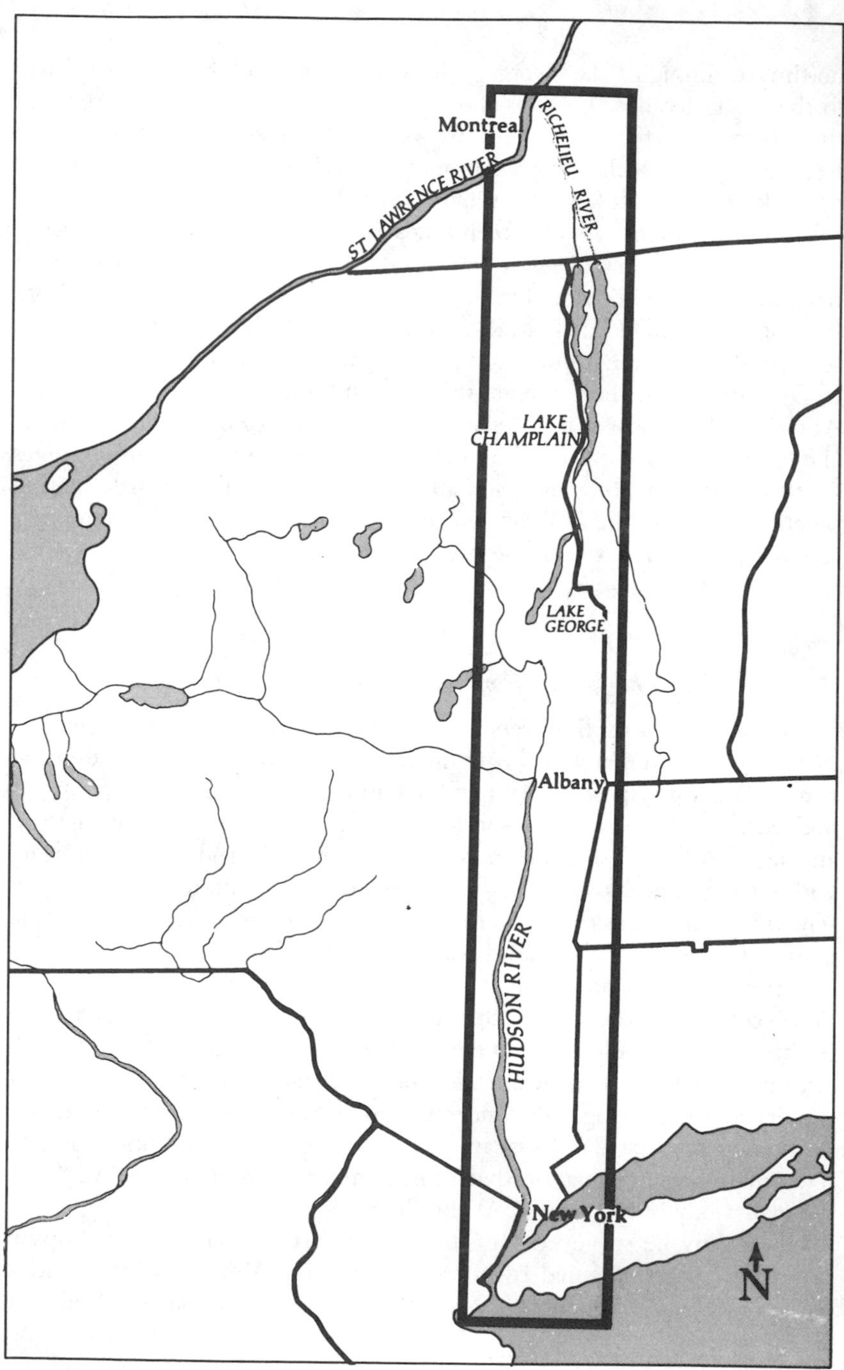

MAP 7. "The Mahican Channel."

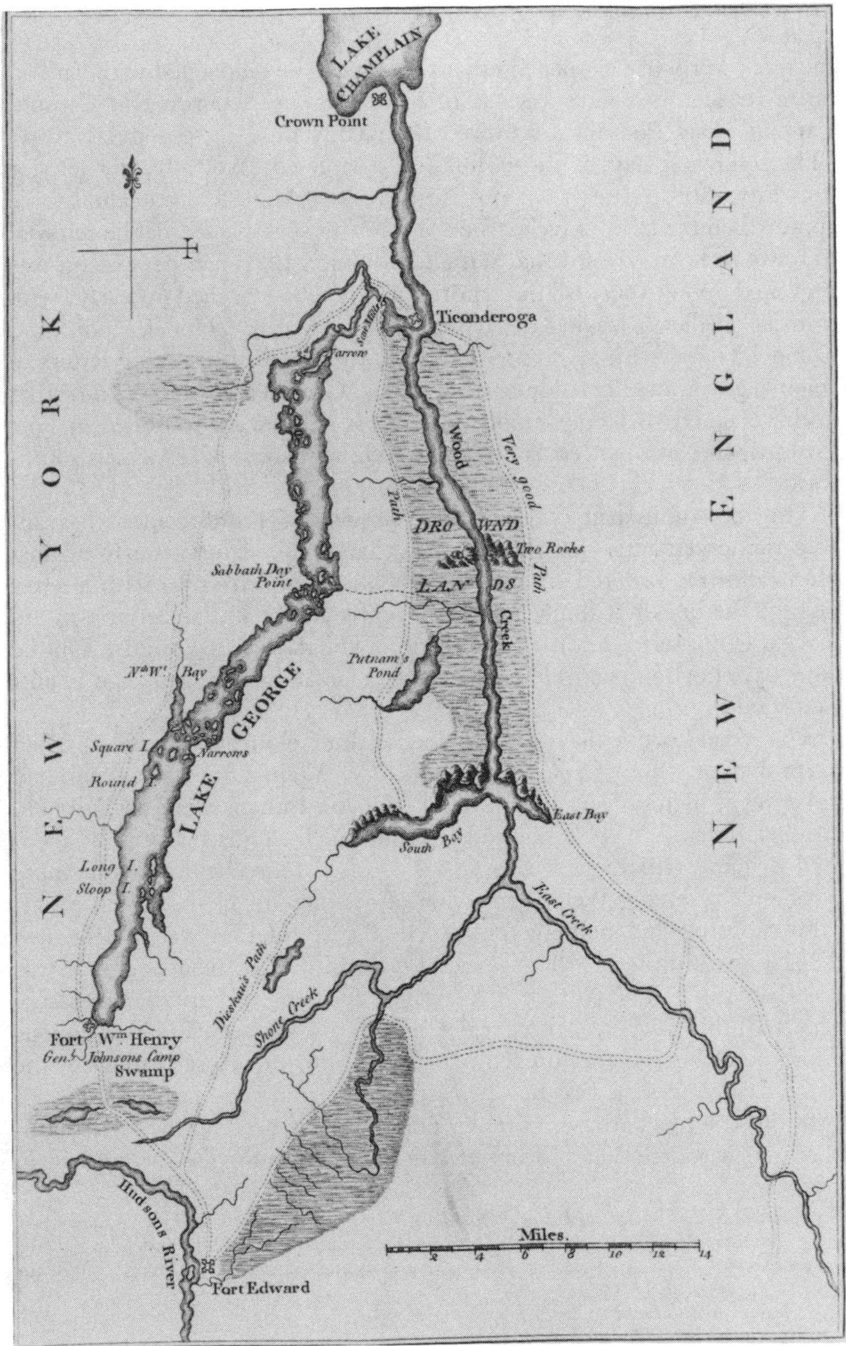

MAP 8. The opposing forts of Lakes George and Champlain. FROM THOMAS MANTE, *The History of the Late War in North-America* (1772). REPRODUCED BY PERMISSION FROM THE COPY IN THE JOHN CARTER BROWN LIBRARY, BROWN UNIVERSITY.

the fort.[3] For what happened next, Gipson can be reconciled with Entick, but a reader must have a sense of black humor. According to Gipson, Captain Israel Putnam discovered the enemy only sixteen miles away. "The following day, with his mission completed, Webb hastily left for Fort Edward."[4] Entick's account is fuller: on 2 August, Montcalm's force appeared on the lake, "which struck Webb with such panic, that he resolved to retire to Fort Edward that same night; but with much persuasion was prevailed upon to stay till next morning: when he marched off early, with a strong artillery, leaving the defence of the fort to Colonel Monro and Colonel Young with 2,300 men."[5] Webb did his bit by writing letters to colonial governors demanding more troops. Gipson observes in a note that Webb claimed that only 1,600 men fit for duty were stationed at Fort Edward, and "if this were so, he must have sent some of his troops southward."[6]

This incredible man *refused* Monro's request for reinforcements—available reinforcements—for the garrison that fought courageously against Montcalm. He ordered an aide to respond to Monro's plea with a letter saying, "he does not think it prudent." His advice in that letter was "to make the best terms left in your power."[7] The date was 4 August. On the same day, Loudoun and Holburne agreed to abandon the campaign against Louisbourg.

To defend Fort William Henry, Lieutenant Colonel George Monro had 2,372 men of whom 1,100 were fit for duty. Against him, Montcalm had 7,626 men, including 1,600 Indians.[8] Monro's Indians were negligible in number because Webb's previous conduct in Iroquoia had totally alienated Britain's tribal allies. Despite the odds, Monro held out four more days after receiving Webb's rejection of his plea for help—which Montcalm captured and politely forwarded. A capitulation was arranged, 9 August 1756, on terms that appeared honorable; but the appearance was less than valid. The pattern of Oswego repeated, and another massacre occurred, this time on a larger scale. As with the Oswego affair, strenuous efforts have been made to exculpate Montcalm, but close reading of the sources convinces me that he was responsible from beginning to end.

In the first place, those Indians would not have been on the scene without French solicitation and organization. As Bougainville made plain in

3. John Entick, *The General History of the Late War: Containing Its Rise, Progress, and Event in Europe, Asia, Africa, and America* . . . 5 vols. (London: Edward Dilly and John Millan, 1763–64), 2:395. I have used the copy of this rare work at Swem Library, College of William and Mary.

4. Gipson, *British Empire* 7:80.

5. Entick, *General History* 2:396.

6. Gipson, *British Empire* 7:81n55.

7. Ibid., 7:80; Entick, *General History* 2:398.

8. The most reliable statistics are in *N.Y. Col. Docs.* 10:620–25.

more than one passage, they required management; and we have Montcalm's word: "I have been obliged here [in Montreal] to gratify the Indian Nations, who will not leave without me, and am obliged to pass my time with them in ceremonies as tiresome as they are necessary."[9] It is a certainty that he promised plunder as he had earlier at Oswego, a certainty made all the surer by Bougainville's acknowledgment at Fort William Henry that everything in the fort except the powder magazine and provision stores "was abandoned to pillage, which it had been impossible to prevent."[10]

Bougainville concocted an alibi, which we shall examine closely. Montcalm hardly bothered: "what would be an infraction in Europe, cannot be so regarded in America," he wrote.[11]

Monro's men were supposed to surrender, not as prisoners of war, but rather on parole to stay out of armed service for eighteen months. They were to march out of the fort with "the honors of war" and continue on to Fort Edward "escorted by a detachment of French troops and some Officers and Interpreters attached to the indians." The sick and wounded unable to march were to "remain under the protection of the Marquis de Montcalm, who will take proper care of them and return them immediately after they are cured."[12]

These stipulations were violated in every respect. Instead of posting guards in the hospital to protect the patients, French officers *withdrew* the sentinels on post there.[13] Just as at Oswego, the massacre started with the helpless.

Whitewash

As for the persons who marched out of the fort—they included many women—Bougainville snidely implied that they were too fearful of the Indians to defend themselves with the arms they had been permitted to take along. One of them has deflated that alibi: Captain Jonathan Carver remarked that "though we were permitted to carry off our arms, yet we were not allowed a single round of ammunition."[14] As is too commonly the case, Bougainville exculpated the guilty French by heaping blame on the victims. Some British soldiers, he wrote, had "given" the Indians rum,

9. Ibid., 10:574–75.
10. Ibid., 10:615.
11. Montcalm to de Paulmy, 15 Aug. 1757, ibid., 10:598.
12. The articles: ibid., 10:617–18.
13. Affidavit of surgeon Miles Whitworth, 17 Oct. 1757, in Parkman, *Montcalm and Wolfe* 2:446–47.
14. Captain J[onathan] Carver, "A detail of the Massacre of the English by the French Indians, at Fort William Henry, in America, in 1757," *Arminian Magazine* 17 (Jan. 1794), 33–38, quotation at p. 34. (NL.)

after which they became uncontrollable.[15] *Given* was certainly as weaselly a word as could be imagined; the French officer Pierre Pouchot noted drily that "those who resisted were killed."[16]

Captain Carver affirmed that the guard promised by Montcalm never appeared. His statement was confirmed by Bougainville, with blame thrown onto the victims again: because of the "inconceivable fear" of the British for the Indians, they "wished to march before our escort was collected and in order." That fear—which drove men to march into danger without a promised guard—must be acknowledged as truly inconceivable.[17]

"All the officers," according to Bougainville, "made the greatest efforts to put a stop" to the "disorder." According to Carver, however, "I could plainly perceive the French officers walking about at some distance, discoursing together with apparent unconcern."[18]

Montcalm stayed well out of sight and hearing—he *knew* what was going to happen—until the Indians had gotten their plunder, after which he made great show of rushing about to "save" the victims. In a scene straight out of classic melodrama he "bared his breast and cried out in midst of the crazed savages: 'Since you are rebellious children who break the promise you have given to your Father and who will not listen to his voice, kill him first of all.' "[19] *Quelle grandeur!*

Bougainville's whitewash includes a statement that Montcalm had gained prior agreement from the Indian chiefs that they approved the terms of capitulation and "would prevent their young men committing any disorder."[20] Probably such a meeting did take place, but for what transpired at it, we have only Bougainville's word, which, in these circumstances, is not worth much. What seems more likely is that Montcalm and the Indians came to an agreement that they could pillage at will and seize prisoners whom he would subsequently ransom as he did, again in the pattern of Oswego.[21] What glaringly exposes all of Bougainville's alibis was the withdrawal of the guards from the hospital after the experience of Oswego had shown that the Indians would rush there first of all.

Fairness requires acknowledgment of the zealous and hazardous endeavors of a missionary priest to mitigate the horrors. Père Roubaud ordered his Abenakis, and got obedience, to abstain from the cannibal feasts of the

15. *N.Y. Col. Docs.* 10:616.
16. Pouchot, *Memoir* 1:89.
17. Carver, "Detail," 34; *N.Y. Col. Docs.* 10:616.
18. Carver, "Detail," 35.
19. Gipson, citing Waddington, *British Empire* 7:86.
20. Bougainville to de Paulmy, 19 Aug. 1757, *N.Y. Col. Docs.* 10:614–15.
21. Entick stated flatly that "the Indian chief insisted upon a previous agreement with M. Montcalm; who had promised him the plunder of the English, and that his men should have their agreement." This is convincing. Why else would the Indians have come? Entick, *General History* 2:401.

Ottawas. He rescued an infant from death and restored it to its mother. He ran everywhere trying to interpose between furious drunken warriors and their helpless captives. But he parrotted Bougainville's line: "The Savages . . . are alone responsible," he wrote, "and it is to their insatiable ferocity and their independence that the cause of it can be ascribed." His narrative distinguishes the mission Indians as less cruel than the non-Christians from the west. As to the French, he could not discover "one single action which would . . . cast upon the French Nation the infamy of that event."[22]

I am obliged to question the candor of this priest. He witnessed the slaughter of hospital inmates without mentioning withdrawal of the guards, and he omitted one item from Bougainville's narrative; to wit, that the Abenakis—Roubaud's own Abenakis—had *begun* the assault upon the British victims.[23]

The casualties

It is impossible to be certain of the number killed in this horror. In its beginning the French Indians massacred Black servants and Indian allies of the British without even a pretense of protection by onlooking Frenchmen. (This on the authority of French historian Richard Waddington.)[24] Nobody counted or estimated those low-caste victims. Nobody counted women and children either. Bougainville wrote that 20 "soldiers" were killed, and 500 "carried off," of whom Montcalm later rescued 400 by ransom as well as exhortation. Captain Carver reported that "it was computed that fifteen hundred persons were killed or made prisoners;" and Pierre Pouchot put the prisoners at "twelve or fifteen hundred" without specifying numbers killed.[25] Gipson thought the dead were "not less than

22. Gipson identifies him as Roubaud though his document dated from St. Francis, 21 Oct. 1757, is anonymous in *The Jesuit Relations and Allied Documents* (1896–1901), ed. Reuben Gold Thwaites, 73 vols., reprinted facsimile in 36 vols. (New York: Pageant Book Co., 1959), 70:90–203, quotation at p. 197.

23. At the hospital: 70:177–78. Roubaud remarked that he arrived next day "in the midst" of the butchery, and acknowledged that "the main part of our troops, occupied in guarding our batteries and the fort [from what?] was, on account of the distance, unable to give them aid." Ibid., 70: 181, 183. He excused Abenaki participation "by the law of retaliation, alleging that more than once in the very midst of Peace, or of conferences, such as that of last winter, their warriors had come to death by treacherous blows in the English Forts of Acadia." This is not incredible. Ibid., 70:195.

24. Gipson, *British Empire* 7: 85, citing Waddington *La Guerre de Sept Ans* 1:263. Francis Parkman described the episode in a famous set-piece in *Montcalm and Wolfe* 1:520–29; his thorough racism was never more evident than in his total disregard of the Black and Indian victims, whose existence he did not bother to notice.

25. Bougainville, *N.Y. Col. Docs.* 10:616; Carver, "Detail," 37; Pouchot, *Memoir* 1:89.

two hundred and may have greatly exceeded that number."[26] [7:87] John Entick calculated that not more than 1,000 men survived, and deducted this from the 2,300 surrenderers "so that they murdered, after the capitulation, 1,300 men besides women, children and other attendants."[27] The calculation is flawed because nobody can possibly know how many British colonials escaped into the woods and made their way *home* (or died in the woods) rather than trust themselves to the honor of Montcalm or Webb. Technically they would have been deserters not eager to stand up and be counted. But Gipson's calculations are persuasive that the casualties were many more than 200, not to speak of Bougainville's lying 20.[28]

In an aside, Gipson noted that British colonial authorities "tended to minimize" the tragedy, "but not for the same reasons" as the French. They were afraid of its effect on recruiting.[29]

It remains only to note that the Indian warriors who took their tokens of bravery from the helpless patients in the hospital and the disarmed prisoners suffered retribution harsher than any court of law could have inflicted. They scalped victims of smallpox, and acquired that fell disease themselves. While it gestated, they went home and spread it among their families and friends, unwittingly creating another massacre that probably killed more of their own peoples than they had murdered among their enemies.[30]

This will serve as occasion to remark that French instigation and pressure could have accomplished nothing with those warriors had they not been culturally and personally prepared to massacre and mutilate. Descendants sometimes try to deny that scalping was "Indian."[31] It won't do. Scalps taken from hospital inmates testify to something other than bravery; but the harshest condemnation that can be made of those Indian warriors is that they acted voluntarily, in a war that was not their own, as "savage" partners in the "civilized" French policy of terror. Morally speaking, the instrument and its employer are as indistinguishable as they are indefensible.

26. Gipson, *British Empire* 7:87.

27. Entick, *General History* 2:401n.

28. In his journal, Bougainville rationalized, "I think that we could have had these troops as prisoners at discretion, but in the first case there would have been two thousand more men to feed, and in the second one could not have restrained the barbarity of the Indians, and it is never permitted to sacrifice humanity to what is only the shadow of glory." I have tried without success to figure out what that last clause was supposed to be saying. [Bougainville], *Adventure*, ed. Hamilton, 170.

29. Gipson, *British Empire* 7:87n81.

30. Carver, "Detail," 37; Edmunds, *Potawatomis*, 55; Clifton, *The Prairie People*, 101–2.

31. See James Axtell, "The Unkindest Cut, or Who Invented Scalping: A Case Study," in Axtell, *European and Indian*, 16–35.

Exposure and denunciation of both commands

There is final irony in the abandonment of Montcalm's army by his Indians after they got their plunder. "Nothing was more critical for us," wrote missionary Roubaud, "than the situation in which the French army then was . . . Hardly a handful of men remained to cope with the enemy if they had assumed the offensive."[32] Governor Thomas Pownall hurried three regiments of Massachusetts men to the scene as fast as they could get past the Berkshires.[33] Besides these, General Webb's own men outnumbered Montcalm's, but Webb sought sanctuary in Albany, and Pownall's troops could not arrive in time. Montcalm prudently decamped with his booty.[34]

In his subsequent communications to Generals Webb and Loudoun, Montcalm practiced what the French call *adresse*, which in these circumstances, translates into English *effrontery*. He confessed no fault, heaped blame on the Indians and the victims, and demanded fulfilment of the capitulation "in every particular." He was "pleased with myself for having exposed my person as well as my officers in the defence of yours." If there were "the least omission" in executing the articles of capitulation "on the slightest pretext," it would be "of still more fatal consequence for you than for us." And he lied boldly about his powerlessness in the face of overwhelming numbers of Indians. Whereas his internal report itemizes 1,600 Indians from 18 nations, in the letters to Webb and Loudoun he magnified his Indian Menace into 3,000 Indians from 33 different nations.[35]

But Pownall at Boston interviewed survivors, so that Montcalm's demand was rejected and the capitulation declared void.

The news of Louisbourg and William Henry reached England almost at the same time. By coincidence, Pitt was now free of the shackles of the duke of Cumberland. (See next chapter.) Furiously he rose in Commons to pronounce "the finest Oration that ever was made in an English Senate." He blistered the military's "Want of Application to Geography, the different Arts of War and Military Discipline; their Insolence to their inferior Officers, and Tyranny over the common Men" and their "Extravagance, Idleness and Luxury." Pitt mourned that "*scarce a Man could be found with whom the Execution of any one Plan in which there was the least Appearance*

32. *Jesuit Relations* 70:197–99.

33. Loudoun Papers, mss., LO 4190, LO 4228, LO 4270, HEH; Pownall to Pitt, 16 Aug. 1757, in [Pitt], *Correspondence*, ed. Kimball, 1:94–98.

34. Itemized in *N.Y. Col. Docs.* 10:626, the plunder included forty-two pieces of artillery. Taken to the French forts on Lake Champlain, this was added to the artillery taken previously from Braddock and Oswego. The accumulation made a formidable armament, which would be used in a few months to inflict yet another terrible defeat on the British regulars.

35. *N.Y. Col. Docs.* 10:618–19, 625, 629–30.

of Danger, could with Confidence be trusted . . . few seem to be affected with any other Zeal than that of aspiring to the highest Posts, and grasping the largest Salaries."[36]

Yet the utmost Pitt could do was to recall Loudoun and Webb, who were given assignments elsewhere. Webb was kept out of command by being given a quartermaster post, from which he complained that his brother officers treated him "like a dog."[37] Loudoun's noble status protected him from any such indignity. Both continued to get promotions.

36. *Pa. Gazette* no. 1525, 16 Mar. 1758, p. 1; Gipson, *British Empire* 7:175n28. Gipson quotes material that does not appear in the *Gazette* extract but he omits a source for it.

37. Gipson, *British Empire* 7:88n86. Webb's utter gall is flabbergasting. *After* he threw away the garrison at Fort William Henry he formed a party of officers against Lord Loudoun by insinuating that Englishmen stood no chance of promotion against the Scots in highest command. Pargellis, *Lord Loudoun*, 349.

Chapter 15 ❧ *STRANGELY BLESSED PEACEMAKERS*

The English, your Brothers, and you are the common Disturbers of this Country. I say, you white People together. We term the English your Brothers as you must have some—We Indians you call Children—You both want to put us Indians a quarreling but we the Six Nations know better. If we begin we see nothing but an entire ruin of us, as we should not leave off till all was gone, so we are resolved to keep Friends on both sides as long as possible and not meddle with the Hatchet but endeavour always to pacifie the white People. Our Arms shall be between you endeavouring to keep you asunder.

Iroquois chiefs to Governor Vaudreuil, 28 March 1757

Blessed are the peacemakers: for they shall be called the children of God.

The Sermon on the Mount

Chronology

November 1755.	Philadelphia families give refuge to women fleeing from stricken backwoods.
December 1755.	Quakers respond to plea for aid by Moravian bishop Spangenberg. They send £267 for refugees.
April 1756.	Publisher Christopher Sauer offers to enlist German support for a "peaceible way" with the Indians.
20 July 1756.	Quakers begin subscription of funds, which becomes the Friendly Association for Regaining and Preserving Peace with the Indians by Pacific Measures.
October 1756.	Newly elected assembly convenes without strict pacifist members and under leadership of Benjamin Franklin.
November 1756.	At Easton treaty, Teedyuscung discloses the Walking Purchase fraud.
December 1756.	George Croghan comes to Philadelphia as Sir William Johnson's deputy. He borrows money from Friendly Association.
December 1756.	Iroquois (without Mohawks) treat with Governor-General Vaudreuil at Montreal.
January 1757.	Friendly Association is denied access to provincial council minutes and is ordered to refrain from doing business with Indians.

March–April 1757.	George Croghan summons a treaty at Harris's Ferry, moved to Lancaster. Delawares and Senecas stay away. Friends pay for the presents.
21 March 1757.	Lord Loudoun advises Denny to agree to assembly's £100,000 supply bill against Thomas Penn's explicit instruction.
May 1757.	Israel Pemberton and Colonel John Stanwix become friendly. Pemberton donates a hogshead of wine for Stanwix's officers.
5 June 1757.	Benjamin Franklin embarks for England as agent for the Pennsylvania assembly. He is accompanied by son William.
10–20 June 1756.	Sir William Johnson summons the Iroquois to a treaty at Fort Johnson. They resist his attempts to give them orders.
10 September 1757.	Johnson tells lords of trade that Pennsylvania's purchase of land at the Albany Congress disgusted the Iroquois and led to hostilities by the Indians living along the Susquehanna River.
September 1757.	William Franklin publishes defense of the Pennsylvania assembly in the *Gentleman's Magazine.*
24 November 1757.	Pennsylvania council sends secret report to the crown, attacking Quakers and exculpating Penns from fraud charge.
December 1757.	Thomas Penn orders his commissioners to make Teedyuscung recant his charge of fraud.
Early January 1758.	Benjamin Franklin confers with Thomas and Richard Penn. They become bitter enemies.
2 February 1759.	Waiting until negotiations in Pennsylvania had run their course, Franklin presents petition to the privy council for an enquiry into Teedyuscung's complaints.

The diversity of purposes among the war's participants shows most clearly in Pennsylvania. There the Quakers and assemblymen, in their distinct ways, ignored Lord Loudoun's bluster, posturing, and incompetence in order to concentrate on their own special battles with their enemy overlord. General Webb could run away from battle, and Loudoun could refuse to commit to it, but Pennsylvanians were not permitted such luxuries. They were committed, willy-nilly and without refuge, so long as Fort Duquesne held a French garrison with Delaware allies. The war had become very much Pennsylvania's own affair; and as the crown's officers created one disaster after another, Pennsylvanians came to understand that they would have to win their own war by their own means—about which they were not at all united.

Instead of genuine help from the crown, they received harassment directed by Proprietary Thomas Penn. Worse, the crown's strategy of support for Iroquois domination over other tribes created especially difficult problems in Pennsylvania where the Delawares intended to achieve full independence. And, after the surrender of Oswego, the Iroquois were no asset to the British.

The divided Iroquois

While Delaware chief Teedyuscung declared fraud at Easton in November 1756, his Iroquois "uncles" were in Montreal explaining the current situation in the Iroquois League. It was far from unity. Speaking for five of the nations, a Cayuga chief told Montcalm "of their having cut off from their cabin the Mohawks, whose heart was wholly English; yet he hoped, by dint of shaking their head, to make them recover their lost senses and to bring them back to their Father [the governor of New France]." Montcalm thought that this embassy was "the môst memorable that ever had been in Canada" in every respect, but especially for "the good dispositions evinced by the Five Nations."[1] Montcalm attributed this cordiality "principally" to the fall of Oswego. We may recall that the Iroquois had made no resistance there. Now, in Montreal, their speaker thanked the French for destroying the English base and reestablishing "the Five Nations in the possession of a place that was their property."[2] That simple remark exposes the long-range strategy of the western Iroquois to get back their own territories from European occupation and to exclude the Mohawks until that nation should cut loose from Sir William Johnson. Exulting Montcalm may not have grasped fully that the strategy was aimed at French Europeans as well as the English variety, and that the Mohawks still had a place in League councils, regardless of internal dissension.

The dissension contributed strongly to the appearance of confusion in Pennsylvania, as it involved contrary Iroquois policies toward the Delawares. In a broad general way, all the Iroquois agreed that Delawares should be made or kept subordinate to the League, but agreement stopped there. Mohawk policy was to enforce Sir William Johnson's orders to Teedyuscung, but this Mohawk policy was opposed by the Senecas, who were pro-French for the time being. The Senecas cooperated with the belligerent Ohio Delawares and protected Teedyuscung's eastern Delawares from Mohawk pressures. The Senecas opposed all efforts to make peace between Pennsylvania and the Ohioans. To speak of "Iroquois" policy in these circumstances is like calling north and south *the* polar direction. What Mohawks tried to do, the Senecas undid, and Teedyuscung

1. Montcalm to de Paulmy, 24 Apr. 1757, *N.Y. Col. Docs.* 10:553, 561. Montcalm apparently referred to the treaty at Montreal, 13–30 Dec. 1756. The official minutes, however, do not include the speech he quotes nor any other speech from a Cayuga chief. Instead they quote Oneida chief Koués as saying, "We shall not lose any time in communicating to the Mohawk that you [Vaudreuil] are willing to pardon him. We shall show him your Belt and will add a word from ourselves to it in order to give him sense and to invite him to withdraw from the English." This is rather different from "cutting off" the Mohawks and "shaking their head" as remembered later by Montcalm. Did a Cayuga chief speak outside the formal sessions? Why is the speech sent to France by Montcalm so much tougher than the speech sent by Vaudreuil? *N.Y. Col. Docs.* 10:499–518, quotation at 513.

2. Ibid., 10:559.

had to keep on terms with both, for he and his people were vulnerable to both, and the more powerful Ohio Delawares showed little concern for his easterners.

Teedyuscung

Teedyuscung added his own complications to the mix. A classic example of ambition exceeding resources, he hoped as mediator to rise to leadership over the Ohio Delawares as well as his easterners. There is not a shred of uncontroverted evidence that he put himself forward as "king" of the Six Nations; that canard was invented by Conrad Weiser to discredit Teedyuscung as a witness to the Walking Purchase fraud and to get him in trouble with the Iroquois. The Iroquois would surely have killed him if he had pretended to lord it over the League. That nonsense aside, he intrigued and maneuvered to make himself indispensable as a spokesman from Pennsylvania to the Ohioans—a position that would have entailed immense prestige if he could have achieved it—and it seems a fair guess that he hoped to become the Ohioans' spokesman to Pennsylvania.

He could not hope to gain such authority by customary means because most of the traditional chiefs had migrated westward, and Teedyuscung belonged to the wrong lineage. He could not achieve the sort of consensus at Ohio that had made him a "pine tree" chief of the eastern Delawares, because the Ohio chiefs would not abdicate in his favor. His greatest asset, besides the support of the eastern Delawares and the Senecas, was Quaker patronage which he exploited skilfully, but he did not want peace as simply as the Quakers did. As their agent to transmit peace messages to the west, he tried to arrange communication to his own advantage, with the result that he became another of the many obstructions to an open channel.

Thomas Penn's obstructionism

The main obstruction was Thomas Penn. When he received the news of Teedyuscung's charge of fraud, Penn reacted immediately. As for peacemaking, he could hardly care less. He concentrated exclusively and intensely on the welfare of Thomas Penn.

He rushed to deflect Delaware negotiations from Pennsylvania, where too many of his enemies could influence them; and to bring them under control. He lobbied Lord Halifax to refer them to Sir William Johnson "with the assistance and concurrence of such Persons as we shall appoint." In his usual smarmy way, he told Halifax that "a more indifferent Place and Person, than our Province, or our Governor would be more satisfactory . . . and more to our honour." and he guaranteed his honor by proposing as "indifferent" commissioners, Richard Peters and Conrad Weiser.[3]

To eliminate Delaware grievances, he proposed a rerun of the Easton affair in 1742 when Onondaga chief Canasatego had bullied Nutimus and the upriver Delawares to dispossess them of their lands. "Sir William Johnson," anticipated Penn, "will no doubt endeavour to strengthen the hands of the Six Nations as much as he can, and those Nations, on hearing the whole Matter, must use all the Interest they have, to settle the Matter between us."[4]

Peters tried faithfully to carry through Penn's strategy. In later proceedings he exhibited an "extract" from this letter to show Penn's desire for justice, and he magnified the desire by certain adjustments to the text. He omitted from his extract Penn's hope that Johnson would crack down on the Delawares through Iroquois instrumentality, and he omitted the names of Weiser and himself as Penn's "indifferent" commissioners. Peters knew well that those names would have given the game away in Pennsylvania.[5]

As encouragement for the Iroquois to "settle this Dispute," Penn offered a bribe. He expected the Six Nations to act "in consideration of our agreeing to consent to the Six nations proposal of releasing them from the Contract at Albany [in 1754]."[6] This typically tightfisted offer could not seem to the Iroquois like much of a quid pro quo since they regarded that Albany deed as a cheat, taking in excessive tracts of land for only half the promised compensation. They did not rise to Penn's bait.

During 1757, Johnson refused to cooperate. Far from directing Iroquois behavior at will, he had trouble enough to keep abreast of developments among the Six Nations. Further, he suspected that Penn's dealings were among the causes of his troubles, and he said as much to the lords of trade.[7] Penn had no alternative except his own men. When the Iroquois failed to perform the repressive function assigned to them, Penn resorted once more to commissioners appointed by himself, this time without reference to Sir William Johnson. His commission, in very specific terms, spells out Thomas Penn's notion of how an enquiry into Delaware grievances should be conducted. The commissioners were to conduct a thorough investigation to find out what person or persons encouraged Teedyuscung to make his assertion of fraud. By means unspecified, they were to convince Teedyuscung of his error, and to require from him an acknowledgment of it. Nothing in the still-extant commission empowers

3. Penn to Peters, 12 Feb. 1757, mss., Penn Ltr. Bks. 5: 75–78, HSP.
4. Loc. cit. See also Penn to Denny, 12 Feb. 1757, mss., Penn Ltr. Bks. 5:78–80, HSP.
5. *Doc. Hist. N.Y.* 2:742. (Q2:431.)
6. Penn to Peters, 12 Mar. 1757, mss., Penn Ltr. Bks. 5:91, HSP.
7. *N.Y. Col. Docs.* 7:329–33.

them to make any satisfaction of Indian grievances. At most, the commissioners were simply to report their findings to Penn himself. No word of peacemaking intrudes in this businesslike, legally binding document.[8]

Therein is the key to the confusion regarding the "enquiry" into Teedyuscung's allegations of grievances. Such an enquiry in good faith could have been completed in a day or two because Richard Peters and Councilor William Logan held all the pertinent documents and Teedyuscung was accompanied in mid-1757 by the affected Delawares. Such an investigation in good faith was what Israel Pemberton and his Quakers had tried to initiate, supported by the assembly's commissioners. But precisely that was what Thomas Penn and his minions dared not permit to happen, so they procrastinated, stalled, equivocated, maneuvered, and lied by every device they could imagine. Their job was to *suppress* an enquiry while giving the appearance of one. No matter the appearance, they must produce complete vindication of Thomas Penn. That was their only task. Making peace was irrelevant; they would rely on Britain's massive power to overwhelm the Indians in due course. Meantime, the proprietary, comfortable in London, and his placemen, secure in Philadelphia, regarded the lives of backwoods rabble as expendable.

In sum, Pennsylvania's most powerful man blocked all negotiations to satisfy Indian grievances, thereby impeding all approaches to peace; and he committed his obstructive strategy to the management of men who had been his associates in creating the grievances. Whatever the Quakers and the assembly tried to do, jointly or separately, Penn's men found ways to frustrate. The year 1757 therefore created a record of initiatives diverted and suppressed.

Franklin's assembly and the Quakers

Because Penn's hirelings knew his general objective, they could stall until he sent specific orders in each case, but distance prevented him from anticipating and forestalling each new move of his antagonists. Optimum turnaround time from the day Richard Peters sent news until he got Penn's response was about three months, and a stormy passage could lengthen that interval greatly so events in the province were always ahead of Penn's directions to cope with them, creating a potential for maneuver that assemblymen well understood. In 1757 the opposition consisted of Anglican followers of Benjamin Franklin in the forefront, supported by "defense" Quakers who had been "disowned" by orthodox Friends. In flat contra-

8. Drafts and signed and sealed commission, Dec. 1757, Penn. Mss., Off. Corr. 3:33–40, 42, HSP. Commissioners finally named were Richard Peters, William Logan, Lyndford Lardner, and Conrad Weiser.

diction to proprietary propaganda, these assemblymen went their own way, distinct from and sometimes conflicting with the Quakers'. The assembly's commissioners had demanded Governor Morris's declaration of war against the Delawares and a bounty on scalps. The assemblymen sympathized and cooperated with efforts to make peace with the Indians, but they also laid out money for arms and troops. They were not opposed to a provincial militia—they willingly organized one—but they would have no part of a "regular" militia controlled by Thomas Penn. They distinguished themselves most sharply in adamant determination to make Penn bear some of the war's costs, and in fierce resistance to enlargement of his powers.

Richard Peters made the distinction carefully in January: "The Assembly want in my Opinion to fasten some Injustices towards the Indians on the Proprietaries. The Quakers would not be displeased with this, but their principal view is to gain Reputation."[9] Characteristically, Peters would not admit that the Quakers' purpose was peace.

About the same time, Israel Pemberton expressed "Apprehension of the Difficulties which may probably arise between the Proprietaries and the Representatives of the People," and offered in behalf of Friends to contribute substantial funds to speed "a final Settlement with the Indians"; but he and his colleagues of the Friendly Association required access to the provincial council minutes in order to distinguish which Indian claims were just.[10] Peters had no trouble with that. A short consultation with Governor Denny produced not only rejection but a flat ban against the Quakers "transacting of Business with the Indians in this Province."[11]

Neither issue died then. Despite Denny's fumings, Quakers continued to deal with Teedyuscung's Delawares informally and at treaty councils. As for access to secret documents, though Peters stonewalled every request, Pemberton organized research that collected old documents from chests and family files; and the assembly pressed Denny for transcripts of council records concerning the lands involved in the Walking Purchase.[12] By pressure of the assembly's (Anglican) commissioners, even Teedyuscung was provided with copies of old deeds of cession.

Early in the year the assembly carried its battle onto Thomas Penn's home grounds by ordering Benjamin Franklin to London as assembly agent. Apprehensive Quakers worried that Franklin's mission might result in a change of Pennsylvania's "constitution".—that is, the loss of its charter

9. Peters to Penn, 10 Jan. 1757, Penn Mss., Off. Corr. 8:219, HSP. See also Minutes of the Meeting for Sufferings, 7 May 1756, mss., 1:24–26, Haverford College Library.

10. Callender and Pemberton to Peters, 21 Jan. 1757, mss., Stauffer Coll. 4:349, HSP.

11. Peters to Callender and Pemberton, 25 Jan. 1757, mss., Minutes of the Proceedings of the Friendly Assn., 306, HSP.

12. *Pa. Council Minutes*, 13 July 1757, 7:635–37.

FIGURE 3. Obverse *(above)* and reverse *(facing page)* of a silver medal used by Pennsylvania Quakers in negotiations with the Delaware Indians, 1757. Barely discernible after much wear are crossed peace pipes held by the symbolic negotiators over a treaty fire. A tree of peace stands behind the Quaker, and the sun that gives life shines over the Indian. The inscription reads, "Let us look to the Most High who blessed our Fathers with Peace." PHOTOGRAPHS BY COURTESY OF THE NATIONAL MUSEUMS OF CANADA.

and consequent conversion to royal government. Far better would it be to make "an amicable Adjustment" with the Penns.[13] Israel Pemberton wrote a carefully qualified letter of introduction, but he thought that there was little the Quakers could expect from Franklin besides "a more candid representation of our conduct."[14]

13. Minutes of the Meeting for Sufferings, 24 Feb. 1757, mss., 1:61–62, Haverford College.

14. Pemberton to Fothergill, 4 Apr., 1 July 1757, mss., Etting Coll., Pemberton Papers 2:21, 24, HSP.

The difference went deep. Franklin was still the imperialist he had been in 1750, more so, indeed, than ever; but the Quakers were devoted to the provincial charter that William Penn had crafted to guarantee their "Liberties and Privileges, civil and religious." Their ancestors had emigrated from vicious persecution in England to enjoy the benefits of that charter, and their families had prospered under it. They were willing to endure the burden of the proprietary family's extortions if that was the price required to maintain freedom.

But—always but—they must have peace, and Thomas Penn would not let them seek peace, no matter how they tried to conciliate him. The rub was that if Penn's misdeeds were exposed, the proprietary charter would probably be revoked in any case. Against their own wish, the Quakers were compelled by Penn's intransigence to make common cause, for the time being, with imperialist Franklin.

Maneuvering in London and Philadelphia

In London, Franklin went through the motions of a visit to the Penns to explore the possiblities of reconciliation, but he had no faith in such a miracle. Quite apart from larger issues, Franklin had a business score with Thomas Penn, whose purchases of books, stationery, and advertisements in Franklin's *Pennsylvania Gazette* dated back to 1734 without any apparent effort to pay. The account was for 57 pounds, 1 shilling, and sixpence, but the twenty-three years overdue caused Penn no shame. He let another year and a half go by before ordering payment.[15]

The Franklin-Penn interview was a total failure. Thomas Penn denied that the Pennsylvania assembly had privileges similar to those of the English House of Commons; he held that the assembly was "only a kind of Corporation acting by a Charter from the Crown and could have no Privileges or Rights but what was granted by that Charter." Franklin retorted that "Your Father's Charter"—distinguishing William Penn's charter to his people from the crown's charter to him—"expressly says that the Assembly of Pennsylvania shall have all the Power and Privileges of an Assembly according to the Rights of the Freeborn Subjects of England, and as is usual in any of the British Plantations in America." Thomas denied that his father had been empowered to make such a grant. Franklin was indignant. "*I said*, If then your Father had no Right to grant the Privileges He pretended to grant, and published all over Europe as granted, those who came to settle in the Province upon the Faith of that Grant and in Expectation of enjoying the Privileges contained in it, were deceived, cheated and betrayed. *He answered* they should have themselves looked to that . . . if, they were deceiv'd, it was their own Fault; and that He said with a Kind of triumphing laughing Insolence, such as a low Jockey might do when a Purchaser complained that He had cheated him in a Horse. I was astonished to see him thus meanly give up his Father's Character and conceived that Moment a more cordial and thorough Contempt for him than I ever before felt for any Man living.[16] To my knowledge this was

15. Penn Papers from Friends House, London, mss., no. 80, photostat in HSP; *Franklin Papers* 7:157–58. Deborah Franklin got the money finally, 30 July 1759, twenty-five years after the account was opened.

16. *Franklin Papers* 7:360–64.

the only insult that ever penetrated the complacent "honour" flaunted by Thomas Penn.

Revealing as it is, the incident was a side issue. Franklin's primary mission was to defend the assembly's case to officialdom and the public, and his followers in the assembly grew tougher, day by day. They sent him instructions to demand a royal investigation into Teedyuscung's charges of proprietary fraud; and after two years of preparation, Franklin duly filed a petition with the privy council. They defied Penn's instructions to governor Denny by presenting Denny with a new tax bill to raise £100,000 on their terms, and they phrased it so carefully that Denny's council advised him to get Lord Loudoun to "extricate" him.[17] Loudoun obliged. "Waive Your [proprietary] Instructions for the present," he directed and to Secretary William Pitt he explained, "had the Bill been neglected, the whole of their Troops would have disbanded immediately."[18] Prerogative man that he was, Loudoun put the crown's interest before Thomas Penn's.

Against all of Penn's attacks, the assembly stood fast, and it won. But in London its provision of £100,000 for defense was somehow twisted to seem like a pacifist Quaker denial of funds for defense. Franklin's task was to counter that propaganda. His son William, who had accompanied him to England, fired a heavy broadside against it in *The Gentleman's Magazine*, the most substantial of London's monthly journals. William totted up the assembly's grants "for the king's use," and described how pacifist Quakers had withdrawn from the assembly and refused to serve when elected. With understandable hyperbole, William asserted that, "more is done for the relief and defence of the country without any assistance from the crown, than is done perhaps by any other colony in America." He persuaded the magazine's influential editor to give a novel twist to the assembly's own arguments: "Neither the proprietaries nor any other power on earth ought to interfere between [the assemblymen] and their sovereign.[19] It was precisely the opposite of Thomas Penn's contention that the sovereign should not interfere with *him*.

Nevertheless, all the skill at maneuver of the Franklins and the Quakers probably weighed less in the balance than the disgrace and downfall of the duke of Cumberland, who had been Thomas Penn's patron at court. (It will be described in chapter 16.) Whatever the cause, Penn remained as determined as ever to save his "honour" and his province from the effects of Teedyuscung's charges.

London's Quakers were much concerned about the campaign against their fellow religionists. "You should know that you are accused, and by

17. *Pa. Council Minutes*, 5 Mar. 1757, 7:430–31.
18. Loudoun Papers, mss., LO 3128, LO 3467, HEH.
19. *Gentleman's Magazine* 27 (Sept. 1757):417–20.

whom you are accused," wrote Dr. John Fothergill to Israel Pemberton, and the good doctor scolded, "if you think it beneath you to clear your selves; at least endeavour to clear us of the imputations we lie under on your account."[20] Something was needed to counter William Smith's *Brief State* and *Brief View. Someone* was needed from Pennsylvania to make instant response to the canards and libels. Pemberton agreed that some Friend should go, but none did.[21]

The Friendly Association's work

While council busied itself with whitewashing Thomas Penn, the members of the Friendly Association rushed frantically about to cope with the other crises of the times. They raised a fund of more than £4,000 for aid to refugees as well as the costs of negotiations with the Indians, and their leaders consulted with German pietists to supplement the fund.[22] The beleaguered Moravians of Bethlehem and vicinity were early beneficiaries of Quaker charity. Besides this outlay in money, Philadelphia families took in refugees from the back country with unstinted hospitality. Richard Peters denounced them for not making "one Effort for the Relief of the Back Inhabitants," but in the same sentence acknowledged that they "receive the Women from Carlisle, Lancaster, and Reading, who are leaving their Families with as much Ease as if they were come upon an ordinary Visit."[23] It may be noted that in all of Peters's papers, I have not come across any reference to charity by himself for the refugees. In contrast, Israel Pemberton extended hospitality to refugees in the city, including Indians, and boarded Cherokee visiting diplomats, including one who recuperated there from a long illness.[24] It appears that Mary Pemberton shared her husband's convictions. Somehow he managed to conduct his mercantile business, raise money, lead the Friendly Association, act as

20. Fothergill to Pemberton, 21 Feb. 1757, mss., Etting Coll., Pemberton Papers 2:20, HSP.

21. Pemberton to Fothergill, 30 May 1757, mss., Etting Coll., Pemberton Papers 2:23, HSP.

22. Samuel Parrish, *Some Chapters in the History of the Friendly Association for Regaining and Preserving Peace with the Indians by Pacific Measures* (Philadelphia: Friends' Historical Association, 1877): 2:48, et passim. See also C. Sowr to T. Pemberton, 25 Apr. 1756, mss., Papers of the Friendly Assn. 1:27.

Bibliographic note: The copy of Parrish in HSP is unique. Its two volumes are interleaved with manuscripts and pasted-in clippings from the journal *The Friend.* Although valuable, it requires supplementation from the manuscript Minutes of the Friendly Association in the Indian Records Collection of HSP and the Papers Relating to the Friendly Association at Haverford College Library. Also the massive collections of Pemberton Papers at HSP.

23. Peters to Penn, 25 Nov. 1755, mss., Peters Ltr. Bk., 197.

24. Thayer, *Israel Pemberton,* 156 and n22.

clerk of the Yearly Meeting and trustee of the Pennsylvania Hospital, and keep up an extensive correspondence; he could not have done it all without the support of a loving, approving partner at home.

In general, hospitality and relief were wholly private. Except for the assembly's provision for subsistence of the Acadians delivered to the province—we cannot forget that they arrived in the time of frontier raids—government gave nothing to the refugees besides arms, and most of the arms seem to have become objects of war profiteering. Undoubtedly other religions besides Quaker gave charity, but to my knowledge only the Friendly Association sent money and goods to the afflicted back country. As noted above, the Association received funds for this purpose from Mennonites and other German pietists. Of these services there are positive records.

But the overriding concern of the Friendly Association was to bring about a negotiated peace, beginning with the eastern Delawares and, through them, drawing in the Ohioans. As we have seen, this purpose created conflict with Thomas Penn and his placemen. As though Penn's forces were not enemies enough, the Friends' purpose necessarily antagonized Sir William Johnson, whose purpose was conquest rather than peace. Though Johnson long remained aloof from and critical of Thomas Penn, he would not tolerate intrusion on his domain, from Quakers or anyone else. Preoccupied by the Iroquois Six Nations on one side, and the demands of the British generals on the other, for the time being Johnson spared little attention for Pennsylvania. He delegated that concern to Deputy George Croghan with results that we shall see.

Lancaster, 1757

Croghan appeared in Philadelphia in his official capacity in December 1756 and quickly pre-empted the function of inquiring into Teedyuscung's grievances. Just as quickly, he borrowed £100 from the Friendly Association.[25] This was for messengers to summon Delawares and Iroquois to a new treaty to be presided over by Croghan. "I will see Justice done you," he promised the Delawares, but Teedyuscung had no faith in that pledge. Teedyuscung remembered that the Iroquois "had abused the Delawares some Years before, greatly in Philadelphia; as if the Delaware and Minisink Indians were their Dogs; and that Canasatego . . . ordered them away from their own Land."[26] And Teedyuscung avoided another meeting with the Six Nations under Croghan's supervision.

25. Warrant to pay, 8 Jan. 1757, mss., Gratz Coll., Commissioners of Indian Affairs Corr., HSP; *Pa. Council Minutes* 7:383–85, 391.

26. *Pa. Council Minutes* 7:429–33; Papers of Frdly. Assn. 1:255.

He may have made a strategic mistake. In February 1757, Lord Loudoun and Sir William Johnson, under pressure of military necessity, seem to have been genuinely intent on satisfying all Indian grievances. According to Richard Peters, Loudoun would do it, if necessary, at the crown's expense, and recover the cost from the offending party.[27] Johnson was certain that "All We Can do will be to no Purpose" unless the "most Prudent, Speedy, and effectual Methods" should be used to make the Delawares "amply Redressed." His sentiments appear genuine. He sideswiped Thomas Penn with an added instruction to promote the crown's Indian interest "only."[28] Croghan himself was well aware of grievances arising from Pennsylvania's policies. Perhaps a real accommodation could have been reached, but Teedyuscung stayed away.

The treaty was set for Harris's Ferry [Harrisburg] where Croghan arrived, 29 March, to find 160 Indians already there, but they were mostly from the Six Nations.[29] The affair was removed to Lancaster where all present killed time waiting for the Delawares, who never came. The Indians expected presents because they had taken time for this journey while planting and politics in Iroquoia demanded their attention, but the expense immediately became an issue. Commissioners from Pennsylvania's assembly thought the costs of an "inter-colony" treaty should be shared. Croghan suggested that Sir William Johnson always gave a shirt to each Indian before beginning a treaty council, but Croghan had neither shirts nor money. In the circumstances Croghan thought "itt wold Nott be a Miss for the frends to Cloath them," including a few laced hats for the principal men.[30] Croghan was always generous with other people's money.

Friends were already being reviled for intruding at Indian councils, and had been forbidden to attend them by Governor Denny and Commander in Chief Loudoun. It is difficult to conceive a legitimate reason why they should have been called on to pay the costs of a council presided over by the crown's agent and attended by governor, councilors, and assemblymen, but the Friendly Association's trustees agreed. "Everything I can do," wrote Pemberton, "to promote a happy Event to this Important Business, thou may'st depend on my Industry in." Ever the merchant, he admonished Croghan to examine the goods carefully and send an inventory.[31]

Everybody came to Croghan's party except the Indians for whom it was

27. Peters to Penn, 10 Jan. 1757, Penn Mss., Off. Corr. 8:219, HSP.

28. Instructions to Croghan, 16 Feb. 1757, mss., Logan Papers 11:45, HSP; Johnson to Denny, 16 Feb. 1757, Pa. Provincial Council Recs., mss., P:171–72, Pa. Hist. and Mus. Comm., Hbg., Pa.

29. Papers of Frdly. Assn., mss., 1:275, Haverford College.

30. Ibid., 1:279.

31. Loc. cit.

given.[32] Everybody rejected or resented paying for it except the persons who were supposed to have nothing to do with it. Governor Denny asked Loudoun to defray the expense of the Indians whom Johnson had invited. Loudoun refused to pay a penny for a meeting "insisted on by Your People and only Aquies'd in by the Kings Servants." Maybe the cost would teach them "not to Interfere with the Prerogative of making Peace and War."[33] At which, Denny angrily proclaimed that the whole expensive business would be turned over to Sir William Johnson and nobody would be "suffered" to treat again in Pennsylvania.[34]

But Denny's eruption blew over because Johnson had become powerless to do anything about Pennsylvania's problems. Johnson's only reliable agents, the Mohawks, confessed their impotence at Lancaster. Mohawk chief Little Abraham acknowledged that the Delawares and Shawnees "would pay no regard" to them, and Denny was obliged to face reality.[35] He told the Penns, "I had there the Mortification to learn from their own Mouths, that these very Delawares, who were lately treated as Women, thrown out of the Council, and order'd to live on Sasquehannah, by their Uncles the Six Nations, as unworthy to live among the Brethren the English, had now put the Six Nations to Defiance, and were so strongly supported by the Senecas, that their other Uncles cou'd not terminate the Differences between them and this Government."[36] Teedyuscung had found protectors who could not be overawed; he would negotiate on his own terms regardless of the demands of the crown's highest officials in America. He would meet only with Pennsylvanians and Senecas, and without Mohawks. When this became quite clear, Denny swallowed his pride, ended the futile mummery at Lancaster, and sent out a new invitation for the Delawares and the Senecas to meet with him at Easton.

Johnson's woes

For the time being, William Johnson showed little concern. His attention was totally absorbed by reciprocal ultimatums between himself and

32. The Delawares consulted the Senecas who forbade attendance because Croghan's wampum belts of invitation were "not proper." Upon this, the Delawares returned the belts and stayed away. *Minutes of Conferences Held with the Indians At Harris's Ferry, and at Lancaster, In March, April, and May, 1757* (Philadelphia: Franklin and Hall, 1757), 8. Copy in NL Iroquois Archive. This is a clear recital of events.

33. Loudoun Papers, mss., LO 3562, HEH.

34. *Pa. Council Minutes* 7:522–24, 527.

35. Ibid., 13 May 1757, 7:521–22.

36. Denny to proprietaries, 30 June 1757, mss., Record Group 21, Exec. Corr., Pa. Hist. and Mus. Comm., Hbg.; printed *Pa. Archives* (1) 3:193. See also draft of governor's speech, 13 May 1757, Chew Papers, Box B., Chew, Ch. Justice, fol. French and Indian War, 1753–1765, mss., HSP.

George Croghan's minutes of these negotiations are in *Johnson Papers* 9:727–65.

the Senecas, Cayugas, and Onondagas. They refused his demand to take up the hatchet against the French on grounds that they feared attack from French-allied Indians, especially the Mississaugas. (They had been beaten down by the Mississaugas once earlier, at the end of the seventeenth century, and they did not believe in the myth of their own invincibility.)[37] They put Johnson in a bind. He was under great pressure from Loudoun who saw that even the Mohawks were wavering and required that "They must either be Friends or Foes." Johnson blustered at the western Iroquois. Their end of the Covenant Chain had become "very rusty," he accused; but an Onondaga chief did not let him get away with that: there were times, responded the Onondaga, when the Senecas and Onondagas had been attacked by the French "while you [English] sat still and smoaked your pipes."

It is a measure of Johnson's astuteness that he recognized the limits of his authority with the Indians. When they stood up to him on this occasion, he backtracked. Accepting their declaration of neutrality, he insisted that they must behave according to rules he prescribed or "we shall look on the Covenant Chain as absolutely broke between us, and you among the number of those enemies whom His Majesty is now at war with." Even this was bluff, but they had not come to pick a fight. They simply ignored it in practice.[38] So did Johnson.

Bankruptcy of British Indian policies

The events at Lancaster and Fort Johnson meant plainly that British officialdom had completely lost control of Indian affairs in Pennsylvania and New York. The concentrated power of great armies had value only in attacks on fixed positions or in combat with other armies fighting by the rules of set battles. Against Indian raids, the troops huddled together for self-protection. At Lancaster, the soldiers shocked Israel Pemberton by their total lack of combativeness when Indians raided "within eighty rods of a fort where the guns could be heard, but not a man went to help." Indignant Pemberton reported that six to eight, at most fifteen, Indians had seized a well-inhabited area and driven out two hundred families while an army of nearly five hundred within twenty-five miles never offered to

37. See Richard Aquila, *The Iroquois Restoration*, ch. 2, and the excellent summary of Iroquois policy on p. 81. See also Leroy V. Eid, "The Ojibwa-Iroquois War: The War the Five Nations Did Not Win," *Ethnohistory* 26:4 (Fall 1979), 297–324; Victor Konrad, "An Iroquois frontier: the north shore of Lake Ontario during the late seventeenth century," *Journal of Historical Geography* 7:2 (London, 1981), 129–44; Donald B. Smith, "Who Are the Mississaugas?" *Ontario History* 17:4(Dec. 1975), 212–22.

38. *N.Y. Col. Docs.* 7:254–66; Loudoun Papers, mss., LO 3809, HEH.

help. "Can such an Instance be produced in the English annals?"[39]

Prerogative men could not solve the problem by familiar procedures. Military solutions required armies that would seek out the enemy instead of cowering behind walls. Authoritarian edicts were just empty noise without means of enforcement. So long as the Indians received food and equipment from the French, they could not be starved into submission. Sheer necessity required British adaptation to Indian requirements instead of Indian compliance with British demands. Gentlemen who knew only how to give commands were helpless. Of all the parties involved, the Quakers were most forthcoming, and in the rebuilding of British credit among Indians, the pariah Quakers were the most effective. Israel Pemberton and his colleagues listened to the Indians instead of trying to dictate to them. As a result the Friends' papers contain a wealth—a neglected wealth—of Indian statements about Indian concerns. Pemberton won their trust and friendship, and because they talked freely to him he knew how little had been accomplished at Lancaster. To his dearest Mary—"My Beloved Spouse"—he confided, "the most difficult parts of our Service are now before us."[40]

Colonel John Stanwix

The troops at Lancaster deserve notice on several counts. Their inactivity led to deaths in the backwoods. Four mutilated corpses were brought into town by a crowd that clamored for Governor Denny to come and see, but Denny stayed out of sight. He was probably well advised to do so, as there were persons in the crowd who "talked publickly of dragging him out and shooting both him and the Commissioners by the Corpses," but the loud talk did not become action. Charles Thomson thought that "extremities" had been prevented by Colonel John Stanwix's British regulars, but Pemberton did not agree. "Especially the Soldiers," he reported, "exclaimed against all that were for making Peace with the Indians," and these were the same soldiers who had abandoned the inhabitants they were supposed to protect.[41]

Indignant though he was, Pemberton had sensed a possible ally in Colonel Stanwix, who was as approachable as Denny was not. Pemberton

39. Pemberton to Fothergill, 30 May 1757, mss., Etting Coll., Pemberton Papers 2:23, HSP.

40. Israel to Mary Pemberton, Lancaster, 20 May 1757, mss., Etting coll., Pemberton Papers 12:23, HSP.

41. Thomson to Wm. Franklin, (June) 1757, mss., Franklin Papers 48:120, APS; Israel Pemberton to Fothergill, 30 May 1757, mss., Etting Coll., Pemberton Papers 2:23, HSP.

reported that he was "at last oblig'd to make Use of Colonel Stanwix . . . to engage him to attend that Treaty," and the maneuver worked well. As we have seen, toward the end of the treaty the frustrated governor Denny threatened to cancel all future negotiations, partly because of cost and partly because of Lord Loudoun's directives, but Colonel Stanwix persuaded him to approach Teedyuscung once more.[42]

It was a strange conjuncture of persons and interests: against the conniving of the proprietary men, who wanted to end all negotiations except their own, were ranged a Mohawk chief, a British army colonel, and the leader of Pennsylvania's orthodox pacifist Quakers. Their ends varied—the Mohawks clearly wanted to preserve a degree of harmony in their League; the colonel wanted a screen of friendly Indians to ward off future raids from the west; and the pacifist wanted peace with all Indians—but their interests coincided for the moment as to means, and they swayed Denny.

It would seem also that Pemberton had learned something from Benjamin Franklin about winning soldiers' good will. As Franklin had provided gourmet food and drink for Braddock's officers on their way to the debacle at Fort Duquesne, so now Pemberton's Friendly Association shipped a hogshead of Madeira to Stanwix. "Common civility" obliged Stanwix to accept this "testimony of their good will," and he further expressed gratitude for the good winter quarters that Philadelphia had provided for his battalion of nearly a thousand men. This was a very different tune from what Lord Loudoun and Penn's men were singing.[43]

It differed also from what Stanwix had to say about Maryland's assembly, which refused not only to maintain Fort Cumberland, but categorically forbade the posting of provincial troops in garrison there. That assembly would not accept the expense of supporting either troops or Indians joining the British. "That set of men has done everything in their power to give the place up to the Enemy," exclaimed Stanwix. "It must be of the highest consequence to prevent such an abominable evil from spreading."[44]

Stanwix was a soldier with a soldier's job to do. Political preconceptions and objectives did not interfere with his ability to distinguish between people who helped him do his job and those who hindered.

42. Loc. cit.

43. Stanwix to Pemberton, 8 Aug. 1757, mss., Papers of the Frdly. Assn. 1:391. The Madeira cost £22.10, ibid., 1:399.

44. Horatio Sharpe to Stanwix, 8 May 1757, mss., Loudoun Papers LO 3578; Stanwix to Loudoun, 12 May, 13 Nov. 1757, ibid., LO 3600, LO 4825, HEH.

Preparing for a treaty

In this respect Stanwix faced 180 degrees away from Thomas Penn, who had sent new instructions to his placemen "*to prevent your holding a Treaty with Teedyuscung and the Delaware Indians.*" Here is an example of the control difficulties imposed by communication delays. Penn wrote a series of letters from 10 to 12 March, which probably reached Philadelphia about mid-May when the Lancaster treaty was already under way. Since Teedyuscung did not attend, the treaty harmed Penn's strategy only—a big *only*—by persuading Governor Denny to invite Teedyuscung to a new treaty. That damage done, the placemen set about minimizing and containing the new treaty's effects.[45]

They could not stop Denny's message from reaching Teedyuscung, because it had gone by way of Bethlehem where the Moravians cooperated as much as they dared with Friends.[46] Teedyuscung, assured that he could bring his protecting Senecas, accepted the invitation and showed up at Bethlehem, 6 July 1757, where he received a wary welcome, and from there he went on to Easton.[47]

Unable to prevent the treaty, Penn's men now knew that they must discredit Teedyuscung thoroughly, and the Quakers also. Their basic objective was to make a favorable record for transmission to the crown—public opinion in Pennsylvania mattered little if at all—and their method was to make Teedyuscung appear to be a crazy sot being manipulated by almost treasonable, power-mad Quakers.

They recruited George Croghan. Up to this time, Croghan had cooperated with the Friendly Association, and his papers show that he understood very well the reality of Delaware grievances, but at Easton he switched sides. His reversal bewildered and disheartened the Friends who had been providing money to him to aid, as they thought, in the royal enquiry into Delaware complaints, but shrewd Isaac Norris, the assembly speaker, had a simple, cynical explanation. Croghan, he knew, owed much money in Philadelphia, and the provincial law to relieve him of his debts for ten years (and keep him out of debtors' prison) had not yet been confirmed in England. Norris passed this information to his respected friend Benjamin Franklin, then in London, who did not need to be told that Thomas Penn

45. Penn to Denny, 10 Mar.; to Peters, 11 and 12 Mar., mss., Penn Ltr. Bks. 5:82–96, HSP.

46. A series of letters shows Bishop Augustus Spangenberg's gratitude for Quaker relief, and his full accord with Quaker objectives. It appears also that a Moravian named William Edmonds acted as confidential go-between. Pemberton Papers, mss., 11:31, 35, HSP; Papers of Frndly. Assn., mss., 1:133, 135, 139, 195, 203; 2:75, Haverford College. I have also seen Edmonds ltrs. in APS, but overlooked their significance at the time.

47. *Pa. Council Minutes* 7:622, 634.

could prevent the relief of Croghan's debts.[48] Croghan did not need to be told either, but I think he was. Thomas Penn had written to Richard Peters that Croghan was "by no means a Person to be depended upon." (Something that Peters did not need to be told.)[49] It is not hard to imagine Peters twisting Croghan's arm with this. Perhaps he did not need to. It is quite clear from Croghan's behavior at Easton and his "report" of it that he fitted himself, hand in glove, into the proprietary strategy.

Easton, July–August 1757

The treaty negotiations continued from 21 July to 7 August 1757.[50] Many Indians attended: 159 of Teedyuscung's company and 119 Senecas "and others of the Six Nations." As usual, these totals included wives and children, who made a picturesque and busy addition to the general scene. Dealing formally with the Indians were Governor Denny, his council, four assembly commissioners, and George Croghan. Informally, a large delegation of Quakers showed up as observers, flouting bans against their presence in any capacity that had been issued at every echelon of authority from Commander in Chief Loudoun, through Proprietary Thomas Penn, to Governor William Denny. Authority was bluffing. The Quakers knew that nobody could prevent them from looking on (Thomas Penn privately acknowledged this);[51] and, as it happened, nobody could prevent the Indi-

48. 17 Oct. 1757, *Franklin Papers* 7:264–70.

49. Penn to Peters, 11 Mar. 1757, mss., Penn Ltr. Bks. 5:88, HSP.

50. Bibliographic note: Three versions of the treaty minutes have survived: George Croghan's in *N.Y. Col. Docs.* 7:280–321; a Pennsylvania version that I take to be Richard Peters's editing, *Pa. Council Minutes* 7:649–714; and Charles Thomson's manuscript version in the library of the American Philosophical Society. They are discrepant with each other in significant detail. The official scribe for Croghan was William Trent who was soon to achieve ill fame for spreading smallpox among the Indians (see ch. 20). Croghan requested that Jacob Duché assist Trent. (Duché was a protégé of Provost William Smith.) Thomson became Teedyuscung's clerk. The Croghan-Trent-Duché version is shorter than the *Pa. Council Minutes* version, which seems to have been edited especially to counteract Thomson's version. I have compared these three versions critically. The original manuscript from which the *Pa. Council Minutes* printed is in Pa. Provincial Records, vol. Q, Pa. Hist. and Mus. Commission, Hbg. Croghan's mss. traveled to England and came to rest in PRO., Co5/1068. Franklin published Croghan's version in *Treaty Held in August 1757, at Easton Between the Province of Pennsylvania and Teedyuscung, King of the Delawares, Representing Ten Tribes of Indians* (Philadelphia: B. Franklin and D. Hall, 1757), reprinted facsimile in *Indian Treaties Printed by Benjamin Franklin, 1736–1762*, ed. Julian P. Boyd (Philadelphia: Historical Society of Pennsylvania, 1938).

The versions may be compared in the Iroquois Archive at the Newberry Library or in the microfilm publication *Iroquois Indians*, eds. Francis Jennings, William N. Fenton, Mary A. Druke, and David R. Miller, reel 21.

51. Penn changed his tune. In February he acknowledged that spectators could not be hindered from attending treaties; he even wished that "every Man of consequence, in the Colonys, was to be present, as the examination must tend to our reputation;" but in Mar. he ordered Governor Denny to forbid any body or society to repair to the place of any treaty

ans from consulting with them after hours and in their private rooms.

Negotiations started with contention over Teedyuscung's demand for a clerk of his own. Denny refused this, whereupon Teedyuscung marched off to the commissioners to say that "he would not enter upon Business, but would go away with all his Men." The Commissioners prevailed on him to press Denny once more, joined with themselves, and Denny capitulated.[52] In anticipation of how this incident would be presented secretly to the crown, we may note that Commissioners Galloway, Masters, and Hughes were Anglicans and Franklin supporters; Commissioner Fox was a disowned "defense" Quaker, also a Franklin supporter. None was a member of the Friendly Association or a colleague of Israel Pemberton. And when Teedyuscung got his way, he appointed as his clerk Charles Thomson, the Presbyterian teacher in the Friends' school who had earlier taught in the Anglican college.

In Croghan's report to William Johnson, who passed it on to the crown, a suggestively equivocal phrase made Teedyuscung choose "a Quaker Schoolmaster for his Clerk;" then, in Croghan's ink, but Conrad Weiser's words, came the denunciation: "Those People, by his having a Clerk, they had a Counsellor for themselves, to put Teedyuscung in Mind what they wanted him to say." Escalating the issue: the Quakers were acting contrary to the king's orders and arrangements for Sir William Johnson to have exclusive jurisdiction over Indian negotiations.[53]

The Quakers denounced

A well-orchestrated anti-Quaker campaign followed up Thomas and Richard Penn's instruction to Governor Denny that he should "not suffer

or to concern themselves with Indians during the treaty or to give presents or to join a present with a public present. Denny tried to enforce this order, but failed. T. Penn to R. Peters, 12 Feb. 1757, mss., Penn Ltr. Bks. 5:76; T. and R. Penn to Denny, 10 Mar. 1757, mss., ibid., 5:95, HSP.

52. The Thomson version at APS recites this incident in matter-of-fact tone, pp. 5–6. Croghan's version omits it, stating only that the Indians "were well satisfied that no Person should take down the Minutes of the Treaty but the One appointed by me." PRO, CO 5/1068, f. 70. This shift was not possible in Pennsylvania because the assembly commissioners had presented their protest formally in writing, so the council's editor narrated the incident with an addition: "The Governor and Council were surprized at Teedyuscung's applying again with so much Warmth for a Clerk after he had expressed himself so well satisfied the Evening before with the Speech made them by the Governor assigning Reasons why he cou'd not comply with his request, and suspected that the Indians had been tampered with on this Occasion by some evil disposed Persons and put on renewing this Demand." *Pa. Council Minutes* 7:654–59, quotation at p. 657. Conrad Weiser pumped a yarn into the minutes also, p. 658, and the council worked up a case of sinister machinations for evil reasons by Israel Pemberton and crew—all because Teedyuscung wanted honest minutes.

53. PRO, CO 5/1068, ff. 96–98.

any body of People to interfere in his Treatys with the Indians nor make them Presents at any such times, or join their Presents with those of the Publick."[54]

At Easton, William Peters and Jacob Duché, Jr., wrote that Israel Pemberton and Joseph Galloway had been "remarkably busy" with Teedyuscung, insinuating that he had been instigated to demand his own clerk. (This was contradicted by Moses Tatamy, one of Denny's Delaware Indian interpreters.)[55] Peters and Duché put a dark construction on an incident that occurred when some frustrated Indians blackened their faces and threatened violence until "when the Quakers came . . . they imediately submitted and deliver'd up their Arms as readily and submissively as common Soldiers would to their Officers." The semantics are wondrous: *Soldiers* and *officers* proved that the peacemaking Quakers were directing the war makers.[56]

Two other deponents swore that Pemberton had "upbraided" Teedyuscung "with being drunk and unfit for Business," saying that he would go home unless Teedyuscung behaved better; after which, Pemberton was seen "seemingly in close and earnest Discourse" with Teedyuscung.[57] The point of this, innocuous though such conduct would appear to be, was that Governor Denny had forbidden the Quakers to transact any business with the Indians. In an age of authority, direct violation of a governor's order was not a slight offense.

A statement in the papers of proprietary lawyer Benjamin Chew avers that Israel Pemberton argued vociferously with Chew and Governor Denny during the treaty proceedings. This seems to have been concocted just to make Thomas Penn love Benjamin Chew as no such incidents were reported in the minutes written by George Croghan's secretaries or Governor Den-

54. Cited n51, above.

55. Moses Tatamy's Account of Indian Complaints, mss., Papers of Frdly. Assn. 1:64–66. Tatamy stated that he had originated the idea for the Indians to have their own clerk, and that the proposal was approved by the Delawares in council at Wyoming before the Easton treaty took place. "This I told to Conrad Weiser at Easton when he accused the Quakers of putting it into Teedyuscung's Head . . . I never heard the Quakers once mention it."

During the treaty conference, Tatamy's son was shot and killed by a colonial while acting as a messenger. Father and son were Presbyterian convert Indians. *Pa. Council Minutes* 7:670, 674–75; Hunter, "Moses (Tunda) Tatamy," 74, 79. Hunter knew Tatamy's accounts, but insinuated Quaker influence over them.

56. Ayer Mss., N.A. 713, NL. William Peters was brother to Richard.

57. Depositions, mss., Roberts Coll., Colonial Papers, Benjamin Shoemaker folder, Haverford College. Apparently there were difficulties in getting the right slant on these depositions. The first was sworn before the governor on 2 Aug. 1757 by John Drake and Benjamin Shoemaker, but the second one, in what looks like Richard Peters's scrawl, is dated 31 Aug., signed only by Shoemaker, and sworn before Chief Justice William Allen. Strikingly it omits all mention of Drake who disappears not only from the signatures, but from the pronouns also. "We" becomes "I" all the way through. It looks as though Drake had withdrawn from the scheme.

ny's or Teedyuscung's, and there is no mention of such an affair in the private correspondence of Pemberton and Thomson. Considering the documents fabricated later by Chew on his way to the provincial chief justiceship, I think he made this one up out of the whole cloth.[58]

Conrad Weiser swore an affidavit (with Thomas McKee) that has been interpreted as meaning that Teedyuscung did not really represent Delaware opinion, with the clear implication that his charges of land fraud had come from persons who were not Indians. Weiser charged that "the Chiefs of the Delawares" were angry with Teedyuscung "for dwelling so long upon the Land Affair . . . which is Dirt." Weiser attributed to a leading man named Lappapitton the demand to "enter upon the Business we came down for, which is for Peace." He quoted Lappapitton as saying that the land issue was "a Dispute we did not hear of till now." and Weiser claimed that Lappapitton had "great Reputation among the Indians."[59] This Delaware did have a reputation, but it was not exactly what Weiser suggested. In 1747, he had been put forward to become paramount chief of the Delawares, but by Weiser rather than the Delawares, and they rejected him. Weiser had had to confess, privately, that Lappapitton was "afraid he will be Envyd and consequently bewitched [i.e., killed] by some of the Indians."[60]

Croghan inserted in his minutes the incident related by Weiser and McKee, but in rather different language. For clarity of exposition, that will be taken up a little further on.

Peace in the east

Thomas Penn's instructions guaranteed that the Easton treaty would not settle the Walking Purchase complaint. Teedyuscung got a runaround, first being introduced to Croghan as Johnson's deputy who had been appointed to adjust all differences to Teedyuscung's satisfaction, then being referred by Croghan to Johnson. Teedyuscung balked. "I do not know Sir William Johnson [i.e., he and I do not have a treaty relationship] . . . as you told us there was nothing in the Way to hinder us from confirming a durable and lasting Peace, I, at present, desire nothing at all of my Brethren, the English, for my Lands, I only want . . . that the Deeds may be produced, and well looked into . . . and true Copies of them taken

58. "Wed., Aug 3d: 1757," mss., boxed, B. Chew, ch. justice, fol. French and Indian War, 1753–1765, HSP. For Chew's later fabrications, see Jennings, *Ambiguous Iroquois Empire*, app. B.

59. 6 Aug. 1757, *Pa. Arch.* (1) 3:256.

60. Weiser to Logan, 15 Oct. 1747, mss., Logan Papers 11:33, HSP; Francis P. Jennings, "The Delaware Interregnum," *Pa. Mag. of Hist. and Biog.* 89:2 (Apr. 1965), 193–94.

. . . let the Copy of the Deeds be sent to Sir William Johnson and to the King, and let him judge. I want nothing of the Land till the King hath sent Letters back."[61]

Nevertheless, Denny made a long, rambling speech repeating that the Walking Purchase charge should be heard by Johnson. Angry Teedyuscung denounced this "Rumbling over the Earth, or Confusion about Lands. I did not want you to make Mention of them . . . I wanted you should come to the main Point, without having so many Words with it."[62]

Here it was that Lappapitton, according to Croghan's minutes, spoke up: "We have been here these twenty Days, and have heard nothing but scolding and disputing about Lands: Settle the Peace, and let all these Disputes stand till after."[63] This was, in fact, just what Teedyuscung wanted to do. He had removed the fraud charge from the agenda because two other issues concerned him much more. He offered formal peace and friendship to Pennsylvania (directly, not through Johnson and the Mohawks) which he did with two wampum belts symbolically tied together in a knot.[64] He was prepared to return captives taken during the hostilities, and subsequent records show that he rounded them up and brought them in. What he wanted for his own people, much more than compensation for the Walking Purchase, was a home and a guarantee against another dispossession. He wanted a permanent community at Wyoming Valley, with English-style houses, a trading center, and missionaries "which may be for our future Welfare, and to instruct our Children in Reading and Writing."[65] When agreement was reached on peace and habitation, though the fraud charge remained unresolved, Teedyuscung responded to Croghan's demand for military alliance in a speech that declared proud independence. "I was stiled by my Uncles, the Six Nations, a Woman in former Years . . . but now, Brethren, here are some of my Uncles, who are present, to witness the Truth of this . . . my Uncles have given me the Tomahawk and appointed and authorized me to make Peace with a Tomahawk in my Hand. I take that Tomahawk and turn the Edge of it against your Enemies, the French."[66]

The meeting ended with something for everybody. Pemberton was encouraged to hope for "a lasting Peace," and he sent to Philadelphia for the Friendly Association's presents. Because the assembly commissioners were, as usual, inadequately supplied, he ordered an extra wagonload "for

61. *Pa. Council Minutes* 7:690–91.
62. Ibid., 7:699.
63. *N.Y. Col. Docs.* 7:311. The incident is wholly lacking from Thomson's mss. at APS.
64. *N.Y. Col. Docs.* 7:310; *Pa. Council Minutes* 7:700; Thomson's mss., p. 30.
65. *Pa. Council Minutes*, 28 July 1757, 7:675–79.
66. Ibid., 7:710, 714.

the Public Interest to spare them to the Commissioners if they should desire it."[67]

Teedyuscung got a promise of houses to be built at Wyoming.

Croghan got the alliance in arms of the eastern Delawares.

The Six Nations kept the eastern Delawares as tributaries, though upgraded to "men."

The proprietary placemen succeeded in stalling the Walking Purchase enquiry.

But the renewed alliance was a rickety structure that also left everyone desiring something more, and distrustful of everyone else. Friends and the commissioners wanted the enquiry as the surest way to reach out to the Ohio Indians. They knew that Indians all the way to the Great Lakes were watching and judging them.

Teedyuscung ran into problems that delayed actual construction of his houses at Wyoming. The land had not been ceded by the Six Nations whose consent was necessary. The man who volunteered to supervise the construction crew (and protect it against hostile Indians) was John Hughes, a hot Franklin man among the assembly commissioners whom Denny and council refused to let go for fear that he might put ideas in the Indians' heads.[68] (Proprietary men were obsessed with the notion that Indians' heads were like bowls full of whatever happened last to be poured in.) The veto of Hughes had to be rescinded because nobody else would volunteer except Isaac Zane, a Friendly Associate, and when funds ran short, the Friends gave the needed money.[69] Without their participation, Pennsylvania would have been seen by Delawares east and west, and all those other Indians all the way to the Lakes, as reneging on the one positive action the government had made at Easton. Denny and council faced alternatives of renewed hostilities or paying out their own money. It is amusing to see how, when faced with such horrid choices, they permitted the Friends to pay instead.

Less amusing is the blow they struck at Friends secretly. The provincial council sent to Thomas Penn, for transmittal to the crown, a formal report attacking persons who "from their unhappy religious Principles or from what other Motive they best knew, refused or declined to concur with the Governor in giving the Hatchet to and joining with those Indians against the Enemy." *From what other Motive*—how sinister! This was presented in the guise of the findings of an exhaustive enquiry into Teedyuscung's charges

67. I. Pemberton, et al. to Joseph Morris, et al., 30 July 1757, mss., Etting Coll., Pemberton Papers 12:50, HSP.

68. *Pa. Council Minutes* 7:734, 736, 754–56.

69. Thayer, *Israel Pemberton*, 150–52.

of fraud for which, council concluded, "there is not the least Shadow of Foundation."[70]

We have seen how Teedyuscung's exposition of his charge was shunted about without ever becoming public. Council's secret report was drafted secretly without the knowledge even of the Quaker members of council. By a maneuver, Denny and the placemen sneaked the paper through when Quaker councilors were not in attendance, and kept it off the minutes.[71] Thus it appeared to have been approved unanimously, and the Pennsylvanians had no inkling of what they needed to defend themselves against. Not until their allies in England learned of the document and sent word did they become aware of its existence.

70. 24 Nov. 1757, Penn Mss., Off. Corr. 3:29–30, HSP; *Pa. Council Minutes*, 20 Jan. 1759, 8:246–61.

71. This is another tale of low chicanery. A committee of council, consisting of James Hamilton, William Logan, and Benjamin Shoemaker had been appointed to make enquiry into Teedyuscung's complaints. It could not agree. Logan reported difficulty getting it to meet whereupon the whole council was joined to the committee. (*Pa. Council Minutes*, 29 Mar. 1757, 7:462) Council discussed the matter four times in April without coming to agreement, the particular stumbling block being the validity of the document of 1686 on which the proprietaries had based their Walking Purchase of Delaware lands. (Ibid., 7:464–65, 468.) A long hiatus ensues in the records. A report purporting to be by a "committee" of council was drawn up and signed on 24 Nov. 1757, but not presented to council at its next meeting on the twenty-seventh when Quaker Benjamin Shoemaker was present. (Ibid., 7:769; see n70 above.) No quorum attended until 6 Jan. 1758. Neither Quaker member, William Logan nor Benjamin Shoemaker, was present, and the "committee report" was adopted unanimously. (Ibid., 7:776.) Though Shoemaker attended the next meeting on the ninth, he was kept ignorant of the transaction by keeping the report out of the minutes. It came to light after London Friends reported the use being made of it, whereupon Logan and Shoemaker protested that "this was a Transaction utterly unknown to them, and that the Secretary had never given them Notice that such Report was Drawn." (Ibid., 8:244–45.) Then it was entered in the minutes (n70 above), but without its fabricated appendices (described in Jennings, *Ambiguous Iroquois Empire*, app. B).

Part Four ❧ VICTORY and MORE WAR

INTRODUCTION ❧

Victory came to Britain as the reward of change in men and policies. William Pitt replaced the duke of Cumberland, and Pitt shook up the army command. Perhaps more important, he ended attempts to order the colonials about by use of the royal prerogative. Instead Pitt solicited cooperation from the colonies, and got it.

A string of triumphs followed: Amherst took Louisbourg; Bradstreet raided Fort Frontenac; Forbes, with astonishing help from the Friendly Association, captured Fort Duquesne; Johnson took Niagara; Wolfe died glamorously in the capture of Quebec; Amherst walked into Ticonderoga, and on to Montreal.

Strongly contributing to this parade of triumph was a massive change in policy by the Indian tribes. Many abandoned their former alliance with New France. Some changed sides to fight against the French. With the loss of Indian advantage, the French lost ability to harry the British off balance, and soon went down under Britain's superior numbers and resources.

Britain promised a price for the tribes' change of sides. Since the war's beginning, the Indians had made very plain their fear of losing their lands. Through complex negotiations beginning in Pennsylvania, British civil and military officials promised to draw a boundary between colonial and tribal jurisdictions, and to prevent settlers from crossing the boundary. But when France surrendered, Britain installed massive garrisons in forts throughout tribal territories.

Against these occupying troops the tribes rose in an angry resistance war in which the Iroquois Senecas played a leading part though the war has been named for Ottawa chief Pontiac. But Indians by themselves could not capture substantial fortifications except by subterfuge and surprise, and the British held on to their major posts until the besiegers dispersed.

"Pontiac's" war must be seen in perspective as an incident in the forty years of on-again, off-again wars by the tribes of the Old Northwest to preserve their lands. Traditional accounts have portrayed these episodes as flare-ups of "savage" emotion lacking rationality, but the land issue was omnipresent in the counciling of the chiefs. When the Delawares and

Shawnees raided Pennsylvania, Virginia, and Maryland in 1755 after Braddock's defeat, they began a sequence of military and political events that continued until the treaty of Greenville in 1795 established a boundary recognized by the United States. In this book, we are able only to examine the first decade of that long resistance, but its totality was one of the most decisive factors in the history of the United States, not to speak of the Indian nations of North America.

Chapter 16 ❧ TURNAROUND

For ultimate decisions [Pitt] appealed over the heads of all politicians to the nation at large, and his greatest distinction lies in the fact that he was the first British statesman to do this. . . . with him the empire in its earlier form reached its culmination. Though he was a thoroughgoing mercantilist, yet under his touch many of the badges of inferiority which the colonists had worn fell away, and for a brief period, till success against the French was won, the realm and the dominions seemed to be one.

Herbert L. Osgood

Chronology

December 1756.	William Pitt becomes leader of the British ministry. He gets information about America from Thomas Pownall and orders aggressive new military measures in America.
5 April 1757.	Because of Cumberland's hostility to Pitt, the ministry falls and a long hiatus ensues.
29 June 1757.	A new ministry is called to office in which Pitt has command and Newcastle supplies the votes in Commons needed for support.
3 August 1757.	Thomas Pownall takes office as governor of Massachusetts. Almost immediately he is required to send troops to relieve Fort William Henry, but the garrison capitulates before relief can arrive.
8 September 1757.	The duke of Cumberland disgraces himself by the Convention of Kloster-Zeven. He is forced to resign as captain general of British armies.
17 October 1757.	Lord Loudoun denounces Pownall to Cumberland.
30 December 1757.	Pitt recalls Loudoun and appoints Abercromby as commander in chief but with reduced powers. Pitt reverses policy of peremptory use of royal prerogative against colonial assemblies, offering cooperation instead. Massachusetts responds instantly on being informed of this by Governor Pownall, and raises a large army.
July 1758.	Abercromby is defeated badly at Ticonderoga. Only British regulars are involved in futile charges. Provincials and Iroquois warriors recruited by Johnson are not committed to the battle.
July 1758.	General Jeffrey Amherst captures Louisbourg.
25–27 August 1758.	Lieutenant Colonel Bradstreet besieges and captures Fort Frontenac with a force made up of ninety-five percent provincials and five percent regulars. Warriors recruited by Johnson refuse to take part when they learn that Fort Frontenac is the objective.

William Pitt came to shaky power in December 1756. Ordinarily the head of government would have operated from the post of first lord of the Treasury, but circumstance dictated otherwise and Pitt's intention was to spend money, not to keep track of it: as secretary of state for the southern department, his primary administrative responsibility (distinguished from policy making) was to supervise the American colonies.[1] In that capacity he had direct charge of Lord Loudoun's operations insofar as he could find out what they were. Loudoun did not help much in the way of information.

He acknowledged Pitt's orders, after typical procrastination, in a long letter full of plans and intentions and motion this way and that; but in this letter that spreads over nine printed pages Loudoun windily managed to say not a word about the fall of Oswego or of his march up the hill to Crown Point and back down the hill again to Albany.[2] With Loudoun as his chief executive Pitt had to plan almost in the dark.

But not quite. Thomas Pownall brought the news of Oswego to London;[3] and Pownall, after sinking Shirley in London,[4] returned to America as Shirley's successor in the government of Massachusetts and, less formally, as Pitt's friend and informer.[5] Pownall's task as governor threw him into the same relationship with Loudoun as all the other governors had; that is, he received Loudoun's more and more peremptory commands.[6] Like the other governors also, Pownall faced an assembly reluctant to truckle to Loudoun's demands for men and money to be used for no visible accomplishments. Though every bit as imperialist as Loudoun (or Pitt), Pownall believed that, as a practical matter of administration, "there cannot be a wiser measure" than to leave all the colonists "in the free and full possession of their several rights and privileges, as by grant, charter, or commission given."[7] To do otherwise might provoke them to unite in opposition to the "mother country." In short, Pownall wanted to negotiate with his assembly while Loudoun demanded that he issue fiats based on

1. Basil Williams, *The Life of William Pitt, Earl of Chatham* (1913), 2 vols. reprinted (New York: Octagon Books, 1966), 1:281–85.

2. Loudoun to Pitt, 10 Mar. 1757, *Corr. of Pitt*, ed. Kimball, 1:14–22.

3. Pownall went to England in Oct. 1756, months after being informed of Oswego's fall. Hallowell to Pownall, 30 Aug. 1756, Loudoun Papers, mss., LO 1630, HEH. Pitt mentioned talking with Pownall in Pitt to Loudoun, 22 Dec. 1756, mss., Loudoun Papers LO 2383, HEH. See also *Corr. of Pitt*, ed. Kimball, 1:87, 132–33; Leonard W. Labaree, "Pownall, Thomas," in *Dict. Amer. Biog.* 15:161.

4. Pownall to Loudoun, 7 Dec. 1756, Loudoun Papers, mss., LO 2321; same to same, 10 Apr. 1757, LO 3333, HEH.

5. E.g., Pownall to Pitt, 15 Jan. 1758, *Corr. of Pitt*, ed. Kimball, 1:161–63; Pitt to Pownall, 9 Dec. 1758, mss., HM 22370, HEH; Pargellis, *Lord Loudoun*, 269.

6. E.g., Loudoun's ltrs. of 15 Nov., 17 Nov., 6 Dec. 1757, in Loudoun Papers, mss., LO 4838, LO 4853, LO 4955, HEH.

7. Thomas Pownall, *The Administration of the Colonies*, 2d ed., revised, corrected, and enlarged (London: J. Dodsley and J. Walter, 1765), 37–38.

the royal prerogative.[8] Neither policies nor personalities could long withstand the strain. Loudoun denounced Pownall to the duke of Cumberland.[9] Pownall, on the other hand, though he has the reputation of a mighty ego, kept his differences with Loudoun to himself.[10] But Pownall became eyes and ears for Pitt, supplying the deficiencies in Loudoun's reports.

Pitt reverses crown policy

Pitt had to fight two battles simultaneously in London. On the one hand, he tried to stir the ossified military structure into aggressive activity; on the other hand, he contended against political intrigues directed against him by Cumberland and Henry Fox. After only four months' tenure in office, Pitt fell victim to Cumberland's hostile influence.[11] Even during that short term, and despite his feeble support by king and Commons, Pitt moved decisively. In less than three weeks after taking office he ordered 2,000 more troops to the port of Halifax in Nova Scotia with the intention to "annoy" the enemy "if possible, in their own Possessions;" that is, to campaign through the St. Lawrence Valley against Quebec.[12]

During his short tenure, Pitt's belligerence signified more than stepped-up activity; it implied a drastic redefinition of war aims. Previously, the ministry had claimed only to be "recovering" territories rightfully belonging to the British crown, such as Acadia and the Iroquois "empire." Such claims were vast enough, but not even the most rabid imperialist had ever suggested that Quebec was British. Impatient Pitt thrust aside the pretences of diplomats. His single-minded purpose was to win the war, never mind the conventions of gentlemen's war, and he chose to accomplish this end by aggressive seizure of New France's heartland. He was not the first to espouse this strategy; Shirley and Pownall, despite their mutual hostility, had recommended it.[13] Pitt's contribution was to make it official crown policy.

Pitt made a new attempt to mobilize colonial resources, bypassing Loudoun with an appeal directly to the colonial governors to raise more pro-

8. LO 4853, HEH.

9. Loudoun to Cumberland, 17 Oct. 1757, mss. Loudoun Papers, LO 4642, HEH.

10. I count thirty letters from Pownall to Pitt between July 1757 and Dec. 1758 in the *Correspondence of Pitt*, ed. Kimball, vol. 1. None contains aspersions on Loudoun.

11. The situation is hugely ironical. Prussia's Frederick II wanted Cumberland in command of the so-called Army of Observation in Europe, and Cumberland refused to serve while Pitt was in the ministry in a position to issue orders to him. Frederick had reason soon enough to regret nominating Cumberland. J. C. Long, *Mr. Pitt and America's Birthright: A biography of the Earl of Chatham, 1708–1778* (New York: Frederick A. Stokes, 1940), 262–63.

12. Pitt to Governor Lawrence, 22 Dec. 1756. *Corr. of Pitt*, ed. Kimball, 1:1–2.

13. Leach, *Arms for Empire*, 379; T. Pownall, *Administration of the Colonies*, 50; J. C. Long, *Mr. Pitt*, 301; C. Pownall, *Thomas Pownall*, 68–70.

vincial troops. In contrast to Loudoun, he avoided invocation of royal prerogative. Instead, as "Encouragement," he undertook payment by the crown for "provisions of all kinds" if the provinces would pay for recruiting and the wages, arms, and clothing of the soldiers.[14] Pitt urged dilatory Loudoun to "vigorous and offensive Measures" and promised 6,000 more regulars from Britain besides the 2,000 being sent to Halifax.[15] But Pitt's energy was not enough to overpower the almost immovable mass that was Loudoun. Neatly shifting the blame for procrastination, Loudoun wrote in late April 1757 that "everything here, must be at a Stand, till Orders arrive with the Plan, you have acquainted me is coming to be Executed by me." That is a very small part of what Loudoun wrote, which fusses on for fifteen pages of print, but it conveyed the essence of his message.[16] Ironically, Loudoun sent it off twenty days after Cumberland's contrivances influenced the king to dismiss Pitt and his ministry from office. That news crossed Loudoun's report at sea.

Then began a game of political hide-and-seek as the strong men in Commons mustered their forces and the king tried to get a ministry that could govern. Testimonials and ceremonial gifts poured in for "The Great Commoner" Pitt from all over the country, but popularity was not the decisive factor in the government of that day.[17]

Eleven weeks went by without a ministry. This in the midst of global war! (Critics of disputatious colonial assemblies might bear it in mind.) At one point, Cumberland and Fox thought they could form a government under Fox by enlisting Halifax as first lord of the Treasury. Halifax played along with them only to betray the plan to Newcastle, who promptly countered by promising him a cabinet post and enlargement of the board of trade's powers if Halifax would support a Pitt-Newcastle ministry. Halifax rose to the bait, and Pitt came back to power. Whereupon Halifax's double-dealing boomeranged to smite himself. For Newcastle had failed to mention to Pitt the promises made to Halifax. When Halifax tried to collect, Pitt stared him down icily. Pitt did not intend to rob his own southern department of patronage in order to enhance Halifax's prestige. To carry this comedy one step further, we may note that Halifax resigned in a huff and went off to sulk in his country estate. Newcastle coaxed him back with a position in the cabinet, but it was as a person rather than as head of the board of trade. From that time forward, Halifax's interest in

14. Pitt to govs. of southern provinces, 4 Feb. 1757, *Corr. of Pitt*, ed. Kimball, 1:5–6. However, regardless of promises and wheedling, there was little recruiting in the southern colonies because of fears of slave uprisings if young men marched off. Such fears "practically prevented [recruiting] altogether" in South Carolina. Pargellis, *Lord Loudoun*, 130.

15. *Corr. of Pitt*, ed. Kimball, 1:15.

16. Ibid., 1:36–51.

17. Peter Douglas Brown, *William Pitt, Earl of Chatham: The Great Commoner* (London: George Allen and Unwin, 1978), 145.

the board declined, and the board reverted to its pre-Halifax function as an instrument of administration instead of policy making.[18]

Incredibly enough, such whimsical spasms determined critical turns of direction in government while great armies and navies grappled to the death. It seems absurd even to chronicle these squabbles for place and personal aggrandizement; but the places at issue were those of power, and Pitt's acquisition of real power (with Newcastle's indispensable help) turned a previously calamitous war into Britain's greatest triumph thus far.

That is not to say that Pitt conquered all by his heroic personality. Behind the personalities were opposed policies and principles of government. In the case of the American colonies, Pitt reversed the Cumberland-Loudoun effort to rule by prerogative. He was not motivated as "a friend of America" nor as a liberal democrat. He was a monarchist, nationalist, imperialist, and Tory. In later years he declared that he would not allow "a nail or a horseshoe" to be made in North America. He reversed the prerogative policy on grounds of practicality rather than ideal principle, because he believed the cooperation of American colonials was essential to winning the war.[19] So doing, he won wholehearted colonial cooperation and guaranteed the conquest of Canada.

Pitt and Newcastle

What made Pitt so popular? His spellbinding oratory explains some of his power in the House of Commons, where the members have always been swayed by good speakers. (It is tempting to compare Commons to the illiterate councils of Indian tribes. How much did the Honorable Members read?) But oratory was not enough even in Commons, where Pitt lost every time he pitted himself against Newcastle's "machine."[20]

Pitt's passionate attacks on the king's devotion to his Electorate of Hanover appealed strongly to the xenophobic English public (though the king became antagonized), but Pitt retained popularity after he switched opportunistically to advocate and provide massive aid to Hanover.[21]

His real base of power, apart from sheer jingoism, seems to have been

18. Arthur Herbert Basye, *The Lords Commissioners of Trade and Plantations, Commonly Known as the Board of Trade, 1748–1782*, Yale Historical Publications, Miscellany 14 (New Haven, Conn.: Yale University Press, 1925), 95–100.

19. H. W. V. Temperley, "The Peace of Paris," in *The Old Empire*, vol. 1 of *The Cambridge History of the British Empire*, gen. eds. J. Holland Rose, A. P. Newton, and E. A. Benians (New York: Macmillan, 1929), 504.

20. See Stanley Ayling, *The Elder Pitt, Earl of Chatham* (London: Collins, 1976), 173–74; Marie Peters, *Pitt and Popularity: The Patriot Minister and London Opinion during the Seven Years' War* (Oxford: Clarendon Press, 1980), 35–40.

21. Ibid., 25–27, 69, 92, 97–101.

FIGURE 4. Monument to William Pitt erected by the merchants of the City of London. COPYRIGHT PHOTOGRAPH REPRODUCED BY COURTESY OF THE GUILDHALL ART GALLERY, CITY OF LONDON.

mercantile. The City of London adored him.[22] After his death the mayor, aldermen, and common council erected in their Guildhall a heroic monument, still standing as the biggest thing in sight, with a tribute of innocently candid revelation.

> In grateful acknowledgment to the Supreme Disposer of events; Who intending to advance this nation, for such time as His wisdom seem'd good, to an high pitch of prosperity and glory . . . *by commerce for the first time united with, and made to flourish by war:*—was pleased to raise up as a principal instrument in this memorable work, WILLIAM PITT.[23]

This seems odd when one considers how Newcastle's Whigs were so warmly supported by the merchants. We have seen, for example, the Hanbury family's association with Newcastle. But the merchants could count. A scholar has computed that British shipping "went up from 451,000 tons in 1755 to 561,000 in 1763; the slave trade had almost doubled in amount between 1758 and 1762."[24] Perhaps Pitt did not deserve credit as much as the royal navy that swept the seas clean of French competition, but Pitt certainly was responsible for what were then vast outlays of public funds to support armies all around the world; and war profiteering then was as lucrative as it is now.

The merchants' support could not by itself give Pitt the majority he needed in Commons, but it made possible, perhaps inevitable, an alliance with Newcastle's Whigs who were so dependent on the City of London's "moneyed men."[25] Thomas Pownall was to theorize in 1765 that the predominant spirit of rule in Europe had been first the *sword*, then *religion*, but was becoming *commerce;* "The rise and forming of the commercial interest is what precisely constitutes the present crisis." Britain was transforming itself by the power of commerce from a kingdom with appendages to a unitary empire.[26] Pitt was the darling of the class making the transformation.

Pitt and Newcastle detested each other personally. At one point Pitt refused to enter a ministry under Newcastle's leadership.[27] Each had enough strength to stymie the other. Newcastle told the king that he could not serve as chief minister "without bringing in my enemy, Mr. Pitt." Pitt confided to a friend that Newcastle was "the wretch who draws the great

22. Ayling, *Elder Pitt*, 207.
23. Peters, *Pitt and Popularity*, frontispiece illustration with text on p. vi. I can testify to the grandiosity of this monument from personal observation.
24. Temperley, "Peace of Paris," 501.
25. Ayling, *Elder Pitt*, 207. A carefully detailed analysis is in the Introduction of Peters, *Pitt and Popularity*, 1–31.
26. Pownall, *Administration of the Colonies*, 3–10.
27. Yorke, *Life of Hardwicke* 2:276–79.

families at his heels."[28] That was sour grapes, for Pitt, despite his popularity, had to face the fact that Newcastle instead of Pitt did have those great families, and they had the seats in Commons. Pitt lacked an *effective* political base. One scholar has remarked that he "could do anything with Parliament except win votes."[29] Pitt always sat for a rotten borough. Sir Lewis Namier has remarked that "at no time during his thirty-one years in the House of Commons did he, the idol of the Empire, represent as many as 100 electors."[30]

When the eleven weeks without an administration had demonstrated conclusively that Pitt could not muster enough votes to govern without a partner, he consented to accept Newcastle in *his*, Pitt's government—Pitt to direct policy and manage great affairs, Newcastle to drum up the necessary support in Commons.[31] Newcastle is generally perceived as corrupt and ditheringly inept, but nothing could have been more realistic or patriotically honorable than the way he swallowed pride on this occasion.

Since Newcastle has fallen into the shadow cast by Pitt, it is well to remember the necessity of his partnership and the efficacy with which he performed his tasks despite his mounting horror at Pitt's free spending. The arrangement between them was a fine example of English muddle-through. Newcastle went to the Treasury as nominal head of the ministry, just as the duke of Devonshire had nominally headed Pitt's first government. Pitt necessarily contented himself with the southern department once more, and the result was that the man who is often called Britain's greatest prime minister does not appear on the formal chronology of prime ministers until 1766, long after his days of glory.[32] The secret is that though no people on earth enjoy pomp and circumstance more than the English, they are sane enough to get on with their real work regardless. As W. S. Gilbert has warbled, "Things are seldom what they seem."

Cumberland's collapse

I am not concerned here to attempt still another biography of William Pitt. It is sufficient to note that the ministry contrived by Newcastle and Pitt had the solid support needed to survive yet more military calamities and the accumulation of unprecedented staggering deficits. Newcastle in

28. Ayling, *Elder Pitt*, 206–8.

29. W. F. Reddaway, "The Seven Years' War," in *The Old Empire*, eds. J. Holland Rose, et al., 470.

30. Sir Lewis Namier, *The Structure of Politics at the Accession of George III*, 2d ed. (London: Macmillan and Co., 1963), 157.

31. Brown, *William Pitt*, 148–51.

32. *Handbook of British Chronology*, eds. F. Maurice Powicke and E. B. Fryde, 2d ed. (London: Royal Historical Society, 1961), 107–8.

the Treasury fretted and wrung his hands but soldiered on.[33] Pitt neutralized the king's hostility by reversing his own earlier policy in order to lavish vast sums on continental allies for the protection of Hanover. The final obstacle to full power disappeared when the duke of Cumberland disgraced himself by losing an entire army without a fight. Pursued by the duc de Richelieu, Cumberland marched and countermarched his men into a hopeless corner, whereupon he signed the Convention of Kloster-Zeven, 8 September 1757. By it, he agreed to disband his army and send the men home; by doing so he effectively handed over to the French the Electorate of Hanover that he was supposed to be protecting. Presented with this fine prize, Richelieu magnanimously agreed not to attack Cumberland's men as they marched off.[34]

Cumberland returned to London where he "pass'd over London-Bridge for Kensington in a very *private manner.*" Pitt disavowed the Convention of Kloster-Zeven, and the king raged against Cumberland, who had to resign his post of captain general and retire for the time being into obscurity.[35]

At almost the same time, more bad news arrived from America. Loudoun retreated from Louisbourg without trying to take the place, and Webb let Fort William Henry fall to Montcalm without even trying to reinforce it. (Maligned Pownall turned Massachusetts upside down to send reinforcements, but he and they were too far away.)[36]

New commanders, new measures

The champions of prerogative had botched every battle. In doing so, they gave Pitt a free hand at last, and he moved swiftly to take advantage of the disasters that were his opportunity. After Cumberland's downfall, Pitt was able to recall Loudoun.[37] Pitt turned over the title of commander in chief in America to General Abercromby, Loudoun's second in command (and soon regretted the act), but once more things were not quite what they seemed. Few of Loudoun's powers descended with the title. The political role disappeared entirely. Even the military functions were divided up as Pitt entrusted a new campaign against Louisbourg to General Geoffrey Amherst, and a campaign against Fort Duquesne to Briga-

33. In 1755 the national debt stood at £72,000,000. By the end of the war it had more than doubled to £147,000,000. Basil Williams, *Life of Pitt* 2:49; see the discussion, 2:47–57. The huge deficits of recent years in the United States may have desensitized American readers to such figures. Englishmen of the eighteenth century thought them a sure road to bankruptcy.

34. E. M. Lloyd, "William Augustus, Duke of Cumberland," in *Dict. Nat. Biog.* 61:346.

35. Loc. cit.; *Gentleman's Magazine* 27 (1757): 424–25, 479.

36. See ch. 14 above, n33.

37. Pitt to Loudoun, 30 Dec. 1757, *Corr. of Pitt*, ed. Kimball, 1:133.

dier John Forbes. Abercromby was left with only his old assignment to force passage through Lakes George and Champlain. His nominal subordinates reported directly to Pitt and took their orders equally directly from the same source.[38] Well that they did. Though Pitt could and did make mistakes, he lacked Abercromby's special ability to do *everything* wrong.

Colonials accepted Pitt's leadership as gladly as the British. Happy as they were to see the end of Loudoun and Loudoun's arrogance, they responded with positive enthusiasm to Pitt's new financial measures. Letters exchanged between Pitt and Pownall explain the new dispensation graphically. Pitt wrote to ask urgently that many thousands of new provincial troops be raised for an "Irruption into Canada." He guaranteed their officers "as high as Colonels inclusive" equal rank with regulars, and the cost-conscious assemblymen heard the following paragraphs of his letter with intense interest:

> *The King is further pleased to furnish* all the Men, so raised as above, with Arms, Ammunition, and Tents, as well as to order Provisions to be issued to the same, *by His Majesty's Commissaries*, in the same Proportion and Manner as is done to the rest of the King's Forces: A sufficient Train of Artillery will also be provided, *at His Majesty's Expense*, for the Operations of the Campaign . . . The Whole, therefore, that His Majesty expects and requires from the several Provinces, is, the Levying, Cloathing, and Pay of the Men; And, on these Heads also, that no Encouragement may be wanting to this great and salutary Attempt, The King is farther most Graciously pleased to permit me to acquaint You, that strong Recommendations will be made to Parliament in their Session next Year, *to grant a proper Compensation for such Expences* as above . . .[39]

Stripped down to terms of accounting, what this meant was that every shilling spent by the province would go to provincials, and that the province would benefit additionally from an inflow of large amounts of specie from the crown.[40] Canny merchants could see at a glance that what had started as a war for the benefit of the crown at great cost to the colonies was being transformed into a war for the benefit and at the expense of both crown and colonies. This understanding is confirmed by the Massachusetts assembly's immediate response to Pitt's letter.

38. Pitt assured Abercromby that the latter's "Commissions and Instructions" were "in every respect the same as was done for Lord Loudoun," but he demonstrated in another letter of the same date that whatever the forms, their meanings had changed. *Corr. of Pitt*, ed. Kimball, 134–35, 143–51.

39. Pitt to governors, 30 Dec. 1757, ibid., 1:136–40.

40. One must distinguish between the finances of governments and those of private persons. Public costs remained high, private profits increased gratifyingly. Anderson, *A People's Army*, 16; Jack P. Greene. "The Seven Years' War and the American Revolution: The Causal Relationship Reconsidered," in *The British Atlantic empire before the American Revolution*, eds. Peter Marshall and Glyn Williams (London: Frank Cass, 1980), 97–98.

Pownall informed him that when the letter arrived Pownall "had been then eight daies labouring to induce the General Court to make Provision for the Raising 2,218 Men as a Quota of 7,000 proposed for all the Northern Governments upon a plan which the Earl of Loudoun had proposed. The matter labour'd greatly, the House seemed to advance in nothing but Difficulties and Objections, Diffidence in the Plan, Objections against the Number as a Quota. Dissatisfaction against a Junction with the Regulars as the Matter of Rank then stood. I was enabled by the Receipt of His Majesty's Commands signifyed by you to take quite different measures as I did instantly that very Night and have the Pleasure to acquaint You that the House of Representatives came into an unanimous Vote next morning to raise a Sufficient Number of Men and determined the Number that they alone wou'd provide for should be 7,000 Men."[41]

Abercromby at Ticonderoga

Pitt's accession to power was certainly the turning point of the war in America as elsewhere, and it cannot be repeated too often or too strongly that his measures and policies were more decisive than his charisma. If he had attempted to continue the Cumberland-Loudoun policy of imposing rule by prerogative, the division and defeat implied by that policy would surely have endured. It is hideous to imagine Abercromby as commander in chief entrusted with the same vast powers that Loudoun had held. Even within the new restrictions, Abercromby managed to be faithful to the Cumberland tradition of ineptitude. Commanded by Pitt to campaign against the French forts, he moved a large army of 16,000 men early in July 1758 into position before Fort Carillon (called Ticonderoga by the British), sending Bradstreet ahead with the vanguard. Bradstreet displayed his usual efficiency by overpowering the outer defenses and urgently requesting permission to attack the fort before the French could call up reinforcements. Permission was denied because Abercromby wanted to bring up the main body of his troops. Grateful Montcalm poured men into the fort from nearby Fort St. Frédéric, and used the day of respite to construct entrenchments and outerwork fascines of fallen trees with branches stabbing outward toward attackers (a predecessor of the barbed wire of World War I). These defenses were vulnerable to artillery fire from a height called Mount Defiance, but Abercromby sent Johnson and his Indians to that height instead of planting there the artillery already at hand. Compounding his mistake, he suddenly became impetuous at exactly the wrong time. Instead of waiting one more day for the rest of his artillery to come

41. Pownall to Pitt, 14 Mar. 1758, *Corr. of Pitt*, ed. Kimball, 1:203–4.

up, with which he could have blasted easily through the French lines and forced Montcalm to evacuate the fort—Montcalm had readied his troops for retreat—Abercromby launched his regulars against the defense lines in a succession of bayonet charges, each of which was bloodily mowed down. Whereupon Abercromby turned his army about and marched back to Albany and his desk where he took up the really skilled occupation of his kind, writing excuses.[42]

That is not all. According to Thomas Mante, Abercromby remained "during the greatest part of the attack, at the Saw-mills, two miles from the scene of action." When disorder increased, he "was not to be found; nor did there, in fact, appear any other officer to do his duty." Mante was a military engineer with a taste for history. We must assume that his information came privately from other officers who had participated in the battle at Ticonderoga, but it accords with data from other sources that identify Bradstreet as the officer who prevented the retreat from turning into panic; Abercromby's whereabouts at that time must be guessed at. Mante adds: "it is still more surprising to think of the steps taken by the General [Abercromby] when he had resumed the command. He ordered the artillery and ammunition to Albany. Nay, as though he did not think them safe even at that place, measures were taken to convey them to New-York."[43]

Casualties of this fiasco included 464 British regulars and 87 provincials killed, with 1,117 regulars and 239 provincials wounded. According to Mante, the French lost about 112 officers and men killed, and about 275 wounded. A French report itemized 106 killed and 268 wounded. Prepared as they had been for sudden evacuation, the French were astounded to find that they had won a great victory against overwhelmingly superior numbers.[44]

Bradstreet at Fort Frontenac

Abercromby's disaster was the nadir of British military fortunes in America, and it demonstrates clearly why Pitt's emergence to power made

42. Godfrey, *Pursuit of Profit*, 120–23; Abercromby to Pitt, 12 July 1758, *Corr. of Pitt*, ed. Kimball, 1:297–302; Gipson, *British Empire* 7:221–36. Excuses have been made for Abercromby, but Bougainville shows still another aspect of his incompetence, *Adventure*, ed. Hamilton, 237.

43. Mante, *History of the Late War* 149–51; Godfrey, *Pursuit of Profit*, 122–23 and n26.
Bibliographic note: Though much of Mante's later sections is lifted from Captain John Knox (q.v.), his material on episodes preceding the siege of Quebec comes from other sources. His large and clear maps are superb. I have used the copy of this very rare book at the John Carter Brown Library.

44. Mante, *History*, 150; *N.Y. Col. Docs.* 10:922; Stanley, *New France*, 181.

a difference in other ways than spending money. If Cumberland had still been in charge of the armies, there can be small doubt that Ticonderoga would have been written off as just another unavoidable incident, and Abercromby would have stayed commander as Webb had kept rank after Oswego. But Pitt was different. Reassuming civil power over the military, Pitt took into his own hands the appointment and assignment of general officers, and he did not accept defeats lightly. Abercromby could feel Pitt's hot breath all the way across the Atlantic.

For the first time in his American career, Abercromby felt genuine pressure to accomplish something in a hurry. Anxiously, he convened a council of war at Bradstreet's urging. Since January 1758, Bradstreet had been aching to take his boatmen across Lake Ontario for a raid on Fort Frontenac. He had proposed the project to Loudoun, who approved it and authorized preparations, but Loudoun's recall interrupted them and Abercromby subsequently concentrated on Ticonderoga. In the wake of that disaster, Abercromby could only do nothing or give Bradstreet free reign. He looked over his shoulder toward London and told Bradstreet to go ahead. Even for this one rational act of his career in America, Abercromby was reluctant. He empowered Bradstreet only after the council of war recommended favorably.[45]

Nevertheless, as Gipson comments, Abercromby "was looking desperately for something that might soften the bitterness of his defeat." When he reported to Pitt, he downgraded the Ticonderoga disaster to a "check," and balanced it with Bradstreet's campaign under way.[46]

Bradstreet was an Anglo-Irish Acadian who differed from the general officers native to the British isles in fundamental ways. Instead of buying his commission, he had served seven years as a volunteer before being commissioned ensign at the age of twenty-two, and he had won promotion thereafter largely by merit and service—helped out, to be sure, by carefully tended contacts. As a colonial he was never fully accepted in the military establishment clique, so he supplemented military service by political and commercial devices not always legitimate but invariably energetic and advantageous. So to speak, he made an end run around the ossified establishment. In 1758 he had risen to the rank of lieutenant colonel with special expertise in logistics.[47] His greatest distinction from the

45. Godfrey, *Pursuit of Profit*, 123–25, 106–10. The assault on Fort Frontenac had been delayed since Mar. 1756 when then-commander Shirley had ordered Bradstreet to make it. Instructions, 17 Mar. 1756, in *Royal Fort Frontenac*, comp. and trans. Richard A. Preston, ed. Leopold Lamontagne, Publications of the Champlain Society, Ontario Series 2 (Toronto, 1958), 249–50.

46. Gipson, *British Empire* 7:238; Abercromby to Pitt, 12 July 1758, *Corr. of Pitt*, ed. Kimball, 1:302.

47. William G. Godfrey, "Bradstreet, John (baptized Jean-Baptiste)," in *Dict. Can. Biog.* 4:83–87; idem, *Pursuit of Profit*, chs. 1–5.

likes of Loudoun, Webb, and Abercromby was an eager desire to engage in battle: though his primary responsibility was to provide supplies, and theirs was to do battle, they organized and organized and marked time until pushed into engagement while Bradstreet looked for opportunities to fight. And he was good at it. We have seen how he converted a French ambush near Oswego into the only British victory in 1756.[48] Now, after Ticonderoga, he was to have the chance to take the offensive on his own initiative.

He summoned his boatmen and accumulated a task force of nearly 3,000 troops. In view of the slurs so frequently cast by regular officers against provincial soldiers, it is instructive that only 135—less than five percent—of this detachment were regulars. The largest contingent, 1,112 were New Yorkers. Massachusetts sent 675 men, New Jersey 412, and Rhode Island 318. The 300 boatmen are not identified by source localities.[49] Sir William Johnson delivered 70 warriors, presumably Iroquois, for Bradstreet's "enterprise," the nature of which was kept efficaciously secret until the last minute—so secret indeed that when the Indians discovered their true objective they promptly walked off. (Johnson had led them to think that the "enterprise" was defensive.)[50] Thomas Mante explains their defection by the special functioning of Fort Frontenac as the site for annual intertribal meetings that "constituted a kind of general council" where alliances were renewed or new ones formed "and plans of operation agreed upon for the ensuing year." In his understanding, Bradstreet's raid "proved the means of dissolving a very powerful confederacy."[51]

It appears that in this instance the Iroquois were quite deceived, for they told Vaudreuil their belief that Bradstreet merely intended to reestablish Fort Bull at the Great Carrying Place on the way from Albany to Oswego. It was a Mississauga party that found two of Bradstreet's marching orders and alerted Vaudreuil to his true purpose.[52]

Too late. Bradstreet's swift efficiency took his men across Lake Ontario and landed them before Fort Frontenac on 25 August 1758.[53] They found the place practically defenseless. Vaudreuil and Montcalm had been so concerned to concentrate force against possible renewed attacks at Fort Carillon (Ticonderoga) that they had neglected Frontenac. Bradstreet's surprise was so complete that his 3,000 men surrounded 110 persons all told—men, women, and children. After a token resistance of two days,

48. Ch. 13, above.
49. Mante, *History of the Late War*, 152.
50. Gipson, *British Empire*, 7:241.
51. Mante, *History of the Late War*, 154–55.
52. Vaudreuil to de Massiac, 2 Sept. 1758, in *N.Y. Col. Docs.* 10:822–23, 826–27.
53. Bradstreet to Abercromby, 31 Aug. 1758, in *Royal Fort Frontenac*, eds. Preston and Lamontagne, 262.

Commandant de Noyan capitulated, Vaudreuil's hurried dispatch of a relief force could not possibly arrive in time, and he was left with the task of explaining away a disaster that was worse for the French than Ticonderoga had been for the British.[54] It is amusing to see the similarity of weasel phrasing in the reports of Vaudreuil and Abercromby. Montcalm also joined in the game by shunting responsibility away from himself: "I have been as much affected at this occurrence . . . as if I had to reproach myself with it."[55] Neat.

Abercromby had lost men, but Britain's superior resources enabled him to maintain his position. Vaudreuil, however, lost his lifeline to Niagara and Duquesne, especially the latter, by losing control of Lake Ontario. He lost besides an immense store of artillery and supplies, including a large stock of the provisions that had become scarce in New France; and this loss not only hurt his western garrisons, but deprived him of the means to maintain tribal alliances. For him, the stroke was fatal. It was compounded by the shipwreck of *L'Aigle,* bound from France and laden with arms and clothing, at the mouth of the St. Lawrence.[56]

Bradstreet reported capture of sixty pieces of cannon and 800,000 livres worth of provisions and goods. "The Garrison made no scruple of saying that their Troops to the Southward and Western Garrisons will suffer greatly if not entirely starve." He captured the whole French navy on Lake Ontario—nine vessels—and loaded two with spoils, burning the rest and all the nontransportable goods. Instead of encumbering himself with prisoners of war (and taking up cargo space that might be used for plunder), he sent the prisoners to Montreal as advance payment for exchange of an equal number of British captives. Six days after landing at Frontenac, his little army arrived back at the site of Oswego, apparently without the loss of a single man. Vaudreuil's relief party found only the smoking ruins of Frontenac.[57]

Amherst at Louisbourg

For the British, 1758 became a very good year in spite of Abercromby's disaster. Bradstreet's raid eased the task of Brigadier General John Forbes, who was hacking his way across Pennsylvania's mountain wilderness toward

54. Frontenac surrendered on 27 Aug. 1758, the same date that a French relief force set out from Montreal's suburb of Lachine. Godfrey, *Pursuit of Profit,* 125–32; documents in *Royal Fort Frontenac,* eds. Preston and Lamontagne, 258–79, 450–64.

55. Quoted in Frank H. Severance, *An Old Frontier of France: The Niagara Region and Adjacent Lakes under French Control,* 2 vols. (New York: Dodd, Mead and Co., 1917), 2:239.

56. Pouchot, *Memoir,* ed. Hough, 1:138.

57. See n53, 54, above.

Fort Duquesne; but Forbes's campaign met with so many of Pennsylvania's peculiar difficulties that it will require its own chapter.[58]

The big news in Britain was General Jeffrey Amherst's sensational capture in July of Louisbourg, the great French fortress that was supposed to guard the entrance to the St. Lawrence River.[59] It did no such thing because British ships could sail through the vast Gulf of St. Lawrence without the garrison at Louisbourg even being aware of their presence; but the fort served as France's base for harassment of British shipping and fishing, and it was a constant threat to Halifax in Nova Scotia.[60] As will be shown, William Pitt intended to keep Louisbourg in any exchange of territory that might be made after the war because he wanted the rich Grand Banks fisheries to become all British.[61] In peace negotiations it was easier to hang on to territory in possession than to bargain for something held by the other side, so the surrender of Louisbourg was greeted by great acclaim and rejoicing, Nova Scotians and New Englanders rejoiced also over the elimination of this base for attacks on their fishing. Thus the fall of Louisbourg overshadowed Bradstreet's triumph at Frontenac, which was a remote place whose importance was not generally understood.[62] To my mind, the destruction of Frontenac seems far more decisive to the outcome of the war than the capture of Louisbourg, but in terms of public relations at the time, Louisbourg did William Pitt a lot of good. Amherst too. Pitt recalled Abercromby and made Amherst commander in chief.[63]

58. Ch. 17, below.

59. Admiral Boscawen to Pitt, 28 July 1758, *Corr. of Pitt*, ed. Kimball, 1:307–8.

60. Discussed in ch. 13, above.

61. See ch. 19, below.

62. Franklin in London, smarting under slurs against provincial soldiers, drew attention in *The London Chronicle*, 10–12 May 1759, to Bradstreet's victory among others. *Franklin Papers* 8:340–56, Bradstreet at p. 344.

This newspaper piece hints at a certain disillusion growing in Franklin's understanding of the workings of the British empire though he continued a strong advocate of it. In 1756 he had judged Lord Loudoun "very well fitted for the Charge he has undertaken" and was sure that the king's affairs in America would "prosper" in Loudoun's hands. By 1759, however, Franklin was disenchanted with Loudoun in more than one way. His *London Chronicle* piece jibes not only at Loudoun's futility at Louisbourg, but also mentions the earl's routed flight at the battle of Prestonpans in 1745. It is fairly sure that Franklin had also learned about more notorious Culloden and Cumberland's devastation of the Highlands. He could not have have failed to hear of these events on his subsequent trip through Scotland in Sept. and Oct. 1759. *Franklin Papers* 6:472; 8:431. But his many friends there were Lowlanders, supporters of the crown.

See also Franklin's letter to Isaac Norris, 19 Mar. 1759, and the editors' headnote, *Franklin Papers* 8:291–97.

63. Ayling, *Elder Pitt*, 232; Pitt to governors, 18 Sept. 1758, *Corr. of Pitt*, ed. Kimball, 1:354. Amherst was recommended by Sir John Ligonier, Cumberland's replacement as commander of the forces in Britain, with Cumberland's concurrence. J. C. Long, *Mr. Pitt*, 293–95, 274.

Chapter 17 ❧ *A GENERAL and HIS FRIENDS*

The withdrawing of the Indians from the French interest by negotiating a peace, is all ascribed to the General, and not a word said to the honour of the poor Quakers who first set those negotiations on foot, or of honest Frederic Post that compleated them with so much ability and success.

Benjamin Franklin

I am convinced that no person understands [Indian negotiations] better or [is] more Zealous to bring them to a speedy and happy conclusion than You are.

Brigadier John Forbes to Israel Pemberton, Jr.

The difficulties Friends have encountered with to bring our rulers to do so much as had been done towards an amicable adjusting [of] difficulties with the Indians is scarce credible, and would take a great deal of time to relate.

Israel Pemberton, Jr.

I dined with Shingas; he told me . . . he would do all in his power to bring about an established peace, and wished he could be certain of the English being in earnest.

Christian Frederick Post

Chronology

30 December 1757.	Pitt commissions John Forbes as brigadier general and assigns him the campaign against Fort Duquesne.
January 1758.	Sir William Johnson sends libel against Quakers, originally fabricated by William Smith, through military channels to Pitt.
January 1758.	Quaker John Hunt returns to England after his mission in Pennsylvania. He brings the manuscript of Charles Thomson, *An Enquiry into the Causes of the Alienation of the Delaware and Shawanese Indians from the British Interest*, and circulates it among officials, but does not publish it.
February 1758.	Quakers Hunt and Wilson report to Thomas and Richard Penn in hopes of reconciling the proprietaries and the Pennsylvania Quakers.
April 1758.	Thomas Penn secretly orders a "stop" to formation of a Quaker company for trading with Indians.
April 1758.	Forbes goes to Philadelphia to prepare his campaign.
April 1758.	George Washington tries to swerve Forbes from Pennsylvania to Virginia. His conspiring continues throughout the campaign until he is sharply reproved by Forbes.

April 1758.	Johnson tells Governor Denny to lose no time inviting Indians to a peace treaty, and appoints George Croghan to act in his behalf, but Croghan does not appear in Philadelphia.
26 April 1758.	Dissension between Governor Denny and Secretary Peters.
4 May 1758.	Forbes complains of lack of cooperation from Johnson.
May 1758.	Forbes conflicts with Pennsylvania assembly commissioners over supply of arms.
May 1758.	More than 700 southern Indians join Forbes's army, but quickly become discontented over lack of action. Their presence alarms the Iroquois.
May 1758.	Israel Pemberton introduces himself to Forbes.
31 May 1758.	Forbes requests Pemberton's help in getting intelligence about Indians.
5 June 1758.	Forbes invites Pemberton to official conference of governor and council members, and insists on acceptance of Pemberton's suggestion of a special conference with Teedyuscung.
12 June 1758.	Charles Thomson and Christian Frederick Post deliver Governor Denny's invitation to Teedyuscung.
June 1758.	Assembly commissioners, reconciled to Forbes, deliver arms and recruits for his campaign.
Late June 1758.	Post goes again to Teedyuscung, meets Ohioans Pisquetomen and Keekyuscung, and they all return to Philadelphia together.
July 1758.	Five hundred southern Indians abandon Forbes. Almost all the rest drop away gradually.
8–12 July 1758.	Denny's conference with Teedyuscung and the Ohio chiefs decides to send Post back with them to propose peace and gather intelligence. Teedyuscung is bypassed.
9 July 1758.	Forbes accuses Johnson of "counter working."
12 July 1758.	The Friendly Association demands that a boundary be fixed between colonial and tribal territories.
22 July 1758.	Johnson asks the Iroquois to attend Pennsylvania's forthcoming treaty.
23 July 1758.	General Abercromby accedes to Forbes, sanctions Pennsylvania's treaty, and asks Johnson to cooperate.
7 August 1758.	Prompted by Quakers, New Jersey holds a treaty at Burlington to assuage complaints of Indians of that region. The province provides a reservation territory.
August–September 1758.	Christian Frederick Post, under Pisquetomen's protection, carries messages from governor Denny and General Forbes to the Ohio Delawares. On his return he carries intelligence to Forbes. Pisquetomen carries the Ohioans' message to the treaty at Easton.
September 1758.	Pennsylvania council's report exculpating Penns and attacking Quakers reaches England.
8–26 October 1758.	A great treaty at Easton includes eastern and western Delawares and Iroquois. Colonials include governors of Pennsylvania and New Jersey, Johnson's deputy George Croghan, and members of the Friendly Association. Peace is agreed by Indians, and promises are made by colonials.
20 November 1758.	Croghan arrives in Forbes's camp with "fewer than fifteen" Iroquois warriors.

July 1759. William Smith, in England fleeing from imprisonment for contempt of assembly, convinces Anglican bishops that Quakers were the sole cause of the war. Oxford University confers Doctor of Divinity degree on him.

We have seen that while William Pitt was still struggling in opposition in Parliament, and Lord Loudoun still crowed from his roost in America. the Quakers of Pennsylvania strove for peace with the Indians harassing the province.* As noted, Israel Pemberton and the Friendly Association forced negotiations in July 1757 that pacified the eastern Delawares under the leadership of Chief Teedyuscung. This was a fair beginning and, considering the obstacles to its achievement not negligible; but the big task was to win over the Ohio Indians who still harassed the back country in 1758 and whose support was vital to the French at Fort Duquesne.

Johnson waffles

Sir William Johnson was the proper official to initiate a peace treaty, but Johnson's first care was for the privilege conferred by his office, which he saw being challenged by "Scheming Quakers" engaged in "interfering Conduct."[1] Perhaps some allowance should be made for Johnson's behavior, because he lacked control over the Indians to such an extent that every remaining bit of influence was precious. So late as November 1758, Johnson confessed that "the Conduct of the Five Nations in general, hath for a considerable time past, been such as to give room for Suspicions of their Fidelity." Though his self-evaluations never erred on the side of humility, Johnson at that time despaired of doing more than holding the line. "Until we repossess our selves of Oswego and by that means establish such a Barrier for them, and that our Success against the French render us so respectable in the Eyes of the Five Nations as to take off their present Dread of the French, and of the extensive Indian Influence, which their unmolested possession of the Lakes gives them. I say until Affairs take this turn, I am of Opinion that the most favorable Expectations we may

* This chapter incorporates and adds to parts of my lecture, "On the Seven Years War in Pennsylvania," presented to the Eighth Lawrence Henry Gipson Institute at Lehigh University, 28 Feb. 1981; and my article, "A Vanishing Indian: Francis Parkman Versus His Sources," *Pa. Mag. of Hist. and Biog.* 87:3(1963), 306–23.

1. Johnson to Denny, 25 Sept. 1757, *Johnson Papers* 2:742.

form of the Five Nations cannot reasonably be for more, than their remaining Neutral between us and the French."[2]

There was no mention of Pennsylvania in this wail, though by that time the Quakers had at last succeeded in getting their great treaty. What follows in the chapter will make sense if we abandon the commonly held notion that Johnson could use the Iroquois as he pleased. To the contrary, the Mohawks especially had considerable success in using him for their purposes, the chief of which was to re-establish the old Iroquois Covenant Chain with the Mohawks in the lead.

It is true that Johnson spurned the Quakers and their intrigues, but his concern was genuine that the Iroquois were going their own way rather than his. He knew that he could not give them orders or simply recruit them with a war dance because those approaches had failed in 1747 and again in 1756. He would have to persuade their chiefs, and they would have to become "of one mind" to follow his lead. A formal treaty would be necessary, and those things took time to prepare. Until the treaty convened, as he told Abercromby, "he looked upon His Majesty's Indian Interest to be in a State of Suspence."[3] He wrote this while General Forbes in Pennsylvania complained about Johnson's obstructionism in Indian affairs.[4]

Events would not await Johnson's convenience. Abercromby demanded warriors for his campaign against Ticonderoga, Teedyuscung "sent a halloo" to the Ohio Indians, and the Pennsylvania assembly proposed a treaty. While Abercromby fretted, governor Denny rejected his assembly's proposal until he could get Johnson's advice, but Johnson stalled both Abercromby and Denny until he could be sure of his Iroquois. Johnson had a low opinion of Teedyuscung—an upstart, all pretense and no substance—but he did second the motion that Governor Denny should "lose no Time" in inviting negotiations with Indians "inclined to Peace."[5] Johnson would send his deputy George Croghan because his own presence was needed at home. This was in April 1758. Whether the promise to send Croghan was genuine or just a smooth way of stalling is not clear, but Croghan did not show up in Philadelphia as promised, and his absence did not sit well with Brigadier General John Forbes, whose new assignment was to capture Fort Duquesne.[6]

An assignment like Forbes's is deceptively simple. To overpower

2. Johnson to Abercromby, 10 Nov. 1758, ibid., 10:53–55. This letter is a fine example of Johnson's ability to seize credit in matters where he deserved little if any.

3. Abercromby to Pitt, 24 May 1758, Abercromby Papers, mss., AB 284, HEH.

4. Forbes to Abercromby, 4 May 1758, in *Writings of General John Forbes Relating to his Service in North America*, comp. and ed. Alfred Procter James (Menasha, Wis.: Collegiate Press, 1938), 85.

5. Johnson to Abercromby, 13 Apr., 17 Apr. 1758, in *Johnson Papers* 2:817, 824–27.

6. Forbes to Stanwix, 29 May 1758, in [John Forbes], *Writings*, ed. James, 103.

Ticonderoga or Duquesne might be difficult or even impossible, as only the effort could prove, but it was not confusing. The generals knew what they had to do—they had to take those places *there*—and every conceivable resource had to be summoned and concentrated upon those plain objectives. Johnson's political functions were more diffuse, and he was caught between two peremptory generals, both of whom wanted Johnson's Indians for their separate purposes; and only Johnson was fully aware of how inadequate his abilities were to respond with those hardheaded Indians to the equally willful generals.

But he understood power, and he knew which of those two generals was commander in chief. When Abercromby insisted, slurringly, on Johnson's appearance with or without Indians (it would have been "no Surprize" to Abercromby if Johnson's "best Endeavours" had been fruitless), Johnson told the Iroquois chiefs that he would have to march, whether or not they joined him. Much to his relief, they went along.[7]

We do not have records of their motive. It was certainly not mere lust for battle, because that could have been gratified as easily on the French side as with the British. Besides, the Iroquois League had tried assiduously to stand neutral between French and British combatants because of the chiefs' soundly based belief that Indians could only lose by joining in the clash of empires. Why, then, did they change policy and march with Johnson? Most likely, they reasoned that if they abandoned him at this juncture, the British would abandon them. Despite British fears and the independent actions of many warriors, the shrewd old politicians of the Iroquois League had no intention of throwing their lot in with the French unless deprived of all choice, because they could not possibly achieve the status of *primary* Indian allies of New France that they held in the Covenant Chain with Britain. Sir William Johnson had become their representative to the British crown. When crisis came, they could expose his unreliability only by demonstrating their own, at peril of being cut adrift.

So they marched with him to Ticonderoga, 400-odd strong. As it happened, they were never committed to the battle. From a hill they observed Abercromby's debacle, very much as the Ohio Delawares had watched Braddock's rout at Duquesne three years earlier.[8] Regardless of admiration for the bravery of British soldiers, Iroquois opinions of British military efficiency were not enhanced by the futile butchery of Abercromby's bayonet charges. In Iroquois military strategy, the unnecessary waste of lives in battle was scandalous. In one respect, however, Ticonderoga was a relief all around, for it reduced Abercromby's peremptory demands. Relieved of that distraction, Johnson turned attention to Pennsylvania.

7. *Johnson Papers* 2:852–53; 9:936–39.
8. Gipson, *British Empire* 7:228.

On 22 July he addressed chiefs of all the six Nations except the Cayugas with a request for "some Wise Men from each of your Nations" to go to Pennsylvania's treaty.[9] They, too, were relieved, and willing enough to restore Iroquois order to a situation that had been getting out of control.

Forbes arrives in Pennsylvania

One of William Pitt's happier appointments was the choice of Brigadier General John Forbes to command the new campaign against Fort Duquesne in 1758. Forbes was a fifty-one-year-old Scottish professional soldier who had, like Loudoun, participated in suppressing the 1745 rising of the Highlanders, and he had been Loudoun's adjutant in New York.[10] He shared little else with Loudoun except the authoritarian outlook natural to his profession and class. Single-mindedly concentrating on his military objective, Forbes lacked Loudoun's overriding political concerns and had none of Webb's pusillanimity. He was certainly more able than Abercromby ("general Nabbycromby" to the provincials), but Forbes was more systematic and less drivingly impetuous than that other able warrior, Bradstreet. When Forbes started to his assignment in Pennsylvania in April 1758, he planned to arrange a solid base for his campaign by "reconciling matters" between Governor Denny and the assembly. Like other officers, he assumed that the assembly was the source of difficulty. He wanted "to convince *them*, how Necessary it is for their own Welbeing, to exert themselves at this Critical Crisis to the Extent of their Abilities."[11] As might be expected, this approach to reconciliation did not get very far. To Forbes's great indignation, commissioners from the assembly blocked his first request for arms from Philadelphia's supply, apparently because they thought he should have applied to them instead of the governor.[12] Fortunately both parties were educable. When they came to understand each other, the commissioners cooperated so well that Forbes's commander in the field wondered at the "miracle" by which they supplied "every thing I had asked to Arm and equip the Pennsylvania Regiment."[13] They also

9. *Johnson Papers* 9:954.

10. A. P. James, "Biographical Sketch," in [Forbes], *Writings*, ed. James, ix–xii.

11. Abercromby to Denny, 20 Apr. 1758, Abercromby Papers, mss., AB 176, HEH.

12. *Pa Council Minutes* 8:79–80, 83–84.

13. Bouquet to St. Clair, 3 June 1758, in *Bouquet Papers* 2:23. At nearly the same time, Joseph Galloway thought that "a very good Understanding has Subsisted between the General and the commissioners," *but* "he hath requested many things of us we cou'd not grant." Understanding or not, Forbes was rankled by what he could not get; the "rubbs and hindrances in every thing depending upon the commissioners" who "meddle, and give orders in the meerest trifles" left him far from content. Galloway to Franklin, 16 June 1758, *Franklin Papers* 8:107; Forbes to Stanwix 29 May 1758, in [Forbes], *Writings*, 102.

recruited 2,700 men for the regiment.[14] Forbes cooperated also. He abandoned hope of imposed "reconciliation," eschewed Loudounesque battering tactics, and studied how to win his needs by indirect means. His opportunity came, strangely enough, when the leading pacifist of the province appeared in his office.[15]

Israel Pemberton desperately wanted to find someone in officialdom who would cooperate with Quaker efforts to negotiate peace with the Indians. Forbes was frantic to find *anyone* working toward that objective. For both of them, an initial reliance on Sir William Johnson had produced only disillusionment. We have seen how ineffectual Johnson was, even with the Iroquois, during the French campaign against Oswego, and how he had used George Croghan to stymie Pemberton (chapters 12 and 15). Now General Forbes discovered the uselessness of relying on him. In response to Forbes's requests for help, Johnson simply did nothing, so far as Forbes could tell.

Within a month after arriving in Philadelphia, Forbes complained to Abercromby, "I am sorry to say and think that Sir William Johnston or his deputies has intirely neglected and disappointed every step that ought to have been taken." Worse, "he sent one Wade here about eight Days ago who in an underhand way was engaging all the Indian Goods in this place," some of which had previously been "bespoke" for Indians Forbes was trying to recruit. "I have been obliged to put a stop to that."[16] From different motives, Forbes and Israel Pemberton joined hands to circumvent Johnson—Forbes to create the prerequisite for taking Fort Duquesne, Pemberton to create a peace based on justice. For a brief while, the interests of the general and the pacifist coincided, and together they managed to overcome almost insurmountable obstacles. But the full evidence for this is to be found only in materials written or preserved by Quakers, and these have been skipped over by most writers. The result has been a historical void where there was, in fact, decisive action at critical moments.

Forbes and Indians

There were Indians, also, who wanted to make peace; otherwise Forbes and Pemberton could have accomplished nothing, no matter how intense their efforts. But Indian politics obstructed negotiations as much as British politics did. Ohio Indians desiring peace seemed to have no way of

14. Gipson, *British Empire* 7:254.
15. Pemberton's ltr. draft, [late May 1758], no address, no signature, boxed with ltrs. to John Hunt, mss., Pemberton Papers, Box 3, HSP.
16. Forbes to Abercromby, 4 May 1758, in [Forbes], *Writings*, 85.

opening discussions except by approaching Sir William Johnson, but to do so would be to have him fasten Iroquois domination upon them. More precisely, the large Seneca nation, as well as Delawares and Shawnees, would have to knuckle under to Johnson's Mohawks. They would not and did not. Some go-between had to be found to make direct contact, bypassing Johnson and the Iroquois.

Further complications involved more tribes. When the fact had become plain to British officials that the Iroquois were disinclined to fight Britain's battles, officialdom turned in another direction to recruit southern warriors for General Forbes. Cherokees and Catawbas came to join Forbes in satisfyingly large numbers, but with large appetites also, and demands much less satisfying. Some who came to Philadelphia presented a problem. Forbes was with his army. Penn's placemen continued as before to spend nothing on Indians, and the assembly's commissioners had run out of funds. Pemberton and his Friendly Association took on the responsibility to feed, clothe, and shelter the Indians whom everybody wanted as allies but nobody wanted to support.

When the Cherokees and Catawbas moved on to join Forbes, friction developed almost instantly. Forbes lacked Quaker patience in dealing with this "very great plague," and the Indians could not bear the slow, systematic inching forward of his army. The two superintendents of Indian affairs, Johnson and Edmund Atkins, stayed home, respectively 500 and 700 miles away, so Forbes was obliged to "amuse" the Indians with promises and presents, which became expensive as there were more than 700 warriors.[17]

The very willingness of the southern Indians to join Forbes stirred hot jealousy among the Iroquois. Despite the advance peacemaking in 1757, the Iroquois feared this great body of warriors from their traditional enemies tramping across territory regarded by Iroquois as their own, and functioning in the role of British allies that the Iroquois had labored over the years to keep for themselves. Even the Quakers' efforts to pacify the Ohio Indians contributed to tension, as rumors of messengers bearing belts came to Cherokee ears so distorted as to arouse suspicions that those belts were intended to mobilize Iroquois warriors to strike the Cherokees. The situation was too unstable to last.

"The Cherokees are now no longer to be kept with us," reported Forbes, 29 May 1758, "neither by promises nor presents. . . . they begin to grow extremely licentious, and have gone so farr as to seize the presents designed for them, and divide it among themselves according to their own Caprice." After which plunder, 500 of them abandoned him. Others trickled off until only 80 were still with him by September. These dwindled further

17. Ibid., 112, 91–92, 103.

to 50 by late October, and most of those left shortly afterward.[18]

Even in leaving they made problems: Forbes ordered all the Virginia and Pennsylvania troops to guard their route "to prevent the Country people and the Cherokees that were returning home from massacring one another."[19] Again he was angered because Johnson and Atkins had ignored his "repeated applications," nor had sent "any one person to look after those Indians," not even George Croghan who had recruited many of them in the first place. Fortunately two southern gentlemen volunteers helped out: Virginia's colonel William Byrd III, and Forbes's kinsman, former governor James Glen of South Carolina, went among the Cherokees and temporarily kept 200 of them steadfast.[20] Forbes would have been a much happier man if the Indian superintendents had done nothing at all instead of starting up trouble for him to handle. He would get no help from them until too late. After the Ohioans were won over by a great treaty at Easton George Croghan promised 50 warriors and arrived in camp, the twentieth of November, with "fewer than" 15. By that time they were no longer needed. "What a sad wretch it is," commented Richard Peters, but very privately.[21]

Forbes's road

Poor Forbes was harried and hounded on every side. So ill that he had to be carried on a litter between two horses, he had to contend with quartermaster Sir John St. Clair, who had bungled Braddock's supplies and was frantically botching Forbes's; at Carlisle early in July, Forbes found "everything a heap of Confusion, and sir John St. Clair at Variance with every mortall." Maryland's assembly refused to vote funds for Fort Cumberland's garrison, so Forbes was obliged to negotiate troops and pay for them. North Carolina sent troops without providing pay or clothes. South Carolina sent none. The troops from Virginia and Pennsylvania were "a gathering from the scum of the worst of people . . . who have wrought themselves up into a panick at the very name of Indians." And the old rivalry between Virginia and Pennsylvania stirred again when Forbes decided to cut his army's road directly through Pennsylvania instead of

18. Ibid., 102, 141, 203, 239.

19. Ibid., 103. Conflicts did break out in Virginia when thirty Cherokees were killed. Post's second journal, App. 2 in Robert Proud, *The History of Pennsylvania in North America*, 2 vols. (1798), reprinted facsimile (Spartanburg, S.C.: The Reprint Co., 1967), 2: p. 100 of separately paged appendices.

20. [Forbes]. *Writings*, ed. James, 141–42.

21. Peters to Weiser, 22 Dec. 1758, Corr. of Conrad Weiser, mss., 2:143, HSP; Wainwright, *George Croghan*, 151–52.

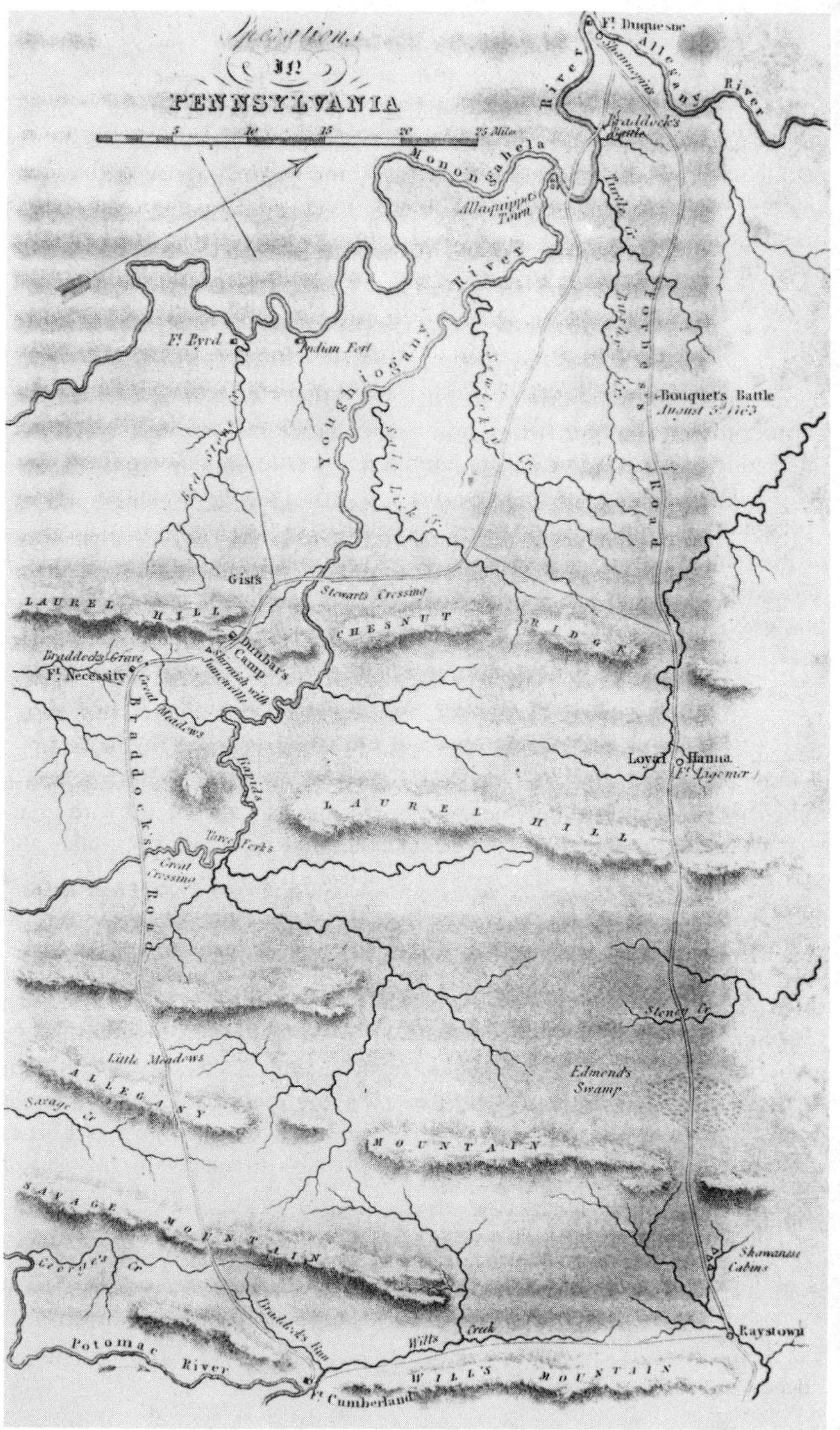

PENNSYLVANIA
5
10
15
20
25 Miles
Ft. Duquesne
Allegany River
Shawnegins
Monongahela
River
Braddock's Battle
Allaquippa's Town
Youghiogany River
Ft. Byrd
Indian Fort
Red Stone Cr.
Sewickly Cr.
Salt Lick Cr.
Turtle Cr.
Bushy Cr.
Forbes's Road
Bouquet's Battle
August 5th 1763
Gist's
Stewarts Crossing
LAUREL HILL
CHESNUT RIDGE
Braddock's Grave
Ft. Necessity
Dunbar's Camp
Skirmish with Jumonville
Great Meadows
Braddock's Road
Loyal Hanna
(Ft. Ligonier)
Rapids
LAUREL HILL
Three Forks
Great Crossing
Braddock's Road
Stoney Cr.
Little Meadows
ALLEGANY
Savage Cr.
Edmond's Swamp
MOUNTAIN
SAVAGE MOUNTAIN
George's Cr.
Shawanese Cabins
Braddock's Run
Wills Creek
Raystown
Potomac River
WILL'S MOUNTAIN
Ft. Cumberland

reopening the more roundabout brush-covered trail cut earlier by Braddock from Virginia. All land speculators knew that new settlers would use the road after the war, so the province that had it would have the way to speculators' wealth. Virginia's officers hatched a conspiracy, led by speculator George Washington, to force Forbes back onto Braddock's road; but Forbes got hold of a revealing letter written by Washington, denounced it as "a shame for any officer to be Concerned in," and "very roundly" let the Virginians know that he would "by no means suffer it."[22]

Quaker scapegoats

In sum, the astounding fact emerges that the only people who gave ailing Forbes unstinted, wholehearted, and trouble-free support were Israel Pemberton and his Friendly Association!

They, however, would have been much less effectual if not for his patronage. On both sides of the Atlantic, the Quakers were not only obstructed; they were reviled (and the habit of castigating them has been continued by historians). The effects still lingered in England of the outrageous libels in William Smith's *Brief State.* Dr. Fothergill wrote that "there is nothing can yet be heard that will convince the generality of the wickedness and falsehood of that representation." In January 1758, Sir William Johnson emulated Smith with a purported "speech" supposed to have been "sent by the Quakers of Pensilvania to the Six Nations." In this the Quakers were made to offer "everything in Plenty" to the warriors if they would "Kill the Soldiers only, and not us . . . You may kill Men enough in other Parts of the Country without coming here." Johnson sent this fabrication to Abercromby, who passed it to Loudoun, who sent it to William Pitt. This libel had been fabricated originally by William Smith, but Johnson's responsibility as abettor is plain; instead of questioning its validity, he threw the whole weight of his authority behind it as fact.

The "Quaker" stick was used by Thomas Penn and his men to beat the assembly dog. Though the assembly had been controlled by Benjamin Franklin and his Anglican supporters for nearly two years, it was called

22. [Forbes], *Writings,* ed. James: St. Clair 139, 168, 189, 287–88, 290; Md. 201; N. Ca. 205; Va. and Pa. 205, 171, 173; Gipson, *British Empire* 7:261–65. Gipson reported the facts about Washington, but followed the custom of bowing to that great name by softening Forbes's indignation.

MAP 9. *(facing page)* The roads of Generals Braddock and Forbes. FROM JARED SPARKS, ED., *Writings of George Washington (1834–37),* 2:38. REPRODUCED BY COURTESY OF THE NEWBERRY LIBRARY FROM THE COPY IN ITS COLLECTIONS.

Quaker in the propaganda barrage, very much as right-wingers have used the terms *Communist* and *Marxist* to smear humanitarians. The Quaker-baiting aroused only indignation in Pennsylvania where public support of the assembly resisted all onslaughts. In England, however, "it is still believed," wrote Dr. Fothergill in June 1758, "that we influence the conduct of public affairs in your Province, and that we have as much influence in them as if we actually composed the majority in Assembly."[23] When the assembly sent Franklin to London to present its case, "great pains" were taken "to render him odious." Franklin reciprocated by conceiving for Thomas Penn "a more cordial and thorough Contempt . . . then I ever before felt for any Man living."[24]

English Quakers agreed on the need to defend their Society and its members, but they seem to have been of several minds about the issue of peace with the Indians under the circumstances as they understood them. Some, however, rallied strongly to the aid of the Pennsylvanians. Especially active was John Hunt one of the two London Friends who had been sent in 1756 to cool the Pennsylvania Quakers battling with the Penns. Hunt's success in that endeavor was matched by their conversion of him on the Indian issues. Hunt was inspired by the treaties with Teedyuscung that he attended; they gave him "the most Satisfaction and best wages" of his visit. Immediately after returning to England late in January 1758, he and companion Christopher Wilson waited on Thomas and Richard Penn to persuade the proprietaries of Friends' desire for an "amicable accommodation," and he noted innocently the cordiality of their reception, somewhat dampened by the Penns' "chagrin" at the Indians' charges of fraud.[25] Hunt gradually learned, to his own chagrin, why the Penns feigned so much cordiality. They gleaned much information from him, including his excited revelation of plans to organize a big Quaker company for trade with Indians, thus to win their friendship. Upon learning which, Thomas Penn wrote to Richard Peters to put a stop to that as "it will be the means of acquiring power to the [Quaker] party."[26] Hunt, along with Dr. Fothergill and four other Quakers who had put up capital, gave up his scheme for a patented company after becoming disillusioned about the Penns,[27]

23. [Fothergill], *Chain of Friendship*, eds. Corner and Booth, 195.

24. *Franklin Papers* 7:362.

25. John Hunt to [Israel Pemberton], 23 Feb. 1758, Pemberton Papers, Box 3, mss., HSP.

26. Penn to Peters, 10 Feb. 1758, Peters Papers 5:31; same to same, 8 Apr. 1758, Peters Papers 5:32, mss., HSP. In the later letter, Penn acknowledged receipt of the Pennsylvania council's report on Teedyuscung's complaints, which contained scurrilous attacks on Quakers: it was "much to our satisfaction."

27. Though London Friends gave up their scheme for a big company, they had quickly bought and sent Pemberton Indian goods to the value of £815.2.3, "bought up in the cheapest manner" and to be sold to the Indians "at as reasonable rates, and as much below the common prices, as to you shall seem expedient." Hunt, Fothergill, and four others to the Trustees of the Friendly Assn., 26 May 1758, in Pemberton Papers, Box 3, mss., HSP.

who were still trying to cozen him in November, nearly a year later: "they propose a nomination of Persons here [in London] to act the part of mediators between them and the people of Pennsylvania, and suggest their readiness to accommodate matters &c." But Hunt had lost his innocence, "I must confess these things look to me like mere pretention and will end in nothing. I cannot discover that thing called sincerity in them."[28]

Hunt seemed to have more luck with Lord Granville whose great estates in North Carolina stimulated interest in peace with Indians. Granville received him several times—more frequently than either Granville or Hunt talked with Benjamin Franklin, then in London as the assembly's agent. Indeed Hunt avoided identification with Franklin and Franklin's assembly. Hunt had a manuscript copy when he came back to England of Charles Thomson's *Enquiry into the Alienation of the Delaware and Shawanese Indians from the British Interest;* instead of immediately transmitting it to Franklin, Hunt took it straight to Granville, and only when Granville had finished was Franklin allowed to see it. It is no wonder that Franklin, who talked to everyone, made no effort to meet with Hunt.[29]

For a while it appeared that Hunt might have chosen the right strategy. Lord Granville promised much. He would aid the trade scheme and try to get a patent for the Friends' company. He would inform the king and Secretary Pitt of the truth about Quaker politics, and he would get Hunt an interview with Pitt. But Pitt was down with gout at the moment, and whatever Granville actually did to fulfill his promises does not appear in any records seen by this writer. Unhappily he aroused great hopes in Israel Pemberton who declared confidently after receiving Hunt's glowing reports that Friends had favor with the ministry.[30] A more sober assessment from Dr. Fothergill convinced Pemberton that his high hopes had been false.[31] Oddly, hostility to Quakers does seem to have slacked off in high places after the almost rabid militarist William Pitt came to power, but enmity heated up again in September when the Pennsylvania council's

28. Hunt to Pemberton, 23 Nov. 1758, Pemberton Papers, Box 3, mss., HSP.

29. Same to same, 23 Feb. 1758, 8 July 1758, Pemberton Papers, Box 3, mss., HSP. The editors of Franklin's papers accuse Hunt of "undercutting" Franklin and deliberately keeping him in the dark to prevent him from getting credit for peacemaking that Quakers wanted for themselves. *Franklin Papers* 7:376n9. This is too simple. The decisive fact was that Franklin and the assembly pursued different policies from the Quakers', and the two groups did not wholly trust each other. Joseph Galloway hoped that "Pennsylvania will regain her lost Credit—and the Quaker Government and Quaker influence be Terms buried in Oblivion and no more remembred." Galloway to Franklin, 16 June 1758, *Franklin Papers* 8:107–08. It should be added that Hunt's snub of Franklin was personal; Pemberton disapproved in his letter to Hunt, 31 May 1758, acknowledged in Hunt to Pemberton, 8 July 1758, Pemberton Papers, Box 3, mss., HSP.

30. Pemberton to Benjamin Horsey and the Menonists in Lancaster County, 29 May 1758, Pemberton Papers, mss., Haverford College.

31. Fothergill to Pemberton, 12 June 1758, in [Fothergill], *Chain of Friendship*, eds. Corner and Booth, 194–98.

secret report reached England. This was the document that Penn's henchmen had slipped through the council without the knowledge of its Quaker members. It responded to Teedyuscung's charges of proprietary fraud by imputing them to "the malicious suggestions and management of some wicked people, enemies to the Proprietaries" who "in disregard of the express injunctions of his Majesty's ministers against it" were "so busy and active in the management and support of the Indians in these affairs against the Proprietaries."

As far as I can make out, this was council's only repayment for the Friendly Association's goods given by governor and council at the treaties with Teedyuscung. Dr. Fothergill sent the passage to Israel Pemberton with the observation that attempts would follow in England "to lay the whole blame of the late Indian ravages in your province upon Friends."[32] He was right. "Parson Smith" was also in England in flight from the imprisonment for contempt of the assembly. Oxford conferred a Doctor of Divinity degree upon him, "to procure which six Bishops, one of 'em an Arch Bishop [of Canterbury] Signed a Letter Recommendatory . . . setting forth that S——h was a true Son of the church and had been persecuted by Dissenters &c. And also that our Society were the Cause of all the Bloodshed both in Europe and America, in Short the sole Cause of the War."[33]

The constant burden of London Friends' advice to those in Pennsylvania was prudence and good behavior. Sooner or later, they thought, the truth of their virtuous motives and proper conduct would come out; patience would discover all. Pemberton and his strict Quakers heeded this advice as well as they could, though it seems anomalous in the circumstances to class Pemberton with the absolute pacifists. Was he responding more to the counsel of London Friends or to the same sort of advice given by his other friend, General Forbes? Whichever, the strict Quakers refrained from direct attack against Thomas Penn *except* on the issue of the fraudulent seizure of Delaware Indian lands. On the other hand, the overtly "defense" Quakers, who remained in the assembly after being disowned by their meetings, followed Franklin's policies of blow-for-blow response to assaults by Penn's placemen. The distinction became a difference. For the time being, Pemberton and Franklin pulled as as team in the same direction; but the Quakers were provincials devoted to the charter that guaranteed religious liberty, and Franklin was an imperialist who saw the proprietary Penns as the enemies of all liberty. Franklin came to think that liberty demanded the revocation of that charter and the dispossession

32. 25 Sept. 1758, in ibid., 204.

33. Hunt to Pemberton, 14 July 1759, Pemberton Papers, Box 3, mss., HSP; Franklin to Galloway, 7 Apr. 1759, in *Franklin Papers* 8:311 and n3.

of the Penns. At that point the Quakers became his antagonists. This process can only be mentioned here to show still another of the underlying complexities of Pennsylvania politics.

For Israel Pemberton in 1758, making peace with the Indians overrode all other concerns. Perhaps he was not quite ready to treat with the devil for that purpose, but he certainly showed eagerness to associate with anyone else going his way. Ordinarily, orthodox religionists shun persons formerly united in faith but newly excomunicated. Not so Israel Pemberton. He kept in close touch with the disowned "defense" Friends in the assembly as well as the stalwart pacifists of the Yearly Meeting and the "weighty" Friends in London—and with Franklin, and Forbes, and Teedyuscung, and the Cherokees, and the Moravians, and the Mennonites and other pietists, not excluding Presbyterian Charles Thomson, Huguenot Daniel Roberdeau, and the anti-proprietary Anglicans. A private merchant without office, Pemberton was the most diversely connected politician in the province; not even Franklin worked with so many various groups and individuals. Pemberton had hoped to pick up information even from within the governor's council by way of councilor, Quaker grandee, and kinsman William Logan, but William liked his position and status, and preferred not to risk them by joining radical agitation. Or, rather, not to be seen as doing so. He shunned Pemberton, but he sent guardedly worded notes to his cousin, and Friends John Smith and Charles Read in New Jersey. Read was official secretary of that province and wholeheartedly working with Pemberton to bring pressure on Pennsylvania's Denny from New Jersey's governor Bernard.[34] (Later, when Logan discovered that the proprietary men were attacking all Quakers, not just the likes of Pemberton, he sent a whole trunkful of documents to James Pemberton through an intermediary.)[35]

It may be seen that though Israel Pemberton lacked official position, he did not lack resource. He had money also—his own fortune, which he did not stint, plus the contributions collected by the Friendly Association. It is quite plain that Pemberton and his associates spent more on the cause of peace with the Indians than the combined payments from the proprietary (zero), the governor, the assembly, and the superintendent of Indian affairs.

34. William Logan's equivocal conduct as he tried to keep well with Thomas Penn and virtuous with his co-religionists would justify a doctoral dissertation, but it was too devious for tracing here. A few references for starters: Thomas Penn Ltr. Bks. 5:137–46, 167, 228–40; Papers of the Friendly Assn. 1:505, 523, 531; 2:231, 235, Haverford College; Pemberton to Read, 19 June 1758, Pemberton Papers, Haverford College; Logan Papers 10:97, HSP; Yi2.7301.F, Library Co. of Phila.; John Smith Mss. 5:83, Library Co. of Phila. All mss.

35. John Smith to James Pemberton, Burlington, 20 Nov. 1758, Pemberton Papers 13:11, mss. HSP.

The partnership of Forbes and Pemberton

Nevertheless, despite his resources and resourcefulness, Pemberton could not convince the Ohio Indians to treat for peace until he could arrange for the invitation to come from proper authority; that is to say, proper authority *in Pennsylvania.* Though Pemberton's message was sent to Ohio, via Teedyuscung, Pemberton could get no response for many months because his message was "only a noise in the woods." Someone had "stopped" it.

Forbes desperately needed intelligence about French numbers and dispositions. Under pressure of necessity he blasted through the obstructionism of Johnson and Penn's men. In June, when Forbes came to understand why no progress had been made toward detaching Indian allies from the French, he summoned a conference attended by Governor Denny, Secretary Peters, interpreter Conrad Weiser (all proprietary men), members of the governor's council, *and* Israel Pemberton. Bluntly, Forbes insisted that official messages *must* be sent to Teedyuscung requesting a parley in Philadelphia about the increasingly dangerous situation in the backwoods; and Forbes joined his own authority to the governor's in issuing the invitation. This was an action proposed by Pemberton, and Forbes overruled all the proprietary men's objections.[36] At last the process of peacemaking got moving again.

Two messengers set off for Wyoming Valley. Christian Frederick Post, a Moravian missionary, had lived among Delawares and could speak their language. His companion Charles Thomson was the Presbyterian master of the Quaker school who had won Teedyuscung's trust by taking honest minutes in 1757. Teedyuscung met with them, 12 June, in the foothills because of worry that his Wyoming village was under a skulking siege by hostile Indians. The precaution was sound; a mason in the construction crew building houses at Wyoming had been killed from ambush, 27 May, by six "enemy Indians" otherwise unidentified. Teedyuscung agreed readily to the proposal for a treaty, but he fretted over the problem of feeding all the visitors he expected from the west.[37]

36. Pemberton to Hunt, 18 June 1758, Pemberton Papers, Box 3, mss. HSP. With great pleasure, I credit Theodore Thayer for leading me to this critical document and the others in Box 3. See *Israel Pemberton,* 154–55. The official account of Forbes's intervention omits Pemberton's presence and is otherwise misleading. *Pa. Council Minutes,* 5 June 1758, 8:128. Forbes had requested Pemberton's help in getting Indian intelligence a week earlier. Papers of the Friendly Assn., 31 May 1758, 1:511, mss. Haverford College.

37. The official records give a confused appearance to Post's and Thomson's journeys. Thayer correctly notes that there were two, but the council minutes acknowledge only one with mixed-up dates. One must go to the Friendly Assn's. mss. for clarification. The first journey occurred early in June, and the messengers gave their report to Pemberton and Denny, 18 June. The second journey was made by Post alone, who started from Philadelphia on the twentieth and submitted his journal on the fourth or fifth of July. Thayer, *Israel Pemberton,* 155–56; *Pa. Council Minutes* 8:128–45; Papers of the Friendly Assn. 2:3, 7, 11,

He had another worry: Could those enemy Indians skulking about Wyoming be the Cherokees who had been brought north in such great numbers? This fear had been foreseen by Pemberton a year earlier when he advised against recruiting the Cherokees. When Post and Thomson reported back to Philadelphia, Pemberton envisioned a dreadful new intertribal war with terrible consequences for Pennsylvanians. With Richard Peters he interviewed the Cherokee chief who had been taken sick in Philadelphia, remaining there when the other warriors marched on. Confusion was never more evident. Far from having hostile intentions, this chief carried a peace message for the Delawares. Unfortunately he also had a mission to the Iroquois that he considered more pressing.[38] *Someone* had to inform the Delawares that the Cherokees were friendly. Post went again to take the news.

This second journey by Post to Teedyuscung was not strictly a negotiation, but it came at a happy moment to speed negotiations along (if *speed* is the right word). Two old Delaware chiefs from the Ohio had come east to ask Teedyuscung about the rumors they had been hearing. Ohio Indians wanted peace, they averred, but had received no reliable information of Pennsylvania's desires; the belts sent to them had been "stopped" somewhere along the way. Now, however, they received Post's messages gladly. Teedyuscung escorted the "Alleghenyans" to Philadelphia.[39] Israel Pemberton forwarded Post's journal to General Forbes.[40]

The party from Wyoming arrived at a propitious moment. The Pemberton-Logan-Read cousinhood had prevailed on New Jersey's newly-arrived governor Francis Bernard to join in the peace campaign, so Bernard's influence was added to the other pressures upon Pennsylvania's Denny.[41] On the eighth of July, Denny and his council met at the State House an assortment of Indians and a sprinkling of "Several Inhabitants of the City."[42] (Read that last as Pemberton and associates.) Richard Peters was very much there in his official capacity, and the importance of the

15–28, 29, mss., Haverford College. Pemberton paid the expenses, £37.10, of the first journey.

38. Ibid., 2:39, *Pa. Council Minutes* 8:135–39.

39. Thayer, *Israel Pemberton*, 157.

40. Papers of the Friendly Assn., 4 July 1758, 2:95.

41. Thayer, *Israel Pemberton*, 156; Pemberton to Charles Read, 19 June 1758, Pemberton Papers, mss., Haverford College; Read to Pemberton, 6 July 1758, Pemberton Papers 12:146, mss., HSP.

42. "Here follows a Blank in Council Book of Five Pages." *Pa. Council Book* 8:145. An official-looking manuscript copy of the treaty minutes 8–12 July 1758, is in Abercromby Papers, AB 422, HEH. Another mss. in Papers of the Friendly Assn. 2:111–24, a copy of which Pemberton sent to Forbes. Ibid., 2:135. Minutes for the eleventh and twelfth of July went to the British Library to become Add. MSS. 21640, f. 83, C, subsequently printed in *Bouquet Papers* 2:187–93 and *Pa. Archives* (1) 3:461–69. My remarks are taken from the HEH mss., except as otherwise noted.

affair is attested by his long report to Forbes written the same evening.[43]

Teedyuscung spoke formally for all the Indians present: a Shawnee and his Delawares from Wyoming, a group of Mahicans, the messengers who had taken belts to the Ohio Delawares, and the two "Alleghenyans." (Peters recognized Pisquetomen and Keekyuscung as "well known to me.") Discrepancies in the surviving accounts indicate that Teedyuscung spoke officially with some discretion but rather deviously. He represented the Alleghenyans as responding to his messages with "now we hear you," but "you have not spoke loud enough." Privately the chiefs told Peters "that none of the Belts designed for them ever reached them, but were detained somewhere." For the moment, we can only guess at the detainer's identity.[44]

Teedyuscung had certain political skills. "Let *us* press heartily on," he urged Governor Denny; and to make his meaning unmistakable, "I don't only press you on alone, but tell you let us press together."[45] What he hoped for was plain enough then as well as now: if Denny were to accept Teedyuscung formally as a partner in the peacemaking with the Ohioans, the chief would become a very big man among the tribes.

Denny answered briefly without commitment. Peters, as already noticed, bypassed Teedyuscung to talk to the Ohioans "in the bushes." Peters's varied motives must be sorted out carefully. As Thomas Penn's dependent and confidante he had no choice but to use every possible device to save Penn's "honor" from exposure of the Walking Purchase fraud; but, unlike Penn, Peters was not indifferent to an Indian peace. Within his permitted limits, Peters cooperated with Forbes's efforts almost as well as Pemberton, and certainly better than that bumbling dunderhead Denny. Well informed and intelligent, Peters extracted from Pisquetomen and Keekyuscung far more information than passed between Teedyuscung and Denny. He learned (and passed on immediately to Forbes) that:

- Ohio Indians were disgusted with the French;
- if they had received a peace belt in the fall of 1757, "they would all have changed sides"(!);
- the Ohioans might still be persuaded to join Forbes, or at least to stand neutral;
- the French at Duquesne were supported by Ottawas, Miamis, "Kuskuski" Delawares, "and two other Nations," but the Wyandots "were averse to the War."

43. Peters to Forbes, 8 July 1758, Penn Mss., Off. Corr., 9:47, HSP.

44. Loc. cit. Ltrs. of Charles Thomson to Wm. Franklin are relevant to this issue: 2 Jan., 12–16 Mar. 1758, Franklin Papers mss., 48, pt. 2, pp. 12, 122, APS.

45. Minutes, 8 July, cited n42.

Most important: Pisquetomen and Keekyuscung would personally take messages to their Delaware "heads" at Kuskuski and Beaver Creek, and they would take intelligence to Forbes. They engaged themselves because "they were afraid future Messages might miscarry as well as past Messages." As events would show, they were faithful to their words.

Among other things, their remarks hint at distrust of Teedyuscung and do more than hint at their intention to negotiate directly rather than through him. When the conference reconvened three days later, Denny responded to Teedyuscung with reiteration of former pledges. Making much ado in acknowledgment of Teedyuscung's good services, he expressed great pleasure that Teedyuscung had "found Openings sufficient to pass thro' with so many of our Indian Brethren, and that you led our old Friends from Ohio so safely thro', for which I thank you very heartily." and he deftly stepped around Teedyuscung to "open a Road from the Ohio to this Council Fire," which meant that he would ignore Teedyuscung in future dealings with the Ohioans.

It is not to be doubted that the words spoken by Denny had been written by Peters. They fitted his strategy perfectly by moving toward western peace while simultaneously suppressing revival of the Walking Purchase contention, and Teedyuscung caught the drift instantly. He rose to tell the governor, "as to the Road we have made now, I sit in the middle of it," which was to assert that the Ohioans could not travel that road without his permission. He invoked higher authority. "I don't sit there on my own Head. *My Uncles the Six Nations have placed me there.*"[46] In subsequent proprietary party efforts to denigrate and downgrade Teedyuscung, he was portrayed as an upstart without genuine tribal support. The situation is murky. Though much has been written about Teedyuscung's clashes with the Six Nations, his first setback came when the Ohioans refused to accept his leadership. Curiously, they seem to have acted partly out of suspicion that he was entirely too close to the Six Nations. They wanted to know why the peace belts entrusted to him had not gotten to them, and they determined not to accept his intermediation for the future.

A boundary demanded

They had another reason for uneasiness, perhaps more important than suspicion of Teedyuscung. It was given voice in a memorial to governor Denny from thirty members of the Friendly Association on 12 July, just as he sat in council preparing for his closing session with the Ohioans.

46. Italics added.

The memorialists protested that Denny had evaded Indian complaints about lands. These had been fundamental to the peace made with Teedyuscung in 1757, and the Indians "expected the faithfull Performance" of the promises then made, but the governor had not even mentioned them in his speech to the Ohioans. Further—and we must attend closely to this point—"the fixing a boundary between the English settlements and the Tract of Land which the Indians desired to be secured to them and their Posterity forever, was another Article of the Peace expressed by them in Strong, Clear and Certain Terms." Beyond abstract justice, a matter of urgent practicality was involved: "the obtaining the Release of our fellow Subjects now in Captivity is immediately concerned in Convincing the Indians that every thing which hath been Solemnly promised by the governour shall be faithfully performed."[47] Denny and Peters ignored the memorial, both in Denny's subsequent remarks at the Philadelphia conference and in the speech he later sent (per wampum belt) to Ohio, but the Indians did not forget; it was one issue on which all the tribes could agree. Regardless of intertribal statuses and rivalries, they had to have a territory of their own.

Peters angrily accused the Friends of having "persuaded" the Indians "that the Governour had not made a true relation of the [1757] Treatie of Easton" (as Teedyuscung, who had been so prominent there well understood). Peters did not allow Teedyuscung a mind of his own: he had been "tutored by Israel" to desire "that a Copy of the Treaties at Easton might be given to the two Alleganians, to carry with them to be read at Ohio, which the Governor was obliged to Comply with." Solemnly, Peters assured General Forbes, "I am sure both Governor and Council want not to screen the Proprietor." From this blunt lie he turned more circumspectly, but no more candidly, to policy: "A Proper Boundary ought and must be fixed with the Indians, but it is neither a preliminary nor ought to be . . . it is nevertheless proper, and what the Proprietors and government have much at Heart as much as these Quakers."[48] Nothing in this letter referred to the Indians' captives.

Pisquetomen takes Frederick Post west

Peters tells us, by way of his minutes of the provincial council, that "great Pains were taken with Pisquetomen and Keekyuscung to prevail

47. Papers of the Friendly Assn. 2:127; *Bouquet Papers* 2:194–96. Missing from *Pa. Council Minutes.*

48. Peters to Forbes, 12 July 1758, in *Bouquet Papers* 2:197–99.

with them to go as quick as possible to the Ohio, and to Observe what was doing at Fort Duquesne, and to send off a trusty messenger from Beaver Creek, with an Account of the Motions of the French and the disposition of the Indians. At length they Consented to go . . . it being a matter of vast Consequence that the Conferences should be known at Ohio, with all possible Care and Dispatch, as well as that the General ought to be furnished with true Intelligence." Post was hired to go with them. He asked for a companion, and Charles Thomson volunteered, but Governor Denny rejected Thomson from a private motive that Thomson might raise the issue of the Walking Purchase. As there were no other volunteers, the rejection of Thomson was also the exclusion of Teedyuscung and Pemberton from any influence on negotiations at Ohio.[49] Written documents and wampum were provided, and the party set off by the roundabout route through Bethlehem and Fort Augusta at the Forks of the Susquehanna because the more direct way along Forbes's road was infested with enemies. Their mission will require special notice below. While they were gone, however, politics continued in the east as exasperatingly as usual.

New Jersey joins the peace effort

Pemberton compensated for his setback in Philadelphia by an end run from New Jersey. Post and Thomson had learned on their first journey to Teedyuscung that 200 hostile Senecas and Minisinks had turned to northern New Jersey. Receiving this information, Pemberton sent it to cousin Charles Read, who was New Jersey's secretary. "The General" wrote Pemberton, "is clearly of this Opinion" that those invading Indians should be placated with a treaty, "and if you were within his District, you would hear it from him."[50] Cousin William Logan wrote to Read also, and Read acted at once. Though much hostility against Indians existed in New Jersey as well as elsewhere, Read prevailed on Governor Francis Bernard to adopt "pacific measures." Bernard sent the Christian converts Moses Tatamy and Isaac Still to Teedyuscung with an invitation for the invaders to treat, Jersey's commissioners of Indian affairs appropriated £1,600 to settle old Indian grievances and buy a new reservation, and a treaty conference con-

49. *Pa. Council Minutes* 8:147–48. Charles Thomson adds motives: "The two Alleghenians expressed a great Desire that some white Man should go with them. By that they said their People would be convinced of the sincerity of the English of their willingness to be at Peace with them . . . I offered my Service . . . However the Governor and Council . . . were of opinion I should not be permitted to go, for fear it seems I should mention something to the Indians of Land Affairs. They are conscious of Guilt and afraid of an Enquiry." Thomson to Susannah Wright, 20 July 1758, Miscellaneous Mss., APS.

50. Pemberton to Read, 19 June 1758, Pemberton Papers, mss., Haverford College.

vened at Burlington on the seventh of August.[51] There is no sign that Pennsylvania officialdom played any part in these proceedings, nor did Sir William Johnson.

Quite apart from whatever may have been justice and equity, £1,600 was cheap compared to what fighting Indians would have cost the Jersey-ites. Place by place, Friends were damping down the fires, but the biggest of all still raged in the west.

Disarray among the obstructionists

Penn's men engaged in what were for them more important matters. Besides their perpetual battles with the assembly, they had begun to fight among themselves. Governor Denny was sore about Thomas Penn's deceitful guarantee of £1,500 sterling per year for Denny's service in government. Denny announced repeatedly that he "would not fight the Proprietary's battles"—absolute anathema to Penn's dependents, who regarded his victories as essential to their welfare—but it was mere bluster in reality because Penn had leashed Denny with a £5,000 bond to do nothing against instructions, and those instructions were as rigid as lawyers could make them. Peters brawled with Denny in council, Denny expelled him, and Peters forced readmission.[52] Benjamin Chew carefully recorded a secret interview between Attorney General Chew and proprietary stalwarts James Hamilton and William Allen, the purpose of which was to prove Denny an enemy of Penn.[53] That "old inveterate scribbler" William Smith continued attacks on Pennsylvania during his enforced exile in England, and his libels excited the apprehension not only of Quakers, but of his own Anglicans at Philadelphia's Christ Church. The rector protested Smith's "endeavours by misrepresenting things (a practice too common with him in this place)" to prejudice the archbishop of Canterbury against himself and vestrymen. "He hath always been exceedingly busy in Politics and very averse to every one of his Brethren who will not fall in with his

51. Thayer, *Israel Pemberton*, 156; Pemberton to Read, 19 June 1758, Pemberton Papers, mss., Haverford College; Read to Pemberton, 6 July, 17 Aug. 1758, Pemberton Papers 12:146, 141; 13:22, mss., HSP; Papers of the Friendly Assn. 2:59, 63, HC; William A. Hunter, "Moses (Tunda) Tatamy," 80–81. And for Tatamy's status as a leading chief and landowner among the New Jersey Delawares see Samuel Smith, *The History of the Colony of Nova-Caesaria, or, New-Jersey* . . . (1756), repr. (Trenton, 1890), 442–46.

52. Draft [never recorded] of minutes of council, 26 Apr. 1758; Peters to James Hamilton, 29 Apr. 1758, Peters Papers 5:40, 42, mss., HSP.

53. "Questions proposed to Benjamin Chew," folder Public Business, 1759–1775, Chew Papers, mss., HSP.

sentiments in that way."[54] But absence prevented Smith temporarily from stirring up more hate in the province.

The peacemakers may have been fortunate to have such concerns distracting the attention of Penn's men from obstructionism, but there was still the looming power of Sir William Johnson to cope with. Forbes took care of that. Johnson, he wrote to General Abercromby, was guilty of "counter working."[55] Everybody in Pennsylvania predicted that he would set up a competing treaty to draw the Indians away from the province's negotiations. Forbes wanted and needed the treaty *there*, with Johnson or without. Lacking a mind of his own, Abercromby bent before Forbes's gale. He tacitly rescinded previous objections to the treaty and asked Johnson to cooperate to the "utmost."[56] Unlike Abercromby, Johnson did possess a mind of his own, a very shrewd one. He had seen the way that wind was blowing and decided not to stand up against it. He told his Iroquois associates to attend Pennsylvania's treaty. At last, the pieces seemed to be falling together in the east. Much now depended on what was happening at Ohio.

Post's party among the Ohioans

The peace mission led by Pisquetomen and Post made its hazardous way toward the Delaware Indian town of Kuskuski.[57] After three weeks the messengers came to French Fort Venango where another of the multiplex peculiarities of backwoods warfare manifested itself when they were able to cross the broad Allegheny River on a ford shown them by the French soldiers in garrison.[58] Three days later they met more Frenchmen "who appeared very shy of us" but made no hostile move. The messengers were lucky to be traveling in more strength than the Frenchmen they encountered—equally lucky that the French did not yet understand their mission. When its full import became clear, the French swore to catch

54. Christ Church rector Dr. Robert Jenney to archbishop of Canterbury, 27 Nov. 1758, discrepant copies in *Historical Collections Relating to the American Colonial Church* vol. 2: *Pennsylvania*, ed. William Stevens Perry (Hartford, Conn.: Church Press, 1871), 273–74; Horace W. Smith, *Life of Smith* 1:185.

55. Forbes was exceptionally tart for a subordinate writing to his commander in chief. [Forbes], *Writings*, 9 July 1758, pp. 134–40.

56. Abercromby to Johnson, 23 July 1758, *Johnson Papers* 9:954–55.

57. The major source for this mission is Post's journal in Robert Proud, *History of Pennsylvania*, App., pt. 2, 65–95. This is available in other publications, so to facilitate checking I cite by date of entry rather than page number.

58. Ibid., 7 Aug. 1758.

Post and "roast him alive for five days."[59] That they never got the chance to perform this "savage" act was entirely owing to the vigilance and protection of the Delawares who had taken him "in their bosom."

Fifteen miles short of Kuskuski, Post paused while Pisquetomen went forward to summon the "kings and captains" to hear Post's "words of great consequence from the Governor and people of Pennsylvania and from the king of England." Post added later that the joyful news came also "from your children, the Friends."[60] Perhaps he remembered that the Friendly Association was paying him, but one should not conclude that money was his primary motive. Like the Friends', Post's Moravian faith was a religion of peace and brotherhood, and Post's dedication to it cannot be faulted.

He needed all the fortitude that faith could provide because he had arrived in the midst of peoples strung to the highest pitch of anxiety, uncertainty, and internecine contention, all exacerbated by the prospect of famine. Indian men could not fight and hunt at the same time; after stored necessities were exhausted, their families became heavily dependent on provision from European allies. Provision had long been short even in Quebec because of the British navy's interdiction of supplies form France, and what was available for shipment from Fort Frontenac had been diverted by Bradstreet's raid. Though the French understood well the need to be generous to their Indian allies, their own garrison in Fort Duquesne was on starvation rations.

Bewildered Indians knew not which way to turn. Who could tell whether France or Britain would win? Certainly, after Indian slaughter and depredation, there could be no hope of a cordial welcome back to the British fold. Equally certainly, the French were known to punish heavily for desertion; the memory of Pickawillany lived on. The polyglot network of western Indian nations were divided against each other and within each community, and French agents were everywhere, constantly and skilfully propagandizing by word and deed. When Frederick Post arrived at Kuskuski he found fifteen Frenchmen building houses for Indians in the town.[61]

Pisquetomen and Keekyuscung understood these circumstances when they journeyed to Wyoming and Philadelphia to initiate negotiations for peace. Pisquetomen has the fuller and more mixed record. He had plenty of reason to hate the British. As a member of the "royal family" of his nation he had been the designated heir apparent to old Chief Sassoonan's chieftainship in the east until a conspiracy between Pennsylvanians and Iroquois blocked his succession. Pisquetomen had interpreted between

59. "Narrative of Marie Le Roy and Barbara Leininger," *Pa. Mag. of Hist. and Biog.* 29 (1905): 412.

60. Post's journal, 12 Aug. 1758.

61. Ibid., 14 Aug. 1758.

the English and Delaware languages at the 1742 treaty when the Iroquois, at Pennsylvania's bidding, had thrown the Delawares off their land. Pisquetomen had lifted the hatchet against Pennsylvanians and taken prisoners; his brother Shingas was the dreaded war chief of the Delawares with a heavy price on his head.[62] Pisquetomen and Keekyuscung made an oddly matched team, yet indisputably they worked together. Unhappily we cannot follow them back into the deliberations of the tribal council as Frederick Post, who wrote our source, was excluded. The consequence of this exclusion is a skewed record in which Post is the central figure. He obviously, if fearfully, enjoyed his prominence in the drama, and his reporting did nothing to reduce it; but while Post manfully endured agonies of apprehension and was shunted sensationally about to escape French plots against his life, decisions were made soberly and quietly in the secret sessions of the tribal councils. With all deference to Post's genuine heroism, his histrionics are a little hard to take. "It is a troublesome cross and heavy yoke to draw this people. They can punish and squeeze a body's heart to the utmost. . . . The Lord knows how they have been counselling about my life; but they did not know who was my protector and deliverer; I believe my Lord has been too strong against them." Post might have shown a little more gratitude to the Delawares, who had indeed been counseling about his life, and how to preserve it at great risk to their own lives. The protection of Post's Lord would have been little use without their care.[63]

French intrigue

Nevertheless there is much information in Post's journal. He reported carefully what the Indians said to him, and one speech especially sets him in his proper role as messenger. In his presence the peace chief Tamaqua (Beaver) and the terrible war chief Shingas spoke formally to their elder brother Pisquetomen: "Brother, you told us that the Governor of Philadelphia and Teedyuscung took this man out of their bosoms, and put him

62. Jennings, "Delaware Interregnum," *Pa. Mag. of Hist. and Biog.* 89:2 (Apr. 1965), 174–98.

63. Post's journal, 17–25 Aug., 7 Sept. 1758. One of Post's journey companions, Shamokin Daniel, after receiving large presents from the commander of Fort Duquesne, tried to deliver Post to the French, but was rebuffed by the negotiating chiefs. Daniel added complications to Israel Pemberton's life because he got back to Easton before Post, so that his self-serving and French-twisted version of the mission was all that Pemberton had to go by in the early days of the great treaty at Easton in October. See "Journal of Daniel's Journey to the Allegheny," Etting Coll., Pemberton Papers 2:29, HSP.

into our bosom, to bring him here; and you have brought him here to us; and we have seen and heard him; and now we give him into your bosom, to bring him to the same place again, before the Governor; but do not let him quite loose; we shall rejoice when we shall see him here again."[64]

The substantive negotiations in the Delaware towns began with an admonition from the chiefs at Kuskuski for Post to say nothing of Teedyuscung. They "had nothing to say to any treaty, or league, of peace, made at Easton [by others than themselves], nor had anything to do with Teedyuscung." They wanted only to hear "from the government."[65] Post complied. He mentioned messages from Denny and Forbes, and the chiefs sent out a summons to "a great many nations." They warned Post that "it is necessary that the whole should join in the peace, or it can be no peace."[66]

These passages confirm the independence of the western Indians from Iroquois domination, and they suggest once more the westerners' suspicions of Teedyuscung's being too close to the Six Nations. Ironically, Teedyuscung had been assailed on the other side by Penn's men and Sir William Johnson for being too close to the Quakers. Though he probably played a double or triple game, and relied heavily on Quaker support, Teedyuscung probably spoke truth when he said that the Six Nations had appointed him to negotiate peace in Pennsylvania. No less a person than William Johnson had taken the petticoat off Teedyuscung's eastern Delawares in 1756 and "made men" of them—that is, qualified them to negotiate independently rather than through Iroquois spokesmen—readmitting them at the same time to the Covenant Chain.[67] So long as Teedyuscung deferred to the Six Nations as his superior "uncles," they could accept him to serve their own purposes. This, I think, was precisely why the Ohio Indians would have nothing to do with him. They were in process of forming a great western confederation alternative to the Iroquois Covenent Chain. In 1758 those allies considered the proposals brought by Pisquetomen and Post without any Iroquois participation except that of the separatist Ohio Mingos and defiant Senecas.

Taken to the vicinity of Fort Duquesne, Post read his messages (slightly altered in accordance with advice) to Delawares, Mingos, and Shawnees in the presence of French observers. It became a matter of life or death with him as the French intrigued desperately to get him across the river and inside the fort, from which he would never have emerged alive; but

64. Post's journal, 6 Sept. 1758.

65. Ibid., 16, 17 Aug. 1758. Notably the chiefs contradicted what Teedyuscung had been saying in Philadelphia: "I read them what Teedyuscung had said . . . They said, they never sent any such advice (as above mentioned) to Teedyuscung, nor ever sent a message at all to the government."

66. Ibid., 18 Aug. 1758.

67. Treaty minutes, 12 July 1756, *N.Y. Col. Docs.* 7:160.

Post's escort "insisted on a hearing on this side of the water" and he "stuck constantly as close to the fire, as if I had been chained there."[68] This dangerous situation has generally been portrayed as a threat from Indian savages, but the menace was French. Post owed his life to the "savages."

In this perilous situation, and before a "great many" French officers who recorded his words, Post presented Pennsylvania's belts without mention of Teedyuscung or previous Easton treaties. He opened the road directly to Pennsylvania's council fire, and he assured that "all past offences shall be forgotten." He made a strong impression, though somewhat dampened by his added demand for return of prisoners. For the moment, that was allowed to pass without protest.

More ominously, the French convened their strongest allies within the fort and proposed an attack upon those worrisome Delawares. "Now all their chiefs are here, and but a handful, let us cut them off, and then we shall be troubled with them no longer." Ottawas stopped that. "No, we cannot do this thing; for though there is but a handful here, the Delawares are a strong people, and are spread to a great distance, *and whatever they agree to must be*." Informed of the plot, the Delawares hastened off with Post to greater security.[69]

Back at Kuskuski the Delawares continued in council while Post fretted to be gone. Shingas explained their hesitation: "We have great reason to believe you intended to drive us away; or else, why do you come to fight in the land that God has given us?" Shingas faced Post bluntly. "This was told us by the chief of the Indian traders . . . the French and English intended to kill all the Indians, and then divide the land among themselves . . . Brother, I suppose you know something about it; or has the Governor stopped your mouth, that you cannot tell us?" Perhaps Post was sincerely deluded about his countrymen's intentions. Perhaps he thought that the great goal of peace justified straying from total candor. Whatever the reason, he responded with more demagogy than accuracy. "I do assure you of mine and the people's honesty. If the French had not been here, the English would not have come," and he ranted against the Irish *papist* traders "who have put bad notions into your heads."[70]

The Indians wanted to believe him, and they almost did, but they still had not heard him "rightly"[71] More negotiations would be needed for confirmation of his assertions, so Pisquetomen would take him back to Philadelphia to make the arrangements. Because the French were now alert to his mission and determined to frustrate it, the return journey was

68. Post's journal, 25 Aug. 1758.
69. Ibid., 26 Aug. 1758. Italics added.
70. Ibid., 30 Aug. 1758. Italics added to show how Post had stressed the term by repetition.
71. Ibid., 3 Sept. 1758.

more dangerous and painful than the way out. Avoiding the common trails, the party made their way over rocks and through swamps by rarely used, hardly distinguishable paths that strained their strength to the utmost, and they had to maintain vigilance every minute. Post's escorting Indians endured more than he did; while he slept soundly through the nights they mounted guard, guns and tomahawks ready. Naively, Post asked what made them fearful. "They said, I knew nothing; the French had set a great price on my head; and they knew there was gone out a great scout to lie in wait for me." They met a raiding party of their own tribesmen who had prisoners and a scalp. "We sat down all in one ring together." Instead of adding Post to their other trophies, the warriors promised, "if you make a good peace, then we will bring all the prisoners back again."[72]

On 22 September, Post's party arrived at Fort Augusta at the forks of the Susquehanna whence they traveled downstream to Harris's Ferry (Harrisburg), at which point certain distinctions became plain. Post immediately turned about to carry intelligence to General Forbes. Pisquetomen continued on to Philadelphia as the Delawares' properly certified negotiator to treat for peace with Pennsylvania.[73]

A great treaty convenes at Easton

At last, everything was coming together at Easton.[74] The governors of Pennsylvania and New Jersey presided. Besides secretaries, interpreters, and provincial counselors and commissioners from both assemblies, members of the Friendly Association appeared in substantial numbers. George Croghan represented Superintendent Johnson. Thirteen nations or bands

72. Ibid., 7–19 Sept. 1758.

73. Forbes to Peters, 16 Oct. 1758, in [Forbes], *Writings*, 235; *Pa. Council Minutes* 8:174, 223. Peters to Chew, Easton, 2 Oct. 1758, folder French and Indian War, 1753–65, Chew Papers, mss., HSP.

Bibliographic note: My first published article, "A Vanishing Indian," was a refutation of Francis Parkman's version of Post's journey: Walter T. Champion, Jr., took issue with some of my interpretations in his "Christian Frederick Post and the Winning of the West," *Pa. Mag. of Hist. and Biog.* 104:3 (July 1980), 308–25. Champion correctly identified "the traitorous Daniel," as I had not, and added considerably to the source evidence. Neither of us attended to the Quakers' role in the proceedings.

74. Treaty minutes, 7–26 Oct. 1758, *Pa. Council Minutes* 8:174–223. These official minutes do not name their scribe. Charles Thomson wrote privately, setting down "nothing but what I heard or saw myself, or received from good Authority." *Franklin Papers* 8:200. Many manuscripts are listed in *Iroquois Indians, A Documentary History*. Benjamin Chew's journal that works up a case for the Penns is in *Indian Treaties Printed by Benjamin Franklin*, ed. Boyd, 312–18, which also prints the official minutes. Israel Pemberton privately wrote that the official minutes were not true in many respects; Indians' expressions of "attachment to and dependence on Friends, as well as the heavy Expenses we have borne on these Occasions [are] carefully suppressed." Pemberton to Samuel Wily, 2 Dec. 1758, Pemberton Papers 13:14, mss., HSP; Pemberton to Franklin, 11 Dec. 1758, in *Franklin Papers* 8:211–13.

of eastern Indians, including all six Iroquois nations, had delegations present when the conference opened, 8 October, and were joined on the thirteenth by Pisquetomen and Thomas Hickman from Post's party. Post did not come until the twenty-second, after the conference business had concluded; negotiation was not included in his role as messenger. Though the immense gathering overstrained the resources of food and shelter available in the young little village of Easton, Israel Pemberton had anticipated such difficulties by sending forward provisions from the Friendly Association. Every building with a roof became a lodging. Dignitaries, including the chief men of the tribes, crowded into innkeeper Vernon's rooms. Indians camped out with their wives and children. One may smile at the image of portly Philadelphians of substance tumbled together in the hay and lining up in the morning at a well. The records do not mention how all those people managed waste disposal.

The motley scene resembled a fair in the Middle Ages. Every type of contemporary costume appeared, and combinations thereof, from the governors' silks and satins through "good" but sober Quaker cloth and Moravian peasant garb to the buckskin leggings of the warriors and the total nakedness of their small children. Men like the synethnic Andrew Montour wore what attracted them from both cultures—leggings topped off with ruffled shirts and laced waistcoats, or knee breeches below and nothing above, and all bedecked with silver and shell ornaments. The women probably contrasted less, though the Indian women's bead embroidery, if nothing else, would have distinguished them from the plain clothes of farmers' wives and the dictated simplicity of Moravian women.

No building could hold all the conferees, so meetings were held "in the bower." One must envision the governors and their entourages at one side with secretaries at tables before them. The Indians faced them in a semicircle, clustering in communal groups with their "great men" dignifiedly squatting in front and the "young" fellows (including forty year olds) standing deferentially behind and women on the outskirts. These participating Indians were disciplined in the total silence that tradition demanded from everyone except the speaker, but out beyond the periphery of the sessions the children played, the servants busied themselves with cooking and cleaning, and intrigues multiplied. Between sessions, action exploded as tribesmen, placemen, Quakers, and hangers-on mixed in all conceivable combinations to wrangle, drink, and plot. The wonder is that in all the confusion anything was accomplished. In fact, however, despite the particularistic conflicting interests of the parties, they all shared, in varying degrees, a desire to patch up some sort of genuine agreement. Unspoken reservations abounded, but somehow the parties pushed and dragged each other into formal agreement. What they did eliminated all possibility of French victory and gestated new British royal policies in Indian affairs.

The immediate consequence was victory for General Forbes at Fort Duquesne. The ironic long-term consequences included temporary reconstitution of the Covenant Chain and motivation for Britain's colonies to secede from the empire. Like most large historical events, the processes were messy and the outcome unforeseen.

Iroquois and Delawares

In this treaty, function diverged from form as the Iroquois took charge of what the governors presided over.

In this situation the Iroquois concerned themselves to insure their own primacy among Indians allied to the British, but they were far from united as to how this primacy was to be exerted. Richard Peters discovered before the official sessions began that "the Senecas and Cayugas insist on being the sole directors of the Munsies and Delawares—exclusive of the other Six Nations . . . the Conoy Indians have thrown themselves upon the Senecas too." Peters sensed correctly that "a mighty difference is likely to arise on this account," but it became one of the matters suppressed from the minutes.[75]

Throughout the conference the proprietary men labored, with George Croghan's help, to reduce the Delawares to subordination to the Iroquois, their hope being to nullify all of Teedyuscung's previous negotiations and start anew. Thomson commented, "In order to gain this Point the Senekas and Six Nations are *privately* treated with and prompted to undo what has been done, in order, as is pretended, to establish their own Authority and gain the Credit of the Peace."[76] This issue came to climax in a private session of the governors with the Six Nations. The official minutes say that Croghan's father-in-law, the Mohawk chief Nichas, demanded to know who had made Teedyuscung "such a great Man . . . we do not know he is such a great Man," and that Nichas was seconded by speakers for the other nations.[77] It may easily be that Teedyuscung, when drunk, had permitted his imagination to embroider his status, and that this would be resented by the Iroquois is certain; but the sound and fury over this issue has been reduced to proper dimensions by Charles Thomson, Governors Denny and Bernard, and Cayuga chief Tokaaion. Thomson: "What concern'd Teedyuscung there, seemed little more than whether he should beconsidered as a King or an Emperor. They did not deny his Power over

75. Peters to Chew, 2 Oct. 1758, mss., cited n74.
76. *Franklin Papers* 8:201.
77. *Pa. Council Minutes* 8:190–91.

his own Nations, and he never claimed (except in his Cups, if then) any Authority over the Six Nations."[78] Denny: Teedyuscung told him "that he acted as a Chief Man for the Delawares, but only as a Messenger for the United Nations, who were his Uncles and Superiors . . . they might do as they saw Cause." Bernard: "I observe in his Treaties . . . he says he was a Woman till you made him a Man by putting a Tomahawk in his hand . . . he calls you his Uncles and professes that he is dependent on you."[79] Tokaaion's comment will be quoted in context below. Though Teedyuscung had tried to remove the lands issue from the agenda, Penn's men kept it going because their assignment was to get Penn vindicated; peace was secondary to that. Israel Pemberton commented caustically, "the time was spent in attempting Teedyuscung's downfall, and silencing or contradicting the complaints he had made."[80]

In a very difficult situation, Teedyuscung tried to maintain good relations with the Iroquois, but he made a slip on the eighteenth of October: "let us not alter what you [of Pennsylvania] and I have agreed. . . . I don't pretend to mention any of my Uncles' Lands. I only mention what we, the Delawares, own, *as far as the Heads of Delaware*." Probably Teedyuscung was thinking of the Minisink country surrounding Port Jervis where the boundaries of Pennsylvania, New York, and New Jersey come to a point; but the Iroquois knew that the "head" of the Delaware River was located in Mohawk territory in present-day Schoharie County, New York. They walked out of council as Teedyuscung spoke. Even the official minutes, read for fact instead of slant, show that the misunderstanding was cleared up quickly: the Six Nations made no claim to Minisink lands, and Teedyuscung "acquainted the Governor [Denny] that "the Delawares did not Claim Lands high up on Delaware River; those belonged to their Uncles."[81]

Later, after further consultation with his uncles, Teedyuscung became precise: since land had become an issue despite his wishes, he defined his complaints as pertaining only to the region "between Tohiccon Creek and the Kittochtinny Hills"—the lands involved in the Walking Purchase of 1737, and precisely what Thomas Penn wanted legitimized. But, in contrast to proprietary propaganda, the Iroquois did not perform as desired.

Tokaaion, the Cayuga Chief, stood up and spoke as follows, addressing himself to Teedyuscung: "Cousin: I thank you for your Openness and Honesty on this Occasion, freely to declare the Truth. We wish our Brethren, the English, naming

78. *Franklin Papers* 8:206.
79. *Pa. Council Minutes* 8:192–94.
80. *Franklin Papers* 8:212.
81. *Pa. Council Minutes* 8:201, 202.

the Governors of Pennsylvania, Virginia, Carolina, and Jersey, were so honest and precise.

They have called us down to this Council Fire, which was kindled for Council Affairs, to renew Treaties of Friendship, and brighten the Chain of Friendship. But here we must hear a Dispute about Land, and our Time is taken up, but they don't come to the Chief point.

The English first began to do Mischief . . . They ought not thus to treat with Indians on council Affairs. . . . I fear they only speak from their Mouth, and not from their Heart."[82]

So far as the Indians were concerned, the proprietary case was dead; the Walking Purchase had been a fraud. (They had known that all along.) But its consequence in the elevation of the Six Nations to superiority over the Delawares had not been rejected along with the land fraud.

When the peacemakers were able to break through the proprietary obstructions, they agreed quickly enough on matters of substance. New Jersey's governor Bernard compensated the Minisink and Wappinger Indians, on the Six Nations' advice, with a thousand Spanish dollars.[83] As noted earlier, the efforts of Israel Pemberton and Charles Read had achieved a reservation for New Jersey's Indians to live in. Teedyuscung's Delawares were not so fortunate. He turned to the Iroquois: "I sit here as a Bird on a Bow: I look about and do not know where to go; let me therefore come down upon the Ground, and make that my own by a good Deed, and I shall then have a Home for Ever; for if you, my Uncles, or I die, our Brethren, the English, will say they have bought it from you, and so wrong my Posterity out of it."[84] To this, Oneida chief Thomas King responded only that "you may make use of those Lands in Conjunction with our People, and all the rest of our Relations."[85] The request for a deed would have to go to the grand council at Onondaga—where it sank into oblivion. The Iroquois knew well that their status as landlords / hosts contributed mightily to their role as *uncles*.

Iroquois and Ohioans

The Ohio Indians were not to be disposed of so summarily. Mystery obscures some details, but the facts of relative strengths stand out. The Iroquois prudently refrained from stretching their pretensions to involvement in combat they could not win. Seneca chief Tagashata, at the head

82. Ibid., 8:211–12.
83. Ibid., 8:209.
84. Ibid., 8:203.
85. Ibid., 8:221.

of the largest delegation in the conference, informed the participants that "we have told all these [on the Ohio] that they must lay down the French Hatchet, and be reconciled to their Brethren, the English," adding anti-climactically, "we hope they will take our Advice."[86] It fell somewhat short of command. Doubt arose also about Tagashata's candor when Teedyuscung indiscreetly blurted out the itinerary of the great peace belt he had sent to the Ohio Delawares in 1757, and why it never reached them. He had been well aware of how it had bogged down, even as he assured Pemberton and other Pennsylvanians how he had sent his "halloo" to the Ohio; he, too, had been keeping some secrets.

For the significance of this issue, one must recall what Pisquetomen had told Richard Peters months earlier: "had the Peace Belt arrived last Fall, they would all have changed sides."[87] Now Teedyuscung revealed where the belt had gone, and why it never reached the Ohioans. It went up the Susquehanna to the Senecas, thence to "all the United Nations"—that is, the Great Council at Onondaga—who "had it almost a Year," after which it was forwarded to Secaughkung (Canisteo, N.Y.), where it stopped.[88] Secaughkung was the village of *eastern* Delawares closest to Iroquoia and obviously most closely controlled by the Iroquois. So the Ohio Delawares had spoken truly when they said that someone had stopped the peace belt sent to them—it was the Iroquois.

The disclosure may have raised eyebrows among the more knowing conferees at Easton, but it was passed over without contradiction, inquiry, or response of any kind. So far as the records show, everyone pretended not to hear. We would be foolish to follow that example, for Teedyuscung's indiscretion, if it was that, penetrates to the heart of secret Iroquois policy. It tells us not only what happened to Pennsylvania's peace belt, but also why Sir William Johnson could not establish contact with the Ohio Indians. The question has to be faced: why did the Iroquois play that game? It seems to be yet another bit of evidence of the policy they had adopted in 1753 when the French first marched toward the Ohio in strength. The chiefs of the League secreted the words of their policy, but they could not mask the testimony of behavior. What that evidences is their intention to *win* the war. They were not fond of the French, but they had thrown themselves against French power in earlier wars and had suffered badly. They preferred their old British alliance, but loyalty to it could cost too high a price, as it had done when they had fought New York's wars. Now the Iroquois would dabble a bit on both sides, just enough to preserve all their options, and make their final commitment

86. Ibid., 8:182.
87. Peters to Forbes, 8 July 1758, Penn Mss., Off. Corr. 9:47, HSP.
88. *Pa. Council Minutes* 8:200.

when the time was right to serve their own purposes. This has been denounced as a policy of sheer opportunism. In the circumstances, it was rationality. The Iroquois had come to understand the hard truth of Shamokin Daniel's furious outburst—"You come here only to cheat the poor Indians, and take their land from them"[89]—and the Iroquois meant to keep their land. No matter which empire triumphed, the Iroquois meant to win—not just to be on the side of the winning empire, but to be winners themselves.

So they had stopped the peace belt from Pennsylvania to the Ohioans until they could see Forbes's army marching determinedly westward. Convinced at last that the British were serious enough to commit their own force for retaking Fort Duquesne, the Iroquois became serious about negotiations. They really had no choice any longer, now that the Ohioans were negotiating directly. If peace should be made without their participation, the Iroquois would sink to unimportance in British policy planning. (Their equivocal role had reduced them pretty far already.) They opted at Easton to take charge of the negotiations that no longer could be stopped, and to use them to re-establish the covenant Chain and Iroquois dominance within it.

The Ohio Delawares had been less than enthusiastic about accepting Iroquois dominance, and they remained so, but the Iroquois had a trump card to play on the territorial stakes. Through Sir William Johnson, they had prevailed on Thomas Penn to renounce part of the cession that Penn's men had brought at Albany in 1754. At Easton, through a power of attorney to Richard Peters and Conrad Weiser, Penn authorized a deed to restore to the Iroquois all the land "Westward of the Allegheny or Appalaccin Hills," precisely the land on which the Ohio Indians were living.[90] Once more the Iroquois created for themselves, by way of the colony's formal recognition, the status of landlord over other tribes which had long been the key to their dominance on the Susquehanna. What were the Ohioans to do about their own claim to own the land being deeded to the Iroquois? For the time being they kept quiet. They were ready to accept the Iroquois in order to get rid of the French, and their readiness increased with Governor Denny's instruction for Peters and Weiser to meet with the Iroquois to "Settle the Boundaries between you." It seemed that when the French had been driven out, the British would be kept out also. Thus was the seed planted for the boundary lines in the Royal Proclamation of 1763 and the Quebec Act of 1774—and the "frontier" boundaries of the United States throughout the nineteenth century.

Pisquetomen apparently stipulated one modification of the peace terms

89. Post's journal, 28 Aug. 1758.
90. *Pa. Council Minutes* 8:204.

which ameliorated the Delawares' re-established tributary status. It appears in Denny's peace message to be carried back to Ohio by Pisquetomen, Thomas Hickman, and (once more) Frederick Post.

> Brethren on the Ohio:
> If you take the Belts we just now gave you, in which all here join, English and Indians, as we don't doubt you will, then by this Belt, I make a Road for you, and invite you to come to Philadelphia to your first Old Council Fire, which was kindled when we first saw one another, which fire we will kindle up again and remove all disputes, and renew the Old and first Treaties of Friendship; . . . we desire all Tribes and Nations of Indians who are in Alliance with you may come.[91]

Translated, this said that Pennsylvania would treat with the Delawares without Iroquois interposition, and would accept the Shawnees allied to the Delawares, equally without Iroquois interposition. Though the Iroquois had become landlords of the Ohio Indians, they had not re-achieved their old status of spokesmen. The unsettled variables of relative powers remained as the objects of future maneuvers. For the time being, if the Ohio council accepted, it was peace.

'Looking around the room," Thomas King "espied Mr. Vernon, the Person who had the Care of furnishing the Indians with Provisions, and he desired that, now Council Business was over, he might be ordered to take the Lock off the Rum, and let it run freely, that, as they were going away, their Hearts might be made glad, and we could very well spare it, as it was of no use to us. Some Wine and Punch was then ordered in, and the Conferences were conducted with great Joy and mutual Satisfaction."[92]

Victory through peace

Few are the celebrations without mornings after. In the sombre dawn, the Indians saw two Cayuga chiefs join the peace party on its way to Ohio, their function being to represent Iroquois authority to those difficult westerners. Israel Pemberton tempered his rejoicing with an awareness of what *yet remained necessary to be done*. Nevertheless, Pemberton would carry on, sustained by the knowledge that "in all the Desolation on our Frontiers, not one Friend we have heard of, has been slain nor carried captive." It is possible, of course, to put a conspiratorial interpretation on this fact, as William Smith and Sir William Johnson had already done, but given all the circumstances a simpler explanation suffices: to wit, that

91. Ibid., 8:207.
92. Ibid., 8:223.

Indians were rational creatures capable of distinguishing Friends from enemies. Pemberton's thankfulness for Indian gratitude to Quakers did not lead to neglect of persons outside the Quaker community; he and associates repeatedly stressed to lackadaisical officials the need to insist upon return of those captives of the Indians, among whom was not a single Quaker. Their struggles to make peace plainly benefited all Pennsylvanians: the benefits were all the greater for those non-Quakers who were being killed and captured. And Pemberton was thoroughly aware of the military implications of his work. Conceiving Indian peace as prerequisite to victory over the French, he wrote: "if General Forbes succeeds, it must be attributed rather to the drawing off the Indians by our pacific Negotiations than anything else . . . [otherwise] I have reason to conclude he would not have ventur'd this Year to Fort duQuesne."[93]

In this war rife with contradiction and paradox, not the least of its ironies was the approach to military triumph through peace.

93. Pemberton to Samuel Wily, 2 Dec. 1758, Pemberton Papers 13:14, mss., HSP.

Chapter 18 ❧ *VICTORIES and MORE VICTIMS*

As . . . [by the capitulation of Montreal] the war in America is at an end, and the Indians will no longer be corrupted by rival interests we shall no more hear of scalping parties, bands of ignorant *Savages*, hired by *Christians*, to murder *Christians* in cold blood; it is to be hoped for the honour of human nature, and for the sake of the poor *Indians*, who have been made both miserable and wicked by our contentions, that whatever may be given up at a peace, *America* will be retained: we shall then possess our colonies there, without the guilt of hired assassinations; without dividing the *Indians* against each other, in a quarrel in which they have no interest; without exciting the thirst of blood amongst them by pecuniary rewards, and entailing upon their posterity the ferocity of fiends, by familiarizing their children to unprovoked barbarity and quenching the compunctions of nature by reiterated murders.

The Gentleman's Magazine 30 (October 1760), 462.

Chronology

22 April 1758.	Governor Denny passes the assembly's tax bill to raise £100,000 after exemption of Penn estates.
25–27 August 1758.	Bradstreet's capture of Fort Frontenac deprives Fort Duquesne of supplies and reinforcements.
August–September 1758.	Christian Frederick Post's first journey to the Ohio Indians.
14 September 1758.	Major James Grant loses a battle near Fort Duquesne, after which the "Far Indian" allies of the French go home with their plunder. Only Ohioans are left.
8–26 October 1758.	Peace treaty at Easton.
27 October 1758.	Pisquetomen and Post set out with the Easton treaty message to the Ohioans.
7 November 1758.	Pisquetomen and Post arrive in Forbes's camp and are given the general's message to add to the governor's.
20 November 1758.	At Kuskuski the Indians reject French commander's request to aid him at Fort Duquesne. French captain sends notice of rejection back to the fort.
24 November 1758.	Commander Lignery destroys Fort Duquesne and retreats to Fort Machault.
25 November 1758.	Forbes seizes ruins of Fort Duquesne. It is renamed "Pittsburgh."
2 December 1758.	Israel Pemberton congratulates Forbes and sends trade goods for the Indians.

"Winter," 1758–59.	Senecas determine to turn against the French.
January 1759.	Iroquois "supplicate" support from Commandant Hugh Mercer at Pittsburgh. They conspire with Mercer to delude the Delawares and Shawnees.
February 1759.	Sir William Johnson proposes expedition against Niagara.
April 1759.	Senecas desire Johnson to reduce Niagara.
June 1759.	George Croghan assumes control over the trade at Pittsburgh. Israel Pemberton persuades General Stanwix to repeal Croghan's powers.
25 June 1759.	General James Wolfe lays siege to Quebec. He bombards the residential city and lays waste the countryside. Montcalm threatens death to anyone who shows timidity.
July 1759.	Delawares become uneasy about Pittsburgh's growing strength.
July 1759.	General Stanwix requests Pemberton to send more trade goods to Pittsburgh.
7 July 1759.	General John Prideaux besieges Niagara. Iroquois on both sides act independently.
19 July 1759.	Prideaux killed, Johnson takes command.
23 July 1759.	Lieutenant Colonel Eyre Massey and Captain James De Lancey rout the French relieving party outside Fort Niagara, and Iroquois pursue the fleeing French.
25 July 1759.	Commander Pouchot surrenders Niagara to Johnson.
July–August 1759.	Amherst takes Ticonderoga and Fort St. Frédéric after the French abandon them.
August 1759.	Senecas begin to plan to oust the British from Niagara.
13 September 1759.	Wolfe defeats Montcalm on the Plains of Abraham outside Quebec. Both generals are killed.
17 September 1759.	Quebec capitulates.
28 April 1760.	After a winter of appalling losses from illness and privation (owing to Wolfe's earlier devastation), General Murray's men march out of Quebec against French besieging force and are badly defeated at Sillery Woods; but they get back within the city walls.
15 May 1760.	British relief ships arrive at Quebec. French lift their siege.
August 1760.	Amherst advances on Montreal.
7 September 1760.	Governor General Vaudreuil surrenders Canada.

After forcing the issue, General Forbes watched and guided the Easton treaty proceedings as well as he could from a distance. The time he spared for them is a gauge of their importance, for Indian relations were only part of the heavy responsibility he carried to form an army, finance it, supply it, train it, and get it intact to Fort Duquesne for an assault. To form it, he had a core of regular troops that he hoped to supplement with provincials, but the supplement required cooperation from provincial assemblies. As the men of New England, New Jersey, and New York had been pre-empted by Abercromby, Forbes had to get his recruits from Pennsylvania and points south. In this instance the South seemed to belie its reputation for martial ardor. South Carolina sent no troops. North Carolina sent 300 without equipment (which Forbes had to find for them), and many of these had deserted by the middle of July. Maryland sent none; its assembly would give no support except for defense of its own territory. Even for defense the assembly refused to pay its garrison at Fort Cumberland, so Forbes had to dig into his crown-supplied funds to prevent the fort from being abandoned. Virginia did better. After urging by Council President Blair, it provided 2,000 men and raised militia to garrison its own frontier forts. Pennsylvania recruited 2,700.[1]

These data do not imply that southerners were cowards. Rather they confirm the provincials' provinciality. Assemblies did not care to support the empire's battles when they saw no advantage to themselves. Massachusetts had become ardent to attack Acadia and Quebec because those places offered prospects of wealth and the end of Indian wars supplied and instigated from thence. Virginia's interest in the Ohio country is plain enough. South Carolinians wanted to campaign on their own colony's frontiers by attacking French settlements on Mobile Bay and the Mississippi River where conquest would have opened a vast new market for Carolina traders; but when their proposal was rejected by Pitt in favor of concentrating against Canada, the Carolinians decided to sit out the war. What was in it for them?[2]

For Pennsylvania, of course, capture of Fort Duquesne would bring pacification of the harassed back country, so it is not strange that the assembly there responded to Forbes's requirements. But the Pennsylvania assembly did not want to give Thomas Penn a free ride. As it pointed out repeatedly, Penn's vast estates would benefit most by expulsion of the French, so the assembly tried to pay part of the war's expense with a tax on lands—including the proprietary lands—to raise £100,000. Penn's ironclad instructions to his governor forbade assent to any tax on Penn property, regardless of circumstance. Denny had other objections also to the assembly's bill, but when the assemblymen removed the tax on Penn estates, he let the bill pass.[3]

The fall of Fort Duquesne

So Forbes got his money, and with much travail he got provisions and supplies. Having won against the provincials, he had still to face the French, but the troops at his advanced base at Loyalhanna literally bogged down

1. Gipson, *British Empire* 7:248–54.
2. Ibid., 7:291–92.
3. *Pa. Council Minutes* 8:63–83.

in the mud, unable to progress farther till the unseasonal rains would stop. Forbes despaired. He had to attack Duquesne before winter set in or run the risk of counterattack.[4] His army would dwindle away when his provincials' terms of enlistment expired and thousands of men departed for home. Worse than this prospect, a disaster occurred. Under orders from Colonel Bouquet, Major James Grant took a detachment of over 800 men on 11 September to reconnoitre the area around Duquesne and take prisoners if possible. When they arrived near the fort, they stumbled about through the dark night of the fourteenth and actually beat their drums at daybreak "to put the troops in spirit." Thus alarmed, French and Indian troops poured out of the fort and routed the intruders who lost a third of their men, including Grant. (As usual in these circumstances, Bouquet blamed Grant, and Grant blamed his subordinate, Major Andrew Lewis.)[5] Once more the unpredictability of this war becomes evident, for this victory cost the French more manpower than a defeat would have done. A prisoner inside the fort relates that the French and Indians quarreled over the division of the spoils, and "the Indians grew so angry that they retired from the Fort, crossed the river and returned to their villages."[6] This seems not to be a highly reliable source, but it is certain that the "far" Indian allies went off after the battle just as they had done after Braddock's defeat. Only Ohio Indians were left.[7]

If Forbes had troubles campaigning against the fort, commandant Francois-Marie Le Marchand de Lignery had even more trouble within it. Forbes's suppliers were a refractory lot, but Lignery's had been entirely cut off by Bradstreet's raid on Fort Frontenac. Lignery would soon be forced by lack of provisions to send away his militiamen from Illinois and Louisiana. Added to the loss of the western Indians, this reduction would leave a precariously small garrison of less than a thousand men to defend against the 5,000 men only forty miles off, with more coming up. Lignery tried to jolt Forbes's troops with a surprise raid on the Loyalhanna camp, 12 October, but the raiders were repulsed and withdrew, angering their Indian allies in the process.[8]

Forbes had been supervising the multitude of tasks required to establish the strongpoints guarding his supply line. He joined the vanguard at Loyalhanna, 2 November, and rejoiced to see Pisquetomen and Frederick Post

4. Forbes to Denny, 9 Sept. 1758, in [Forbes], *Writings*, 206–8; Forbes to Abercromby, 24 Oct. 1758, ibid., 244–47.

5. Gipson, *British Empire* 7:268–70; *Bouquet Papers* 2:499–505, 517–22. The quotation is Gipson's remark.

Adding to Forbes's other troubles, smallpox had broken out among the troops and Indians in his Maryland base at Fort Cumberland. *Bouquet Papers* 2:61, 89, 96.

6. *History of David Boyd* p. 36.

7. Gipson, *British Empire* 7:273.

8. Ibid., 7:273–74.

arrive with their party on the seventh. "We were gladly received" wrote Post, and next day Forbes made much of them in formal ceremony. When they went forward on the eleventh, to Kuskuski, they carried Forbes's message as well as those from the Easton treaty.[9] Lignery launched another harassing raid on the twelfth, which turned into a boon for Forbes when his men took three prisoners while chasing the French away. By the carrot and club technique, Forbes extracted information about the fort's weakness that moved him to order an immediate advance. Lignery had already come to understand that he was "in the saddest situation one could imagine."[10] The remainder of his Indians abandoned him to attend the great peace council at Kuskuski where a French captain labored in vain to disrupt the proceedings.[11] On the twenty-fourth of November, Lignery burned and blew up the fort, sent his arms and most of the garrison downriver in boats to the Illinois country, and retired up the Allegheny to Fort Machault (Franklin, Pa.). There he planned to mount a counterattack against Forbes's force when conditions became ripe.[12]

Pittsburgh founded

Forbes marched into the burning ruins next day and was sobered by what he saw. "After reviewing the Ground and Fort," he wrote, "I have great reason to be most thankful for the part that the French have acted."[13] Bouquet was more explicit: "After God the success of this Expedition is intirely due to the General, who by bringing about the Treaty of Easton, has struck the blow which has knocked the French in the head, in temporizing wisely to expect the Effects of that Treaty, in securing all his posts, and giving nothing to chance; and not yielding to the urging instances for taking Braddock's Road, which would have been our destruction."[14] Colonel Washington was more reserved: he told Virginia's new governor Francis Fauquier that, "the possession of this fort has been matter of great surprise to the whole army, and we cannot attribute it to more probable causes than those of weakness, want of provisions, and desertion of their

9. Post's second journal, 6–9 Nov. 1758, in Proud, *History of Pa.* 2, app. part 2, pp. 100–102; [Forbes], *Writings*, 252–53.

10. Gipson, *British Empire* 7:282–83; Frégault, *Canada*, 224.

11. Post's second journal, 19–29 Nov. 1758, in Proud, *History of Pa.* 2:106–24.

12. Gipson, *British Empire* 7:284; Frégault, *Canada* 257.

Bibliographic note: I have cited Gipson frequently for discrete facts, but he leaves out as much as he has put in. For him the conquest of Fort Duquesne "came about as the result of Forbes's close study of French military science" (7:285). He gives no credit to Indian diplomacy, and he does not even notice the Quaker role.

13. [Forbes], *Writings*, 264.

14. *Bouquet Papers* 2:611.

Indians."[15] In this description, no person is meritorious. Nose out of joint, Washington marched his Virginia troops back to Winchester where he resigned his commission, 9 December.[16]

It is essential to an officer's advancement in military hierarchies that blame for battles lost be shifted to shoulders other than his own, and that all credit be seized for battles won. Forbes followed the rule, with certain consequences for the historical record. "I do myself the Honour" he wrote to William Pitt, "of acquainting you that it has pleased God to crown His Majesty's Arms with Success over all His Enemies upon the Ohio, by my having obliged the Enemy to burn and abandon Fort Du Quesne . . . the Enemy . . . being abandoned by their Indians, whom I had previously engaged to leave them."[17] It may be affirmed without reservation that Forbes's accomplishment, given his physical condition and the snakepit politics he had to deal with, was almost superhuman. Yet it does seem reasonable and proper to note that some credit is due to Israel Pemberton and his Friendly Association for withdrawing those Indians from French alliance. The exhausting and hazardous journeys of Christian Frederick Post may be noticed also. Nor may we overlook the decisive influence of Pisquetomen, Keekyuscung, Tamaqua, and Shingas. They, however, held strong suspicions still about British intentions, with good reason.

Forbes's army had no sooner taken Fort Duquesne than it began falling apart. Maryland's troops at Fort Cumberland deserted "in great numbers" and Maryland's assembly refused maintenance. Provision shortages dictated sharp reduction of the forces at Fort Duquesne, renamed Pittsburgh. Forbes believed that a garrison of no more than 250 men could be subsisted through the winter. When the Virginia troops departed, he saw "a risque of being without troops if Pensilvania recalled theirs . . . I shall soon be greatly difficulted how to maintain our new conquest should the Enemy return." Forbes himself would soon have to return to Philadelphia to look after his health and interest.[18] He knew he could not keep possession of the fort's smoking ruins without the good will of the surrounding Indians, for which he would have to supply what they needed and wanted. Negotiations first, goods soon afterward. If the English did not provide trade goods, the Indians would turn by necessity to the French who were not far away. Some had not really turned away from the French; led by Chief Custaloga they still maintained ties with Lignery at Fort Machault.[19]

15. [Washington], *Writings*, ed. Fitzpatrick, 2:308.
16. Gipson is full of praise. *British Empire* 7:293–94.
17. [Forbes], *Writings*, 267, 280–82.
18. Ibid., 272, 268, 280–82, 289.
19. "Casteogain's [Custaloga's] Report," *Wilderness Chronicles of Northwestern Pennsylvania*, eds. Stevens and Kent, 134–38. Cf. Bouquet's version of the same event. *Bouquet Papers* 2:621–24.

Forbes still needed the services of Israel Pemberton. When news reached Pemberton of Forbes's victory, he sent warm congratulations on "this glorious Event . . . a greater and more compleat Victory . . . than a bloody Battle could have produc'd," and he quickly loaded four wagons with £1,400 worth of trade goods. He hoped to meet Forbes at Lancaster "to receive thy directions in what manner to employ them most Effectually."[20] But Pemberton had rushed ahead of his colleagues in the Friendly Association. They remonstrated that "bad Consequences" might ensue, and asked him to bring back his goods. Perhaps they worried about possible accusations from detractors that Quakers would be profiteering in competition with the markets set up by the provincial commissioners, but they did not specify, and Pemberton rejected their protest as bluntly as if it had come from Penn's men. Tartly, he told the Friends that none of their money had been used for his stock of goods, and his business was none of theirs. Forbes, arrived at Lancaster, applauded his "Zeal for the service" and sent orders to pass his goods along the road. (Like other correspondence between them, these letters exist only in manuscripts.)[21]

The evidence is undeniable that the pacifist and the general collaborated closely to gain peace with the Indians, but they aimed at quite different goals. For Pemberton, peace was an end in itself to be preserved perpetually by guaranteeing a boundary line between colonial and tribal territories. Forbes, however, aimed to make the Indians "our friends as long as we please to keep them." Pragmatically "those Scoundrals" had to be placated because of their capacity to do harm. Peace with them, therefore, was but a means to the end of bringing "this noble, fine Country, to all Perpetuity, under the Dominion of Great Britain."[22] Curiously both men achieved their immediate aims, and in so doing both failed in the long run. Pemberton got his boundary, but it wobbled continually westward. Forbes got Britain's dominion, but not quite in perpetuity.

Pittsburgh after conquest

What happened at "Pittsburgh" after Forbes left was a mass of confusion and conflicting purposes. The garrison dwindled to 200 men in December 1758, far too few to protect the place against the counterattack

20. Pemberton to Forbes, 2 Dec. 1758, Friendly Assn. Mss., Friends Historical Library, Swarthmore College. Assembly commissioners also sent £800 worth of goods. Forbes, *[Writings]*, 277.

21. Frdly. Assn. to Pemberton, 25 Dec. 1758, Pemberton Papers 13:20, mss., HSP; Pemberton to Friends, 15 Jan. 1759, ibid., 13:26; Forbes to Pemberton, 15 Jan. 1759, Papers of the Friendly Assn. 3:351, HC.; Parrish, *Some Chapters . . . of the Friendly Assn.* 2:110–11.

22. [Forbes], *Writings*, 283, 289–90, 265.

that Lignery at Fort Machault prepared to make. Lignery sent out a call to the "far" tribes—Potawatomis, Ottawas, Mississaugas—upon whom he could depend, but who could not appear until spring. Meantime he sent out raiding squads to probe the British supply line.

Fortunately for the garrison, Israel Pemberton's wagons appeared with the goods required to set up a market in the goods upon which peace had been premised. Apparently some other free enterprisers came also—the usual ragtag of rum dealers and the like—but the substantial trade authorized under supervision of the assembly's commissioners came into existence very slowly. When it started, the commissioners were surprised to find that George Croghan, as deputy superintendent of Indian affairs, had "assumed a power of licensing such persons to trade with the Indians at Pittsburg, as he thinks proper; and also to fix the prices."[23] They complained to the governor that Croghan's prices were more favorable to the Indians than theirs. The same news stirred Pemberton, but instead of going to the powerless governor, Pemberton used his undiminished influence with Forbes's successor, Brigadier General Stanwix, and obtained an order for Croghan to cease and desist. Whereupon Pemberton sent £3,000 more of goods. Again these were on his own account; he held up the Friendly Association's at Carlisle until reconciliation could be worked out with the "sour'd" provincial commissioners.[24]

Croghan took charge of political negotiations with the Indians, who were far from satisfied as they saw Pittsburgh's garrison increase to 350 men in January 1759. It was well for that outpost that the Indians remained ignorant of William Pitt's orders to build a new fort strong enough "to maintain His Majesty's Subjects in the undisputed Possession of the Ohio."[25]

Regrettably, even the trusted Quakers contributed to the deception practiced on the Indians (whether wittingly or otherwise does not appear). Pisquetomen came in July to Pemberton's storekeeper James Kenny and wanted to know "what the English or the General Meant by Coming here with a Great Army." As Pisquetomen and his brothers had been the very architects of the peace, his question betokened massive unrest. Kenny's answer may have been strictly true, but it was certainly misleading. Quakers knew only "what we hear'd," he responded, adding "which we believ'd to be true." This was that the army's purpose was to drive off the French

23. Hanna, *Wilderness Trail* 2:20; James Kenny, Journal to the Westward, 1758–59, mss., 23 June, 26 June, 6 July 1759, HSP. Printed, ed. John W. Jordan, *Pa. Mag. of Hist. and Biog.* 32(1913), 395–449; journal for 1761–63 printed ibid., 1–47, 152–201.

24. Pemberton to Lightfoot, 19 July 1759, Pemberton Papers 13:90, mss., HSP. Stanwix requested goods from Pemberton, 2 July 1759, observing, "I know of no body . . . I can depend on so well." Frnds. Hist. Lib., Swarthmore College.

25. Gipson, *British Empire* 7:332–33.

and protect the trade, "and when they were subdued the Army would be Called away Home."[26] This was not what William Pitt intended, but it was what Pisquetomen wanted to hear, so he departed mollified, unaware that even as the interview took place, General Stanwix was assembling an army of 3,500 men for Ohio duty and complaining that lack of provincial support prevented him from making up the full number of 7,200 men that he wanted.[27] That secret could not be kept long, but events moved swiftly now to put the British in control.

Iroquois intrigue

An understanding of subsequent events requires attention to intertribal relations as well as those between the tribes and the empires. The whole situation was described by Commandant Hugh Mercer to General Forbes, 8 January 1759, in a report so perceptive and so concise that it merits quotation in full.

> I have Sent inclosed for your Excellencies perusal, the minutes of Conferences held here with nine Chiefs of the Six Nations, Shawneese and Delaware Indians.
>
> What the Chiefs of the Six Nations delivered by themselves in private appeared to be of Such Consequence that I have lost no time in communicating it, and as Captain Ward is the only Person here, that understands any thing of their Language, he accompanies two of these Chiefs as Interpreter.
>
> The Intelligence they bring is, that twelve considerable Nations of Indians, inhabiting on the other Side of Lake Erie are intirely in the French Interest, and engaged by them to cut off the Six Nations as Allies to the English.
>
> This Stroke they have reason to dread, as they are by no means that powerfull and Warlike People they were on our first Settling America: and should the Shawanese and Delawares Join in the Confederacy against them, their ruin would soon be compleated, unless a very powerfull aid is afforded them by the English.
>
> This Support from us they come now to Supplicate but are obliged to cover this design of waiting on your Excellency, as well from the Shawanese and Delawares, as from the French, for they observe too great an intimacy Still Subsists between these. At the Same time they appear to be convinced that the French may be easily drove from this Country; that one or two Defeats will make their Indians drop their Alliance, and universally join the English.
>
> The Strength of the Ennemy at Wenango [Fort Machault] does not amount to one Hundert; at the Carrying Place, and Presque'Isle both the Garrisons don't make up that number: Their Magazines of Provisions, and arms is forming a little

26. Kenny's journal, 24 July 1759. Pisquetomen reminded Kenny that "Quakers always should Speak truth and not Lye (the Old man some times Calls himself a Quaker)."

27. Gipson, *British Empire* 7:333–34.

above Kuskuski, as most convenient for assembling the Lake Indians, to fall down on this Place. They may from thence move in Concert with a body from Vinango if they propose bringing artillery, for the two Places are about an equal distance from us.

Not a word of this we have heard from the Delawares, tho' Hundreds of them from that Place have been here, living upon us at a very great Expense of Provisions, and pretending the utmost friendship; they have alarmed us by their account of the force at Vinango ready to fall down the River, but carefully concealed every Circumstance that would make their own vilainy, and treachery appear.

It is however necessary to Keep fair with them, till Such a time as a Sufficient Force is Sent to defeat any designs the Ennemy can form on this River: Then and not before, the Delawares and Shawnee Indians, from pretended, will become real Friends. I mentioned in my letter to Col. Bouquet the necessity of Sending an Interpreter here, with a large quantity of Indian Goods, the Constant Sollicitations of all our Friends obliges me again to repeat it, as a measure equally necessary to gain the Indian Interest, as a Body of Troops is to Secure the Country.

Give me leave to hint to your Excellency that these Chiefs of the Six Nations expect some genteel Presents, rather to testify the generosity of the English to their Country men at their Return home, than to satisfy their own avarice.

I am &ca,
H. Mercer.[28]

This is the plainest speaking to emerge from the welter of intrigue at Pittsburgh. Among other things, it explains the rumors about Iroquois ostensible anger against the British—they needed "cover" for their "design." More than any single factor, it pictures the universal distrust of each party for all the others, their temporary interdependence, and their discordant purposes. Such volatility could not long hold to a stable state, but the British were lucky this time, and for once it was by their own doing. Aided, to be sure, by Iroquois policy.

The Iroquois at Niagara

Since the beginning of the war, a main British goal had been the capture of Fort Niagara, the guardian of New France's lifeline to the west. Braddock and Shirley had it on their campaign plans. Bradstreet thirsted frustratedly for the assignment, but Loudoun and Abercromby would not trust their troops that far through the territory of the Iroquois whose loyalties were so doubtful. Now, in 1759, General Amherst deemed conditions ripe to march against Niagara as William Pitt had proposed. More than Pitt's urging moved the prudent commander. What finally convinced

28. *Bouquet Papers* 3:25–26.

Amherst, who never stirred two inches without massing his forces, was the turned-about desire of the Iroquois League.

That this arose partly as response to the fall of Fort Duquesne can hardly be doubted. Colonel Mercer's letter, quoted above, describes Iroquois anxiety about the French-allied western Indians. Johnson later confirmed it: the Iroquois were "but a handfull" in comparison with those western tribes.[29] In a more general way, all Indians were disgusted with French inability to supply enough trade goods "at a reasonable price, or good in quality."[30] What was to be done?

The Senecas concluded that the time had come to drive the French out of their territory, a process that required the destruction of Fort Niagara; but long experience had shown that Indians could not capture a properly built European fort except by subterfuge. Niagara's commandant Pouchot was competent and alert, and had loyal Indians in service, so the prospects of successful subterfuge were dim. The alternative was for the Iroquois to sic on the British to do what they wanted done, but could not do by themselves. Johnson quickly caught wind of something stirring. In mid-February he proposed an expedition against Niagara "thro' the Country of the Six Nations," giving assurances that he could "prevail" upon them to join it.[31]

This would be an astonishing tribute to Johnson's powers of persuasion (as he meant it to be), for only three months earlier his fondest hope had gone no further than to keep the Iroquois from joining the French.[32] He had not suddenly acquired new powers during the intervening months. Rather, the French-occupied Senecas had observed how the Delawares had cooperated with Forbes to get rid of French occupation at the forks of the Ohio. "Last winter," they told Johnson in April 1759, they had determined "among themselves" to turn against the French, and now they asked that the English "proceed to the reduction" of Fort Niagara "with all possible speed." They promised to assist.[33]

Johnson's style of reporting has gained for himself the credit for a decision he gladly accepted. He told Amherst that the Indians had accepted the war hatchet "which *I* threw down to them in Your Name," and he told the board of trade, "*I* could not only prevail on those Indians of the

29. Johnson to lords of trade, 17 May 1759, *N.Y. Col. Docs.* 7:236.
30. Oneida chief Conochquieson, treaty minutes, 18 Apr. 1759, ibid., 7:390.
31. Johnson to Amherst, 16 Feb. 1759, *Johnson Papers* 3:19–20.
32. Johnson to Abercromby, 10 Nov. 1758, ibid., 10:55.
33. Treaty Minutes, *N.Y. Col. Docs.* 7:391. In May, Niagara's commandant Pouchot picked up a rumor that "Some Iroquois told the Hurons . . . that they had resolved to keep their country quiet, and that they wished first to drive off the French, who were the bravest, and then the English." He challenged Iroquois at Niagara "who denied having ever thought of such an explanation." Pouchot, *Memoir*, tr. Hough, 1:148–49.

five Nations . . . but *I* could also prevent many if not most of those Northern and Western Indians who form the Ottawawa confederacy from joining the French against us, and which they have hitherto done."[34] To mix metaphors,it was sheer moonshine but good press. Johnson was actually so uncertain at the beginning of his April conference with the Iroquois that he complained of their attitudes. "We know, and you know, that some of every one of the Six Nations have privately spilt our Blood . . . we have great reason to be suspicious and provoked," and he wanted to know why they had taken eighty days to respond to his summons that had specified a meeting date two months earlier. For once the chiefs scanted ceremony and got straight to the point. Astonished Johnson heard his protégé, Oneida sachem Conochquieson, declare that all the warriors of all the nations were "ready to join and revenge both Your Blood and ours upon the French." But Johnson recovered quickly. Next day, he responded that "All that remains for me to do at present is to offer You this General's Hatchet, which I now do," and the war dance began.[35] This was enough to satisfy Amherst. He set the campaign in motion.

Amherst gave command to Brigadier General John Prideaux, an experienced officer newly arrived from England, and made Johnson his second in command. The troops and warriors mobilized at Oswego where a flotilla of small craft awaited to carry them near to Niagara. They arrived, 7 July, and promptly next day presented a demand for the fort's surrender. Commandant Pouchot adopted the debonair attitude customary in such cases. "He did not understand English," and both sides settled down for the siege. Pouchot, however, did understand English armament and numbers very well, and his interior apprehensions belied his exterior confidence. Though his was the strongest French fort at the time, the besiegers had plenty of artillery and they greatly outnumbered his garrison. Pouchot quickly came to understand that this English army knew what it was about. A zigzag trench opened closer to the fort every day; it was only a matter of time until the English would get close enough to mine the walls and batter through.[36]

Pouchot also understood his business. Not being addicted to futile heroic gestures, he sent out a call for help to Lignery at Fort Machault who had just succeeded in massing an army of more than a thousand men for his campaign against Pittsburgh. Everything was ready there. Lignery had danced the war dance, and he would have been on the march except for a protest from two Iroquois warriors that delayed the undertaking one day, just time enough for Pouchot's plea to arrive. Lignery immediately can-

34. *Johnson Papers* 3:27–30; *N.Y. Col. Docs.* 7:376. Italics added.
35. Ibid., 7:381, 386, 389.
36. Gipson, *British Empire* 7:344–48; Pouchot's journal of the siege, *N.Y. Col. Docs.* 10:979.

celed his own expedition, turned his men around, and hurried off to succor Niagara. Doing so, he very efficaciously saved Pittsburgh.[37]

Always there were the Iroquois. How should one interpret the action of those mysterious unnamed warriors who delayed Lignery until he was obliged to abandon his project against Pittsburgh? Did they know about the English advance on Niagara in spite of Amherst's strenuous efforts to keep it secret until the last moment? Were they simply stalling? Were they trying to help the English at Pittsburgh or the French at Niagara? They appeared as enigmatically as messengers from the ancient Greek gods, and they disappeared afterward without trace. Certainly their errand was every bit as decisive as though it had been divinely ordained.

The Iroquois at Niagara engaged in maneuvers almost equally inexplicable. From within the fort, Seneca chief Kaendaé opened negotiations with the Iroquois in the English camp, and Iroquois good will was so essential that Johnson permitted the council to be held in his own presence—or so Kaendaé reported to Commandant Pouchot. According to Pouchot's memoir, Kaendaé "reproached" Johnson "with having plunged his Nation into bad business. Johnson smiled, and took this reproach as a joke." But it could hardly have been funny when Johnson's Iroquois cohorts announced "we abandon the English army" and said they would prove it by going a distance off to camp by themselves. Johnson's surviving papers do not report the incident—they are remarkably taciturn about the whole Niagara expedition—but the Iroquois did move off to a place called La Belle Famille.[38]

So far, Pouchot seemed to be ahead, but the Iroquois made their gesture more dubious by reciprocally asking all the Iroquois within the fort to join them at La Belle Famille. And the Mahicans with them sent a wampum belt to the Ottawas and other Algonquians to withdraw also from the fort. Though the belt was Mahican, its message was the one formed by the Iroquois League at the war's beginning: "leave the Whites to fight." Pouchot considered these efforts to steal his warriors "to be inspired by the English," and he cut off further negotiations."[39]

Johnson's pen is mightier than the sword

An accidental shot from one of his own guns killed General Prideaux, 19 July, whereupon Johnson assumed command over protest by Lieuten-

37. Severance, *An Old Frontier of France* 2:313–14.

38. Pouchot, *Memoir*, tr. Hough, 11–14 July 1759, 1:171–78.

39. Pouchot's journal, *N.Y. Col. Docs.* 10:982. Pouchot's *Memoir* seems to be the source for this journal. I took notes from them at different times, and the rare *Memoir* is not accessible at time of writing.

ant Colonel Eyre Massey who, as a regular, believed he outranked Johnson. While this dispute still simmered, Lignery's relief party appeared on the horizon, and the British prepared to intercept it. What happened then depends a little on whose account one reads. Pouchot got only a confused view from his battlements. Johnson wrote a masterpiece of ambiguity which could be, and has been, interpreted as putting him in the midst of the fray where he definitely was not; his device was the deft omission of names of officers who really were there, especially rival Eyre Massey.[40] Lieutenant Moncrieff, who had been aide-de-camp to General Prideaux, commented that Johnson had "made a disposition" of the forces, putting them under Massey's command.[41] Johnson also used the phrase "made a disposition" without mentioning Massey. This careful phrase was transformed by Johnson's biographer William L. Stone, who wrote that Johnson "marched out with his army to meet the enemy."[42] By far the most specific and detailed report is that of Captain James De Lancey (son of New York's governor) which is corroborated by Pouchot insofar as the latter could see what happened.[43]

In Captain De Lancey's report, we see him, 23 July, setting up a barricade across the road leading to the fort. Next day he forwarded the news of Lignery's approach to Johnson at headquarters, on which he was given reinforcements. Lieutenant Colonel Massey arrived with more men and took charge. Was this by his own volition? No orders to Massey appear in Johnson's orderly book. Johnson stuck to his command post at headquarters. The Indians acted independently of all and sundry officers except their own chiefs. About a hundred took up positions by the side of the road in position to outflank the advancing attackers. Some others, however, "went to the Enemy's Indians to prevail on them not to fight. But the French told them, they did not want to fight with our Indians but with us. On this our Indians returned and told us, the Enemy was coming, which they soon did with a very great noise and shouting." It looks as though the French hoped to repeat their success against Braddock's men on the road before Fort Duquesne, but this time the British were not surprised, did not panic, and stopped the advance with volley fire. De Lancey led a bayonet charge that routed the enemy, and the flanking Indians descended upon the fleeing French to complete the rout. De Lancey

40. Johnson to Amherst, 25 July 1759, *Johnson Papers* 3:108–10; Gipson, *British Empire* 7:354n93.

41. Coventry to De Lancey, 2 Aug. 1759, in *The Seven Years War in Canada, 1756–1763*, comp. Sigmund Samuel (Toronto: Ryerson Press, 1934), 72.

42. William L. Stone, *The Life and Times of Sir William Johnson, Bart.*, 2 vols. (Albany: J. Munsell, 1865), 2:97.

Bibliographic note: Stone's biography generally is so unreliable that no use of it has been made for this study.

43. *N.Y. Col. Docs.* 7:402–3; 10:988.

estimated that the attackers had numbered 850 French and 350 Indians. "We killed 200 and took 100 prisoners," among whom were five senior French officers. (Of all this there is not a word in Johnson's orderly book or any of his reports. The orderly book records only his thanks to "the troops"—anonymous.)[44]

A day later, beleaguered Pouchot capitulated—to Johnson, naturally, whose name became very prominent indeed in consequence. The Iroquois were content: at very small cost, they had not only achieved their objective of driving the French away, but had managed the affair so as to get much of the credit for doing so. Yet this was only the first step toward their ultimate goal, which was to drive all Europeans out of their territory. Captive, and transethnic adoptee, Mary Jemison heard that the Senecas began to plan to oust the British within a month after the French surrendered.[45]

Quebec besieged

Pitt's grand strategy for 1759 had aimed in three directions, allowing necessary discretion to commanders in the field. He had listed Niagara as a desirable objective for Amherst, and Ticonderoga as a definite one, but against Quebec he concentrated an amphibious force that was effectively independent under Major General James Wolfe and Vice Admiral Charles Saunders. This great force ascended the hazardous St. Lawrence without losing a single ship—a splendid display of seamanship—and assembled before Quebec, 25 June, two weeks before Prideaux and Johnson appeared at Niagara.[46] After that superior achievement, however,it accomplished very little during the next two and a half months except to harass the countryside and bombard the city. Montcalm turned back Wolfe's probes of the city's defenses. One achievement was substantial: the navy sustained itself intact against massive French assaults with fire ships and rafts chained together—sailors in small boats towed the floating conflagrations to shore where they burned out uselessly. The seamen were jaunty about it. "Damme, Jack," cried one to his mate, "did'st thee ever take hell in tow before?"[47]

44. *Johnson Papers* 3:81.
45. James E. Seaver, *A Narrative of . . . Mrs. Mary Jemison*, 55.
46. Gipson, *British Empire* 7:375–80.
47. Knox, *An Historical Journal* 1:445.
Bibliographic note: This is a basic source by a military engineer with professional expertise and classic condescension to colonials. I can't resist his account of a crisis when his transport was in danger of running on the rocks. The master, a devout Massachusetts man, "instantly fell upon his knees, crying out,—'what shall we do? I vow, I fear we shall be all lost, let us go to prayers; what can we do, dear Jonathan?'—Jonathan went forward, muttering to him-

For Wolfe, as William J. Eccles has observed, Canada presented the same problems, to be solved by the same means, as Scotland during the Jacobite rising.[48] Genocide was not unthinkable. John Prebble reports that when Wolfe was stationed in Scotland in 1751, "he believed that lingering resistance among the clans might be finally crushed by a contrived massacre, that the deliberate sacrifice of one of his patrols in the killing of the Macphersons' chief would justify the extirpation of the whole clan in reprisal. 'Would you believe that I am so bloody?' he asked his friend William Rickson." As events were to demonstrate, his coyness was only assumed; Wolfe *was* bloody.[49]

So much romantic gush has been spilled over his Quebec campaign that a cool appraisal seems like an attack on motherhood; but many mothers are bad ones, and Quebec was not won by brilliant tactics. After several futile efforts to penetrate the city's defenses, Wolfe turned to terror. His cannon played on the city day and night, on its residential areas more than its military defenses.[50] Wolfe was perfectly clear that no military purpose was served by this bombardment because "the upper batteries cannot be affected by the [fire from the] ships," and the destruction of the lower, residential town gave little advantage to "the business of an assault."[51]

He ordered scouting parties to "burn and lay waste the country."[52] For Wolfe, this was already a familiar procedure: he had previously devastated the Gaspé region while Amherst besieged Louisbourg.[53] Wolfe professed humanitarianism toward women and children, but it did not stop him

self, 'Do—I vow, Ebenezer, I don't know what we shall do, any more than thyself; when fortunately one of our soldiers (who was a thorough-bred seaman . . .) hearing and seeing the helpless state of mind which our poor New-England-men were under, and our sloop driving towards the shore, called out, "Why, d[am]n your eyes and limbs, down with her sails, and let her drive a[rs]e foremost; what the devil signifies your praying and canting now?'—Ebenezer, quickly taking the hint, called to Jonathan to lower the sails, saying, 'he vowed he believed that young man's advice was very good, but wished he had not delivered it so profanely.' . . . the soldier gave directions, and, seizing the helm, we soon recovered ourselves, cleared the streight, and drove into the bay stern foremost." Ibid., 1:283–84.

48. W. J Eccles, *France in America*, New American Nation Series (New York: Harper and Row, 1972), 200. Angus Calder thought that "this priggish young man . . . despised most sections of the human race," and after setbacks, Wolfe "began to seek solace in cruelty. He had not served under 'Butcher' Cumberland for nothing." *Revolutionary Empire: The Rise of the English-Speaking Empires from the Fifteenth Century to the 1780's* (New York: E. P. Dutton, 1981), 607, 610.

49. Prebble, *Mutiny*, 94. Wolfe was also a little strange. See Gipson, *British Empire* 7:374n8.

50. Knox, *Historical Journal* 2:8–9, 11, 60–61, 133n3, 135.

51. Wolfe to Pitt, 2 Sept. 1759, *Gentleman's Magazine* 29 (1759), 467, 469.

52. Knox, *Historical Journal* 1:438; "Copy of a Letter from an Officer to his Friend," *Gentleman's Magazine* 29 (1759), 556; *An Accurate and Authentic Journal of the Siege of Quebec, 1759* (London: J. Robinson, 1759), 18–19.

53. Details of these ravages in mss. [Henry Fletcher?], [Seven Years' War Journal of the proceedings of the 35th regiment of Foot . . .] British North America, the Caribbean and England, Aug. 1757–Dec. 1765, JCB. Service casualties of this regiment were so great that only 100 survived to return to England. See also Knox, *Historical Journal* 1:275.

from sending out the ruthless rangers who killed everyone they could reach.[54] More directly he threatened to Montcalm that "if the enemy presume to send down any more fire-rafts, they are to be made fast to two particular transports, in which are *all* the Canadian and other prisoners, in order that they may perish by their own base inventions."[55] Wolfe's mercy extended only to surrenderers.

Naturally, the civilian population wanted to escape Wolfe's fury by capitulation, but Montcalm also understood the uses of terror—against his own people as well as enemies. When Quebec residents suggested surrender, "he threatened them with the savages."[56] This was Acadia and Abbé Le Loutre all over again.

By mid-September, Wolfe despaired of winning, and ordered a general attack that appears to have been for cosmetic reasons; he had to defend himself back in England against the inevitable criticism that he had not even tried. Admiral Byng had been executed on such a charge.

We know that Wolfe won after all, and it might seem that he was supremely lucky, but something more than luck contributed to the outcome. Certainly tribute is due to Admiral Saunders and his seamen, who performed flawlessly. Something should be said for Wolfe's perfectionist training of his soldiers. The very qualities that were useless in wilderness warfare served admirably in set battle where disciplined volley fire was essential. And Wolfe's junior officers were steady, competent professionals.

On the other side, French resources had been strained to the utmost by the prolonged effort to defend against forces many times as great as New France could possibly mobilize. A sort of domino effect had set in, almost like the old chant, "for want of a nail the shoe was lost, for want of a shoe the horse was lost . . ." Without attributing determinative causation, let us consider how each event in the series created conditions favorable to continuing the succession. Bradstreet seized Fort Frontenac and the supplies necessary to maintain Indian alliance in the west, and a French ship was wrecked carrying Indian trade goods to make up the shortfall. Indian unrest grew to the point where the Ohio tribes sought peace at Easton, whereupon Duquesne had to be abandoned. Pouchot sent troops from Niagara to the expedition to retake Duquesne, and thereby so weakened himself that he could not effectively defend Niagara. Niagara fell while

54. Examples: British North America mss. cited n53, entry of 6 Mar. 1759; Knox, *Historical Journal* 1:410. Knox interpreted his reported atrocity as proceeding "from that cowardice and barbarity which seems so natural to a native of America, whether of Indian or European extraction." Then he went back to his cannonading.

55. Knox, *Historical Journal* 1:445.

56. Ibid., 1:441. French regulars were intermixed with Canadian troops and ordered to shoot "any of them that should betray the least timidity." Ibid., 2:6n.

Wolfe stood before Quebec. The losses of Duquesne and Niagara cut off all French communication to the west, which meant also that supplies and manpower could not be summoned to the relief of Quebec; and the news of Niagara's fall, which came in the midst of the siege, cast a pall of gloom on the city.

Ticonderoga falls

While Wolfe hammered at Quebec, Amherst started to march against Ticonderoga, and the French were forced to shorten their overextended lines as Montcalm had long advocated. Astonished and delighted, Amherst marched into the ruins of Ticonderoga, and of Fort St. Frédéric at Crown Point also, without firing a shot. All of Lake Champlain came into British possession.[57] The resources of its countryside were lost, and none of the men stationed at Isle-aux-Noix for last-ditch defense could be rushed to the defense of Quebec. In preceding years, Montcalm's trump card had been his ability to move men swiftly about from one threatened point to another: now he was pinned down and isolated except from Montreal, which could not be stripped of the means for its own defense.

The Plains of Abraham

Nonetheless Quebec's position was so strong that so long as Montcalm fought from behind his walls and trenches he seemed invincible. Technically, Quebec was in the classic European mode of sieges. The British force, though mighty, was not large enough to surround the city completely and thus cut off its supplies, which, though minimal, were still enough to keep the defenders alive. What Wolfe had to do was to draw Montcalm out into the open for a battle in which the fear-inspired discipline of British soldiery could prevail over the individualism learned by Canadians in wilderness fighting. Montcalm refused to give up his defensive advantage until the thirteenth of September, when luck at last played into Wolfe's hand. It should be known as "the day of errors," according to Guy Frégault whose phrase recalls the axiom familiar to chess players that games are lost rather than won.[58] Wolfe's decisions were potentially disastrous, Montcalm's actually so.

Stripped of the aura of romance, what happened can be told briefly. Wolfe landed a detachment in the middle of the dark night at l'Anse au

57. Gipson, *British Empire* 7:360–68.
58. Frégault, *Canada*, 253.

Foulon, upstream of the city. They fooled a sentry in the dark with a cock and bull story by an officer who spoke fluent French. After landing, glamorously (and foolishly) led by Wolfe himself, they scrambled up the high bluff, deluded another sentry and established a position. Even then, Wolfe was so unsure of himself that he sent orders to prevent landing of more troops. His behavior, together with his previous despondency, suggests intention to seek heroic death with minimum sacrifice of other men, thus to overcome the stigma of failure.[59]

Never was a general more fortunate in his choice of officers: Adjutant General Isaac Barré simply disregarded Wolfe's order and continued to send up more soldiers. As Gipson has commented, Wolfe "was permitted to obtain his objective and undying fame as the result of disobedience to his orders on the part of those who were eager to second his efforts."[60]

When the news of Wolfe's upstream landing reached Montcalm, he refused at first to believe it. His rigidly fixed idea was that Wolfe would strike again downstream of the city at a place called Beaumont, and in fact Wolfe had wanted to do just that but had been dissuaded by the unanimous opinion of his senior officers. Montcalm, therefore, was ready at the wrong place. When he finally became convinced that the British really had mounted up that "impossible" bluff, he rushed to face them on the Plains of Abraham, where he compounded being at the wrong place by doing the wrong things. He might have charged Wolfe's troops while their numbers were small, but he waited until they increased to formidable size and shifted to a more favorable position. Then, instead of waiting for his own reinforcements—Bougainville was on the way from Montreal with 3,000 men and was due to arrive in a couple of hours—Montcalm ordered the charge. His wilderness fighters rushed forward in motley formation, formidable as individuals, disorganized as a mass. The British waited until their volley could take maximum effect, fired into the screaming mass, and threw it into utter confusion; then fixed bayonets and countercharged in an implacable, inexorably advancing line. In fifteen minutes the battle was over.[61] Wolfe and Montcalm were both fatally wounded. When Bougainville came on the scene, he saw that the battle had been decided and that British troops held the high ground. He pulled back. Four days later, another of New France's dominos went down when the city surrendered.[62]

59. Editor Doughty comments that Wolfe, "contrary to the advice of one of his officers, had that morning donned a new uniform, and it is probable that he was particularly conspicuous and an easy mark." Knox, *Historical Journal* 2:115n.

60. Gipson, *British Empire* 7:415–16.

61. Ibid., 7:416–18.

62. That Wolfe seems to have had a death wish is further evidenced by his placing himself in his bright new uniform, "at the head of Bragg's and the Louisbourg grenadiers, advancing with their bayonets." Who ever heard of a major general leading a bayonet charge? Town-

A French victory too late

In effect, the war in America had been decided. The French still held Montreal and the Richelieu River up to Isle-aux-Noix at the bottom of Lake Champlain. (The stream flows northward; on a Mercator map projection the position appears to be at the top of the lake.) Perhaps Amherst might have rolled over the remaining strongpoints, but he chose instead to consolidate, and New France's leaders opted for a desperate defense in the forlorn hope of saving something in the peace negotiations, but events elsewhere prolonged hostilities. Winter passed uneventfully except for privation, and the French took heart from the departure of Wolfe's fleet and most of his troops before the St. Lawrence froze over. They tried to retake the city, not without hope of success because of its weak garrison.

There was justification for their hope. The very strategy of devastation by which Wolfe had weakened Quebec's defenses now weakened the British garrison left behind under General James Murray. An officer reported that "near one third of the houses were reduced to ashes, and what remained were so shattered by the cannon during our besieging it, that very few were fit to be inhabited."[63] In consequence, Commandant Murray could not strengthen the city's fortifications because he had to put his men to building shelter against the Canadian winter, and to fall and haul timber for firewood from the surrounding forests. This was hazardous work as the firewood parties were prey for Indians still faithful to the French.

Another consequence for the garrison was poor nutrition because of Wolfe's destruction of outlying farms and villages. Forced to fall back on a diet of salt pork, the soldiers succumbed to disease in appalling numbers. Fewer than 250 men had died during the entire siege and assault on Quebec, but a thousand died of scurvy in the triumphant garrison; and General Murray reported to Pitt that more than 2,000 of the rest became "unfit for any service." Thus, when he marched out in May 1760 to try to spoil the mounting French effort to retake Quebec, he had lost half his strength before the battle began. He was badly defeated by overwhelming French odds, and he lost another thousand men killed or wounded—a third of the troops still fit for service.[64]

But he was lucky. Hasty retreat to the shelter of the city's walls enabled

shend to Pitt, 20 Sept. 1759, in *Gentleman's Magazine* 29(1759), 472. On the surrender, see the slur in Pouchot's *Memoir* (1:220): "The commandant of Quebec could not refuse the solicitations of the inhabitants, who sought rather to save their goods than their country."

63. *Gentleman's Magazine* 30(1760), 311.

64. Alfred Le Roy Burt, *The Old Province of Quebec* (Toronto: Ryerson Press, 1933), 15–16; Murray to Pitt, 25 May 1760, in *Gentleman's Magazine* 60 (1960), 295–96.

him to hold out just long enough until a new British fleet came up the river to his rescue.[65]

Farther south, Amherst at last felt that he had consolidated enough and decided to seek battle. He organized a systematic, three-pronged campaign against Montreal from Oswego, Quebec, and Lake Champlain. Against such force, Governor Vaudreuil could mount only token defense. His men struggled until Amherst reached Montreal and the British vise could no longer be evaded. Vaudreuil surrendered Canada on 7 September 1760.[66]

65. Gipson, *British Empire* 7:440–43.
66. Ibid., 7: ch. 14.

Chapter 19 ❧ *UNRAVELING*

One good treaty is worth ten good fights. These fighting fellows lose all on the treaties that they gain on the fights.

George Bernard Shaw, *Saint Joan*

George III and Bute were anxious to have the war off their hands in order to break the power of the great Whig houses, and consequently the treaty of peace was inadequate in many points.

George Louis Beer, *British Colonial Policy*

Chronology

26 November 1758.	After the Easton treaty, Iroquois and Delawares renew Covenant Chain links.
28–29 November 1758.	Western Delawares tell Frederick Post that the British should retire east of the Appalachians.
5 December 1758.	Western Delawares tell Colonel Bouquet to take his troops back east, but the British prepare to build and garrison Fort Pitt.
January 1759.	Iroquois and Fort Pitt commandant Mercer conspire to delude Delawares and Shawnees.
2 February 1759.	Franklin files petition with the privy council for enquiry into Penns' conduct of Indian affairs.
March 1759.	Franklin arranges publication of Charles Thomson's *Alienation of the Delawares and Shawnese.*
July 1759.	Pennsylvania assembly, resentful of Penns' propaganda against them, seize the Penns' land office records.
25 October 1760.	Great Britain's king George II dies. Grandson George III mounts the throne.
5 October 1761.	William Pitt resigns from the ministry.
3 November 1761.	John Stuart, third earl of Bute, becomes prime minister.
January 1762.	Bute declares war on Spain.
May 1762.	Duke of Newcastle resigns from the ministry.
May 1762.	The Susquehannah Company sends settlers into the Wyoming Valley. They conflict with Teedyuscung's Delawares residing there by agreement of Iroquois and Pennsylvania.
June 1762.	Sir William Johnson holds a hearing at Easton, as instructed by the privy council, on Teedyuscung's charge of fraud in the Walking Purchase. After much palaver, Teedyuscung is paid off and withdraws his charge.

January 1763.	Thomas Penn offers gratitude and alliance to Johnson.
10 February 1763.	By the peace treaty at Paris, France cedes Canada to Britain, and Spain cedes Florida. France compensates Spain by ceding Louisiana to Spain.
8 April 1763.	Lord Bute resigns from the ministry under heavy opprobrium.
19 April 1763.	Unidentified arsonists, probably the Susquehannah Company's men, burn the cabins of the Delaware Indians at Wyoming. They flee. Teedyuscung is burned to death in his cabin.

Victory meant different things to different people. The governing class in England had suppressed its differences in the struggle against the foreign foe, but the triumph of arms brought a reversion to normal politics. Some statesmen worried that France would fight on if the terms of peace were too drastic, and then the great costs of war would continue to mount. In the words of Pitt's biographer, "the fear became common that even complete victory might leave England bankrupt. The dissatisfaction thus caused centred on Pitt."[1]

Pitt wanted to break France's power completely, but he could not get his way. It was agreed that France would have to give up some part of its empire, but which? Pitt summarized in characteristically colorful terms: "Some are for keeping Canada; some Guadeloupe; who will tell me which I shall be hanged for not keeping?"[2]

King George III

In hopes of salvaging something out of British dissension, the French fought on elsewhere than in America. The crisis intensified in 1760 when George II died and was succeeded by grandson George III whose policies took a new turn. As heir apparent he had learned how the great Whig families had governed Britain since George's family had been brought from Hanover to reign. Though he conceived himself as a Whig in principles, he determined to restore the royal prerogative to full strength, and to rule as well as reign.

1. Basil Williams, *Life of Pitt* 2:57.

2. Ibid., 2:82. An influential pamphleteer suggested that Parliament should let the ministry handle peace negotiations without a debate, thus to avoid factionalism. This was hotly opposed, and according to the editors of *Franklin Papers* (9:47–48), "at least sixty-five pamphlets had been published on this one topic, besides uncounted articles and letters in the newspapers." One of the most important was by Benjamin Franklin. [Anonymous], *A Letter Addressed to Two Great Men, on the Prospect of Peace; And on the Terms necessary to be insisted upon in the Negociation* (London: A. Millar, 1760); Benjamin Franklin, *The Interest of Great Britain Considered, With Regard to her Colonies, And the Acquisitions of Canada and Guadaloupe* (1760), in *Franklin Papers* (with informative headnote) 9:47–100.

Three requirements stood in his way. He had to break Pitt's power, to make peace with France, and to beat the Whigs at their own game of controlling Parliament by means called variously "patronage" by its advocates, "corruption" by its opponents. George concentrated immediately on Pitt. Through his favorite John Stuart, earl of Bute, George drove Pitt out of office in 1761, despite Pitt's enormous popularity, but did not thereby solve the problems of peacemaking.[3] On the contrary, the war widened as Spain soon came into it on France's side. Victories by the British navy quickly reduced Spain's belligerence, whereupon the questions of peace re-emerged in even greater complexity.

The West Indian island of Guadeloupe seemed a great prize because of its cheap production of great quantities of sugar, far more valuable than the tobacco staple of Virginia and Maryland, but Britain's West Indian planters lobbied fiercely against the introduction within the empire's closed commercial system of a competitor that could undersell them.[4] On the other side were aristocrats like the duke of Bedford who worried more about the power of the colonials than that of the French. Bedford objected to the acquisition of Canada *and* Guadeloupe because "we have too much already—more than we know what to do with." More ominously, "the neighbourhood of the French to our North American colonies was . . . the greatest security for their dependence on the mother-country, which I feel will be slighted by them when their apprehension of the French is removed."[5]

Peace between Britain and France

What probably decided the issue was the general concern for naval power.[6] On this score, Pitt and Bute could see eye to eye; and it was clear to everyone that seamen were made from fishermen. Pitt would not tolerate continuance of a French presence in the fisheries off Newfoundland and along the continental shelf at the mouth of the St. Lawrence. Nearly

3. G. F. Russell Barker, "Stuart, John, Third Earl of Bute (1713–1792)" in *Dict. Nat. Biog.* 55:93–94.

4. The arguments are reviewed in William L. Grant, "Canada Versus Guadeloupe, an Episode of the Seven Years' War," *Am. Hist. Rev.* 17:4 (July 1912), 735–43, For belief that the West India planters in Parliament controlled the decision see Eric Williams, *Capitalism and Slavery* (Chapel Hill: University of North Carolina Press, 1944), ch. 4. This idea is heavily discounted in Namier, *England in the Age*, *235*. Clarence Walworth Alvord identifies larger membership in the Scottish bloc than Namier counts among West Indians, *The Mississippi Valley in British Politics* (1916), 2 vols. reprinted (New York: Russell and Russell, 1959), 1:38.

5. Basil Williams, *Life of Pitt* 2:85; Alvord, *Mississippi Valley* 1:55–56.

6. Alvord thought that a changing conception of the value of colonies—from sources of raw materials to markets for finished products—was decisive. *Mississippi Valley* 1:52.

3,000 vessels and 15,000 Frenchmen had been engaged in that industry before the war, which, besides functioning as a training school for the French navy, produced an annual income calculated at half a million pounds sterling. English competition in the same seas came to about half these figures.[7] Intent on destroying French naval power and building England's, Pitt adamantly rejected all suggestions to return fishing bases and rights to France.[8] Bute, though ready to make small concessions, agreed in substance.[9] Their objective implied seizure of all coastal territories useful as fishing bases. Thus, with the gateway to Canada closed, its value as a French deterrent to colonial independence diminished to the vanishing point. Why not take it all?

So it was Canada, after all, and many a French official was not sorry to see it go, for Canada, excepting the fisheries, had been a constant drain on French finances and military manpower.[10] On the map its vast expanse was the stuff of imperial dreams, and perhaps future generations would see it emerge in glory, but at that time it seemed to Frenchmen a wilderness inhabited mostly by savages and peasants almost as savage. (French officers described it so in their letters home.)[11] As for those savages and peasants, in the manner customary in empires, they were not consulted. Minister Courcelles wrung a fisheries concession out of Minister Bute, so the two tiny islands of St. Pierre and Miquelon in the Gulf of St. Lawrence remained French; all the rest of French North America, after the compensatory cession of Louisiana to Spain, became British in jurisdiction.[12] Cultures, however, do not change at the direction of two men signing a treaty, so what was solemnly subscribed at Paris, 10 February 1763, left Canada culturally Indian and French Canadian—potentially a bigger political headache than Ireland. And there were headaches enough already in Britain's old colonies.

On the other side of the mountain

Let us return to the situation in Pennsylvania after the treaty at Easton in 1758 and the subsequent fall of Fort Duquesne. At that time, as previously, Pennsylvania's segment of the Ohio Valley had only slight communication with the Susquehanna and Delaware valleys east of the

7. Basil Williams, *Life of Pitt* 2:84.
8. Ian R. Christie, *Wars and Revolutions; Britain, 1760–1815* (Cambridge, Mass.: Harvard University Press, 1982), 45; Alvord, *Mississippi Valley* 1:69.
9. Bute: "if we had not the fishery, we really got nothing." Sherrard, *Lord Chatham*, 401,n3.
10. Frégault, *Canada*, 319–26; Gustave Lanctot, *A History of Canada*, 3:199–200; Stanley, *New France*, 268.
11. [Bougainville], *Adventures*, ed. Hamilton, 331; Frégault, *Canada*. 61–62.
12. Gipson, *British Empire* 8:309–10.

Appalachian mountains, with the consequence that the two regions evolved historically almost independently of each other. Politically the driving forces in the west centered in the tribes and in the forts occupied by British garrisons—forces that by their nature must come into collision sooner or later.

Three days after General Forbes marched into abandoned Fort Duquesne, Frederick Post heard the Indians' desire expressed in very plain terms at Kuskuski. "Brother," said Delaware chief Beaver in formal treaty conference, "I would tell you, in a most soft, loving and friendly manner, to go back over the mountain and to stay there." Noted counselor Kittiuskund confirmed the message privately with explanatory detail:

> all the nations had jointly agreed to defend their hunting place at Alleghenny, and suffer nobody to settle there; and as these Indians are very much inclined to the English interest, so he begged us very much to tell the Governor, General, and all other people not to settle there. And if the English would draw back over the mountain, they would get all the other nations into their interest; but if they staid and settled there, all the nations would be against them; and he was afraid it would be a great war, and never come to a peace again.[13]

Kittiuskund's revelation, though highly informative, told only part of what was happening west of the mountains. Another part concerned the omnipresent Iroquois. No matter where one turns in the sparse documents of the era, there is strong distrust of the Iroquois by the other tribes, jealous of their own independence. In form, the Delawares renewed the Covenant Chain with Iroquois ambassadors at Kuskuski, and the formal relations were as of old: "uncles" on the Iroquois side, "cousins" on the Delaware side. Cayuga chief Petiniontonka gave orders and Delaware chief Beaver assented meekly. Observed carefully, however, Beaver's remarks show implicit reservations: "Our uncles have made an agreement . . . and we likewise agree"—not we *therefore* agree. More explicitly, "*whatever I agree with*, they will assist me." This is not the language of subservience.[14]

In fact, Delawares and Iroquois dealt with each other at arms' length, apparently because the issue of land ownership rose between them almost as strongly as between the western tribes and the English. The Iroquois clung to their century-old claim to have "conquered" all that territory, and the English recognized the claim as legitimate because of its usefulness in diplomacy; but the Indians living on the land rejected all such notions

13. Post's "second journal," entries of 28, 29 Nov. 1758, in Proud, *History of Pa.* 2: app., 121, 124.

14. Ibid., 26 Nov. 1758, 2: app. 117–21. Italics added.

because they were there and had not been conquered—nor were they ready to let themselves be subjugated, whether by fiat or by arms.

Forks in pen and tongue

We owe much to Frederick Post's honest writing. He set down plainly how the Delawares insisted that the English leave their territory. The demand displeased Colonel Bouquet, but Chief Beaver repeated that the troops "should go back over the mountains; we have nothing to say to the contrary." Sly George Croghan made him say otherwise in the official minutes of the same conference; to wit, "the General has left Two hundred Men here . . . we assure you it is agreable to us."[15]

The Iroquois on the scene did not read or pay attention to Croghan's version. There is no record, but it seems likely that they summoned help as a delegation of more than forty Indians came to Pittsburgh early in January 1759. A mixture of Senecas, Onondagas, Shawnees, and Delawares, they were led in Covenant Chain fashion by the Iroquois, who spoke for all of them. Regrettably, so far as the other Indians were concerned, the Iroquois spoke with forked tongue. Five of them met secretly with Colonel Mercer and told him that "the Delawares and Shawnees are not yet to be Depended upon." In total contradiction to the Delawares' expressed demands, these chiefs urged Mercer, "let your men come soon . . . Come Immediately with a great many men." Otherwise, they feared, "both you and we Will be Killed." A word of caution: they would present a demand in open meeting on the morrow; "you are not to mind what is Said then, it is Outside my lips; . . . I will give you that Belt to Return home to your Own country, but you are to Return it back to me, and tell me at the Same time that you are Resolved to Stay here, and fight the French till they are drove off from this Country," And so it was done. In front of the Delawares and Shawnees, the Iroquois and Mercer acted out the drama precisely according to scenario, whereupon the Iroquois capitulated immediately to Mercer's stern rejection of their overt demand.[16] In sports parlance, they "took a dive."

Were the others fooled? Perhaps so. In any case they were unable for the moment to do more than bide their time and cherish a grudge. As the eastern Delawares had been subjugated by a combination of Pennsylvania and the Iroquois, so now the Iroquois displayed by their behavior a plan to join Britain's armies for the reduction of the westerners. The scheme

15. Ibid., 4 Dec. 1758, 2: app. 127; *Bouquet Papers* 2:623. Note the contradiction of Croghan by Chief Custaloga, 2:624n2.

16. Conference at Pittsburgh, 8 Jan. 1759, *Bouquet Papers* 3:26–32.

was subtle and simple enough to work, and it was gladly seized upon by the British. For several years it did seem to work as the Delawares kept the peace despite much grumbling and protest. But the Iroquois were unable to maintain unity within their own League. As the Senecas watched more and more British forts and garrisons spring up in territory they regarded as their own, they came to think more like the Delawares than like their eastern brethren in the League. Many wampum belts circulated among the western tribes, all bearing variants of the same message: "let us liberate our land."[17] For that purpose it did not matter which particular tribe or tribes owned the land according to custom. The essential point was the British presence and the need to make it an absence. Intertribal differences could be settled afterwards.

Franklin and Washington react to peace

In eastern Pennsylvania the fall of Fort Duquesne produced a sense of security that intensified rather than relaxed the conflict between assembly and proprietaries. Relieved of the fear of Indian attacks, assemblymen now concentrated their attention in earnest on Thomas Penn and his placemen.[18] Assemblymen eschewed Quaker tactics of negotiation and conciliation by striking back at Penn in the most direct way possible. They seized the Penns' private land office and copied for record its warrants and surveys documents, which exposed much illegality in land transactions.[19] Franklin pushed through the board of trade and the privy council the assembly's demand for an inquiry into the Penns' Walking Purchase fraud,

17. Howard H. Peckham, *Pontiac and the Indian Uprising* (1947) repr. (Chicago: University of Chicago Press, 1961), 74, 88, 106 (General Forbes played no role in the developing new crisis in the west. He died in Philadelphia, 11 March 1759. Obituary in [Forbes], *Writings*, 301–02.

18. Until the American Revolution, assembly policies were set by Joseph Galloway in partnership with Benjamin Franklin. Galloway was, like Thomas Penn, an Anglican with Quaker ancestry. However, he was a royalist/imperialist implacably hostile to Penn. Historian Richard Bauman classes the much-divided Quakers into "reformers," "politiques," and "worldly politicians." Benjamin H. Newcomb, *Franklin and Galloway; A Political Partnership* (New Haven: Conn. Yale University Press, 1972); Richard Bauman, *For the Reputation of Truth; Politics, Religion, and Conflict among the Pennsylvania Quakers, 1750–1800* (Baltimore: Johns Hopkins Press, 1971), 103–6, 235–45, ch. 4.

19. The Archives Division, Philadelphia City Hall, has nine manuscript volumes with card index of the transcribed Warrants and Surveys of the Province of Pennsylvania, 1682–1759, supplemented by other volumes in the Pa. Dept. of Internal Affairs, Harrisburg. Vol. 1 of the Philadelphia set has a mss. "Historical Background." Joseph Galloway drafted the act for seizure of the Land Office records. Controversy over enactment runs through minutes of the assembly and the governor's council from Apr. to July 1759. Newcomb, *Franklin and Galloway*, 61–62, 65–66, 87; the act, 7 July 1759, in *The Charters and Acts of Assembly of the Province of Pennsylvania*, 2 vols. (Philadelphia: Peter Miller and Co., 1762) 2:110–13. Crown's repeal noted at 2:162, 164.

and conducted his own propaganda campaign in the metropolis. Then, after much hesitation, he aimed directly at the Penns' lordship by committing himself to a campaign to take Pennsylvania away from its proprietaries and make it a royal province.[20] It was not an easy decision for Franklin. Despite his cosmopolitanism, he thought that "Pennsylvania is my darling,"[21] and the imperialist royalist side of him clashed with the pride of the provincial. But Thomas Penn's personality and practices settled the issue for a time. It is another irony of those unpredictable times that the effort to make Pennsylvania royal gained force from the great leader of the colonies' future secession from the empire.

In the wake of the Seven Years War, however, Franklin's imperialism was still very much in the ascendant. Grandly visionary, he joined in schemes to create new colonies in what is now called the Old Northwest—colonies that would violate by their very existence the promises of territory to be reserved for Indians. Such schemes revived the old rivalry between Virginians and Pennsylvanians for western lands.[22] George Washington also continued to be fascinated by the lure of the west, to an extent that flouts traditional views of his incorruptibility. Less adulatory scholars have found him involved in shady transactions that even their softened terminology does not prettify: Washington "evaded" Pennsylvania's law and "infringed" Virginia's in order to get hold of lands intended as bounty for the enlisted men who had been his comrades in arms. As Bernhard Knollenberg has observed, "the more he got of the allotted 200,000 acres, the less was available for the enlisted men to whom it was promised."[23]

It would be a number of years yet before Washington and Franklin joined on the same side of an issue of empire. In the meantime, however much they may have rationalized behavior with abstract notions of liberty, it is clear that there were concrete, material connotations to that abstraction. It is also clear that, no matter how high-flown the rhetoric

20. *Franklin Papers*. 8:264–76; Newcomb, *Franklin and Galloway*, chs. 3, 5. Hutson's entire *Pennsylvania Politics, 1746–1770* is devoted to the issue.

Bibliographic note: Hutson is superior in analysis of the technical implications of the issues, but his work is marred by tendentious reporting motivated by evident pro-Penn, anti-Quaker, and anti-Franklin biases, and his semantics are slippery. Newcomb presents the political maneuverings more clearly. The inability of the divided Quakers to take a united stand was interpreted by the pro-proprietary *Pennsylvania Journal* as "disapprobation' of the movement for royal government. *Franklin Papers* 11:376n2.

21. *Franklin Papers* 6:217.

22. The schemes for trans-Appalachian colonies are surveyed in Abernethy, *Western Lands and the American Revolution*. Supplement, for the imperial approach to such colonies, with Alvord, *Mississippi Valley*, and Jack M. Sosin, *Whitehall and the Wilderness: The Middle West in British Colonial Policy, 1760–1775* (Lincoln: University of Nebraska Press, 1961).

23. Washington to William Crawford, 21 Sept. 1767, in [Washington] *Writings*, ed. John C. Fitzpatrick, 39 vols. (Washington, D.C., 1931–32), 2:468; Bernhard Knollenberg, *George Washington: The Virginia Period, 1732–1775* (Durham, N.C., 1964), 93–100, quotation at p. 99.

describing their motives, morality was either irrelevant or conceived in a manner strange to modern understanding.

Teedyuscung beaten down and assassinated

At Wyoming, Teedyuscung had little time to enjoy the land assigned by the Iroquois League and the houses built by the Quakers for his people. Colonials from Connecticut claimed the land as their own by right of the Susquehannah Company's irregular Iroquois deed and the sea-to-sea charter of Connecticut. For once a sort of unity prevailed among all the other claimants to Wyoming. Teedyuscung's Delawares, the Iroquois, and Thomas Penn agreed that Connecticut's people had no business there, and Teedyuscung was encouraged to stand pat.[24]

This agreement, though genuine, was limited in scope. It did not signify recognition of Delaware right to Wyoming— only that Teedyuscung should hold off the intruders to preserve the rights of the Iroquois and the Penns.[25] Sir William Johnson joined the agreement in 1762 after solicitation by the others and a certain amount of equivocation.[26] Thereby began a process of rapprochement that eventuated in Johnson and Thomas Penn becoming close political allies. This was a new development. A few years earlier, the temperature between Fort Johnson and Philadelphia had been distinctly chilly, what with Johnson making caustic reports to England about Penn's abuses of Indians, and Pennsylvanians telling General Forbes to expect no help from Johnson for the campaign against Fort Duquesne— both of which censures had the merit of truth.[27] But Johnson and Penn had a common enemy—the Friendly Association—and a common purpose to suppress it and all Quakers. Another common enemy was John Henry Lydius, who guided the Susquehannah company's invasion of the Wyoming Valley from Connecticut and who was deemed a "very dangerous man" in New York.[28] Johnson's equivocation was not matched by the Iroquois: a Mohawk chief assured him that if Connecticut settlers came into the Wyoming Valley the Iroquois League and their confederates would

24. Hamilton to Johnson, 10 Feb. 1761, in *Johnson Papers* 10:210–13; *Pa. Council Minutes* 8:563–72.

25. A. F. C. Wallace, *King of the Delawares*, 241.

26. Solicitation: Hamilton's ltr. cited n24 above; R. Peters's ltrs., 12 Feb. and 18 May 1761, *Johnson Papers*, 10:213–16, 266–68. Evasion: Johnson to Hamilton, 4 Mar. 1761, ibid., 230–31.

27. Johnson's mss. strictures on the Penns were lost in a fire at Albany. References to them can be followed in *Johnson Papers* 2:657, 685, 741, 743; *Doc. Hist. N.Y.* 1:412–20. For Pennsylvanians' attitudes toward Johnson, see ch. 15, above.

28. Cadwallader Colden to Johnson, 6 June 1762, mss., HM 8231, HEH.

"commence hostilities."[29] In this tense situation, Johnson summoned Teedyuscung to the Walking Purchase inquiry that the privy council had referred to him in 1759.[30]

The inquiry took the form of a hearing at Easton in June 1762. Conducted superficially along the familiar lines of treaty conference, it differed in substance as the Indians appeared as plaintiffs before a judge rather than peers negotiating a settlement.[31] Penn's lawyers, the assembly's commissioners, and Friendly Association members attended. Teedyuscung's Delawares were also there, of course, but no Iroquois were recorded present. Johnson stuck to proper legal form in a way that recalls the comment of a lawyer friend of mine that "you can hang a man with due process." Johnson listened to Teedyuscung's complaint and the defenses offered by Penn's men. (These defenses had been adjusted with fabricated new documents to plug the holes in earlier explanations.)[32] Pemberton's excited intervention was squelched so that the Quakers could present their evidence only through Teedyuscung himself. Much of this consisted of elaborate analyses of deed transactions, partly extracted from the warrants and surveys previously seized by the assembly from the Land Office; and the proprietary lawyers countered with their own intricate collection of references—all of which was obviously far more than illiterate Teedyuscung could carry in his memory. Johnson's hostile manner made the Indians desperate as they saw their last chance of restitution, on which they had pinned all their hopes, slip away.

Johnson's luck held good once more as the Indians' apprehensions enabled him to conclude the hearing on a happy note. He recessed the hearing from Thursday, 24 June, to Sunday, 27 June, and a miracle happened in

29. Johnson to Connecticut governor Thomas Fitch, 30 Mar. 1762, *Johnson Papers* 3:660–61.

30. As of May 1761, Penn was still so dubious that he told Peters, "We must not be too fond of leaving everything to Sir Wm. Johnson, he cannot have anything to do in Affairs between us and the Indians unless we refer it to him." This although "it was first at my desire that Johnson was ordered to hear Teedyuscung's complaint." The actual hearing was precipitated by Teedyuscung himself. Thomas Penn's Ltr. Bks., mss., 7:30–31, HSP; A. F. C. Wallace, *King of the Delawares*, 242–43. *Pa. Council Minutes* 8:707–9.

31. Sources are scattered. Johnson's report to the lords of trade, 1 Aug. 1762, is in *Johnson Papers* 3:837–51. His minutes are in ibid., 760–818, including one document submitted by assembly commissioners (described as "Quakers, and others") and two long arguments from proprietary advocates Richard Peters and Benjamin Chew. Various supporting affidavits and deeds are in manuscript at Kew, England: PRO, CO 5/1276:141 ff. I have used transcripts of these at Hist. Soc. of Pa.: Board of Trade Papers, Proprietaries XXI–I, indorsed x–12. There are also short manuscripts in Friendly Assn. Papers at Haverford College Library. One is a memorandum signed by Delaware convert Isaac Still, 23 June 1762; three, of 24 June 1762, are messages from Teedyuscung to Johnson. In certain particulars they contradict Johnson's report of the hearing.

32. See Jennings, *Ambiguous Iroquois Empire*, ch. 17, app. B.

the interval. No document tells explicitly what guiding spirit wrought the transformation, but Teedyuscung's vision of a new light had been hinted at on an earlier occasion when he told Governor Hamilton that £400 would be adequate compensation for his lost lands.[33] When Johnson's hearing reconvened after the interval of official silence, Teedyuscung contritely acknowledged that a "cousin" had written his legal papers, which he did not understand; and on the day following that he retracted all his charges, buried underground "all Controversies about Land," and offered to sign a release for all the lands formerly in dispute. Whereupon Governor James Hamilton offered a generous present from the proprietaries "as a Mark of their Reconciliation with you, and a Token of their affection for you."[34]

It was neatly done. The Indians got the compensation they desired, the Quakers were outwitted,[35] and Thomas Penn ecstatically promised to render Johnson any service in his power.[36] Penn meant it. He was well aware of the advantages of a partnership with Johnson. Soon the two great magnates began to work as a team for mutual benefit.[37]

Teedyuscung was not so fortunate. When the settlers of Connecticut's Susquehannah Company returned to Wyoming in force, they drove his people away and burned his cabin with him in it.[38] (No one was caught handling a smoking brand, but their motive is very clear.) Sorrowful Quakers reorganized to help Indians by charitable means, which they have done ever since.[39]

On the other hand, Sir William Johnson, fortified by the prestige of victory at Niagara and the lobbying expertise of Thomas Penn, rose to new heights of power and glory from which he *used* Indians—all Indians—as means to his and the empire's advancement. That his conduct and verdict were preordained in the hearing of Teedyuscung's case is amply clear from his candid private expression of principle to an English army officer.

I have laid it down as an invariable rule, from which I never did, nor ever shall deviate, that wherever a Title is set up by any Tribe of Indians of little conse-

33. *Pa. Council Minutes* 8:708.

34. *Johnson Papers* 3:781–89.

35. But James Pemberton thought the issue settled "to tolerable satisfaction." Ltr., 1 July 1762, in Parrish, *Some Chapters of the Friendly Association* 2, unpaged, HSP.

36. Penn to Johnson, 8 Jan. 1763, mss., Penn Papers, Thomas Penn (boxes), HSP.

37. *Johnson Papers* 11:347–48; 13:324–25; and see index references for "Penn, Thomas, Canajoharie grant and," ibid., 14:456. In return for Penn's effective lobbying, Johnson guarded Penn's landed interest.

38. P. A. W. Wallace, *Indians in Pennsylvania*, 156; A. F. C. Wallace, *King of the Delawares*, 258–61.

39. Bauman, *For the Reputation of Truth*, ch. 13. An older survey is Rayner Wickersham Kelsey, *Friends and the Indians, 1655–1917* (Philadelphia: Associated Executive Committee of Friends on Indian Affairs, 1917). The mss. records of Friends' Indian Committee, including the Papers of the Friendly Assn., are at Haverford College. These have been microfilmed in 12 reels by APS.

> quence or importance to his Majesty's Interest, and who may be considered as long domesticated, that such Claim unless apparently clear, had better remain unsupported than that Several old Titles of his Majesty's Subjects should thereby become disturbed—and on the contrary, Wherever I found a Just complaint made by a People either by themselves or connections capable of resenting, and who I knew would resent a neglect, I Judged it my Duty to support the same, altho it should disturb the property of any Man whatsoever.[40]

Translated into operational terms, this meant that Johnson would help the Mohawks in their protests against land frauds in New York because he needed them (and as long as he needed them); but in his court the Dela wares were lucky to get anything at all.

40. Johnson to Roger Morris, 26 Aug. 1765, *Johnson Papers* 11:911–12.

Chapter 20 ❧ *THE WAR CALLED "PONTIAC'S"*

As I think it likely Peace May be concluded with some of the [Indian] Nations next year; I would submit to your Consideration the best Manner of Making Peace with Indians Whether by Assembling the Several Nations together; or treating as much as possible with each of Them Separately; by the first Method, it appears to me, that we should Strengthen their Confederacys, and cement their Alliances. By the last That we should raise up Jealousies of each other and kindle those Suspicions So natural to every Indian, and which it's now our Business to encourage, and foment as much as possible.

Sir William Johnson to General Thomas Gage, 26 December 1763

Chronology

22 February 1761.	Amherst forbids presents of food and arms to Indians.
3 July 1761.	Senecas present a war belt to Detroit Indians, but it is rejected and disclosed to the fort commandant.
Summer 1762.	War belts circulate among western Indians, encouraged by Senecas and Frenchmen.
23 August 1762.	Major Henry Gladwin takes command at Detroit.
27 April 1763.	Pontiac proposes to Ottawas, Potawatomies, and Hurons near Fort Detroit that they attack and plunder the fort. He inspires them with the teachings of the revivalist Delaware prophet Neolin.
9 May 1763.	Pontiac lays siege to Fort Detroit with a force composed of Ottawa, Chippewa, Potawatomi, Huron, Shawnee, and Delaware warriors.
Summer 1763.	Tribal allies destroy forts at Venango, LeBoeuf, and Presque Isle. Senecas wipe out a convoy near Niagara. Forts at Detroit, Pittsburgh, and Niagara hold out against besiegers.
July 1763.	On their own initiative, but with sanction from Amherst and Bouquet, the garrison at Fort Pitt start an epidemic among the Indians by infecting besieging chiefs with blankets from the smallpox hospital.
1 August 1763.	Indians withdraw from siege of Fort Pitt.
5 August 1763.	Colonel Bouquet fights off an attack at Bushy Run and forces attackers to withdraw.
1–28 September 1763.	Sir William Johnson treats with the Iroquois and admits Senecas back in the Covenant Chain with only nominal punishment.

31 October 1763.	Pontiac lifts the siege of Detroit.
17 November 1763.	Amherst embarks on return to Britain. He is succeeded as commander in chief by General Thomas Gage.
Early April 1764.	Iroquois attack eastern Delawares and turn prisoners over to Johnson.
12 August 1764.	Bradstreet, on his way to Detroit, treats with Delawares and Shawnees at Presque Isle.
7 September 1764.	Bradstreet treats with Detroit chiefs (but not Pontiac) for peace under Britain's sovereignty. He immediately applies for a grant of lands to make a new colony.
July 1766.	Pontiac treats with Johnson for peace.
March 1767.	Johnson joins with William Smith in a campaign to establish Anglican bishops in American colonies.

After the surrender of Canada in 1760, fighting ceased in North America, although the war continued elsewhere in the world and French forces in the west remained ready to resume hostilities if given opportunity. In military calculations the western garrisons of the French represented a threat to security that Amherst with habitual thoroughness determined to eliminate by systematically replacing French troops with British. Few events better illustrate the shortcomings of military solutions to political problems, for Amherst's blinkered policies led straight to disaster as he set in motion a train of consequences, each pulling another along after it. In part, one must concede, Amherst was listening to a different drummer, heeding the politics of economy in Parliament.[1]

Delawares and Shawnees had been promised withdrawal of British troops; instead, garrisons were increased. Senecas had fought to free their territory of Fort Niagara; instead, the British presence there became more oppressive than the French had ever been as Amherst made grants of Seneca lands to his officers. Farther west, Ottawas, Potawatomies, and Chippewas, though accustomed to forts housing traders and small French garrisons, took alarm as they heard distress stories from Forts Pitt and Niagara and watched the British dig in at Detroit. Sensitivities already raw were scraped painfully by British officers; unlike the preceding French whose need for Indian support had made them accommodating, the British treated Indians contemptuously and made quite clear that their purpose was control.[2]

1. Alvord, *Mississippi Valley* 1:185–87; Randolph C. Downes, *Council Fires on the Upper Ohio: A Narrative of Indian Affairs in the Upper Ohio Valley until 1795* (Pittsburgh: University of Pittsburgh Press, 1969), 106–11; Sosin, *Whitehall and the Wilderness*, 35–38; Bernhard Knollenberg, *Origin of the American Revolution: 1759–1766* (1960), rev. ed. (New York: Collier Books, 1961), ch. 8. Gipson's strong anglophilia softens Amherst's disaster to "a profound effect upon the Indians." *British Empire* 9:91.

2. Peckham, *Pontiac*, 102.

The Iroquois plan an uprising

By 1761 the Senecas' resentment at Fort Niagara spilled over to Onondaga where the Iroquois League chiefs laid plans for a simultaneous uprising of all the tribes against the British. Two Seneca chiefs bore a war belt to Detroit with an invitation to the western tribes to unite with the Iroquois for the war of liberation, but the local Indians at Detroit rejected the demand and disclosed it to the fort's commandant.[3] From this time forward, Johnson altered his own fundamental strategy. Whereas he formerly had worked to fasten the League's domination on other tribes, he now deliberately aimed to stir up intertribal discord, encouraging a western confederation as counterweight to the League and promoting jealousy between them. There is no need to infer this policy from circumstance; Johnson stated explicitly to Gage, "the great pains I have been constantly at in dividing them and preventing their unanimity." Even more explicitly: "The Six Nations on the one side and the Indians of [eastern] Canada on the other may be made an usefull barrier and Check upon the Western Indians, and the fomenting a Coolness between them and Jealousy of each others power will be the surest means of preventing a Rupture [with us], dividing them in their Councils, and rendering an union impracticable which cannot be too much guarded against."[4]

Among other things, this implies that Johnson's reputation as a friend of the Iroquois is in need of reformulation. He was their friend and advocate as long as their policies coincided with his, and at such times he enriched himself with their trade and with vast cessions of their territory; though only a baronet, Johnson acquired an estate (on paper) equal to any English duke's, and the Iroquois League was the direct or indirect source of all of it.[5] (It seems equally true that the Iroquois submitted to Johnson's will only so long as it suited their own purposes.) Johnson never for a moment "crossed over" to identify himself as an Iroquois. He was self-consciously an imperialist British lord *over* the Indians, in imitation of his forebears in Ireland. He did not hesitate to betray those Indians by the classic technique of dividing to rule, and he was clever enough to succeed—or, at least, to achieve personal success.

3. Ibid., 74–75.

4. Johnson to Gage, 27 Jan., 16 Mar. 1764, *Johnson Papers* 4:308, 368.

5. Sung Bok Kim, "A New Look at the Great Landlords of Eighteenth-Century New York," *Wm. and Mary Qtly.*, 3d ser., 27(1970): 586; Edward Countryman, *A People in Revolution*, 16, 21, 23, 117–18. Examples of Johnson's land acquisitions: *Collections of the New-York Historical Society*, publication fund series 9(1877), 130–32, 324–25.

Amherst's Indian policies

Unlike bullheaded Amherst, Johnson paid attention to Indian attitudes and tribal diplomacy. These could be called his bread and butter (though caviar and champagne come closer to the mark). When Amherst ordered disastrous policies, Johnson tried to reason with him, but Amherst had lost prudence as he gained glory. In regard to Indians, Amherst disdained logic. To save money he banned presents to the Indians on the theory that he would thereby compel them to go off the dole and subsist themselves by hunting. But he made hunting impossible by withholding ammunition on the theory that he thereby protected his soldiers from potential enemies.[6] What he did in fact was to convert potentiality into actuality. Because the overriding fact of life for Indians at the time was disruption by war of their subsistence practices, they needed help until they could resume normal routines. The denial of such help, especially of the ammunition needed for hunting, condemned them to go hungry. If Amherst observed the fact, or if the contradictions in his Indian policies occurred to him, he shrugged off the irritants with a classic expression of military contempt for occupied peoples. He boasted of his "power" over Indians "to punish the delinquents with entire destruction, which I am firmly resolved on whenever any of them give me cause."[7] The statement presaged atrocity to come.

One must recall also that Indians regarded British troops as being in their debt. The "presents" that Amherst conceived as bribes appeared to the Indians as a form of rent for the land occupied by British forts, and as tolls for passage by troops and traders over tribal territories. French officials had tacitly deferred to the Indian understanding by producing presents regularly. When Amherst stopped the practice, he was seen by the Indians as violating yet another compact.[8]

The effect of Amherst's attitudes and policies was what Johnson had foreseen—what anyone could have foreseen. As the tribes became aware of Amherst's many sins against them, they plotted to overthrow his vaunted power. Some Frenchmen abetted the plots and may have had part in insti-

6. Peckham, *Pontiac*, 70–72, 81. To Cornelius J. Jaenen, presents represented acknowledgment of interdependency. For Wilbur R. Jacobs they were "an important issue in controlling the Indians during the last phases of the struggle for empire." This was true for Europeans. For Indians, however, presents were an essential element of their ceremonial and diplomatic culture. Cornelius J. Jaenen, "The Role of Presents in French-Amerindian Trade," in *Explorations in Canadian Economic History: Essays in Honour of Irene M. Spry* (Ottawa: University of Ottawa Press, 1985), 231–50, esp. 249–50; Wilbur R. Jacobs, *Diplomacy and Indian Gifts* (Stanford, Calif.: Stanford University Press, 1950), quotation at 161–62.

7. Peckham, *Pontiac*, 88.

8. Jaenen, "Role of Presents," 241–49; W. J. Eccles, "Sovereignty-Association, 1500–1783," *Canadian Historical Review* 65:4 (1984), 498–99, 507.

gating them. The ensuing hostilities were not racial war as traditionally imagined, because Indians did not attack Frenchmen.[9] Instead they solicited aid from the French and permitted them to move about at will.[10]

Pontiac in the Forty Years' War

In Francis Parkman's murky mind the backwoods plots emanated from one savage genius, the Ottawa chief Pontiac, and thus they became "The Conspiracy of Pontiac," but Pontiac was only a local Ottawa war chief in a "resistance" involving many tribes spread over the vast region now known as the Old Northwest. By Pontiac's own declaration, he waged war "solely on repeated invitations made me by the Delawares, Iroquois, and Shawnees."[11] In the brief account allowable here, the resistance is seen as integral to the series of wars waged by tribes of the Old Northwest from 1755 to 1795 against first Britain and then the United States. The common objective of these wars was to force the aliens to withdraw, and they were marked commonly by horrid practices of utmost cruelty and ferocity on all sides. From the Indians' viewpoint, the great world wars in which France lost Canada and Britain lost its thirteen seaboard colonies were but components of the tribes' forty-year struggle to liberate themselves and their lands. In that perspective, "Pontiac's" war is an episode—the resistance of 1763.[12] In these also, the expansion of empire had aroused such passionate mutual hatred that the quality of mercy was abandoned and atrocity became the rule.

Indian political motives gained fervency from the teachings of revivalist prophets among the Delawares and Senecas, whose messages from "The Master of Life" denounced the "dogs clothed in red." A curious reversal of our traditional associations with menaces colored red: Delaware prophet Neolin believed that those red menaces came only to trouble the lands. "Drive them out," he demanded, "make war upon them." The messages spread westward and were received eagerly by Pontiac and others.[13]

Ironically it was the triumphant end of Britain's war with France that triggered the tribes' liberation war against Britain. In February 1763,

9. Francis Parkman, *The Conspiracy of Pontiac and the Indian War after the Conquest of Canada* (1870), 2 vols., repr. New Library ed. (Boston: Little, Brown and Co., 1909), 1:193. For Parkman's biases and falsehoods see Jennings, "Francis Parkman: A Brahmin among Untouchables."

10. Parkman, *Pontiac* 1:194; Peckham, *Pontiac,* 192–93, 203, 230, 235, 240.

11. Parkman, *Pontiac* 1:190–96; Peckham, *Pontiac,* 272.

12. Eccles has conceived the war as "a pre-emptive strike by the Indians to defend their lands," and he insists that the British had not established duly constituted authority. Eccles, "Sovereignty-Association," 507.

13. Peckham, *Pontiac,* 115; Anthony F. C. Wallace, *The Death and Rebirth of the Seneca* (New York: Alfred A. Knopf, 1970), 115–21.

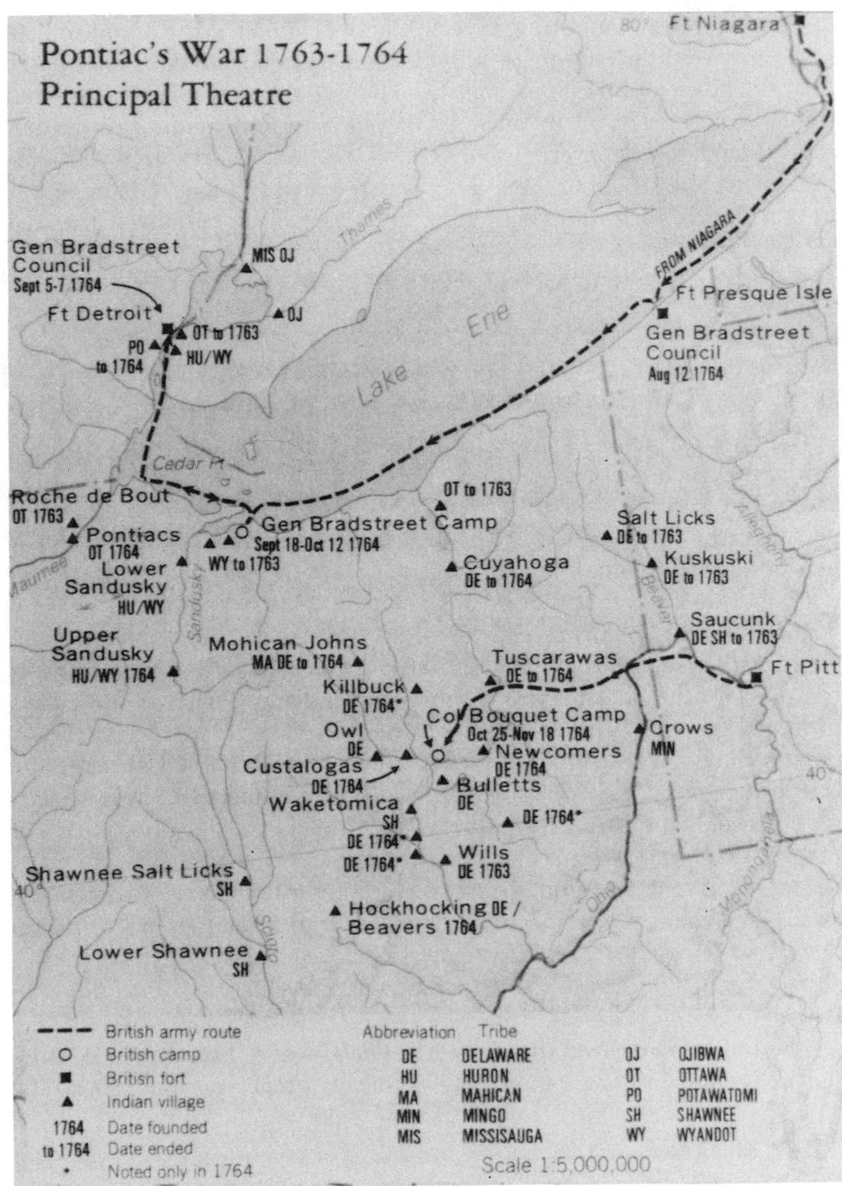

MAP 10. Sites of major events in the Indian war called Pontiac's. REPRODUCED FROM THE *Atlas of Great Lakes Indian History* BY PERMISSION OF OKLAHOMA UNIVERSITY PRESS.

Detroit's commanding major Henry Gladwin announced the end of hostilities between the empires and the beginning of negotiations for a peace treaty. The news did not go down well among the assembled Indians and some of the French inhabitants. In this locality Pontiac did take leadership, though it was never absolute command, and he organized a scheme to take the fort by subterfuge. This was revealed to Major Gladwin, but to this day the identity of the secret informant is not certain. Frustrated by Gladwin's immediate precautions, Pontiac laid siege to the fort on 9 May 1763 and began to harass backwoods settlers of British extraction.

The siege of Detroit

With few exceptions (those who were identified as too friendly with the British,) French persons remained unharmed.[14] The French were in an anomalous position, and they were far from agreed on anything except personal survival. One of them, Robert Navarre, wrote a journal that vividly portrays the complexity of the situation at Detroit when Pontiac laid siege.[15] It discloses that the Indians comprised Ottawa, Chippewa, Potawatomi, Huron, Shawnee and Delaware warriors, and even some from the Erie tribe (supposed by scholars to have been extinguished after Iroquois conquest a century earlier).[16] Among the Indians, Pontiac's leadership prevailed generally—he must have had a truly dominating personality—but unanimity was definitely not the rule. The chiefs vied for prestige; Chippewa great chief Wasson, whose men outnumbered Pontiac's Ottawas, insisted on the authority due to such numbers. One "bad" band of Hurons (in Navarre's phrase) joined the siege enthusiastically, but another "good" band took part under duress, waiting for the chance to get safely away. The younger warriors did as they pleased; when they got drunk on plundered liquor, not even the greatest chiefs could stop them from rampaging through the camps to torture and kill prisoners and sometimes each other.

The Indians conceived themselves in one aspect as Frenchmen fighting the battles of their distant monarch. Ethnically French persons ranged the

14. Peckham, *Pontiac*, 112–13, 116–26, 130–44.

15. *The Siege of Detroit in 1763*, xiii–206.

16. Peckham knew the Navarre journal, but at the time he lacked the background in tribal history required to recognize the significance of the mention of Eries. Understandably, other students seem to have relied on him without going back to the original manuscript, which was written in archaic and almost illegible French. Ford's English translation, first published in 1912, got little notice because it came out in a few copies and without an index. My cited Lakeside Press edition was a presentation copy given at Christmas to R. R. Donnelley's customers and friends, therefore never advertised, reviewed, or marketed. I came across it by chance in a used book stall.

gamut from full cooperation with the Indians to full cooperation with the besieged Britons. Some Frenchmen stayed within the fort and labored on its defenses. (Our journal writer Navarre was one of these.) Some traders continued to try to do business, but came to grief. The *habitants* living in the surrounding farm community were completely vulnerable to the Indians who demanded provisions and livestock and plundered at will. Some of the *habitants* secretly sold provisions to the fort. An astonishing amount of traffic moved in both directions through the fort's gates. Some of the French helped Pontiac plan tactics, but only a few young men actually joined the warriors, and they were "have-nots." The propertied French, anchored to their lands, understood acutely how high they could hang if the British should triumph, and they evaded Pontiac's demands to be as belligerently "French" as himself.

Only the beleaguered British were unified in outlook and command. The prospect of torture and mutilation concentrated their minds and wills to the point where they performed prodigies of labor and valor through a siege that lasted from May until September. Theirs was not a passive defense. The fort's sloops cruised along Detroit River and Lake Erie for provisions and reinforcements. Sortie after sortie destroyed buildings and walls, and cut down trees that offered cover to the attackers. Captured Indians were exchanged for captured Britons at the favorable rate of one for three. There were some among the defenders whose ethnocentric contempt for the savages led them to fatal episodes of bravado, especially in the battle of Bloody Run, which taught (in editor Quaife's words) "something about the red man's capacity for strategy."[17] But Commandant Henry Gladwin held steady, neither venturing foolhardy escapades nor letting morale deteriorate through idleness. Marvelously, the fort's band gave concerts through it all! The British upper lip was never stiffer.

On the other side, Indian morale deteriorated as time wore on. Relief came for the fort from Fort Niagara, and the Indians learned through trusted French channels that their great king at Versailles really had ceded Canada to the British. Pontiac was compelled to lift his siege in disgrace, and Fort Detroit emerged triumphant, stronger than ever. Of all the Indian leaders of that misnamed "Pontiac's Conspiracy," Pontiac was almost the least successful.[18] After failing to reanimate the western tribes to war, Pontiac finally, in 1766, submitted to his "father," Sir William Johnson: "we shall do every thing you have desired of us, we shall do nothing but what is good and reject every thing bad." By that time he had become so

17. *Siege of Detroit*, 137–38, 208.

18. Even the relatively unimportant Erie chief criticized Pontiac caustically in the midst of the siege: "because thou hast begun the war ill-advisedly and art now in a rage at not having been able to take the English in the Fort thou art bound to have our brothers, the French, feel thy bad humor." Ibid., 145. This is not the language of a fellow conspirator.

insignificant that Johnson barely mentioned his name in the letter transmitting the treaty minutes.[19]

Atrocities

Other leaders and other tribes had varied success. A surprise attack captured the westernmost French post of Michilimackinac at the junction of Lakes Superior, Michigan, and Huron. Tiny garrisons of outposts on the supply line to Detroit fell to stratagem and surprise. The Senecas took Forts Venango, LeBoeuf, and Presque Isle, and Delawares laid siege to Fort Pitt as the Senecas besieged Niagara. In retrospect, the Senecas achieved greatest success, both militarily and politically. Though the British garrison of Fort Niagara held out against them, they ambushed and slaughtered seventy-two soldiers at the Devil's Hole road along the Niagara chasm.[20] How much of their fighting had Iroquois League approval is difficult to say, but in 1764 Johnson and the League chiefs maneuvered the Senecas back into the Covenant Chain without serious penalty. The Senecas won forgiveness by ceding the Niagara carrying place tract and by taking up the hatchet against the Delawares and Shawnees.[21]

In this war, civilians suffered greatest casualties. Rampaging warriors killed an estimated 2,000 colonial settlers (as compared to 400-odd soldiers), inflicting horrible tortures and forcing survivors to flee to refuge in the town and forts. This was something more than the satisfaction of bloodlust; though there was plenty of that, a Frenchman's blood presumably would have sated it as well as an Englishman's. The settler victims were mostly persons who had violated bans against invading Indian territory. If British officialdom would not or could not fulfill its pledges against such settlement, the Indians reasoned that they would have to use their own force to maintain their territorial integrity. Nation-states do the same thing.[22] To say this does not explain the frightful cruelties of backwoods war, of course, and no effort will be made here to palliate or excuse them. Even so, distinctions must be made; among the Indians themselves the Delawares were disgusted by the cannibalism practiced by some other tribes.[23] The Ottawas' ritual cannibalism was denounced to Pontiac's face

19. Minutes and ltr. to lords of trade, 28 July, 20 Aug. 1766, *N.Y. Col. Docs.* 7:861, 851.

20. Wallace, *Death and Rebirth*, 115–16.

21. General Gage wanted strong punishment for the "Chenussios" (Genesee Senecas). Johnson agreed in principle but diluted the terms in specifics. *Johnson Papers*, 4:274, 4:290–93, 307–310, 11:105–15, 134–61.

22. *Pontiac*, 239–40, ch. 15, et passim.

23. The Unami (Delaware) contemptuous name for the people who called themselves Kanienkahaka was "Maqua" meaning "cannibal monsters." The English corrupted this to "Mohawk." Ives Goddard in *Northeast*, 478.

by Chippewa chief Kinonchamek, and the chief of the Eries who spoke also for Delawares. Pontiac "was like a child surprised in some fault with no excuse to give, and he did not know what to say. . . . Kinonchamek, the Eries, and the Delawares withdrew without receiving any reply from Him."[24]

Germ warfare at Fort Pitt

The fallacy of homogenizing all Indians as identical "savages" can be seen most clearly by turning the same sort of logic around to apply it to their British adversaries. Suppose that all Englishmen and English colonials were to be defined by the standard set by their highest authority in America, Commander in Chief Amherst. When the news of the rising reached Amherst, he raged without restraint. Demonstrating that he had attended closely to the methods of his former commander, "Butcher" Cumberland, Amherst ordered "extirpation" of the Indians and "no prisoners" to be taken. "Put to death all that fall into your hands," he ordered Captain Lieutenant Valentine Gardiner, and he asked Colonel Bouquet "to send the small pox among the disaffected tribes of Indians."[25]

Bouquet passed Amherst's directive along to Captain Simeon Ecuyer commanding Fort Pitt. Ecuyer summoned besieging Delaware chiefs into the fort for parley—a common occurrence in backwoods warfare—and presented them with tokens of his personal esteem: blankets infected with smallpox from the fort's hospital. "I hope it will have the desired effect," gloated Captain William Trent, who provided the blankets; and so it did by his standards.[26] An epidemic raged among the Delawares, after which

24. *Siege of Detroit* 143–45.

25. Peckham, *Pontiac*, 226–27.

26. Amherst's and Bouquet's intentions in this matter have been fully documented, but dates indicate that the idea to infect the Indians occurred independently to Fort Pitt's officers. Smallpox broke out at the fort in June 1763. An account book for the same month bears the item, "To sundries got to Replace in kind those which were taken from people in the Hospital to Convey the Small-pox to the Indians," listing two blankets and two hankerchiefs. These were presented to two Delaware chiefs in the fort on 24 June. Amherst apparently was unaware of the event when he ordered the same practice on 7 July, and Bouquet wrote agreement on 13 July. The account mentioned above was later approved for payment by General Thomas Gage with a notation that it should be posted to "extraordinaries."

The situation raises more questions than if Amherst and Bouquet were to be singled out as exceptional criminals. To what extent was germ warfare against Indians accepted as legitimate, though covert, in "frontier" war? Rumors of widespread acceptance were hinted in the nineteenth century, but I have not seen other evidence as explicit and irrefutable as that of Fort Pitt.

All the Fort Pitt evidence is itemized and discussed in Bernhard Knollenberg, "General Amherst and Germ Warfare," and Knollenberg and Donald H. Kent, "Communications," *Miss. Valley Hist. Review* 41 (Dec. 1954), 489–94, and ibid. (Mar. 1955), 762–63. For the rumors see "News and Comment," ibid., 12 (925–26), 295–96; and Randolph C. Downes's review in ibid., 32 (1946), 627–28.

some familiar chiefs appear no more in any account: Great Chief Shingas, for example, and his brother Pisquetomen.[27]

Should Pennsylvania's Quakers be homogenized with Amherst, Bouquet, Ecuyer, and Trent under one judgmental identifying epithet?

Thinking persons must constantly ask themselves what they admire and what they want to be. What, then, do they think about this matter of germ warfare that was unquestionably effective at Fort Pitt? If it is admired, or even merely accepted as superior to the "savage" way of hacking at bodies, is there not a dead certainty that military advantage will provide sufficient motive for practicing it again? And for overlaying the enormity with cant phrases about civilization triumphing over savagery, or something of the sort?

A righteous mercenary

Bouquet went on to relieve Fort Pitt after a battle nearby at a place called Edge Hill, though the battle is named for the creek called Bushy Run. The besiegers of Fort Pitt had withdrawn from the fort in order to ambush Bouquet's approaching force, and they did surprise it but failed to panic the troops, who kept good order. Bouquet feinted by pulling back two companies, luring the Indians to charge, and then flung his reserves at their flanks. Had the Indians been willing to take heavy losses for the sake of victory, they might have overwhelmed the soldiers, but the Indian way of war gave top priority to preservation of one's own men. Recognizing the new danger, the attackers fled and the drawn battle was subsequently trumpeted as a great triumph. In the sense that it permitted Bouquet to raise the siege, it accomplished his purpose, and that is victory enough; but its limits should be noted. The battle was not a rout. Bouquet did not try to pursue the retreating Indians, and the battle did not destroy their capacity to fight.[28] Smallpox was doing that, and a question seems legitimate as to how much effect the smallpox had already taken on Indian forces before the battle. There are no statistics. Peckham remarks that "it certainly affected their rigorous prosecution of the war."[29]

27. Shingas: C. Hale Sipe, *The Indian Chiefs of Pennsylvania* (Butler, Pa.: Ziegler Printing Co., 1927), 304. Pisquetomen: my own observation.

28. Peckham, *Pontiac*, 212–13. The presumptuous punditry of provost William Smith (an "authority" on everything as soon as he noticed it) is usually cited for Indian military strategy and tactics. [William Smith], *An Historical Account of the Expedition against the Ohio Indians in the Year 1764* (1765) reprinted facsimile (Readex Microprint, 1966). Long overdue correction is in Leroy V. Eid, " 'National' War Among Indians of Northeastern North America," 125–54. Professor Eid's research has required some revision of my own earlier views on this subject.

29. Peckham, *Pontiac*, 170.

Before leaving this subject entirely, we may notice Colonel Bouquet's comment in 1764 when an organized lynch mob from Paxton, Pennsylvania, massacred the few peaceful Indians—men, women, and children—at Conestoga and those that had been taken for protection into the jail at Lancaster.

> After all the noise and bustle of our young men on the Frontiers, Every body expected that they would have offered their Services, as soldiers or Volunteers, for the defence of their Country, as being the fittest men for an Expedition against Indians, and as the best way to wipe off the Reproaches cast upon them for the violences committed, and offered to defenceless Indians;
>
> Instead of such honourable conduct . . . they go as Pack Horse Drivers and Waggoners, Employs for which a Coward is as fit as a brave man;
>
> Will not People say that they have found it easier to kill Indians in a Gaol, than to fight them fairly in the Woods?

Though Bouquet's righteous aura dims when one remembers that these so-proper sentiments were expressed by a man who had left his own country to fight for pay in a succession of others, and that this gentleman mercenary practiced fair fighting in the woods with, among other weapons, infected blankets, his letter is worth notice for the light it casts on the passionate rhetoric of militarists who denounced Quakers for pacifism. It seems that there was considerable "mean Spirited behaviour" among their own kind that was inspired by something other than principle: "I make no doubt that when his Majesty is informed what little assistance I have had from the Frontier Inhabitants, and that hardly any men of Property and character have joined the Expedition that they will hereafter be left to fight their own Battles themselves."[30]

But Bouquet was mistaken in attributing the reluctance of the westerners to cowardice. The immediate danger to themselves was past. Why should they venture their lives and endure the hardships of campaigns in far-off places for the gain of king and proprietary? They were to prove their courage soon enough when they volunteered in masses to fight *against* that king in the American Revolution.

We must get on with the story. General Amherst's appeal for return to England was granted, and he embarked, 17 November 1763, but his reception at home was not what he had anticipated. As Howard H. Peckham has written, "A new king was on the throne, a new ministry in power, . . . the Indian revolt in the West was in the news, and Amherst was pointed out as the general who had failed to subdue it."[31]

30. Bouquet to John Harris, 19 July 1764, Add. MSS. 21,650, ff. 349–50, Bouquet Papers, British Library.

31. Peckham, *Pontiac*, 242.

Bradstreet again

The new commander, General Thomas Gage, sent two expeditions westward in the summer of 1764. Colonel Bouquet drove through the Delaware and Shawnee country at the Ohio while Nova Scotian Colonel John Bradstreet led a large force from Niagara to Detroit. Bradstreet was in a tearing hurry. Usually eager to rush into battle, his great goal this time was to get to Detroit for purposes other than combat. Instead of beating down the Delawares and Shawnees along his road, he made a peace with them at Presque Isle that Bouquet immediately denounced as insufficiently punitive. It did not hold, but Bradstreet blamed the Indians' return to the warpath on the provocation of Bouquet's belligerent advance.[32]

Bouquet and Johnson criticized Bradstreet's Delaware treaty harshly, but a contemporary chronicler attributed their strictures to conflicts of ambition. In Thomas Mante's view, the Indians who treated with Bradstreet genuinely wanted to get "a state of tranquillity" after long warring, "but Colonel Bouquet's pressing in upon them robbed Colonel Bradstreet and his army of the honour of concluding a work which they had commenced on Lake Erie and which would have been effected without Colonel Bouquet's assistance."[33] Most writers have preferred the view of our old friend Parson Smith, who glorified Bouquet for showing "by what methods these faithless savages are to be best reduced to reason."[34]

No less than others, Bradstreet was certainly motivated by ambition. His treaty enabled him to achieve what he most wanted: he got to Detroit and took command long enough to negotiate another treaty with the western tribes. Afterwards he suffered calamities on his return to Niagara, and he met sharp reproof from Gage, but he had his Detroit treaty, and it explains his otherwise uncharacteristic conduct.

He made the Detroit treaty, 7 September 1764, with a congeries of hostile chiefs, (without Pontiac) by which he forced the Indians to accept England's king as their *father* rather than just their *brother*. That is, he made them accept Britain's sovereignty over their lands and people, upon which he promptly applied for a royal grant of lands and a charter for a new colony, promising to settle 600 people in it.[35] It appears also that Bradstreet picked up a little income on the side by collaborating with certain traders while suppressing their competitors.[36] No one ever accused

32. Godfrey, *Pursuit of Profit*, ch. 9. Copy of the treaty, 12 Aug. 1764, Penn Papers, Off. Corr. 9:246, mss., HSP.

33. Mante, *History*, 329–32.

34. [William Smith], *An Historical Account of the Expedition against the Ohio Indians, in the Year 1764 . . . by a Lover of his Country* (Philadelphia: William Bradford, 1765), 6 et passim.

35. Godfrey, *Pursuit of Profit*, 206–7.

36. Ibid., 107–10.

Bradstreet of lack of enterprise, but in this case his ambition collided head-on with royal policy, as will be shown. He was not alone, however, in trying to acquire Indian lands. Commander in Chief Thomas Gage made discreet arrangements through Sir William Johnson.[37]

Meantime, Johnson labored with the Iroquois, who were by no means losing the war regardless of damages inflicted on other Indian nations. When they met with Johnson in September 1763, Mohawk chief Abraham (Tiyerhasere) spoke "in behalf of all the Confederacy consisting of Eighteen Nations including seven in Canada." As salvagers of tribes damaged by war, the Iroquois had no superiors. Historically the Senecas had been most successful of all the Iroquois nations. Now they were admonished, scolded, and threatened by Johnson and their Iroquois brethren, but aside from verbal punishment they suffered only the cession of their carrying place at Niagara.[38] Bernhard Knollenberg contrasts their treatment with that allowed to "the ravaged frontier settlers" for whom "no indemnity whatever was demanded or received." On the whole, "it was perfectly clear that the British army had dismally failed not only to protect the colonial frontiers but even to punish the Indians promptly."[39] Backwoods people had reason to think that Britain fought for the empire, not for them.

Iroquois attack Delawares

The Iroquois seized war's opportunities to re-establish their dominance within their confederation. Since the founding of Pennsylvania in 1681 had put Iroquois and Delawares under separate colonial protectorates, they had competed for status and prestige, but until 1764 their competition had been bloodlessly political. However, when Johnson demanded that the Iroquois take up the hatchet to show loyalty, they were not difficult to persuade. "The first Party," according to Cadwallader Colden, "consisting of 200 came up with a party of Delawares consisting of 41, surprised them and brought them in Prisoners of which 14 were delivered up to Sir William and are now in the Jail of this City, among them their Leader Captain Bull [Teedyuscung's son] who had lately done much mischief on the Frontiers." Another party killed one Delaware and took three prisoners. "This is the first blood shed by Indians in our favor," Colden commented. He added a wistful note: "People in general are in hopes of Peace

37. See index listing "Gage, Thomas, land purchases," *Johnson Papers* 14:214.
38. Ibid., 10:845; and see n21 above.
39. Knollenberg, *Origin of the American Revolution*, 121.

with them; for I find any Service against Indians is disagreeable."[40]

Once more a distinction must be made between east and west; and the reason, I think, is that the Iroquois could count. They had no difficulty attacking the fragmented bands of Delawares and Shawnees on the Susquehanna River, but they would not go out against the powerful western tribes unless British troops moved with them. Caughnawaga chief Tahaghtaghquisere explained their attitude bluntly. He gave the lie to Colonel Bradstreet's statement that the Indians had been unwilling to fight. "We were always ready, had he shewn us where, and set the Example: but all he wanted was, that some of us Indians should go, and try to Scalp one of the Shawanese, or Delawares, and he lye in his Camp idle. . . . We all expected there would be an Opportunity of distinguishing ourselves, and of getting some Prisoners and Scalps to shew our People that we had been at War, but instead of that, on his meeting two, or three little Canoes with a few Ottawas, and talking a little with them (which he never communicated to us) he dropt his first Resolution of fighting them, and set off for Detroit."[41]

The threat of religious establishment

Johnson came out of the war a clear winner by any standard. He was confirmed as *the* authority on Indian affairs. He acquired Iroquois grants to yet more vast estates. he achieved glory as the victor of Lake George and Niagara. Parliament voted him thousands of pounds as reward, and the king knighted his dubiously legitimate son and gave Sir William himself the coveted order of the garter—an honor for which English noblemen struggled bitterly (Lord Halifax, for example).[42] An indeterminate part of Johnson's success in England was due to the efforts of Thomas Penn.[43] Johnson also became close with Penn's chief hatchet man, Provost William Smith, and the two men campaigned for the establishment of Anglican

40. Colden to Amherst, 13 Apr. 1764, and to lords of trade, 14 April, *Colls. of the N.-Y. Hist. Soc.* 9 (1877), 319–23; Governor John Penn (nephew) to T. Penn, 17 Mar. 1764, mss., Penn Papers, Off. Corr. 9:220; unidentified newspaper clipping, 23 Apr. 1764, ibid., 9:296, HSP. Iroquois attacks, however, were notably restrained and highly directional. For the somewhat confused situation see the papers cited in index listing: "Delaware Indians, Iroquois recruitment (1764) to punish," *Johnson Papers* 14:160.

41. Ibid., 11:401–2, 504–5.

42. Halifax's alternate sulking and hounding of the duke of Newcastle over "one of the vacant Garters" runs as a comic refrain for years through the British Library's Newcastle Papers. See it flaunted in his portrait, p. 12 above.

43. Penn to Peters, 11 Nov. 1764, mss., Gratz Coll., Govs. of Pa., Case 2, Box 33-a, HSP.

missions among the Indians and bishops among the colonials, coordinating their efforts at the desire of the archbishop of Canterbury.[44]

Their motives had much in common. Both saw opportunity in the missions to acquire lands. Both were avowedly imperialist and authoritarian. Smith wanted more power in Pennsylvania and a bishopric for himself. Johnson wanted to fend off the Dissenter missions from New England and the Jesuits from Canada to assure greater control over the Iroquois source of all his power and wealth. They agreed on a political objective with a religious pretense, and they seemed to think that their major task was simply to win crown support. What they overlooked was what the ministry well understood; that is, that the establishment of bishops would arouse fury among the colonials who had emigrated to America to escape the English establishment. Ministers knew as well as Johnson and Smith the political value of bishops, but ministers had not forgotten Oliver Cromwell, so the American bishops never materialized. However, the campaign to appoint them became public knowledge that aroused almost as much hostility as though it were the accomplished fact.[45] Johnson had the good luck to die in 1774 before the storm struck.[46] Smith lived on to become a battered, humiliated, friendless old drunk.[47]

44. Smith to Johnson, 16 Mar. 1767, mss., SPG Papers 15:185–87, Lambeth Palace Library, London, printed with minor variations in *Johnson Papers* 5:510–14, Johnson to Smith, 10 Apr. 1767, ibid., 5:528–32; The Correspondence of General Thomas Gage with the Secretaries of State, 1763–1775, ed. Clarence Edwin Carter, 2 vols. (1931–33), repr. (Hamden, Conn.: Archon Books, 1969), 1:26–27.

45. See the excellent account of the general crisis, including the roles played by Smith and Johnson, in Bridenbaugh, *Mitre and Sceptre*.

46. Johnson died in harness during a treaty conference with the Iroquois, 12 July 1774. He was spared the odium acquired by his son for whipping the Indians up against outlying communities during the American Revolution. There can be no doubt that Johnson would have undertaken that task without hesitation. *N.Y. Col. Docs.* 8:479.

47. Smith wrote to Benjamin Rush in 1793, calling him "my only Friend," mss., Wm. Smith Papers 3:52, HSP. This was surely an odd couple—High Tory and Revolutionary—but Rush was Smith's physician, and his comments after Smith died, 14 May 1803, suggest that the "friendship" was professional and its temperature cool: "We are struck by the great contrariety of his morals to his religious principles," wrote Rush. "He descended to his grave . . . without being lamented by a human creature . . . not a drop of kindred blood attended his funeral . . . he appears to have been a nondescript in the history of man." [Benjamin Rush], *Autobiography*, ed. George W. Corner, published for the American Philosophical Society (Princeton, N.J.: Princeton University Press, 1948), 262–65.

Part Five ❧ *THE EMPIRE OF FORTUNE*

INTRODUCTION ❧

My purpose in these brief concluding chapters is to tie up some loose ends and to make explicit the destinations of historical journeys reported throughout the book. Irony is omnipresent. Proof is not attempted.

The British crown's peace with the French crown did not imply peace with the peoples under British rule. Instead of disbanding his armies, George III persuaded Parliament to authorize maintenance of the troops at full strength. Parliament acceded readily because place-hungry military members identified their own prosperity with the king's program.

Armies must be paid and equipped. King and Parliament tried to tax Britain's colonies to support the troops occupying Indian territory "ceded" by France. When the colonists resisted, taxation was added to the heavy burden already borne by Englishmen to pay for the Seven Years War debt. Englishmen added their resistance to the colonials', whereupon king and Parliament instituted repression on both sides of the Atlantic. The colonists observed that the troops occupying Indian territory were shifted to occupy colonial towns, and they rose in revolt.

Unlike their earlier resistance, the Revolutionaries opposed the sovereignty of king *and* Parliament, and they established their own sovereign governments. Whereupon, to complete the cycle of irony, they set out to expand their own empire over Indian territories and peoples—in the name of liberty.

Chapter 21 ☙ *REPRESSION of COLONIALS*

All artful rulers, who strive to extend their own power beyond its just limits, endeavour to give to their attempts, as much semblance of legality as possible.

John Dickinson

The peacetime army

Several events coincided in the year 1763 so that their sequence must be observed closely to avoid confusing cause and effect. It would be natural, for instance, to assume that the Indian rising stirred British statesmen to decide to keep a large military establishment and an army of occupation to protect the colonials. Indeed, this excuse was often advanced; but, in fact, Parliament voted a big army *before* the Indians rose in arms, and the reasons had more to do with suppressing colonials than protecting them.

As the treaty of Paris was being negotiated, early in 1763, Parliament took up the issue of the size of the peacetime army. Obviously great economies could be made by reducing the military establishment, but to do so would be to reduce the king's patronage, which Cumberland had made absolute in the military establishment.[1] Prerogative men took the alarm. Led by King George III personally, they schemed to maintain a big army with many royal perquisites, which the duke of Newcastle correctly perceived as "an Extensive Plan of Power, and Military Influence . . . never thought of before, in this Country." But Newcastle's power had been eroded by the war so that he and his Old Whigs could only look on helplessly when that frenetic militarist William Pitt emerged from seclusion to breathe fire in the House of Commons, 4 March 1763. As noted above, Pontiac did not lay siege to Detroit until 9 May, and the news could not reach London till months later. Historian John Shy remarks, "the decision to maintain a garrison in North America had been accepted without

1. Yorke, *Life of Hardwicke* 2:256.

scutiny or criticism, primarily for reasons that had nothing to do with North America.[2]

The king and his ministers had more in mind than enjoying the perquisites of that expensive big army. They aimed at restoring royal power through the use of the royal prerogative in the colonies as well as the homeland, and the Indian rising came as an interruption, though not unwelcome, to their plans. Their goals were suspected in London. One opposition pamphleteer fretted over the "infinite Dependance upon the Crown" created by the war. "Too many" of those servants of the crown, civil and military, "might be tempted to assist in extending the Influence of the Prerogative to the Prejudice of public Liberty." He lamented to see the nation "so amazingly reconciled" to a large standing army in peacetime.[3] Another pamphleteer denounced "the present extravagant Fondness for military Establishments of every Kind."[4] But Pennsylvania's Joseph Galloway actually endorsed a standing army to keep order against Indians and violent frontiersmen.[5] Benjamin Franklin was told bluntly by a London friend that the army's purpose in America was "to preserve a Military Awe over you,"[6] but Franklin kept quiet for four years on the issue; in 1768 he broke silence to threaten civil war for seventy-five years, if necessary, to prevent military domination—but in the guise of an anonymous Englishman writing in the *London Public Advertiser* to deplore such an eventuality.[7] For most Londoners, a few hundred warriors in a wilderness 6,000 miles away constituted an irritant rather than a threat. Far from sharing Amherst's desire to "extirpate" the Indians, his majesty's ministers in 1764 had an eye cocked toward the uses that those Indians might serve. Their trade in peltry, entirely lost during hostilities, was a matter of concern. So also was the Indians' function as a barrier to westward expansion of the seaboard colonials, much feared by prerogative politicians and some others who projected their own logic as an image of colonial thinking. With France out of the way, these men reasoned that the colonies had become less dependent on Britain's protection and would therefore become more assertive. Subministers John Pownall and Maurice Morgann conceived a ban on further western colonization, with a reservation of territory for Indians "encouraged to support their own sovereignty," as a means of coercing the colonies into obedience.[8]

2. Shy, *Toward Lexington*, 78–79; Knollenberg, *Origin of the American Revolution*, 93.
3. *Letter to Two Great Men*, 43–46.
4. *Reasons Why the Approaching Treaty of Peace Should Be Debated in Parliament . . .* (London: R. Griffiths, 1760), 41.
5. Newcomb, *Franklin and Galloway*, 89.
6. Alexander Small to Franklin, 1 Dec. 1764, in *Franklin Papers* 11:482.
7. On Civil War, 25 Aug. 1768, in ibid., 15:191–93.
8. Knollenberg, *Origin of the American Revolution*, 91–92; Marshall, "Imperial Regulation," 31–35; Wickwire, *British Subministers*, 91–96.

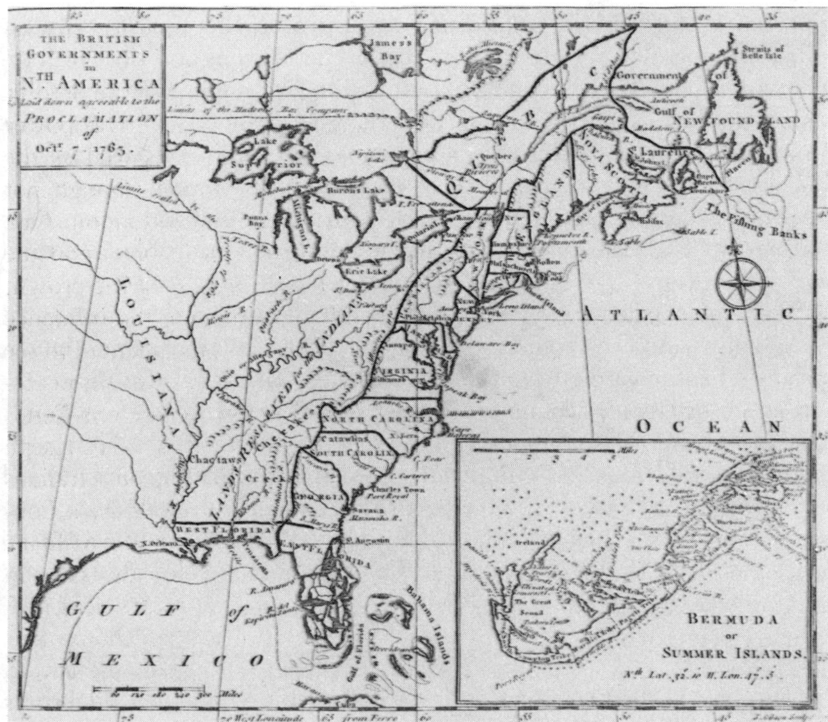

MAP 11. The Proclamation Line of 1763. REPRODUCED BY PERMISSION FROM THE COPY OF *The Gentleman's Magazine* IN THE JOHN CARTER BROWN LIBRARY, BROWN UNIVERSITY.

The Royal Proclamation of 1763

For imperialists far from the blood and destruction, the Indian rising was not inconvenient: the warriors drove back colonials to the protection and control of royal officials, and the fighting seemed to teach the desired lesson that an army of occupation was a necessity for colonial security. In the tumult of Indian war, the motives of royal patronage and royal controls associated with military power disappeared temporarily from sight.

The ministers desired to pacify those Indians in order to make them serve royal purposes, and were willing therefore to make concessions rather than seek revenge. They seized upon the device of a boundary, first broached at Easton in 1758, and promulgated it in the famous Royal Proclamation of 7 October 1763.[9] This seemed to offer the tribesmen their primary war

9. Stagg, *Anglo-Indian Relations in North America*, 284–348.

aim, but it had a catch. Instead of decreeing a line between British and tribal sovereignties, it ordered that "the several Nations or Tribes of Indians with whom We are connected, and who live under Our Protection should not be molested or disturbed in the Possession of such Parts of *our* Dominions and Territories as, not having been ceded to, or purchased by Us, are *reserved* to them, or any of them, *as their Hunting Grounds.*" A further qualification declared this to be "Our Royal Will and Pleasure for the present."[10] Events quickly demonstrated the impermanence of the royal will and pleasure.

When the hostile tribes finally laid down their arms, they were amused by promises and even some actual surveys of the boundary line, though always it bent inward farther than the Indians wanted. Even as these proceedings ostentatiously continued, however, land speculators swarmed over London, clamoring for grants to create new colonies in the "reserved" lands; and noblemen with influence joined the speculating companies.[11] Naturally this activity was not advertised to Indians solemnly engaged in negotiations about their boundary, but they were not the only persons to lose sight of the direction of affairs. For eleven years, colonials excitedly

10. Italics added. A comprehensive study with contemporary maps is in Louis De Vorsey, Jr., *The Indian Boundary in the Southern Colonies, 1763–1775* (Chapel Hill: University of North Carolina Press, 1961). The proclamation line on modern maps is in *Atlas of Early American History*, eds. Lester J. Cappon, et al., published for the Newberry Library and the Institute of Early American History and Culture (Princeton, N.J.: Princeton University Press, 1976), 15, 16, 92. Detailed analysis and text of the proclamation's terms are in Jack Stagg, *Anglo-Indian Relations in North America To 1763 And An Analysis of The Royal Proclamation of 7 Oct. 1763* (Ottawa: Research Branch, Indian and Northern Affairs Canada, 1981), 350–400. Many associated papers are in *Documents Relating to the Constitutional History of Canada, 1759–1791*, eds. Adam Shortt and Arthur G. Doughty, Canadian Archives Sessional Paper 18 (Ottawa, 1907), 119–23. The proclamation continues to have importance as a judicial precedent in Canada and Australia. For example, see Kenneth M. Narvey, "The Royal Proclamation of 7 Oct. 1763, The Common Law, and Native Rights to Land within the Territory Granted to Hudson's Bay Company," *Saskatchewan Law Review* 38 (1974), 124–233. Thanks for this to Professor Imre Sutton, and see his comment in *Indian Land Tenure: Bibliographical Essays and a Guide to the Literature* (New York: Clearwater Publishing Co., 1975), 210.

Bibliographic note: The proclamation's legal boundary line was the reality behind Frederick Jackson Turner's mythical abstraction of a frontier line between "civilization" and "savagery." Apparently Turner paid no attention to the proclamation line while he "built his hypothesis on theories borrowed from biologists, geographers, and statistical cartographers, each providing an essential brick for its foundations." Bernard DeVoto illustrated the power of Turner's creation by publishing a book in 1952 without a mention of the proclamation or its line in his chapter on "Converging Frontiers," or anywhere else in the book.

F. J. Turner, *The Frontier in American History* (1920, but the essay in question was written 1893), repr. (New York: Holt, Rinehart and Winston, 1962), 2–3; Ray Allen Billington, *The Genesis of the Frontier Thesis: A Study in Historical Creativity* (San Marino, Calif.: The Huntington Library, 1971), 7; Bernard DeVoto, *The Course of Empire* (Boston: Houghton Mifflin Co., 1952).

Please note that Billington meant his quoted remark and his book's title as compliments.

11. Abernethy, *Western Lands*, chs. 2–12. Maps in Alvord, *Mississippi Valley*, 1: frontispiece, 97, 317; 2: frontispiece.

pursuing gold at the end of the rainbow overlooked the Royal Proclamation's quality as an act of high prerogative that sharply curtailed the practical effect of the sea-to-sea charters of Massachusetts, Connecticut, Virginia, and North Carolina. Virginians consoled themselves that the proclamation's limits on their expansion were temporary.[12] The lure of potential great wealth was so great that when crown and colonies soon came to conflict they disputed on grounds other than the proclamation.

The stamp tax

Sooner or later, someone had to pay for the royal army of occupation, and in 1765 Parliament submitted a bill for part of the cost in the shape of a tax. Its worst feature, in colonists' eyes, was enforcement of collectibility. There could be no smuggling to evade the tax on stamped paper without which no contract nor deed would be legal, nor any newspaper published (among many other transactions). There was more in this law than just collecting money. Violations might be tried in Admiralty courts of royal jurisdiction, without juries. The law hinted also, by its mention of courts "exercising ecclesiastical jurisdiction," at appointment of Church of England bishops—anathema in New England most of all. As Edmund S. Morgan and Helen M. Morgan observe, "the colonists would find themselves taxed without consent for purposes of revenue, their rights to common-law trial abridged, the authority of one prerogative court (admiralty) enlarged, and the establishment of another (ecclesiastical) hinted at."[13]

The crown attempted to justify all this as necessary to maintain a standing army for the protection of the people, but that excuse did not wash among the people supposedly benefited. Massachusetts's agent protested that "sending troops to defend America . . . has great appearance of care over them, but really is as absurd as it is needless;" Americans, he averred, could defend themselves. An officer in New Jersey declared, with some reason, that garrisons and forts in Indian country were "so far from protecting that they are the very cause of our Indian wars." Philadelphia's Charles Thomson objected that no army had been needed during New France's existence, but after its demise "we are burthened with a standing

12. George Washington, for example, wrote that "the nominal line, commonly called the Ministerial Line . . . seems to have been considered by government as a temporary expedient . . . and no further regard has been paid to it by the ministers themselves." Quoted in Alvord, *Mississippi Valley* 2:186; ch. 3. But the Quebec Act nullified Washington's grants of western lands.

13. Edmund S. and Helen M. Morgan, *The Stamp Act Crisis*, 96–98. For the great importance of smugglers see John W. Tyler, *Smugglers and Patriots Boston Merchants and the Advent of the American Revolution* (Boston: Northeastern University Press, 1986).

army and subjected to insufferable Insults from any petty officer."[14] The cities erupted in violent opposition that need not be retold here. It is enough to say that merchants boycotted English goods while organized mobs persecuted the tax collectors and prevented the distribution of their stamped papers.

Whereupon the basic function of a standing army was revealed. General Gage moved his troops from the western forts to the coastal towns. From being an army to control Indians, it became the crown's agency to enforce controls over colonials. In the words of Clarence Edwin Carter, "The convergence of so many powers and responsibilities into this single authority, which was given frequent impetus by royal decrees and parliamentary action, points unmistakably to a trend towards imperial union, based upon military foundations. . . . In laying the foundation for the ultimate exercise of coercive authority, it represents a new phase of British policy."[15]

The new policy contradicts the frequently expressed assertion that the conquest of Canada, by removing colonists' fears of the French, had stimulated them to revolution. Rather, with the French gone, the British crown felt free, at last, to bear down on the colonies, and did so with the enforcing power of its occupying army. Not the Canadian conquest, but rather the new British policy and its instruments were the stimuli that finally determined the colonists for liberation.

The Quebec Act

When New France's officials returned to Europe, French Canadians remained in Canada. So did all the Indians, and for these peoples left behind the conquest dictated new futures, necessarily still interlinked. British officials, anxious to forestall new uprisings by their old enemies,

MAP 12. Distribution of British troops in North America, 1766. DETAIL ADAPTED FROM ADD. MSS. 11288 AND REPRODUCED BY COURTESY OF THE BRITISH LIBRARY. This was included in the exhibition and catalog *The American War of Independence, 1775–1783* (London: British Library, 1975), with the comment: "During the Stamp Act crisis, 1765–66, Thomas Gage, Commander-in-Chief in North America, began to withdraw troops to the Atlantic colonies, with the evident intention of using military force to support civil rule. . . . Troops were withdrawn from all but the largest forts in the interior, and quartered on the unwilling colonists in the provinces of New York and Pennsylvania" (p. 17).

14. Shy, *Toward Lexington*, 141–42.

15. Troop movement: map, "Cantonment of His Majesty's Forces in N. America," Add. MS. 11288, British Library, reproduced in *The American War of Independence, 1775–83*, catalog for a commemorative exhibition (London: British Museum Publications, 1975), 17.
Quotation: "Introductory Note," *Correspondence of General Thomas Gage*, ed. Carter, 1:xii.

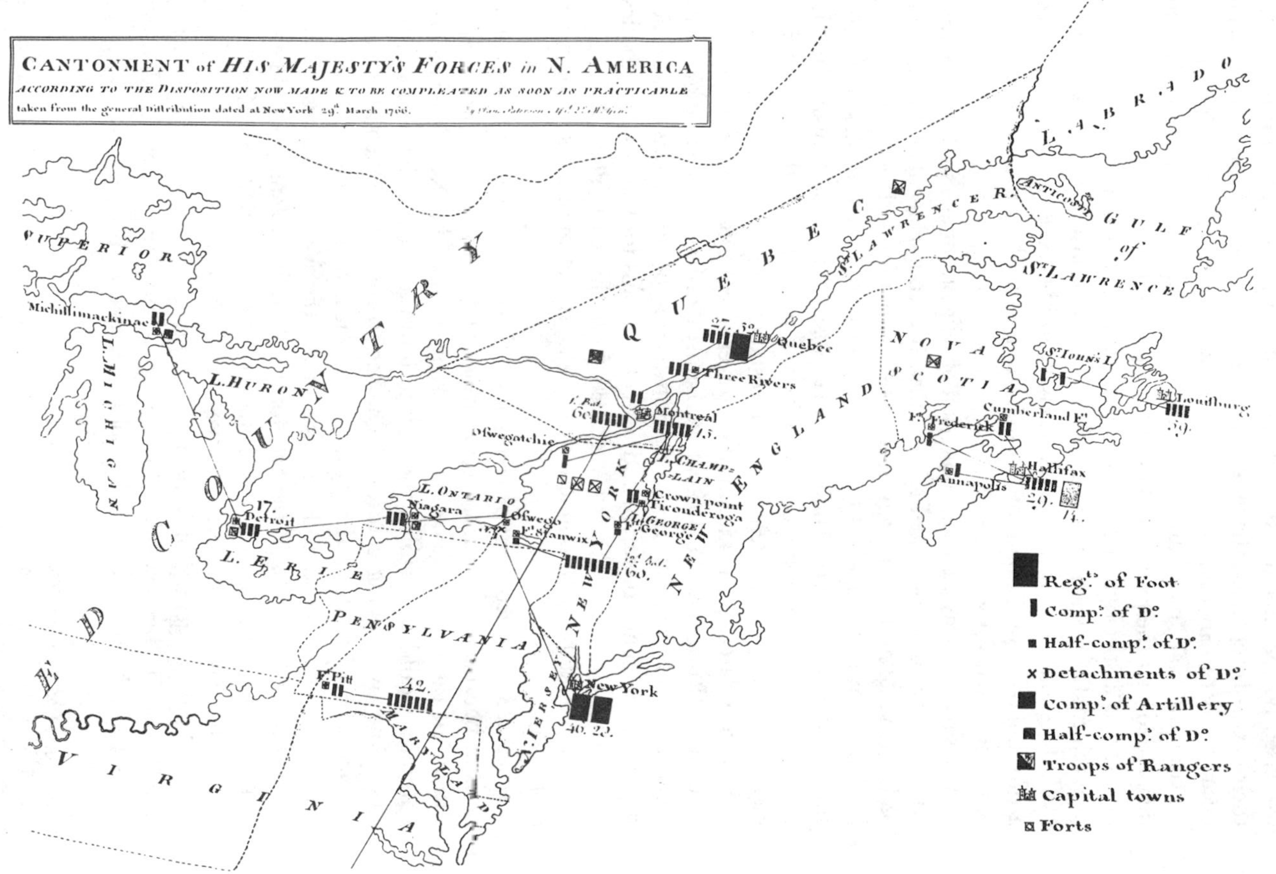
CANTONMENT of HIS MAJESTY'S FORCES in N. AMERICA
ACCORDING TO THE DISPOSITION NOW MADE & TO BE COMPLEATED AS SOON AS PRACTICABLE
taken from the general Distribution dated at New York 29th March 1766.
LABRADO
GULF of St. LAWRENCE
ANTICOSTI
St. LAWRENCE R.
QUEBEC
COUNTRY
SUPERIOR
L. MICHIGAN
L. HURON
L. ONTARIO
L. ERIE
NOVA SCOTIA
NEW ENGLAND
NEW YORK
PENSYLVANIA
VIRGINIA
Michillimackinac
Detroit
Niagara
Oswego
Ft. Stanwix
Oswegatchie
Montreal
Quebec
Three Rivers
CHAMPLAIN
Crown point
Ticonderoga
Ft. George
St. Johns I.
Louisburg
Cumberland Ft.
Ft. Frederick
Halifax
Annapolis
New York
Ft. Pitt
Regts. of Foot
Compy. of Do.
Half-compy. of Do.
x Detachments of Do.
Compy. of Artillery
Half-compy. of Do.
Troops of Rangers
Capital towns
Forts

exercised power leniently in Canada. Indeed they were forced to protect their new subjects from the greed and bigotry of some of the old ones who became what in another era would be called carpetbaggers.[16]

After the war, merchants from New England rushed to Quebec and demanded that the province should have the "liberty" of a colonial assembly. It was a specious liberty that native Canadians and the British military rejected, for such an assembly could only consist of, and be elected by, Protestants so that it would automatically become the instrument for a tiny minority of immigrants to impose their will on the great majority of Catholic natives.[17]

The situation was a curious inversion of religious affairs in New England where "Dissenters" protested against British encouragement of the Church of England. The terminology has an Alice in Wonderland quality. The Dissenters in fact belonged to the churches established in Massachusetts and Connecticut where Anglicans were dissenters and Roman Catholicism was illegal. In Quebec, royal power protected Catholic establishments against encroachment of all Protestants.

Sooner or later in Canada, military government would have to give way to civil institutions. The British Parliament ordained the change in its Quebec Act of 1774, but not to the satisfaction of Protestants, for the act stipulated religious toleration and provided means for Canadian Catholics to govern themselves in accustomed ways. On this basis alone, New Englanders would have responded to the act as yet another sort of royal repression.

It seemed like encouragement of popish threats, worse even than Anglicanism, because of the act's extension of Quebec's jurisdiction down the "backs" of the seaboard colonies; surely, reasoned the New Englanders, Catholics would be enabled thereby to infiltrate their colonies from the west. And by denying control of Quebec to the Protestant immigrants, the act seemed to deny the fruits of conquest to the colonies who had poured out most blood and treasure during the war of conquest. There was yet more bitterness in the act, for it definitely violated, permanently and beyond appeal, the sea-to-sea charters of Connecticut and Massachusetts with a consequent barrier to westward expansion.[18]

The Anglican gentry of Virginia were not overfond of the New Englanders, whom they considered to be bigots, but Virginia also had a sea-to-sea charter. Whereas the Royal Proclamation of 1763 had been an

16. Burt, *Old Province of Quebec*, ch. 6.

17. Ibid., 92–93; Sir Reginald Coupland, *The Quebec Act: A Study in Statesmanship* (Oxford: Clarendon Press, 1925), 43–47.

18. Ibid., ch. 3, app. B: Sosin, *Whitehall and the Wilderness*, 244–49; Charles H. Metzger, S. J., *The Quebec Act: A Primary Cause of the American Revolution*, United States Catholic Historical Society Monograph Series 16 (New York, 1936), 149–50.

expedient that temporarily forbade westward expansion but stimulated schemes for new western colonies when the ban should be lifted, the Quebec Act destroyed such schemes permanently. It became plain that new colonies, when founded, would benefit English projectors instead of Virginians, and the reaction was swift and strong.[19]

Thomas Jefferson displayed his ability to define words to suit his purposes by writing hotly that a people had the inherent right to circumscribe their own boundaries.[20] He omitted Indians from the ranks of "people" as he would later speak of the equality of all men without including Black slaves, but he spoke for the expansion-minded Virginians, high and low, and his remark was as treasonable in intent as Patrick Henry's more notorious outbursts.

Setting aside the other causes or factors involved in the American Revolution, we must recognize that Britain's conquest of New France stimulated opposed motives in the British crown and its American colonies. The king and his ministers determined to prevent expansion westward until they could establish stronger rule within the colonies, but royal restrictions aroused hot anger among colonials dreaming of western empire—their own empire—and that anger became fury when the crown enforced its restrictions with an alien occupying army.

19. Samuel W. Jones, "Memoir of the Hon. James Duane," in *Doc. Hist. N.Y.* 4:1071; Declaration of Resolves of the First Continental Congress, 14 Oct. 1774, in *Documents of American History*, ed. Henry Steele Commager, 7th ed., 2 vols. (New York: Appleton-Century-Crofts, 1963), p. 83, resolution 7.

20. Thomas Jefferson, *A Summary View of the Rights of British America* (1774), in *Tracts of the American Revolution, 1773–1776*, ed. Merrill Jensen (Indianapolis: Bobbs-Merrill Co., 1967), 273.

Chapter 22 ❧ *REPRESSION of ENGLISHMEN*

The corrupt influence of the crown, by having all the places in its disposal, hath so effectually swallowed up the power, and eaten out the virtue of the House of Commons (the republican part in the Constitution) that the government of England is nearly as monarchical as that of France or Spain. . . . Why is the Constitution of England sickly, but because monarchy hath poisoned the Republic; the crown has engrossed the Commons.

Tom Paine

A critical debate in Parliament was held on the eighth and ninth days of May 1770. On the eighth, Thomas Pownall moved for an enquiry into contradictions and discrepancies between the commissions of civil and military officers in America, especially to correct those that "contain any powers and authorities that are not warranted by law and the constitution." What Pownall said may well be taken to heart today. Defending the people of Massachusetts shortly after news of the "Boston Massacre" had reached England, he denounced "military discipline for the specious pretence of assisting the civil government when it is upon no other pretence but the increasing of your army."[1]

Pownall protests

Much has been written about Pownall's vanity and egotism, perhaps with half truth; to complete the truth, one must recognize his courage and clarity in the crisis.

"They believe, they feel, that you not only mean to alter their constitution, but to establish a military government . . . this is the way that every free government upon the continent of Europe has lost its liberty.

1. *Proceedings and Debates*, eds., Simmons and Thomas, 3:272.

Their apprehensions are well-founded." Pownall did not pretend that he was only citing the opinions of others.

This is the material point. The rest are only doubts, but here they say, are certainties. They know you mean to establish a military government there. They have remonstrated against it. They have petitioned against it. The Council will not act. The magistrates will not quarter them. They will do no one act, by which you can say they recognize the right of the troops being there, under that establishment that they are there. The consideration of this point is the great occasion of the whole.[2]

Many a history has been written to insist that the American Revolution was the product of misunderstanding on both sides. They are dead wrong. George III's minions, in full control of Parliament, intended to help him use the authority of Parliament to whip the colonists into submission, and the colonists understood this very well. They had no options but to submit or rebel. Even the concession that some of the crown's servants had made "mistakes" was denied them. On the next day after Pownall lost his motion for an enquiry, Edmund Burke filed eight motions in Commons censuring the administration on particular issues of practice. He had as little success as Pownall. The crown's voting machine rolled right over him with such a display of power that he called for a division of the house on only one of the eight resolutions which went down by 197 votes to 79.[3]

There is no doubt of the king's direct, personal complicity. Each day, Lord North rushed to George III to inform about the resolutions and their rejection; and North "informed" also in a more sinister meaning of the word. He carefully listed the names of speakers for and against the motions.[4] What was spoken then between the king and his first minister cannot be documented, but it does not seem hard to guess.

As these events proceeded, North and the king were also engaged in formally rebuffing a remonstrance from the City of London (whose lord mayor William Beckford was one of Pownall's supporters, among other things).[5] The king and his servants had equally authoritarian notions at home and abroad. Their logic, considering their intentions, was impeccable. Repression in England was necessary. As Lord Mayor Beckford cried out in Commons, "If you draw the sword in America, half the people of this country will be against you."[6]

2. Ibid., 3:273.
3. Ibid., 3:296–99, 327.
4. *The Correspondence of King George the Third from 1760 to December 1783*, ed. John Fortescue, 6 vols. (London: Macmillan and Co., 1927–1928), 2:144–46. North reported 199 votes against Burke.
5. Ibid., 2:143, 147–51.
6. *Proceedings and Debates*, eds. Simmons and Thomas, 3:279.

"Wilkes and Liberty!"

John Wilkes led the general protest from his place in the House of Commons and in the pages of his periodical pamphlet *The North Briton*, whereupon Lord Halifax (who had trimmed his way into the new ministry) closed down Wilkes's paper with a libel charge and tried futilely to jail him on more serious accusations.[7] (Wilkes sued Halifax and won £4,000 damages.) The royalists in Commons expelled Wilkes, and a total stranger challenged him to a duel, plainly intending to separate him from politics by the quickest, most permanent means.[8]

Wilkes fled to France. His Middlesex constituents re-elected him to Commons, and George's minions expelled him again. The routine was repeated twice more when, hoping to put an end to the scandal, the royalists simply seated Wilkes's defeated (and corrupt) opponent. Support came for Wilkes from Americans who perceived that his fight was theirs. They raised a large fund—thousands of pounds—that enabled him to pay his large debts and keep up his struggle until finally those determined Middlesex voters elected him again and he entered Commons in muted triumph. (Middlesex was not a rotten borough; it came closer to democracy than most English constituencies of the time.)[9]

Wilkes was an unlikely hero. Flamboyant, rakish, violent in temper, he has won many sneers from commentators who put manners higher than matter. Edmund Burke thought that the Middlesex voters had become "unfastened from their usual moorings," but, when the City's guildsmen chose Wilkes as lord mayor, Burke could only wonder.[10] What Wilkes did, more than any other Englishman, including Burke, was to challenge the crown's repression. His constituents and the colonials paid homage to his bold courage and principled struggle in their behalf. So should we. In an age when politicians unscrupulously truckled and trimmed for place and profit, Wilkes's political integrity was unique. That was precisely why he drew lightning from an administration determined to suppress all such manifestations of independence.

7. [John Wilkes], *The North Briton, Revised and Corrected by the Author*, 2 vols. bound together (London: n.p., 5 June 1762–23 Apr. 1763); *Gentleman's Magazine* 33 (1763), 239–46. Halifax's "messengers" arrested the *North Briton*'s printer and were brought to trial for doing so; judge and jury concurred that the whole proceeding was illegal and fined the "messengers" £300 and costs. Ibid., 33:341–48.

8. "Wilkes, John (1727–1797)" in *Dict. Nat. Biog.* 61:242–50.

9. Loc. cit. Wilkes' opponent in the Middlesex election was Colonel Henry Laws Luttrell, who polled 296 votes against Wilkes's 1,143. "Wilkes, John," *Encyclopaedia Britannica*, 11th ed., 28:642–43.

10. Burke to O'Hara, ca. 1 Apr. 1768, in *Edmund Burke, New York Agent*, ed. Ross J. S. Hoffman (Philadelphia: American Philosophical Society, 1956), 430; same to same, 19 Nov. 1773, ibid., 551.

Militarism creates disorder

Having such views I am at odds with the Tory historians whose most famous spokesman was Sir Lewis Namier. Namier's politics are openly reflected in his work. He was a conservative and a Conservative, evidently incapable of conceiving government other than that of the rich and well born; anything else would be anarchy or chaos. He put his conception of democracy in a capsule: "there is no free will in the thinking and actions of the masses, any more than in the revolutions of planets, in the migrations of birds, and in the plunging of hordes of lemmings into the sea."[11] He accompanied that attitude with the Tory sort of cynicism justifying whatever usurpations of power the right people might find necessary to take charge and keep control. It was quite easy for Namier to forgive the maneuvers and manipulations of his side—the right side, naturally—which he surveyed with an amused and deceptive air of being above the battle. He could maintain this specious appearance by concentrating exclusively on the machinery of politics, avoiding notice of issues, programs, and policies. His writing is an account of means without ends.

Thus Namier could present George III, Lord Bute, and Lord North as the successor generation and mirror image of Newcastle and the Old Whigs, but the falsity of this view becomes instantly apparent when programs are compared. Certainly all of these gentry used patronage to win power and dominate Parliament; just as certainly they called it corruption when used by their opponents. Namier was at his best when describing and characterizing the methods of this system of patronage/corruption. As he rightly declared, the system was integral to government in the conditions of that era.[12] But on issues, George's Tories went in different directions from the Old Whigs.

The big dividing issue was militarism. Newcastle had wanted a small army and no militia at all, partly because of the expense of a military establishment, partly because he correctly foresaw its use to inflate royal power. In George's calculations, the inflation of royal power was worth the extra expense, and he got his way. It makes little difference in outcome that he manipulated Parliament to win instead of triumphing by overt appeal to prerogative.

But we must not regard prerogative as a thing abandoned. It was very much at work within Parliament through the military members, not to speak of the beneficiaries of other patronage; and when George got his big

11. Herbert Butterfield, *George III and the Historians*, rev. ed. (New York: Macmillan, 1969), 206; Sir Lewis Namier, *England in the Age of the American Revolution*, 2d ed. (London: Macmillan and Co., 1961), 40–41.

12. Sir Lewis Namier, *The Structure of Politics at the Accession of George III*, 2d ed. (London: Macmillan and Co., 1963), 9, 17, 25–28, 163–64, 176, 234, et passim.

army, it was by his prerogative that it became an army occupying the colonies. Can this policy be compared without absurdity to the decades of Newcastle's "salutary neglect"?

Apart from personalities, that big army had to be paid for. It is not true, as has sometimes been said, that the stamp tax was imposed on colonials in order to help defray the costs of the Seven Years War; it was intended to maintain the postwar army, and when Americans resisted it successfully, the money had to be found elsewhere.[13] Englishmen were taxed instead, and resented it no less, but without the same success.

The "cyder" tax

When colonials refused to pay for their army of occupation, Parliament imposed a heavy excise tax at home to pay for it, and gave the excise collectors power to enter and search any householder's premises, business or domestic, and seize whatever the searcher chose to call suspect.[14] Abuses were made all the more likely because even the collectors were exploited by salaries so low that they joined to send one of their number to Parliament for redress. He was Thomas Paine, but his argument that "poverty and opportunity corrupt many an honest man" failed to convince the gentlemen in power. For this, his first venture into political agitation, Paine was sacked.[15] He emigrated to America, where he found solace and opportunity to speak his full mind about the government of England. That government's use of arbitrary search and seizure methods on both sides of the Atlantic aroused furious opposition on both sides. In America the opposition grew into revolution and eventually was embodied in the Bill of Rights of the Constitution of the United States.

In Britain, however, the opposition was suppressed. Government designated it a libel against government, and prosecuted its spokesmen. The transition from Newcastle to Bute was bridged by our old, prerogative-minded war hawk, Lord Halifax, who personally warranted the seizure of John Wilkes and his papers, and tried to get Wilkes hanged by stretching libel to treason.

13. Wilkes berated the government for its extravagance and corruption: e.g., by floating a loan of £3,500,000 among the ministry's friends at ten percent. *North Briton* no. 42. A writer in *Gentleman's Magazine* 33 (1763), 523 (possibly Wilkes) commented that "the nation now owes 140 millions, for which it never received more than 100 millions, and one fourth of that has been squandered in jobbs and contracts." Such complaints seem relevant to the righteous denunciations of colonial assemblies for not bearing their share of the financial burdens.

14. *Gentleman's Magazine* 33 (1763), 447.

15. Ed. intro., *The Complete Writings of Thomas Paine*, ed. Philip S. Foner, 2 vols. (New York: Citadel Press, 1969), 1:xi, 2:10.

The members of Parliament had Wilkes's example before them when considering whether to speak and vote against the crown's wishes. In an earlier trial, Law Lord Mansfield had carried the libel law to a new extreme by ruling that it applied to *dead* monarchs as well as the living.[16] Had that ruling existed in Shakespeare's day, could he have survived *Richard III?*

In sum, the crown's devotion to militarism required oppression, and I am inclined to believe that this is a general rule in history, not excepting our own times. Details vary according to circumstance, and conquest radiates glory, but sooner or later the price in blood and treasure makes the military burden too painful to bear. Then the generals must step aside or try to conquer their own people.

16. "Shebbeare, John, 1709–1788," in *Dict. Nat. Biog.* 52:2.

Chapter 23 ❧ *LIBERATION AND REPRESSION*

> We hold these truths to be self-evident, that all men are created equal, that they are endowed by their Creator with certain unalienable Rights, that among these are Life, Liberty and the pursuit of Happiness.
>
> The Declaration of Independence of The United States of America

> Although the leaders of the American government had qualms of conscience, the frontiersmen saw no inconsistency in expanding the area of freedom across the land of dead or dispossessed Indians.
>
> Reginald Horsman, *The Frontier in the Formative Years*

Sir Lewis Namier destroyed the old notion that good Whigs fought against repression by bad Tories, but he did not thereby destroy also the fact of repression. The clear implication of his findings (and all the sources) is that Whigs and Tories joined forces to put down groups outside the oligarchy who were struggling for participation in government—that is, those who could not legally vote for members of Parliament. Such groups included the large majority of British males and all females and all colonials of both sexes. Whig proclamations of devotion to "liberty" were meant to apply to Whigs' liberties, which included privilege to rule over lower classes and colonial appendages. Tories had the same objective, but with their own great families in the driver's seat instead of Whigs. With allowances for adjustment and compromise, Whigs and Tories could get along, and did. Their joint statement of principle was the Declaratory Act of Parliamentary supremacy of 1766, which followed upon repeal of the Stamp Act. The Declaratory Act passed without a division in the House of Commons; at most, only about half a dozen members had spoken against it.[1]

In strictly legal reasoning, Parliament's declaration was faultless because it was based on the assumptions and categories created by lawyers and judges in the service of the crown. By the logic of the legal fiction of sovereignty, wedded to theological reasoning from the assumption of one

1. Gipson, *British Empire* 10:386–414, ch. 17.

omnipotent deity also in the service of the crown, all power must derive from the crown. When George III gained control of Parliament, colonials lost ability to resist repression by maneuver within the empire's power structure.

Pennsylvania appeals

Pennsylvania tried. While other colonies protested and rioted, the solid citizens of Pennsylvania, led by imperialists Benjamin Franklin and Joseph Galloway, tried by the most respectful behavior to persuade crown and Parliament to concede self-government in the manner prevailing before the Seven Years War. Pennsylvania's assembly even petitioned to be released from the rule of hated proprietary lords and taken under the crown's direct government. To this end, Franklin exerted all his wiles as the assembly's agent in London, only to meet frustration and eventual insult.[2] All the colonies were to be treated alike (excepting the new conquest in Canada) regardless of variations in behavior, because the king was determined to coerce the colonists into subjection rather than mere loyalty. The king's political machine ground out measure after measure, which his officials enforced until finally Massachusetts exploded and was singled out to be "coerced" as an example.

Faced with such determination and power, the colonists had no alternatives but subjection or revolt. It was not an easy decision and they were not unanimous. Contrary to the fantasies of authoritarians, revolutions are not made by fickle mobs swayed by crackpot agitators. The very sober gentlemen who committed their lives and fortunes to this one recognized that "Prudence, indeed, will dictate that Governments long established should not be changed for light and transient causes; and accordingly all experience hath shewn, that mankind are more disposed to suffer, while evils are sufferable, than to right themselves by abolishing the forms to which they are accustomed." It was "a long train of abuses and usurpations, pursuing invariably the same Object" that forced the issue.

The dictatorship of the presbyteriat

It is absolutely necessary, however, to clarify what those gentlemen meant when they spoke grandly of liberty: they did not mean equal liberties for all people. Again, Pennsylvania is a touchstone. There, the American Revolution became also an internal revolution in which political leaders changed sides bewilderingly. The proprietary lords were overthrown at last, but the king went down with them and so did the assem-

2. Newcomb, *Franklin and Galloway*, chs. 3–5, pp. 241–42.

bly. Joseph Galloway along with Benjamin Chew went off to English exile, but Benjamin Franklin switched sides to ally with the Presbyterian politicians whom he had excoriated all his life,[3] and he accepted the dictatorship of the presbyteriat that they imposed on the new state. They had revenge on the Quakers at last by enacting a loyalty oath that no Quaker or pietist could reconcile to religious belief, as Thomas Penn had tried and failed to do in 1756, and the oath laws not only disfranchised a large mass of the state's population, but resulted in harassment and persecution of Quakers such as they had not experienced in Britain since the seventeenth century.[4]

Franklin made no protest that I have seen against the banishment by Pennsylvania's Revolutionary government of Israel Pemberton and other Friends to internal exile in West Virginia. John Hunt died there, and Pemberton survived the hardships only a short while after being permitted to return home. Though much harsh criticism has been made of Quaker "rule" in the province, the rise to power of the Quakers' enemies introduced an era during which a smaller proportion of the population could vote than ever was true during provincial times.

Written documents must be read in context of reality. The Pennsylvania Constitution, often touted as the high water mark of democracy during the Revolution, guaranteed religious freedom, but the loyalty oath legislation permitted under that constitution was sanction for religious persecution. Under these laws some people were more equal.[5]

What did the Declaration of Independence mean then by its pronouncement that the "just powers" of government are derived "from the consent of the governed"? One cannot reconcile that principle to what existed in Pennsylvania. The revolutionaries were concerned with power rather than justice.

Who were the Revolutionaries?

There has been much controversy as to whether the Revolution involved a rising of the masses against the classes. I do not propose to settle this

3. See Melvin H. Buxbaum, *Benjamin Franklin and the Zealous Presbyterians* (University Park, Pa.: Pennsylvania State University Press, 1975). All but the last two pages is devoted to the hostility between Franklin and the Presbyterians. Franklin's change of sides is omitted from the biographical studies I have seen, but is very evident from listings of names in the sources.

4. Philip S. Klein and Ari Hoogenboom, *A History of Pennsylvania* (New York: McGraw-Hill Book Company, 1973), 94, 97–98; Jackson Turner Main, *The Sovereign States, 1775–1783* (New York: New Viewpoints, 1973), 277, 292. And see ch. 11, n67, above.

5. For other devices of repression as well as the test oaths, see Anne M. Ousterhout, "Controlling the Opposition in Pennsylvania During the American Revolution," *Pa. Mag. of Hist. and Biog.* 105:1 (Jan. 1981), 3–34.

vexed issue in a sentence or two. Most historians agree that the Revolution stimulated movements in the direction of democracy, regardless of causes and motivation. I think, however, that ethnicity and religion were at least as much involved as social class in the outbreak of the war for independence. Calvinist ministers exhorted to revolt from New England's pulpits. Observably, south of New England, the Scotch-Irish Presbyterians of the western counties provided more than their proportionate share of the revolutionary armies; and in Pennsylvania their leaders pushed through the loyalty oaths that put pietists beyond the pale of citizenship. Tom Paine and the Pennsylvania Line were not gentry, nor were the Minutemen who rallied at Concord's North Bridge. On the other hand, Washingtons and Lees in Virginia, Livingstons in New York, Hancocks and Mayhews in Massachusetts—these, among others, were not peasants rising against landlords. Nor were they English, despite all their protestations about "Home" and the "rights of Englishmen." They had become distinctively American in their own comprehension, and certainly in that of supercilious British officers.

The Revolutionaries included every class of people from lowly Crispus Attucks to great planter and slave owner George Washington, but it was not a war of the whole people. Because American histories rarely let the Loyalists speak for themselves, it seems important to balance this analysis with the eloquent statement of the exiles who fled to Ontario, where a monument stands in front of Hamilton-Wentworth Court House.

> For the Unity of Empire
>
> The United Empire Loyalists, believing that a monarchy was better than a republic, and shrinking with abhorrence from a dismemberment of the empire, were willing, rather than lose the one and endure the other, to bear with temporary injustice. Taking up arms for the King, they passed through all the horrors of civil war and bore what was worse than death, the hatred of their fellow-countrymen, and when the battle went against them, sought no compromise, but, forsaking every possession excepting their honour, set their faces toward the wildernesses of British North America to begin, amid untold hardships, life anew under the flag they revered.

Empire and colonialism

Devotion to the king did indeed set the Loyalists against the Revolutionaries, but all articulate parties were equally determined in principle in favor of empire—and of colonialism. The Revolutionaries fought to be the rulers rather than the ruled.

It is instructive that the emigrants from Connecticut, who had driven

Teedyuscung's Delawares out of Pennsylvania's Wyoming Valley, honored John Wilkes in the name of their new town of Wilkes-Barre.

We must remember that colonialism was two-faced in Britain's American colonies. In one aspect the colonies were communities of Europeans reproducing, with modifications, the cultures and communities of their parent lands. In their other aspect, however, these colonists exerted power over indigenous communities of American Indians and imposed their own cultures upon the weaker peoples; in the process seizing lands, exploiting persons, and inflicting great harm. American Indians suffered every "colonialist" abuse from the European colonists in America that those colonists complained of in their Declaration of Independence, and more.

When the American war for independence ended, the problems of peacemaking echoed those of the end of the Seven Years War. As France had given up territory in 1763, so Britain did in 1783, and it is instructive that what changed sovereignties in 1783 was the Mississippi Valley land that the Quebec Act had sliced off the charter grants of Britain's older colonies. New post-treaty issues emerged. Were the new territories to come under the sovereignty, and therefore the granting power, of the states individually? Or were the new lands to be under the federal government directly? Restated, the question became: Were the crown lands reserved for the Indians to become the lands of the new empire or of its constituent states—and what about those Indians?

The new empire could not ignore the Indians, for the same reasons that had preoccupied the old empire. In an era when the existence of the United States of America was still shaky and problematical, its government understood acutely how troubles in Indian country could explode into full-scale international war, as the Seven Years War had started. And the end of the American states' war for independence did not mark the end of the Indians' war for tribal independence.

The tribes east of the Appalachian mountains were beaten into submission or driven into Canada; but west of the mountain range a new tribal confederation, wholly, independent of the old Iroquois Covenant Chain, fought on. After they defeated two major expeditions sent against them—Harmar's Humiliation in 1790 and St. Clair's Shame in 1791—the Indians forced reversal of United States policy concerning tribal territory. The assumption proclaimed in the Fort Stanwix treaty of 1784, that the defeat of Britain implied conquest of the Indians, was abandoned.[6] In its place, the federal government recognized tribal territorial rights under an overarching sovereignty of the United States, precisely the sort of legal fiction that crown lawyers had formerly concocted for Great Britain. In 1795, at

6. Graymont, *The Iroquois in the American Revolution*, 276–82; treaty text at 297–98; Jones, *License for Empire*, 173–75.

the treaty of Greenville, General Anthony Wayne convinced the hostile tribes to accept the new policy. (He had humbled but not conquered them in the battle of Fallen Timbers.) The tribes of the Old Northwest retreated behind their recognized boundary, within which they governed themselves as they pleased, and the lands east and south of the boundary became the American National Domain in fact as well as law.[7]

The statesmen of that era had more sense of reality than most imperialists. They saw Euramericans filling up their own new colonies, which they called "territories" in distinction from their "states"—and they realized that those westerners were as independent minded as themselves. Foresightedly they provided for those colony / territories to become states as peers in every respect of the thirteen founder states.[8] This was perhaps the greatest political invention of modern times, but the Indian tribes were left out of it.

The Delaware Indians had tried to negotiate an Indian state with themselves at its head in 1778, but Congress refused even to consider the treaty.[9] The event demonstrates that the founding statesmen never intended to let Indians become the peers of Euramericans. Indians were consigned deliberately to the social status of a lower caste in the political conditions of colonialism.

The romantic theory of revolution, in which all the lowly unite to rise against the oppressors, is embarrassed by the American Revolution's multiplicity of variously oppressed and exploited peoples who preyed upon each other; what most aggrieved the poor frontiersman was his sovereign's ban on robbing the even-poorer Indian, and the first target of the Indian's hatchet was the frontiersman's skull. Realism must also contemplate the disparity between upper-class rhetoric and conduct. The gentry cried out passionately for liberty in general, but itemized it as rights for themselves to hold slaves and seize land from Indians.

Heedless of theories, Americans began the building of their empire with an inheritance of ethnocentric semantics that made logic valid to themselves out of the strange proposition that invasion, conquest, and dispossession of other peoples support the principle that all men are created equal.

7. Earlier writers have refused to recognize the significance of tribal land cessions. See, for example, *The Public Lands: Studies in the History of the Public Domain*, ed. Vernon Carstensen (Madison: University of Wisconsin Press, 1968) xiv, 3–34. For welcome improvement see *Irredeemable America: The Indians' Estate and Land Claims*, ed. Imre Sutton (Albuquerque: University of New Mexico Press, 1985), 65–66, 212–15.

8. *Documents of American History*, ed. Commager, 1:121–24, 128–32.

9. Treaty text, 17 Sept. 1778, in *The American Indian and the United States: A Documentary History*, ed. Wilcomb E. Washburn, 4 vols. (Westport, Conn.: Greenwood Press, 1973), 3:2263–66. See also Downes, *Council Fires*, 216–17; Harvey H. Jackson, *Lachlan McIntosh and the Politics of Revolutionary Georgia* (Athens: University of Georgia Press, 1979), 79–80.

EPILOGUE

Civil history, particularly so called, is of prime dignity and authority among human writings; as the examples of antiquity, the revolutions of things, the foundations of civil prudence, with the names and reputations of men, are committed to its trust. But it is attended with no less difficulty than dignity; for it is a work of great labor and judgment, to throw the mind back upon things past, and store it with antiquity; diligently to search into, and with fidelity and freedom relate, 1, the commotions of times; 2, the characters of persons; 3, the instability of counsels; 4, the courses of actions; 5, the bottoms of pretences; 6, the secrets of state; and 7, to set all this to view in proper and suitable language . . . in short, nothing is so seldom found among the writings of men as true and perfect civil history.

Sir Francis Bacon, *The Advancement of Learning*, ch. 5

This is the culminating volume of a work begun more than thirty years ago in reaction to, and as a replacement for, Francis Parkman's multivolume *France and England in North America*. I have explained elsewhere why Parkman's work is fiction rather than history. My three volumes and supporting journal articles have all been based on principles diametrically opposed to his, of which the most important is candor. Parkman was a liar. He fabricated documents, misquoted others, pretended to use his great collection of sources when he really relied almost entirely on a small set of nastily biased secondary works, and did it all in order to support an ideology of divisiveness and hate based on racism, bigotry, misogyny, authoritarianism, chauvinism, and upper-class arrogance. These charges are demonstrated in two articles that need not be reprinted here.[1] Parkman's admirers have not risen to challenge my evidence, though they object to its presentation.

Who does not have biases? The issue is what kind. I do not subscribe to the view that objectivity requires a blandly even handed discussion of the villain and his victim in the same polite terms: a murderer is not just a person who was present when another person died. Let me recall the scene in Charlie Chaplin's film *The Great Dictator* in which dictator Hinkel screams and froths in a violent diatribe against "die Juden! *die Juden!!* DIE JUDEN!!!" His radio commentator interprets this maniacal outburst into

1. "A Vanishing Indian: Francis Parkman Versus His Sources"; "Francis Parkman: A Brahmin among Untouchables."

one English sentence: "Der Fuehrer referred to the Jews." This is not objectivity.

A double relationship is at issue: on the one side, between the writer and his materials; on the other, between the writer and his readers. Fidelity to source materials must be matched by candor of utterance, including honest statement of one's own values and judgments. Restraint of language is not a mandate to prettify truth; it is a tactic to maintain readers who would be put off by invective. Something seems to depend, however, on the values and preconceptions of readers; I have noticed that Parkman's invective and vilification are hailed by some critics as great style.

On the whole I am happy with the reception given my work. Fortunately it has been done during a general movement of criticism and revision of traditional mythology. Except where ideological priesthoods defend the old faith, historians now generally accept that the European colonization of America was an invasion rather than a mere settlement. There are exceptions, to be sure. But, like myself, many scholars now see "frontiers" as regions of mingling peoples rather than lines between myths of *savagery* and *civilization*. The Covenant Chain central to my research is now so standard that a new book is entitled *Beyond the Covenant Chain*.[2] (Obsolescence is swift nowadays.)

In some respects the present volume may be criticized, like its predecessors, as an "old-fashioned sort of political history." I can accept this with a slight modification; to wit, that political history is very new-fashioned for Indian tribes who have generally had only a sort of social history, when it deserved to be called history at all.

To portray the tribes' politics and diplomacy required me to attend also to the struggles of colonists and imperialists to acquire power of various kinds. Colonists defined their desire for power as a means of achieving *liberty*, recognizing that without the power to make it effective, liberty is only a noise. Indians also understood this hard fact and also participated in power struggles, with each other as well as by mingling in colonists' contests. Historiographical fossils have created the assumptions that Indian struggles consisted solely of armed combat, but the real people who were Indians understood political means to achieve their ends. They, too, wanted liberty, but they defined it in different terms than the colonists.

All the participants in this political history competed for *liberties* (as noted for example in the Magna Charta). Politics in this sense is the means for determining persons' shares of work, wealth, and privilege; tangibles that make empirical, inductive investigation possible. And that, to my mind, is the most illuminating kind of history.

2. *Beyond the Covenant Chain: The Iroquois and Their Neighbors in Indian North America, 1600–1800*, eds. Daniel K. Richter and James H. Merrell (Syracuse, N.Y.: Syracuse University Press, 1987).

In my field of work critics have strong notions of right and wrong, and express them with few inhibitions. As I have followed the prevailing custom, I can't complain at receiving some hostile reviews along with the kinder variety. What I did not expect—and it has bloodied my head and humbled my pride—is the criticism that comes from some younger scholars. From this side comes no effort to justify the actions or outlook of conqueror types, but its protagonists call me to task for paying insufficient attention to the internal development of Indian tribes and the personal biographies of Indian leaders. As the evidence is against me, I may as well plead guilty. An excuse might be that I do not like to write what I don't know, but that would only raise the question why I did not search harder for more as some of these critics are busily doing, blessings on them.

Forced to the wall, I confess (and will probably rue it) that my underlying motive for studying the history of Amerindians and Euramericans has been to discover my own people. Their dealings with Indians have made possible a propaganda of American exceptionalism from the patterns of human behavior elsewhere; a dogma, in short, that Americans are and have been God's Chosen People. It is a lethal delusion, a mythology that can be maintained only by false history and bullying policy. It must be challenged and exposed because its implications have spilled too much blood in our own land and all over the world. I found it necessary and truthful to show that Indians were human, rather than savage, in order to clarify that Europeans also remained human in America instead of acquiring divine Election here. All this is hindsight, of course. What I had in advance was curiosity and a strong sentiment against racism.

In extenuation, I plead only that I have done better than most predecessors in respect to Indian participation in historical events. My privilege, it seems, has been to do a certain amount of indispensable groundwork. As mentioned earlier, I have had to change my mind about a startling number of matters in response to unanticipated discoveries: neither the Indians nor the Euramericans of this work are quite the same people that I thought I knew when starting it. It is pleasing that I can still learn.

Besides my debts to colleagues in history, I must acknowledge a deep one to good friends in anthropology who have instructed me in the use of ethnohistorical concepts and methods. We sometimes exasperate each other—why can't they attend more to textual validation and chronological sequence? (Why can't he be more careful about the subtler workings of cultures?)—but their help has been indispensable to analysis of Indian cultural responses to European contact, which often included Indian initiatives requiring European responses.

Although my motive in writing seemed at the time to be simply rejection of deception and falsity in the historical literature, I perceive in retrospect a greater debt to anthropologists than was clearly apparent during the work. This was the substitution of a basic concept—a new *Weltanschauung*—for the ideas of race that patterned the histories I was challenging. In science this process of substituting concepts of culture for those of race would be called seeking a new paradigm to establish dimensions of future research. More plainly, since what one learns must be fitted somehow into what one already knows, too many bad fits require creation of a new paradigm capable of assimilating new data.

Within a bounded area of research, I have demonstrated a great many bad fits of facts to the paradigm of race, confirming the invalidity of that paradigm already demonstrated by many colleagues, especially in the field of Black history. It now seems necessary and desirable to explore more historical dimensions of the substitute paradigm of culture. If health and longevity permit, I hope, within a few years, to present an essay on a larger scale of American Indian history, with considerable attention to its historiographical implications.

I have *not* tried to write definitive history in any of my books, among other reasons because I think it impossible except for small subjects, tightly limited in purpose. As my studies range across immense spaces and centuries of time, selectivity of data and theme have been necessary, but far more evidence than was used remains available to demonstrate my theses. (My editor bursts into tears when he sees the size of my typescript piles.) Critics who think I have selected wrongly should write the corrections instead of carping that *I* should write *their* books.

Again and again in the course of research, I have been struck by modern parallels to the processes and events of my subject. A few of these instances have compelled recognition in the text, but I have been mindful that "history teaches" whatever the historian wants to teach. It seemed best therefore to present the subject as straightforwardly as my own understanding permitted. Readers who know that history has functions beyond entertainment will draw their own parallels from their own experience and knowledge.

On a pedestal placed modestly among the shrubbery behind the University of Pennsylvania's College Hall stands a bust of Mr. Charles Lennig, erected by his son. Its inscription is my favorite in contrast to the pomposities of most monuments. It states simply that Mr. Lennig bequeathed his fortune to the university "as a contribution to the advancement of his fellows in consideration of means acquired with and by their aid."

I have no fortune, but I am keenly aware that what I have done in scholarship would have been impossible without generous aid from many sources, institutional and personal. Having been critical in many respects of my countrymen and their political and cultural institutions, I acknowledge with grateful pride how they have supported my work nonetheless. Beyond personal gratitude, my tribute is for the traditions of unfettered scholarship and freedom of discussion that permit challenge to ideological dogmas. These traditions have been struggled and sacrificed for, generation after generation. They can be preserved only by constant exercise.

APPENDIX ❧

An early political paper of Benjamin Franklin

This document seems to have been the first state paper prepared by Benjamin Franklin specifically for submission to the English government. It is printed here because it was overlooked by the editors of the *Franklin Papers*, whose catch-up volume of such materials is unlikely to appear for several years. I published the paper previously in the *American Journal of Legal History* 8 (1964), 264–66.

Franklin's document was written nearly two years before he set sail for London on his first tour of duty as agent for the Pennsylvania assembly, and it shows the skills which had brought him to leadership in the assembly and which were to make him the most successful of the colonial agents. For the circumstances that moved Franklin to write, see chapter 7 above.

The document was found in the manuscript transcripts of *Board of Trade Papers, Proprietaries* in the Historical Society of Pennsylvania, volume 19, numbered V:145 and indorsed, "Read Decr. 6, 1755." (These transcripts are unpaged.) The reading is confirmed by the December 6, 1755, entry in *Board of Trade Journals* (also transcripts), volume 63, p. 353, in the same society's library.

Extract of a Letter from Benjamin Franklin dated Philadelphia 28th Augst 1755 to Richard Partridge Esqr Agent for Pennsylvania

You will receive by this Ship the Speeches & Messages that have passed between the Governour and Assembly in the late Sitting, which ended on Friday last. Also a Copy of the Bill for granting £50,000 to the Kings Use which he refused to pass. It is Expected that the Proceedings of the Assembly will be much misrepresented and therefore I am directed by the House to State Matters clearly in their due light to you that you may be able to justify the Assembly so far as they are fairly & rightly justifiable.

At the opening of the Sessions the Govr. made a Speech to the House, acquainting them with the unhappy Situation of Publick Affairs by the Defeat of General Braddock, & recommending the Grant of a Supply for the King's Service, withall cautioning them to avoid every Thing that might revive any former dispute between him & them; The House accordingly voted a Supply of £50,000 for the King's

Use, to be raised by an equitable Tax on all Estates Real & Personal, which was thought a great Sum for this Province, tho perhaps it may appear otherwise in England where 'tis said we have been invidiously represented as vastly Rich & able. In observance of the Gov^{rs} Caution to avoid all former Disputes about extending the Excise Act, the House Chose to raise the Money by a Tax.

To avoid all Disputes about suspending Clauses, in Paper Money Acts, and the Royal Instruction enjoining such Clauses, They chose to make no Paper Money.

To avoid all Disputes about the Disposition of the Money arising by the Tax, & yet to Secure a right Application, they proposed by the Bill to put it into the Hands of Commissioners to be disposed of by them for the Kings Service, with the Consent & approbation of the Govr or of Commander in chief of the Kings Forces in North America.

But to obtain a Credit for imediate use, as Collecting the Tax w^{d} require some Time they empowered ye said Comm^{rs} to draw Orders on the Treasurer (not exceeding ye Sum granted) payable out of the Tax as it sh^{d} come into his hands which Orders it was presumed w^{d} have at least a short Credit as Orders on our Treasury have always been paid wth punctuality & hon^{r}.

Lest ye Issuing of these Orders sh^{d} be considered as a making of Money To avoid all disputes on that head the Orders were not proposed a Legal Tender.

And to secure their Credit & give the Creditor a Compensation for ye Credit he afforded, the Orders were to bear an Interest till paid at ye Rate of 5 / cent / Annum.

To avoid all disputes concerning the Propriety of extending hither an Act of Parliam^{t} expressly made for other Colonies instead of taking more than 5 years for ye Sinking these Orders, the House chose to have them sunk in Two years & so it was ordered in the Bill.

Thus all former Disputes & every thing that might seem to interfere wth Royal Instructions, Old or new, or Acts of Parliam^{t} in Force, or not in Force here & the like were carefully avoided by the House in the formation of their Bill. And the Govern^{r} not being able to make any Objections to the passing of it on those acco^{ts} was driven to the Necessity of Saying That he was restrained by the Proprietors & accordingly refused his assent.

BIBLIOGRAPHY

Materials cited in the notes

The list is divided into the following sections: (I) manuscript materials (classified by locations); (II) printed source materials originating before 1800 (in alphabetical order); and (III) printed materials originating after 1800 (in alphabetical order).

A few works have been commented upon in "bibliographic notes" scattered at appropriate places throughout the book. Such comments are cited as "Bib. n.: ch. —, n—."

I. Manuscript Materials

California

San Marino

Henry E. Huntington Library: (1) Abercromby Papers; (2) Brock Collection; (3) Huntington Manuscripts; (4) Loudoun Papers.

England

Kew

Public Record Office: Colonial Office Papers.

London

British Library: (1) Bouquet Papers; (2) Hardwicke Papers; (3) Newcastle Papers.
Lambeth Palace Library: SPG Papers.
Friends House Library: mss.

Illinois

Chicago

Newberry Library: (1) Ayer Manuscripts; (2) Iroquois Treaty Archive. Bib. n.: ch. 15, n50.

Pennsylvania

Bethlehem

Moravian Archives: (1) Conrad Weiser, "observations, made on the Pamphlet, intituled 'An Inquiry into the Cause of the Alienation of the Delaware and Shawano Indians from the British Interest' "; (2) Treaty held at Easton, 28 July 1756.

Harrisburg

Pennsylvania Historical and Museum Commission: Pennsylvania Provincial Records.

Haverford

Haverford College: (1) Minutes of the Meeting for Sufferings for Pennsylvania and New Jersey; (2) Miscellaneous Manuscripts; (3) Papers Relating to the Friendly Association; (4) Pemberton Papers; (5) Roberts Collection.

Philadelphia

American Philosophical Society: (1) Council at Easton, July 1756; (2) Council at Easton, July 1757; (3) Indian and Military Affairs of Pennsylvania; (4) Miscellaneous Manuscripts. Bib. n.: ch. 15, n50, 52.

City Hall Archives Division: Warrants and Surveys of the Province of Pennsylvania, 1682–1759.

Historical Society of Pennsylvania: (1) Cadwalader Collection; (2) Chew Papers; (3) Correspondence of Conrad Weiser; (4) Etting Collection; (5) Gratz Collection; (6) Indian Records Collection; (7) Isaac Norris Letter book; (8) James Kenny Journals; (9) Logan Papers; (10) Minutes of the Friendly Association; (11) Pemberton Papers; (12) Penn Papers; (13) Penn Papers from Friends House, London; (14) Pennsylvania Miscellaneous Papers; (15) Peters Papers; (16) Stauffer Collection; (17) Transcripts of Board of Trade Papers and Board of Trade Journals; (18) William Smith Papers.

Library Company of Philadelphia: John Smith Manuscripts.

University of Pennsylvania: Archives.

Swarthmore

Friends Historical Library at Swarthmore College

Rhode Island

Providence

John Carter Brown Library, Brown University: [Henry Fletcher?], [Seven Years' War Journal of the Proceedings of the 35th regiment of Foot . . .] British North America, the Caribbean and England, August 1757–December 1765.

Virginia

Richmond

Virginia State Library: Colonial Papers.

II. Printed Materials Originating before 1800

"The Acadians in Pennsylvania Ordered to Be Dispersed in 1756," *Records of the American Catholic Historical Society of Philadelphia* 5 (1894), 353–56.

An Account of Conferences held, and Treaties made, Between Major-general Sir William Johnson Bart. and the chief Sachems and Warriours of the . . . Indian Nations in North America . . . in the Years 1755 and 1756. With a Letter from the Rev. Mr. Hawley to

Sir William Johnson, written at the Desire of the Delaware Indians . . . London: A. Millar, 1756. Reprinted facsimile, Lancaster, Pa.: Lancaster Press, 1930.

An Accurate and Authentic Journal of the Siege of Quebec, 1759. By a Gentleman in an eminent Station on the Spot. London: J. Robinson, 1759.

An Accurate Description of Cape Breton. London: M. Cooper, 1755.

Adair, James. *History of the American Indians* (1755). Reprinted as *Adair's History of the American Indians*. Ed. Samuel Cole Williams. New York: Promontory Press, 1973.

[Allen, William]. *The Burd Papers: Extracts from Chief Justice William Allen's Letter Book . . . Together with an Appendix Containing Pamphlets in the Controversy with Franklin*. Pottsville, Pa., 1897.

[Almon, John]. *A Review of the Reign of George II*. 2d ed. London: J. Wilkie, 1762.

The American Indian and the United States: A Documentary History. Ed. Wilcomb E. Washburn. 4 vols. Westport, Conn.: Greenwood Press, 1973.

The American War of Independence, 1775–83: A Commemorative Exhibition Organized by the Map Library and the Department of Manuscripts of the British Library Reference Division, 4 July to 11 November 1975. Published for the British Library. London: British Museum Publications, 1975.

The Appalachian Indian Frontier; The Edmond Atkin Report and Plan of 1755 (1954). Ed. Wilbur R. Jacobs. Reprinted Lincoln: University of Nebraska Press, 1967.

[Bollan, William]. *The Importance and Advantage of Cape Breton*. (1746). Reprinted Toronto: S. R. Publications, 1966.

[Bougainville, L. A. de]. *Adventure in the Wilderness: The American Journals of Louis Antoine de Bougainville, 1756–1760*. Tr. and ed. Edward P. Hamilton. Norman: University of Oklahoma Press, 1964.

[Bouquet, Henry]. *The Papers of Henry Bouquet*. Eds. S. K. Stevens, et al. Harrisburg: Pennsylvania Historical and Museum Commission, 1951–.

Bowen, Emanuel. *An Accurate Map of North America*. London: Robert Sayer, 1763.

Brebner, J. B. "Subsidized Intermarriage with the Indians." *Canadian Historical Review* 6 (1925), 33–36.

[CANADA]

Documents Relating to the Constitutional History of Canada, 1759–1791. Eds. Adam Shortt and Arthur G. Doughty. Canadian Archives Sessional Paper 18. Ottawa, 1907.

Papiers Contrecoeur et Autres Documents concernant le Conflit Anglo-Francois sur l'Ohio de 1755 a 1756. Ed. Fernand Grenier. Quebec: Les Presses Universitaires Laval, 1952.

Carver, Captain J[onathan]. "A detail of the Massacre of the English by the French Indians, at Fort William Henry, in America, in 1757." *Arminian Magazine* 17(1794), 33–38.

[CONNECTICUT]

The Public Records of the Colony of Connecticut. Ed. J. Hammond Trumbull. 15 vols. Hartford, 1850–90.

[Cross, ?]. *An Answer to an invidious Pamphlet intitled, A Brief State of the Province of Pennsylvania*. London: S. Bladon, 1755. Bib. n.: ch. 7, n7.

Documents of American History. Ed. Henry Steele Commager. 7th ed., 2 vols. New York: Appleton-Century-Crofts, 1963.

Eastburn, Robert. *A Faithful Narrative of . . . his late Captivity among the Indians* . . . Philadelphia, reprinted Boston: Green and Russell, 1758.

Edmund Burke, New York Agent. Ed. Ross J. S. Hoffman. Philadelphia: American Philosophical Society, 1956.

[ENGLAND]

Acts of the Privy Council of England, Colonial Series, 1613–1783. Eds. W. L. Grant and James Munro. 6 vols. Hereford, 1908–12.

The Correspondence of General Thomas Gage with the Secretaries of States, 1763–1775. Ed. Clarence Edwin Carter. 2 vols. (1931–33). Reprinted Hamden, Conn.: Archon Books, 1969.

The Correspondence of King George the Third from 1760 to December 1783. Ed. John Fortescue. 6 vols. London: Macmillan and Co., 1927–28.

Correspondence of William Pitt, Earl of Chatham. Edited by the executors of his son, John, Earl of Chatham. 4 vols. London: John Murray, 1838–40.

Military Affairs in North America, 1748–1765; Selected Documents from the Cumberland Papers in Windsor Castle. Ed. Stanley Pargellis. Published under the direction of the American Historical Association. (1936) Reprinted Hamden, Conn.: Archon books, 1969. Bib. n.: ch. 1, n8.

Proceedings and Debates of the British Parliaments Respecting North America, 1542–1754. Ed. Leo Francis Stock. 5 vols. Washington, D.C.: Carnegie Institution of Washington, 1924–41.

Proceedings and Debates of the British Parliaments Respecting North America, 1754–1783. 3 vols to date. Eds. R. C. Simmons and P. D. G. Thomas. Millwood, N.Y.: Kraus International Publications, 1982–.

Entick, John. *The General History of the Late War: Containing Its Rise, Progress, and Event in Europe, Asia, Africa, and America* . . . 5 vols. London: Edward Dilly and John Millan, 1763–64.

Forbes, John. *Writings of General John Forbes Relating to his Service in North America*. Ed. Alfred Procter James. Menasha, Wis.: Collegiate Press, 1938.

Forbes, Robert. *The Lyon in Mourning*. Ed. Henry Paton. 3 vols. Publications of the Scottish History Society 20–22. Edinburgh: T. and A. Constable, 1895.

Fothergill, John. *Chain of Friendship: Selected Letters of Dr. John Fothergill of London, 1735–1780*. Eds. Betsy C. Corner and Christopher C. Booth. Cambridge, Mass.: Belknap Press, 1971.

[FRANCE]

[Moreau, Jacob Nicolas]. *The Conduct of the Late Ministry, or, A Memorial Containing A Summary of Facts with their Vouchers, in Answer to the Observations, sent by the English Ministry, to the Courts of Europe*. Tr. from *Memoire contenant* . . . London: W. Bizet, 1757.

———. *Memoire contenant le Precis des Faits avec leurs Pieces Justificatives.* Paris: De L'Imprimerie Royale, 1756.

Relation de la prise du Fort Georges, ou Guillaume-Henry, situé sur le Lac Saint-Sacrament, & de ce qui se'est passé cette année en Canada. Paris: Bureau d'Adresse aux Galleries de Louvre, 18 Octobre 1757.

Relation De la prise des Forts de Choueguen, ou Oswego & de ce qui s'est passe cette annee en Canada. N.p., 1756.

Franklin, Benjamin. *The Autobiography of Benjamin Franklin.* Eds. Leonard W. Labaree, et al. New Haven, Conn.: Yale University Press, 1964.

———. *The Papers of Benjamin Franklin.* Eds. Leonard W. Labaree, et al. New Haven, Conn.: Yale University Press, 1959–.

[Galloway, Joseph]. *A True and Impartial State of the Province of Pennsylvania.* Philadelphia: W. Dunlap, 1759.

The Garland Library of Narratives of North American Indian Captivities. Comp. Wilcomb E. Washburn. 111 vols. New York: Garland Publishing, Inc., and the Newberry Library, 1975–79.

The Gentleman's Magazine, London.

George Mercer Papers Relating to the Ohio Company of Virginia. Comp. and ed. Lois Mulkearn. Pittsburgh: University of Pittsburgh Press, 1954.

[Gibson, Hugh]. "Account of the Captivity of Hugh Gibson." *Collections of the Massachusetts Historical Society*, 3d ser., 6(1837), 141–53.

Gist, Christopher. *Christopher Gist's Journals.* Ed. William M. Darlington. Cleveland: Arthur H. Clark Co., 1893.

Gist, Thomas. "Thomas Gist's Indian Captivity, 1758–1759." Ed. Howard H. Peckham. *Pennsylvania Magazine of History and Biography* 80(1956), 258–311.

Held Captive by Indians: Selected Narratives, 1642–1836. Ed. Richard Van Der Beets. Knoxville: University of Tennessee Press, 1973.

Historical Collections Relating to the American Colonial Church, II, "Pennsylvania." Ed. William Stevens Perry. Hartford, Conn.: Printed for the Subscribers by the Church Press, 1871.

The History of an Expedition Against Fort Duquesne in 1755; Under Major-General Braddock. Ed. Winthrop Sargent. Memoirs of the Historical Society of Pennsylvania 5. Philadelphia, 1855.

Hollister, Isaac. *A Brief Narration of the Captivity of Isaac Hollister Who was taken by the Indians, Anno Domini, 1763* (1767). Reprinted facsimile in *The Garland Library*, q.v., 10. Separately paged.

Hutchinson, Thomas. *The History of the Colony and Province of Massachusetts-Bay* (1764–1828). Ed. Lawrence Shaw Mayo. 3 vols. Cambridge, Mass.: Harvard University Press, 1936.

[ILLINOIS]

Anglo-French Boundary Disputes in the West, 1749–1763. Ed. Theodore Calvin Pease. Collections of the Illinois State Historical Library 27, French Series 2. Springfield, 1936. Bib. n.: ch. 6, n49.

Illinois on the Eve of the Seven Years' War, 1747–1755. Eds. Theodore Calvin Pease and Ernestine Jenison. Collections of the Illinois State Historical Library 29, French Series 3. Springfield, 1940.

Indian Treaties Printed by Benjamin Franklin, 1736–1762. Ed. Julian P. Boyd. Philadelphia: Historical Society of Pennsylvania, 1938.

Ingles, John Sr. *The Story of Mary Draper Ingles and Son Thomas Ingles*. Eds. Roberta Ingles Steele and Andrew Lewis Ingles. Radford, Va.: Commonwealth Press, 1969.

"Intercepted Letters, 1756." *American Historical Association Annual Report for the Year 1896*. 2 vols. Washington, D.C.: Government Printing Office, 1897. 1:662–85.

Iroquois Indians: A Documentary History of the Diplomacy of the Six Nations and Their League. Eds. Francis Jennings, William N. Fenton, Mary A. Druke, and David R. Miller. 50 microfilm reels and a printed guide. Woodbridge, Conn.: Research Publications, 1985.

[Jackson, Richard]. *An Historical Review of the Constitution and Government of Pennsylvania, From its Origin; So far as regards the several Points of Controversy, which have, from Time to Time, arisen between The several Governors of that Province, and their Assemblies*. London: R. Griffiths, 1759.

Jefferson, Thomas. *A Summary View of the Rights of British America* (1774). In *Tracts of the American Revolution, 1773–1776*. Ed. Merrill Jensen. Indianapolis: Bobbs-Merrill Co., 1967.

The Jesuit Relations and Allied Documents. (1896–1901). Ed. Reuben Gold Thwaites. 73 vols. Reprinted facsimile in 36 vols. New York: Pageant Book Co., 1959.

[Johnson, William]. *The Papers of Sir William Johnson*. Eds. James Sullivan, et al. 14 vols. Albany: University of the State of New York, 1921–65.

[Kennedy, Archibald]. *The Importance of Gaining and Preserving the Friendship of the Indians to the British Interest, Considered*. New York: James Parker, 1751.

Kenny, James. Journals, 1758–59, 1761–63. Ed. John W. Jordan. *Pennsylvania Magazine of History and Biography* 32(1913), 395–449, 1–47, 152–201.

King, Titus. *A Narrative of Titus King of Northampton, Mass.: A Prisoner of the Indians in Canada, 1755–1758* (1938). Reprinted facsimile in *The Garland Library*, q.v., 109. Separately paged.

Knox, Captain John. *An Historical Journal of the Campaigns in North America, For the Years 1757, 1758, 1759, and 1760*. (London, 1769). Reprint ed. Arthur G. Doughty. 3 vols. Publications of the Champlain Society 8, 9, 10. Toronto, 1914. Bib. n.: ch. 18, n47.

Lafitau, Joseph Francois, S.J. *Customs of the American Indians Compared with the Customs of Primitive Times*. Ed. and tr. by William N. Fenton and Elizabeth L. Moore. 2 vols. Publications of the Champlain Society 48–49. Toronto, 1974, 1977.

A Letter Addressed to Two Great Men, on the Prospect of Peace; And on the Terms necessary to be insisted upon in the Negociation. London: A. Millar, 1760.

[Livingston, William]. *A Review of the Military Operations in North America; from The Commencement of the French Hostilities on the Frontiers of Virginia in 1753, to the Surrender of Oswego, on the 14th of August, 1756*. London: R. and J. Dodsley, 1757.

Mante, Thomas. *The History of the Late War in North-America, and the Islands of the West-Indies, including the Campaigns of 1763 and 1764 against this Majesty's Indian enemies*. London: W. Strahan and T. Cadell, 1772. Bib. n.: ch. 16, n43.

Minutes of Conferences Held with the Indians At Harris's Ferry, and at Lancaster, In March, April, and May, 1757. Philadelphia: Franklin and Hall, 1757.

Mitchell, John. *The Contest in America between Great Britain and France . . . By an Impartial Hand*. London: A. Millar, 1757.

———. *A Map of the British and French Dominions in North America, with the Roads, Distances, Limits, and Extent of the Settlements*. London: Andrew Millar, 1755.

Morris, Robert Hunter. "An American in London, 1735–1736." Ed. Beverley McAnear. *Pennsylvania Magazine of History and Biography* 64(1940), 356–406.

"The Narrative of Marie Le Roy and Barbara Leininger, for Three Years Captives among the Indians." Tr. Edmund de Schweinitz. *Pennsylvania Magazine of History and Biography* 29(1905), 407–20.

[NEW YORK]

Collections of the New-York Historical Society. Publication Fund Series 9. New York, 1877.

The Documentary History of the State of New-York. Ed. E. B. O'Callaghan. 4 vols. Albany: Weed, Parsons and Co., 1849–51.

Documents Relative to the Colonial History of the State of New York. Eds. Edmund B. O'Callaghan and Berthold Fernow. 15 vols. Albany: Weed, Parsons and Co., 1856–87.

New-York Mercury.

[NOVA SCOTIA]

Selections from the Public Documents of the Province of Nova Scotia. Ed. Thomas B. Atkins. Halifax: Charles Annand Publisher, 1869.

Paine, Thomas. *The Complete Writings of Thomas Paine*. Ed. Philip S. Foner. 2 vols. New York: Citadel Press, 1969.

The Paxton Papers. Ed. John R. Dunbar. The Hague: Martinus Nijhoff, 1957.

[PENNSYLVANIA]

The Charters and Acts of Assembly of the Province of Pennsylvania. 2 vols. Philadelphia: Peter Miller and Co., 1762.

The Charters of the Province of Pensilvania and City of Philadelphia. Philadelphia: B. Franklin, 1742.

A Collection of all the Laws of the Province of Pennsylvania Now in Force. Published by order of the assembly. Philadelphia: B. Franklin, 1742.

Minutes of the Provincial Council of Pennsylvania. [Spine title: *Colonial Records*.] Ed. Samuel Hazard. 16 vols. Harrisburg and Philadelphia, 1838–53. Vols. 1–3 printed in two editions with different pagination.

Pennsylvania Archives. 9 series 138 vols. Harrisburg and Philadelphia, 1852–1949.

Votes and Proceedings of the House of Representatives of the Province of Pennsylvania,

1682–1776 (1752–76). 8 vols., continuously paged. 8th ser., *Pennsylvania Archives*. Harrisburg, 1931–35.

Wilderness Chronicles of Northwestern Pennsylvania. Eds. Sylvester K. Stevens and Donald H. Kent. Harrisburg: Pennsylvania Historical Commission, 1941.

Pennsylvania Gazette.

Pennsylvania Journal and Weekly Advertiser.

"Personal Accounts of the Albany Congress of 1754." Ed. Beverly McAnear. *Mississippi Valley Historical Review* 39(1953), 727–46.

Post, Christian Frederick. Journals. In Robert Proud, *The History of Pennsylvania in North America* (1798). Reprinted facsimile Spartanburg, S.C.: The Reprint Co., 1967. Vol. 2, Appendix 2.

Pouchot, [Pierre]. *Memoir upon the Late War in North America, Between the French and English, 1755–60* (1781). Tr. and ed. Franklin B. Hough. 2 vols. Roxbury, Mass.: W. Elliott Woodward, 1866.

Pownall, Thomas. *The Administration of the Colonies* (1764). 2d ed., revised, corrected and enlarged. London: J. Dodsley and J. Walter, 1765. Bib. n.: ch. 5, n80.

———. *A Topographical Description of Such Parts of North America as are Contained in The (Annexed) Map of the Middle British Colonies, &c. in North America* (1776). Reprinted as *A Topographical Description of the Dominions of The United States of America*. Ed. Lois Mulkearn. Pittsburgh: University of Pittsburgh Press, 1949.

Reasons Why the Approaching Treaty of Peace Should be Debated in Parliament. London: R. Griffiths, 1760.

Relations Diverses sur La Bataille du Malangueule [Monongahela] *Gagne le 9 Juillet 1755* . . . Recueillies par Jean Marie Shea. Shea's Cramoisy Press series 14. Nouvelle York: De La Presse Cramoisy, 1860.

Rogers, Robert. *Journals of Major Robert Rogers* (1765). Readex Microprint, 1966.

Royal Fort Frontenac. Comp. and tr. Richard A. Preston. Ed. Leopold Lamontagne. Publications of the Champlain Society, Ontario Series 2. Toronto, 1958.

Rush, Benjamin. *The Autobiography of Benjamin Rush: His "Travels Through Life" together with his Commonplace Book for 1789–1813*. Ed. George W. Corner. Published for the American Philosophical Society. Princeton, N.J.: Princeton University Press, 1948.

The Seven Years War in Canada, 1756–1763. Comp. Sigmund Samuel. Toronto: Ryerson Press, 1934.

[Shebbeare, John]. *A Letter to the People of England on the Present Situation and conduct of National Affairs, Letter I*. London, 1755.

[Shirley, William?]. *The Conduct of Major Gen. Shirley, Late General and Commander in Chief of His Majesty's Forces in North America. Briefly Stated*. London: R. and J. Dodsley, 1758.

[Shirley, William]. *Correspondence of William Shirley, Governor of Massachusetts and Military Commander in America, 1731–1760*. Ed. Charles Henry Lincoln. 2 vols. New York: Macmillan, 1912.

The Siege of Detroit in 1763: The Journal of Pontiac's Conspiracy and John Rutherfurd's Narrative of a Captivity. Ed. Milo Milton Quaife. Lakeside Classics. Chicago: R. R. Donnelley and Sons, 1958.

Smethurst, Gamaliel. *A Narrative of an Extraordinary Escape out of the Hands of the Indians* . . . (1774). In *The Garland Library*, q.v., 10. Separately paged.

Smith, Samuel. *The History of the Colony of Nova-Caesaria, or, New-Jersey*. . . . (1765). Reprinted Trenton, 1890.

[Smith, William, Provost]. *A Brief State of the Province of Pennsylvania*. London: R. Griffiths, 1755. Bib. n.: ch. 11, n39.

———. *A Brief View of the conduct of Pennsylvania For the Year 1755*. London: R. Griffiths, 1756.

———. *A Letter from a Gentleman in London, To his Friend in Pensylvania; with a Satire; containing some Characteristical Strokes upon the Manners and Principles of the Quakers*. London: J. Scott, 1756.

———. *A Letter from Quebeck, in Canada, to M. L'Maine, a French Officer*. Boston: Thomas Fleet, 1754.

———. *An Historical Account of the Expedition against the Ohio Indians in the Year 1764* (1765). Reprinted facsimile, Readex Microprint, 1966.

———. *Some Account of the North-America Indians . . . To which are added, Indian Miscellanies . . . Collected by a learned and ingenious Gentleman in the Province of Pensylvania*. London: R. Griffiths, 1754.

———. Supplement to *New-York Mercury* No. 168, 27 October 1755.

Smith, William, Jr. *A History of the Province of New York* (1757, 1826). Reprint ed. Michael Kammen, 2 vols. Cambridge, Mass.: Belknap Press, 1972.

[SOUTH CAROLINA]

Colonial Records of South Carolina: Documents Relating to Indian Affairs, 1750–54. Ed. William L. McDowell, Jr. Columbia: South Carolina Archives Dept., 1958.

Documents Relating to Indian Affairs, 1754–1765. Ed. William L. McDowell, Jr. Published for the South Carolina Department of Archives and History. Columbia: University of South Carolina Press, 1970.

Stuart, Charles. "The Captivity of Charles Stuart, 1755–57." Ed. Beverley W. Bond, Jr. *Mississippi Valley Historical Review* 13(1926–27), 58–81.

The Susquehannah Company Papers. Eds. Julian Parks Boyd and Robert J. Taylor. 11 vols. Wilkes-Barre, Pa., and Ithaca, N.Y., 1930–71.

Thomson, Charles. *An Enquiry into the Causes of the Alienation of the Delaware and Shawanese Indians from the British Interest*. London: J. Wilkie, 1759. Thomas Penn's annotated copy is in John Carter Brown Library. Mss. copies are at Haverford College. Bib. n.: ch. 12, n25.

T. W. *Two Letters to a Friend on the Present Critical Conjuncture of Affairs in North America* (Boston, 1755). Reprinted London: T. Jeffreys, 1755.

[VIRGINIA]

"The Treaty of Logg's Town, 1752; Commission, Instructions, &c., Journal of Virginia Commissioners, and Text of Treaty." *Virginia Magazine of History and Biography* 13(1905–6), 148–74.

The Virginia Soldiers' Claim to Western Lands Adjacent to Fort Pitt. Intro. by Willis Van Devanter. New York: privately printed at Spiral Press, 1966.

Walpole, Horace. *Memoirs of the Reign of King George the Second*. Ed. Lord Holland. 2d ed. rev. 3 vols. London: H. Colburn, 1847.

[Washington, George]. *The Diaries of George Washington, 1748–1794*. Ed. John C. Fitzpatrick. 4 vols. Boston: Houghton Mifflin Co., 1925.

———. *George Washington's Expense Account*. Ed. Marvin Kitman. New York: Ballantine Books, 1970.

———. *The Journal of Major George Washington* (1754). Reprinted facsimile Williamsburg, Va.: Colonial Williamsburg Foundation, 1959.

———. *The Papers of George Washington, Colonial Series*. Eds. W. W. Abbott, et al. Charlottesville: University Press of Virginia, 1983–.

———. *The Writings of George Washington*. Ed. John C. Fitzpatrick. 39 vols. Washington, D.C., 1931–44.

Westcott, Thompson. *Names of Persons Who Took the Oath of Allegiance to the State of Pennsylvania Between the Years 1777 and 1789, with a History of the Test Laws of Pennsylvania*. Philadelphia, 1865.

[Wharton, Samuel]. *Plain Facts: Being an Examination into the Rights of the Indian Nations of America to their respective Countries . . .* Philadelphia, 1781.

[Wilkes, John]. *The North Briton, Revised and Corrected by the Author*. 2 vols. bound together. London: n.p., 5 June 1762–23 April 1763.

Williamson, Peter. *French and Indian Cruelty; Exemplified in the Life and Various Vicissitudes of Fortune of Peter Williamson, A Disbanded Soldier* (1757). In *The Garland Library*, q.v., 9. Separately paged.

[WISCONSIN]

Collections of the State Historical Society of Wisconsin 18. Ed. Reuben Gold Thwaites. Madison, 1908.

Wraxall, Peter. *An Abridgment of the Indian Affairs* (1754). Ed. Charles Howard McIlwain. Harvard Historical Studies 21(1915). Reprinted New York: Benjamin Blom, Inc., 1968.

III. Printed Materials Originating after 1800

Abernethy, Thomas Perkins. *Western Lands and the American Revolution* (1937). Reprinted New York: Russell and Russell, 1959.

Alberts, Robert C. *The Most Extraordinary Adventures of Major Robert Stobo*. Boston: Houghton Mifflin Co., 1965. Bib. n.: ch. 7, n52.

Alden, John R. "The Albany Congress and the Creation of the Indian Superintendencies." *Mississippi Valley Historical Review* 27 (1940), 193–210.

———. *Robert Dinwiddie, Servant of the Crown*. Williamsburg in America series 9. Williamsburg, Va.: Colonial Williamsburg Foundation, 1973.

Alvord, Clarence Walworth. *The Mississippi Valley in British Politics: A Study of the Trade, Land Speculation, and Experiments in Imperialism Culminating in the American Revolution* (1916). 2 vols. Reprinted New York: Russell and Russell, Inc., 1959.

Ambler, Charles H. *George Washington and the West* (1936). Reprinted New York: Russell and Russell, 1971.

The American Indian and the American Revolution. Ed. Francis Jennings. D'Arcy McNickle Center for the History of the American Indian Occasional Papers 6. Chicago: Newberry Library, 1983.

Anderson, Fred. *A People's Army: Massachusetts Soldiers and Society in the Seven Years' War*. Published for the Institute of Early American History and Culture. Chapel Hill: University of North Carolina Press, 1984.

Andrews, Charles M. *The Colonial Period of American History* (1934–38). 4 vols. Reprinted New Haven, Conn.: Yale University Press, 1964.

Aquila, Richard. *The Iroquois Restoration: Iroquois Diplomacy on the Colonial Frontier, 1701–1754*. Detroit: Wayne State University Press, 1983.

Axtell, James. *The European and the Indian: Essays in the Ethnohistory of Colonial North America*. New York: Oxford University Press, 1981.

———. *The Invasion Within; The Contest of Cultures in Colonial North America*. New York: Oxford University Press, 1985. Bib. n.: ch. 8, n28.

Ayling, Stanley. *The Elder Pitt, Earl of Chatham*. London: Collins, 1976.

Bailey, Alfred Goldsworthy. *The Conflict of European and Eastern Algonkian Cultures, 1504–1700* (1937). 2d ed. Toronto: University of Toronto Press, 1969.

Bailyn, Bernard. *The Ideological Origins of the American Revolution*. Cambridge, Mass.: Belknap Press, 1967.

Baker-Crothers, Hayes. *Virginia and the French and Indian War*. Chicago: University of Chicago Press, 1928.

Basye, Arthur Herbert. *The Lords Commissioners of Trade and Plantations, Commonly Known as the Board of Trade, 1748–1782*. Yale Historical Publications, Miscellany 14. New Haven, Conn.: Yale University Press, 1925.

Bauman, Richard. *For the Reputation of Truth; Politics, Religion and Conflict among the Pennsylvania Quakers, 1750–1800*. Baltimore: Johns Hopkins Press, 1971.

Beard, Charles A. and Mary R. *The Rise of American Civilization (1927). Rev. ed. New York: Macmillan, 1939.*

Beer, George Louis. British Colonial Policy, 1754–1765 (1907). Reprinted facsimile, Gloucester, Mass.: Peter Smith, 1958.

Bell, Whitfield J., Jr., and Leonard W. Labaree. "Franklin and the 'Wagon Affair.' " *Proceedings of the American Philosophical Society* 101 (1957), 551–58.

Berkeley, Edmund, and Dorothy Smith Berkeley. *Dr. John Mitchell: The Man Who Made the Map of North America*. Chapel Hill: University of North Carolina Press, 1974.

Bibliotheca Americana: A Dictionary of Books Relating to America from Its Discovery. Eds. Joseph Sabin, Wilberforce Eames, and Robert W. G. Vail. 29 vols. New York, 1868–1936.

Billington, Ray Allen. *The Genesis of the Frontier Thesis: A Study in Historical Creativity*. San Marino, Calif.: The Huntington Library, 1971.

Blackey, Robert Alan. "The Political Career of George Montagu Dunk, 2nd Earl of Halifax, 1748–1771: A Study of an Eighteenth Century English Minister." Ph.D. diss., New York University, 1969.

Bloch, Marc. *Feudal Society*. Tr. L. A. Manyon. 2 vols. Chicago: University of Chicago Press, 1964.

Bonomi, Patrica U. *A Factious People: Politics and Society in Colonial New York*. New York: Columbia University Press, 1971.

Boorstin, Daniel. *The Americans: The Colonial Experience.* New York: Random House, 1958.

Brasseaux, Carl A. *The Founding of New Acadia: The Beginnings of Acadian Life in Louisiana, 1765–1803.* Baton Rouge: Louisiana State University Press, 1987.

Brebner, John Bartlet. *The Neutral Yankees of Nova Scotia: A Marginal Colony during the Revolutionary Years.* New York: Columbia University Press, 1937.

———. *New England's Outpost: Acadia before the Conquest of Canada.* Studies in History, Economics and Public Law of Columbia University 293. New York: Columbia University Press, 1927.

Brewster, William. *The Pennsylvania and New York Frontier, 1700–1763.* Philadelphia: George S. McManus Co., 1954.

Bridenbaugh, Carl. *Mitre and Sceptre: Transatlantic Faiths, Ideas, Personalities, and Politics, 1689–1775.* New York: Oxford University Press, 1962.

Brown, Peter Douglas. *William Pitt, Earl of Chatham: The Great Commoner.* London: George Allen and Unwin, 1978.

Browne, James. *A History of the Highlands and the Highland Clans.* 4 vols. Glasgow: A. Fullerton and Co., 1840.

Browning, Reed. *The Duke of Newcastle.* New Haven, Conn.: Yale University Press, 1975. Bib. n.: ch. 6, n3.

Burt, Alfred LeRoy. *The Old Province of Quebec.* Toronto: Ryerson Press, 1933.

Bushman, Richard L. *King and People in Provincial Massachusetts.* Published for the Institute of Early American History and Culture. Chapel Hill: University of North Carolina Press, 1985.

Butterfield, Herbert. *George III and the Historians.* Rev. ed. New York: Macmillan, 1969.

Buxbaum, Melvin H. *Benjamin Franklin and the Zealous Presbyterians.* University Park: Pennsylvania State University Press, 1975.

The Cajuns: Essays on Their History and Culture. Ed. Glenn R. Conrad. 2d ed. Lafayette: Center for Louisiana Studies, University of Southwestern Louisiana, 1978.

Calder, Angus. *Revolutionary Empire: The Rise of the English-Speaking Empires from the Fifteenth Century to the 1780s.* New York: E. P. Dutton, 1981.

Callender, Charles. "Shawnee." in *Northeast,* q.v. Pp. 622–35.

Cappon, Lester J., et al. *Atlas of Early American History.* Published for the Newberry Library and the Institute of Early American History and Culture. Princeton, N.J.: Princeton University Press, 1976.

Carter, Mary F. "James Glen, Governor of South Carolina." Ph.D. diss., University of California, Los Angeles, 1951.

Champion, Walter T., Jr., "Christian Frederick Post and the Winning of the West," *Pennsylvania Magazine of History and Biography* 104:3 (July 1980), 308–25. Bib. n.: ch. 17, n74.

Chandler, R. E. "The St. Gabriel Acadians: the First Five Months." *Louisiana History* 21 (1980), 287–96.

Chidsey, A. D., Jr. *The Penn Patents in the Forks of the Delaware.* Publications of the Northampton County Historical and Genealogical Society 2. Easton, Pa., 1937.

Christie, Ian R. *Wars and Revolutions; Britain, 1760–1815.* Cambridge, Mass.: Harvard University Press, 1982.

Clark, Andrew Hill. *Acadia: The Geography of Early Nova Scotia to 1760.* Madison: University of Wisconsin Press, 1968.

Clayton, T. R. "The Duke of Newcastle, the Earl of Halifax, and the American Origins of the Seven Years' War." *The Historical Journal* 24 (1981), 571–603. Bib. n.: ch. 6, n43.

Clifton, James A. *The Prairie People: Continuity and Change in Potawatomi Indian Culture, 1665–1965.* Lawrence: Regents Press of Kansas, 1977.

Conkey, Laura E., Ethel Boissevain, and Ives Goddard. "Indians of Southern New England and Long Island, Late Period." In *Northeast,* q.v., 177–89.

Coolidge, Guy Omeron. *The French Occupation of the Champlain Valley from 1609 to 1759* (1938). Reprinted Harrison, N.Y.: Harbor Hill Books, 1979.

Cooper, Johnson Gaylord. "Oswego in the French-English Struggle in North America, 1720–1760." D.S.S. diss., Syracuse University, 1961.

Corkran, David H. *The Cherokee Frontier: Conflict and Survival, 1740–62.* Norman: University of Oklahoma Press, 1962.

Countryman, Edward. *A People in Revolution: The American Revolution and Political Society in New York, 1760–1790.* Studies in Historical and Political Science, 99th ser. Baltimore, Md.: Johns Hopkins University Press, 1981.

Coupland, Sir Reginald. *The Quebec Act: A Study in Statesmanship.* Oxford: Clarendon Press, 1925.

Crane, Verner W. *The Southern Frontier, 1670–1732.* Ann Arbor: University of Michigan Press, 1929.

Cuneo, John R. *Robert Rogers of the Rangers.* New York: Oxford University Press, 1959.

Daiches, David. *The Last Stuart: The Life and Times of Bonnie Prince Charlie.* New York: G. P. Putnam's Sons, 1973.

Day, Gordon M. *The Identity of the Saint Francis Indians.* National Museum of Man Mercury Series, Canadian Ethnology Service Paper 71. Ottawa, 1981.

———. "Rogers' Raid in Indian Tradition." *Historical New Hampshire* 17 (1962), 3–17.

De Vorsey, Louis, Jr. *The Indian Boundary in the Southern Colonies, 1763–1775.* Chapel Hill: University of North Carolina Press, 1961.

DeVoto, Bernard. *The Course of Empire.* Boston: Houghton Mifflin Co., 1952.

Dictionary of American Biography. Eds. Allen Johnson and Dumas Malone. 22 vols. New York: Charles Scribner's Sons, 1928–44.

Dictionary of Canadian Biography. Eds. George W. Brown, et al. Toronto: University of Toronto Press, 1966–.

Dictionary of [British] National Biography. Eds. Leslie Stephen and Sidney Lee. 63 vols. plus supplements. London, 1885–1903.

Dolan, Jay P. *The American Catholic Experience: A History from Colonial Times to the Present.* Garden City, N.Y.: Doubleday and Co., 1985.

Douglas, David C. *William the Conqueror: The Norman Impact upon England.* Berkeley: University of California Press, 1964.

Downes, Randolph C. *Council Fires on the Upper Ohio: A Narrative of Indian Affairs in the Upper Ohio Valley until 1795.* Pittsburgh, Pa.: University of Pittsburgh Press, 1969.

Doyle, J. A. *The Colonies under the House of Hanover.* London: Longmans, Green and Co., 1907.

Eccles, W. J. *The Canadian Frontier, 1535–1760.* Histories of the American Frontier series. New York: Holt, Rinehart and Winston, 1969.

———. "The French forces in North America during the Seven Years' War." In *Dictionary of Canadian Biography*, q.v. 3:xv–xxxiii.

———. "Sovereignty-Association, 1500–1783." *Canadian Historical Review* 65 (1984), 475–510.

Eckert, Allen W. *Wilderness Empire: A Narrative.* Boston: Little, Brown and Co., 1969.

Edmunds, R. David. *The Potawatomis: Keepers of the Fire.* Norman: University of Oklahoma Press, 1978.

Eid, Leroy V. " 'National' War Among Indians of Northeastern North America." *Canadian Review of American Studies* 16 (1985), 125–54.

———. "The Ojibwa-Iroquois War: The War the Five Nations Did Not Win." *Ethnohistory* 26 (1979), 297–324.

Ellis, John Tracy. *Catholics in Colonial America.* Benedictine Studies 8. Baltimore, Md.: Helicon Press, 1965.

Encyclopaedia Britannica, 11th ed.

Fenton, William N. "Introduction" to *Parker on the Iroquois.* Ed. Fenton. Syracuse, N.Y.: Syracuse University Press, 1968.

Ferguson, E. James. "Currency Finance: An Interpretation of Colonial Monetary Practices." *William and Mary Quarterly*, 3d ser., 10 (1953), 153–80.

Flexner, James Thomas. *Mohawk Baronet: Sir William Johnson of New York.* New York: Harper and Brothers, 1959.

Fortier, John. *Fortress of Louisbourg.* Toronto: Oxford University Press, 1979.

Frégault, Guy. *Canada: The War of the Conquest.* Tr. Margaret M. Cameron. Toronto: Oxford University Press, 1969.

Gegenheimer, Albert Frank. *William Smith: Educator and Churchman, 1727–1803.* Philadelphia: University of Pennsylvania Press, 1943.

Gipson, Lawrence Henry. *The British Empire Before the American Revolution.* 15 vols. New York: Alfred A. Knopf, 1958–70. Bib. n.: ch. 18, n12.

———. *Lewis Evans, to which is added Evans' A Brief Account of Pennsylvania Together with Facsimiles of His* Geographical, Historical, Political, Philosophical, and Mechanical Essays, *Numbers I and II* . . . Philadelphia: Historical Society of Pennsylvania, 1939.

Goddard, Ives. Synonymy for *Mohawk.* In *Northeast*, q.v. Pp. 478–79.

Godfrey, William G. *Pursuit of Profit and Preferment in Colonial North America: John Bradstreet's Quest.* Waterloo, Ont.: Wilfrid Laurier University Press, 1982.

Grant, William L. "Canada Versus Guadeloupe, an Episode of the Seven Years' War." *American Historical Review* 17 (1912), 735–43.

Graymont, Barbara. *The Iroquois in the American Revolution.* A New York State Study. Syracuse: Syracuse University Press, 1972.

Greene, Jack P. " 'A Posture of Hostility': A Reconsideration of Some Aspects of the Origins of the American Revolution." *Proceedings of the American Antiquarian Society* 87 (1977), 27–68. Bib. n.: ch. 6, n86.

———. *The Quest for Power: The Lower Houses of Assembly in the Southern Royal Colonies, 1689–1776.* Published for the Institute of Early American History and Culture. Chapel Hill: University of North Carolina Press, 1963. Bib. n.: ch. 6, n2.

———. "The Role of the Lower Houses of Assembly in Eighteenth-Century Politics." In *The Reinterpretation of the American Revolution, 1763–1789.* New York: Harper and Row, 1968. Pp. 86–109.

———. "The Seven Years' War and the American Revolution: The Causal Relationship Reconsidered." In *The British Atlantic Empire before the American Revolution.* Eds. Peter Marshall and Glyn Williams. London: Frank Cass, 1980.

Greiert, Steven G. "The Earl of Halifax and British Colonial Policy: 1748–1756." Ph.D. diss., Duke University, 1976.

Griffin, Marvin I. J. "Why Old St. Joseph's, Philadelphia, Was Not Founded until 1733." *American Catholic Historical Researches* 9 (1892), 17–24.

Hamilton, Milton W. *Sir William Johnson: Colonial American, 1715–1763.* Port Washington, N.Y.: Kennikat Press, 1976.

Handbook of American Indians North of Mexico. Ed. Frederick Webb Hodge. 2 vols. Washington, D.C.: Government Printing Office, 1907.

Handbook of British Chronology. Eds. F. Maurice Powicke and E. B. Fryde. 2d ed. London: Royal Historical Society, 1961.

Hanna, Charles A. *The Wilderness Trail, or The Ventures and Adventures of the Pennsylvania Traders on the Allegheny Path.* 2 vols. New York: G. P. Putnam's Sons, 1911. Bib. n.: ch. 3, n9.

Hanna, William S. *Benjamin Franklin and Pennsylvania Politics.* Stanford, Calif.: Stanford University Press, 1964.

Heard, J. Norman. *White into Red: A Study of the Assimilation of White Persons Captured by Indians.* Metuchen, N.J.: Scarecrow Press, 1973.

Heckewelder, John. *Narrative of the Mission . . .* (1820). Extracted in *Thirty Thousand Miles with John Heckewelder.* Ed. Paul A. W. Wallace. Pittsburgh: University of Pittsburgh Press, 1958. Bib. n.: ch. 9, n47.

Henretta, James A. *"Salutary Neglect": Colonial Administration under the Duke of Newcastle.* Princeton, N.J.: Princeton University Press, 1972.

Higonnet, Patrice Louis-René. "The Origins of the Seven Years War." *Journal of Modern History* 40 (1968), 57–90. Bib. n.: ch. 6, n43.

History of the Capture and Captivity of David Boyd from Cumberland County, Pennsylvania (1931). Ed. Marion Morse. In *The Garland Library,* q.v. 109. Separately paged.

The History and Culture of Iroquois Diplomacy: An Interdisciplinary Guide to the Treaties of the Six Nations and Their League. Eds. Francis Jennings, William N. Fenton, and Mary A. Druke. Published for the Newberry Library Center for the History of the American Indian. Syracuse, N.Y.: Syracuse University Press, 1983.

Howard, James H. *Shawnee!: The Ceremonialism of a Native Indian Tribe and Its Cultural Background.* Athens: Ohio University Press, 1981.

Hunter, William A. "Documented Subdivisions of the Delaware Indians." *Bulletin of the Archaeological Society of New Jersey* 20 (1978), 20–40.

———. *Forts on the Pennsylvania Frontier, 1753–1758*. Harrisburg: Pennsylvania Historical and Museum Commission, 1960.

———. "History of the Ohio Valley." In *Northeast*, q.v. Pp. 588–93.

———. "Moses (Tunda) Tatamy, Delaware Indian Diplomat." In *A Delaware Indian Symposium*. Ed. Herbert C. Kraft. Anthropological Series 4. Harrisburg: Pennsylvania Historical and Museum Commission, 1974.

Huston, Charles. *An Essay on the History and Nature of Original Titles to Land in the Province and State of Pennsylvania*. Philadelphia: T. and J. W. Johnson, 1849.

Hutson, James H. "Benjamin Franklin and Pennsylvania Politics, 1751–1755; A Reappraisal." *Pennsylvania Magazine of History and Biography* 93 (1969), 303–71.

———. *Pennsylvania Politics, 1746–1770: The Movement for Royal Government and Its Consequences*. Princeton, N.J.: Princeton University Press, 1972. Bib. n.: ch. 5, n37; ch. 19, n20.

Irredeemable America: The Indians' Estate and Land Claims. Ed. Imre Sutton. Albuquerque: University of Mexico Press, 1985.

Jackson, Harvey H. *Lachlan McIntosh and the Politics of Revolutionary Georgia*. Athens: University of Georgia Press, 1979.

Jacobs, Wilbur R. *Diplomacy and Indian Gifts: Anglo-French Rivalry Along the Ohio and Northwest Frontiers, 1748–1763*. Stanford, Calif.: Stanford University Press, 1950.

Jaenen, Cornelius J. *The French Relationship with the Native Peoples of New France and Acadia*. Ottawa: Research Branch, Indian and Northern Affairs Canada, 1984.

———. "The Role of Presents in French-Amerindian Trade." In *Explorations in Canadian Economic History: Essays in Honour of Irene M. Spry*. Ottawa: University of Ottawa Press, 1985.

James, Alfred Procter. *The Ohio Company: Its Inner History*. Pittsburgh, Pa.: University of Pittsburgh Press, 1959.

Jennings, Francis. *The Ambiguous Iroquois Empire: The Covenant Chain Confederation of Indian Tribes with English Colonies from its beginnings to the Lancaster Treaty of 1744*. New York: W. W. Norton and Co., 1984.

———. "The Delaware Interregnum." *Pennsylvania Magazine of History and Biography* 89 (1965), 174–98.

———. "Francis Parkman: A Brahmin among Untouchables." *William and Mary Quarterly*, 3d ser., 42 (1985), 305–28.

———. "Incident at Tulpehocken." *Pennsylvania History* 35 (1968), 335–55.

———. "The Indians' Revolution." In *The American Revolution: Explorations in the History of American Radicalism*. Ed. Alfred F. Young. DeKalb: Northern Illinois University Press, 1976. Pp. 319–48.

———. "The Indian Trade of the Susquehanna Valley." *Proceedings of the American Philosophical Society* 110 (1966), 406–24.

———. *The Invasion of America: Indians, Colonialism, and the Cant of Conquest*. Published for the Institute of Early American History and Culture. Chapel Hill: University of North Carolina Press, 1975. Reprinted New York: W. W. Norton and Co., 1976.

———. "Miquon's Passing: Indian-European Relations in Colonial Pennsylvania, 1674 to 1755." Ph.D. diss., University of Pennsylvania, 1965.
———. "Thomas Penn's Loyalty Oath." *American Journal of Legal History* 8 (1964), 303–13.
———. "A Vanishing Indian: Francis Parkman Versus His Sources." *Pennsylvania Magazine of History and Biography* 87 (1963), 306–23. Bib. n.: ch. 17, n74.
Jones, Dorothy V. *License for Empire: Colonialism by Treaty in Early America*. Chicago: University of Chicago Press, 1982.
Katz, Stanley Nider. *Newcastle's New York: Anglo-American Politics, 1732–1753*. Cambridge, Mass.: Harvard University Press, 1968.
Kawashima, Yasuhide. *Puritan Justice and the Indian: White Man's Law in Massachusetts, 1630–1763*. Middletown, Conn.: Wesleyan University Press, 1986.
Kelch, Roy A. *Newcastle, A Duke without Money: Thomas Pelham-Holles, 1693–1768*. Berkeley: University of California Press, 1974. Bib. n.: ch. 6, n3.
Kelsey, Rayner Wickersham. *Friends and the Indians, 1655–1917*. Philadelphia, Pa.: Associated Executive Committee of Friends on Indian Affairs, 1917.
Kennedy, J. H. *Jesuit and Savage in New France* (1950). Reprinted Hamden, Conn.: Archon Books, 1971.
Kent, Donald H. *The French Invasion of Western Pennsylvania, 1753*. Harrisburg: Pennsylvania Historical and Museum Commission, 1954.
Ketcham, Ralph L. "Benjamin Franklin and William Smith: New Light on an Old Philadelphia Quarrel." *Pennsylvania Magazine of History and Biography* 88 (1964), 142–63.
———. "Conscience, War, and Politics in Pennsylvania, 1755–1757." *William and Mary Quarterly*, 3d ser., 20 (1963), 416–39.
Kettner, James H. *The Development of American Citizenship, 1608–1870*. Published for the Institute of Early American History and Culture. Chapel Hill: University of North Carolina Press, 1978.
Kim, Sung Bok. "A New Look at the Great Landlords of Eighteenth-Century New York." *William and Mary Quarterly*, 3d ser., 27 (1970), 581–64.
Kistler, Ruth Moser. *William Allen*. Rev. ed. Proceedings of the Lehigh Valley Historical Society. Allentown, Pa., 1962.
Klein, Philip S., and Ari Hoogenboom. *A History of Pennsylvania*. New York: McGraw-Hill Book Co., 1973.
Klinefelter, Walter. *Lewis Evans and His Maps*. Transactions of the American Philosophical Society, new series 61:7. Philadelphia, 1971.
Knollenberg, Bernhard. "General Amherst and Germ Warfare." *Mississippi Valley Historical Review* 41 (1954), 489–94. Bib. n.: ch. 20, n26.
———. *George Washington: The Virginia Period, 1732–1775*. Durham, N.C., 1964.
———. *Origin of the American Revolution, 1759–1766*. New York: Macmillan, 1960.
———, and Donald H. Kent. "Communications." *Mississippi Valley Historical Review* 41 (1955), 762–63.
Konrad, Viktor. "An Iroquois Frontier: The North Shore of Lake Ontario during the Late Seventeenth Century." *Journal of Historical Geography* 7 (1981), 129–44.
Kopperman, Paul E. *Braddock at the Monongahela*. Pittsburgh, Pa.: University of Pittsburgh Press, 1977.
Krugler, John D. "Lord Baltimore, Roman Catholics, and Toleration: Religious

Policy in Maryland During the Early Catholic Years, 1634–1649." *Catholic Historical Review* 65 (1979), 49–75.

Labaree, Leonard Woods. *Royal Government in America: A Study of the British Colonial System Before 1783.* Yale Historical Publications, Studies 6. New Haven, Conn.: Yale University Press, 1943.

Lanctot, Gustave. *A History of Canada.* Tr. Josephine Hambleton and Margaret M. Cameron. 3 vols. Cambridge, Mass.: Harvard University Press, 1963–65.

Leach, Douglas Edward. *Arms for Empire: A Military History of the British Colonies in North America, 1607–1763.* New York: Macmillan, 1973.

Lemisch, Jesse. "Jack Tar in the Streets: Merchant Seamen in the Politics of Revolutionary America." *William and Mary Quarterly*, 3d ser., 25 (1968), 371–407.

Lenman, Bruce. *The Jacobite Risings in Britain, 1689–1746.* London: Eyre Methuen, 1980.

Locke, Amy Audrey. *The Hanbury Family.* London: Humphries, 1916.

Long, J. C. *Mr. Pitt and America's Birthright: A biography of the Earl of Chatham, 1708–1778.* New York: Frederick A. Stokes, 1940.

McCardell, Lee. *Ill-Starred General: Braddock of the Coldstream Guards* (1958). Reprinted Pittsburgh: University of Pittsburgh Press, 1986. Bib. n.: ch. 7, n52.

McLennan, J. S. *Louisbourg from Its Foundation to Its Fall, 1713–1758.* London: Macmillan and Co., 1918.

MacNutt, W. S. *The Atlantic Provinces: The Emergence of Colonial Society, 1712–1857.* Canadian Centenary Series. Toronto: McClelland and Stewart, 1965.

Main, Jackson Turner. *The Sovereign States, 1775–1783.* New York: New Viewpoints, 1973.

Marietta, Jack D. "Conscience, the Quaker Community, and the French and Indian War." *Pennsylvania Magazine of History and Biography* 95 (1971), 3–27.

Marshall, Peter. "Imperial Regulation of American Indian Affairs, 1763–1774." Ph.D. diss., Yale University, 1959.

Metzger, Charles H., S. J. *The Quebec Act: A Primary Cause of the American Revolution.* United States Catholic Historical Society Monograph Series 16. New York, 1936.

Morgan, Edmund S. *The Puritan Family: Religious and Domestic Relations in Seventeenth-Century New England* (1944). Rev. ed. New York: Harper and Row, 1966.

———, and Helen M. *The Stamp Act Crisis: Prologue to Revolution.* Rev. ed. New York: Collier Books, 1963.

Morison, Samuel Eliot, Henry Steele Commager, and William E. Leuchtenburg. *The Growth of the American Republic.* 6th ed. 2 vols. New York: Oxford University Press, 1969.

Morrison, Kenneth M. *The Embattled Northeast: The Elusive Ideal of Alliance in Abenaki-Euramerican Relations.* Berkeley: University of California Press, 1984.

Morton, Richard L. *Colonial Virginia.* 2 vols. Published for the Virginia Historical Society. Chapel Hill: University of North Carolina Press, 1960.

Namier, Sir Lewis. *England in the Age of the American Revolution.* 2d ed. London: Macmillan and Co., 1961.

———. *The Structure of Politics at the Accession of George III.* 2d ed. London: Macmillan and Co., 1963.

Nammack, Georgiana C. *Fraud, Politics, and the Dispossession of the Indians: The Iro-*

quois Land Frontier in the Colonial Period. Norman: University of Oklahoma Press, 1969.

Narvey, Kenneth. "The Royal Proclamation of 7 October 1763, the Common Law, and Native Rights to Land within the Territory Granted to Hudson's Bay Company." *Saskatchewan Law Review* 38 (1974), 124–233.

Newcomb, Benjamin H. *Franklin and Galloway: A Political Partnership.* New Haven, Conn.: Yale University Press, 1972.

Northeast. Ed. Bruce G. Trigger. Vol. 15 (1978) of *Handbook of North American Indians.* Gen. ed. William C. Sturtevant. 20 vols. Washington, D.C.: Smithsonian Institution, 1978–.

Norton, Thomas Elliott. *The Fur Trade in Colonial New York, 1686–1776.* Madison: University of Wisconsin Press, 1974.

O'Donnell, James Howlett, III. *Southeastern Frontiers: Europeans, Africans, and American Indians, 1513–1840; A Critical Bibliography.* Newberry Library Center for the History of the American Indian Bibliographical Series. Bloomington: Indiana University Press, 1982.

Olson, Alison Gilbert. "The British Government and Colonial Union, 1754." *William and Mary Quarterly.* 3d ser., 17 (1960), 22–34.

Origins of the 'Forty-Five.' Ed. Walter Biggar Blaikie. Publications of the Scottish History Society. 2d ser., 2. Edinburgh: T. and A. Constable, 1916.

Osgood, Herbert L. *The American Colonies in the Eighteenth Century* (1924). Reprinted, 4 vols. Gloucester, Mass.: Peter Smith, 1958.

Ousterhout, Anne M. "Controlling the Opposition in Pennsylvania During the American Revolution." *Pennsylvania Magazine of History and Biography* 105:1 (Jan. 1981), 3–34.

Pargellis, Stanley McCrory. *Lord Loudoun in North America.* Yale Historical Publications, Studies 7. New Haven, Conn.: Yale University Press, 1933. Bib. n.: ch. 13, n5, 59.

Parker, Arthur C. *The Constitution of the Five Nations, or the Iroquois Book of the Great Law* (1916). Reprinted facsimile (separately paged) in *Parker on the Iroquois.* Ed. W. N. Fenton. Syracuse, N.Y.: Syracuse University Press, 1968.

Parkman, Francis. *The Conspiracy of Pontiac and the Indian War after the Conquest of Canada* (1851). Rev. New Library ed. 2 vols. Boston: Little, Brown and Co., 1909.

———. *Montcalm and Wolfe* (1884). New Library ed. 2 vols. Boston: Little, Brown and Co., 1909.

Parrish, Samuel. *Some Chapters in the History of the Friendly Association for Regaining and Preserving Peace with the Indians by pacific Measures.* Philadelphia, Pa.: Friends' Historical Association, 1877. Unique, interleaved copy at Historical Society of Pennsylvania. Bib. n.: ch. 15, n22.

Parsons, William T. "The Bloody Election of 1742." *Pennsylvania History* 36 (1969), 290–306.

Peckham, Howard H. *Pontiac and the Indian Uprising* (1947). Reprinted Chicago: University of Chicago Press, 1961.

Pencak, William. "Warfare and Political Change in Mid-Eighteenth-Century Massachusetts." In *The British Atlantic Empire before the American Revolution.* Eds. Peter Marshall and Glyn Williams. London: Frank Cass, 1980. Pp. 51–73.

Perdue, Theda. *Slavery and the Evolution of Cherokee Society, 1540–1866*. Knoxville: University of Tennessee Press, 1979.

Peters, Marie. *Pitt and Popularity: The Patriot Minister and London Opinion during the Seven Years' War*. Oxford: Clarendon Press, 1980.

Plumb, J. H. *England in the Eighteenth Century*. Pelican History of England. Baltimore, Md.: Penguin Books, 1950.

Pole, J. R. *Political Representation in England and the Origins of the American Republic*. London: Macmillan and Co., 1966.

Pownall, Charles A. W. *Thomas Pownall*. London: Henry Stevens, Son and Stiles, 1908.

Prebble, John. *Culloden* (1961). Reprinted Harmondsworth, England: Penguin Books, 1967.

———. *Mutiny: Highland Regiments in Revolt, 1743–1804*. New York: Penguin Books, 1977.

Price, Jacob M. "The Great Quaker Business Families of Eighteenth-Century London." In *The World of William Penn*, q.v., 363–99.

The Public Lands: Studies in the History of the Public Domain. Ed. Vernon Carstensen. Madison: University of Wisconsin Press. 1968.

Radabaugh, Jack Sheldon. "The Military System of Colonial Massachusetts, 1690–1740." Ph.D. diss., University of Southern California, 1965.

Raistrick, Arthur. *Quakers in Science and Industry; Being an Account of the Quaker Contributions to Science and Industry During the 17th and 18th Centuries*. London: Bannisdale Press, 1950.

Reddaway, W. F. "The Seven Years' War." In *The Old Empire:* vol. 1 of *The Cambridge History of the British Empire*. Gen. eds. J. Holland Rose, A. P. Newton, and E. A. Benians. New York: Macmillan, 1929. Ch. 16, pp. 460–84.

Reed, William B. "The Acadian Exiles, or French Neutrals in Pennsylvania." In *Contributions to American History*. Memoirs of the Historical Society of Pennsylvania 6. Philadelphia, Pa.: J. B. Lippincott and Co., 1858. Pp. 283–313.

Reid, John Phillip. *In Defiance of the Law: The Standing-Army Controversy, the Two Constitutions, and the Coming of the American Revolution*. Studies in Legal History series of the American Society for Legal History. Chapel Hill: University of North Carolina Press, 1981.

———. *A Law of Blood: The Primitive Law of the Cherokee Nation*. New York: New York University Press, 1970.

Ritzenthaler, Robert E. "Southwestern Chippeawa." In *Northeast*, q.v., 743–59.

Robertson, Sir Charles Grant. *England Under the Hanoverians* (1911). Reprinted London: Methuen and Co., 1958.

Rogers, Alan. *Empire and Liberty: American Resistance to British Authority, 1755–1763*. Berkeley: University of California Press, 1974.

Rothermund, Dietmar. "The German Problem of Colonial Pennsylvania." *Pennsylvania Magazine of History and Biography* 84 (1960), 3–21.

———. *The Layman's Progress: Religious and Political Experience in Colonial Pennsylvania, 1740–1770*. Philadelphia: University of Pennsylvania Press, 1961.

Russell, Peter E. "Redcoats in the Wilderness: British Officers and Irregular Warfare in Europe and America, 1740 to 1760." *William and Mary Quarterly*, 3d ser., 35 (1978), 629–52.

Rutman, Darrett Bruce. "A Militant New World, 1607–1640: America's First Generation, Its Martial Spirit, Its Tradition of Arms, Its Militia Organization, Its Wars." Ph.D. diss., University of Virginia, 1959.

Savelle, Max. *Seeds of Liberty: The Genesis of the American Mind.* New York: Alfred A. Knopf, 1948.

Schutz, John A. *William Shirley, King's Governor of Massachusetts.* Published for the Institute of Early American History and Culture. Chapel Hill: University of North Carolina Press, 1961.

Seaver, James E. *A Narrative of the Life of Mrs. Mary Jemison, Who was taken by the Indians in the year 1755 . . .* (1824). Reprinted New York: American Scenic and Historic Preservation Society, 1950.

Sener, S. M. "The Catholic Church at Lancaster, Penna." *Records of the American Catholic Historical Society of Philadelphia* 5 (1894), 307–38.

Severance, Frank H. *An Old Frontier of France: The Niagara Region and Adjacent Lakes under French Control.* 2 vols. New York: Dodd, Mead and Co., 1917.

Sherrard, O. A. *Lord Chatham: Pitt and the Seven Years' War.* London: Bodley Head, 1955.

Shotwell, J. T. "Foreword." In Harold A. Innis, *The Cod Fisheries: The History of an International Economy.* Published for the Carnegie Endowment for International Peace. New Haven, Conn.: Yale University Press, 1940.

Shy, John W. "A New Look at Colonial Militia." *William and Mary Quarterly.* 3d ser., 20 (1963), 175–85.

———. *Toward Lexington: The Role of the British Army in the Coming of the American Revolution.* Princeton, N.J.: Princeton University Press, 1965.

Sipe, C. Hale. *The Indian Chiefs of Pennsylvania.* Butler, Pa.: Ziegler Printing Co., 1927.

Smith, Donald B. "Who Are the Mississauga?" *Ontario History* 17 (1975), 211–22.

Smith, Horace Wemyss. *Life and Correspondence of the Rev. William Smith, D.D.* 2 vols. Philadelphia, 1879, 1880. Bib. n.: ch. 11, n9.

Snow, Dean R. "Eastern Abenaki." In *Northeast*, q.v., 137–47.

Sosin, Jack M. *Whitehall and the Wilderness: The Middle West in British Colonial Policy, 1760–1775.* Lincoln: University of Nebraska Press, 1961.

Speck, W. A. *The Butcher: The Duke of Cumberland and the Suppression of the 45.* Oxford: Basil Blackwell, 1981.

Stagg, Jack. *Anglo-American Relations in North America to 1763, and an Analysis of The Royal Proclamation of 7 October 1763.* Ottawa: Research Branch, Indian and Northern Affairs Canada, 1981.

Stanley, George F. G. *New France: The Last Phase, 1744–1760.* Canadian Centenary Series. Toronto: McClelland and Stewart, 1968.

Stone, William L. *The Life and Times of Sir William Johnson, Bart.* 2 vols. Albany: J. Munsell, 1865. Bib. n.: ch. 18, n42.

Sutton, Imre. *Indian Land Tenure: Bibliographical Essays and a Guide to the Literature.* New York: Clearwater Publishing Co., 1975.

Tanner, Helen; Adele Hast; and Jacqueline Peterson. *Atlas of Great Lakes Indian History.* Published for the Newberry Library. Norman: University of Oklahoma, 1986.

Temperley, H. W. V. "The Peace of Paris." In *The Old Empire:* vol. 1 of *The*

Cambridge History of the British Empire. Gen. eds. J. Holland Rose, A. P. Newton, and E. A. Benians. New York: Macmillan, 1929. Ch. 17, pp. 485–506.

Thayer, Theodore. "The Army Contractors for the Niagara Campaign, 1755–1756." *William and Mary Quarterly*. 3d ser., 14 (1957), 31–46.

———. *Israel Pemberton, King of the Quakers*. Philadelphia: Historical Society of Pennsylvania, 1943.

———. *Pennsylvania Politics and the Growth of Democracy, 1740–1776*. Harrisburg: Pennsylvania Historical and Museum Commission, 1953.

Turner, Frederick Jackson. *The Frontier in American History*. New York: H. Holt and Co., 1920. Bib. n.: ch. 21, n10.

Tyler, John W. *Smugglers and Patriots: Boston Merchants and the Advent of the American Revolution*. Boston: Northeastern University Press, 1986.

Upton, L. F. S. "Indian Policy in Colonial Nova Scotia, 1783–1871." *Acadiensis* 5 (1975), 3–31.

———. *Micmacs and Colonists: Indian-White Relations in the Maritimes, 1713–1867*. Vancouver: University of British Columbia Press, 1979.

Van Alstyne, Richard W. "Impressment of Seamen." In *Dictionary of American History*. Ed. J. T. Adams. 5 vols. New York: Charles Scribner's Sons, 1940. 3:80–81.

Van Doren, Carl. *Benjamin Franklin*. New York: Viking Press, 1938.

Volwiler, Albert T. *George Croghan and the Westward Movement, 1741–1782*. Cleveland, O.: Arthur H. Clark Co., 1926.

Waddington, Richard. *La Guerre de Sept Ans: Histoire Diplomatique et Militaire*. 5 vols. Paris: Firmin-Didot et Cie., 1899.

Wainwright, Nicholas B. *George Croghan: Wilderness Diplomat*. Published for the Institute of Early American History and Culture. Chapel Hill: University of North Carolina Press, 1959.

Wallace, Anthony F. C. *The Death and Rebirth of the Seneca*. New York: Alfred A. Knopf, 1970.

———. *King of the Delawares: Teedyuscung, 1700–1763*. Philadelphia: University of Pennsylvania Press, 1949.

Wallace, Paul A. W. *Conrad Weiser, 1696–1760, Friend of Colonist and Mohawk*. Philadelphia: University of Pennsylvania Press, 1945.

———. *Indian Paths of Pennsylvania*. Harrisburg: Pennsylvania Historical and Museum Commission, 1965.

———. *Indians in Pennsylvania*. Harrisburg: Pennsylvania Historical and Museum Commission, 1961.

Webb, Stephen Saunders. *The Governors-General: The English Army and the Definition of the Empire*. Published for the Institute of Early American History and Culture. Chapel Hill: University of North Carolina Press, 1979.

———. *1676: The End of American Independence*. New York: Alfred A. Knopf, 1984. Bib. n.: ch. 5, n30.

Webster, John Clarence. *The Career of the Abbe Le Loutre in Nova Scotia with a Translation of his Autobiography*. Shediac, N.B.: Privately printed, 1933.

Wells, Robert V. *The Population of the British Colonies in America before 1776: A Survey of Census Data*. Princeton, N.J.: Princeton University Press, 1975.

Weslager, C. A. *The Delaware Indian Westward Migration*. Wallingford, Pa.: Middle Atlantic Press, 1978.
White, Richard. "Red Shoes: Warrior and Diplomat." In *Struggle and Survival in Colonial America.*" Eds. David G. Sweet and Gary B. Nash. Berkeley: University of California Press, 1981. Pp. 49–68.
Wickwire, Franklin B. *British Subministers and Colonial America, 1763–1783*. Princeton, N.J.: Princeton University Press, 1966.
Williams, Basil. *The Life of William Pitt, Earl of Chatham* (1913). 2 vols. Reprinted New York: Octagon Books, 1966.
———. *The Whig Supremacy, 1714–1760*. 2d ed., rev. by C. H. Stuart. Oxford History of England. Oxford: Clarendon Press, 1962.
Williams, Eric. *Capitalism and Slavery*. Chapel Hill: University of North Carolina Press, 1944.
Winzerling, Oscar William. *Acadian Odyssey*. Baton Rouge: Louisiana University Press, 1955.
Wood, George Arthur. *William Shirley, Governor of Massachusetts, 1741–1756*. Studies in History, Economics and Public Law 92. New York: Columbia University, 1920.
The World of William Penn. Eds. Richard S. Dunn and Mary Maples Dunn. Philadelphia: University of Pennsylvania Press, 1986.
Wright, J. Leitch, Jr. *The Only Land They Knew: The Tragic Story of the American Indians in the Old South*. New York: The Free Press, 1981.
Wroth, Lawrence C. *An American Bookshelf, 1755*. Philadelphia: University of Pennsylvania Press, 1934.
Yorke, Philip C. *The Life and Correspondence of Philip Yorke, Earl of Hardwicke, Lord High Chancellor of Great Britain*. 3 vols. Cambridge, Eng.: Cambridge University Press, 1913. Bib. n.: ch. 6, n6.
Zoltvany, Yves F. *Phillippe de Rigaud de Vaudreuil, Governor of New France, 1703–25*. Carleton Library 80. Toronto: McClelland and Stewart, 1974.

Note: A review essay containing some references to studies that escaped my attention has been published since the completion of my text. The serious student may wish to consult the varied views surveyed by Don Higginbotham in "The Early American Way of War: Reconnaissance and Appraisal," *William and Mary Quarterly*, 3d ser., 44:2 (April 1987), 230–73.

See also: *Beyond the Covenant Chain: The Iroquois and Their Neighbors in Indian North America, 1600–1800*. Eds. Daniel K. Richter and James H. Merrell. Syracuse, N.Y.: Syracuse University Press, 1987.

INDEX